Our United States

Silver Burdett Ginn
Parsippany, NJ • Needham, MA
Atlanta, GA   Deerfield, IL   Irving, TX   Santa Clara, CA

PROGRAM AUTHORS

Juan R. García
Associate Professor of History and Associate Dean
  of the College of Social and Behavioral Sciences
University of Arizona
Tucson, AZ

Daniel J. Gelo
Associate Professor of Anthropology, Division of
  Behavioral and Cultural Sciences
University of Texas at San Antonio
San Antonio, TX

Linda L. Greenow
Associate Professor and Acting Chair,
  Department of Geography
S.U.N.Y. at New Paltz
New Paltz, NY

James B. Kracht
Professor of Geography and Educational
  Curriculum and Instruction
Texas A&M University
College Station, TX

Deborah Gray White
Professor of History
Rutgers University
New Brunswick, NJ

Silver Burdett Ginn
A Division of Simon & Schuster
299 Jefferson Road, P.O. Box 480
Parsippany, NJ 07054-0480

UNIT 6 · INTO THE TWENTIETH CENTURY

UNIT 7 — MODERN TIMES 480

R REFERENCE 584

MAPS

ATLAS MAPS

MAP ADVENTURES

TIME LINES

GRAPHS, TABLES, CHARTS, AND DIAGRAMS

SKILLS

LITERATURE

The following books are recommended for optional reading and research.

Map Handbook

CONTENTS

A MAP: When Is It Better Than a Photo?

If a picture is worth a thousand words, how many words would a map be worth? How many words would it take to describe going by land from one state to another or from one country to another? Luckily, you can use maps instead of words!

A map shows what Earth, or a part of it, would look like if seen from overhead. It gives you a picture that is very useful if you are trying to get from one place to another.

The photograph on this page was taken from about 1,500 feet above Earth's surface. In the map on page M3, a cartographer (kahr TAHG ruh-fur), or mapmaker, shows the same scene.

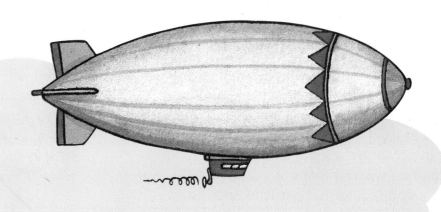

	KEY
	KEY
	Highways
	Other roads
	Buildings
	Parking lots
	Tennis courts
	Pond
	Trees
	Other land

Unlock the meaning.

The key on a map helps you to read the map. Another name for the key is the legend.

◆ What does this color symbol [ ] stand for?

◆ What color stands for trees?

Go from one kind of picture to another.

◆ Find a parking lot in the photograph. What color stands for it?

◆ Now find the parking lot on the map. Find a highway and the tennis courts, too.

Now Try This!

◆ Draw a map that shows what the top or the inside of your desk would look like if seen from above. Make up symbols to stand for books, rulers, pencils, and so on.

MAPS: Get the Most out of Them!

Maps are the most important tools we have for finding out where places are located. People use maps to help them understand the world around them. Maps are so much a part of our lives that we seldom stop to think about them. But, without maps, it would be difficult to plan a vacation or find out where Kenya is!

You will see many maps in this book. Each one has symbols that show different information. A symbol may look like the thing it stands for. For example, symbols for roads and mountains usually look like those things. Often, colors are used as symbols on maps.

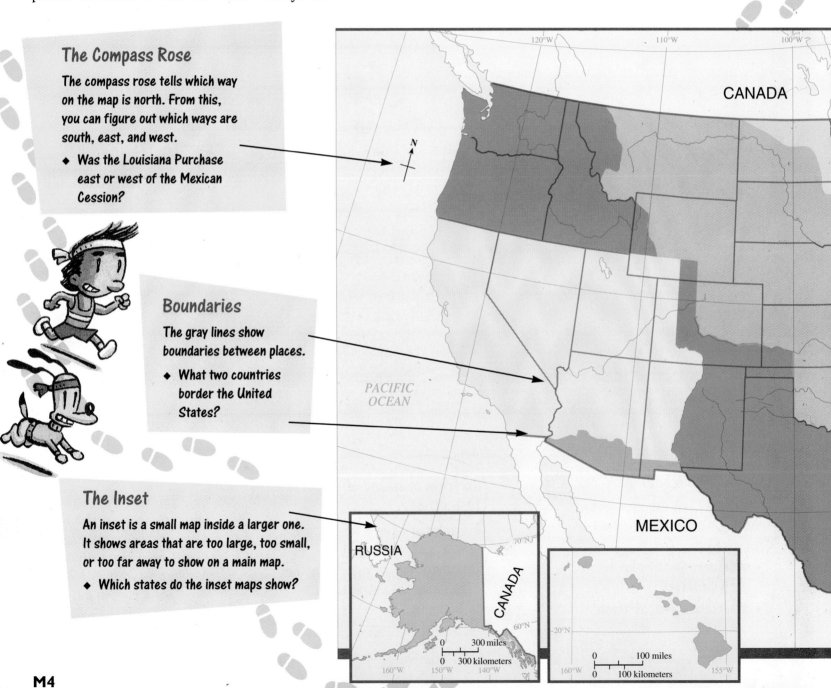

The Compass Rose

The compass rose tells which way on the map is north. From this, you can figure out which ways are south, east, and west.

◆ Was the Louisiana Purchase east or west of the Mexican Cession?

Boundaries

The gray lines show boundaries between places.

◆ What two countries border the United States?

The Inset

An inset is a small map inside a larger one. It shows areas that are too large, too small, or too far away to show on a main map.

◆ Which states do the inset maps show?

CANADA

PACIFIC OCEAN

MEXICO

RUSSIA

CANADA

| 0 | 300 miles |
| 0 | 300 kilometers |

| 0 | 100 miles |
| 0 | 100 kilometers |

The Scale

The scale allows you to tell the distances between places.

◆ How many miles does this scale show?

Latitude and Longitude

Maps have lines to help locate places.

Latitude lines run east and west.

Longitude lines run north and south.

The latitude and longitude of a place tells exactly where it is located.

◆ Name two latitude lines that cross the Texas Annexation.

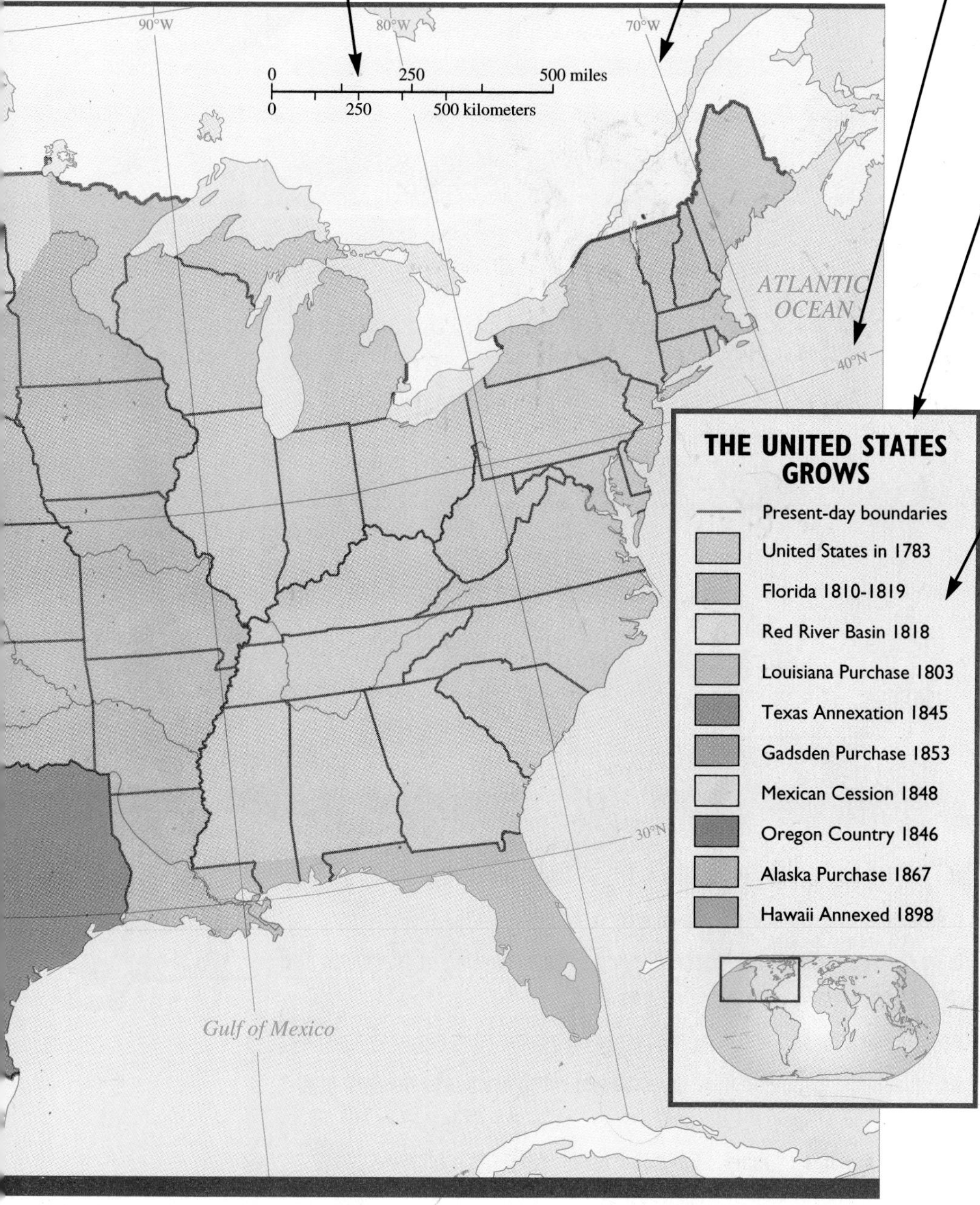

Map Titles

In this book, map titles are located at the top of the map key. The title tells you what kind of information you can find on the map.

◆ What is the title of this map?

The Key

On most maps, a box called a key, or legend, explains the symbols. Often, the key also contains a locator map. This helps you locate the area in relation to a larger area.

◆ What larger area is shown on this locator map?

90°W 80°W 70°W

0   250   500 miles
0   250   500 kilometers

ATLANTIC OCEAN

40°N

30°N

Gulf of Mexico

THE UNITED STATES GROWS

— Present-day boundaries
United States in 1783
Florida 1810-1819
Red River Basin 1818
Louisiana Purchase 1803
Texas Annexation 1845
Gadsden Purchase 1853
Mexican Cession 1848
Oregon Country 1846
Alaska Purchase 1867
Hawaii Annexed 1898

Now Try This!

Draw a map of your neighborhood or town. First, sketch out the major streets. Then add places of interest. Later, as you master map skills, you will revise this map, using your new skills.

M5

SCALE: How Far is It?

How long is a soccer field? How far is it from Phoenix to Chicago? To find out, you need a sheet of paper and a map that has a **distance scale**.

Distances on maps are smaller than the real distances on Earth. The distance scale shows how much smaller. A certain number of inches on a map stands for a certain number of feet, yards, or miles on Earth. If the map uses the metric system, centimeters stand for meters or kilometers.

Study the distance scale below. How many miles does one inch stand for? How many inches would show 400 miles? How many kilometers does one centimeter stand for?

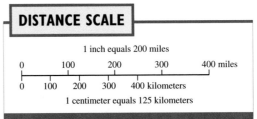

DISTANCE SCALE

1 inch equals 200 miles

| 0 | 100 | 200 | 300 | 400 miles |

| 0 | 100 | 200 | 300 | 400 kilometers |

1 centimeter equals 125 kilometers

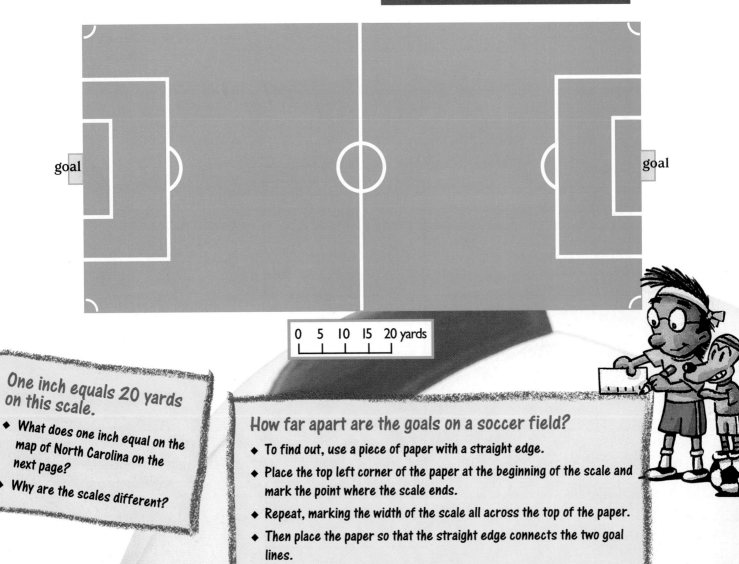

goal   goal

0 5 10 15 20 yards

One inch equals 20 yards on this scale.

- What does one inch equal on the map of North Carolina on the next page?
- Why are the scales different?

How far apart are the goals on a soccer field?

- To find out, use a piece of paper with a straight edge.
- Place the top left corner of the paper at the beginning of the scale and mark the point where the scale ends.
- Repeat, marking the width of the scale all across the top of the paper.
- Then place the paper so that the straight edge connects the two goal lines.
- Count the number of marks between them. How far apart are they?

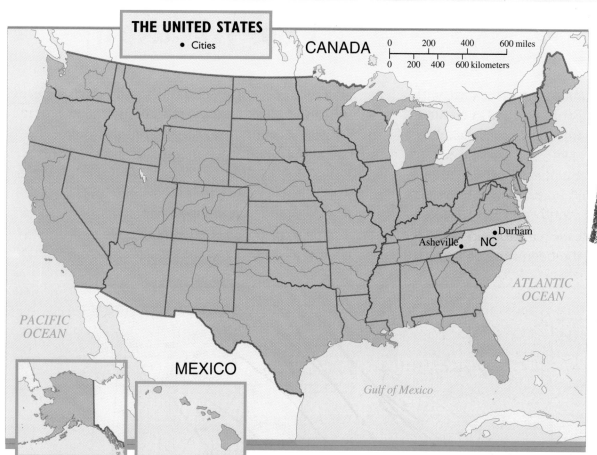

THE UNITED STATES

• Cities

CANADA

0	200	400	600 miles
0	200	400	600 kilometers

• Durham
Asheville • NC

ATLANTIC
OCEAN

PACIFIC
OCEAN

MEXICO

Gulf of Mexico

Use your ruler.

◆ About how many miles are represented by one inch on the U.S. map?

◆ About how many miles are represented by two inches on the map of North Carolina?

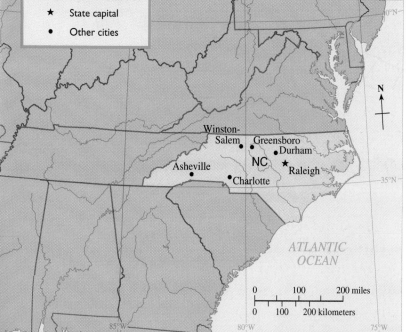

NORTH CAROLINA

★ State capital
• Other cities

40°N

N

Winston-Salem • Greensboro
• Durham
NC
Asheville • ★ Raleigh
• Charlotte

35°N

ATLANTIC
OCEAN

0	100	200 miles
0	100	200 kilometers

85°W   80°W   75°W

Large scale, small scale

◆ Use the scale on the map of North Carolina to find out how far it is from Asheville to Durham.

◆ Do this again, using the map of the United States. Did you get the same distance?

Now Try This!

With a group of classmates, map your classroom. Use a yardstick or tape measure to measure the room's length and width. Decide what scale of feet you will use to fit the map on a sheet of paper. Draw the map. Show windows, desks, and other features.

An INSET Map: Why Use It?

If all countries were about the same size, with even boundaries, it would be easy to create maps. Unfortunately, countries do not always cooperate with a mapmaker. Some countries have parts that do not touch each other. Other countries have some large parts and some small parts.

One nation that makes it hard for a mapmaker is the United States. At the beginning of 1959, the United States consisted of 48 states. Each state touched at least one other state. By the end of 1959, Alaska and Hawaii entered the Union, causing problems for mapmakers. Alaska and Hawaii are located far away from the other states. And Alaska is more than 400 times as large as Rhode Island, our smallest state!

This map shows the United States today, with Hawaii and Alaska in their correct locations.

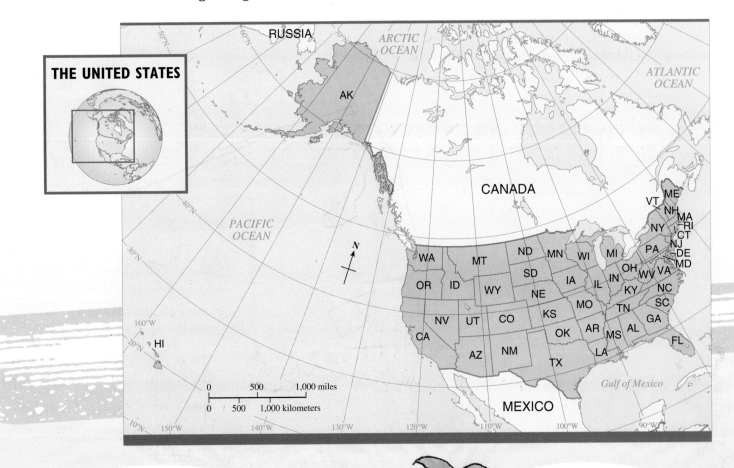

Find Alaska on the map.
- What other country has been included in order to show all of Alaska?

Find Hawaii on the map.
- Use the scale of miles to find the distance between Hawaii and its nearest neighbor in the United States.

The map on this page shows Alaska and Hawaii in a different way than the map on page M8 does. On the map below, Alaska and Hawaii are shown on **inset maps.**

To make the map fit, a different scale of miles is used for the main map and each inset. Alaska is shown much smaller than it actually is. It looks about the same size as Arizona, but it is actually much larger.

Hawaii appears in a small inset, close to the other states. This makes it hard to tell where Hawaii is in relation to the other states. To figure this out, you must use lines of latitude and longitude. You'll learn more about latitude and longitude on pages M14 through M16.

Use the scale of miles.

Using the scale on the inset map of Alaska, measure the distance from its northern to its southern boundaries. Now measure the distance from the northern to the southern boundaries of California.

◆ If you didn't understand scale, which distance would seem greater? Which is actually greater?

Now Try This!

On what floor of your school is your classroom? Draw a map of that floor, labeling the rooms. Then draw an inset map that shows your classroom. Work with a group of classmates to figure out two different distance scales for your main map and your inset.

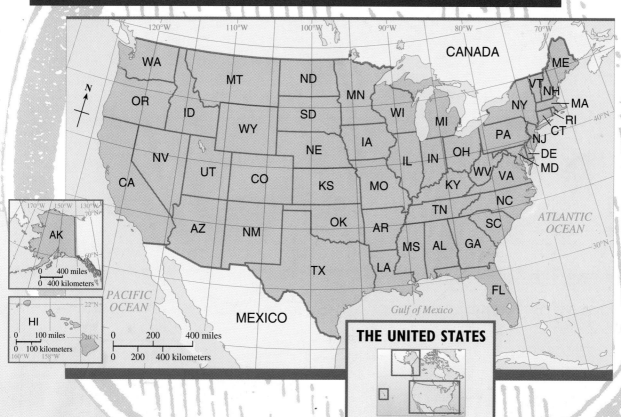

THE UNITED STATES

The COMPASS ROSE:

How Do I Get There From Here?

The tips of the compass rose on the map below point to the four **cardinal**, or main, directions: north, south, east, and west, marked N, S, E, and W. Between these directions are four **intermediate**, or in-between, directions. For example, in between north and east is northeast.

NE stands for northeast. What do NW, SE, and SW stand for?

The map below shows Harlem, a section of New York City. There, in the 1920s, many African American artists, writers, and musicians lived and created great works.

Visit Harlem in the 1920s.

Go from the Apollo Theater to Garvey's Liberty Hall.

◆ In which direction are you walking?

Which way is in-between?

From Garvey's Hall, go to Langston Hughes's home.

◆ In what intermediate direction are you walking?

Now Try This!

Use cardinal and intermediate directions to tell a partner how to get from one place to another on this map. Give a starting point, and give the directions. Did your partner end up in the right place?

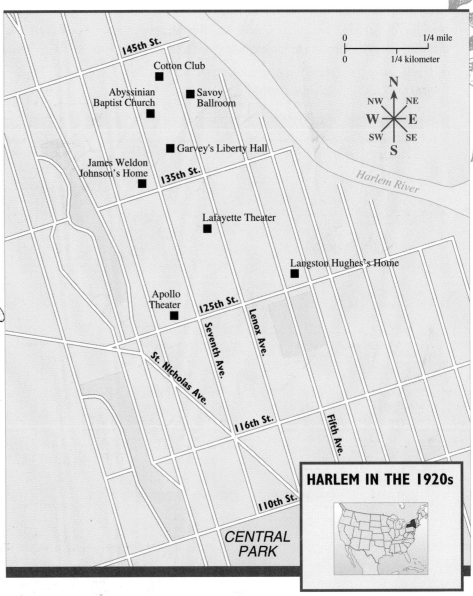

Map labels: 145th St., Cotton Club, Abyssinian Baptist Church, Savoy Ballroom, Garvey's Liberty Hall, James Weldon Johnson's Home, 135th St., Lafayette Theater, Langston Hughes's Home, Apollo Theater, 125th St., Seventh Ave., Lenox Ave., St. Nicholas Ave., 116th St., Fifth Ave., 110th St., Harlem River, CENTRAL PARK

Scale: 0 — 1/4 mile, 0 — 1/4 kilometer

Compass: N, NW, NE, W, E, SW, SE, S

HARLEM IN THE 1920s

An ELEVATION Map:
What Do All Those Colors Mean?

A map has its own language. The "words" of this language are the symbols on the map. The mapmaker puts all the symbols together in one place. This part of a map is called the **key**, because it unlocks the meaning of the symbols.

Another term for the key is the **legend**.

On the **physical map** below, the symbols are colors that show differences in the **elevation**, or height, of land. Elevation is the height of land above or below sea level.

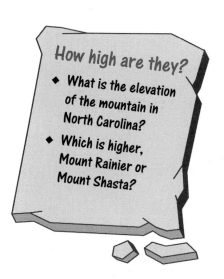

How high are they?

- What is the elevation of the mountain in North Carolina?
- Which is higher, Mount Rainier or Mount Shasta?

Now Try This!

- Find the place where you live. Use its color to find its elevation.
- Name two places that have a higher elevation than your home.
- Which color on the map stands for the lowest elevation?

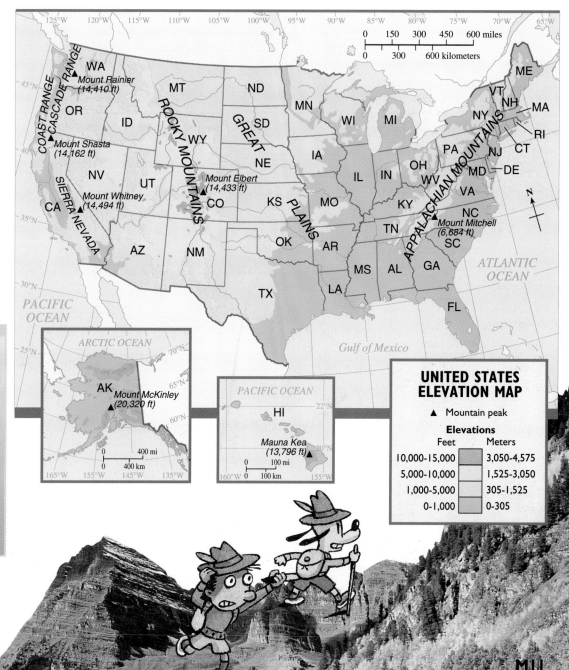

UNITED STATES ELEVATION MAP

▲ Mountain peak

Elevations

Feet		Meters
10,000–15,000		3,050–4,575
5,000–10,000		1,525–3,050
1,000–5,000		305–1,525
0–1,000		0–305

Places of interest are shown on the map of Anytown below. This map has a **grid**, or a set of crossed lines that form boxes on the map. The grid system helps you find places on street maps. Numbers run along the top, and letters run down the sides, giving each box an "address."

One museum in Anytown is called the Museum for the Study of Knockwurst. To find it, put a finger on the letter C, then put a finger of your other hand on the number 5. Move your fingers, one across and the other down, until they meet. Here you will find the box whose address is C5. Somewhere in that box is the museum.

Use the map key and the grid.

- What symbol stands for schools? How many schools are on the map?

- Is the library in box C2, or is it in box E5?

- The Chili Conservatory school is in box D3. What is the grid address of the other school?

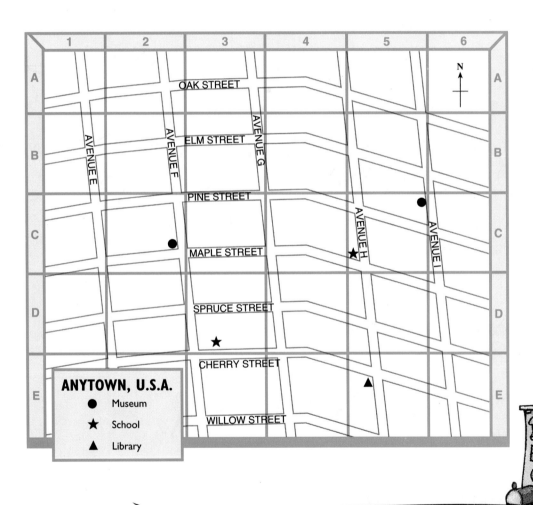

ANYTOWN, U.S.A.

- ● Museum
- ★ School
- ▲ Library

OAK STREET
ELM STREET
PINE STREET
MAPLE STREET
SPRUCE STREET
CHERRY STREET
WILLOW STREET

AVENUE E
AVENUE F
AVENUE G
AVENUE H
AVENUE I

Road Maps

- On a road map the map key explains each symbol.
- The area is divided into squares that are identified at the top and left side of the map. The letter and number next to the name of each city listed in the **city index** identify the square in which that city is located.

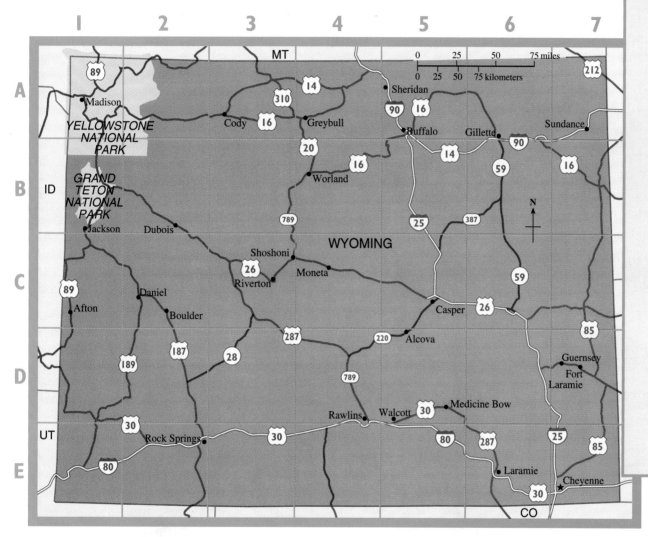

WYOMING ROAD MAP

★	State capital
•	Cities
(90)	Interstate highways
(16)	U.S. highways
(59)	State highways

Cities and Towns

Afton. C1
Alcova. D5
Boulder. C2
Buffalo. A5
Casper. C5
Cheyenne. E7
Cody. A3
Daniel. C2
Dubois. B2
Fort Laramie. . . D7
Gillette. A6
Greybull. A4
Guernsey. D7
Jackson. B1
Laramie. E6
Madison. A1
Medicine Bow. . D5
Moneta. C4
Rawlins. D4
Riverton. C3
Rock Springs. . . E2
Sheridan. A5
Shoshoni. C3
Sundance. A7
Walcott. D5
Worland. B4

Use the map tools.

- Find Routes 16, 59, and 90. Which one is an interstate highway?
- Find Cody in the city index. Then find it on the map.

Now Try This!

- Get out the map you drew of your neighborhood.
- Add a grid system to it.
- List places of interest in an index, giving each place an address.

M13

LATITUDE and LONGITUDE:
Use Them to Find Places!

Mapmakers have created a special kind of grid system that gives us a way of finding the exact location of any place on Earth. This system uses two sets of lines that cross, called lines of **latitude** and **longitude**.

Latitude is the position of a place north or south of the equator. Lines of latitude run east and west around Earth. The **latitude** line that circles Earth at its center is called the **equator**.

North Pole

75°N
60°N
45°N
30°N
15°N
0° Equator
15°S
30°S
45°S
60°S

San Diego
Minneapolis
San Antonio
New Orleans
Jacksonville

Use lines of latitude.

Jacksonville, Florida, is near the 30° latitude line north of the equator (30°N). Find it on the map.

◆ What other U.S. cities are located near 30°N?

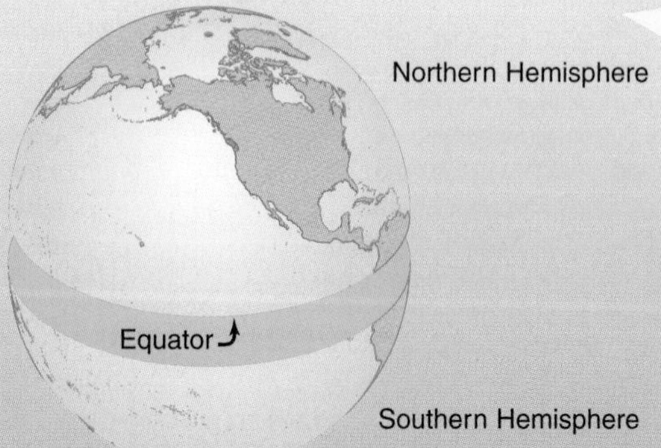

Consider the length.

◆ Do lines of latitude become shorter or longer near the North Pole?

◆ What is the longest line of latitude?

Northern Hemisphere

Equator

Southern Hemisphere

The equator divides the Earth into a Northern Hemisphere and a Southern Hemisphere.

Another set of lines runs north and south on the globe. These are called **meridians**, or **lines of longitude**. They meet at the North Pole and the South Pole.

The line numbered 0° longitude runs through Greenwich, England. It is called the **prime** **meridian**. Lines east of the prime meridian, marked 20°E, 40°E, and so on, are called lines of east longitude. Lines west of the prime meridian, marked 20°W, 40°W, and so on, are called west longitude.

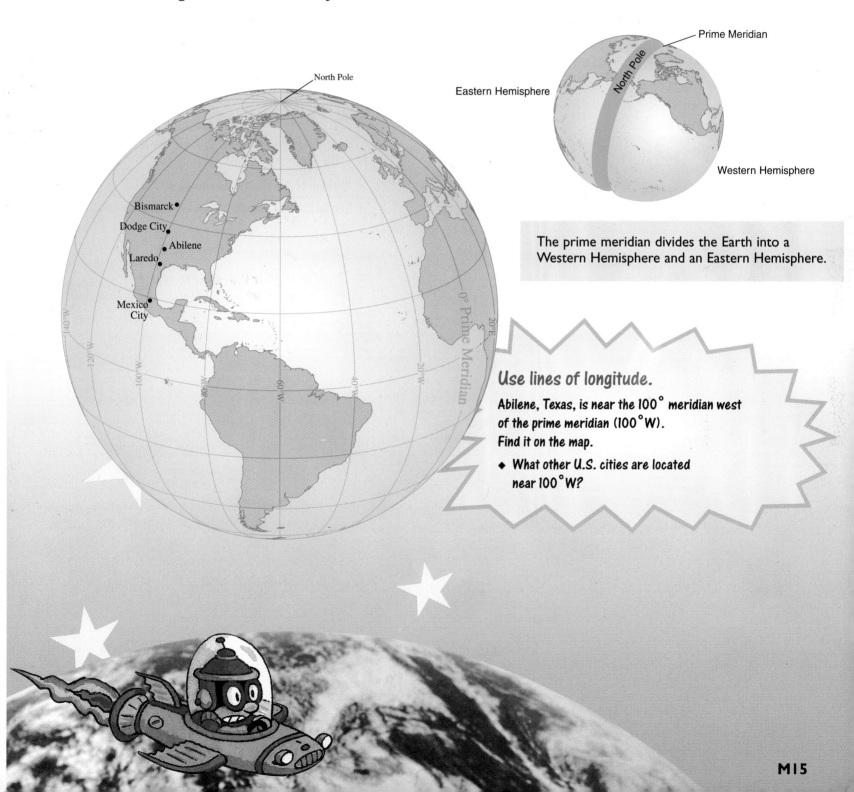

The prime meridian divides the Earth into a Western Hemisphere and an Eastern Hemisphere.

Use lines of longitude.

Abilene, Texas, is near the 100° meridian west of the prime meridian (100°W). Find it on the map.

◆ What other U.S. cities are located near 100°W?

Using Latitude and Longitude

Using latitude and longitude lets you give any place on Earth an exact "address." Jacksonville, Florida, is at 30°N. But so is New Orleans, Louisiana. Since the two cities are in different places, they can't have the same address. Combining latitude and longitude gives each city its own address. Use the map to see that Jacksonville's address is 30°N latitude, 82°W longitude. This address is written as 30°N/82°W. How would the location of New Orleans, Louisiana, be written?

Listen to an urgent message!

"This is the captain of the S.S. Peril. We are sinking fast. We are at 45°N/40°W. Help!"

◆ In which ocean should the rescue ship look?

◆ Should it look in the Northern Hemisphere or the Southern Hemisphere?

◆ What continent is west of the ship?

San Diego

Abilene

New Orleans

Jacksonville

Mexico City

60°N

45°N

30°N

ATLANTIC OCEAN

15°N

0° Equator

PACIFIC OCEAN

120°W

100°W

80°W

60°W

40°W

20°W

0° Prime Meridian

Now Try This!

Use an atlas to locate the route of a hot-air balloon trip. Start at 60°N/70°W, and end at 30°N/100°W. Then write a travel brochure that tells

◆ what continent you will fly over

◆ what countries you will be in

◆ what cities you might see.

What's So Special About SPECIAL-PURPOSE Maps?

A Precipitation Map

There are many kinds of maps. The most familiar is a **political map**. A political map uses color to show different countries or states.

The map below has a special purpose. It is a **precipitation map**. **Precipitation** is the amount of moisture that falls as rain, snow, sleet, or hail. However, since much of it falls as rain, this is also called a **rainfall map**. Color is used to show average precipitation over a one-year period.

How to read a rainfall map:

Match the color on the map with the key.

◆ What color is used for Minnesota? Find that color in the map key.

◆ How much precipitation does Minnesota get in an average year?

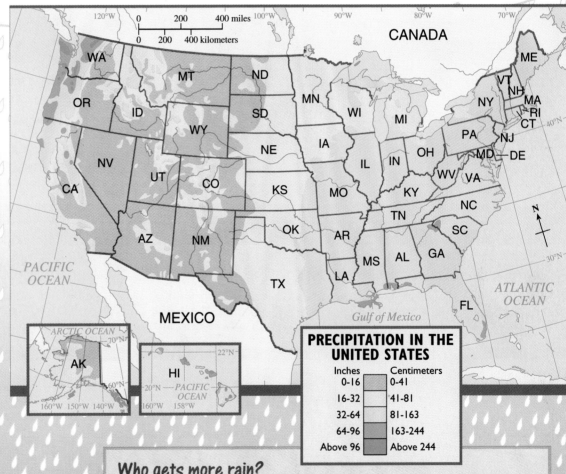

PRECIPITATION IN THE UNITED STATES

Inches		Centimeters
0-16		0-41
16-32		41-81
32-64		81-163
64-96		163-244
Above 96		Above 244

Who gets more rain?

Annual precipitation is different from one place to another.

◆ Which state receives more precipitation, Pennsylvania or New Mexico?

◆ In general, which section of the United States is drier, the west or the east?

◆ Which areas tend to get more precipitation, coastal areas or inland areas?

Routes on a Map

Every map tells a story. This map tells how the explorers Lewis and Clark found their way across North America to the Pacific Ocean. How much of the story can you tell just by looking at the map?

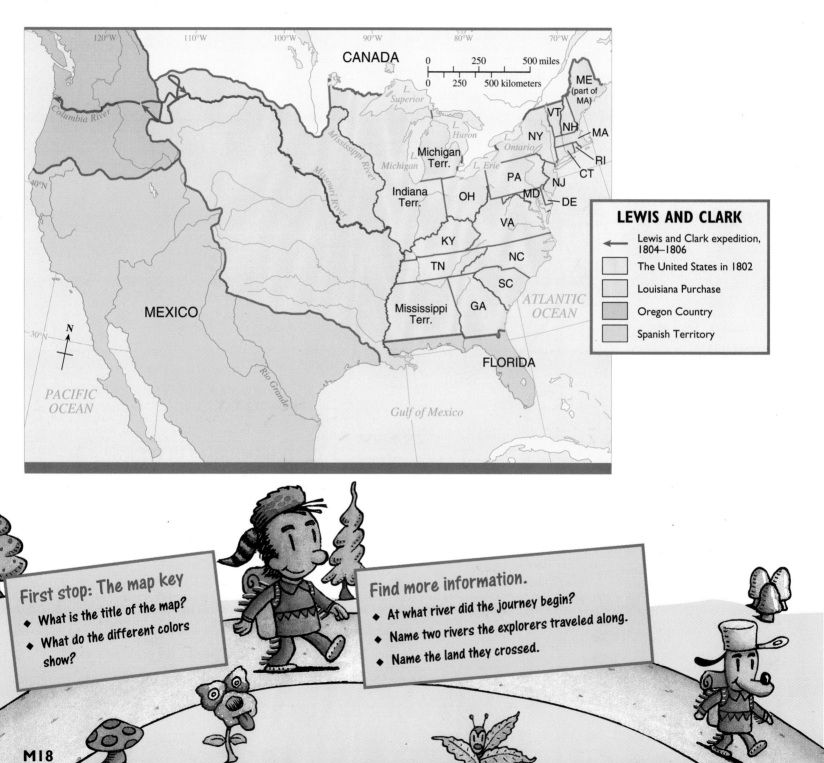

First stop: The map key
- What is the title of the map?
- What do the different colors show?

Find more information.
- At what river did the journey begin?
- Name two rivers the explorers traveled along.
- Name the land they crossed.

An Election Map

The **election map** below shows the results of the 1964 election for President. Presidential election maps show which states each candidate won.

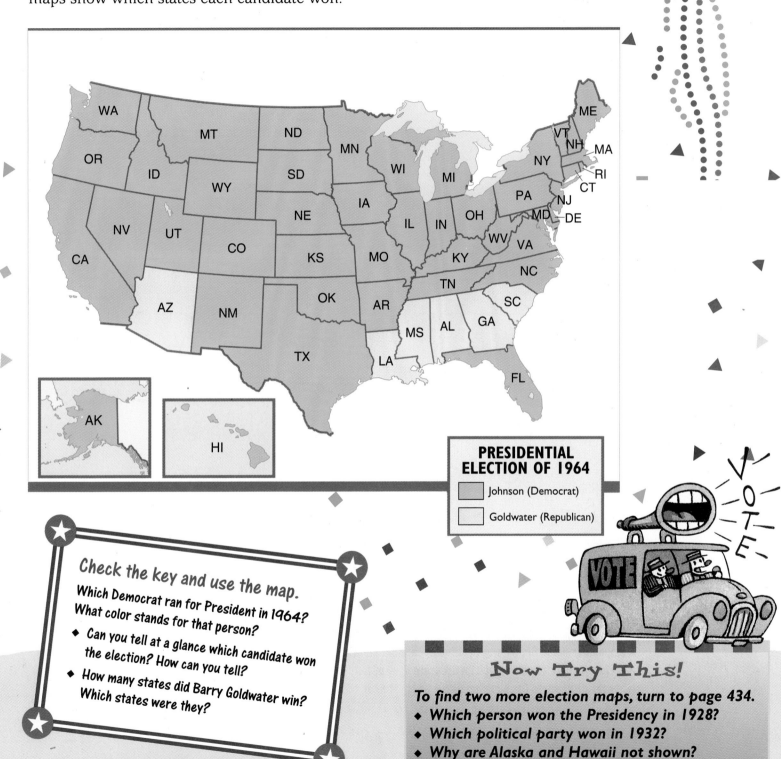

PRESIDENTIAL ELECTION OF 1964

- Johnson (Democrat)
- Goldwater (Republican)

Check the key and use the map.

Which Democrat ran for President in 1964? What color stands for that person?

- ◆ Can you tell at a glance which candidate won the election? How can you tell?
- ◆ How many states did Barry Goldwater win? Which states were they?

Now Try This!

To find two more election maps, turn to page 434.

- ◆ Which person won the Presidency in 1928?
- ◆ Which political party won in 1932?
- ◆ Why are Alaska and Hawaii not shown?

PROJECTIONS: Why Do Different Maps Show the Earth in Different Ways?

Maps are useful tools, but they all have one big problem. Maps are flat and Earth is curved. This means that maps are not entirely accurate. Globes are accurate, but what a problem you would have if you wanted to get from Elm Street to Spruce Avenue with only a globe to guide you!

Over the years, mapmakers have developed many map **projections**, ways of showing the curved Earth on a flat surface. Each projection is useful. However, each distorts, or changes, the shape of Earth in some way. Some maps are better for showing *shapes* accurately. Others show *distances* accurately.

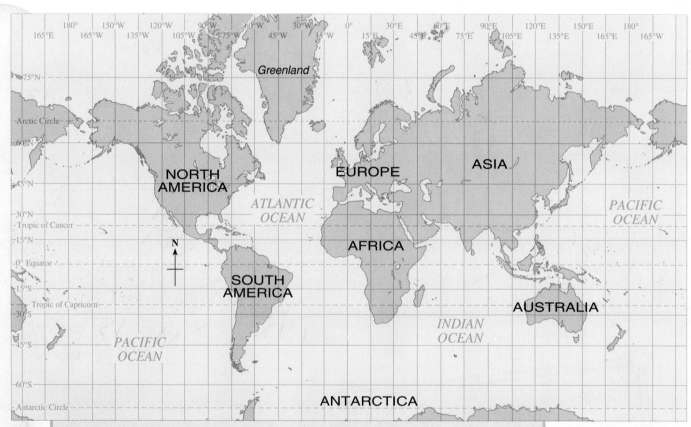

Mercator Projection

In the 1500s, sailors from Europe were exploring the oceans. They needed better maps. A mapmaker named Mercator created a map that shows direction accurately. The Mercator projection also gives an accurate view of land areas near the equator. However, it distorts the size and shape of lands near the Poles.

◆ How is longitude shown on this map? How is it different from longitude on a globe?

◆ Which is bigger on the map, Greenland or South America?

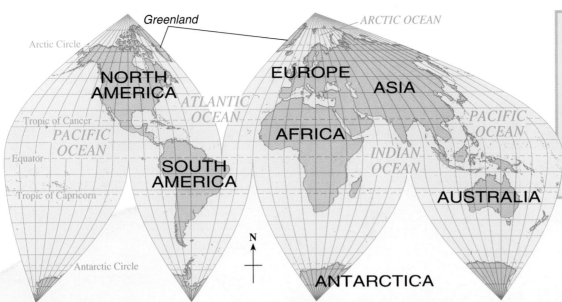

Greenland

ARCTIC OCEAN

Arctic Circle

NORTH
AMERICA

EUROPE

ASIA

ATLANTIC
OCEAN

PACIFIC
OCEAN

Tropic of Cancer

PACIFIC
OCEAN

AFRICA

INDIAN
OCEAN

Equator

SOUTH
AMERICA

Tropic of Capricorn

AUSTRALIA

Antarctic Circle

N

ANTARCTICA

Interrupted Projection

An interrupted projection shows the correct sizes and shapes of land. To do this, parts of oceans are separated.

◆ Can you measure the distance between the U.S. and Europe on this map?

Robinson Projection

This projection shows the correct sizes and shapes of most landmasses. It gives a fairly accurate view of the sizes of oceans and of distances across land.

◆ How does the Robinson projection show Greenland? How does the Mercator projection show it? How does the interrupted projection show it?

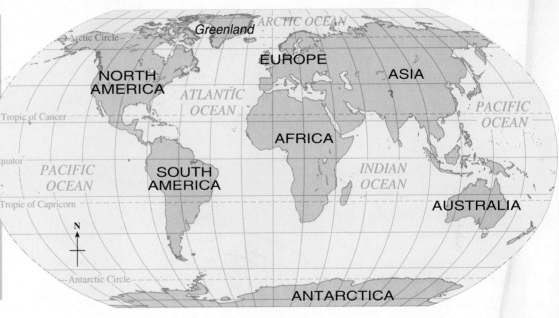

Greenland

ARCTIC OCEAN

Arctic Circle

NORTH
AMERICA

EUROPE

ASIA

ATLANTIC
OCEAN

PACIFIC
OCEAN

Tropic of Cancer

AFRICA

Equator

PACIFIC
OCEAN

SOUTH
AMERICA

INDIAN
OCEAN

Tropic of Capricorn

AUSTRALIA

N

Antarctic Circle

ANTARCTICA

Now Try This!

Trying to make a flat map out of a globe is like wrapping a round object in a piece of paper without making any creases. Try it with a small ball. Use scissors to cut out any bulges, creases, or bumps. Then unfold the paper. Does it look something like the interrupted projection on this page?

Photos taken of Earth from outer space seem to show a surface that is very much alike from one place to another. However, the closer one gets to the surface, the more differences one sees. On the surface itself, Earth is a complex, interesting place.

The diagram on these pages shows common forms of land and water. To find out about a certain form, check the number next to its description and find it on the diagram.

1 **bay**   A bay is a part of an ocean or lake that is partly enclosed by land.

2 **coast**   Coast is land that borders on the sea or ocean.

3 **delta**   A delta is an area formed by soil washed downstream by a river.

4 **glacier**   A glacier is a huge body of ice that moves slowly over land.

5 **island**   An island is an area of land surrounded by water.

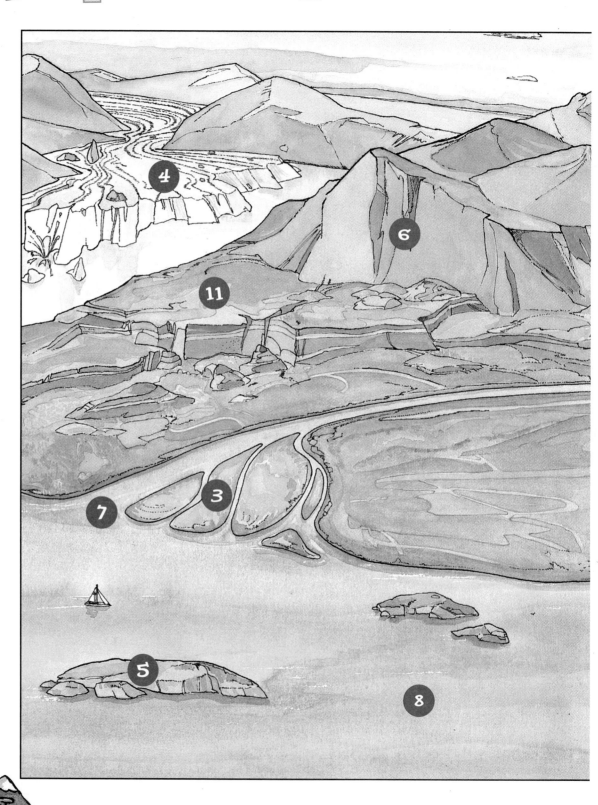

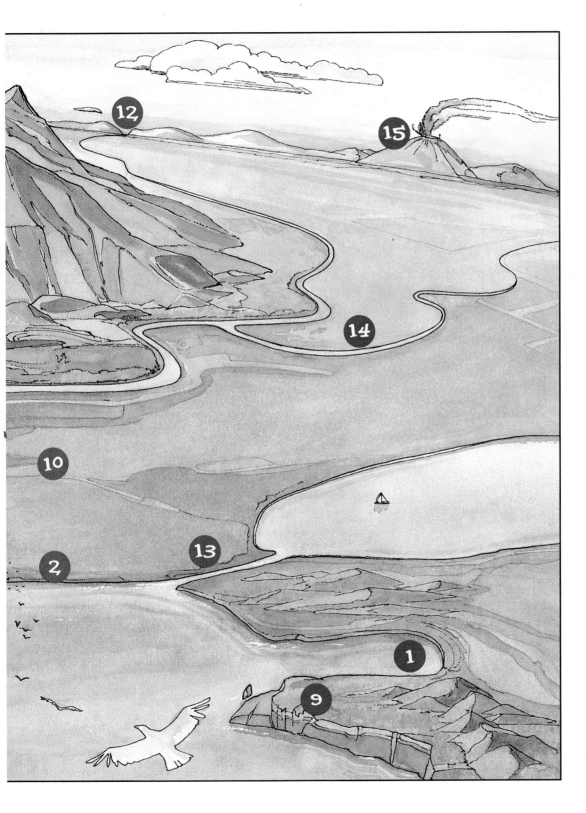

6 **mountain range** A mountain range is a group of connected mountains or steep, high land areas.

7 **mouth of a river** A river mouth is the place where a river flows into a larger body of water.

8 **ocean** The oceans are the entire body of salt water that covers almost three fourths of Earth's surface.

9 **peninsula** A peninsula is a piece of land that is surrounded by water on three sides.

10 **plain** A plain is a broad stretch of level or nearly level land.

11 **plateau** A plateau is a large, level area of high land.

12 **source of a river** A river source is the place where a river begins.

13 **strait** A strait is a narrow waterway that connects two larger bodies of water.

14 **tributary** A tributary is a stream or river that flows into a larger river.

15 **volcano** A volcano is a mountain that builds up around an opening in Earth's surface. Under the opening is hot, melted rock.

Land AND People

How Do People in Different Places Live?

Explore the land that is America. Then learn how some Native Americans, Africans, and Europeans lived before they were thrust together in the Americas.

A LAND OF

The physical features of the United States affected the way our nation has developed and grown since it was first explored and settled.

▼ Find out what parts of America you can explore on page 12.

CONTENTS

GREAT VARIETY

These books tell about some people and places that are part of the story of our nation's geography and natural resources. Read one that interests you and fill out a book-review form.

READ AND RESEARCH

Adventures in Your National Parks edited by Donald J. Crump (National Geographic Society, 1988)
America's national parks help to preserve the country's natural beauty for all of us to see. Breathtaking photos show people taking part in park activities, such as wading in the Everglades and exploring Crater Lake. *(nonfiction)*

Going Places: The Young Traveler's Guide and Activity Book by Harriet Webster, illustrated by Gail Owens (Macmillan Publishing Co., 1991)
Reading this book will be fun as you learn tips on how to become a successful traveler in the United States. You will also learn much about what makes our country fascinating to explore. *(nonfiction)*

John Muir by Eden Force (Silver Burdett Press, 1990)
When you are thrilled by the sight of California's towering redwoods and struck by the majesty of Yosemite's granite cliffs, you can thank John Muir. Read how he heroically fought to save our wilderness areas for future generations. *(biography)*

The Nystrom Atlas of Our Country edited by Charles Novosad (Nystrom, 1996)
Use the variety of maps contained in this atlas to learn about the history and geography of the United States. With the help of photographs, time frames, art, and graphs, your knowledge of our country will grow. *(nonfiction)*

Reading a Temperature Map

You can use a temperature map to help you learn about different sections of the United States.

UNDERSTAND IT

Has your family ever taken a trip to another part of the United States? If so, how did you decide on what kind of clothes to pack? Did you take T-shirts and shorts? Or did you take a warm jacket and a sweater? Your decision probably depended on what your family knew about the average temperature of the place you were going to for the time of year in which you were traveling.

MESA VERDE NATIONAL PARK COLORADO

EXPLORE IT

Temperature measures the amount of heat in the air. A *temperature map* gives the average temperatures in an area over a period of time, such as a month. The map of the United States on the next page gives the average temperatures in July. The map key uses colors to show degrees Fahrenheit. Use the map and the map key to answer these questions.

1. What is the average July temperature in Indiana?

2. What are the average July temperatures in Texas?

3. What two states have areas that have average July temperatures above 90°F?

4. Which state has the lowest average July temperatures?

MOUNT RUSHMORE
BLACK HILLS SOUTH DAKOTA

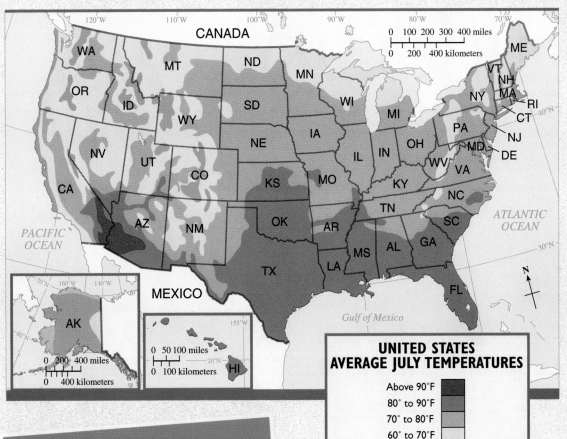

UNITED STATES
AVERAGE JULY TEMPERATURES

Above 90°F
80° to 90°F
70° to 80°F
60° to 70°F
50° to 60°F
40° to 50°F

TRY IT

Look at the map above and the map on page 10 that shows average January temperatures. Choose a part of the country that has average January or July temperatures that are different from the area in which you live. Plan a trip to that part of the country. Describe the kinds of clothes you would take. Include clothing you would take in case the actual temperature is 20° cooler or warmer than the average.

SKILL

POWER SEARCH
Use the temperature map on page 10 to write five questions. Trade questions with a classmate and answer them.

1 Setting the Scene

★ **KEY TERMS**

history
geography
metropolitan area
natural resource
region
climate

OUR COUNTRY

FOCUS *The United States has spectacular mountains, lakes, rivers, valleys, deserts, and plains. People from many different cultures live and work together here.*

This land is your land, — This land is my land
From California — to the New York island;
From the redwood forest — to the Gulf Stream waters;
This land was made for you and me.

Woody Guthrie

Our Wonderful Land

Look around you—at your city or town, your county, your state, your country. Just by looking, you can tell that the United States is a land of great variety. Your community is not exactly like any other community in your state. And your state does not look just like the state next to it.

That is because the United States contains seacoasts, mountains, lakes, rivers, marshes, valleys, deserts, canyons, and grasslands. Each of these landforms features different kinds of plant and animal life. The area in which you live has grown and developed differently than other areas of our nation. Our country's landforms have affected our country's **history** in many ways. But before we begin to study our country's history, we must first understand its **geography**.

 history The study of past events and people
geography The study of the earth and how people use it

A Snapshot of America

A snapshot is a photo. Could you take *one* photo to show what our country looks like? As you have read, the country is different in different areas. You might be able to take a picture of your neighborhood or a natural wonder. But it would be hard to capture the country's variety in just *one* photo.

One reason is that our country is very large. Find the United States on the world map on pages 586–587 in the Atlas. With its 3.6 million square miles, the United States takes up about 6 percent of the world's land area. That makes it the fourth largest country, after Russia, Canada, and China.

More than 250 million people live in the United States. That's about 5 percent of the world's 5.4 billion people. Only China and India have larger populations. Compared with its neighbors, the United States has a huge population. It has about three times as many people as Mexico and nearly ten times as many people as Canada.

Who We Are

The United States is a diverse country made up of people from many different backgrounds. Many thousands of years ago the first Americans came here from Asia. Beginning in the late 1400s, people began arriving here from Europe. Over the years, people came here from many countries throughout the world. Immigrants, or people who were born in other countries, continue to come to the United States. Almost 20 million people living here today were born in other countries. That's 8 percent of the population. The largest group of immigrants in the 1980s and 1990s has come from Mexico. The second largest group immigrated from the Philippines. Between the 1970s and the 1990s large numbers of immigrants also came from Cuba, Vietnam, China, Korea, and Russia.

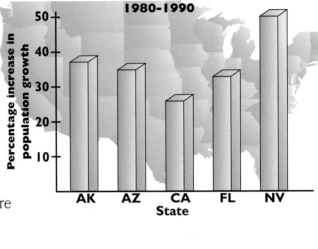

Fastest Growing States in the United States 1980-1990

(Bar graph. Y-axis: Percentage increase in population growth, from 10 to 50. X-axis: State — AK, AZ, CA, FL, NV)

- AK: about 37
- AZ: about 35
- CA: about 26
- FL: about 33
- NV: about 50

Emma Lazarus's poem "The New Colossus" is inscribed on the Statue of Liberty.

Give me your tired, your poor,
Your huddled masses yearning to breathe free,
The wretched refuse of your teeming shore.
Send these, the homeless, tempest-tost to me.
I lift my lamp beside the golden door!
—Emma Lazarus, 1883

Where We Live

Americans have always been on the move. Up until the 1800s, many Americans made their living farming, hunting, and fishing. Then some Americans moved to cities as industries grew there. Although farming is still a major occupation in the United States, today about 80 percent of all Americans live in or near cities. About half of them live in **metropolitan areas**.

In recent years, Americans have been moving to southern and western states. These areas have experienced more population growth than the North or the East. This movement has resulted in rapid population growth in states such as Alaska, Arizona, California, Florida, and Nevada. Today about 56 percent of the population lives in either the West or the South.

metropolitan area An area made up of a large city or several large cities and the surrounding towns, cities, and other communities

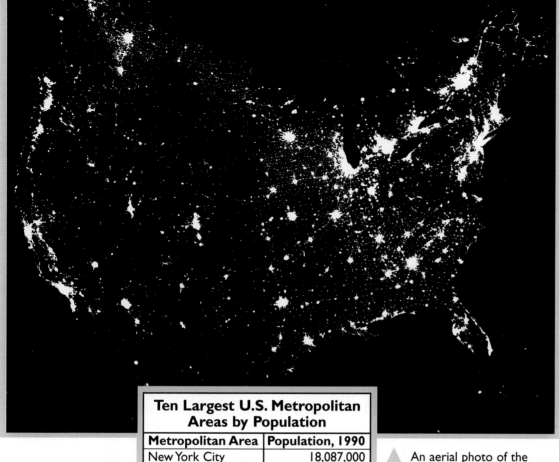

Ten Largest U.S. Metropolitan Areas by Population	
Metropolitan Area	Population, 1990
New York City	18,087,000
Los Angeles	14,532,000
Chicago	8,066,000
San Francisco	6,253,000
Philadelphia	5,899,000
Detroit	4,665,000
Boston	4,172,000
Washington	3,924,000
Dallas	3,885,000
Houston	3,711,000

An aerial photo of the United States taken at night

Population Regions

Look at the photo of the United States on the top of this page. It was taken at night from a satellite in space. The lighted spots in the photo show the areas in which the greatest number of people live. Even though the photo isn't labeled, you can easily see where the largest cities are. The brightest glow on the Atlantic Coast includes Boston, New York City, Philadelphia, and Washington, D.C.

There are good reasons that people choose to live in certain places. Many American cities are located on the seacoast, along major rivers, or on the Great Lakes. These waters provide transportation, which is essential for trade. Take a look at the list of the top ten metropolitan areas. Four of the top five cities are located on either the East Coast or the West Coast. The other city, Chicago, is located on Lake Michigan. Some cities also grew because they were located close to natural resources needed to fuel industry.

SHOW WHAT YOU KNOW!

REFOCUS
COMPREHENSION

1. Where do most Americans live?

2. Name three kinds of regions.

THINK ABOUT IT
CRITICAL THINKING

Why is it important for our country to have resources?

WRITE ABOUT IT
ACTIVITY

Describe the climate of your state and tell how it affects the way you live. Use the maps on pages 5 and 10 for reference.

REGIONS OF THE UNITED STATES

FOCUS *The United States has nine physical regions. Each has unique features that distinguish it from other regions of the nation.*

Nine Special Regions

You have already learned about some ways to study regions of the United States. Another common way to study the country is to look at its distinct landforms, or physical regions. Geographers have identified seven physical regions within the 48 contiguous (kun TIHG yoo us), or adjoining, United States, shown on the large map on page 13. These regions are the Coastal Plain, the Appalachian (ap uh LAY chun) Highlands, the Interior Lowlands, the Great Plains, the Rocky Mountains, the Intermontane West, and the Pacific West. In addition, the United States includes two other distinct regions—Alaska and Hawaii. They are shown in the two inset maps on page 13.

Most of the early Europeans and Africans who came to North America arrived on the Atlantic Coast. They moved westward over the years, eventually reaching all of the landform regions of the United States. Native Americans, who reached America long before Europeans and Africans, arrived in present-day Alaska and moved east and south from there.

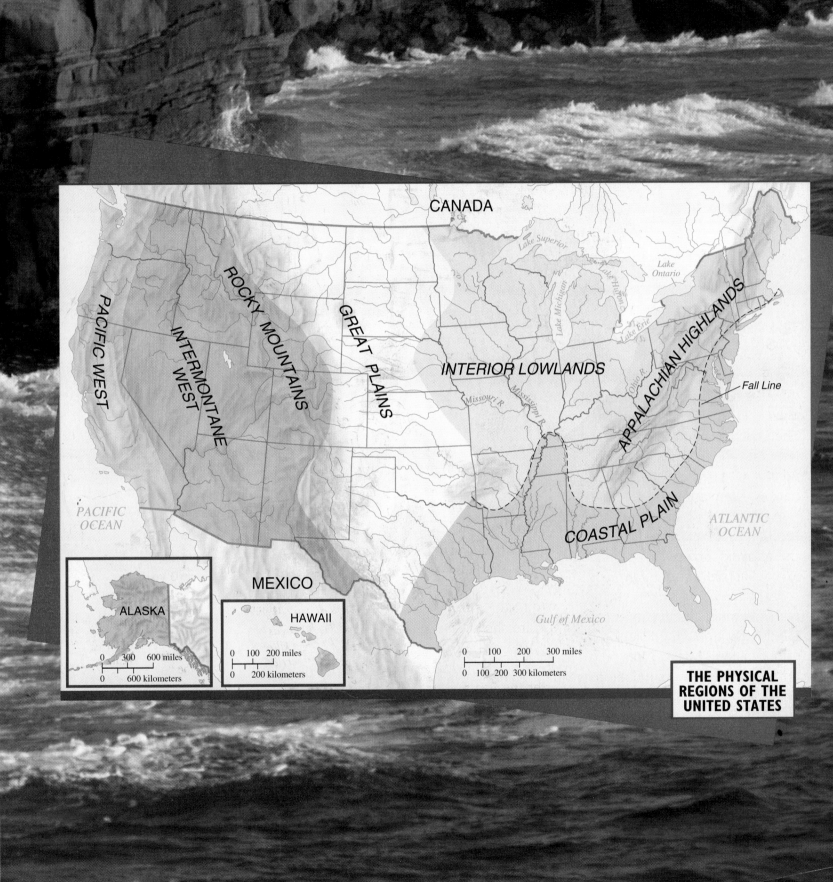

CANADA

Lake Superior

Lake Ontario

Lake Michigan

Lake Huron

Lake Erie

PACIFIC WEST

ROCKY MOUNTAINS

INTERMONTANE WEST

GREAT PLAINS

INTERIOR LOWLANDS

APPALACHIAN HIGHLANDS

Fall Line

Missouri R.

Mississippi R.

Ohio R.

PACIFIC OCEAN

COASTAL PLAIN

ATLANTIC OCEAN

MEXICO

Gulf of Mexico

ALASKA

0   300   600 miles

0   600 kilometers

HAWAII

0   100   200 miles

0   200 kilometers

0   100   200   300 miles

0   100   200   300 kilometers

THE PHYSICAL REGIONS OF THE UNITED STATES

13

The Coastal Plain

As you can see from the regional map on page 13, most of the land along the Atlantic Ocean and the Gulf of Mexico is a plain, or area of flat land. The Coastal Plain reaches from southern New England to Texas. Along the Atlantic Ocean the plain is often very narrow—sometimes only 20 or 30 miles wide. Along the Gulf of Mexico, it is much wider, reaching several hundred miles inland. The soil in this region is sandy and makes good farmland.

Many rivers, such as the Potomac (puh TOH muk) and the Savannah (suh-VAN uh), cut through this region. Several of our nation's largest cities began as ports where the rivers meet the ocean. The Coastal Plain has fine beaches along the Atlantic and the Gulf of Mexico. The region's low elevation gives it many swamps, marshes, and lagoons. One of the world's best-known wetlands is the Everglades in Florida.

> plain   A wide area of flat or gently rolling land
> elevation   The height of land above sea level

▲ Alligators call the southern part of the Coastal Plain home.

▼ The Appalachian Mountains are popular with hikers.

The Coastal Plain also includes the most southerly part of the Mississippi River. This part of the plain, known as the Mississippi Delta, is a vast area of sand, silt, and mud. Because the land is so low, it is in constant danger of flooding.

Appalachian Highlands

Find the Appalachian Highlands on the map on page 13. The mountains in this region have different names in different states. They are the Green Mountains in Vermont, the Catskill Mountains in New York, and the Blue Ridge Mountains in Virginia and North Carolina. A few peaks are over 5,000 feet high. The Appalachians were a major barrier to transportation and moving west for early settlers.

The population of the Appalachian Highlands is fairly low. That's because

Wheat grows in the Interior Lowlands.

cattle, and dairy cows.

The region is also rich in natural resources such as coal and petroleum. Such resources are essential for the development of heavy industry. Two great cities in the Interior Lowlands grew up around railroads or industry. Chicago's growth revolved around railroads. And Detroit's growth came from manufacturing automobiles.

the land is rugged and the soil is poor for farming. But it does have grazing land for cattle and sheep. Also, parts of the region are rich in resources such as coal, oil, and timber.

Interior Lowlands

The Interior Lowlands covers the center, or *interior*, of the United States and is lower than the regions around it. The great feature of this region is the Mississippi River. Several other large rivers cut through the region and empty into the Mississippi. These include the Ohio and Missouri rivers.

Sediment from these rivers has helped to enrich the soil. This, plus a humid climate and flat land, makes the region one of great agricultural productivity. Farmers here specialize in raising crops such as corn, wheat, and soybeans. In addition, they raise hogs,

Great Plains

The Great Plains is a large, flat, fairly dry area between the Rocky Mountains and the Interior Lowlands. The land's elevation rises gently as you travel westward. Near the Rockies, the Great Plains reaches more than 5,000 feet in elevation. The region gets less than 20 inches of rain a year, and there are few trees except along the edges of rivers. The region's grassland, however, is ideal for grazing cattle.

Rodeos are common in the flat Great Plains.

 sediment Matter that settles to the bottom of a liquid

"Old Faithful" is one of the natural wonders in Yellowstone National Park.

Large rivers, such as the Platte and the Kansas, flow west to east from the Rockies. Some of these rivers were followed by early settlers heading westward in covered wagons. The dryness of the Great Plains kept most people from settling there. That's why today the region has few large cities. Denver began as a small mining town but became a major city. It is on the Great Plains and also on the edge of the Rocky Mountains.

Rocky Mountains

Many peaks in the Rocky Mountains, such as Pike's Peak and Snowmass in Colorado, are over 14,000 feet in elevation. The Rocky Mountains, like the Appalachians, were a barrier to transportation. Severe, unpredictable weather made the Rockies a hazard to pioneers trying to move west. Early adventurers came to the Rockies to mine the region's rich deposits of gold, silver, and copper.

The rugged land and cold weather have kept this region sparsely settled. Some small cities have grown up as important ski resorts. These include Vail and Aspen in Colorado and Sun Valley in Idaho. Tourists flock to the Rockies to enjoy skiing, hiking, and backpacking. Two famous **national parks** are found here—Yellowstone, mostly in Wyoming, and Glacier in Montana.

Intermontane West

The Intermontane West is located between the Rocky Mountains and the mountains of the Pacific West. *Intermontane* means "between the mountains." This region is a vast area of deserts and dry lands. In this region, mountains alternate with flat areas called **basins**.

These areas are flat because over the ages they filled with sediment. When it

---

national park   An area of scenic beauty maintained by the federal government for the public to visit

basin   A wide, deep area bounded by higher elevations

A cactus blossoming in the desert ▶

rained, many streams overflowed into the deserts and then dried up, leaving the sediment behind. The Great Salt Lake in Utah formed in this way.

Only a few rivers cut through this region. But the results can be spectacular. The Colorado River, for example, has carved out the Grand Canyon. Some of the nation's largest dams, including the Hoover Dam on the Colorado River, are here. They provide a steady source of water, making it possible for cities such as Las Vegas and Phoenix to grow.

Pacific West

The Pacific West is a region of mountains and valleys. The Coast Ranges are located near the Pacific Ocean and extend through Washington, Oregon, and California. Farther inland there are more mountains—the Cascades in the north and the Sierra Nevada in the south.

In between the mountain ranges are some of the most fertile valleys in the world. These include the Willamette Valley in Oregon and the Central Valley in California. The Pacific West region is also rich in resources such as petroleum, fish, minerals, and forests.

Alaska and Hawaii

Alaska and Hawaii are two regions that are not located in the contiguous United States. Alaska is a vast,

Redwood trees are found only in the Coast Ranges ▶

mountainous region that lies far to the north. The climate is very cold, with long, bitter winters. In the summer, temperatures rise well above freezing. Most people who live in Alaska live in the southern part of the state where temperatures are warm enough in summer to allow for some farming.

Hawaii is made up of a series of islands in the Pacific Ocean. These islands are the tops of volcanic mountains that rise from the floor of the ocean. Much of Hawaii's income comes from tourists who enjoy its warm climate, pretty scenery, and beautiful beaches. Sugar, pineapple, and coffee are also important sources of income.

SHOW WHAT YOU KNOW!

REFOCUS
COMPREHENSION

1. List nine regions of the United States.

2. Compare and contrast the Coastal Plain and the Appalachian Highlands.

THINK ABOUT IT
CRITICAL THINKING

National parks are public property—they belong to all Americans. Why is it important to take care of and preserve these areas?

WRITE ABOUT IT
ACTIVITY

Which region do you live in? Describe its landforms and natural resources.

Citizenship

KEY TERMS
conservation
nonrenewable
resource
fossil fuel

CONSERVING OUR RESOURCES

FOCUS *More and more Americans have begun to realize the importance of conserving our country's resources.*

▲ Students in Los Angeles found ways to recycle plastic and build a playground.

Testing riverbeds for pollutants ▶

Taking Action

You have learned about the great natural beauty and variety of the United States. All over the country, people are now taking action to preserve that beauty and variety. In Everett, Washington, they have stopped companies from dumping waste into a nearby creek. In West Milford, New Jersey, they have convinced schools not to use disposable plastic food trays in cafeterias. In Austin, Texas, they have organized the Children's Alliance for Protection of the Environment to clean up local beaches.

conservation The care, protection, or management of natural resources

Why Conservation Is Important

These people—adults as well as children—are part of a growing movement to preserve the environment. As they have shown, this movement is not limited to powerful lawmakers or wealthy foundations. It has been started and helped along by people of all ages.

Conservation is important in assuring that our nation's natural resources are not being wasted or destroyed. Many natural resources are **nonrenewable resources**. *Nonrenewable* means we can't make any more of

nonrenewable resource A resource of which there is a limited supply

Conserving Resources

Here are a few simple things that you can do to help save the environment and our natural resources.

● Recycling aluminum cans, glass bottles, plastic bottles, and paper products reduces what we throw away.

● Conserving water helps save our limited usable water supply.

● Disposing of trash properly keeps the environment clean and safe for animals.

● Joining an organization or writing a letter to your representative or senator will let people know your concerns about the environment.

● Planting a tree provides homes for birds and animals and air for people and animals to breathe.

SHOW WHAT YOU KNOW!

REFOCUS
COMPREHENSION

1. List some examples of renewable resources and nonrenewable resources.

2. Although trees are a renewable resource, why is it important for us to be careful about how we use them?

THINK ABOUT IT
CRITICAL THINKING

Why is it the responsibility of all Americans to preserve natural resources?

WRITE ABOUT IT
ACTIVITY

Make a list of ways people can conserve both renewable and nonrenewable resources.

them. Once they are used up, they are gone from our lives forever. All **fossil fuels**—coal, petroleum, and natural gas—are nonrenewable resources.

Some resources are *renewable*. Renewable energy sources include water power, wind, and the sun. Although some resources are renewable, they must still be used wisely. For example, forests are renewable, but if we cut down too many trees at once, we may later face wood and paper shortages. Trees provide oxygen, which is necessary to maintain life on the earth.

fossil fuel　A nonrenewable energy source found underground

Saving Our Natural Resources

The chart above offers some simple ideas for conserving the earth's resources. Consider how you might use these ideas in your own life. After all, the earth belongs to all of us. We share the responsibility of caring for it.

As you read the remaining chapters in this book, think about how well the land and its resources have served us over the many years of our nation's history. Remember that if we use resources wisely, they will provide for us long into the future.

Map Adventure

LINKING OUR LAND

FOCUS In the 1950s, President Eisenhower began the Interstate Highway System to link the nation's regions. The resulting **interstate highways** made cross-country travel easier and safer, so Americans could explore their country.

NATIONAL PARKS AND INTERSTATE HIGHWAYS

- National parks
- 90 Interstate highways
- ⊛ National capital
- ★ State capitals

Adventure in Our National Parks

The Interstate Highway System stretches from the Pacific Coast to the Atlantic Coast and from our border with Canada to our border with Mexico. Each highway has a number and passes through many different states. By learning the way the highways are numbered, you can travel around the nation. Use the interstate highways on the map to reach many national parks.

Map Legend

1 Everglades National Park Created in 1934, this park is responsible for protecting the endangered ecosystem of southern Florida. Visitors take nature walks and boat rides to see exotic plants and animals.

2 Great Smoky Mountains National Park This is the nation's busiest national park, with over 8 million visitors a year. It covers 800 square miles and has over 270 miles of roads and 900 miles of trails. Hiking the trails, you can see the homes of people who lived here before the area became a park.

3 Badlands National Park This park is famous for its 100-mile strip of cliffs known as "the Wall." Carved over many years by water, these cliffs attract hikers and campers year-round. The park also has 35-million-year-old fossils embedded in its cliffs.

4 Yellowstone National Park Almost as big as the state of Rhode Island, Yellowstone National Park is the site of Old Faithful, the world-famous geyser. Near Old Faithful is the Upper Geyser Basin, a one-mile-long trail of geysers and boiling hot springs.

5 Grand Canyon National Park Every year over 4 million people visit the Grand Canyon. This park offers a 277-mile long canyon, hiking, mule trails, museums, and Native American ruins.

6 Redwood National Park This park has 110,000 acres of redwood trees, some of which are over 200 feet high. The federal government created it in 1968 to preserve the redwood trees, estimated to be over 400 years old.

⭐ **interstate highway** One of the network of highways connecting the regions of the United States
ecosystem A group of plants and animals and their environment
geyser A hot spring that shoots steam

MAP IT

Your family in Boston is planning to visit some national parks.
1. What interstate highways will you take to get to the Great Smoky Mountains National Park? In what direction will you travel on each road?
2. You are now on Interstate 40, headed from the Great Smoky Mountains to Badlands National Park. What are some north-south routes you could take to get from Interstate 40 to Interstate 90? What pattern do you see in the numbers of the north-south routes as you travel toward Badlands?
3. After you leave Badlands National Park, your next stop is Yellowstone National Park. What points of interest will you see there?
4. You are on your way to Redwood National Park from Yellowstone. You want to visit relatives in Olympia, Washington, on the way. What interstates will you take to Redwood National Park?

EXPLORE IT

Plan a route from Redwood National Park to the Everglades. Choose the national parks you want to visit on the way and the interstate highways that can take you there.

SUMMING UP

1 DO YOU REMEMBER . . .
COMPREHENSION

1. How does the United States compare in size and population with other countries?

2. Give some examples to show that the United States has many kinds of landforms.

3. You can divide a climate region into two other kinds of regions. What are they?

4. Name the physical regions of the United States.

5. Name three features of the Coastal Plain.

6. What is the most important river in the Interior Lowlands?

7. Why does the Great Plains region have few large cities?

8. What two regions are not located in the contiguous United States?

9. What might happen if Americans do not practice conservation?

10. Which national park is home to alligators? Where could you see 400-year-old trees?

2 SKILL POWER
READING A TEMPERATURE MAP

In this chapter you have learned to read temperature maps. Work with a small group to make your own temperature map. Use your local newspaper or television station to track the daily temperatures in several communities in your state for one month. Then make a map that shows the average temperatures in those communities for that month. Repeat your project in six months.

3 WHAT DO YOU THINK?
CRITICAL THINKING

1. Why have Americans been moving to the southern and western states recently?

2. Which natural resources found in the United States do you think early settlers considered most valuable? Would a person today have a different answer? Why?

3. Why are both the Appalachian Mountains and the Rocky Mountains no longer barriers to settlement?

4. If you could live in any of the nine physical regions of the United States, which would you choose? Why?

5. The President of the United States has appointed you head of a commission to decide what qualifies a place to become a national park. What will your rules be?

4 SAY IT, WRITE IT, USE IT
VOCABULARY

You are the teacher. Make up a quiz to test your students' understanding of the words below. Give your quiz to classmates and see how they do.

basin	interstate highway
climate	metropolitan area
conservation	national park
ecosystem	natural resource
elevation	nonrenewable resource
fossil fuel	plain
geography	region
geyser	sediment
history	

5 GEOGRAPHY AND YOU
MAP STUDY

Use the maps on pages 13 and 20 to plan a two-week automobile trip for your family.

1. You have decided to visit three places in three different physical regions. What are they? Where are they located?

2. What highways will you take to your first stop?

3. What highways will link the three places you want to visit?

4. List the states you will go through on your trip.

6 TAKE ACTION
CITIZENSHIP

It is very important to protect the environment and help with conservation. With a small group of classmates, find out about organizations in your community that work to save natural resources and preserve the environment. Choose an organization that you would like to work with. Call and ask what you can do to help. With permission, volunteer to work with the organization of your choice.

7 GET CREATIVE
SCIENCE CONNECTION

Find out more about conservation and find a subject that interests you. (An environmental organization in your community will help you find a subject of interest.) With a partner or by yourself, create a poster that promotes conservation in your school or community. You can use original art, take photographs, or create a collage to emphasize your message. Present your poster with other posters made by your classmates.

LOOKING AHEAD

In Chapter 2, learn about life in Europe, Africa, and the Americas before 1500.

CHAPTER 2

THREE

The first people to live in North America began to migrate from Asia many thousands of years ago. People from Europe and Africa also came here, but only after 1500. What was life like for some of these people before 1500?

CONTENTS

◀ What is this girl holding? Turn to page 30 to find out.

HOMELANDS

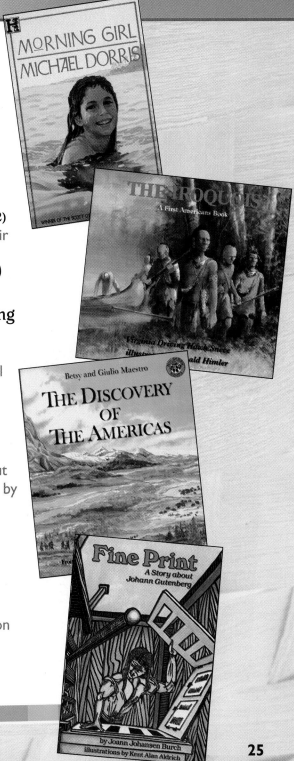

These books tell about some people, places, and important events before 1500. Read one that interests you and fill out a book-review form.

READ AND RESEARCH

Morning Girl by **Michael Dorris** (Hyperion Books for Children, 1992)
Listen to 12-year-old Morning Girl and her brother, Star Boy, describe their peaceful lives on an island in the Bahamas just before the arrival of Columbus in 1492. What will happen when the explorers arrive? *(fiction)*

The Iroquois: A First Americans Book by **Virginia Driving Hawk Sneve, illustrated by Ronald Himler** (Holiday House, 1995)
Among the first people to live in what is now New York State were the Iroquois. From the peacemaker Hiawatha to women in the nation, you will learn about many different people in the Iroquois society. *(nonfiction)*

The Discovery of the Americas
by **Betsy and Giulio Maestro** (William Morrow & Co., 1991)
At least 20,000 years ago, the discovery of the Americas began. Read about the groups of people and explorers who found their way to the Americas by land and by sea. *(nonfiction)*

Fine Print: A Story About Johann Gutenberg
by **Joann Johansen Burch, illustrated by Kent Alan Aldrich**
(Carolrhoda Books, 1991)
For over 30 years Johann Gutenberg struggled to invent a machine that would print books faster. Find out how important Gutenberg's contribution was to the world. *(biography)*

Writing a Research Report

Learning some simple steps to write a report will make your work easier and faster.

UNDERSTAND IT

You have to write a two-page social studies report. You've decided to do it on *Native American Ways of Life*. Right away, though, you have a problem. The encyclopedia article on *Native Americans* is 70 pages long, and you don't see anything about *ways of life*. What should you do?

Step 1 in writing a report is finding a suitable topic. *Native American Ways of Life* is too big and general for two pages. You have to narrow the topic.

To narrow a topic, get more specific. What group of Native Americans most interests you—the Hopis, Cheyennes, Iroquois, Seminoles? What is it about this group's way of living that gets your attention—their hunting or farming methods, their houses or religions or weapons? You can't cover them all in a short report, so choose one—Iroquois houses—and check the encyclopedia again.

EXPLORE IT

Once you've narrowed the topic, you're ready for *Step 2*—gathering information.

• Remember, your information should come from a variety of sources. Encyclopedias—in book version or on CD-ROM—are good places to start. Then check the library for other books and magazines. Your librarian can help you use databases, too.

• As you read, take notes on index cards. Write down any information that you might need. Don't copy anything word for word. Use your own words. On each index card, be sure to give the source of the information.

• Keep a list of the sources you use. Write the name of the source, the author, the publisher, the date of publication, and the page reference.

Step 3 is organizing your information. Organize ideas and information into categories. Then write a heading for each category: *Materials for Long Houses, How They Were Built,* and so on.

Step 4 is writing a first draft. Get your ideas down on paper in an order that makes sense.

Step 5 is the final draft. Make sure every sentence says exactly what you want it to say. Also be sure to check your spelling and punctuation.

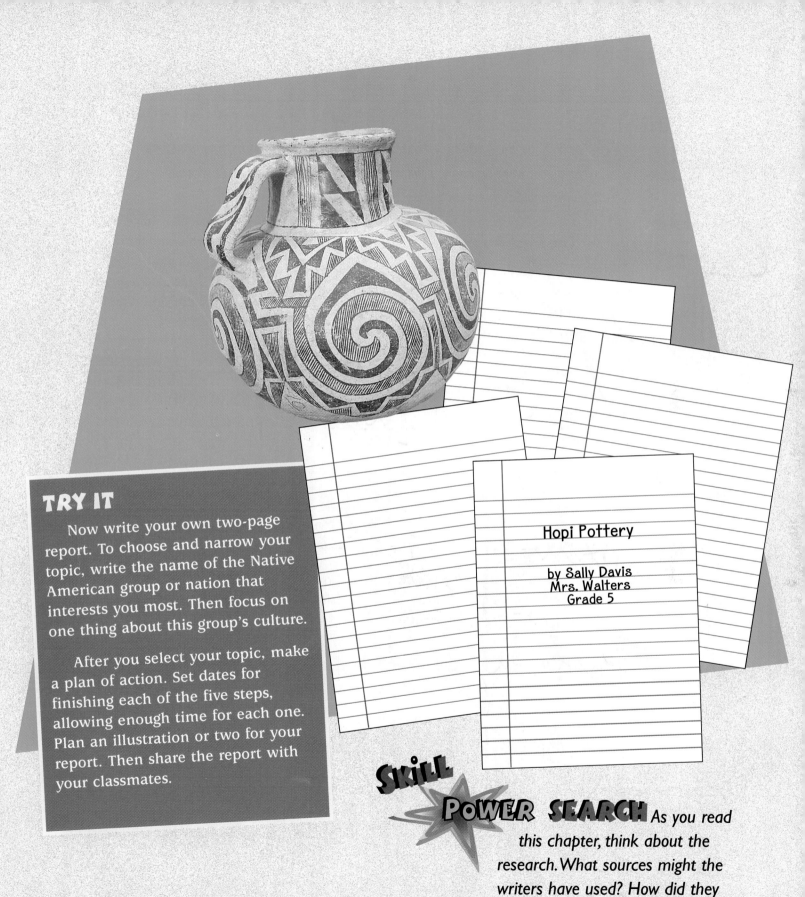

TRY IT

Now write your own two-page report. To choose and narrow your topic, write the name of the Native American group or nation that interests you most. Then focus on one thing about this group's culture.

After you select your topic, make a plan of action. Set dates for finishing each of the five steps, allowing enough time for each one. Plan an illustration or two for your report. Then share the report with your classmates.

Hopi Pottery

by Sally Davis
Mrs. Walters
Grade 5

SKILL POWER SEARCH As you read this chapter, think about the research. What sources might the writers have used? How did they organize their information?

KEY TERMS

migrate
nomad
environment
culture
mesa
long house

NATIVE AMERICANS

FOCUS *By the 1400s the Pueblos of the Southwest and the Iroquois of the Northeast were among the more than 500 nations of Native Americans living in North and South America.*

The First Americans

In Chapter 1 you looked at the geography of the United States. Now you will find out about the people. But there was a time, many thousands of years ago, when no people lived in the Americas. Over a very long period of time, people came here from Asia and then from Europe and Africa. In this chapter you will read about how some of these people lived in their homelands before 1500. In later chapters you will explore how, why, and when some of these diverse people left their homelands and came to the Americas.

The first people who came to North America **migrated** from Asia between 20,000 and 36,000 years ago. As shown on the map, Asia and North America are separated by a body of water called the Bering Strait. But 36,000 years ago, land connected Asia and North America.

This land bridge was over 1,000 miles wide. People crossed into North America on foot, looking for plants to

⭐ **migrate** To move from one place to another

Map: ROUTES OF THE FIRST AMERICANS

ASIA
ALASKA
Bering Strait
Bering Sea
NORTH AMERICA
ATLANTIC OCEAN
PACIFIC OCEAN
SOUTH AMERICA
Equator
ARCTIC OCEAN

ROUTES OF THE FIRST AMERICANS

→ First Americans

☐ Present-day land area

☐ Bering Strait Land Bridge

☐ Other land area during Ice Age

☐ Ice sheet

Hunters killed animals with sharp stone points attached to wooden handles.

eat and animals to hunt. Over thousands of years these people spread out through North and South America. You can see their migration routes on the map. Because they were the first people to populate the Americas, we refer to them as Native Americans or American Indians.

Nomads and Farmers

Early Native Americans were **nomads**, people who wander in search of food. They knew how to make spear points from hard stones. Their tools helped them hunt large animals, such as the woolly mammoth.

About 10,000 years ago the climate gradually became warmer. Much grassland turned to desert or forest, and many large animals didn't survive. Native Americans had to hunt smaller animals, fish, and gather fruits, nuts, and other vegetation. In time, some learned to farm, and this allowed them to become settled.

Native people lived in many areas of North America. Four of the major groups are shown on the map on page 30. Different **environments** greatly affected the way each group lived. As the members of each group found ways to cope in their new environment, they formed a unique **culture**.

Eventually there were more than 500 groups or nations of Native Americans. By the 1400s these nations totaled about 10 million people. Two groups who lived in very different environments were the Pueblos of the Southwest and the Iroquois of the Northeast.

Pueblo ruins at Mesa Verde, Colorado

The Pueblo People

Native Americans who were later called Pueblos lived in permanent villages. In fact, the word *pueblo* comes from the Spanish word meaning "village." The Pueblos built their homes, groups of which were also called *pueblos*, from materials found in their environment. Walls were made of local stone, and roofs were made of timber covered with tree branches and

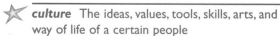

nomad A person who moves from place to place
environment The physical setting of a place, including everything that affects the way people live there: the land, air, water, plants, animals

culture The ideas, values, tools, skills, arts, and way of life of a certain people

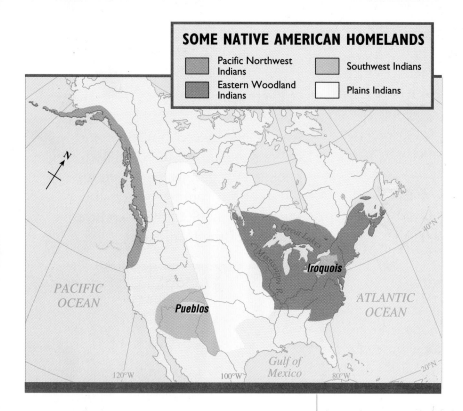

PACIFIC OCEAN

Great Lakes

Mississippi

Iroquois

Pueblos

ATLANTIC OCEAN

Gulf of Mexico

120°W   100°W   80°W   40°N   20°N

Pueblo Farming

The dry land and rocky cliffs made the Southwest a difficult place in which to live. But the Pueblos found ways to farm the land successfully. They watered their crops to make up for the lack of rain. People who didn't live near rivers made reservoirs to collect and store rainwater and mountain runoff. They even rolled huge snowballs off the mountains to melt in the reservoirs.

This water was used for growing crops such as corn, beans, peppers, and squash. Corn was the most important crop. Most days, and especially at times of celebration, Pueblos ate a corn bread called *piki* (PEE kee). They also grew cotton, which they wove into cloth for blankets and clothing.

Women and Men Share Work

Women made grinding stones, pottery, and baskets. Women also prepared and stored the food. Food storage was important because lack of rain could ruin crops. Men worked in the fields, collected building stones, and in many pueblos did the weaving, knitting, and embroidery. They also made arrows and other necessary tools.

earth. In some areas the Pueblos built their homes on top of flat plateaus or hills, called **mesas**. Houses were box-shaped, and as more houses were needed, they were built next to or even on top of others.

In areas where stone was scarce, houses were built out of a clay mixture called adobe (uh DOH bee). These homes, too, were built side by side and stacked on top of each other. Homes built closely together helped make villages safe from enemy attacks. Cliff-top locations, small doorways, and removable ladders made pueblos easier to defend.

mesa A flat-topped hill or small plateau with steep sides

Pots like this one were used to store food and water. Squash and beans were Pueblo crops.

◄ A reconstructed Iroquois long house

The Iroquois

The Iroquois also began building permanent homes and growing crops. The map on page 30 shows the extent of their territory. The Iroquois lived in long rectangular buildings called long houses. These were made of poles covered with bark shingles and were about 60 feet long, 18 feet wide, and 18 feet high. As many as 10 to 12 related families, each with its own living space and fire, occupied a long house. Usually a woman and her husband, their unmarried children, and their married daughters and families made up the household. When a son married, he moved into his wife's long house.

Sharing Responsibility

Iroquois divided work between men and women. Women grew corn and other crops, gathered wild vegetation, cooked, and prepared animal skins to make clothes and moccasins. Men fished and hunted for deer and elk.

Women and men shared political power. Women headed each household, but they chose male leaders to represent their households in village meetings. Men were the warriors, but women could prevent military excursions by withholding food and moccasins.

An Iroquois mask, ► or false face, worn for prayers and offerings

⭐ *long house* A large house built by Native Americans in which a number of families lived

SHOW WHAT YOU KNOW!

REFOCUS
COMPREHENSION

1. How did people first arrive in North and South America?

2. How did the environment of the Southwest affect the Pueblos' way of life?

THINK ABOUT IT
CRITICAL THINKING

What were some benefits for Native Americans of learning to farm?

WRITE ABOUT IT
ACTIVITY

Do some research to find out more about the Iroquois. Write about their family life.

LIVING IN A HOPI PUEBLO

Map Adventure

★ **KEY TERM**

topsoil

FOCUS *The Hopis were a Pueblo group living in an arid section of the Southwest. Finding water for crops in this region was difficult. However, the Hopis succeeded in building villages and growing a variety of crops.*

WHERE PUEBLO INDIANS LIVED

Pueblo peoples

Hopi pueblos

Adventure in a Hopi Pueblo

Hot days, cold nights, and about ten inches of rain each year made life difficult in a Hopi (HOH-pee) pueblo. The sun sucked up each drop of water, leaving the earth dry and lifeless. Summer rainfalls brought water, but their floods often spelled doom for young unprotected corn plants. The Hopis walked miles to their fields and toiled for hours, hoping that some of these plants would survive.

Map Key

1 **Pueblo** To protect themselves from attack, the Hopis built their pueblos on top of high mesas. Hopi pueblos were as large as five stories high. As many as 1,000 people might call a pueblo home.

2 **Corral** Here the Hopis kept animals, including wild turkeys. They also kept eagles. Corrals were made of either stones and mud or wooden posts.

3 **Rainwater pools** The Hopis dug pools in the top of the mesas to collect rainwater. In the winter, snowballs were put into the pools to melt.

4 **Gardens** Each family had a garden, where beans, peppers, and onions were planted. Small walls were built around each plant to keep in the water. Gardens were often located at the base of the mesas to catch the rain running down from the top.

5 **Underground spring** Underground springs were often found where the rain running down from the top of the mesa landed. Finding the underground water was difficult. Digging up too much of the hard topsoil might cause the underground water to dry up.

6 **Corn** The Hopis traveled miles to find the best places to plant corn and other crops. These were often at the base of mesas or near small streams. Corn was the most important crop. It was grown in the summer to take advantage of rainstorms. Seeds were planted deep into the ground so that roots could reach the underground springs.

7 **Field Shelters** Shelters were built on the edges of fields to provide shade from the sun. Many were built out of tree branches or stones. If fields were far from home, farmers built small pueblos to live in until the harvest.

⭐ **topsoil** The upper layer of soil

8 **Storage** Storing food was important for the Hopis, who faced cold winter months and frequent droughts (drouts), or dry spells. Each family had a room in the pueblo where a two-year supply of food was dried and stored.

MAP IT

Think about being a Hopi child living in a pueblo. Your mother is grinding corn into meal, using her metate (muh TAHT ay), or stone. She asks you to get more corn from your father, who is out in a field. Describe what you see as you go to find him.

1. As you near the fields, you hear men talking about planting a new field. Where might be a good spot? Why?

2. You cannot find your father. The villagers tell you he is resting from the hot sun. Where will you find him?

3. Your father tells you that the family's garden needs water. Where are you likely to find water for the plants? Trace the route you will take to get the water.

EXPLORE IT

The pueblo is getting crowded. Some people decide to build a new pueblo and plant their own cornfields. Look at the drawing and locate a good place for a new pueblo. Explain why you chose that spot.

PEOPLE OF WEST AFRICA

FOCUS *By the 1400s, kingdoms such as Ghana, Mali, and Songhai were among several large kingdoms that had flourished in West Africa.*

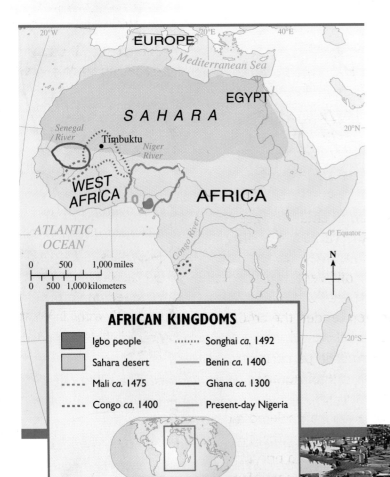

AFRICAN KINGDOMS

■ Igbo people	⋯⋯ Songhai ca. 1492
☐ Sahara desert	— Benin ca. 1400
----- Mali ca. 1475	— Ghana ca. 1300
····· Congo ca. 1400	— Present-day Nigeria

An Ancient Society

The first people who lived in Africa, about 2 million years ago, were nomads. Around 7,000 years ago they learned how to farm and raise animals. Although some groups remained nomadic, many settled to farm in small villages.

By the 1400s several great kingdoms had arisen in West Africa. You can find some of them on the map. The supply of gold and ivory in West Africa helped form these wealthy and powerful kingdoms. There were extensive trading networks and large cities where the arts and education flourished. Scholars studied science, law, and religion. Artists created sculptures, ceramics, and metalwork.

The Kingdom of Ghana

The first of these great kingdoms was Ghana. It controlled an important trade route through the Sahara Desert between West Africa, northern Africa,

► Present-day salt market on the Niger River

34

This head, made of zinc and brass, represents a king from West Africa.

and southern Europe. Ghana traded items within Africa, such as gold and salt. In fact, salt was so important that it was literally worth its weight in gold. In hot climates, people needed salt in their bodies to keep from losing too much water. Salt was also needed to season some foods and preserve others, especially meats.

In addition, the traders of Ghana exchanged gold, ivory, salt, and other objects for European clothes, horses, glassware, swords, and books. Ghana traders also bartered enslaved people, who were **slaves**.

Mali and Songhai

In the mid-1000s, Ghana was conquered. Soon, Mali replaced Ghana as the largest kingdom in West Africa. Like Ghana before it, Mali controlled important Saharan trade routes. In Mali, the city of Timbuktu (TIM buck TOO), was a center of culture and learning.

Mali eventually lost control of its outermost regions and by the early 1400s was replaced by Songhai (SAWNG-gye), the largest and most powerful of the three kingdoms. Other kingdoms of this time period were Congo and Benin. Congo reached its height between the 1300s and 1600s. Benin, known for its brass work, survived well into the 1800s.

slave A person who is enslaved and owned by another person

Life in West Africa

Farmers lived in small villages, growing rice and yams and raising cattle. Men and women were responsible for different kinds of work. Both worked in the fields, breaking up the soil. Women tended the crops and traded food and goods in the marketplaces and prepared meals. Men were in charge of hunting, fishing, and warfare.

Some people were considered more important than others. The most respected were nobles and priests, usually elderly men. Next came farmers, the largest category. Least respected were the slaves. People became enslaved in different ways. Some were captured in war, others were criminals, and still others sold themselves into slavery to repay debts. By the early 1600s, enslaved Africans were being forced on ships headed to the Americas.

SHOW WHAT YOU KNOW!

REFOCUS
COMPREHENSION

1. Name the three largest West African kingdoms.

2. Describe Ghana trade and trade routes.

THINK ABOUT IT
CRITICAL THINKING

Why were many people in these kingdoms farmers?

WRITE ABOUT IT
ACTIVITY

Make a chart showing the differences between men's and women's work in West African villages in the 1400s.

GROWING UP IN AN IGBO VILLAGE

FOCUS *Like children everywhere, African children had to learn many things on the road to adulthood.*

This mask is for a play in Igbo villages.

A Child's Life

What would it be like to grow up in West Africa in the 1400s? The answer would depend, in part, on which African **society** you lived in. Just as there were many groups of Native Americans, each with their own way of life, so too were there many African communities. One group, called the Igbo (IHG boh), lived in what is now Nigeria.

Suppose you were born into an Igbo family. Your first three years of life would be spent surrounded by family and friends and being showered with affection. Adults let you do just about anything you want.

West African girl carrying sticks

Soon, though, your carefree life comes to an end. By the age of three or four, you have chores to do. If you are a boy, you carry messages for your father. If you are a girl, you collect firewood for cooking. By age five or six, boy or girl, you also work in the fields. You spend long hot hours helping your parents grow yams and rice for the village.

As a young child, much of your free time is spent in the center of the village, mixing with other children. You do not go to a formal school. You often play games in the sand or wrestle with your friends.

 society People living together as a group with the same way of life

West African mother and child gathering rice

Girls Learn From Their Mothers

As Igbo children grow older, boys and girls begin to be separated from each other. Igbo girls spend much time with their mothers. They learn to sweep floors, prepare food, and polish the clay walls of their homes by using wet banana leaves. Since women do the trading, girls accompany their mothers to market, where they learn to bargain for oils, peppers, fish, and other goods.

Beginning at age four, girls also have to learn to carry water. No village can survive without fresh water, and often the nearest supply is a long way off. To bring water back, girls have to balance water pots on their heads. Imagine trying to carry a full pot of water on your head. Now imagine doing it while walking two miles through the hot morning sun in bare feet as insects swarm all around you!

Secret Societies for Girls

Mothers are not the only ones who teach Igbo girls. Some training comes from so-called secret societies. These groups, led by older unmarried girls, teach girls to make up songs, create new dances, sew special costumes, and prepare elaborate feasts. Igbo girls also take part in wrestling matches to see who is the strongest and most powerful among them.

These secret societies have rules governing girls' behavior. If you are an Igbo girl and you break the rules, you are fined. Did you leave trash lying around? Were you too lazy to help polish the walls of

Woman and child from Mali carrying water on their heads

a neighbor's new home? Did you skip some of your cleaning duties? If so, it will cost you. After paying a few fines, you will probably change your ways. This is how you will learn appropriate behavior.

Calabash, or gourd, carver of West Africa

Boys' Societies

Boys, meanwhile, have secret societies of their own. The boys' groups are even more organized and more secret than the girls' societies are. The boys' groups are set up in a separate part of the village and are off-limits to all girls and women—no sisters,

girlfriends, or mothers are allowed to visit here.

Boys learn many things in their secret societies, including archery and wrestling. They also learn the rules of fighting and become experts at using a long sharp knife called a machete (muh SHET ee).

From age five, boys spend most of their time in these secret societies. Their mothers still feed them. Their fathers still expect them to help with farm work and to carry clay from nearby pits so that new houses can be built. But beyond that, parents have little control over their sons. Whatever a boy needs to know, he learns from the other boys in his society.

Boys quickly figure out that life in a secret society is tougher than life with parents. If you are an Igbo boy and you misbehave around your parents, they may smile or shake their heads. But discipline is strong in your secret society. You need to learn how to behave before you can take your place as an adult in the village.

SHOW WHAT YOU KNOW!

REFOCUS
COMPREHENSION

1. What chores did Igbo boys do?

2. What chores did Igbo girls do?

THINK ABOUT IT
CRITICAL THINKING

Why were the secret societies so important to the Igbo people?

WRITE ABOUT IT
ACTIVITY

Write a paragraph telling what chores you are expected to do and how these differ from those of an Igbo child.

LIFE IN EUROPE

FOCUS *Europeans in the 1400s had clear ideas about how the world was ordered. By the end of the century, they were also developing national identities.*

Kings and Peasants

Europeans in the 1400s had different lives according to their rank, or position, in society. A person's position was based on wealth, political power, and the status of his or her parents.

Most powerful and important were kings. With the help of soldiers, kings tried to acquire territory.

People in a king's territory were expected to pay taxes, increasing his wealth. A king's power depended on the support of rich men who ran the local governments.

Most people were peasants, who had the lowest rank in society. Peasants were farmers who either owned or rented land in villages. But because farming was such hard work, villagers shared the work of

plowing, planting, and harvesting crops such as wheat, rye, barley, and oats. Many villages also had some land for grazing cattle and other livestock that everyone shared.

Work for Men and Women

Men were responsible for much of the work in the fields. At planting and harvest time, however, women helped,

▼ Working in the fields is the subject of this painting from the 1400s.

EUROPE IN 1450
- Major cities
— National boundaries

ENGLAND
London
Antwerp
Paris
FRANCE
HOLY ROMAN EMPIRE
Milan
Venice
SPAIN
Lisbon
Seville
Rome
Constantinople
Naples
PORTUGAL
AFRICA
ASIA
Black Sea
Mediterranean Sea

0° 10°E 20°E 30°E 40°E

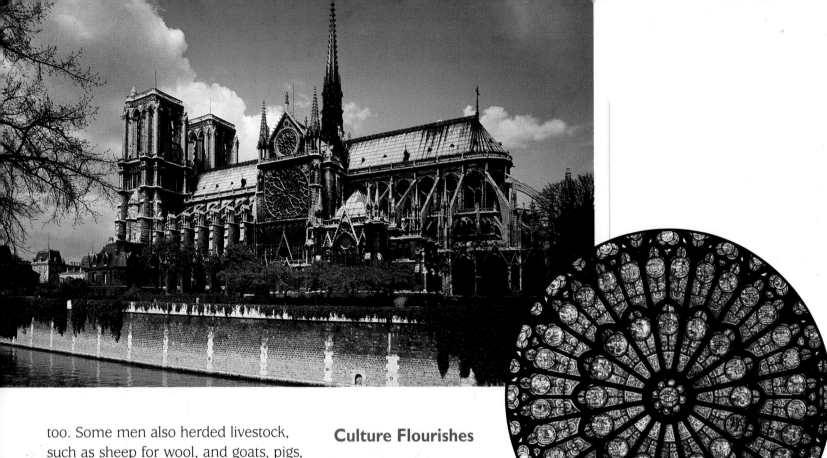

too. Some men also herded livestock, such as sheep for wool, and goats, pigs, and cattle for food.

Peasant women worked hard, milking cows and raising poultry. They cared for children, preserved food, cooked, spun thread for making clothing, and did other jobs necessary for maintaining the household.

Some poor peasants moved from the country to the cities in search of a better living. But even if they found jobs, they often remained poor.

Whether peasant or royalty, women in Europe had less status than men. Most Europeans believed that men were better suited than women to be political and religious leaders. Even though peasant women had huge responsibilities, men were considered heads of households.

Culture Flourishes

Important changes in education, art, architecture, and literature took place in Europe before 1500. Johann Gutenberg invented a printing press with moveable type in the 1440s. Within 50 years many presses were built. Now books and other printed materials were available in European cities.

Art and architecture flourished, often around religious themes. Huge cathedrals were built to glorify Christianity. These buildings had stained-glass windows that often depicted biblical scenes. Since most people couldn't read or write, they could "read" the Bible by looking at the windows. Elaborate paintings and **tapestries** served a similar purpose.

▲ Cathedral of Notre Dame de Paris and a stained-glass window from the cathedral

 tapestry An elaborate, heavy cloth with designs and scenes woven into it

Many fine works of literature were also produced. Some, called illuminated manuscripts, were hand-written, with decorative initial letters, designs in gold and silver, and miniature pictures.

Europe in a State of Change

Europe was emerging from a difficult period in the 1400s. During the 1300s there was not only widespread starvation but also a terrible plague, a deadly disease that travels from person to person. This Black Death killed one third of Europe's population.

Warfare, too, took its toll. Between 1337 and 1453, France and England, in a struggle for territory, fought a series of wars known as the Hundred Years' War. But this warfare helped

nationalism   A feeling of pride, loyalty, and devotion to one's country

bring about great changes in Europe. People began thinking in terms of national, rather than local, interests. A feeling of **nationalism**, or pride in one's country, developed. With this new way of looking at themselves, and with the years of famine and plague behind them, Europeans soon looked beyond their own borders and set out to explore other parts of the world.

Three Cultures Meet

As a result of exploration, Native Americans and Europeans came into contact for the first time in the Americas. Eventually, enslaved Africans were also forced to come. By the 1600s, Native Americans, Europeans, and Africans were living side by side in the Americas.

This page from a French book of the 1400s shows the activities of the farm year.

SHOW WHAT YOU KNOW!

REFOCUS
COMPREHENSION

1. What kind of work was done by peasant men and women?

2. Describe some ways in which culture flourished in Europe before 1500.

THINK ABOUT IT
CRITICAL THINKING

Why was the availability of books, made possible by Gutenberg's printing press, an important development?

WRITE ABOUT IT
ACTIVITY

Write a paragraph telling why a person might be proud of his or her nation.

SUMMING UP

1 DO YOU REMEMBER . . .
COMPREHENSION

1. When did the first Native Americans settle in North America?

2. About how many Native Americans lived in North America in the 1400s?

3. How were Pueblo houses different from Iroquois houses?

4. Why were Hopi homes built on mesas?

5. What led Ghana to become a great kingdom in Africa?

6. What types of work did women do in West Africa? What work did men do?

7. If you were an Igbo girl, what might you learn in your secret society?

8. What did Igbo boys learn in their secret societies?

9. Why was Johann Gutenberg's invention so important?

10. What serious disease killed one third of Europe's population in the 1300s?

2 SKILL POWER
WRITING A RESEARCH REPORT

In this chapter you read about many possible topics for a research report. Choose three topics you've read about and narrow them to about the right size for a report. Then list three likely sources you might use to find out more information about each topic.

3 WHAT DO YOU THINK?
CRITICAL THINKING

1. The land bridge crossed by the first Native Americans is no longer there. (See map on page 28.) Tell what you think happened to it.

2. Would you rather live in a Hopi village or in an Iroquois village? Give reasons for your choice.

3. Why did trade instead of farming lead to the rise of large kingdoms in Africa?

4. What institutions in your community might play some of the same roles that secret societies did for the Igbo?

5. Why do you think Europeans wanted to explore other parts of the world?

4 SAY IT, WRITE IT, USE IT
VOCABULARY

You've just traveled by time machine to North America in the 1400s to visit Iroquois and Hopi settlements. In a letter to a friend, describe what you see. Try to include most of the vocabulary words in your letter.

culture	nomad
environment	slave
long house	society
mesa	tapestry
migrate	topsoil
nationalism	

5 GEOGRAPHY AND YOU

MAP STUDY

Use the map below and the ones on pages 28, 30, and 34 to answer the following questions.

1. Name the major cities in Europe in 1450.

2. What body of water now separates Asia and North America?

3. Which Native American group lived near the Pacific Ocean?

4. In what direction would you travel to go from West Africa across the Sahara Desert to Europe?

6 TAKE ACTION

CITIZENSHIP

Taking pride in one's country is very important. With a group of classmates, make a list of things about the United States that make you very proud. Tell what it is about each item that gives you this sense of pride. What other things make you proud?

7 GET CREATIVE

LANGUAGE ARTS CONNECTION

Look at the traditional designs on the Pueblo pot and the African calabash in this chapter. Or find other traditional Native American and African designs in library books. Choose one design and describe something about that design.

LOOKING AHEAD In the next chapter you will learn more about why Europeans set out to explore other parts of the world.

UNIT 2

Exploration AND Colonization

Why Do People Explore and Colonize?

Go back in time and find out what made people explore and colonize. Learn what happened when people from different cultures encountered one another and how people adapted to a new environment.

EXPLORATION

By the 1400s, Europeans' desire for riches had inspired them to travel to unknown places. At first the goal was to find a water route to Asia. In 1492, Christopher Columbus reached the Americas, and Europeans' knowledge of the world changed forever.

▼ This girl is holding a sextant. Find out what it was used for on page 52.

CONTENTS

These books tell about explorers and explorations of the 1200s, 1400s, and 1500s. Read one that interests you and fill out a book-review form.

READ AND RESEARCH

Pedro's Journal **by Pam Conrad** (Scholastic, 1992)
Pedro de Salcedo is a ship's boy aboard Christopher Columbus's *Santa María.* Read Pedro's journal about the excitement of finally reaching land.
(historical fiction)
• *You can read a selection from this book on page 58.*

Around the World in a Hundred Years: From Henry the Navigator to Magellan **by Jean Fritz** (G. P. Putnam's Sons, 1994)
In 1400 all maps had a space at the edge representing the "Unknown," a dangerous area that no one could explore and hope to return from. Travel with many different explorers on their journeys to find out more about the "Unknown." *(nonfiction)*

Marco Polo **by Zachary Kent** (Childrens Press, 1992)
Read about the life and journeys of the remarkable Marco Polo. Use the map at the end of the book to follow him as he travels through China and other Asian lands. *(biography)*

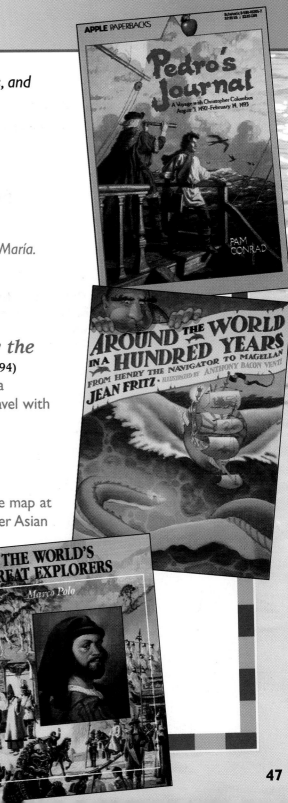

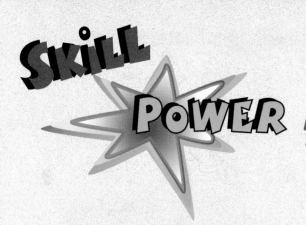

SKILL POWER
Tracing Routes on a Map

Knowing how to trace routes on a map can help you understand important information about the past.

UNDERSTAND IT

Have you ever had to explain to a friend how to get to your home or tell a new student where the cafeteria is? Then you know what a difference a map can make. Even if it's just a rough sketch on a scrap of paper, a good map clears up the confusion over where you're going in no time.

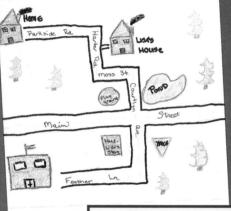

At one time there were very few maps. There was even a time when there weren't any maps of the continent of North America. That was the case when Spaniards began to explore what is now America. As explorers, part of their job was to create the first maps.

This is a modern-day map showing the routes that Cabeza de Vaca took. ▶

EXPLORE IT

Álvar Núñez Cabeza de Vaca (AHL vahr NOO nyethh kah BE thhah thhe VAH kah) could have used a good map. In 1528, after sailing across the Gulf of Mexico from Florida, he was shipwrecked near what is now Texas. Hoping to find a Spanish settlement, Cabeza de Vaca wandered for eight years across unmapped territory. Eventually, he reached a Spanish settlement in Mexico.

Cabeza de Vaca's route is shown on the map below. How many present-day states did he pass through during his long journey? According to the map key, when did his exploration take place?

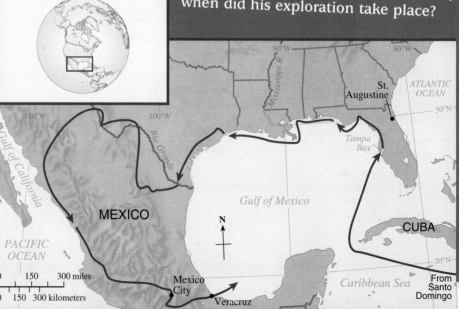

CABEZA DE VACA'S EXPLORATION

← Cabeza de Vaca, 1528–1536

— Present–day boundaries

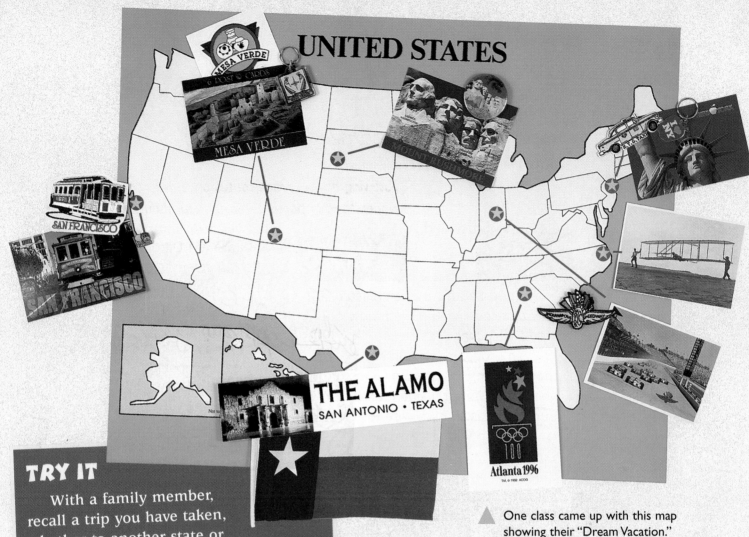

UNITED STATES

THE ALAMO
SAN ANTONIO · TEXAS

Atlanta 1996

One class came up with this map showing their "Dream Vacation."

TRY IT

With a family member, recall a trip you have taken, whether to another state or simply in your neighborhood. You might have made the trip by car, bus, train, or plane. On a local map, state map, or map of the United States, mark the two locations between which you traveled. Then draw in the route you followed between the two places.

With a group of classmates, create a "Dream Vacation" map. Each member of your group should first name one place in the United States that he or she would like to visit. Mark these locations on a map of the United States. Then trace the best route to follow to visit all these places and return home. You can decorate your map with pictures of the things you would see at each place.

SKILL POWER SEARCH

Can you find other maps in this book that show the routes of different explorers?

Setting the Scene

KEY TERMS

Crusade
empire
cartographer
northwest passage
conquistador
economy

EXPLORING THE WORLD

FOCUS *In the 1400s and 1500s, Europeans discovered that the world was a much larger place than they had previously imagined.*

Looking Outward

In the early 1400s, most Europeans had no idea that the continents of North and South America existed. It was by accident that their view of the world was changed forever.

Even though they didn't know about the Americas, Europeans were curious about the world outside their borders. European fascination with foreign lands began with the Crusades, a series of wars fought between Christians and Muslims. Muslims are followers of the religion of Islam. Christians believe in the religion of Christianity. The two groups were fighting over the Holy Land—a wide area around Damascus, Bethlehem, and Jerusalem, along the eastern coast of the Mediterranean (med ih tuh RAY-nee un) Sea. For many years Muslim rulers from Arabia had allowed Christians to travel to Jerusalem, a city sacred to Christianity. But in the late 1000s, Turkish Muslims conquered the area and cut off Christians' access to the city. For the next 200 years, thousands of Christian soldiers joined the Crusades to take the Holy Land from the Muslims.

Muslim Trading Centers

The tales that these crusaders brought back to Europe taught Europeans about the Muslims, who knew much about science, geography, and medicine. Europeans were also dazzled by news of Muslim trading centers full of exciting goods.

In the late 1200s the stories of an Italian merchant named Marco Polo again captured the

This map, made for Columbus, shows how some Europeans thought the Earth was shaped.

Crusade A Christian expedition to take the Holy Land from Muslims

1298	1394	1488	1492	1507
Marco Polo first tells about his journeys	Prince Henry is born	Bartholomeu Dias rounds the tip of Africa	Columbus reaches North America	America is named

1300   1375   1400   1450   1475   1500

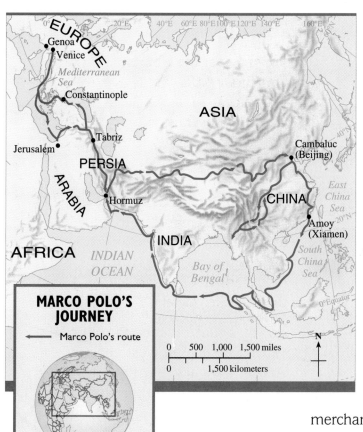

MARCO POLO'S JOURNEY

← Marco Polo's route

0   500   1,000   1,500 miles

0   1,500 kilometers

N

widely throughout Europe and influenced explorers for 200 years.

The Silk Road

For many years there had been a long overland trade route between Asia and some Arab and European cities on the Mediterranean Sea. Camels were used to carry goods 4,000 miles across mountains and deserts. This route is known as the Silk Road, for Asian silk was one of the main goods traded. The stories of crusaders and Marco Polo heightened the demand for Asian goods. But the few merchants who controlled the trade routes charged high prices for their

imagination of Europeans. Polo had traveled from Europe to China, India, and other places in Asia between 1271 and 1295. The map above shows the routes he took. Polo told of rich Asian **empires**, brilliant scholars, golden palaces, spices, silks, and jewels. A book describing his journey was read

 empire The lands and peoples ruled by a powerful ruler or group

▼ One artist of the 1300s depicted Marco Polo greeting China's ruler, Kublai Khan.

51

An artist of the time painted this portrait of Prince Henry the Navigator.

goods in the rest of Europe.

In the 1400s, parts of the Silk Road were blocked by Muslims, making the movement of goods along the route even more difficult. Europeans all over the Continent wanted easier access to Asia and its wealth. Would it be possible to *sail* there? Prince Henry of Portugal wondered.

Henry the Navigator

Born in 1394, Prince Henry was fascinated with ships, maps, and riches. And he had a dream—he wanted the Portuguese to find a water route east around Africa to Asia.

Prince Henry started a school to teach navigation, the science of figuring the course of a ship. Students at his school learned how to use a compass, which shows direction, and an astrolabe, an instrument used for determining location. They learned how to use a sextant, which measured distance to determine latitude and longitude. They learned how to read a map, and they learned about ocean currents. Students also learned how to use these skills to sail farther and farther away from the sight of the coast without getting hopelessly lost. By the late 1400s

new and better ship designs made ships faster and easier to sail. Sea captains then began to make voyages that reached farther and farther down the west coast of Africa. In 1488, Bartholomeu Dias (bahr too loo ME OO DEE us), who studied at the school, was the explorer who first rounded the southern tip of Africa.

Sailing West

Another of Prince Henry's students was Italian navigator Christopher Columbus. Columbus had read Marco Polo's stories of Asia. He hoped to find a water route to Asia, but he wondered: why not sail *west* to get there?

In 1492, Christopher Columbus sailed westward across the Atlantic Ocean.

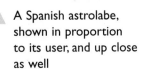

A Spanish astrolabe, shown in proportion to its user, and up close as well

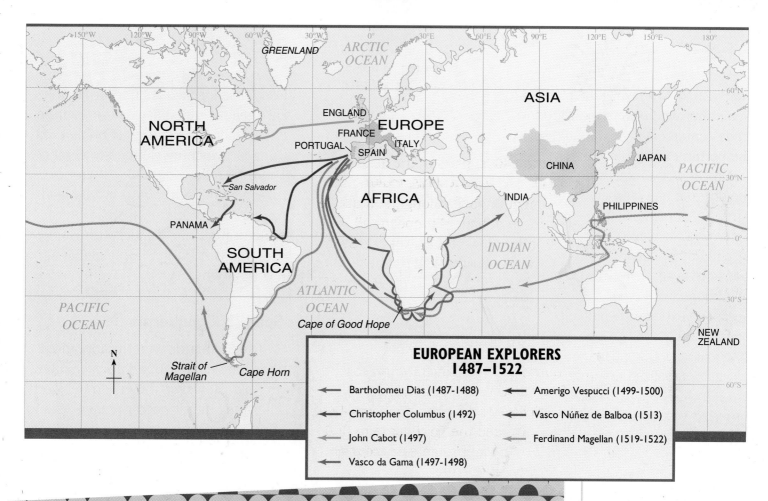

EUROPEAN EXPLORERS
1487–1522

⟵ Bartholomeu Dias (1487-1488)   ⟵ Amerigo Vespucci (1499-1500)

⟵ Christopher Columbus (1492)   ⟵ Vasco Núñez de Balboa (1513)

⟵ John Cabot (1497)   ⟵ Ferdinand Magellan (1519-1522)

⟵ Vasco da Gama (1497-1498)

EXPLORER	SPONSORING COUNTRY	PLACE REACHED
Bartholomeu Dias	Portugal	Rounds the southern tip of Africa
Christopher Columbus	Spain	Bahamas
John Cabot	England	North America
Vasco da Gama	Portugal	India
Amerigo Vespucci	Spain	South America
Vasco Núñez de Balboa	Spain	Reaches the Pacific Ocean by crossing Central America
Ferdinand Magellan	Spain	Philippines; His expedition is the first to sail around the globe

We were three months and twenty days without fresh food. We ate biscuit, which was no longer biscuit, but powder of biscuit swarming with worms. —**Pigafetta**, shipmate of Magellan

He reached land, which he claimed for Spain. But where were the glittering trade centers? Where were the spices, the perfumes, the silks?

Although Columbus didn't know it at the time, he had reached North America, not Asia. Still, Columbus's achievement inspired other countries to sponsor voyages west. You can read more about other European explorers beginning on page 60.

Eventually, European navigators realized Columbus's error. In 1500, Italian sailor Amerigo Vespucci (ah me REE-goh ves POOT chee) reached the coast of South America. His journey helped convince Europeans that a huge landmass lay between Europe and Asia. In 1507 a **cartographer**, or mapmaker, honored Vespucci by putting his first name, Amerigo, on this land. From then on, this landmass would be known as North America and South America.

A Northwest Passage?

Europe was still interested in finding a water route to Asia. Some explorers hoped they could sail around North America to get there. France sponsored several voyages in search of a **northwest passage** to Asia. In 1534,

A SHORTE AND briefe narration of the two Nauigations and Difcoueries to the Northweaft partes called NEWE FRAVNCE:

First tranflated out of French into Italian, by that famous learned man Gio: Bapt: Ramufius, and now turned into Englifh by Iohn Florio: Worthy the reading of all Venturers, Trauellers, and Difcouerers.

IMPRINTED AT LONdon, by H. Bynneman, dvvelling in Thames ftreate, neere vnto Baynardes Caftell.

Anno Domini. 1580.

This pamphlet is an English translation of the story of Jacques Cartier's journeys in America.

French sailor Jacques Cartier (zhahk kahr tee AY) sailed across the Atlantic and reached the shores of present-day Canada, which he claimed for France. There he followed the St. Lawrence River for miles, hoping it would lead him to Asia. It didn't. Instead, it brought him into contact with Native Americans from the Iroquois (IHR uh-kwoi) nation.

Spanish Conquerors

The Spaniards were disappointed that they hadn't found a water route to Asia. However, they soon decided that they didn't need to reach Asia to find riches. The American continents had treasures of their own. Beginning in the early 1500s, Spanish explorers came to South America searching for gold and silver. Some of the routes they took are shown on the map on page 55.

As you learned in Chapter 2, America was already home to a great many peoples. To get to the gold and silver, the Spanish explorers attacked many Native American societies and claimed their lands for Spain. These explorers were called **conquistadors**, which is Spanish for "conquerors."

The Columbian Exchange

Columbus's voyage brought together two worlds—Europe and the Americas. By

---

cartographer A person who makes maps
northwest passage A water route from the Atlantic Ocean to the Pacific Ocean through the arctic islands of Canada

conquistador Spanish conqueror of America in the 1500s

This Portuguese ship, painted by an artist of the day, was one that participated in the Columbian exchange.

the 1600s the relationship between Europeans and Native Americans had changed the way both groups lived. The exchange of goods and ideas between these two worlds became known as the Columbian exchange.

From Native Americans, Europeans learned to grow potatoes, corn, squash, pumpkins, and beans. These new sources of nutrition led to rapid population growth in Europe. Also, Europe's **economy** became stronger with the new supply of American gold and silver.

Native Americans, meanwhile, saw a new side to farming when Europeans arrived with cattle, pigs, and horses. The native people also learned to grow wheat,

rice, sugar, coffee, and bananas. But more than goods and ideas were exchanged. Disease, too, traveled across the sea. Native Americans had no resistance to European diseases, such as smallpox, chicken pox, whooping cough, and measles. These and other diseases killed hundreds of thousands of Native Americans.

SPANISH EXPLORERS 1539–1543

← Francisco Vásquez de Coronado, 1540–1542

← Hernan de Soto/ Luís de Moscoso, 1539–1543

0   200   400   600   800 miles
0   400   800 kilometers

NORTH AMERICA

Grand Canyon

Mississippi River

St. Augustine — 30°N

Tampa

Rio Grande

Gulf of Mexico

N

Cuba

PACIFIC OCEAN

Tenochtitlán

Caribbean Sea

110°W   105°W   100°W   95°W   90°W   85°W   — 20°N
— 25°N
— 35°N

⭐ **economy** The way in which natural resources and workers are used to produce goods and services

SHOW WHAT YOU **KNOW!**

REFOCUS
COMPREHENSION

1. What were some ways in which Europeans learned about Asia?

2. Why were Europeans looking for a water route to Asia?

THINK ABOUT IT
CRITICAL THINKING

Which of the explorers you read about do you think had the greatest impact on history? Give reasons for your answer.

WRITE ABOUT IT
ACTIVITY

Use pictures and words to describe the Columbian exchange.

55

CHRISTOPHER COLUMBUS

FOCUS *The voyages of Christopher Columbus opened new doors to European exploration of the world.*

A Teenage Boy, A Bold Idea

Christopher Columbus was born in Genoa in 1451. At that time Genoa was one of the great Italian port cities that traded goods arriving from the Silk Road. At the age of 14, Columbus took a job on a ship, and from then on the sea was his life.

By the late 1400s all the countries of Europe were competing to find an easy route to Asia—one that wasn't controlled by a few greedy merchants like those in Genoa and other Mediterranean ports. Many hoped to find a water route to Asia. Columbus took a fresh look at this idea. While everyone else was looking *east* to reach Asia, he looked *west*.

▲ Portrait of Columbus and one of several versions of his signature

The First Voyage

Columbus eventually found sponsors to pay for his exploratory voyage—King Ferdinand and Queen Isabella of Spain. In return he promised to bring them back great riches. In August 1492, Columbus set sail with three small ships—the *Niña,* the *Pinta,* and the *Santa María*—and a crew of about 90 sailors.

Early on the morning of October 12, one of his men spotted the small island that Columbus called San Salvador. After reaching the island, Columbus and his men were greeted by the local people, the Arawaks. Because Columbus believed he had reached the East Indies, he called these people "Indians." Columbus had actually come upon an island in what we now call the Bahamas, close to present-day Florida. Unknown to him, or to any other Europeans, two large continents lay between Europe and Asia—North America and South America.

Columbus presented the Arawaks with gifts of blue glass beads, red cloth caps, and small copper bells. The Arawaks gave gifts to Columbus, but none of these were the spices and gold he expected.

Columbus sailed on through the Caribbean Sea, searching for the great Asian cities described by Marco Polo. Though he found no gold and had not yet found China or Japan, he was sure he had reached Asia.

 East Indies The islands of Indonesia; in older times the East Indies also included India, Indochina, and the Malay Peninsula

This painting shows Columbus and his crew leaving Spain. ▶

A Colony in the Caribbean

In 1493, Columbus returned to the Caribbean and set up a Spanish colony on the island of Hispaniola (hihs pun-YOH luh). The Arawaks who lived there were described by Columbus as "very gentle." But Columbus believed that the Arawaks were inferior to Europeans, partly because he thought they had no religion.

The Arawaks did "not know what it is to be wicked, or to kill others, or to steal," wrote Columbus—but the sailors did. They stole from the Arawaks. Many Arawaks were enslaved and sold in Spain. An enslaved person is someone who is forced to work for another, often under brutal conditions.

From the sailors, the Arawaks also caught European diseases, which their bodies could not fight. Fifty years after Columbus's arrival, nearly all the Arawaks of Hispaniola were dead.

The Final Voyages

Columbus made two more voyages between 1497 and 1502, still looking for the fabulous cities of Asia. He sailed to Central America and South America, but he never reached his goal.

Although Columbus never found Asia, explorers from many European countries followed his route west, exploring what was to them a "new world." This world, however, had been home to many peoples for a great many years. The presence of Europeans in the Americas changed the lives of the native people forever as Europeans began to claim these lands as their own. The Americas would never be the same again.

The land is "full of trees of endless varieties, so high that they seem to touch the sky, and I have been told that they never lose their foliage. I saw them as green and lovely as trees are in Spain in the month of May."—Christopher Columbus, 1493, on the land he sighted that he named San Salvador

Pedro's Journal

by Pam Conrad

APPLE PAPERBACKS

Pedro's Journal
A Voyage with Christopher Columbus
August 3, 1492–February 14, 1493

PAM CONRAD

■SCHOLASTIC

Pedro de Salcedo worked aboard Christopher Columbus's Santa María *in 1492. He captured major events of the voyage in his journal.*

October 10: I am certain of this. . . . There is nothing out here. Surely we are lost. . . . This morning the men responded slowly to orders, scowling and slamming down their tools and lines. They whispered in pairs and small groups on deck and below. The air was thick with mutiny and betrayal, until finally everything came to a dead stop. . . .

"Enough," one of the men said. . . . "This is enough. Now we turn back."

Columbus paced the deck, telling them how close he figured we must be, that land could be right over the next horizon. He told them again of the fame and fortune that would be theirs if they could only last a little longer. And they laughed at him, the cruel laughter of impatient and defeated men.

"Let me offer you this," Columbus finally said. "Do me this favor. Stay with me this day and night, and if I don't bring you to land before day, cut off my head, and you shall return."

The men glanced at each other. Some nodded. "One day," they said. "One day, and then we turn around."

October 11 Through the day, the day that was to have been our last day traveling westward, many things were seen floating in the water, things that stirred everyone's hopes and had the men once again scanning the horizon. We saw birds in flocks . . . and even a stick was recovered that had iron workings on it, obviously man-made.

No one asked about turning back. . . . The men dispersed to their watches and their bunks, and the Captain paced the deck. I don't know why, but this night I stayed with him. I stayed still by the gunwale, watching over the side. Once in a while he would stand beside me, silent, looking westward, always westward.

Then, an hour before moonrise, the Captain froze beside me. "Gutierrez!" he called to one of the king's men on board, who came running. He pointed out across the water. "What do you see?"

Gutierrez peered into the west. "I don't see anything," he said. "What? What? What do you see?"

"Can't you see it?" the Captain whispered. "The light? Like a little wax candle rising and falling?"

The man at his side was quiet. I was there beside him, too, straining my own eyes to the dark horizon.

Suddenly another seaman called out across the darkness, "Land! Land!"

"He's already seen it!" I shouted. "My master's already seen it!" And the Captain laughed and tousled my hair.

Want to find out more about Pedro and Christopher Columbus? Check the book out of your school or public library.

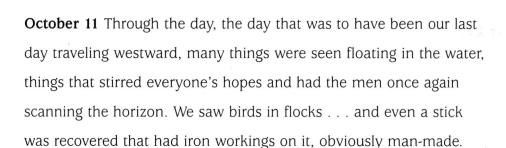

SHOW WHAT YOU KNOW!

REFOCUS
COMPREHENSION

1. How was Columbus's plan for finding a water route to Asia different from other people's plans?

2. Why did Columbus call the Arawaks "Indians"?

THINK ABOUT IT
CRITICAL THINKING

Why did Europeans claim lands in the Americas even though people already lived there?

WRITE ABOUT IT
ACTIVITY

Write how you would have felt about "turning back" on October 11, 1492, as a mate on Columbus's voyage.

WORLD EXPLORERS

FOCUS *During this period, Europeans set out to explore the world beyond their borders. Although they didn't always reach their goals, their journeys vastly expanded European knowledge of the world.*

FAILURE FOR ENGLAND

Like Spain, England sought a western route to Asia. In 1497, England paid for Italian John Cabot's trans-Atlantic voyage. Cabot and his crew spotted what they thought was Asia, but it was actually an island off Canada.

In 1498, Cabot headed west again, this time with a fleet of four ships in which to take home the riches he expected to find. But something went terribly wrong with Cabot's voyage. No one knows exactly what happened, but John Cabot and his small crew were never seen again. Disappointed, England sponsored no more westward journeys until the late 1500s.

TO AFRICA, AGAIN

In 1497, Portuguese sailor Vasco da Gama picked up where Bartholomeu Dias had left off. With a fleet of four ships, Da Gama rounded the southern tip of Africa, as Dias had done, and sailed on to reach India in 1498. At last, a water route to Asia had been found.

BRAZIL, NOT AFRICA

In 1500, Portuguese navigator Pedro Cabral was instructed by his king to duplicate Da Gama's voyage. Cabral set out from Portugal to sail down the west coast of Africa. But tradewinds directed his ship away from Africa's coast, and he landed on the east coast of South America in the present-day country of Brazil. Cabral claimed this land for Portugal.

1498	1498	1500	1513	1519–1522	1524
Da Gama reaches India	Cabot lost at sea	Cabral claims Brazil for Portugal	Balboa sees the Pacific Ocean	Magellan's crew sails around the world	Verrazano looks for northwest passage

1495   1500   1505   1510   1515   1520   1525

PANAMA TO PACIFIC

In 1501, conquistador Vasco Núñez de Balboa (VAHS-koh NOONyethh thhe bahl-BOH ah) sailed from Spain to the Americas in search of gold. He settled on the island of Hispaniola.

In 1513, Balboa sailed from Hispaniola to explore present-day Panama. Slashing through jungles and climbing over mountains, he crossed over Panama and was amazed to see a great ocean—the Pacific!

AROUND THE WORLD

In 1519, Ferdinand Magellan set out from Spain to reach Asia by sailing around South America. Over a year later he found the waterway he was looking for. His ships sailed on for three months without seeing land and with no fresh supplies. The sailors were so hungry they became ill and weak. Many died.

They eventually reached the Asian islands called the Philippines. Magellan planned to sail west all the way back home, but he was killed in a battle with the local people.

Magellan's crew continued on to Indonesia, where they traded for spices. From there they followed the route that Da Gama had discovered 25 years earlier. They arrived back in Spain in 1522, three years after they had left. Of the five ships and nearly 240 sailors that had started the voyage, one lone ship with 18 crew members made it home. But those 18 were the first people to have sailed around the world.

NO WATERWAY TO ASIA

Of course, no one who wanted to go from Europe to Asia would choose Magellan's route. It was far too long and dangerous. Some European rulers, however, hoped to find a northwest passage around *North* America that would lead to Asia.

One of these rulers was the king of France, who in 1524 hired Italian sailor Giovanni da Verrazano (joh VAHN nee duh vayr raht SAHN OH) to find such a route. Verrazano explored the coast of North America from what is now North Carolina northward to Canada. But to his great disappointment, he found no sign of a waterway to Asia.

61

| 1528-1539 | 1539–1542 | 1540–1542 | 1610 | 1673 |
| Estevan explores America | De Soto explores America | Coronado explores America | Hudson explores Hudson Bay | Marquette and Joliet explore America |

1530 — 1540 — 1550 — 1610 — 1670 — 1680

SEARCH FOR CITIES OF GOLD

Estevan, an enslaved person of African descent, was a guide to Spanish explorer Álvar Núñez Cabeza de Vaca. Their group was part of a failed 1528 trip to explore Florida. Most were killed, but Estevan, Cabeza de Vaca, and two others were captured by Native Americans in what we now call Texas.

The four men later escaped and headed south to Mexico. They heard stories of golden cities that sounded like an old Spanish legend about bishops who had left Spain to found the Seven Cities of Gold, Cíbola (SEE buh luh), across the ocean. The search for Cíbola began.

LAND CLAIMS

Conquistador Hernando de Soto had heard that what we call Florida was a land of gold. Perhaps, he thought, that's where Cíbola could be found.

In 1539, De Soto began exploring much of what is now the southeastern United States. He and his men killed many Native Americans in their search for gold.

De Soto died in 1542, having found no gold. He did, however, claim the lands he explored for Spain.

MORE LAND FOR SPAIN

In 1540, Spain's Francisco Vásquez de Coronado began exploring the American Southwest. Like De Soto, who at the same time was exploring the American Southeast, he was looking for the legendary Cíbola.

Coronado and his men found many things, including the Grand Canyon and Pueblo Indian villages, but no golden cities. Coronado took a Native American, called Turk, prisoner. Turk told Coronado what he wanted to hear—that cities of gold did exist. So in 1541, Coronado continued his search, exploring what would later become New Mexico, Texas, Oklahoma, and Kansas. Though he found no gold, Coronado did claim these lands for Spain.

ENGLAND TRIES AGAIN

In 1610, Henry Hudson of England still believed in a northwest passage to Asia. He thought he had found it in what is now Canada. He sailed through what was later named Hudson Strait. This waterway led to Hudson Bay.

But the bay was just that—a bay. It did not lead to Asia. Hudson's men, weary of the harsh winter voyage, took control of his ship. They set Hudson, his son, and seven others adrift in a small boat with no food. Then the crew sailed back to England. No one ever heard from Hudson again.

DOWN THE MISSISSIPPI

In 1673 a French explorer, Father Jacques Marquette (zhahk mahr-KET), and a French Canadian fur trader, Louis Joliet (lwee JOH lee et), set off to search for a western river to Asia. Traveling by canoe, they reached the Mississippi River, which they thought was that route. They found catfish so large that when one struck their canoe, Marquette thought they had hit a big tree. Joliet and Marquette traveled as far south as the Arkansas River. They discovered that the Mississippi flowed to the Gulf of Mexico, not to the Pacific Ocean.

SHOW WHAT YOU KNOW!

REFOCUS
COMPREHENSION

1. What did Magellan's crew accomplish?

2. How were Native Americans treated by some of these explorers?

THINK ABOUT IT
CRITICAL THINKING

If you could travel with one of these explorers, which one would you choose? Explain your choice.

WRITE ABOUT IT
ACTIVITY

Describe the effects the European explorers might have had on the native people.

THE MAYA, INCAS, AND AZTECS

FOCUS *The Americas were home to several highly developed, complex cultures before Europeans arrived in the 1500s.*

Maya Civilization

Hundreds of years before the arrival of the Spaniards, three great civilizations flourished in Central and South America. Find them on the map on page 65. The earliest of these was the Maya (MAH yuh) Empire. The Maya moved south into the green valleys of Mexico and Guatemala (gwah tuh-MAH luh) more than 1,500 years ago.

They found that corn grew well there—so well that they raised more than they could eat. They stored away their extra corn so that they would be sure of a food supply.

Since they no longer had to worry about finding food, the Maya settled down and built permanent homes. They began creating works of art from wood and stone. They learned to make beautiful pottery, jewelry, and statues.

Maya Achievements

The Maya civilization reached its height between A.D. 300 and 900. During that time the Maya built more

▲ A Maya stone sculpture, A.D. 500–800

▲ What does this look like to you? It is a stucco mask on a Maya stone temple now covered by jungle plants.

than 40 cities. These cities were home to great pyramid-temples, with which the Maya honored their gods. The temples were made of huge blocks of stone atop large mounds of earth. Some rose more than 150 feet high. No one today knows exactly how the Maya were able to create such gigantic structures.

The Maya had a remarkable understanding of mathematics and astronomy. By carefully observing the movement of the sun, planets, and stars, they were able to create a very accurate calendar—far better than any calendar used in Europe at the time.

The Maya also developed a system of writing. Using pictures and symbols, they began recording information about their history, calendar, mathematics, and religious ceremonies. They carved these symbols on stone or painted them on strips of plant fiber.

By the early 1100s, the Maya world had fallen apart. No one knows why, but the Maya left their cities. Their wooden art works began to rot. Their fields were overgrown with vines and trees. When Europeans arrived in the 1500s, even the great Maya temples were crumbling.

The Inca Empire

The Incas settled along the western coast of South America during the 1100s, as you can see on the map on the right. They built dozens of cities along 2,500 miles of Pacific Ocean coastline. They conquered other societies to build an empire of perhaps 7 million people.

The region they settled was both dry and mountainous. In the desert lowlands there was not enough water to grow crops. Although plenty of rain fell in the mountains, it washed the soil away, down the steep hillsides. Despite this, the Incas used their remarkable skills to prosper in this difficult land.

Developing the Land

To water the deserts, they built **aqueducts** that carried water from mountain streams. Some of these aqueducts were 500 miles long. To keep soil from washing down the steep mountains, they cut terraces, or rows of wide steps, into the mountainsides. The edge of each step was walled with stone for support. Rain now fell gently from terrace to terrace, watering the soil but not washing it away. The Incas used their now fertile land to grow potatoes, beans, corn, and squash.

The rugged land also made travel difficult. Again the Incas put their skills to work. The Incas built paved roads that stretched up to 2,000 miles. They created sophisticated rope bridges to cross the deep canyons and built **causeways** over swamps and streams. This great road system was used for travel, trade, and even as a postal highway.

MAYA, AZTEC, AND INCA EMPIRES

- Aztec Empire
- Maya Empire
- Inca Empire
- ← Pizarro's route
- ← Cortés's route

The Incas honored their gods by creating tapestries, such as this one, and other images of them.

⭐ **aqueduct** A structure that carries water to an area from a distant site
causeway A roadway built above water

The Incas were also great architects. They carved up huge blocks of stone for use in building homes and temples and to surround their capital city, Cuzco. Using rope, rollers, and human muscle power, they moved blocks as heavy as 200 tons. These blocks were cut so precisely that they fit together perfectly.

End of the Inca Empire

The Incas worshiped a sun god. They mined large amounts of gold, a symbol for the sun, to use in religious ceremonies and for decoration. They also worshiped a moon god, represented by silver.

In 1532 a conquistador, Francisco Pizarro (frahn THHEES koh pee THHAHR-roh) and his small army attacked the unsuspecting Incas with guns and cannons. They killed thousands and kidnapped the Inca ruler, Atahualpa (ah-tuh WAHL puh). The Incas gave Pizarro huge amounts of gold and silver, for which Pizarro had agreed to release

The Incas made this counting device, or *quipu*, out of strings made to look like gold and silver.

Atahualpa. But instead, Pizarro murdered him. Soon Pizarro's army overran the Inca capital. The beautiful gold and silver statues and ornaments meant to save Atahualpa were melted down into bars. The Inca Empire had been crushed.

Aztec Culture

In the 1200s the Aztecs, or Mexica (me CHEE cah), settled in what is now central Mexico. By the 1500s they had conquered enough neighboring societies to claim a dazzling empire of 10 million people.

The Aztec capital was called Tenochtitlán (te nawch tee TLAHN). It was built on an island in Lake Texcoco (tay SKOH koh). People and goods moved along the city's many roads and canals. Aqueducts brought water from distant freshwater lakes. Long causeways connected the island city to the shore.

Although it was one of the world's biggest cities, Tenochtitlán was clean and orderly. Every day the streets were swept and washed, and garbage was hauled away.

Tenochtitlán buzzed with activity. Thousands gathered daily to trade at its great marketplaces. Towering above all this bustle were glorious pyramids. These temples were as central to the city as religion was to Aztec life.

The Aztecs believed in many gods, but the most important was

An Aztec urn being restored by an archaeologist, who studies the remains of early civilizations

Huitzilopochtli (wee-tsee loh POHCH tlee), the god of sun and war. Because Aztecs believed that the first gods sacrificed themselves to create the world, sacrifice was important to their religion. Warriors could gain honor by capturing prisoners to offer as sacrifices. These sacrifices were thought to be honorable and welcomed by the gods.

The Aztecs were great astronomers and created accurate calendars. They also knew how to set broken bones, fill dental cavities, and even do brain surgery. They used hundreds of herbal medicines, some of which are still used today. Anything they couldn't make from local resources they got by demanding payments from the cities they conquered.

The Aztecs believed they could appease their gods by making masks such as this.

An Empire Disappears

In 1519 the Spaniards, led by Hernán Cortés, marched toward Tenochtitlán in search of gold. Helping him were warriors from neighboring cities that were tired of making payments to Tenochtitlán.

Aztec warriors were no match for Spanish guns and cannons, which they had never seen before. And Aztecs had never battled soldiers mounted on horses, huge beasts the Spaniards had brought with them. In just two years Aztec gold was in the hands of Europeans, and the mighty Aztec Empire was gone forever.

Mexican painter Diego Rivera's vision of Tenochtitlán

SHOW WHAT YOU KNOW!

REFOCUS
COMPREHENSION

1. What were some results that followed after the Maya had built a food supply?

2. How were the Incas able to farm, even though they lived in a mountainous area?

THINK ABOUT IT
CRITICAL THINKING

Compare the accomplishments of the Maya, the Incas, and the Aztecs.

WRITE ABOUT IT
ACTIVITY

What would you do if you were an Aztec living in Tenochtitlán in 1519? Write a journal entry about the advance of the Spaniards.

SUMMING UP

1 DO YOU REMEMBER . . .
COMPREHENSION

1. What effect did Marco Polo and the Crusades have on Europeans in the 1200s?

2. What was the Silk Road?

3. Why did Europeans want to find easy access to Asia?

4. What was Prince Henry the Navigator's dream?

5. What were French and English explorers looking for on their first voyages to the New World?

6. What important discovery did Jacques Marquette and Louis Joliet make?

7. What did early Spanish explorers—Balboa, De Soto, Coronado—most want to find?

8. Describe the Columbian exchange.

9. What were some achievements of the Maya, Inca, and Aztec cultures?

10. What were some similarities in the way the Incas and the Aztecs were conquered?

2 SKILL POWER
TRACING ROUTES ON A MAP

In this chapter you used maps to trace the routes of explorers. Work with other students to draw a larger version of the map on page 53. The map should be large enough to display in your classroom. Be sure to include the routes of the explorers. Then have each member of your team choose one or more of these explorers to write a report about. Display your reports with your map.

3 WHAT DO YOU THINK?
CRITICAL THINKING

1. Why might Native Americans have wished that the Europeans had never come to their land?

2. Who do you think made the greater contribution—Columbus or Magellan? Explain.

3. Why do you think people want to become explorers? What are people exploring today?

4. No one knows why the Maya abandoned their cities about 900 years ago. List three possible reasons why they did so.

CHAPTER 3

4 SAY IT, WRITE IT, USE IT
VOCABULARY

Write a paragraph about the world's explorers as discussed in this chapter. Try to use as many vocabulary words as possible. If you include four or more, you are a very talented word worker!

aqueduct	East Indies
cartographer	economy
causeway	empire
conquistador	northwest passage
Crusade	

5 GEOGRAPHY AND YOU
MAP STUDY

Use the map and chart on page 53 to answer the following questions.

1. Which explorers sailed for Spain?

2. Whose voyage was longer—Vespucci's or Da Gama's?

3. Which explorer traveled along the coast of South America?

4. In what year did Balboa cross Panama?

6 TAKE ACTION
CITIZENSHIP

Explorers expanded their knowledge of the world by going beyond borders. With videotapes you can go beyond the borders of your school and community. Make a poster, audio tape, or videotape about your class, showing your special projects and interests. Then send it to a class in another community or state. Include a note that asks the class to reply with information about themselves. By being a "pen pal," you will expand your knowledge of the world.

7 GET CREATIVE
ART CONNECTION

With a group of classmates, create a mural that shows scenes of the Maya, Inca, and Aztec cultures. Begin by drawing a giant map of Central and South America. Place the scenes of each culture in the correct region. Use the illustrations on pages 64–67, encyclopedias, library books, and other resources for art ideas.

LOOKING AHEAD In the next chapter you'll find out what happened as Europeans began to settle the lands they explored.

CHAPTER 4

Early European

Spain, France, England, and the Netherlands had all established settlements in North America by the 1600s. Each nation had different goals for its settlements and treated the Native Americans they encountered in different ways.

CONTENTS

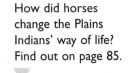

How did horses change the Plains Indians' way of life? Find out on page 85.

Settlements

These books tell about some people, places, and events of interest during the time of the early European settlements. Read one that interests you and fill out a book-review form.

READ AND RESEARCH

St. Augustine: America's Oldest City by Linda R. Wade
(Rourke Enterprises, 1991)
Travel back 400 years and find out about the history of America's oldest city. Notice how the past affects life in the city today. *(nonfiction)*

North American Indian Sign Language by Karen Liptak
(Franklin Watts, 1992)
Without sign language, Plains Indian nations would not have been able to communicate so easily. Explore the world of symbols that many of these people used to express their feelings and ideas. *(nonfiction)*

The Jews of New Amsterdam by Eva Deutsch Costabel
(Simon and Schuster Children's Publishing, 1988)
What historical events led to the arrival of 23 Jews in the Dutch colony of New Amsterdam? Find out about their contributions to the colony. *(nonfiction)*

Reading a Time Line

Knowing how to read a time line will help you understand when different events happened.

UNDERSTAND IT

When you're really busy, it's easy to lose track of the time. That's why people use calendars like this to show when things are planned to happen.

Saturday, May 13

9:00 A.M.   Soccer game

11:30 A.M.   Orthodontist

2:00 P.M.   Help Dad at store

4:30 P.M.   Guitar lesson

6:00 P.M.   Pizza party at Eric's

When keeping track of past events, people use a time line, which is similar to a calendar. A time line organizes historical information by putting events in sequence.

EXPLORE IT

The city of St. Augustine, Florida, has been governed by many nations, including Spain and the United States. Who first settled the city? When did it become part of the United States?

1565 The Spaniards settle St. Augustine

1586 The English sack and burn St. Augustine

1672 The Spaniards begin building San Marcos, a fort, to protect the city

1763 Britain gains control of Florida

Look at the time line on page 73. Since the earliest date is on the left, the first event took place in 1565—the Spaniards settled St. Augustine.

The second date, 1586, is placed to the right of the first event. When making a time line, it is important to have a scale for the number of years. For instance, every one-inch space might represent 20 years.

Look at the time line again. When did Britain gain control of St. Augustine? How long had the Spaniards been in St. Augustine before they built San Marcos? Time lines can answer many questions about the order of events in history.

History of St. Augustine

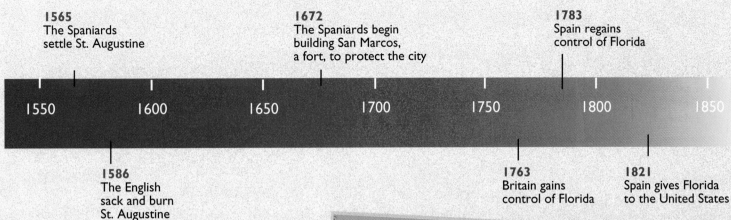

1565
The Spaniards
settle St. Augustine

1672
The Spaniards begin
building San Marcos,
a fort, to protect the city

1783
Spain regains
control of Florida

| 1550 | 1600 | 1650 | 1700 | 1750 | 1800 | 1850 |

1586
The English
sack and burn
St. Augustine

1763
Britain gains
control of Florida

1821
Spain gives Florida
to the United States

TRY IT

With a group of your classmates, create a time line. Here are some topic ideas.

- The history of your town or city

- The history of your school

- Figure skating from 1945 to the present

- The life of a famous person

- The history of desktop computers

When all the groups have finished, all the time lines can be combined in a booklet.

Fort at St. Augustine ▶

SKILL POWER SEARCH

Look for other time lines in this chapter. How many years are shown on each one?

Europeans Settle in America

FOCUS *Various groups of Europeans settled in North America for different reasons. They often pursued their goals at the expense of the Native Americans.*

Spaniards in America

The Spaniards who settled the islands of the Caribbean, shown on the map below, were looking for gold. But they were unwilling to do the dangerous work of mining for gold themselves. Instead, they enslaved the local Native Americans, the Arawaks. The terrible working conditions and European diseases caused the Arawaks to die at a horrifying rate. Soon the Spaniards were using enslaved Africans to replace the Arawak slaves who died. By the end of the 1500s, most of the enslaved workers were African.

As Spanish explorers pushed northward during the 1500s, they

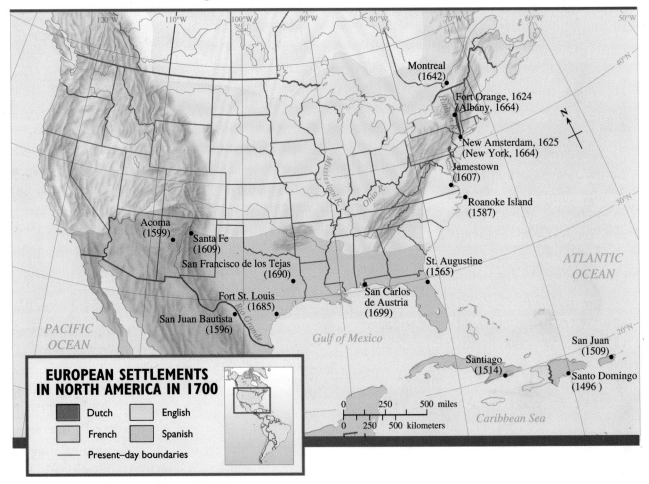

EUROPEAN SETTLEMENTS IN NORTH AMERICA IN 1700

- Dutch
- English
- French
- Spanish
- —— Present–day boundaries

Montreal (1642)

Fort Orange, 1624 (Albany, 1664)

New Amsterdam, 1625 (New York, 1664)

Jamestown (1607)

Roanoke Island (1587)

Acoma (1599)

Santa Fe (1609)

San Francisco de los Tejas (1690)

St. Augustine (1565)

Fort St. Louis (1685)

San Carlos de Austria (1699)

San Juan Bautista (1596)

Rio Grande

PACIFIC OCEAN

Gulf of Mexico

San Juan (1509)

Santiago (1514)

Santo Domingo (1496)

Caribbean Sea

ATLANTIC OCEAN

0   250   500 miles

0   250   500 kilometers

1565
Spaniards settle
St. Augustine

1585
England sends first
settlers to Roanoke

1613
Dutch establish
New Netherland

1682
La Salle claims
Mississippi Valley for France

1560   1580   1600   1620   1640   1660   1680

claimed more and more land for Spain. Spain soon began to establish colonies in present-day Mexico, New Mexico, Texas, and California.

Many Spaniards came to North America with an *encomienda,* or royal grant. The grant gave the holder control over a certain number of Native Americans in a particular area. The grant holder could demand payment from the Native Americans in the form of gold, goods, or labor. In return, the grant holder was supposed to protect the Native Americans and teach them Catholicism, the religion of Spain.

This *encomienda* system was created by Spain, not by the Native Americans. It let Spaniards take over Native American lands and became, in practice, a form of slavery.

Catholicism Spreads

Gold was not the only reason Spain settled North America. The Catholic church of Spain wanted to spread Catholicism. The Spanish government saw the spreading of Catholicism as a way to expand its

Native Americans and Spaniards building a settlement

empire. Spain sought to convert Native Americans into tax-paying Christians under Spanish rule.

Spanish priests worked as **missionaries** to convert Native Americans to Catholicism. They built **missions** in which to carry out their work.

These missionaries wanted not only to spread Catholicism but also Spanish culture—they expected Native Americans to give up their own religion and culture. Missionaries also taught European methods of farming and cattle raising. But they forced Native Americans to do the work needed to keep the missions running. Sometimes mission life for Native Americans was little better than slavery.

Presidios Protect Spain's Claims

Many Native American groups, such as the Apaches, Comanches, and Navajos, resisted Spanish rule and sometimes fought missionaries and settlers. Other Europeans, such as the French and the English, also disliked

missionary A person sent to teach religion to people of a different faith
mission A settlement of religious teachers

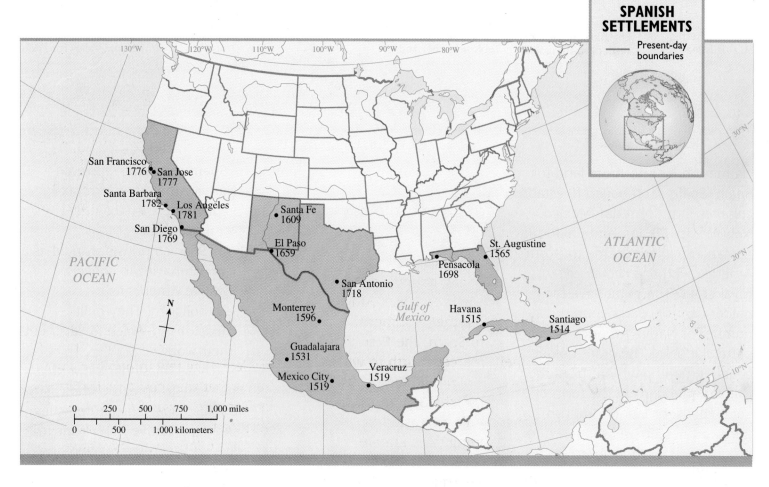

Present-day boundaries

San Francisco 1776
San Jose 1777
Santa Barbara 1782
Los Angeles 1781
San Diego 1769
Santa Fe 1609
El Paso 1659
St. Augustine 1565
Pensacola 1698
San Antonio 1718
Monterrey 1596
Havana 1515
Santiago 1514
Guadalajara 1531
Veracruz 1519
Mexico City 1519

PACIFIC OCEAN

ATLANTIC OCEAN

Gulf of Mexico

N

0   250   500   750   1,000 miles
0   500   1,000 kilometers

Spain's presence in North America and envied the gold and silver that Spain was accumulating. To help protect their claims in North America, Spaniards built fortified settlements called **presidios**.

Spain claimed a large part of North America, and its many presidios helped it protect those claims. In the western part of North America, Spain had settlements, missions, and presidios as far south as Mexico and as far north as California. In the east, Spain claimed part of the Caribbean and took over French settlements in Florida.

In 1565, the Spaniards built St. Augustine in a spot where they had destroyed a French settlement. St. Augustine is today the oldest European settlement still standing in North America.

As you can see on the map above, Spaniards were building settlements in North America for over 250 years. What were some of Spain's earliest settlements? What were some of the latest settlements?

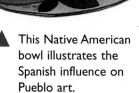

This Native American bowl illustrates the Spanish influence on Pueblo art.

presidio   A Spanish military base on the edge of a settlement

It is likely that the floral design on these Iroquois moccasins was learned from French nuns in Quebec. ▽

French Settlements

Although Spain claimed a huge portion of the Americas, other European countries laid claim to North America. Having lost their southern settlement to Spain, the French took their interests north to what is now Canada. Unlike the Spaniards, the French weren't interested in expanding their empire. Instead, they wanted to trade with the Native Americans. They set up **trading posts**, where they could get beaver and other furs that they could sell in Europe for a huge profit. Furs were used for hats, coats, and other clothing and were in great demand in Europe. The French traded beads, tools, firearms, brass and iron kettles, and rum in exchange for furs.

Relations With Native Americans

The French took care to establish good relations with Native Americans because the French depended on

them to obtain the valuable furs. The fur traders were few in number and knew that they could easily be defeated in a war with Native Americans. It was to their advantage to stay friendly with the Native Americans. Because the French didn't want Native American land, the Native Americans didn't see them as a threat.

France soon discovered, though, that without colonies it couldn't protect its trading posts. In 1608 the French founded the settlement of Quebec. Later they established Montreal. In 1682, French explorer Robert Cavelier, Sieur (syoor) de La Salle, claimed the Mississippi River valley for France. He named it Louisiana after the French king, Louis XIV.

Like the Spaniards, the French also sought religious converts. But instead of trying to wipe out Native

▲ A French fur trader

★ **trading post** A place where people trade goods with the people who live in the area

James Fort

Built in the period of
May 14 to June 15, 1607.

A painting of early Jamestown

American beliefs, the French missionaries studied those beliefs and tried to blend them with Catholicism. As a result, French missionaries had better relationships with Native Americans than Spanish missionaries did.

Early English Settlements

England also began establishing North American settlements during this time. The English first tried to set up a colony in 1585. Sir Walter Raleigh sent 108 men and boys to Roanoke Island, off the coast of present-day North Carolina. Unprepared for the hard work needed to maintain a settlement, the colonists gave up and returned to England after 10 months.

Raleigh tried again in 1587. He sent 91 men, 17 women, and 9 children to Roanoke. But when supply ships returned to the island three years later, the colony had vanished.

Twenty years after the Roanoke disaster, the English tried yet again. This time they started a settlement, called Jamestown, on an island in the James River in present-day Virginia. The first 104 settlers arrived in May 1607. They had high hopes of finding large supplies of gold, as Spaniards had found in Mexico and South America. And they expected to make the Native Americans who lived there do all the hard work, as the Spaniards often did. But there was no gold to be found, no empires to conquer.

A helmet from Jamestown

Lacking eager missionaries and government and military support, the English were unable to enslave the Native American population.

Jamestown Survives

Being aristocrats who were not used to doing hard work, the English were unwilling to do the labor needed for successful farming. As winter arrived, food supplies decreased. Many settlers died from disease and malnutrition. By January 1608 only 38 were still alive. Things didn't look good for the settlement. Yet a few years later, Jamestown found a way not only to survive but to prosper.

Although local Native Americans taught English settlers how to grow new crops, relations between the two groups rapidly grew worse. The English, like most Europeans, believed Native Americans were inferior and not worthy of respect. Europeans felt that if land was not heavily farmed, it belonged to no one. So they settled on lands the Native Americans used for hunting and growing crops. Conflicts over land occurred again and again as more and more English settlers arrived in America.

The Dutch Arrive

In the early 1600s the Dutch came to America. They were interested in the area explored by Henry Hudson, who was working for a Dutch company when he explored the Hudson River.

Like the French, the Dutch wanted to trade with local Native Americans for furs. But they, too, found that trading posts needed the support of colonies. In 1613 they therefore started the colony of New Netherland.

New Netherland had trouble attracting settlers, for the Dutch enjoyed prosperity at home. So the Dutch invited others to come to their settlements, including Germans, Swedes, and Norwegians seeking religious freedom. Still, Dutch settlements remained small.

Dutch relations with Native Americans were peaceful until the Dutch began settling Native American land. Native American groups also started fighting with each other for control of the fur trade. By 1664 few Native Americans remained in New Netherland.

Dutch traders took furs back to the Netherlands for use in clothing, such as this coat.

SHOW WHAT YOU KNOW!

REFOCUS
COMPREHENSION

1. What were the purposes of the Spanish missions and presidios?

2. How was the French treatment of Native Americans different from the treatment of other Europeans?

THINK ABOUT IT
CRITICAL THINKING

If you were a leader of the Jamestown colony, what would you do to make it more successful?

WRITE ABOUT IT
ACTIVITY

Look at the map on page 74. Make a time line showing when the different European settlements shown on the map were established.

Spanish Culture in America

FOCUS *As Spaniards settled in America, they set up several different kinds of communities. They brought Spanish life to the Americas, but in some ways they adapted their culture to the new area.*

Transplanting Spanish Culture

For Spanish settlers, life in America often proved extremely difficult. In Florida, settlers struggled with isolation, harsh conditions, pirate raids, and hostile relationships with other European settlers. For instance, French and English ships sometimes cut St. Augustine off from Cuban supply ships. The Spaniards would then face hunger and hardship. Settlers in Texas, New Mexico, and California faced similar problems. Throughout the Southwest they dealt with dry, dusty climates. And

almost everywhere they dealt with poor soil, angry Native Americans, and a lack of supplies.

Spaniards who came to America didn't plan to change their lifestyle. They wanted to live as they had in their homeland. Spanish settlers tried to transplant as much of their culture as they could, including their language, religion, traditions, architecture, and social class structure.

They even dressed as they had in Spain. They wore ruffled shirts, leather

▼ Father Ignacio Tirsch returned to Spain in 1768 with this drawing of a California mission.

This drawing explains the different parts of the soldier's outfit.

boots, and Spanish suits. They used linen handkerchiefs and fancy hats.

Settlers also hauled Spanish furniture to America. They brought Spanish kitchen items, paintings, and jewelry. They also planned settlements to look like towns back in Spain.

Adjusting to a New Land

Despite their best efforts, however, settlers could not duplicate Spain on this side of the Atlantic Ocean. Things simply were not the same. When leather boots wore out, there were no shoemakers around to make new ones. So Spanish settlers wore Native American moccasins. They needed to eat, so they learned to like corn, beans, and squash. They didn't always have enough silverware, so they began scooping up food with tortillas.

Similarly, the Spaniards soon gave up on European-style towns. Settlers needed to live out in the countryside. They needed to be near their animals, fields, and water supply.

In addition, the houses varied from settlement to settlement, based on the climate or environment. In Florida, houses had big windows to catch the cooling breezes. In the Southwest they had small windows to keep out the sun. In Florida, roofs were made with palm leaves. In New Mexico, roofs were made of wood and dirt.

In all the settlements the homes were small and simple. Often there was not much furniture. Many settlers slept on mats on the floor. The settlers quickly learned to do without many things, especially since they had to make whatever they lacked.

Life in the Presidios

Even more difficult than a civilian's life in a settlement was a soldier's life in a presidio. Soldiers lived with bare walls, dirt floors, and little furniture. While all faced death from disease or enemy arrows, soldiers were at greater risk from enemy attacks.

In addition, soldiers dressed very uncomfortably. They wore long leather coats and carried lances and leather shields. The coats were heavy—about 18 pounds each. The coats protected soldiers from arrows, but in the heat of the desert, they were brutally hot.

Spanish soldiers also faced loneliness. Most of them were unmarried men who came to the **frontier** alone. Some eventually married Native American women and set up their own huts near the presidio. Others, however, lived and died without any family nearby.

 frontier A newly settled area that separates older settlements from the wilderness

Establishing Missions

Since the Spanish people believed that Native American souls were at risk, they sent priests to become missionaries and to build missions. In the missions the priests would teach Spain's religion, Catholicism, and culture to the Native Americans.

Once the priests had converted enough people, they could begin building a mission. This would include a church, workshops, housing for the priests, and separate housing for the "mission Indians." Some Native Americans liked mission life. They learned to speak Spanish. They learned Spanish methods of sewing, farming, and pottery making. However, mission Indians had to give up their old customs and beliefs.

Not all Native Americans wanted to give up their beliefs. Some didn't want to wear European clothes. Either way, many Native Americans didn't like being ordered around all day long.

In missions Native Americans learned skills such as black-smithing.

Some mission Indians tried to run away. The ones who were caught were locked up or whipped. Other Native Americans tried to drive priests out by attacking the missions.

In the end, missions did not do well in Arizona, New Mexico, and Texas. But they did succeed in California. And some California missions, such as San Diego and San Francisco, eventually grew into major cities.

A mission bell

SHOW WHAT YOU KNOW!

REFOCUS
COMPREHENSION

1. How did the Spaniards try to recreate their old lifestyle?

2. What were some ways in which they learned to adapt?

THINK ABOUT IT
CRITICAL THINKING

Why do you think the Spaniards insisted on wearing clothes from their homeland when they moved to a very different climate?

WRITE ABOUT IT
ACTIVITY

Draw a picture or diagram showing what a Spanish settlement house might have looked like on the inside.

Living on America's Plains

FOCUS *Plains Indians lived on the land that stretches from present-day Canada to Texas and from the Rocky Mountains to the Midwest. At their height the Plains Indians numbered around 250,000.*

The Plains Indians

In the 1600s and 1700s, some Plains Indians lived in settled farming villages and hunted during different seasons. They lived in grass houses or earthen lodges.

Other Plains Indians were truly nomadic hunters. They did not live a settled life at any time of the year. Nomadic Plains Indians lived in **tipis** (TEE peez). Read about life growing up as a nomadic Plains Indian.

Searching for Food

You certainly put a lot of miles on your moccasins. Every few months, as the seasons change, your family packs up and moves—and you walk every step of the way. You do have some dogs that are harnessed to pull your belongings, but there are no animals to carry you.

The reason for all your traveling is simple: food. In the summer your family may gather wild fruits and roots. But you mostly eat buffalo meat.

So each year, as the buffalo herds migrate, or move, the people in your camp migrate, too.

Hunting buffaloes on foot requires great skill. Hunters must either **stampede** the buffalo off a cliff or drive the animal into a trap. To get the buffalo over the cliff or into the trap, hunters will sometimes disguise themselves with animal skins. This way the hunters will look and smell like animals the buffalo is used to.

You will want to set up camp near where you will hunt, because buffaloes weigh more than 1,000 pounds each.

Plains Indians often disguised themselves with animal skins when hunting buffalo.

⭐ **tipi** A Native American tent made of animal skins

⭐ **stampede** To cause a herd of animals to panic and run

How will you carry all that weight? You will cut up the buffalo to make it easier to carry. And you will not waste any parts of the buffalo.

On a good day you eat buffalo meat. But on a bad day you may not eat at all. With food supplies so scarce, you can't be a picky eater. You are expected to eat whatever is given to you, whether you like it or not.

There are other rules to follow as well. You are not allowed to sit down inside your tipi until an adult gives you permission. And you cannot interrupt older people when they talk.

Time to Play

You will probably take a toy or two with you wherever you move. The first present girls get is a doll made of wood or animal skin. Boys receive a bow and arrow. Later on, both boys and girls are given puppies. Sometimes these animals are raised as pets, but often they are used to do work.

You may also play games with other children in your nation. You might play war or you might pretend to hunt buffaloes, with some of the children acting as the animals. In the winter you probably sled on the ice, using animal bones for runners.

▼ This picture, from a later time period, shows Native American children with their dogs.

A Social People

In your community there are social rules to follow. When you are a guest in someone else's tipi, you take your own bowl and spoon. When your host cleans his pipe, it is time for you to leave.

You do not spend all your time with people of your own nation. You may get together with other Plains Indians. Sometimes your meetings are friendly. Other times there are disagreements.

▲ The pictures on this buffalo skin tell a part of Plains Indian history.

Most of the people you meet speak different languages. So how do you communicate with each other? You use sign language. The Plains Indians have a highly developed system of signs that enable you to share stories, ideas, and warnings with each other.

Help From Horses

When the Europeans arrive with horses, your way of life as a Plains Indian completely changes. On horseback your hunters can travel faster and farther than ever before. This gives Plains Indians a new freedom. It is now easier to reach fresh water supplies. And your next meal of buffalo meat is just a horseback ride away.

Horses also enable you to carry much more weight when you move around. In fact, one horse can carry up to 250 pounds. It doesn't take many horses to enable your hunters to bring a buffalo back to the camp. Moving your tipi is much easier, too. So your home gets bigger and more comfortable.

Not every Native American nation gets horses right away, of course. The northernmost nations do not get horses until 1800. Since the horse makes living on the plains easier, other Native American groups from the east and west move onto the plains. The map above shows some Plains Indian nations after the arrival of the horse. By the mid-1700s, horses are a central feature in the lives of most Plains Indians.

PLAINS INDIAN NATIONS

Present-day boundaries

REFOCUS
COMPREHENSION

1. How did the buffalo affect the way the Plains Indians lived?

2. How did the people of different Plains Indian nations communicate with each other?

THINK ABOUT IT
CRITICAL THINKING

How did the horse change the Plains Indians' hunting and living patterns?

WRITE ABOUT IT
ACTIVITY

Your nation has just been introduced to the horse. In your journal describe your reaction to this new animal.

85

March of Time
1590 TO 1769

From Roanoke to California

FOCUS European settlements were scattered across the continent of North America, from east coast to west coast. Not all settlements were successful, but some developed quickly and grew stronger over time.

ROANOKE SETTLERS LOST

In August 1590, John White brought fresh supplies for English settlers who had come to Roanoke Island three years earlier.

As he walked along the shore, White saw footprints in the sand. But he found no other sign of life. The houses were torn down, and some rusty armor was lying among the weeds.

White saw the word CROATOAN carved on a tree. Did this mean that the settlers had fled to the nearby island where the Croatoan Indians lived? Bad weather kept White from going to the island to find out. So the lost colonists of Roanoke are still a mystery.

THE DUTCH BUY AN ISLAND

Peter Minuit was looking for land. As director of a Dutch trading company, he wanted to expand New Netherland. In 1626 he asked the Canarsie Indians if they would sell him the island of Manhattan.

It wasn't the Canarsies' land to sell. It really belonged to the Manhattan Indians. Nonetheless, the Carnarsies and Minuit made a deal. Minuit gave the Canarsies $24 worth of beads and trinkets. Today that $24 would really be thousands of dollars.

Minuit then founded New Amsterdam on the island. Later the Dutch did pay the true owners of Manhattan.

TROUBLE IN NEW MEXICO

Pueblo Indians were furious with Spaniards who were charging them taxes. In addition, the Spaniards were whipping—even hanging—Pueblos who practiced their native religion.

Finally, one Pueblo man, named Popé, had had enough. He gathered his people and planned a revolt. On August 9, 1680, the Pueblos attacked Santa Fe. Of the 2,800 settlers, 400 were killed, and 2,000 fled to El Paso, Texas. No one knows what happened to the other 400. The Pueblos controlled Santa Fe until Spain regained control after Popé's death in 1692.

1590	1626	1680	1701	1769
John White brings supplies to Roanoke	Peter Minuit pays the Carnarsies for Manhattan	The Pueblos attack Santa Fe	Cadillac founds Detroit	Junipero Serra leaves for California

1590   1610   1630   1650   1670   1690   1710   1730   1750   1770

NEW MISSIONS IN CALIFORNIA

Father Junípero Serra (hoo NEE pay-roh SER rah) desperately wanted to bring Catholicism to Native Americans. He spent 20 years as a missionary in Texas and Mexico. Then he had an opportunity to spread his faith even farther. The king of Spain asked him to establish missions in California.

In 1769, Serra, who had been sickly throughout his whole life, had an infection in his left leg that wouldn't heal. But he set out for California anyway. On some days he couldn't walk at all and was carried on a stretcher. Still, by 1782, Serra had founded nine missions throughout California, in places such as San Diego and San Francisco.

CADILLAC BUILDS DETROIT

Detroit's founder had quite a name—Antoine de La Mothe Cadillac (ahn twahn duh lah mawt kah dee YAHK). Actually, when he was born, he was named Antoine Laumet. But as a young man, he changed his name so that people would think he was more important.

Cadillac loved money, sword fights, and his country—France. In 1701 he was sent to start a French fur settlement on the Detroit River. Cadillac headed off with 102 men. After 49 days of canoeing, on July 24, they reached what is now Detroit. Cadillac made friends with local Native Americans, and soon the settlement of Detroit was thriving.

SHOW WHAT YOU KNOW!

REFOCUS
COMPREHENSION

1. Why did Peter Minuit want to buy Manhattan?

2. How did Father Junípero Serra go about bringing Catholicism to Native Americans?

THINK ABOUT IT
CRITICAL THINKING

Why do you think the Spaniards tried to stop the Pueblos from practicing their own religion?

WRITE ABOUT IT
ACTIVITY

Suppose it is 1590 and you are John White. Write a letter to a relative in England and describe what you discovered when you arrived in Roanoke.

87

SUMMING UP

1 DO YOU REMEMBER . . .
COMPREHENSION

1. Why was the death rate of Native Americans so high in Spanish settlements?

2. In what part of North America did France set up its first colony?

3. What colony did the English try unsuccessfully to start in 1585 and again in 1587?

4. Why did the Dutch set up the colony of New Netherland?

5. What type of lifestyle did the early Spanish settlers try to create in the New World?

6. Why did the Spaniards want Native Americans to live in missions?

7. Why did Plains Indians move so often?

8. How did horses change the way of life of the Plains Indians?

9. Why did the Pueblo Indians revolt in 1680?

10. Who was Antoine de La Mothe Cadillac?

2 SKILL POWER
READING A TIME LINE

In this chapter you learned how to make and use time lines. Make a time line of the last ten years. At the top, place important events from your own life. At the bottom, place major events that have happened in our nation and in the world.

3 WHAT DO YOU THINK?
CRITICAL THINKING

1. Which Europeans seemed to have the best relationships with Native Americans? Explain.

2. What do you think might have happened to the early settlers at Roanoke?

3. Why do you think some Native Americans resisted mission life?

4. Not all Plains Indians had contact with European settlers. How do you think they got horses?

5. What do Peter Minuit's experiences in buying Manhattan Island tell you about early land deals between Europeans and Native Americans?

4 SAY IT, WRITE IT, USE IT
VOCABULARY

Write a conversation that might have taken place between an early Spanish settler and a Native American. Have the characters describe their ways of life. Use as many of the vocabulary terms as you can.

frontier	stampede
mission	tipi
missionary	trading post
presidio	

5 GEOGRAPHY AND YOU
MAP STUDY

Use the map below and the map on page 74 to answer these questions.

1. What European nations had settlements along the east coast of the United States?

2. What river connected the Dutch settlements of Fort Orange and New Amsterdam?

3. Name five present-day states that have land once claimed by Spain.

4. Which European nation settled in the area around the Great Lakes?

6 TAKE ACTION
CITIZENSHIP

In 1680 the Pueblo Indians were angered by Spanish taxes, and they revolted against Spanish rule. Almost one hundred years later, antitax feelings on the part of British colonists led to the American Revolution. Taxes are still a necessary part of citizenship. Talk to adults at home and school to find out more about taxes. Is there a state income tax where you live? Are the schools in your community funded with real estate taxes? Make charts to show the different taxes that people pay and what people get in return for these taxes.

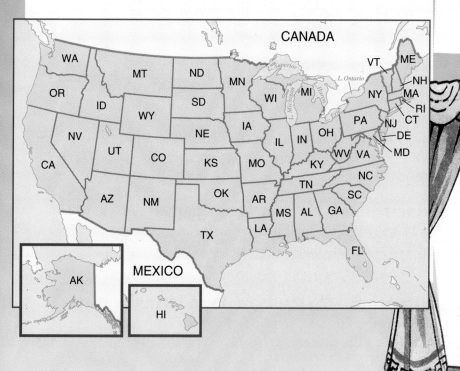

7 GET CREATIVE
LANGUAGE ARTS CONNECTION

Create a short skit based on one of the events in this chapter. Your skit could show a Spanish family trying to adjust to life in the Southwest, a group of Plains Indians learning to use horses, or Peter Minuit trying to buy Manhattan Island.

LOOKING AHEAD In the next chapter, read about English settlements that were started by Pilgrims and Puritans.

CHAPTER 5

THE NEW

Pilgrims and Puritans left "old" England and settled in New England, with strong religious beliefs. They produced a close-knit, structured society, but their society was soon threatened by problems of disease, hunger, conflict, and rebellion.

How can a gravestone tell you about early New England? Find out on page 103.

CONTENTS

Here lyes y Body of Stephen Cooke Dec'd Dec'r y 14ᵗʰ 1749 in y 19 year of his Age

ENGLAND COLONIES

These books tell about people, places, and events of interest in New England in the 1600s. Read one that interests you and fill out a book-review form.

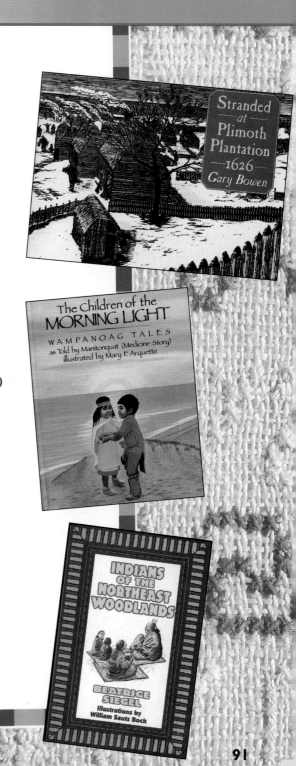

READ AND RESEARCH

Stranded at Plimoth Plantation, 1626 by Gary Bowen
(HarperCollins, 1994)
Christopher Sears is 13 and an orphan at the struggling Plymouth Colony in 1626. No wonder he feels stranded! In his journal he recounts the details of his life in one year at Plimoth Plantation. *(historical fiction)*

The Children of the Morning Light: Wampanoag Tales
as told by Manitonquat (Simon & Schuster Books for Young Readers, 1994)
An Assonet Wampanoag storyteller retells tales and legends of his people, including stories of the creation of the world and of how the Wampanoags ended up near Plymouth in 1620. *(folk tales)*

Indians of the Northeast Woodlands by Beatrice Siegel
(Walker, 1992)
Northeast Woodland Indians—the Wampanoags, Narragansetts, and Pequots—lived and still live in New England. Find out all about their history, culture, language, and art. *(nonfiction)*

Reading a Table

Tables organize information so that it is easier to understand.

UNDERSTAND IT

Do you have a paper route? If so, how do you organize information about your customers? Do you organize it by the order in which you deliver papers or by the customers' last names? Whichever way you use, a table would help you organize the information. A table has a title, columns, and rows to make information easier to find and use.

CUSTOMER LIST

Name	Address	Instructions
Chan, Lu	12 Park St.	none
Johnson, Sam	16 Park St.	Leave at door
Doty, Ellen	24 Park St.	Inside gate
East, Olivia	110 East St.	none
Dughan, Sam	124 East St.	Inside door
Goldman, Sol	130 East St.	Leave at door

▲ This table is organized by order of delivery.

EXPLORE IT

When you have to organize names, dates, sizes, or locations, a table may be a good way to do so. When you read a table, first look at its title to see what information is included in it. To find information, you can look for the **row** you want and move your finger across it until you find the **column** you want. Another way is to look for the column you want and run your finger down it until you find the row you want. Use the table below to answer these questions.

● Was Rhode Island the first, second, third, or fourth place shown to become a colony?

● On what date did Connecticut become a state?

● Which other colonies in the table also became states in 1788?

● What is the nickname for New Hampshire?

TITLE

SUMMARY OF NEW ENGLAND COLONIES

	SETTLED BY EUROPEANS	BECAME A COLONY	BECAME A STATE	RANK OF STATEHOOD	NICKNAME TODAY
Connecticut	1636	1639	Jan. 9, 1788	5th	Constitution State
Massachusetts	1620	1630	Feb. 6, 1788	6th	Bay State
New Hampshire	1623	1679	June 21, 1788	9th	Granite State
Rhode Island	1636	1663	May 29, 1790	13th	Ocean State

ROWS

COLUMNS

◄ This table gives a lot of information about early New England colonies.

TRY IT

Try your hand at making a table. First, think of information that could be put in the form of a table. Perhaps your family needs to keep track of phone numbers. Maybe your baseball card collection needs to be sorted so that you know if you have duplicates. Or maybe your class wants a list of who plays what position on your softball team, and their birthdays.

How will you organize your table? You could list the names in alphabetical order, like the table on the above right, so that it would be easy to look up the names of your teammates. But maybe you're really interested in when the team members' birthdays are. The table to the right shows you one way to do that.

When your table is finished, make up questions based on the information it includes. Then trade your table and questions with a classmate.

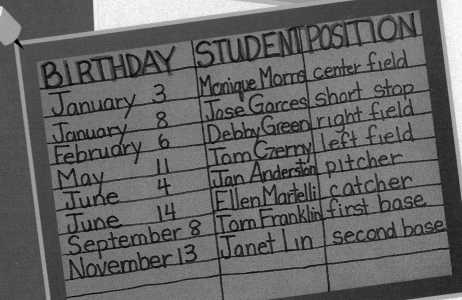

STUDENT	POSITION	BIRTHDAY
Anderson, Jan	Pitcher	June 4
Czerny, Tom	left field	May 11
Franklin, Tom	first base	September 8
Garces, Jose	Short stop	January 8
Green, Debby	right field	February 6
Lin, Janet	second base	November 13
Martelli, Ellen	Catcher	June 14
Morris, Monique	Center field	January 3

BIRTHDAY	STUDENT	POSITION
January 3	Monique Morris	center field
January 8	Jose Garces	short stop
February 6	Debby Green	right field
May 11	Tom Czerny	left field
June 4	Jan Anderson	pitcher
June 14	Ellen Martelli	catcher
September 8	Tom Franklin	first base
November 13	Janet Lin	second base

SKILL POWER SEARCH

As you read this chapter, think about how information about the New England colonies could be organized in a table.

KEY TERMS

Puritan
separatist
Pilgrim
Mayflower Compact
charter
delegate

SETTLING NEW ENGLAND

FOCUS *The people who settled New England hoped to create a model society. In some ways they succeeded beyond their wildest dreams. In other ways they fell short of their goals.*

Trouble in England

By 1600, life in England had become particularly difficult for many groups of people, including those known as Puritans.

What was so bad about life in England for people at that time? Cities were growing rapidly. Prices were rising. Unemployment was high, and wages were low. But for Puritans, life was also difficult because they didn't like many things about the Church of England. They felt that the church encouraged people to ignore the rules of the Bible as the Puritans interpreted them. People danced and played cards. Worship services were elaborate. The Church of England was the official church—the *only* legal church in the country. So Puritans saw it as responsible for what was wrong with England.

In truth, the country was ripe for change. But James I,

THE NEW ENGLAND COLONIES

★ Colony capitals
● Other settlements
── Present-day boundaries

king of England, and his successor, Charles I, were resistant to Puritan demands for change. James didn't like the way the Puritans spoke out against the Church of England. He did whatever he could to make their lives miserable. He even had some Puritans thrown in jail.

Most Puritans believed they could change the church and still remain a part of it. But a small group of them wanted to form their own church, *separate* from the Church of England. People in this group were known as **separatists**. For them, it was time to leave England and move to a new land, where they could worship as they believed. If they could create a truly religious society, perhaps other English people would recognize their accomplishments and follow their examples.

★ **Puritan** A person in the 1600s in England who thought the English church should be made "pure"

★ **separatist** A person who wished to separate from the Church of England

Leaving Home

In 1608 the separatists left England for the Netherlands, where they could worship as they pleased, without interference from a church. By 1620, though, this group had returned to England because they were not comfortable with Dutch ways and customs. They set their eyes on America. Their ship, the *Mayflower,* set sail from Plymouth, England, in September 1620.

Not all 101 passengers on board were separatists, however. About half were *strangers*—the English term for those who were unfamiliar. Generally these men and women were farmers who simply hoped to get a fresh start, away from England. Together the people on the *Mayflower* became known as the **Pilgrims.** For two months the Pilgrims sailed west, expecting to go to Virginia, where the English had already settled. When at last they spotted land, it was the coast of New England, not Virginia! But they could not turn back—this was to be their new home.

The Mayflower Compact

The Pilgrims had to deal with two problems right away. They needed a government, and they had to make it through the winter.

They tackled the first problem before they got off the ship. Separatist Puritans and strangers naturally might have had different ways of seeing things, but they were able to agree to make rules for their new colony in the **Mayflower Compact.** Those who signed the compact agreed to live by the rules and to work together to

 Signing the Mayflower Compact

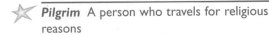 **Pilgrim** A person who travels for religious reasons

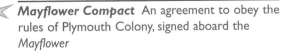 **Mayflower Compact** An agreement to obey the rules of Plymouth Colony, signed aboard the *Mayflower*

A high chair like this was brought to America for the first Pilgrim child born at Plymouth, Peregrine White.

support them. Their settlement was called Plymouth because that is what Captain John Smith, who had mapped the coast of New England, named it.

The next problem for the Pilgrims was how to survive a cold winter that was much harsher than England's. They barely had time to throw together shelters before the first snow came. More than half of the Pilgrims died during the winter of 1620–1621. They *all* might have died if it hadn't been for Native Americans. The Wampanoags (wahm puh NOH agz) lived near Plymouth Colony. They taught the colonists where to plant corn and where to fish.

By the fall of 1621, the Pilgrims were still facing tough times. But they had made it through one whole year in Plymouth. To show their gratitude, they held a three-day harvest festival, known to us today as the feast of Thanksgiving.

The Massachusetts Bay Colony

By the late 1620s another, larger group of English settlers began to talk of heading for America. The Puritans, like the Pilgrims, were fed up with things in England. Unlike the Pilgrims, these Puritans did not believe that they had to *separate* from the Church of England. They hoped to create a Puritan society in the new Massachusetts Bay Colony.

More than 1,000 Puritans founded the Massachusetts Bay Colony in 1630. John Winthrop was the colony's governor for most of its first 20 years. Winthrop believed that Boston, the heart of the colony, should be a "City of God." It would show the world how society should be run. This colony and other New England colonies are shown on the map on page 94.

Plymouth Colony has been recreated as Plimoth Plantation. ▶

Many Puritans who settled in the Massachusetts Bay Colony shared Winthrop's vision. They expected to work hard and live a pure life. If they did, they hoped that God would bless their colony with economic success. They thought that their success might be proof that God's grace had been given to them. Puritans believed that only with God's grace would they enter heaven.

How the Colony Worked

The Puritans who set up the Massachusetts Bay Colony had to deal with many of the same hardships the Pilgrims had endured. They suffered through long winters and struggled farming rocky soil. Still, this second group of settlers didn't have to worry about creating a new government. They already had one in place.

Back in England the king had granted these Puritans a **charter** allowing them to settle in Massachusetts. The charter, which they brought with them, gave them the right to elect their own leaders.

Puritans expected their government to support their church. They expected, for instance, that government leaders would pass a law requiring everyone to go to church. But Puritans did not want the government to *control* the church, as it did in England.

Laws for the Massachusetts Bay Colony were made in Boston. At first a

"*Whatsoever we did or ought to have done when we lived in England, the same must we do, and more also, where we go. . . . We must bear one another's burdens. . . .*" *--John Winthrop, 1630*

▲ John Winthrop

small group of men made the laws. But as the colony grew, people in new towns wanted input. So each town was allowed to send a **delegate** to Boston to help make laws. Towns voted on who would be sent.

However, only free white men were allowed to vote. And they had to be members of the Puritan church. To join the church, a person had to pass a test by standing up in front of fellow churchgoers and describing how he or she had experienced God's grace.

Complaints

Almost from the beginning many settlers had problems with some of the colony's rules. For example, a Puritan minister named Roger Williams didn't like the idea that only church members could vote. He thought that this rule too closely linked the government and the church. In 1635, Williams was forced out of the Massachusetts Bay Colony. The next year he established a settlement that later became the colony of Rhode Island.

Thomas Hooker had similar complaints and left Massachusetts. In 1636 he founded what became the colony of Connecticut. Anne Hutchinson also spoke up. She saw no reason why church members always had to agree with their ministers. In 1637 she was put on trial for her ideas and was banished from Massachusetts. She fled to Rhode Island.

★ **charter** An official paper in which rights are given by a government to a person or company

★ **delegate** A representative

Changing Times

As time passed, more people arrived in Massachusetts. Many were single people, not people with families. They came not for religious reasons but to make money.

These settlers helped build the farming colony into a center for fishing, shipbuilding, and trading. The map on this page shows some of the trade routes that developed and the goods traded between the colonies and other places. Frontiers were extended as older settlements along the coast became overcrowded. People moved from Boston to lands farther north, west, and south, across hills and rivers into western Massachusetts and into what became Maine and New Hampshire. They also moved into Rhode Island and Connecticut.

But it wasn't just strangers and newcomers who caused change. The children of the original settlers found some Puritan rules too rigid. For example, they weren't interested in taking a test to join the church. In 1662 the Puritans changed

Cod, important to New England's economy, was traded for goods from other countries.

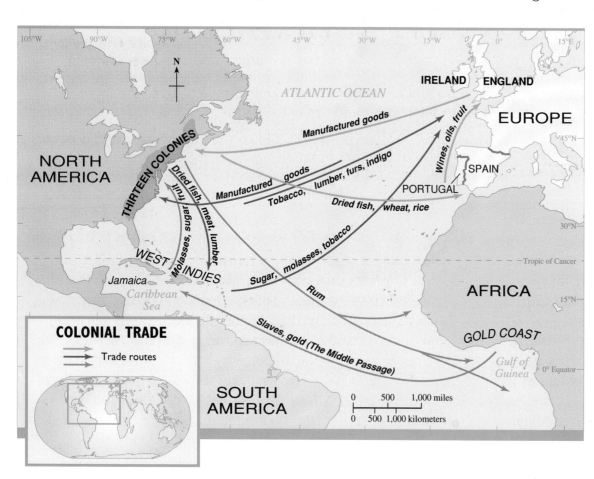

COLONIAL TRADE

→ Trade routes

98

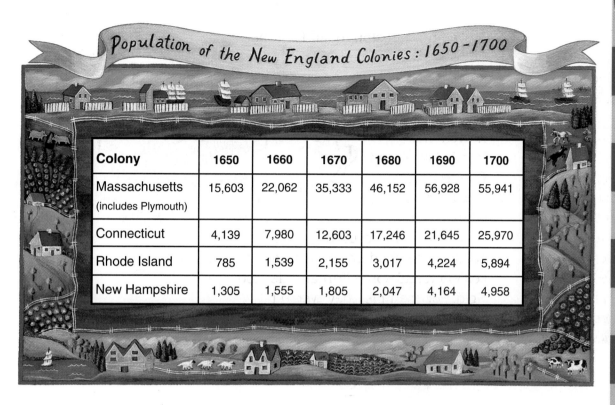

Population of the New England Colonies: 1650-1700

Colony	1650	1660	1670	1680	1690	1700
Massachusetts (includes Plymouth)	15,603	22,062	35,333	46,152	56,928	55,941
Connecticut	4,139	7,980	12,603	17,246	21,645	25,970
Rhode Island	785	1,539	2,155	3,017	4,224	5,894
New Hampshire	1,305	1,555	1,805	2,047	4,164	4,958

this rule, allowing children of the original Puritan settlers to become church members, even if they hadn't experienced grace. The importance of the Puritan church began to decline.

Relations With Native Americans

Over the years the settlers' dealings with Native Americans also changed. At first, relations with Native Americans had been quite friendly. The Wampanoags, after all, had assisted the settlers that first year.

But things soon turned ugly. Native Americans were hurt by diseases brought from Europe. They were angry that colonists were settling more and more land. In 1636 the Pequots (PEE-kwahts) fought to keep colonists off Pequot land. The Wampanoags did the same thing in 1675. Many Native Americans were killed in the fighting; others lost all of their lands.

Growing by Leaps and Bounds

The colonies grew rapidly after the English colonists took control of what had been Native American lands. Massachusetts swallowed up Plymouth Colony in 1691 and also claimed land that later became Maine and New Hampshire. By 1700, Massachusetts had more than 50,000 settlers. New England as a whole had about 90,000.

SHOW WHAT YOU KNOW!

REFOCUS
COMPREHENSION

1. Most people who settled New England in the 1600s came from what country in Europe?

2. What New England colony was settled first?

THINK ABOUT IT
CRITICAL THINKING

Compare New England in 1635 with New England in 1700. What major changes took place? Why?

WRITE ABOUT IT
ACTIVITY

If you were a settler who did not agree with the Puritan rules in Boston in 1650, what would you do? Where would you go?

LIFE IN A NEW ENGLAND VILLAGE

FOCUS *People in Puritan New England had a strong sense of family and community. These values were evident in many aspects of everyday life.*

Nosy Neighbors?

If you suddenly found yourself transported from your home today to a Puritan village of the 1600s, you would think that your neighbors were pretty nosy. They would be watching every move you made. But if you felt as if your privacy were being invaded, you'd be missing the point. In Puritan society your neighbors were *supposed* to watch you.

As you have learned, Puritans believed that you needed God's grace to get into heaven. You and your Puritan neighbors cannot be sure how to obtain it, but you feel it can't hurt to try to live a perfect life. That means following every rule. It means you have to read the Bible and listen to your minister. It means doing plenty of good deeds. By keeping an eye on you, your neighbors are really trying to help you make sure that you live as good a life as possible.

▲ A meeting house built in the 1700s in Sudbury, Massachusetts

Much in Common

To watch over each other, Puritans have built their houses close together. The fields you farm might lie on the outskirts of your village, but chances are your home is right in the center of town. You see your neighbors every day. You also see your neighbors at your village's **meeting house**. Every village has one or more of them. Meeting houses are simple wooden buildings, sometimes called Lord's barns. Across from or near the meeting house is the **common**, where

▶ Meeting houses were simple, but communion cups, such as this one that belonged to John Winthrop, were fancy.

meeting house A building used for both public and religious meetings
common Land available for use by all people of a village or town

villagers meet to discuss events of the day, as well as to graze their animals.

At the meeting house, townspeople gather at least twice a week—every Sunday, plus one day in the middle of the week. You listen for hours as the minister tells you what God expects of you. And then you are expected to go back home and do it!

Most Puritans, of course, like being part of a strong community. On the map on this page, you can see that Boston is an example of a Puritan community. Its meeting house and common are right in the middle of town! You enjoy being with neighbors who care about and think like you. If you get sick, neighbors will bring you meals. If your barn burns down, neighbors will help you rebuild it. Often the people who settled a town were relatives. But even those who were not related were, in a way, like brothers and sisters.

Family All Around

If you lived in Puritan New England, you would not only be part of the community but you would also be part of a family. Family life isn't just nice; it is necessary.

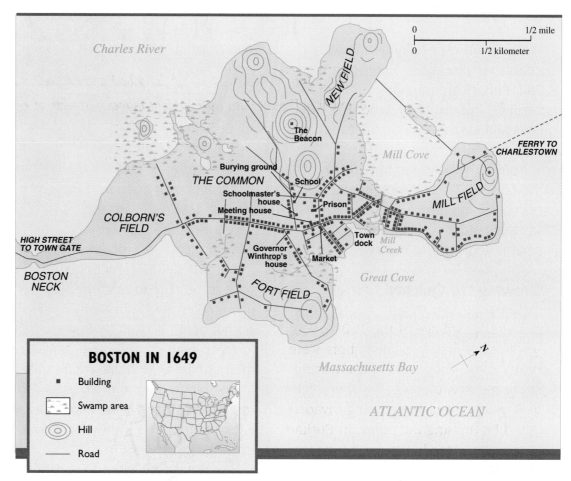

BOSTON IN 1649

- ■ Building
- Swamp area
- ◎ Hill
- —— Road

Only families are granted land. In fact, single people aren't welcomed into early Massachusetts at all. They aren't allowed to move to the colony unless they can find a family to live with. This is because New Englanders think single people are more likely to cause trouble than married people or family members. They might break laws and live lives different from those lived by families. They might gamble or dance, for example.

Both mothers and fathers play important roles in family life. Puritan mothers handle household chores. They take loving care of their children.

Mothers are especially gentle with infants, as disease is a constant worry. Still, fathers are in charge of Puritan families. Puritan men, who make the laws and cast the votes, believe that men are wiser than women.

Your father decides how much of the family's land or money you will get when you grow up. And he has to say yes before you can marry the person you want to marry.

Growing Up Quickly

Childhood for Puritans didn't last as long as it does for people today. Today most people consider you to be an adult when you reach age 21. But in the 1600s you were expected to act like an adult at the age of 6 or 7. You have to dress like an adult. You work alongside your parents. Girls begin cooking, spinning, and making soap. Boys work outdoors, tending to farming chores, such as caring for animals, planting crops, and making and mending fences.

When you are just a little older, you might become an **apprentice**. This means leaving your home and spending several months or even years learning a

skill from an experienced laborer. Skills such as barrel making, cabinet making, and silversmithing are commonly taught.

Chances are your father will teach you to read and write. There are very few schools in early New England. Yet reading is an important skill in New England. You have to be able to read the Bible. A **primer** (PRIHM ur), an early version of a school book, is used by Puritan fathers to teach reading and other skills to their children. Mothers are less likely to be able to read and write.

Ministers have to be especially well educated. After all, they have to explain God's word to the community. No one is more important to a town than its minister. In 1636, Puritans start Harvard College to train these ministers.

Staying Healthy . . .

With their emphasis on reading, New Englanders are very well educated settlers. They are also very

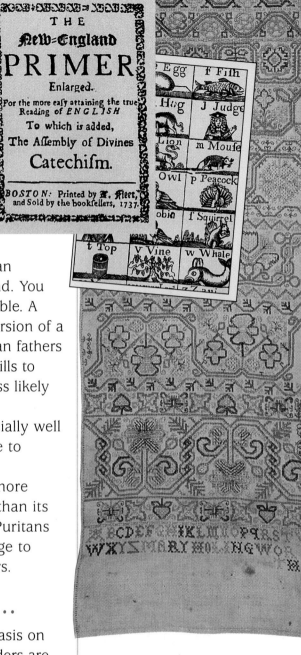

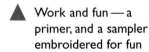

▲ Work and fun — a primer, and a sampler embroidered for fun

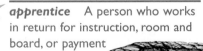

★ **apprentice** A person who works in return for instruction, room and board, or payment

★ **primer** A simple book for teaching reading to beginners

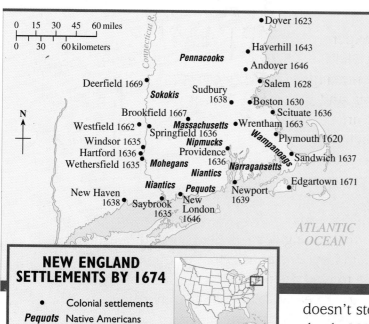

NEW ENGLAND SETTLEMENTS BY 1674

- Colonial settlements
- *Pequots* Native Americans

Map labels: Connecticut R., Dover 1623, Haverhill 1643, Pennacooks, Andover 1646, Salem 1628, Deerfield 1669, Sokokis, Sudbury 1638, Boston 1630, Brookfield 1667, Scituate 1636, Westfield 1662, Massachusetts, Wrentham 1663, Springfield 1636, Wampanoags, Windsor 1635, Nipmucks, Plymouth 1620, Hartford 1636, Providence 1636, Sandwich 1637, Wethersfield 1635, Mohegans, Niantics, Narragansetts, Niantics, New Haven 1638, Pequots, Newport 1639, Edgartown 1671, Saybrook 1635, New London 1646, ATLANTIC OCEAN

sweep through whole towns. (Many of the early towns are shown on the map on this page.) Finally, everyone around you has enough land to grow plenty of food. With a healthy diet, your body can fight off diseases.

healthy. As a New England settler—if you have survived childhood—you are likely to live a long, healthy life. One reason for this is New England's cold climate. For nearly half the year, bad weather keeps you from traveling far. If you don't move around, you don't carry disease with you. Also, your town is not as crowded as European cities are. This means that diseases tend not to

...But Accepting Death

Puritans are generally pretty healthy, but that doesn't stop them from thinking about death. Most Puritan families experience the death of at least one or two children. And they know that New England, as good as it is, is not perfect. They feel that heaven is the only perfect place. Therefore Puritans work hard at gaining God's favor so that they might enter heaven after they die. You and your family and friends also spend much of your life wondering what heaven is like.

Gravestones show this interest in life and death. Their inscriptions tell stories of people who lived, worked, and died for faith.

◀ In New England you can find gravestones from the 1600s.

SHOW WHAT YOU KNOW!

REFOCUS
COMPREHENSION

1. How was life in a Puritan village different for boys and girls?

2. Why was education so important to Puritans?

THINK ABOUT IT
CRITICAL THINKING

What aspects of life in a New England village might have made an outsider feel unwelcome? What about it made others feel right at home?

WRITE ABOUT IT
ACTIVITY

If you lived in a New England village of the 1640s instead of in your town or city today, how would life be different for you?

March of Time
1621 TO 1676

NEW ENGLAND CHANGES

FOCUS *Some of New England's first settlers had strong Puritan beliefs. The beliefs began to change over time as people challenged them.*

SQUANTO'S HELP

In early 1621 the Pilgrims were cold, sick, and hungry. They wouldn't have survived had it not been for Squanto. This Native American had been captured by European explorers some years earlier. He had been taken to England, but he was back now, living with the Wampanoags and their leader, Massasoit (MAS uh-soit). As a result of his captivity, he spoke English. Squanto was willing to live with the Pilgrims, teaching them how to survive in a land that was strange to them. He introduced them to new methods of farming and fishing. When he died in 1622, many in Plymouth Colony felt the loss.

ROGER WILLIAMS'S TROUBLES

When Roger Williams settled Rhode Island in 1636, he did so fuming over the Massachusetts rule that only church members could vote. It was a law, he said, that "stinks in God's nostrils." Williams wouldn't have that kind of rule in his colony. In Rhode Island, the government would not make *any* laws about religion.

As a result, people in Rhode Island were free to worship any way they wanted to. The colony encouraged people of different faiths to live together.

ANNE HUTCHINSON'S QUESTIONS

Anne Hutchinson was in big trouble. She had questioned the wisdom of ministers in the Massachusetts Colony. She held meetings in her home to discuss the ministers' sermons. Soon she started to express opinions about religion that differed from those of the colony's ministers. The ministers weren't used to anyone—especially a woman—challenging what they taught. At Hutchinson's trial, in 1637, ministers and lawmakers tried to show that she was wrong. Hutchinson knew the Bible so well that she tripped them up. But they didn't care. They decided she was "a woman not fit for our society." When they forced her out of the colony, she fled to Rhode Island with her husband and children.

1621	1636	1637	1662	1675–1676
Squanto begins helping the Pilgrims	Roger Williams settles Rhode Island	Anne Hutchinson is put on trial	Puritans adopt Halfway Covenant	King Philip's War fought

1620	1630	1640	1650	1660	1670	1680

THE HALFWAY COVENANT'S COMPROMISE

Children and grandchildren of the original Puritan settlers weren't eager to join the church. Many of the rules for joining—and maintaining church membership—were very strict. And these second and third generations of Puritans didn't like what had happened to people who had questioned church authority—people such as Roger Williams and Anne Hutchinson.

As a result, church membership was down. This worried the original Puritan settlers. To get their children to join the church, they adopted the Halfway Covenant in 1662. This allowed children of church members to join the church, even if they hadn't experienced grace. So original church members could pass on membership to their children, who in turn could pass it on to their children. But what kind of church would those children want? Something much different from that of 1630, for sure.

KING PHILIP'S SAD END

It was a sad time for Metacomet (met uh KAHM iht), known as King Philip, leader of the Wampanoags. For 60 years his people had been friends with New Englanders. His father was the legendary Massasoit. But times had changed since his people were so generous to the Pilgrims and the Pilgrims were so thankful in return. Throughout the 1600s, Puritan settlers had taken Wampanoag land and brought much disease. Anger and distrust now filled the air.

In June 1675, King Philip led a war against the colonists, in which both sides committed terrible acts. By the end of 1676, hundreds of settlers had been killed.

Most significantly, though, *40 percent* of the Native American population in New England—including King Philip himself—had been killed.

SHOW WHAT YOU KNOW!

REFOCUS
COMPREHENSION

1. Why did Anne Hutchinson leave Massachusetts Bay Colony?

2. Why was King Philip's War fought?

THINK ABOUT IT
CRITICAL THINKING

How would you compare Roger Williams's Rhode Island Colony with the Massachusetts Bay Colony?

WRITE ABOUT IT
ACTIVITY

Make a map that shows where the major events in New England took place between 1621 and 1676. Then write a key that works with your map.

Citizenship

KEY TERMS

majority rule
direct democracy

WHY WE HAVE TOWN MEETINGS

FOCUS *Starting with the Mayflower Compact, New Englanders developed a tradition of self-government. That tradition can still be seen in town meetings across New England and America.*

The Roots of Self-government

The Pilgrims hadn't planned on governing themselves. If their ship hadn't strayed off course, they wouldn't have had to. Remember, they thought they were going to Virginia. There an English settlement was already in place, with a charter and rules of order clearly spelled out.

But the Pilgrims had landed in a very different place from Virginia! Luckily they didn't panic. Before leaving their ship, they wrote the Mayflower Compact. It wasn't very long—only about 200 words. Yet it was a great accomplishment. It contained the seeds of self-government that would, years later, help America become independent. It proved that separatists and strangers on board the *Mayflower* could agree on basic ideas about how their new homeland would be run.

▲ People have been speaking out at town meetings for centuries.

Rules of the Compact

The Mayflower Compact set the stage for town meetings at which everyone who could vote would play a part in making laws. At these meetings, decisions would be made by **majority rule**. In other words, if most people voted in favor of an idea, that idea would become law.

The Mayflower Compact worked! It kept everyone, separatists and strangers alike, united in the new colony. The compact remained in place until 1691, when Plymouth became part of the larger, more powerful Massachusetts Bay Colony. The Pilgrims then came under that colony's rules. But the idea of town meetings didn't die. In fact, many laws and rules in the Massachusetts Bay Colony were similar to those of Plymouth. All across New England settlers picked up on this form of

majority rule Rule by more than half the population

TOWN MEETING
8 P.M.

government. It became the way New Englanders made their local laws. Many New Englanders took this form of government with them when they went on to settle in other areas.

Town Meetings Live On

Even today, town meetings are alive and well in many communities across the country. Once a year, or more often if necessary, people gather at a public place, such as a school or town hall. They talk, debate, and sometimes even shout at each other. Should the town pass a leash law for dogs? Should it spend money constructing new basketball courts? Each townsperson might have his or her own point of view on issues such as these. And each townsperson has the right to express that point of view, just as the people are doing in the picture on these pages. After all the talk a vote is taken. The decision is made by majority rule, just as it was in Plymouth Colony.

Town meetings remain popular because they allow for **direct democracy**. This means that the people vote on laws. Town meetings are about the only places left where Americans get to do this. Americans don't vote directly on state or national laws. Instead, we vote to elect lawmakers, and the lawmakers actually make the laws.

Will town meetings always be around? It's hard to say. As towns become larger, it gets harder to make town meetings work. Many towns have gotten so big that it's impossible to fit all the voters into one meeting hall. Still, town meetings are such an important part of New England's—and America's—history that it's unlikely they will disappear anytime soon.

⭐ **direct democracy**   A principle of American government that allows citizens to participate in making laws

SHOW WHAT YOU KNOW!

REFOCUS
COMPREHENSION

1. Where did the tradition of town meetings begin?

2. What is the major reason town meetings remain popular?

THINK ABOUT IT
CRITICAL THINKING

What are some possible problems with town meetings?

WRITE ABOUT IT
ACTIVITY

Write a letter to your newspaper saying whether you believe your town should have town meetings. If so, why? If not, why not?

SUMMING UP

1 DO YOU REMEMBER . . .
COMPREHENSION

1. Why did the Puritans come to America?

2. What was the Mayflower Compact?

3. How did the English colonists depend on Native Americans at first?

4. What did economic success prove to the Puritans?

5. What rights did their royal charter give the Puritans?

6. How were Roger Williams's and Anne Hutchinson's ideas different from those of most Puritans?

7. Why did Puritan townspeople gather at meeting houses?

8. Who could vote in Puritan villages?

9. How did the Puritans make decisions at town meetings?

10. What was the Halfway Covenant?

2 SKILL POWER
READING A TABLE

Make a table that shows the accomplishments of John Winthrop, Roger Williams, and Thomas Hooker. List the colonies they started. Also give their reasons for starting these new colonies.

3 WHAT DO YOU THINK?
CRITICAL THINKING

1. The Puritans wanted to show the world how society should be run. Tell whether you think they succeeded.

2. Would you have wanted to live in Massachusetts when the Puritans ruled the colony? Explain your answer.

3. Would you say the Massachusetts colony was run in a democratic or undemocratic fashion? Explain.

4. How do you think Puritan beliefs influenced daily life in early New England?

5. Why, do you think, did the Massachusetts colony grow so rapidly?

4 SAY IT, WRITE IT, USE IT
VOCABULARY

If you were a tour guide in a typical Puritan village in 1650, how would you tell a group of visitors from another country about what they see as they ride through town? Use as many of the vocabulary words below as you can.

apprentice	Mayflower Compact
charter	meeting house
common	Pilgrim
delegate	primer
direct democracy	Puritan
majority rule	separatist

CHAPTER 5

5 GEOGRAPHY AND YOU
MAP STUDY

Use the map below and the map on page 94 to help you answer the following questions.

1. What New England river ran through two colonies, splitting each in half?

2. Name the capitals of the New England colonies.

3. What settlements, established by very small groups, were founded between 1620 and 1630?

4. List the ten earliest New England settlements on this map.

6 TAKE ACTION
CITIZENSHIP

You probably agree that it was unfair that only white male church members could vote in Massachusetts Bay Colony. Over the centuries the vote has been given to all American citizens over 18. Yet in many elections, less than half of all eligible voters bother to go to the polls!

Make a poster that tells why you think voting is important. Include information about how people can register to vote. Hang your poster in a place where adults will see it.

7 GET CREATIVE
HEALTH CONNECTION

With room enough to fish, hunt, and grow plenty of food, New Englanders had a healthy diet. Do some research to find out about the typical foods that New Englanders ate in the 1600s and 1700s. Then make a chart that compares their typical meals with those of your family. Finally, decide who ate the healthier foods.

LOOKING AHEAD   Find out in the next chapter why the Southern Colonies were different from those in New England.

CHAPTER 6

The Southern

The English began settling the Southern Colonies in the early 1600s. The settlers grew tobacco and rice, which required many workers and lots of land. The need for both land and workers greatly impacted the lives of Native Americans and Africans.

Where might you see a weather vane like this? Look on page 124 for one example. ▶

CONTENTS

Colonies

These books tell about some interesting people, places, and events during the settlement of the Southern Colonies. Read one that interests you and fill out a book-review form.

READ AND RESEARCH

An Introduction to Williamsburg by Valerie Tripp
(Pleasantry Press, 1985)
Picture yourself living 200 years ago in Colonial Williamsburg. Find out about the daily lives and activities of various people at that time. *(nonfiction)*
* *You can read a selection from this book on page 126.*

Pocahontas and the Strangers by Clyde Robert Bulla
(Scholastic, 1987)
Trouble starts for Pocahontas and her nation when the Europeans arrive. After her people capture Captain John Smith, Pocahontas saves his life. Will her life change forever? *(biography)*

Who Owns the Sun? by Stacy Chbosky (Landmark Editions, 1988)
A father and son have a conversation about beautiful things in the world that belong to no one. Read slowly as the boy sadly discovers the truth about his own situation. This book was written by a 14-year-old. *(historical fiction)*

SKILL POWER — Making an Outline

Writing an outline can help you organize information for a report.

UNDERSTAND IT

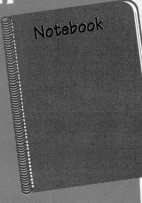

Notebook

Are you an organized person? If you are, your loose-leaf notebook is probably organized according to subjects—social studies, science, and so forth.

How can you organize your thoughts and ideas before writing a report? A good way is to use an outline, organizing your information into a title, main ideas, and supporting ideas.

To make an outline:

• Center the title at the top.

• Label each main idea, or topic, with a Roman numeral and a period. List the topics in a logical order.

• Indent the supporting ideas, or subtopics. Label each subtopic with a capital letter and a period.

• Use a capital letter for the first word of each main topic and subtopic.

EXPLORE IT

American colonists in the 1600s, especially in what is today South Carolina, grew rice. The outline below describes this kind of farming.

Rice Farming

I. Conditions for growing

   A. Type of soil

   B. Temperature

II. Planting and cultivating

   A. Sowing the seeds

   B. Water supply

   C. Weed control

Where would you add the subtopic *Rainfall?*

Which would be a good topic for the next entry—III—Making rice pudding or Harvesting the crop?

Work in groups of four. As a group, decide on a topic you all know about, such as "An Ordinary Day" or "Planning a Surprise Party." Have each person, without consulting the others, make an outline to organize information about the topic. When everyone in the group has finished, compare your outlines. Are they different in some ways? Do they all work? Do they all organize information in a clear and logical way?

Guest List
Music
Food
Balloons
Games

Planning a Surprise Party

I. Guest list

  A. Relatives

  B. Friends

  C. Neighbors

II. Decorations

  A. Crepe-paper streamers

  B. "Congratulations" banner

  C. Balloons

  D. Paper plates, cups, and napkins

III. Food

  A. Appetizers

  B. Main dishes

  C. Desserts

IV. Entertainment

  A. Music

  B. Games

SKILL POWER SEARCH *As you read the next lesson, Setting the Scene, make an outline of the main topics.*

Setting the Scene

⭐ **KEY TERMS**

work ethic
export
cash crop
indentured servant
buffer zone
plantation

People in the South

FOCUS *The development of the Southern Colonies was often slow and painful. It was hard for the settlers, but it was worse for Africans and Native Americans.*

Trouble in Jamestown

As you read in Chapter 4, the early years of the Jamestown settlement in Virginia were not easy. Many of the settlers died, and others wasted their time looking for gold. These early settlers also made enemies of the Algonquian Indians in the area. The settlement seemed unlikely to survive.

However, things changed in 1608, when Captain John Smith took control of Jamestown. Smith brought a new **work ethic** and announced a new rule—only people who worked would get food. It was a tough policy, but it worked. People stopped digging for gold and started planting crops. Smith also improved relations with the Algonquians. He met with their powerful chief, Powhatan, and traded with him for corn.

Despite Smith's new plan, there were still problems. Many settlers were weakened by a mosquito-borne disease called malaria. And during the winter of 1609–1610, the settlers ran out of food. They had to eat dogs, rats, and snakes. So many people died that the population of Jamestown dropped from 500 to 60 within a few months.

Again help came. In the summer of 1610, a ship

▼ This picture shows early settlers arriving in Jamestown.

⭐ **work ethic** A belief in working hard

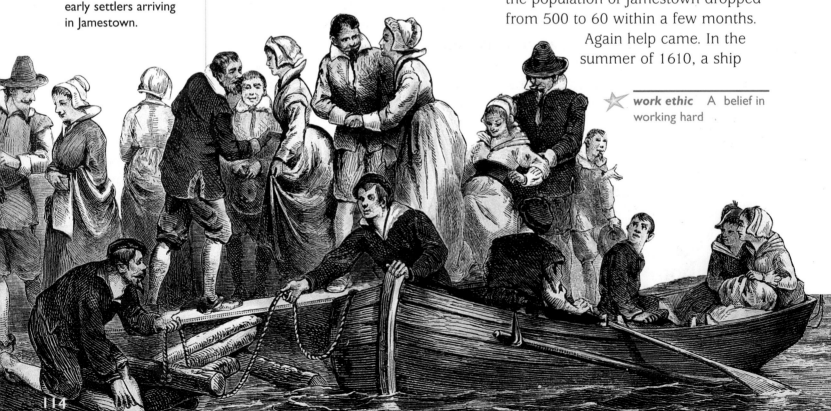

| 1610 | 1619 | 1634 | 1680 |
| 300 more English settlers arrive in Jamestown | The first African slaves are brought to Virginia | The first settlers arrive in Maryland | Algonquian population drops below 1,000 in Virginia |

1600   1610   1620   1630   1640   1650   1660   1670   1680

arrived from England bringing food, supplies, and 300 more settlers. Virginia would soon become the first English colony in America to succeed. Find Virginia and the other Southern Colonies on the map on this page.

An Important Crop

In 1612, John Rolfe made a discovery that would dramatically affect the settlement of Jamestown and the colony of Virginia. He learned that tobacco would grow in Virginia. Settlers then began to grow tobacco and **export** it to Europe.

Tobacco became popular in Europe after explorers took it home from North America in the 1500s. However, not everyone liked tobacco. Even King James I of England said, "Smoking is a custom loathsome to the eye, hateful to the nose, harmful to the brain, [and] dangerous to the lung." Many people disagreed with the king. And by 1638, Virginians exported 3 million pounds of this **cash crop** annually.

A Need for Workers

Tobacco helped Virginian colonists but not Native Americans. To grow tobacco, settlers needed lots of land and workers. The colonists took land from Native Americans. They also tried to force Algonquians to work in tobacco fields. The Algonquians fought successfully to keep their freedom, but they were still devastated by war

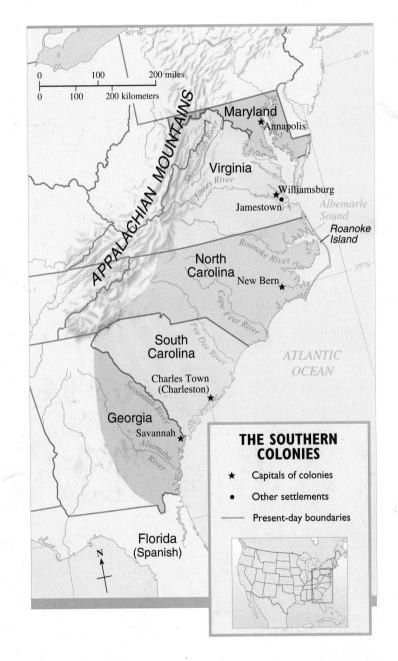

THE SOUTHERN COLONIES

★ Capitals of colonies
● Other settlements
— Present-day boundaries

---

 export To ship a product to another country to sell it there
cash crop Something that is grown for a profit

and European diseases. The Algonquians had never been exposed to European diseases, such as smallpox. As a result, many of them died from these diseases. By 1680 there were fewer than 1,000 Algonquians left in the colony of Virginia.

Failing to get the Native Americans as laborers, the colonists tried using **indentured servants.** These were mostly Europeans who couldn't afford the trip to America. So they worked for planters for up to seven years in exchange for passage to Virginia. They left Europe and were willing to become servants because they hoped for a good life in America after their years of service were over.

However, indentured servants worked long hours in hot mosquito-filled fields day after day. Some servants didn't get enough to eat, and many died before earning their freedom.

Those who did become free couldn't afford land. Most did not find the prosperity they sought. By 1660 few people wanted to come to Virginia as indentured servants.

The Slave Trade

The planters still needed workers to plant and harvest their tobacco. So they turned to Africa to find those workers. Unlike indentured servants who had come to America voluntarily, these Africans were brought here against their will. And unlike indentured servants who rode as passengers on boats, these Africans traveled like cargo beneath the decks of ships. Also, unlike indentured servants who could eventually gain freedom, most of these Africans would never become free.

The process of enslaving Africans began in Africa. Often European slave traders, armed with guns, crept into African villages and forests. They captured unarmed men, women, and even children. Sometimes Africans were captured and enslaved by rival African groups.

After being captured, enslaved Africans were chained together, forced to march to the west coast of Africa, and sold to the highest bidder. The map on page 117 shows how many Africans were forced into slavery.

Once they reached the coast of Africa, these captives were forced into

▲ An announcement of a slave auction

---

indentured servant A person who sold his or her services for a certain period of time in exchange for free passage to America

ships that would take them across the ocean. Called the *Middle Passage*, this voyage took from four to six weeks.

For the Africans, every moment was torture. There were so many people forced into the bottom of the ship that they had no room to move. The high waves of the open sea made many of them seasick. The conditions were so bad that many Africans did not survive the trip. Those who did survive were forced to lie in filth at the bottom of the ship. They did not know why they had been ripped from their families or where they were going.

The Life of a Slave

When Africans arrived in America, they were treated like animals and sold at auctions. Their masters now completely controlled their lives and their children's lives. Any baby born to an enslaved woman automatically became a slave.

In the 1600s most enslaved people had masters, or owners, who did not give them enough food, decent clothing, or shelter. Many slaves were also whipped. Some slaves fared better, depending on their masters.

Africans had been torn from their homelands and confronted with a new language, a new culture, and a grim new life. However, they adapted to this life and used their skills to help build the colonies.

Over time the Southern Colonies purchased even more Africans. In

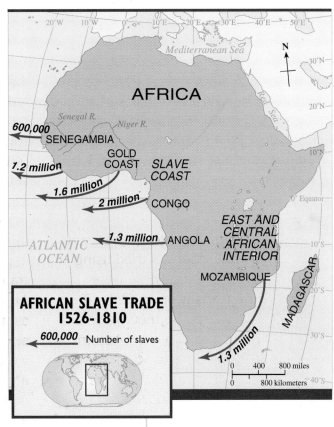

AFRICA

AFRICAN SLAVE TRADE
1526-1810

← 600,000   Number of slaves

600,000 SENEGAMBIA
1.2 million GOLD COAST
1.6 million SLAVE COAST
2 million CONGO
1.3 million ANGOLA
1.3 million MOZAMBIQUE

EAST AND CENTRAL AFRICAN INTERIOR

MADAGASCAR

ATLANTIC OCEAN

Mediterranean Sea

Senegal R.   Niger R.

0   400   800 miles
0   800 kilometers

Slaves on a forced march to the African coast

the Chesapeake area alone there were 4,000 enslaved people in 1675, and by 1760 there were over 185,000.

Maryland and the Carolinas

As Virginia became more established, other Southern Colonies were settled. Find Maryland on the map on this page. In Maryland, settlers learned from Virginia's mistakes. They planted food crops and developed good relationships with the Native Americans.

Another colony took a very different approach. In Carolina, settlers didn't want friendship from Native Americans. Instead they wanted land and workers because they grew tobacco and rice, which required a great deal of land and labor.

The Carolinians used force to take the lands they wanted from Native Americans. Fierce fighting broke out

between the two groups.

Carolinians, like Virginians, turned to Africans for labor. By 1720, enslaved people outnumbered free colonists two to one in the southern part of Carolina.

Since most of Carolina's settlers lived near Albemarle Sound in the north or near Charleston in the south, they considered splitting into two colonies. In 1729 the colony was split into North Carolina and South Carolina.

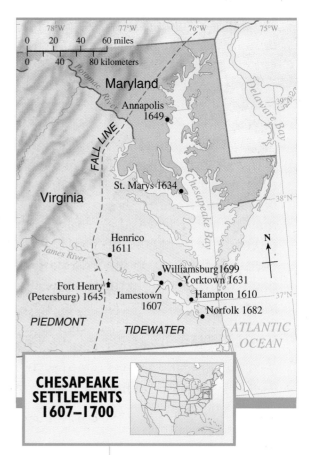

CHESAPEAKE SETTLEMENTS 1607–1700

The Georgia Colony

Georgia was the last English colony to be established in America. It grew much more slowly than the other colonies. One reason was that Georgia was too hot for many Europeans.

The few colonists in Georgia created a great problem for Native Americans. Before the colonists arrived, the area that was later called Georgia was used as a **buffer zone** for Native Americans. When settlers were fighting the Yamasees (YAH muh seez) in Carolina, some Yamasees fled south, retreating into the area of Georgia. It wasn't

Population of the Southern Colonies 1630 – 1750				
	1630	**1670**	**1710**	**1750**
Virginia	2,500	35,309	78,281	231,033
Maryland		13,226	42,741	141,073
North Carolina		3,850	15,120	72,984
South Carolina		200	10,883	64,000
Georgia				5,200

 buffer zone An area of safety between people in conflict

the best land, but it was safe. When English settlers moved into Georgia, these Native Americans had to face Spanish settlers in Florida if they moved farther south.

Plantations and Farms

Throughout the Southern Colonies most farms were small. The farmers worked the land themselves, growing a few crops, raising a few animals, and basically surviving year to year.

Over time, farming in the Southern Colonies changed. There were always many small farms in the South. But later, planters set up some very large farms, called **plantations**. Often on a plantation, only one main crop, such as tobacco, would be grown.

⭐ *plantation* A large farm where one main crop is grown

Many people in the Southern Colonies lived more isolated lives than people in the New England Colonies. In New England, many people lived in towns and farmed fields on the edge of town. New Englanders might have friendly conversations with neighbors on the way out to the fields each morning. Many southerners lived on farms or plantations that were widely scattered. So they often had few neighbors. Also, since the Southern Colonies didn't have many towns, many Southerners didn't have the opportunity to go to weekly church services or attend town schools as New Englanders did. Life on plantations was not as lonely as on small farms, since plantations had more people.

▼ Cultivating tobacco on a Virginia plantation

SHOW WHAT YOU KNOW!

REFOCUS
COMPREHENSION

1. How did John Smith improve the work ethic in Jamestown?

2. What were the major differences between indentured servants and enslaved people?

THINK ABOUT IT
CRITICAL THINKING

In what ways did the African slave trade affect the development of the Southern Colonies?

WRITE ABOUT IT
ACTIVITY

It is 1695 and you live in Carolina. Write a letter to a friend in England explaining how the colonists' relationship with the Native Americans has deteriorated in the Carolinas.

Colonizing the South

FOCUS *The story of the Southern Colonies was full of false starts and dashed hopes. Still, some important lessons were learned, and the colonies survived.*

50 ACRES FREE

It was difficult to get people to move to Virginia. In 1618 the Virginia Company of London, which owned the colony, introduced the *headright system*.

This meant that the company would give 50 acres to every person who paid for his or her own passage to America and then settled in Virginia. The company also would give these settlers an extra 50 acres of land for every person they brought with them.

Since thousands of people lived in overcrowded cities in England, many people were attracted to Virginia through this plan, and the colony grew.

THAT WAS QUITE A GIFT

In 1632, King Charles I gave George Calvert a gift—the large territory around the Chesapeake Bay. It was named Maryland, in honor of the king's wife, Henrietta Maria. Being Catholic, Calvert wanted Catholics to be able to worship in public and to hold public office in his colony.

Calvert died before anyone moved to Maryland. But his son, Lord Baltimore, carried out his father's plans by offering land to wealthy English people who would settle the land. In 1634 the first 200 settlers arrived in Maryland.

Fewer Catholics came than Baltimore had hoped for, so he invited Protestants. Before long, more Protestants than Catholics lived in Maryland. In 1649 they passed the Toleration Act, which allowed all Christians—Catholic or Protestant—to worship as they pleased.

1618	1649	1663	1732
The Virginia Company introduces the headright system	Toleration Act is passed in Maryland	The King approves plan for colony of Carolina	Parliament charters colony of Georgia

1600   1620   1640   1660   1680   1700   1720   1740

RAISING SILKWORMS IN CAROLINA

Eight rich Englishmen planned to earn a fortune by starting a colony in America. They hoped to send other people to live in the colony and raise silkworms for silk, olives for oil, and grapes for wine. Then the Englishmen thought they could sell the products in Europe.

The king of England approved the plan for the colony of Carolina in 1663. But things didn't go the way the Englishmen had hoped. Few Carolina settlers wanted to raise silkworms, olives, or grapes. Instead they grew rice, indigo, and tobacco.

In 1670 the settlers built Charles Town, which attracted people from England, Scotland, and English colonies in the West Indies. Huguenots (HYOO-guh nahts), or French Protestants, also came to Carolina. They had been persecuted in France, and Carolina offered them religious freedom.

GEORGIA

James Oglethorpe wanted to help give released prisoners a second chance. In 1732, Parliament chartered the colony of Georgia as a refuge for people who had been jailed for not paying their debts. In Georgia, Oglethorpe hoped these people would live reformed lives. He also planned for them to raise silkworms and make him rich.

And Oglethorpe didn't want slavery in his colony. So Georgia became the only colony where slavery was illegal.

Oglethorpe had good intentions, but his plans mostly failed. The silkworms didn't survive in Georgia, the settlers didn't change their ways, and in 1750, slavery was legalized.

SHOW WHAT YOU KNOW!

REFOCUS
COMPREHENSION

1. What were some reasons that people came to the Southern Colonies?

2. How did the colonies of Maryland and Georgia turn out differently than their founders had planned?

THINK ABOUT IT
CRITICAL THINKING

If you were to move to the Southern Colonies, which colony would you choose? Why?

WRITE ABOUT IT
ACTIVITY

Make an outline for the March of Time: 1617 to 1732.

Africans in Carolina

FOCUS *Africans who came to America as slaves brought skills they had learned in their homelands. By using these skills, Africans helped the colony of Carolina survive and develop.*

A Struggling Colony

During colonial times the southern coastal area of the colony of Carolina was miserable, especially in the summer. There was no relief from the heat and humidity. Mosquitoes buzzed over the swampy land, carrying a variety of diseases, including yellow fever and malaria.

By the 1680s, new settlers avoided the southern region of the colony. Some settlers who were already there left. Many who stayed were sickly. However, the southern region of the colony did survive and even flourished due to the hard work and abilities of the settlers and the African slaves.

To begin with, Africans didn't get as sick as European settlers. Having come from lands where malaria and yellow fever were common, they were often **immune** to these diseases. Thus, Africans were able to work more days than the European settlers.

Cultural Influences

In addition, enslaved Africans brought from Africa many skills that were useful in Carolina. For instance, in the southern region of Carolina there were many rivers and few roads. So travel was easiest by boat. The Africans knew how to handle boats, and they knew how to hollow a canoe out of a single cypress tree log. Africans taught settlers how to make these **dugout canoes**.

A region full of rivers also meant that fishing was a good source of food. Africans made fishing nets that worked better than the ones the English made. Africans also knew more efficient ways of catching fish.

▼ Fishing with a net in Albemarle Sound

immune To be protected from an illness because of previous exposure to it
dugout canoe A boat that is made by hollowing out a log

One way was to dam up a river. Then the Africans added a mixture to the water that calmed the fish and made them easier to catch.

Another skill the Africans brought with them was cattle-herding. In Europe, cattle grazed in closed areas. In Africa they grazed in open fields. Since the colonists were from Europe, they tried to have their cattle graze in closed areas, as they had done in Europe. However, when this practice didn't work, the Africans showed the colonists how to graze cattle in open fields. The cattle thrived.

Having grown rice along the West African coast, Africans were able to teach the colonists more efficient ways of planting, hoeing, and processing rice. In addition, Africans designed baskets for "fanning" the grain in the sun. Carolinian colonists,

▲ *The Banjo Lesson* was painted by Henry O. Tanner in 1893.

with the Africans' help, were able to turn rice into a profitable **staple crop**.

Africans also wove baskets and mats out of reeds and grass. And they carved out gourds that could be used to hold drinks and food.

Cultures Are Blended

Africans also made other important contributions to American culture. Some Africans crafted musical instruments, such as the banjo, based on similar instruments they had played in their homeland.

They also had a long tradition of storytelling. By passing along old stories and folk tales, Africans were able to keep their history alive. Folk tales have long been appreciated as a special form of American literature.

As African traditions were adapted to an American setting, something new began to develop—an African American culture.

 staple crop The most important crop grown in an area

SHOW WHAT YOU KNOW!

REFOCUS
COMPREHENSION

1. How did Africans use their skills to help the colony survive?

2. What are some ways that Africans preserved their past and their culture?

THINK ABOUT IT
CRITICAL THINKING

How might life have been different in Carolina without the Africans and their contributions?

WRITE ABOUT IT
ACTIVITY

Write a short story about something that has happened in the history of your family or write your own folk tale.

4

Citizenship

★ **KEY TERMS**
legislature
veto
represent

📖 **LITERATURE**
An Introduction to
Williamsburg

The House of Burgesses

FOCUS *In 1619, Virginia settlers elected people to the House of Burgesses. It began a tradition of representative government in America that continues today.*

Governing a Colony

How do you run a colony? The Virginia Company of London was a small group of merchants who had provided the money to start the colony of Virginia. The company planned to keep all the lawmaking power for the colony in England. A few colonists would set things up without making any laws. Then these colonists would carry out instructions sent from England.

When the Virginians needed a law changed, they had to send a request to England and wait for someone to bring back the news of the change (if it was granted). It became obvious that the colonists really needed local leaders who had power. In 1610 the Virginia Company sent a governor with more power to Jamestown.

Nine years later the Virginia Company decided to give the settlers a voice in the colony's government. Then Virginians set up their own **legislature**. This legislature would share power with the governor. The

---

★ **legislature** A group of people who make laws

legislature could create laws, and the governor had the right to **veto** any laws passed by the legislature.

The First Legislature

Virginia's new legislative body was named after Parliament, the lawmaking body in England. Since members of the English Parliament were called burgesses, the new legislature in Virginia was named the House of Burgesses.

Members of the House of Burgesses were elected by the "free men" of the colony. These did not include enslaved people or women. The first assembly had 22 elected burgesses to **represent** the colonists. They met for the first time on July 30, 1619, in a little church near the James River.

It could be brutally hot in the Tidewater, or lowland, of Virginia. The burgesses made it worse by wearing the same kinds of robes and felt hats as members of the English Parliament did. The heat was so bad that several burgesses fell ill, and one died. After six hot, sweaty days, the burgesses ended the very first legislative meeting in the English colonies.

The burgesses passed a series of laws about distributing land. They also passed laws against drunkenness, gambling, and idleness. And they set penalties for "excess in apparel," meaning that settlers had to dress properly.

A reenactment of a meeting at the House of Burgesses

They also made it a law that everyone had to attend church twice on Sunday. Also, anyone who owned a gun or sword had to take it to church. This was a time of peace with the Native Americans, but this law showed that the settlers weren't quite sure it would last.

Creating a Tradition

As the years passed, the House of Burgesses continued to meet. The idea that people could govern themselves had taken hold, and colonists didn't want to give it up.

This independent spirit would, in time, lead Americans to fight for their own nation. And when the United States of America was established, it would be based on the same kind of representative government that began with the House of Burgesses.

---

veto   To reject a proposed law
represent   To act and speak for another in a lawmaking body

This is the capitol in Williamsburg, Virginia. Note the flag of England and the weather vane.

An Introduction to Williamsburg

by Valerie Tripp

Colonial Williamsburg in Virginia is a living museum, where people experience colonial America. Williamsburg was a very important colonial city, especially during the American Revolution. Most of Colonial Williamsburg represents the late 1700s. Read about Colonial Williamsburg and enjoy the sights, smells, and sounds of this exciting town as if you were actually taking a tour there.

Walk down Williamsburg's deep-shaded streets and walk back into history. Back to the eighteenth century, when ladies in elegant gowns and gentlemen in powdered wigs rode in horse-drawn carriages down the dusty streets. Back to colonial times, when the king of England ruled America and the British flag flew above the housetops you pass.

Williamsburg was born as the eighteenth century dawned. The original capital of Virginia had been located in the crowded village of Jamestown. When the statehouse there burned in 1699, the legislators voted to rebuild it in a new place. They named the new town Williamsburg in honor of their king, William III. Here was a chance for a fresh start, the opportunity to create a noble capital city where before there had been little more than fields and forests. To guard against haphazard growth, a town plan was drawn up that was both practical and artistic. Williamsburg's main street was to be long and broad, skirted by wide greens and open spaces. Houses were to be set back six feet from the streets on lots of one-half acre. The main street, named for the Duke of Gloucester, would stretch nearly a mile from the College of William and Mary, past the church and the market square, to the new statehouse called the Capitol. Soon there would be an elegant Palace for the governor of the colony, who was the king's appointed representative there.

By 1750 Williamsburg had become the most important city in Virginia. People came here from remote parts of the colony to learn of the latest fashions from England and Europe in clothing, furnishings, music, amusements, and ideas. It was a major business center where tobacco planters, farmers, craftsmen, shippers, and merchants came to buy, sell, and trade. And because Williamsburg was the capital of Virginia, it was the political center of the colony where affairs of government were conducted. Laws made in the Capitol and enforced in the courts here affected everyone in Virginia and even influenced other colonies far beyond its borders.

Want to read more? You can continue exploring Colonial Williamsburg by checking the book out of your school or public library.

SHOW WHAT YOU KNOW!

REFOCUS
COMPREHENSION

1. How was power divided between the governor and the House of Burgesses?

2. Who could and who couldn't vote for members of the House of Burgesses?

THINK ABOUT IT
CRITICAL THINKING

Why is it important to have people who represent us in our government?

WRITE ABOUT IT
ACTIVITY

Make a brochure that would encourage people to visit Colonial Williamsburg.

SUMMING UP

1 DO YOU REMEMBER...
COMPREHENSION

1. What rule did John Smith announce to make sure Jamestown would survive?

2. What important product did Jamestown settlers export to Europe?

3. What was the Middle Passage?

4. What caused the fighting between early Carolinian settlers and Native Americans?

5. Why was life on a southern farm lonelier than life in a New England village?

6. What was the *headright system*?

7. What did James Oglethorpe hope to achieve in Georgia?

8. What important skills of Africans helped the Carolina colony survive?

9. Describe the first government of the Virginia colony.

10. Who could vote in Virginia's first elections?

3 WHAT DO YOU THINK?
CRITICAL THINKING

1. Do you think the work ethic that John Smith imposed on the first Virginians was fair? Why or why not?

2. In what ways was farming in the Southern Colonies different from farming in the New England Colonies?

3. What skills might be needed to settle a colony on the moon?

4. How might the Southern Colonies have developed differently if slavery had been outlawed from the beginning?

5. What makes the founding of the House of Burgesses so important?

2 SKILL POWER
MAKING AN OUTLINE

Make an outline showing what you learned in this chapter. For each main topic, list at least three subtopics. These subtopics should be the important supporting ideas in the chapter. You can use each of the Southern Colonies as a main topic for your outline.

4 SAY IT, WRITE IT, USE IT
VOCABULARY

Write sentences that show what you've learned in this chapter. Include at least two of the vocabulary words in each sentence. Try to use as many of the words as you can.

buffer zone	legislature
cash crop	plantation
dugout canoe	represent
export	staple crop
immune	veto
indentured servant	work ethic

5 GEOGRAPHY AND YOU
MAP STUDY

Use the map below and others throughout this chapter to answer these questions.

1. What present-day states made up the Southern Colonies?

2. What borders the western edge of the Southern Colonies?

3. From what part of Africa were the most African slaves taken?

4. How far was Charles Town from New Bern?

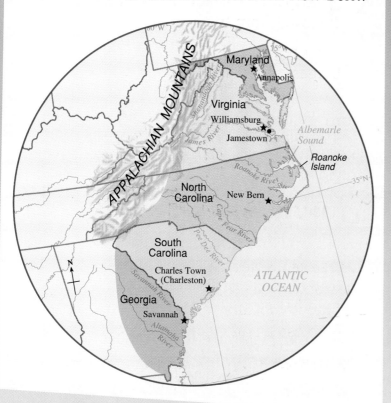

6 TAKE ACTION
CITIZENSHIP

The House of Burgesses provided Virginians with local leaders who had power. With a group of classmates, find out who the local elected leaders are in your community. Is there a mayor, a town supervisor, or a town council? Draw a chart that identifies some local officials and the powers they have.

7 GET CREATIVE
HEALTH CONNECTION

In the United States, people rarely get diseases such as polio and smallpox because of vaccines. In tropical areas of the world, some people still get yellow fever, even though a vaccine is available.

Research how a vaccine works. What are some reasons that people don't get vaccines for diseases that are prevalent in their part of the world?

LOOKING AHEAD In the next chapter read about the rest of the English colonies in North America—the Middle Colonies.

The Middle

New Jersey, New York, Pennsylvania, Delaware—do you know anyone who lives in one of these states? If you do, you already know something about the Middle Colonies. Clearing forests, planting crops, trading, learning from other groups—that's what this chapter is all about.

◄ Can you guess what he's holding? You can find out on page 144.

CONTENTS

Colonies

These books tell about some people, places, and events of interest during the settlement of the Middle Colonies. Read one that interests you and fill out a book-review form.

READ AND RESEARCH

Night Journeys by Avi (William Morrow & Co., 1994)
In this story Peter York has a chance to help two young indentured servants. Will he lose his own freedom if he chooses to help them? *(historical fiction)*
• *You can read a selection from this story on page 150.*

The Lenape Indians by Josh Wilker (Chelsea House, 1993)
The Lenapes are a peaceful people who struggle for survival when Europeans settle on their land. Their feelings after they are scattered across many states and Canada are part of their story. *(nonfiction)*

Charlie's House by Clyde Robert Bulla (Alfred A. Knopf, 1993)
This is the story of a boy who is tricked into becoming an indentured servant but remains determined to fulfill his dream. *(historical fiction)*

They Led the Way: 14 American Women
by Johanna Johnston (Scholastic, 1987)
Included in this book about great women in America is the story of Lady Deborah Moody. You might be surprised to learn what Moody does with the land she buys from the governor of New Amsterdam. *(biography)*

Using Primary and Secondary Sources

Knowing how to identify and use a primary source can give you important information about the past.

UNDERSTAND IT

Historians rely on two kinds of sources to get information about the past. The kind they prefer is called a primary source. This can be a firsthand account of an event by an eyewitness. It can be a letter, a book, or a newspaper article. Photographs that have not been tampered with and artifacts such as tools can also be primary sources.

Secondary sources use facts from other books to describe or interpret an event. These sources are written by people who did not witness the event.

If you have old photographs, you have primary sources that tell about your own history.

This family photograph was taken in 1921.

EXPLORE IT

William Penn wrote this letter from Pennsylvania in 1683. As the governor of the new English colony of Pennsylvania, Penn wanted to attract settlers. He tried in this letter to convince people that Pennsylvania was a better place to live than Europe. Penn's colorful words and detailed descriptions give us a good idea about the climate of Pennsylvania more than 300 years ago!

Is Penn's letter an example of a primary or a secondary source?

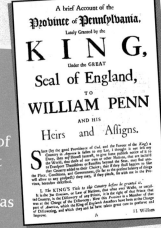

A brief Account of the
Province of Pennsylvania,
Lately Granted by the
KING,
Under the GREAT
Seal of England,
TO
WILLIAM PENN
AND HIS
Heirs and Assigns.

"The air is sweet and clear, rarely overcast. The waters are generally good, for the rivers and brooks have mostly gravel and stony bottoms.... From December to the beginning of March, we had sharp frosty weather; not foul, thick black weather, as in England. The air [is] dry, cold, and piercing, yet I [did not wear] more clothes than in England. From [March] to June, we enjoyed a sweet spring, no gusts, but gentle showers and a fine sky.... And whatever mists or fogs foul the heavens, in two hours time [they] are blown away."

Letters written by William Penn spread the word about the benefits of Pennsylvania.

TRY IT

Ask family members to help you find primary sources that tell about your family. You might bring in printed material, such as a newspaper clipping, postcard, or photograph, or an artifact, such as baby shoes or a medal. Share your primary source with your classmates and tell what you learned from it.

As a class you could create a display that shows what everyone has brought in (a bulletin board is good for this). You could call the display "Exploring Our Past" or whatever title the class chooses. Small cards that tell about each primary source would help visitors understand the display.

▲ This Civil War medal was awarded to a soldier in 1865.

EXPLORING OUR PAST

My great-grandparents' wedding day (1914)
Jamie Mahoney

A hand-carved wooden toy (1921)
Carmine Ferraro

Family picture (1921)
Alethia Carter

A Civil War medal (1865)
Megan Honeyman

St. Mary's Hospital
Aunt Judy's birth certificate (1938)
Jennie Bracken

A shoe-buttoner (1890s)
Elissa Knoerr

My grandma came to America as a war bride. (1946)
Ryan Tettemer

Baby shoes worn by a relative (about 1904)
Lee Chin

My aunt's family (1955)
Elaine Soares

SKILL POWER SEARCH

There are more primary sources in this chapter. How many can you find?

Setting the Scene

★ **KEY TERMS**

Frame of
  Government
Iroquois League
gristmill
cooper
cultural borrowing

WHEN CULTURES MEET

FOCUS *Many different groups of people helped create the Middle Colonies. To survive in their new surroundings, they borrowed and learned from each other.*

Coming to a New Land

William Penn's letters advertising his colony were a great success. By the late 1600s, thousands and thousands of European settlers were packing their belongings and sailing to the Middle Colonies. These colonies were called Pennsylvania, New York, and New Jersey. At that time the present-day state of Delaware was part of the Pennsylvania colony. Locate the colonies on the map on this page.

The Middle Colonies offered several advantages over New England and the Southern Colonies. For one thing, the climate was more inviting. Much of the Middle Colonies did not have the scorching heat of the South or the bone-chilling cold of New England. In addition, the land was rich and fertile, perfectly suited for farming. It was better than the hard, rocky soil of Massachusetts and better than the swampy fields of the Carolina colony.

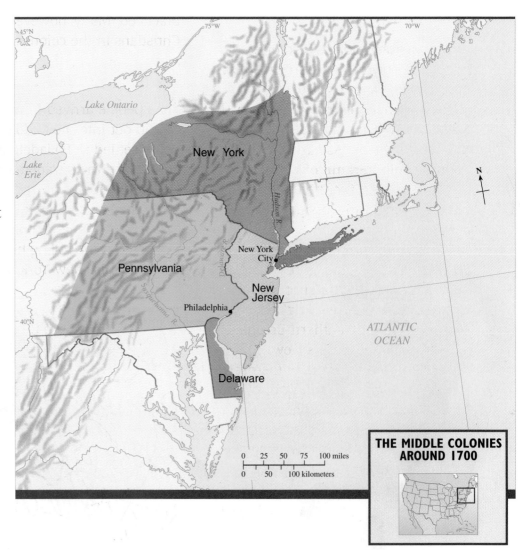

THE MIDDLE COLONIES AROUND 1700

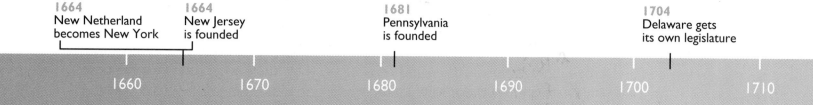

1664	1664	1681	1704
New Netherland becomes New York	New Jersey is founded	Pennsylvania is founded	Delaware gets its own legislature

1660   1670   1680   1690   1700   1710

Freedom of Religion

The Middle Colonies also offered religious freedom, which means that people were free to practice the religion of their choice. Pennsylvania especially welcomed settlers of different religions. As early as 1682, Pennsylvania's **Frame of Government**, or plan of government, guaranteed people the right to worship God as they saw fit.

The settlers did not think of their new homeland as the Middle Colonies. That label was used later to distinguish the area from the New England Colonies and the Southern Colonies.

So how did the settlers view themselves? Most thought of themselves as members of a religious group. They were Quakers, Jews, Mennonites, or Anglicans. They were Presbyterians, Dunkards, Moravians, or Baptists. Almost every settler felt a burning commitment to his or her religion. It was a central feature in people's lives.

Africans who came to America as enslaved persons had not lived in areas of Africa where Christianity was practiced. Many, however, became Christians in the colonies.

Furs, Farms, and Cities

As people arrived from Europe, they spread out into the Middle Colonies. Some settled in Philadelphia or New York City. Others traded for furs with Native Americans at trading posts along the Hudson River in the New York colony. Other people looked for farmland in the rolling hills of Pennsylvania, New York, and northern

Colonists traded with Native Americans in New York.

★ **Frame of Government** William Penn's plan for the government of the Pennsylvania colony

135

New Jersey. These settlers had to clear the forests before they could plant crops in the rich soil. The sandy soil of Delaware and southern New Jersey also proved good for farming.

The Native Peoples

As the settlers of the Middle Colonies spread out across the land, they cut deeper and deeper into Native American territory. Several Native American nations lived in this region. The Lenapes (LEN uh peez) made their home in what is now New Jersey and in nearby parts of New York, Pennsylvania, and Delaware. Farther south, in southern Delaware, lived the Nanticokes (NAN tih-kohks). The Susquehannocks (sus kwuh HAN uks) lived in southern Pennsylvania. And the Iroquois had settled in northern Pennsylvania and New York.

There were important differences among these Native American nations. But they all shared a respect for the land. Their families had lived here for centuries. They knew where the best hunting grounds were and how to travel the complex network of trails through the forests. They knew how to live on the land without changing it very much. Yet change was on its way. As the number of European settlers in the Middle Colonies grew, some Native Americans must have sensed that things would never again be the same.

The Iroquois League

While the Middle Colonies were just beginning, the **Iroquois League** had been running smoothly for well over a hundred years. This league consisted of five Indian nations: the Oneidas, Onondagas, Mohawks, Cayugas, and Senecas. According to legend, two heroic Indians—a Huron named Dekanawidah and a Mohawk named Hiawatha—took a stand for peace. They convinced five warring Indian nations to join together to form the Iroquois League, also called the League of the Great Peace. The result was an effective and democratic system.

The people in the league were governed by a council of chiefs. The chiefs had the power to settle disagreements, make treaties, and declare war. They were chosen by important women of the clans that made up each nation. These women could also remove the chiefs from

A painting created in 1946 by Tom Two-Arrows Dorsey, an Onondaga artist, showed respect for the earth.

The Iroquois League

Oneidas (oh NYE duz)
Onondagas (ahn un DAW guz)
Mohawks (MOH hawks)
Cayugas (kay YOO guz)
Senecas (SEN ih kuz)
Tuscaroras (tus kuh RAWR uz)

Iroquois League A political union of five, and later six, Iroquois nations who were governed by a council of chiefs

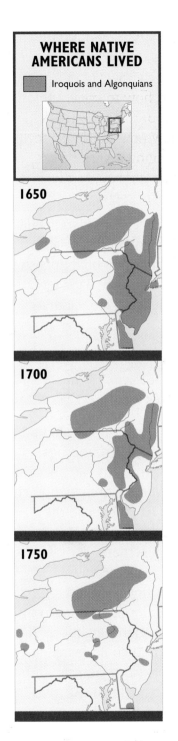
power. Iroquois women owned the cornfields, and they had an equal say with men in making important decisions, such as when to harvest crops.

About 1722 a sixth nation, the Tuscaroras, joined the league. The Iroquois League worked so well that some Americans later studied it as a model when they were creating the United States government.

Impact on Native Americans

Over time, more and more Europeans moved into areas where Native Americans lived. The European colonists came to view Native Americans as obstacles to expansion and settlement. The maps on this page show where Native Americans lived in the years 1650, 1700, and 1750. As you can see on the maps, by 1750, Native Americans had been forced to move to the north and west of where they had been in 1650.

Forcing them off their land was not the only effect that the arrival of Europeans had on Native Americans. Smallpox and other diseases brought by the Europeans spread like wildfire through Native American communities. Native Americans had never been exposed to these diseases before, and their systems could not handle them. As a result, the death rate from disease was very high.

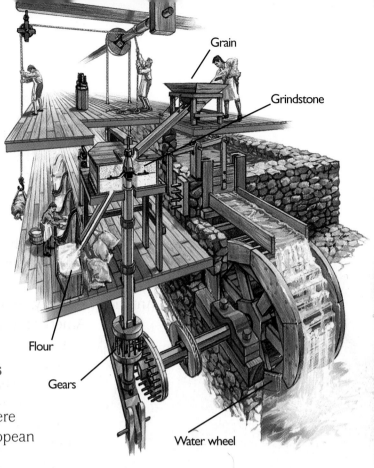

Grain

Grindstone

Flour

Gears

Water wheel

▲ **GRISTMILL**
The river current turned the water wheel, providing the power to turn the gears. The gears operated the grindstone, which then ground the grain into flour.

"The Bread Colonies"

It didn't take long before settlers in the Middle Colonies were able to grow all the food they needed and more. They had enough left over to sell. Farmers began taking wheat and rye to **gristmills** that sprang up along the rivers. At these mills the grains were ground into flour. Then the flour was sold to settlers throughout the English colonies. This is how the Middle Colonies earned the nickname "the bread colonies."

 gristmill A structure where grain is ground into flour

A Need for Workers

Throughout the Middle Colonies there was a shortage of workers to farm the land and to do the many other jobs that needed to be done. As you learned in Chapter 6, a need for labor was sometimes met by indentured servants. In exchange for having his or her passage to America paid, a person agreed to work as an indentured servant for a period of five to seven years. Indentured servants lived with the families they worked for. Most indentured servants in the Middle Colonies were English, Scots-Irish, and German.

Africans in the Middle Colonies

Some indentured servants came from Africa. Other Africans came to the Middle Colonies as enslaved persons. They were all brought to this area to supply much-needed labor.

Africans did many kinds of jobs. Some worked as skilled artisans or craftspersons. Some worked as farmhands. Others did household chores. Those who lived in cities often labored alongside the people they worked for and learned a trade. They might have worked as carpenters, coopers, or tailors. Other Africans worked on the wharves, loading and unloading ships.

Africans learned trades, like soap making, by laboring alongside skilled workers.

Ties to the Past

At first the European colonists identified with the countries from which they had come. They clung to customs and manners from their homeland. Settlers from France wore distinctive wigs. Settlers from the Netherlands built Dutch-style homes and barns. English settlers tried to plant traditional English flower gardens. In addition, each group brought its own style of food, clothing, and entertainment.

Learning to Change

These distinctions began to fade as time passed. Life in the colonies demanded a new outlook. People had to adapt to their new surroundings. They needed to learn from each other's mistakes and to take advantage of each other's successes. In that sense the great variety of people in the Middle Colonies helped all settlers.

Some Swedish settlers showed Welsh newcomers how to build log homes. English settlers might learn to bake pies from German neighbors. A farmer from Scotland could learn new farming techniques from German neighbors on the next farm. After a

cooper A person who makes or repairs wooden barrels, tubs, or casks while, Dutch families might begin to dress more like the English families they met.

Cultural Borrowing

Again and again different groups borrowed and learned from each other. Before long, even differences in religion and language began to blur. Some Quakers became Lutherans. Some Germans turned to the Dutch Reformed Church. Children from different backgrounds learned to speak English. These are all examples of **cultural borrowing**—that is, learning new ideas, customs, languages, and ways of doing things from different groups of people.

Settlers also learned from Native Americans who lived in the area of the Middle Colonies. These people already knew how to live on this land. They taught settlers to grow corn and beans, eat a kind of fish called sturgeon, and make dugout canoes, as shown below. Settlers also learned to like Native American dishes, such as succotash, a mixture of corn and beans. Popcorn covered with maple syrup was a popular dish, too.

▲ Native Americans carved bowls and spoons from wood.

A New Culture

By 1750 most of the settlers living in the Middle Colonies had been born there. The American colonies were the only homes they knew. Most who had a European background had never seen Europe. Although they still valued their European roots, they were becoming less European with each passing generation. Some Africans, however, still wanted to return to their homeland.

The mixing and blending of cultures was changing the way people in the Middle Colonies lived and worked. By 1750 a new, distinctive culture was beginning to emerge. Whether they knew it or not, the settlers were becoming less European and African and more what we would eventually call American.

⭐ *cultural borrowing* The exchange of ideas, languages, customs, and ways of doing things among different groups of people

▼ A dugout canoe was hollowed out of a large log.

SHOW WHAT YOU KNOW!

REFOCUS
COMPREHENSION

1. What different groups of people helped create the Middle Colonies?

2. What did the different groups learn from one another?

THINK ABOUT IT
CRITICAL THINKING

What, do you think, were the most important lessons the settlers had to learn to survive?

WRITE ABOUT IT
ACTIVITY

It is April 4, 1724. You came to the Middle Colonies three years ago from France. Write a letter to a friend you left behind, telling about your new life and the adjustments that you've had to make.

Spotlight

KEY TERMS

Quaker

pacifist

WILLIAM PENN

FOCUS *William Penn founded Pennsylvania on his belief in the value of peace and toleration. Part of his plan was a government that reflected democratic ideals.*

An English Quaker

In the late 1670s, William Penn was a wealthy Englishman living on his country estate. Yet he was not happy. He constantly had to defend his religious views. Penn had joined the Society of Friends. The Friends claimed that the spirit of God lay inside every person. This spirit was so strong, some said, that it made them quake. The Friends were called **Quakers**.

If God's spirit lay inside *everyone*, then no one was better than anyone else. So the Quakers saw no reason to give special treatment to the rich or powerful. For example, they did not tip their hats when they met a wealthy man. Quakers were also **pacifists**— they did not believe in fighting or going to war. Many people in England despised the Quakers and considered them to be troublemakers. They feared the spread of Quaker beliefs.

A Pennsylvania Governor

Penn wanted to form a perfect Quaker society in America. He asked the king of England to give him land there. To pay a debt owed to Penn's father, the king agreed. In 1681, Penn became owner and governor of a new colony named Pennsylvania—"Penn's Woods"—in honor of his father. He set up a government that allowed settlers to choose their own lawmakers and to practice their own religion.

William Penn advertised far and wide for settlers from different backgrounds and countries. He believed everyone could thrive in his colony if people treated each other fairly and with respect.

Penn also wanted to treat Native Americans fairly. He viewed them as people with rights and ideas of their own. His attitude toward

I am very sensible of the unkindness and injustice that has been too much exercised towards you by [Europeans]. . . . But I am not such a man. . . . I have great love and regard toward you, and I desire to win and gain your love and friendship by a kind, just, and peaceable life. . . . I am your friend.

William Penn

A silver friendship collar was given by Penn as payment for Indian lands.

A wampum belt honors a 1682 treaty of friendship between the Delaware Indians and William Penn.

 Quaker A member of a religious society whose beliefs include equality and nonviolence
pacifist A person who does not believe in fighting or going to war

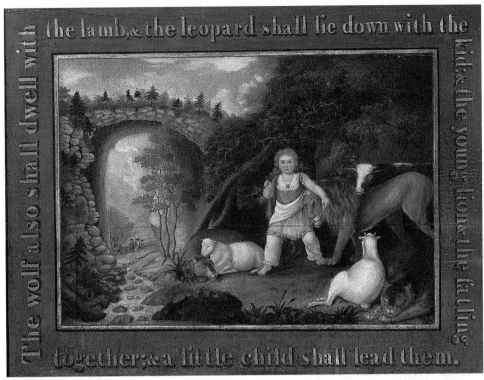

The Peaceable Kingdom of the Branch was painted in 1830 by Edward Hicks, a Quaker minister.

SHOW WHAT YOU KNOW!

REFOCUS
COMPREHENSION

1. How did William Penn put his beliefs into action?

2. How did William Penn view Native Americans?

THINK ABOUT IT
CRITICAL THINKING

What was William Penn's dream for Pennsylvania? Why did he have difficulty putting his dream into practice?

WRITE ABOUT IT
ACTIVITY

How would William Penn have felt about the role his sons played in the Walking Purchase of 1737? You can use Penn's letter, a primary source, to help you write an answer.

Native Americans is evident in a letter he wrote to the Lenape nation. You can see part of his letter on page 140.

Within a few years Pennsylvania was booming. But the results of this prosperity did not always please Penn. He feared that Quaker ideas were slipping away. He thought the settlers now had too much interest in money and not enough interest in God.

After Penn's Death

In fact, after Penn's death, his own sons cheated the Lenapes of almost 1 million acres of land. In the Walking Purchase of 1737, the Native Americans agreed to give up the amount of land that a man could cover *walking* in a day and a half from a certain tree. Penn's sons hired athletes to *run* the distance, much of it on roads.

Generally, Pennsylvania was a success. It became the fastest-growing of the 13 colonies. It produced some of the best craftspersons, farmers, and merchants. It also had a public library, a general hospital, and an organized postal service. And Quaker ideas had made a difference. They led to 40 years of peace with local Native Americans and to the first written protests against slavery in America.

141

SETTLING THE MIDDLE COLONIES

FOCUS *The years 1664 to 1750 saw the emergence of the Middle Colonies—New York, New Jersey, Pennsylvania, and Delaware. As the colonies grew in size, Native Americans were forced to give up their lands.*

ENGLAND GAINED NEW YORK

For 40 years the Netherlands had controlled New Netherland, the area between New England and Maryland. In Europe the Netherlands and England were often at war. In 1664, England's Duke of York sent warships to take over New Netherland. The ships sailed into the port city of New Amsterdam. New Netherland's cruel governor, Peter Stuyvesant, wanted to fight. But he had few weapons, and his colonists refused to fight. Stuyvesant surrendered. The colony was renamed for the Duke of York. The English now controlled the Atlantic coast from Maine to Carolina.

TROUBLE IN NEW JERSEY

The Duke of York, feeling generous, gave part of the New York colony to his friends John Berkeley and George Carteret. They called their new colony New Jersey, after the English island of Jersey.

By 1676, trouble was brewing in the colony. Some thought the land belonged to Berkeley and Carteret. Others said it belonged to settlers from New York. Finally, the king of England declared that Berkeley and Carteret were the rightful owners. The men divided the colony into East and West Jersey. Carteret kept East Jersey. Berkeley sold West Jersey to a group of Quakers.

PENNSYLVANIA NEEDED DELAWARE

William Penn, governor of the new colony of Pennsylvania, had a problem. The colony had no direct access to the ocean. In 1682 the Duke of York solved the problem by giving Penn the area called Delaware. Now Penn's colony had access to the Atlantic Ocean by way of Delaware Bay. Delaware got its own legislature in 1704.

In 1682 an Irishman named Thomas Holme worked with William Penn to design a new city on the Delaware River. This city would have a logical design for streets. Penn called it Philadelphia, "the city of brotherly love."

1664	1676	1682	1686	1702	1750
England controls New Netherland	New Jersey is divided	William Penn gains Delaware	Mennonites protest slavery	East and West Jersey are rejoined	Nearly 30 percent of Middle Colonists are Africans

| 1660 | 1670 | 1680 | 1690 | 1700 | 1710 | 1720 | 1730 | 1740 | 1750 |

A PROTEST AGAINST SLAVERY

The Mennonites, a religious group in Pennsylvania, believed that slavery was wrong. In 1686 the Mennonites wrote an important document addressed to the Quakers of Pennsylvania, some of whom owned slaves. It stated the following.

We should do to all men [as we would have them do to us]; making no difference of what generation, descent or colour they are. . . . To rob and sell [people] against their will, we stand against.

The statement was the first protest against slavery in the English colonies. The protest embarrassed many Quakers. In 1696 the Quakers themselves passed a resolution saying that slavery violated the teachings of the Bible.

NEW JERSEY AGAIN

People in East Jersey and West Jersey were still arguing over who owned what. In 1702, King William III of England rejoined the two colonies, once again calling the area New Jersey. This time it became a royal colony. However, New Jersey continued to have two capital cities—Perth Amboy in the east and Burlington in the west.

A GROWING POPULATION

Between 1680 and 1750 the population of the Middle Colonies grew considerably. A mix of people from all over Europe flocked to these colonies for a better life.

By 1750 almost 30 percent of the people in the Middle Colonies were Africans. The proportion of Native Americans to white settlers had changed dramatically. As more and more white settlers moved to the Middle Colonies, Native Americans were forced to give up their land.

143

LIVING IN A NEW LAND

FOCUS *A new life in a strange land was filled with challenges and new experiences. From letters and journals that settlers wrote, we know what ordinary people faced when moving to the Middle Colonies.*

Leaving Home

If you think about leaving your home in Europe, traveling across an ocean, and carving out a new life in a strange land, it may sound exciting. In fact, it probably was for the settlers who came to the Middle Colonies in the late 1600s. But it was also scary and dangerous. The map below shows the areas in Europe and Africa from which people came to the Middle Colonies.

Crossing an Ocean

The ocean voyage itself is a challenge. It is probably your first journey out onto the open sea. Feel the spray of salt water on your face. Enjoy the power of the wind and the waves as they move you along. After a while, though, the rolling of the ship might make you sick. You might experience headaches, fever, or vomiting. Even if you don't get sick on the voyage, other people probably will. Some might even die. Their bodies will be buried at sea.

The ship is crowded and dirty. The meat you eat has been heavily salted to keep it from rotting. It burns your mouth and leaves you with sores on your tongue. By now, every inch of the ship smells. Bugs are everywhere. They even crawl over your face as you sleep. At last, after six or seven weeks at sea, you arrive in America.

A New Land

When you reach your new land, many things look strange but wonderful. You see animals you've never seen before. Imagine seeing a raccoon for the very first time! You might catch a glimpse of a wild turkey, a wood turtle,

▲ The oak footwarmer had hot coals inside. You would rest your cold feet on top.

The long-handled pan filled with embers would be used to warm your bed.

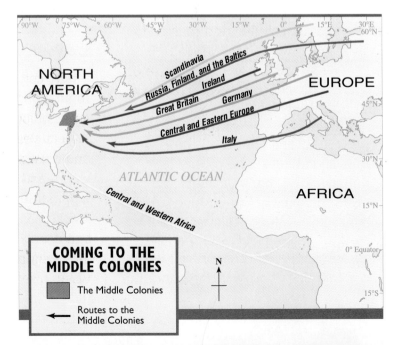

COMING TO THE MIDDLE COLONIES

■ The Middle Colonies

← Routes to the Middle Colonies

or a white-tailed deer. Don't forget all the new kinds of flowers, bushes, and trees you can discover.

Building a Home

You and your family will probably build your new home. You might even live in a cave until a hut can be put up. When the hut is finished, it is small— perhaps only 18 feet by 20 feet. Your entire family—father, mother, and several brothers and sisters—live in one room. A fire in the fireplace is the only source of heat and the only way to cook your food. Clouds of smoke from the fire hang in the room, and you can't draw a breath without taking in dry, dusty air. But outside, the air is crystal clear—far better than the smoke and smog of European cities, like London, England.

What's for Dinner?

You eat some of the same foods you had back in Europe. Day after day you eat bread, buttermilk, and roasted or boiled meat. Some food, though, is new to you. You get your first taste of corn, potatoes, pumpkins, and squash. You might also taste Native American dishes, such as the flavorful mixture called succotash.

What Will You Wear?

Boys and girls in the colonies are dressed alike, often in long gowns, until they are about five or six years old. Then they start wearing hand-me-

This reconstructed hut was made from materials at hand—branches, sticks, and leaves.

down clothes from their parents or older brothers or sisters. At about this same age, children are given duties and chores.

Do Your Chores!

The colonists never run out of work to do. Everybody in the family has chores. Boys spend hours helping their fathers clear trees, plow the land, plant and harvest crops, build fences, chop wood, and care for livestock.

Most of what is used in the home is made there. Girls help plant gardens and care for the younger children. The girls help prepare food, preserve vegetables, smoke meats, milk cows,

Children in the colonies played with dolls made from corn husks.

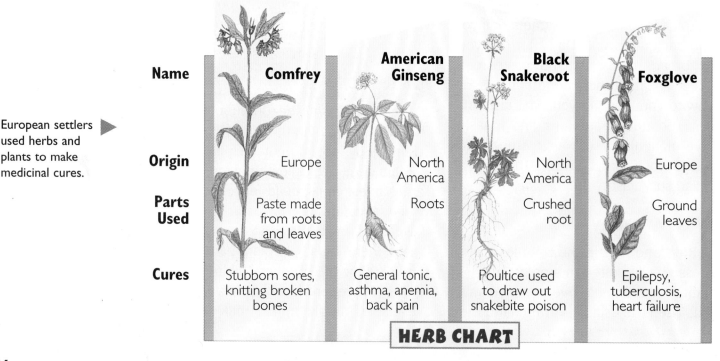

Women and girls spent hours at spinning wheels.

make butter and cheese, and make clothes. Before you can make clothes, you first have to spin the thread, weave the thread into cloth, and then dye the cloth. Once a month, girls help gather up all the dirty clothes in the house and wash them, using homemade soap. Three or four times a year, girls help pluck the feathers off the geese to get goose down for feather beds. The geese put up a terrible fight. You might have to pull a stocking down over each bird's head to keep it from biting you. Although the chores might seem difficult at times, children go to bed at night knowing that their family can take care of themselves.

Do You Have a Cure?

There are very few trained doctors in the colonies. If you get sick, you will probably be cared for by your mother or some other female settler. Sometimes she uses cures brought over from Europe. Many of these are herbal cures. Your mother might learn more about herbal medicines from local Native Americans. They know which plants can ease the pain of a sprained ankle and which soothe an upset stomach.

The colonists don't know what causes certain illnesses. But they use a variety of remedies to treat various symptoms. Feeling feverish? Eat seven insects. Depressed? Go gather ants by the light of the moon. If that doesn't work, some people think that letting a person bleed will get the sickness out of the body.

European settlers used herbs and plants to make medicinal cures.

Name	Comfrey	American Ginseng	Black Snakeroot	Foxglove
Origin	Europe	North America	North America	Europe
Parts Used	Paste made from roots and leaves	Roots	Crushed root	Ground leaves
Cures	Stubborn sores, knitting broken bones	General tonic, asthma, anemia, back pain	Poultice used to draw out snakebite poison	Epilepsy, tuberculosis, heart failure

HERB CHART

Still, your best hope is to stay healthy. For many diseases there is no effective treatment. Diseases such as smallpox, yellow fever, and malaria are passed easily from person to person. They pose a special threat in the cities, where living conditions are the most crowded. You might step on a rusty nail and die of blood poisoning. You could die from rabies after being bitten by a rabid animal. You could die from bee stings or snakebites. With no fire departments in existence until 1736, your entire family could die in a house fire.

A Little Learning

Chances are you won't have much schooling, especially if you live in the country. Maybe your parents will use a **hornbook**, such as the one shown here, to teach you to read the Bible. The rest of your education is learning to follow in your parents' footsteps. Boys usually learn their father's trade—farming, woodworking, or other crafts. Girls usually master the many skills needed to run a household.

Life in a City

You and your family might make your way to a city in search of work. Although America in colonial times is mostly countryside dotted with farms and small villages, a few cities are thriving. You might choose to make your home in New York City or in Philadelphia (the biggest city of the time). As you arrive, you see a built-up area, a busy harbor with ships of all sizes coming and going, and streets lined with dwellings, shops, and churches. And on those streets you hear many languages spoken.

One of your chores might be to walk to a main street of the city to buy fruit for your family. As you approach the marketplace, you see hundreds of farmers, fishers, fur traders, and sellers of all kinds.

Before journeying home, you stop to visit your older brother, who is working as an apprentice for a printer. Your brother and his master have signed a contract. The master feeds, clothes, and trains your brother. In exchange, your brother works hard until he is experienced and old enough to open his own shop.

SHOW WHAT YOU KNOW!

REFOCUS
COMPREHENSION

1. What challenges and new experiences did the Middle Colonists face?

2. What were some of the cures the colonists used for injury or sickness?

THINK ABOUT IT
CRITICAL THINKING

If you were a Middle Colonist, would you rather live in a city or out in the country? Why?

WRITE ABOUT IT
ACTIVITY

What have you done today—plucked a goose or made soap? Write a journal entry as a Middle Colonist might have written it.

hornbook A piece of wood with the letters of the alphabet, often protected by a thin layer of transparent horn

147

DELAWARE RIVER VALLEY

FOCUS *The Delaware River valley provided waterways for transportation, lands for farming, and an abundance of food sources.*

7

Fort Delaware

Minisink

Milford

1

Easton

2

PENNSYLVANIA

8

Bridgeport

Germantown

5

Trenton

Morrisville

6

Bordentown

Bristol

Burlington

Philadelphia

Wilming

3

New Castle

Salem

4

enwich

Delaware River

NEW

Delaware Bay

DELAWARE

JERSEY

Adventure on the Delaware

The Delaware River begins its life in the high hills of southern New York. It then flows south, zigging and zagging its way through hills, valleys, and lowlands. After a 280-mile journey, the river reaches the Delaware Bay. The river forms part of the border between Pennsylvania and New York, the entire border between Pennsylvania and New Jersey, and—for a few miles—the border between New Jersey and Delaware.

Map Legend

1 **Delaware Water Gap** This beautiful gorge is two miles long, with steep stone wall cliffs on both sides.

2 **Woodland** Trees provided the settlers with logs for buildings and wood for fuel.

3 **Crops and livestock** Throughout the Delaware Valley, settlers grew wheat (the most important crop), rye, potatoes, and corn. They also raised pigs, cattle, and horses.

4 **Fish and crustaceans** The waters of the valley were an important source of food for the Native Americans and the European settlers. The Delaware Bay provided oysters, crabs, and clams. The Delaware River provided trout, bass, and shad.

5 **Small industry** Sawmills, gristmills, and ironworks built along the Delaware River and its tributaries supplied lumber, flour, and iron for the settlers.

6 **Towns and cities** Towns sprang up along the Delaware River, often near the site of a mill or ironworks. Trade spurred the growth of some towns into cities.

7 **Lenape villages** The Lenapes used saplings and trees to build their homes.

8 **Animals in the forests** Europeans saw strange new animals, such as the white-tailed deer, the red squirrel, and the passenger pigeon. Settlers trapped or shot wild animals for their meat and fur.

---

gorge A narrow pass or valley between steep heights

tributary A stream or river that flows into a larger one

MAP IT

What if you lived in the village of Minisink, which is north of the Delaware Water Gap? Locate the village on the map with your finger. You have trapped beaver and mink all winter, and now the skins can be taken by boat down the Delaware River.

1. Use your finger to trace your boat journey on the map. Traveling south, what is the name of the first town you reach? What do you see near that town?

2. Passing the town of Easton, you begin paddling southeast. What do you see as you make your way to Burlington?

3. You are headed to Wilmington to sell your furs. In what direction must you travel as you leave Burlington? What settlements do you pass along the way?

EXPLORE IT

You could design a travel plan for a partner, using the map as your guide. Invite your partner to follow your directions and explore your route, making observations along the way.

ATLANTIC
OCEAN

Night Journeys

by Avi

During the 1700s a child just about your age has an adventure on the Delaware River. Read about Peter, an orphan taken into the home of a Quaker, Mr. Everett Shinn. Mr. Shinn and his family live about 60 miles north of Philadelphia. Mr. Shinn and Peter are helping to search for two escaped indentured servants. Join Peter and Mr. Shinn as they keep watch at Morgan's Rock, an island that lies between Pennsylvania and New Jersey.

At that point the Delaware River is fairly wide, almost a quarter of a mile, wider than anywhere else for some miles north or south. There in the river lies Morgan's Rock, set at unequal distances from the river's banks: fifty yards from the Pennsylvania side and perhaps three hundred or so from Jersey.

A narrow island, Morgan's Rock is much in the shape of a teardrop, its pointed end to the south. At the northern end a mass of rock thrusts against the river's flow like the prow of a great ship, making the river split into two different paths.

On the eastern—Jersey—side of the island the water runs wide and fairly shallow, making it wild and fierce. On the western—Pennsylvania—side, it's the reverse. There the narrow channel runs to a greater depth but is quiet as church. But on that side a line of broken rock juts halfway into the river: the dangerous Finger Falls.

Thus, while one side of the island is rough and fast, there is no obstruction; the other side is soft but obstructed. Boats coming down the river must decide which route to take. To the unknowing, the silent side looks easier. To those who know, the rough side is the wiser choice. Too late a decision is the greatest danger of all, for at the dividing point, where the rock stands, the river is at its worst, tearing itself like mad dogs in battle. Many a boat has broken there; and men have drowned. The island's very name—Morgan—recalls a man who so drowned.

The land directly behind the rock itself is an island clear of water. The northern section, some sixty yards or more, is solid and fertile, being heavily overgrown with trees, bushes, and whatever else can grow there. Indeed, the foliage is so thick that it's hard to enter. Moreover, it holds masses of logs and branches, hurled up on the island by the rolling waters around the rock.

The island's southern end is but an ever narrowing strip of sand and silt, which lengthens and shortens depending on the river's height.

Curiously, the island is known as a good place to ford the river. Indeed, it *is* a good place, but only when the river is low, such as might occur in summer. Then one can drive a wagon across the shallow side, cross the island, and float across the narrow channel.

At one place near the middle the sand and trees commingle. Mostly

open and easy to cross, it was there we meant to take our watch.

We tied Jumper loosely to a tree, but kept her saddle on, not knowing when, or if, we would be called upon to use her.

The place to which we had come was a little landing area. There, a small flat-bottomed boat was kept, which belonged to a man who fished for shad. A low-sided craft (no more than eight inches in height), it was steady but so easily swamped as to make it useless for anything except the calm waters we intended to cross. At the bottom of the boat lay the two poles used to push it.

Having set the lantern at one end of the boat, I fixed the rifle on Mr. Shinn's back, then each of us took up a pole. Standing on either side we edged off into the channel and began to push.

As I have said, the western channel of the island is far calmer than the eastern. Even so, with the water rising, the river ran swiftly. We had to work in unison, Mr. Shinn and I, or else the boat would most certainly have spun.

Beginning at the prow, we pushed the poles into the river bottom, and firmly holding the poles, walked toward the stern. This moved the boat forward and kept it on an even course. We reached the other side in moments.

I leaped ashore and tied the boat's rope securely to a nearby tree.

"The water's still rising," I said to Mr. Shinn.

"That will make it easier for us," he answered.

"Why?" I asked.

"I'll show thee." Still holding his lantern carelessly, he led me over the narrow width of the island across the slight rise in its center. We stood then upon the eastern side.

It was yet night, but the high half-moon was bright and unobstructed so that I could look across. The Jersey side was a black mass of trees. The river before us, swollen and shapeless, had flecks of foam that caught the moonlight, revealing the water's speed.

What I saw made my heart sink. Anyone attempting to cross the river there and then would have to be a fool. He would be swept away, never to reach the island.

"We'll win no rewards here," I complained.

Mr. Shinn shrugged.

Swinging about, he moved a few feet up the island's rise to a place where we could look down on the river, keep our feet from getting wet, yet lean comfortably against the trees.

"Now," he whispered, settling his back and trimming the lantern to a lower light so that the night seemed to come that much closer. "Let us wait and hope that no one comes. Thee wished to come, Peter. Look to thy silence."

Want to read more? You can find out what becomes of Peter by checking the book out of your school or public library.

SHOW WHAT YOU KNOW!

REFOCUS
COMPREHENSION

1. Why did so many people choose to settle in the Delaware River valley?

2. What was the most important crop grown in the Delaware Valley?

THINK ABOUT IT
CRITICAL THINKING

What do you think might happen next to Peter and Mr. Shinn? Share your prediction with your classmates.

WRITE ABOUT IT
ACTIVITY

Suppose that you are a Lenape on a scouting mission to observe the newcomers and their activities along the Delaware River. Report your findings to a partner.

SUMMING UP

1 DO YOU REMEMBER...
COMPREHENSION

1. Describe the climate and land of the Middle Colonies.

2. What groups of people made up the population of the Middle Colonies?

3. What happened to Native Americans as more and more settlers came to the Middle Colonies?

4. What kinds of work did Africans in the Middle Colonies do?

5. What was William Penn's purpose in founding Pennsylvania?

6. How was each of the Middle Colonies started?

7. Tell about the chores boys and girls performed in the Middle Colonies.

8. How were children educated in the Middle Colonies?

9. Describe city life in the Middle Colonies.

10. What were the food sources for settlers in the Delaware River valley?

2 SKILL POWER
USING PRIMARY AND SECONDARY SOURCES

In this chapter, primary sources helped provide you with information. Can you find more examples of primary sources that tell about the Middle Colonies? How many can you find? Team up with a partner. Set a time limit. Then begin the search! Track down magazines, like *Cobblestone;* books with historical paintings; and other sources. Share what you find.

3 WHAT DO YOU THINK?
CRITICAL THINKING

1. How did the settlers learn to survive? What were the most important lessons they had to learn?

2. Based on what you have read, rate William Penn on a scale of 1 to 10 as a leader of Pennsylvania. Write a short defense of your rating.

3. Why, do you suppose, were the Native Americans willing to teach the settlers how to hunt, trap, fish, make canoes, and grow crops?

4. How do you think the Middle Colonies would be different if the region had been settled by people from only one European country?

5. Many settlers saw themselves as members of religious groups from countries with different customs. How do you see yourself? Write a brief description.

4 SAY IT, WRITE IT, USE IT
VOCABULARY

Write a short paragraph that summarizes what you learned about the Middle Colonies. Try to include as many vocabulary words as possible. If you include four or more, you are a very talented word worker!

cooper	hornbook
cultural borrowing	Iroquois League
Frame of Government	pacifist
gorge	Quaker
gristmill	tributary

5 GEOGRAPHY AND YOU
MAP STUDY

Use the map below and others throughout this chapter to answer these questions.

1. What four present-day states made up the Middle Colonies?

2. What are the three main rivers found in the Middle Colonies?

3. Which river forms the border between Pennsylvania and New Jersey?

4. In what colony were Trenton and Burlington located?

6 TAKE ACTION
CITIZENSHIP

Think about how hard it is to start a new life in a strange land. Welcome newcomers to your school or community by thinking of helpful things that you could do. You might offer to help with school work or point out the bus stop. You can think of lots more! As you get to know your new friends, you will learn new ideas and ways of doing things from them, too!

7 GET CREATIVE
COMPUTER CONNECTION

On the computer create an advertisement that encourages others to settle in your community. Use William Penn's letter as an example. You might want to decorate your advertisement by hand or with a graphics program, if you have one.

LOOKING AHEAD

Find out in the next unit what happened when the colonies take a stand and declare their independence from England.

War AND Independence

What Is a Revolution?

How far would you go to support a cause you believed in? Would you be willing to fight a war? Explore the revolution that changed the world and has an impact even today.

THE WAR

After the French and Indian War, the colonists were upset by changes in British policy. Peaceful colonial protests gave way to battles at Lexington and Concord. The War for Independence, or the Revolutionary War, had begun.

CONTENTS

◀ To find out what this tool is used for, turn to page 172.

FOR INDEPENDENCE

These books tell about some people, places, and events of interest during America's struggle for independence. Read one that interests you and fill out a book-review form.

READ AND RESEARCH

Hand in Hand: An American History Through Poetry
collected by Lee Bennett Hopkins (Simon & Schuster, 1994)
As you read poetry, you will travel back to many different periods in history. Find out about Molly Pitcher and other people and places of the Revolutionary War. Read these poems aloud with your classmates. *(poetry)*
•*You can read a poem from this book on page 180.*

George Washington: The Man Who Would Not Be King
by Stephen Krensky (Scholastic, 1991)
Learn how George Washington became general of the colonial troops during the Revolutionary War. See how his courage and leadership inspired the new nation when he was made President. *(biography)*

Phillis Wheatley **by Victoria Sherrow** (Chelsea House, 1992)
In 1761, Phillis Wheatley, a young African girl, arrived in Boston and served as a domestic slave. Find out how she later became known as a poet. *(biography)*

The Fighting Ground **by Avi** (HarperTrophy, 1984)
When the tolling of a bell is heard throughout the New Jersey countryside, Jonathan hopes for a battle against the British and the Hessians. But when he becomes a soldier in that battle, he learns more about war than he ever could have known. *(historical fiction)*

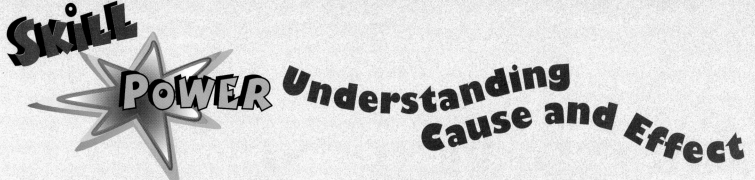

Understanding Cause and Effect

Identifying the relationships between causes and effects can help you understand history better.

UNDERSTAND IT

If you touch a hot stove, you'll burn your hand. You know this so well that you don't even think about it anymore. That is because you've learned a lesson in cause and effect. The cause of the burn is touching the hot stove. The effect is a burned hand. Here is another cause and its effect: If you work hard at something, you improve at it. The cause is that you work hard. The effect is that you improve.

In many ways, history is the study of cause and effect. For example, a historian looking at the Revolutionary War has to study many causes and their effects. Each action (or cause) by the British resulted in a reaction (or effect) by the colonists. The string of causes and effects led to war.

EXPLORE IT

On the night of April 18, 1775, Paul Revere was one of two riders who crept out of Boston to warn their neighbors of the British advance on Concord, Massachusetts. Because of their warning, the farmers and militia weren't caught by surprise. They prepared to fight.

In a famous poem the poet Henry Wadsworth Longfellow describes Paul Revere's historic ride. Part of the poem appears on this page. It describes a cause and effect. If the lantern is hung in the belfry (cause), Boston will know that it is in danger (effect).

He said to his friend, "If the British march
By land or sea from the town tonight,
Hang a lantern aloft in the belfry arch
Of the North Church tower
as a signal light—
One, if by land, and two, if by sea;
And I on the opposite shore will be,
Ready to ride and spread the alarm
Through every Middlesex village and farm,
For the country folk to be up and to arm."

TRY IT

Recall at least five things you have learned about the American colonies in Chapters 5, 6, and 7. Then, using large index cards, make a cause-and-effect quiz. On one side of each card, write an action (cause) you learned about. On the other side, write the action's effect.

With a group of your classmates, take turns displaying one side of a card, either a cause or its effect. Let group members give a cause for each effect and an effect for each cause.

CAUSE

The British were taxing tea.

EFFECT

The Boston Tea Party!

Stamp Act!

CAUSE & EFFECT FLASH CARDS

SKILL POWER SEARCH You'll find many examples of cause and effect in this chapter. Think about how history would be changed if any of the causes and effects had been different.

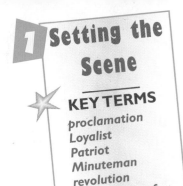
1 Setting the Scene

⭐ **KEY TERMS**

proclamation
Loyalist
Patriot
Minuteman
revolution
Declaration of
Independence

MAKING A NEW NATION

FOCUS *After 1763, Americans grew increasingly angry about British rule. Finally, they declared their independence and waged a successful war to guarantee it.*

French and Indian War

You have already learned that England had established colonies in America. By 1750, Great Britain, of which England was now a part, still had those 13 colonies. The population in these colonies was growing and so was the need for land. By 1754, colonists tried to expand into the Ohio River valley, but France already claimed this area for itself. French trappers and traders did not welcome the British settlers.

This dispute over land led to a war between France and Great Britain. For nine years, French and British troops

fought this war in America. Because some Native Americans fought on the French side, colonists called the war the French and Indian War.

Britain won the war in 1763, and France lost most of its land in North America. The cost of the war had been high. Thousands of British

◀ Soldiers carried gunpowder in powderhorns like this.

▲ Young Washington meets with Iroquois chiefs during the French and Indian War.

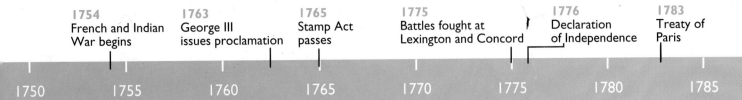

1754	1763	1765	1775	1776	1783
French and Indian War begins	George III issues proclamation	Stamp Act passes	Battles fought at Lexington and Concord	Declaration of Independence	Treaty of Paris

| 1750 | 1755 | 1760 | 1765 | 1770 | 1775 | 1780 | 1785 |

soldiers had been killed. There were also casualties among Americans who had fought in the war.

Proclamation of 1763

In 1763, Britain's King George III issued a proclamation. He called for a line to be drawn on a map along the top of the Appalachian Mountains, from New York to Georgia. The colonists were to stay on the east side of the line; Native Americans would stay on the west side.

The king and his ministers felt that keeping the colonists east of the line would make them easier to control. The colonists were angered. They had fought for the land west of the line. Now their king was telling them they couldn't use it. Their anger grew when British soldiers were sent to the colonies to enforce the proclamation.

New Taxes

A second event made colonists even angrier. Parliament announced it was imposing new taxes. This made sense to the British government. The war had cost a lot of money. Since the war had been fought to help the colonists, it was only fair that the colonists should

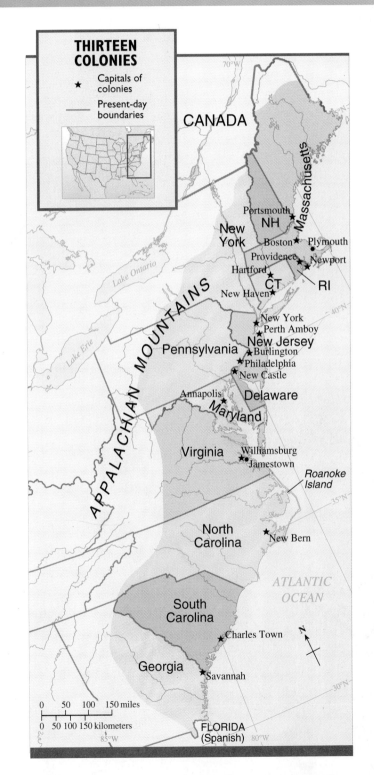

⭐ **proclamation** An official announcement

help pay for the war. Americans saw things differently. They felt they *had* paid for the war—with their blood.

As the colonists grumbled, it became clear that many didn't think of themselves as British anymore. Also, for years they had pretty much governed themselves. What made Britain think it could step in and push them around?

Few people realized it, but Great Britain and the colonies were now on a collision course. Britain was determined to remind the colonies who was boss. Americans were determined not to buckle under to some distant king. Within a dozen years these two sides would be at war.

Boston citizens, angered by the Stamp Act, burned the stamps.

Colonists Revolt

Between 1764 and 1775 the colonists felt increasing pressure from the British. By means of the Stamp, Sugar, and Townshend acts, Parliament imposed new taxes on such items as paper, sugar, and tea. Some Americans vowed to fight back. In Boston, Sam Adams and John Hancock spoke out strongly against the new taxes. Patrick Henry did the same in Virginia.

Some of these colonists joined the Sons of Liberty, a group formed to fight British control. These men held rallies, gave speeches, and sang songs. They also harassed British tax collectors, dumped British tea into Boston Harbor, and set fire to the house of a British customs official.

Colonial women protested, too. They formed the Daughters of Liberty to show that Americans could survive without British goods. Daughters of Liberty set up spinning wheels in public places, spinning wool hour after hour to prove they could get along without British cloth. They stopped buying British tea and began drinking tea made from local herbs.

Not all colonists wanted to break away from Britain. Some, called **Loyalists** or Tories, wanted to stay under British control. But as time passed, more and more Americans were convinced that they could not be happy under British rule. They joined the side of the **Patriots**.

Loyalist   A colonist who was a supporter of Great Britain and King George III

Patriot   A person who supported the American cause for independence from Britain

Preparing for the Worst

By the spring of 1775, tempers were flaring. Britain had sent thousands of soldiers to America. Dressed in their fancy red coats and polished black boots, these "redcoats"—as the colonists called them—tried to calm the restless Americans. This only made the colonists angrier.

The colonists meanwhile were building up militias, groups of ordinary Americans who agreed to act as soldiers if the need arose. In Massachusetts, militiamen were especially active. Some of them were called **Minutemen**, as they were to be ready to fight at a minute's notice.

The Shot Heard Round the World

The fighting began on April 19, 1775, as British troops marched from Boston toward the town of Concord, 20 miles away. Find Concord on the map on the right. There they planned to seize weapons belonging to the Massachusetts militia. The militia rushed to block their way. The two sides met in the town of Lexington, east of Concord. As they stood face to face, a pistol shot rang through the early morning air. No one knows who fired the weapon, but it later became known as "the shot heard round the world." A **revolution**—the American

Revolution—had begun. By the end of the day, 50 Americans had been killed. Another 39 had been wounded. The British casualties were much worse, with 73 dead and 174 wounded.

THE WAR IN MASSACHUSETTS 1775

North Bridge
REVERE CAPTURED
Concord
Lexington
Lexington Green
REVERE AND DAWES
Medford
REVERE
Arlington (Menotomy)
Cambridge
Bunker Hill
Old North Church
DAWES
Boston
Boston Harbor
Brookline
Roxbury
Mystic River
Concord River
Charles River

N

* Battle site, American victory
* Battle site, British victory
- - - Dawes's route
- - - Revere's route
→ British route

0 — 5 miles
0 — 5 kilometers

▼ A Minuteman is plowing, ready to move out with his weapon on a moment's notice.

Minuteman   A member of a militia of citizens who claimed to be ready to fight the British at "a minute's notice"
revolution   A sudden, complete change

Declaring Independence

By 1776 many Americans had shaken off their lingering loyalty to the king. Thomas Paine, who had moved to America from England, helped with a pamphlet he wrote called *Common Sense*. In the pamphlet he argued that it was wrong for kings to be in charge just because they were born into a certain family. True power to govern, Paine suggested, came only when people gave that power to someone.

By the summer of 1776, Americans were ready to break from Britain. A group of colonial leaders called on Thomas Jefferson to write the **Declaration of Independence**. This was America's formal announcement that it was becoming a separate nation—the United States of America. The Declaration of Independence was signed on July 4, 1776.

Advantages and Disadvantages

Americans had declared themselves an independent nation. Now they had to fight a war with Great Britain to make that independence a reality. Several things, however, were working in America's favor. Great Britain had plenty of resources, but they were all thousands of miles away. Weapons, soldiers, ammunition—everything had to be shipped across the Atlantic Ocean.

In addition, while British soldiers were better trained than Americans, they were not as determined. British soldiers fought because it was their job. Americans fought because their homes, their families, and their beliefs were at stake.

Americans adopted a Native American style of fighting. This was guerrilla warfare, sneaking up on the enemy to stage hit-and-run attacks. George Washington, the leader of America's Continental army, taught this

You can read the Declaration of Independence on pages 612–615.

THE ILLUSTRIOUS PATRIOTS OF 1776 AND AUTHORS OF THE DECLARATION OF INDEPENDENCE. 1844

In UNITY there is STRENGTH

The signing of the Declaration of Independence, painted in 1844 by American artist Edward Hicks

Declaration of Independence The document that stated the reasons for the desire of the American colonies to be independent of British control

approach to his men. Francis Marion's use of this style of fighting in the swamps of South Carolina gained him the nickname Swamp Fox.

Perhaps the biggest boost to the Patriots came in 1778, when France agreed to help the United States fight the war. France had no particular reason to do this other than that it disliked having the British in North America. Great Britain and France had fought many wars over the years, including the French and Indian War just a few years earlier. To help the new nation defeat Britain, France provided the Americans with troops, money, and supplies.

Surrender!

By 1781 the British were growing weary. On October 19, British general Charles Cornwallis found himself outnumbered and trapped on a small peninsula on Chesapeake Bay in Yorktown, Virginia. Knowing that it was useless to keep fighting, Cornwallis surrendered his troops. Yorktown was the last great battle of the war. Peace talks began the next year, and in 1783 the Treaty of Paris was signed. Great Britain agreed that its colonies were now "free and independent states."

▲ British troops surrender to General George Washington at Yorktown. The British general, Lord Cornwallis, did not attend this ceremony.

SHOW WHAT YOU KNOW!

REFOCUS
COMPREHENSION

1. What were some effects of the French and Indian War?

2. Name some advantages and disadvantages for both the British and the Americans during the Revolutionary War.

THINK ABOUT IT
CRITICAL THINKING

Why, do you think, did the British fight a war with the Americans after the Declaration of Independence was issued?

WRITE ABOUT IT
ACTIVITY

Write a letter to a relative in Great Britain about American reactions to the new taxes. Describe some of the ways in which the colonists protested the taxes.

STEPS TO INDEPENDENCE

FOCUS *From 1765 to 1776 there was a steady stream of stern British actions and bitter American reactions. American anger built until it exploded in revolution.*

STAMP ACT

The colonists were angry. It was bad enough when the British Parliament put taxes on goods coming into the colonies. But the Stamp Act of March 22, 1765, was something new. Now a tax was added to things made right here in America. Some 50 kinds of paper used in the colonies were to be taxed. To prove that the tax had been paid, a special stamp was placed on everything from calendars and newspapers to playing cards.

STAMP ACT CONGRESS

Furious about the Stamp Act, nine colonies decided to send representatives to New York to talk things over. At this Stamp Act Congress, held in October 1765, Americans declared the new tax illegal. They said that only colonial legislatures had the power to tax them.

On March 11, 1766, Parliament backed down. It got rid of the Stamp Act. But Parliament warned the colonists that it did indeed have the power to pass any laws it wanted to for the colonies— including tax laws.

BOSTON MASSACRE

On a cold winter night, five people died in the streets of Boston, Massachusetts. The incident began as a kind of one-sided snowball fight. Bostonians didn't like having British soldiers stationed in their city. On March 5, 1770, they expressed their disgust by throwing snowballs at the soldiers. Some colonists turned mean and started throwing rocks.

A few redcoats lost control and fired into the crowd. One of those killed was Crispus Attucks, a runaway slave who worked as a sailor. Attucks was the first African American to die for the cause of American liberty but not the last. The incident became known as the Boston Massacre.

1765
Stamp Act
Congress

1770
Boston
Massacre

1772
Committee of
Correspondence formed

1773
Boston
Tea Party

1765 | 1766 | 1767 | 1768 | 1769 | 1770 | 1771 | 1772 | 1773

COMMITTEES OF CORRESPONDENCE

Samuel Adams worked hard to build Patriot support in Boston. But local efforts were not enough, and Adams knew it. Other towns and colonies needed to be involved. In November 1772, Adams formed a Committee of Correspondence. Whenever something happened in Boston, this group sent messages out across the colonies.

Soon other areas set up similar committees to send and receive messages. A network was created from New England to the Carolinas. Now all Americans could be kept informed of British actions.

BOSTON TEA PARTY

Americans loved their tea. They drank it morning, noon, and night. But when Britain tried to collect a tax on tea, the Americans took a stand. They wanted nothing to do with taxed tea. When three ships brought a new supply of tea into Boston Harbor, the Sons of Liberty took action. On December 16, 1773, about 60 of them disguised themselves as Mohawk Indians. They crept onto the ships and dumped 342 chests of tea overboard.

INTOLERABLE ACTS

King George was furious about the Boston Tea Party. He wanted to punish the entire city of Boston. Parliament agreed. In the spring of 1774, it passed a series of tough acts. It closed Boston Harbor until the tea that had been dumped was paid for. Another law took away most of the colony's rights of self-government.

Americans labeled the measures the "Intolerable Acts." The British hoped that the measures would teach the colonists a lesson. Instead, the acts simply stirred up more anti-British feelings. Until now, the trouble had been confined mostly to Massachusetts. But now, people in all 13 colonies were angry.

| 1774 | 1774 | 1775 | 1775 | 1775 | 1775 | 1776 |
| Intolerable Acts | First Continental Congress | Paul Revere's ride | Battles of Lexington and Concord | Second Continental Congress | Battle of Bunker Hill | Declaration of Independence |

1774   1775   1776

FIRST CONTINENTAL CONGRESS

The Committees of Correspondence called for action. They felt that the Intolerable Acts were simply—well—intolerable! On September 5, 1774, representatives from 12 colonies met in Philadelphia. Among the representatives were Samuel Adams, Patrick Henry, and George Washington.

These men wrote down their complaints and sent the list off to the king, asking him for help. They also agreed to meet again in May 1775.

THE MIDNIGHT RIDE OF PAUL REVERE

Paul Revere jumped onto his horse and galloped off through the night. Revere was a Boston silversmith and one of the Sons of Liberty. On the night of April 18, 1775, he learned that the British were headed to Concord. Revere rushed to warn local leaders and military commanders that their supplies were about to be seized. He and a man named William Dawes rode like the wind. Thanks to them, and other riders, the militia was ready and waiting when the British reached Lexington the next morning.

BATTLES OF LEXINGTON AND CONCORD

Things hadn't gone well for the Americans in Lexington on April 19, 1775. Eight Patriots were killed and nine were wounded.

But things changed as the day went on. In Concord the British destroyed some of the Patriots' military supplies. But the militia continued to advance toward the British, and more fighting broke out. Soon the British turned and headed back to Boston. Americans hid behind trees, fences, and stone walls. They shot at the redcoats all along the way, picking them off one by one. By the time the British reached Boston, they had suffered defeat. The day was considered a big victory for the colonists.

SECOND CONTINENTAL CONGRESS

As planned, representatives met for the Second Continental Congress on May 10, 1775. But things had changed since their first meeting. Now war had broken out. John Adams told his fellow representatives that they must rise to the challenge. At his urging, they created an official American army, called the Continental army. To lead the new army, Adams said, Congress was fortunate to have the right man for the job in that very room—George Washington. With his military experience in the French and Indian War, his ability to remain calm, his strong will, and his determination, George Washington was indeed the perfect man for the job.

THE BATTLE OF BUNKER HILL

Before Washington could take command of his new army, more fighting broke out near Boston. On June 17, 1775, the British tried to drive Americans off Breed's Hill and Bunker Hill. Americans had no ammunition to waste, so Israel Putnam, a major general in the Continental army, cried out, "Don't fire until you see the whites of their eyes!" The Americans obeyed. When British soldiers got close, militiamen fired.

The British managed to capture the hill, but more than 1,000 redcoats were killed or wounded in the process. The battle of Bunker Hill convinced Americans that they *did* stand a chance against the mighty British army.

DECLARATION OF INDEPENDENCE

Americans wanted the world to know why they were breaking away from Great Britain. So in 1776, when Thomas Jefferson wrote the Declaration of Independence, he listed the "long train of abuses" the colonists had suffered. He said that governments didn't have the right to interfere with "Life, Liberty, and the pursuit of Happiness." Because Britain had done this, Americans had a duty to revolt.

SHOW WHAT YOU KNOW!

REFOCUS
COMPREHENSION

1. What led to the Boston Massacre?

2. How did Parliament punish the colonists for the Boston Tea Party?

THINK ABOUT IT
CRITICAL THINKING

Find some examples of cause and effect in events discussed in this lesson.

WRITE ABOUT IT
ACTIVITY

Look up the word *taxes* in the dictionary. With another student discuss items that are taxed today and what the tax money is used for. Write a paragraph explaining what you like and dislike about taxes.

Citizenship

KEY TERM

surveyor

GEORGE WASHINGTON

FOCUS *Americans were fortunate to have George Washington on their side. This bold, brave leader saw Americans through some of their bleakest moments.*

Nerves of Steel

George Washington was a brave, determined man. He faced many dangers in his life, yet he seldom panicked and never gave up. Instead, he worked his way through each problem as calmly and bravely as possible.

As a boy in Virginia, Washington learned to love music, drama, and books. But he also loved adventure. In 1749, at the age of 17, he became a **surveyor**. As part of his work, he traveled through tangled wilderness for weeks at a time. Washington fed himself by

▼ Washington surveys a tract of land, using measurements known as chains and links.

shooting wild turkeys, and at night he slept under the stars.

Then came the French and Indian War. Washington was a young man—just 22 years old. Still, he took charge of more than 150 men and headed off to face the French. He ended up fighting hundreds of enemy soldiers in the pouring rain. Two horses were shot out from under him. Four bullets whizzed through his coat. Washington lost the battle, but he had survived. By the time he left the army four years later, he had earned a reputation as a man who could deal with anything.

Peaceful Years

In 1759, Washington married a widow, Martha Dandridge Custis. He lived the life of a Virginia planter at his Mount Vernon plantation, attending the theater and going on fox hunts and fishing trips. He danced, played cards, and watched horse races.

But the Revolutionary War changed Washington's life. Americans needed an army, and they needed someone to lead it. On June 15, 1775, the Second Continental Congress appointed George Washington to lead the Continental army.

surveyor A person who determines the location, form, and boundaries of a tract of land

General and Mrs. Washington attend a formal reception in 1789.

Doing His Duty

Washington agreed to take the job, but he refused a salary. He believed in the American cause. More than that, he believed in doing his duty.

For eight years Washington led the American forces. He led them on long marches through snow and rain. Like his troops, he sometimes went without food or rest. During the frightful winter of 1777–1778 at Valley Forge, Pennsylvania, he was the strength that held the army together. Men watched him to see if his spirits sank. When they saw he wasn't giving up, some decided they could hang on, too.

An American Hero

In the end George Washington became a hero. He was more than just a good general. He had the ability to take command and inspire his soldiers to do the impossible. Also, as commander of the revolutionary army, he was quick to understand the importance of geography in a way that the British never did. He learned the dangers of having his soldiers in any location where their retreat or escape might be cut off. When Americans were looking for their first President, it is no wonder they turned to George Washington.

SHOW WHAT YOU KNOW!

REFOCUS
COMPREHENSION

1. What were some skills that Washington developed as a young man?

2. Why did Washington agree to lead the American forces during the Revolutionary War?

THINK ABOUT IT
CRITICAL THINKING

What, do you think, are some essential qualifications that a military leader needs?

WRITE ABOUT IT
ACTIVITY

You are a soldier in the Continental army. Write a letter home telling your family why you think George Washington is the right person to lead the army.

Spotlight

KEY TERMS

Hessian
mercenary
privateer

WINNING THE WAR

FOCUS *Showing remarkable grit and determination, the American troops defeated the more powerful British army. As a result, the colonies had truly gained their independence.*

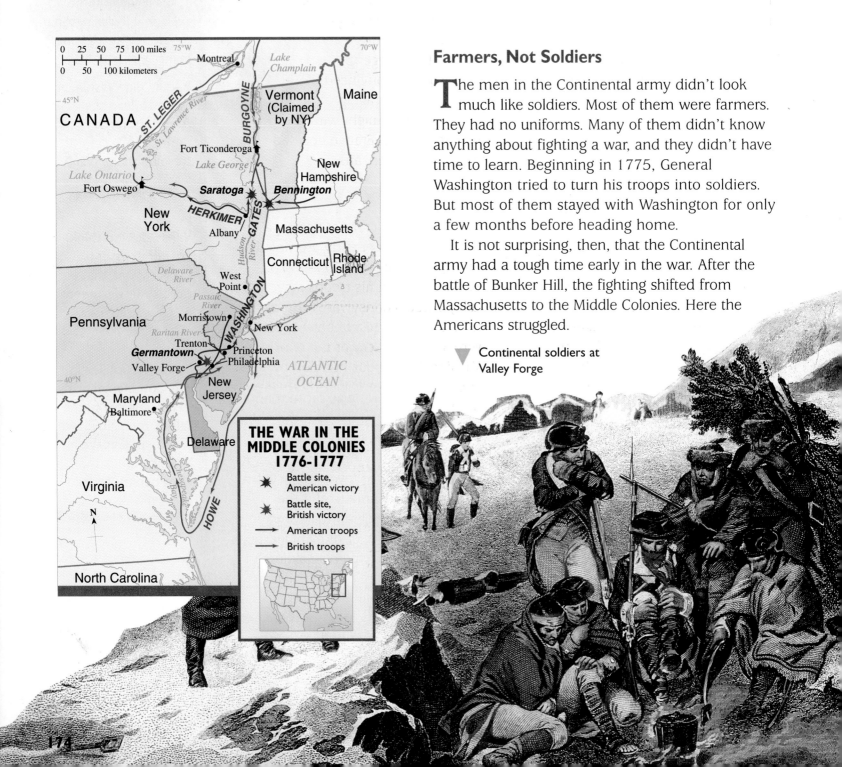

THE WAR IN THE MIDDLE COLONIES 1776-1777

✳ Battle site, American victory

✳ Battle site, British victory

→ American troops

→ British troops

Farmers, Not Soldiers

The men in the Continental army didn't look much like soldiers. Most of them were farmers. They had no uniforms. Many of them didn't know anything about fighting a war, and they didn't have time to learn. Beginning in 1775, General Washington tried to turn his troops into soldiers. But most of them stayed with Washington for only a few months before heading home.

It is not surprising, then, that the Continental army had a tough time early in the war. After the battle of Bunker Hill, the fighting shifted from Massachusetts to the Middle Colonies. Here the Americans struggled.

▼ Continental soldiers at Valley Forge

In August 1776 the two sides met near New York City. By December, Washington's troops had been pushed back across New Jersey all the way into Pennsylvania. Washington looked at his tired, confused men. "The spirits . . . [are] quite shrunk," he told a friend. "Without fresh troops . . . I think the game is pretty near up."

Glimmers of Hope

Washington knew he had to do something fast. On Christmas night, 1776, he led his men across the icy Delaware River. They staged a lightning-quick early-morning raid at Trenton, New Jersey. Find Trenton on the map on page 174.

The attack was not on British soldiers but on **Hessians.** These German soldiers earned money by fighting for any country that would pay them. Since the British had the cash, the **mercenaries** had signed on with them.

Washington's plan worked. The Americans overwhelmed the enemy troops. A few days later Washington's men scored again by taking control of Princeton, New Jersey.

These successes kept Americans going. But the war was far from over, and it still looked to many as though Britain would ultimately win.

Victory at Saratoga

In the spring of 1777, British troops moved into northern New York. They planned to take control of the Hudson River, cutting New England off from the other colonies. But the redcoats didn't coordinate their attack. On October 17, 1777, they lost a huge battle at Saratoga.

This was the biggest victory yet for the struggling Americans. It convinced France that the ragtag Americans just might win the war. As a result, France decided to help the Americans.

Hard Times at Valley Forge

Despite the victory at Saratoga, the Continental army nearly crumbled during the winter of 1777–1778. Washington and his troops stayed in Valley Forge, Pennsylvania. Nearly 20 miles away, in Philadelphia, the British were snugly settled for the winter. Washington's troops huddled in crudely built huts, shivering their way through bitterly cold nights.

The troops ate stew "full of burnt leaves and dirt." Many had worn-out boots, so they wrapped rags around their bloody feet to keep them from freezing.

Many Continental soldiers died from disease that winter. Others deserted the army. Those who stayed had such trust in General Washington that they were willing to put up with almost anything.

▲ Drums such as this were played to summon troops.

▼ A press to make musket balls

Hessian A German soldier hired to fight for the British in the Revolutionary War
mercenary A person hired to be a soldier

War in the West and South

While Washington was at Valley Forge, a young Virginian, George Rogers Clark, was preparing to attack British forts in the West. The British wanted to stir up the Indians against the Americans.

In the summer of 1778, Clark and his men took the British fort at Kaskaskia, in present-day Illinois. Later, Clark also took a fort at Vincennes

The first Purple Heart, a military decoration awarded to those wounded or killed in action, was designed by Washington and established in 1782. Today's Purple Heart is shown on the right.

(vihn SENZ) in what is now Indiana. Locate Kaskaskia and Vincennes on the map below. Clark's victories gave the United States control of much land between the Appalachian Mountains and the Mississippi River.

In 1778, fighting also shifted to the South. For the next two years, American forces suffered their worst defeats. The British captured Savannah, Georgia, and Charleston, South Carolina. They won control over a large part of the South.

Victory at Sea

The Patriots had only a small navy. To help it, Congress allowed private owners of ships to arm their own vessels with cannons. These ships were called **privateers**. By the end of the war, American privateers had sunk or captured more than 600 British ships.

Although there were not many American warships, the privateers could put up a good fight against one British ship at a time.

One such battle came on September 23, 1779. The American warship *Bonhomme Richard* was fighting the British warship *Serapis* off the coast of

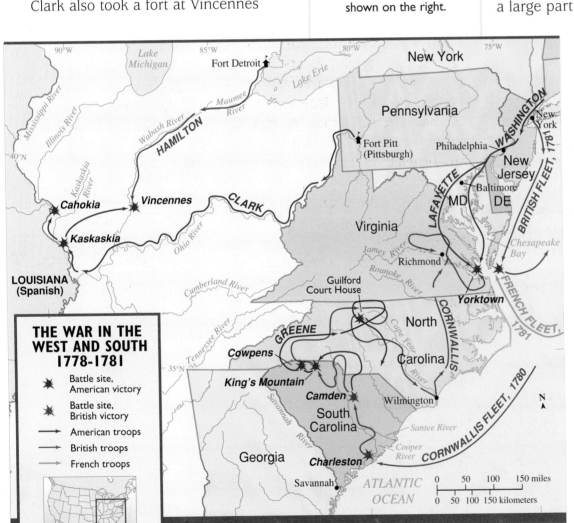

THE WAR IN THE WEST AND SOUTH 1778–1781

- ✴ Battle site, American victory
- ✴ Battle site, British victory
- → American troops
- → British troops
- → French troops

⭐ *privateer* A privately-owned armed ship having a government's permission to attack enemy ships

This painting shows the battle between *Bonhomme Richard* and HMS *Serapis*.

Washington, the British band played "The World Turned Upside Down."

It did seem that everything had been scrambled. A scrawny string of colonies had taken on one of the world's great powers—and won! It was the first time in history that colonists had successfully broken away from their home country.

Freedom—But Not for All

Americans had won their freedom, but not for everyone. Few people talked about freeing the enslaved Africans. In the Declaration of Independence, Thomas Jefferson wrote, "All men are created equal. . . ." But most Americans thought that meant "all *white* men are created equal."

About 5,000 African Americans had fought on the American side. At least that many had fought for the British, because the British were the first to promise freedom in return for fighting. But no matter which side they chose, African Americans didn't have much hope for a better life.

Native Americans didn't have much to look forward to either. Many Native Americans stayed away from the fighting. Others, such as the Iroquois, fought for the British. They figured the British couldn't be any worse than the Americans who wanted to take over their land.

Britain. It seemed certain that the heavily armed *Serapis* would win. The British gave the *Bonhomme Richard's* captain, John Paul Jones, a chance to surrender. But Jones cried out, "I have not yet begun to fight!" After several more hours of bitter fighting, Jones and his men won.

Americans Win the War

Faced with such determination, the British finally gave up. They could hardly believe that the weak American army had beaten them. When General Cornwallis's troops surrendered to George

SHOW WHAT YOU KNOW!

REFOCUS
COMPREHENSION

1. What were some challenges that George Washington faced as head of the Continental army?

2. What was the significance of the victory at Saratoga?

THINK ABOUT IT
CRITICAL THINKING

What were some qualities that Americans had that helped them win the war?

WRITE ABOUT IT
ACTIVITY

Suppose you are a soldier spending the winter at Valley Forge. Write a letter home describing your living conditions. Reference and trade books may help give you more accurate detail.

WOMEN DURING THE REVOLUTION

FOCUS *During the time of the Revolutionary War, women were important participants in social, economic, political, and military activities.*

Women at Work

During the war, women took care of their families. Some also ran farms and businesses while their husbands were away at war. If her husband died on the battlefield, a woman would often carry on her husband's occupation.

Jane Burgess, a Maryland widow, advertised in a local paper in 1773 that she still carried on "the Blacksmith Business" of her husband. Women ran inns and were barbers and apothecaries (pharmacists) in the 1700s. In many cases women carried on trades their fathers or husbands had practiced. But women began to be recognized for their own accomplishments as well.

The Goddards were an interesting family of business women. Sarah Goddard of Providence lent her son William money to start the *Providence Gazette* in 1765, on the condition that she would be his partner. Several years later William and his sister Mary Katherine moved to Maryland and started a printing business as well as Baltimore's first newspaper. Because of Mary's skill, she was selected by the Congress to print the official copy of the Declaration of Independence.

▼ Making cannon balls

Volunteers and Activists

Women also played other important roles. Most women did not work outside the home and often spent time together spinning and sewing. Their hands were busy, but their minds were free to think about issues of the day. Since clothing for soldiers was needed, spinning became vital. Betsy Ross and others like her used their sewing skills to produce banners and flags.

The Daughters of Liberty, which you read about on page 164, organized **boycotts** of textiles and tea. In 1770 over 300 women in Boston vowed not to drink tea. They made and sold teas instead. Made from herbs or fruit leaves, these "liberty teas" were described as "bad-tasting." But people loved the idea of the boycotts, and the liberty teas were popular.

Poets and Playwrights

During this time period there were some well-known women writers. Phillis Wheatley, although enslaved, was treated well by her owners in Boston. She eventually became famous as America's first-known African American poet. In 1776 she wrote a poem praising George Washington and even met him when he camped nearby.

Mercy Otis Warren wrote popular political plays during the 1770s. Nasty

Phillis Wheatley was born in Africa around 1753. Captured by slave traders in 1761 and taken to Boston, she eventually became a celebrated poet.

characters in Warren's plays were Loyalists; nice ones were Patriots.

On the Battlefield

Some women became directly involved in the war. Women who were gunsmiths and blacksmiths helped make weapons. One group of women got hold of the statue of George III that had been pulled down by the Sons of Liberty. They melted it down to make bullets.

In 1777, Colonel Ludington, a local militia leader, heard that British troops were raiding a supply center in Danbury, Connecticut. Sybil Ludington, his 16-year-old daughter, volunteered to warn the militia. Despite the danger of being stopped by a British patrol, she rode many miles on horseback to spread the news.

Many women served as nurses and seamstresses. Others helped on the battlefield, carrying food and drink and comforting soldiers.

One woman, Mary "Molly" Hays, was at her husband's side during the battle at Monmouth. Because she brought pitchers of water to other Continental soldiers, she got the nickname Molly Pitcher. When Mary's husband was wounded during the fighting, she bravely took his place, firing the cannon.

 boycott An organized campaign in which people refuse to have any dealings with a particular group or business

Hand in Hand:
An American History Through Poetry

Collected by Lee Bennett Hopkins

During the Revolutionary War some women went to the front. One of them was Mary "Molly" Hays, known as Molly Pitcher, who was at her husband's side during the battle at Monmouth.

Molly Pitcher

All day the great guns barked and roared;

All day the big balls screeched and soared;

All day, 'mid the sweating gunners grim,

Who toiled in their smoke-shroud dense and dim,

Sweet Molly labored with courage high,

With steady hand and watchful eye,

Till the day was ours, and the sinking sun

Looked down on the field of Monmouth won,

And Molly standing beside her gun.

Now, Molly, rest your weary arm!

Safe, Molly, all is safe from harm.

Now, woman, bow your aching head,

And weep in sorrow o'er your dead!

HAND IN HAND
AN AMERICAN HISTORY THROUGH POETRY
COLLECTED BY LEE BENNETT HOPKINS
ILLUSTRATED BY PETER M. FIORE

Next day on that field so hardly won,

Stately and calm stands Washington,

And looks where our gallant Greene doth lead

A figure clad in motley weed—

A soldier's cap and a soldier's coat

Masking a woman's petticoat.

He greets our Molly in kindly wise;

He bids her raise her tearful eyes;

And now he hails her before them all

Comrade and soldier, whate'er befall,

"And since she has played a man's full part,

A man's reward for her loyal heart!

And Sergeant Molly Pitcher's name

Be writ henceforth on the shield of fame!"

Oh, Molly, with your eyes so blue!

Oh, Molly, Molly, here's to you!

Sweet honor's roll will aye be richer

To hold the name of Molly Pitcher.

Laura E. Richards

You can read other poems about the history of the United States by checking the book out of your school or public library.

SHOW WHAT YOU KNOW!

REFOCUS
COMPREHENSION

1. In what ways did women contribute to the war effort?

2. Who were the Daughters of Liberty and what did they do?

THINK ABOUT IT
CRITICAL THINKING

Why do you think so many women actively supported the revolution?

WRITE ABOUT IT
ACTIVITY

Read the poem "Molly Pitcher." Write a paragraph that summarizes the meaning of the poem.

SUMMING UP

1 DO YOU REMEMBER...
COMPREHENSION

1. Why did Great Britain raise taxes in 1763?

2. How did the first fighting of the revolution break out?

3. What did the Declaration of Independence formally announce?

4. What was the purpose of the Committees of Correspondence?

5. What did the Second Continental Congress accomplish?

6. What were some of George Washington's strengths as a leader?

7. What problems did Washington have as general of the American army?

8. Why was the American victory at Saratoga so important?

9. Why was the final outcome of the war surprising to so many people?

10. In what important ways did women help win the war?

2 SKILL POWER
UNDERSTANDING CAUSE AND EFFECT

List three examples of cause and effect in the events leading up to the start of the Revolutionary War. Then give three examples of cause and effect during the war itself.

3 WHAT DO YOU THINK?
CRITICAL THINKING

1. Could the differences between Great Britain and the colonies have been resolved without a war? Explain.

2. Why was the first shot fired at Lexington said to be "heard round the world"?

3. Washington had the ability to inspire his soldiers to do the impossible. What are some ways in which a leader inspires people?

4. What, do you think, was the greatest American advantage in the Revolutionary War? What was the greatest British advantage?

5. In what ways was being a soldier in the revolution different from being a soldier today?

4 SAY IT, WRITE IT, USE IT
VOCABULARY

Write newspaper headlines that might have appeared in a newspaper during revolutionary times. Use one or more of the vocabulary words in each headline, showing that you know the meanings of these words.

boycott	Minuteman
Declaration of Independence	Patriot
	privateer
Hessian	proclamation
Loyalist	revolution
mercenary	surveyor

5 GEOGRAPHY AND YOU
MAP STUDY

Look at the maps on pages 163 and 165 and below to answer the following questions.

1. List the 13 colonies.

2. Use the scale of miles and measure the distance from Boston to Concord.

3. Identify the battle sites of the war in Massachusetts.

4. What colonies did Cornwallis pass through as he went from Charleston to Yorktown?

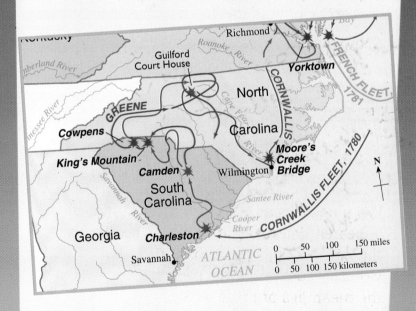

6 TAKE ACTION
CITIZENSHIP

Independence meant that the United States needed its own flag. With a group of classmates, draw pictures of some of our nation's early flags. Find out what the parts and colors of the flags stand for. Then make a list of rules that tell how we should honor and display our flag.

7 GET CREATIVE
LANGUAGE ARTS CONNECTION

The Declaration of Independence was written in beautiful handwriting on special parchment paper. Look at the text of the Declaration of Independence on pages 612–615. Find a passage from the declaration that means a lot to you. Use pen and ink to create a copy of the passage that you can post in your classroom.

LOOKING AHEAD

In the next chapter you will find out how the new nation set up a new government.

CHAPTER 9

The New

Passing laws, raising taxes, making treaties—have you ever wanted to know how the government goes about accomplishing these things? Or have you ever wondered about the beginnings of our government? This chapter is about all that and more.

▲ How do the branches of our government balance each other? Find out on page 201.

CONTENTS

Nation

These books tell about some people, places, and events of interest during the time when the Constitution was written. Read one that interests you and fill out a book-review form.

READ AND RESEARCH

Shh! We're Writing the Constitution by Jean Fritz
(G. P. Putnam's Sons, 1987)
Did you know that Benjamin Franklin arrived at the Grand Convention for the Constitution in a sedan chair carried by four prisoners from a Philadelphia jail? Read all about the serious and ridiculous details involved in the making of the United States Constitution. *(nonfiction)*

Martha Washington by Joan Marsh (Franklin Watts, 1993)
Read about the life of Martha Washington from her childhood to her time as First Lady of the United States. *(biography)*

Benjamin Franklin, Scientist and Inventor by Eve B. Feldman (Franklin Watts, 1990)
Did you know that people once thought that lightning was caused by magic or heavenly powers? Find out about Benjamin Franklin's scientific experiments with electricity and his many practical inventions. *(biography)*

The Constitution by Marilyn Prolman (Childrens Press, 1995)
Journey back to 1787, when the 13 states were not in agreement about what the new government should be, and when a strong national government did not exist. Learn all about the making of the Constitution, a document that continues to guide our nation. *(nonfiction)*

SKILL POWER
Using a Flowchart

Knowing how to read a flowchart will help you understand the order of the steps in a process.

UNDERSTAND IT

People often use diagrams to explain how something works. One type of diagram, a flowchart, shows the steps involved in a process. Flowcharts are often used to explain how to do something or how a complicated system works.

If you have ever seen a chart of how to help a choking victim in a restaurant, you have seen a flowchart. You might also have seen flowcharts that show how newspapers can be recycled into paper that can be used again.

Flowcharts are also used to explain how different parts of our government work.

EXPLORE IT

The flowchart below shows how the President of the United States is elected. Study the flowchart for a minute. Are there some things that surprised you? Did you think, for example, that the citizens actually elect the President directly?

Look again at the chart. What problem might arise in this system? How do people know that an electoral college representative will vote for their candidate?

How the President Is Elected

In November, people vote for the candidate of their choice. Each candidate is represented by members of the electoral college.

In December the electoral college members vote for the President. In January the votes are counted.

The candidate with the majority vote becomes President.

If there is no majority, the House of Representatives decides which candidate will be President.

186

TRY IT

With a group of your classmates, learn more about how your local government operates. Talk with parents and other adults in your community to find out as much as you can about one government task or operation. For example, you might look into how your community

- responds to a fire or medical emergency
- builds a new school or park
- recycles and/or disposes of trash
- puts in a new road
- hires a new school principal
- decides how much property tax to charge homeowners

Take notes on all the information you learn. Then make a flowchart to arrange the steps of the task or operation in order. Show what may or may not happen at each step. Include small drawings.

Collect all the flowcharts and fasten them together at the top. You can display your Flowchart Flip Book in your classroom.

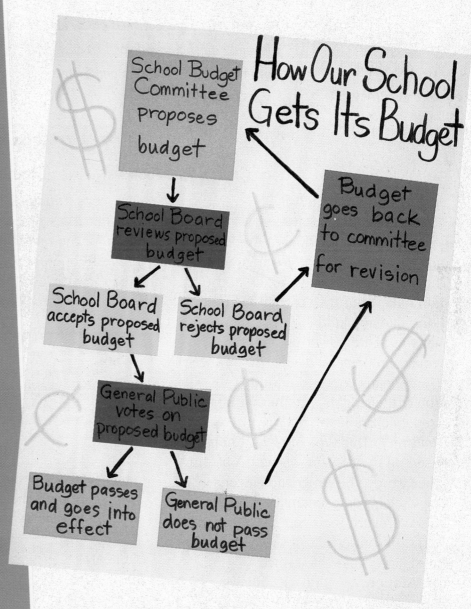

How Our School Gets Its Budget

School Budget Committee proposes budget

↓

School Board reviews proposed budget

School Board accepts proposed budget

School Board rejects proposed budget

Budget goes back to committee for revision

General Public votes on proposed budget

Budget passes and goes into effect

General Public does not pass budget

SKILL POWER SEARCH *What other flowcharts can you find in this chapter? What processes do they show?*

1 Setting the Scene

KEY TERMS
republic
constitution
ratify
Bill of Rights
Cabinet
political party

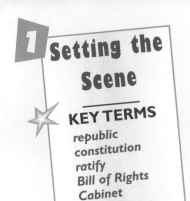

A New Government

FOCUS *Americans designed a new kind of government. Through trial and error, hard work, and creative thinking, they wrote a constitution that still guides and protects us.*

Americans Create a Republic

Now that America was independent, what kind of government would it have? Americans didn't want a king and a parliament. They had seen those in action and didn't like what they saw. In fact, they didn't like any kind of government that was more powerful than the people it represented.

Americans chose a **republic** to protect their rights. Another name for a republic is a *representative democracy*. This type of government is based on the consent of the people. In other words, the American citizens would elect representatives to pass laws or govern their country.

The 13 former colonies were now states. Each state had its own **constitution**, or written set of laws. These constitutions told the exact powers of state governments. Most states also had bills of rights added to their constitutions so that Americans could have their freedoms written down.

A Weak Government

State constitutions seemed fine, but Americans also wanted a written constitution for the national government. In 1777, a Congressional committee created the Articles of Confederation. This document provided for the first

▲ Each state printed its own money. But money from one state might not be accepted in another.

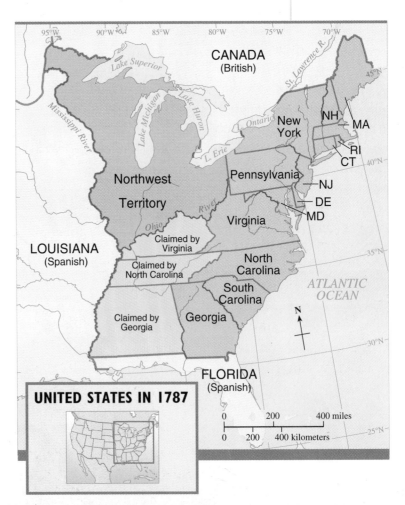

UNITED STATES IN 1787

CANADA (British)

Lake Superior · Lake Michigan · Lake Huron · Lake Erie · Lake Ontario

St. Lawrence R.

NH · MA · RI · CT

New York

Pennsylvania · NJ · DE · MD

Northwest Territory

Ohio River

Virginia

Claimed by Virginia

LOUISIANA (Spanish)

Mississippi River

Claimed by North Carolina

North Carolina

South Carolina

ATLANTIC OCEAN

Claimed by Georgia

Georgia

FLORIDA (Spanish)

0   200   400 miles
0   200   400 kilometers

---

republic A government in which the power to govern comes from the people, not a king

constitution A set of laws governing a state or nation

1777	1787	1789	1791
Articles of Confederation are created	Constitutional Convention meets in Philadelphia	George Washington is elected President	Bill of Rights is added to the Constitution

1775   1780   1785   1790   1795

government of the United States. There was to be no king and no parliament, and the national government was to be weaker than the state governments. Americans wanted state governments to have more power because they were considered closer to the people than the national government.

How weak was the first national government? It had no army, no court system, and no President. It did have a weak Congress that had to beg the states for money because it had no power to collect taxes. Usually the states refused, and Congress went further and further into debt. Congress couldn't even settle disputes between states. And if people wanted to make Congress stronger, *all* the states had to agree. One state could block the will of all the others.

Congress did have some accomplishments, one of which dealt with the Northwest Territory. Find this area on the map on page 188. Passed in 1787, the Northwest Ordinance divided the territory into "not less than three nor more than five states." (In fact, it became five states—Ohio, Indiana, Illinois, Michigan, and

Wisconsin.) The ordinance said that the new states would be equal to the original 13 states. And these new states would not have slavery.

Shays's Rebellion

Soon Congress's weaknesses outweighed its accomplishments. Massachusetts farmers had a hard year in 1786, and they couldn't pay their taxes. Judges ordered them to sell their land to get the tax money.

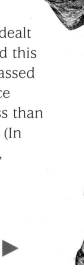

Shays's Rebellion ▶

A reenactment of the 1787 Constitutional Convention

You can read the United States Constitution on pages 616–635.

These delegates met throughout the summer. They argued back and forth. They fought bitterly with each other. In the end they wrote a new constitution, which made the national government more powerful. Now the government could raise an army and collect taxes. Still, the Constitution left the states with a great deal of power.

Constitutional Genius

This was the first time a nation had written its own constitution. No other nation had one. Even Great Britain didn't have a written constitution. Later our Constitution became a model for other nations to use. Today it remains the oldest constitution in use in the world.

The writers of the Constitution knew they weren't perfect. So they made it possible to *amend*, or change, the Constitution. This enabled future Americans to change part of the Constitution instead of getting rid of the whole thing.

Not everyone was pleased by the new Constitution. Some people didn't want power taken away from the states and given to the national government. This opposition didn't surprise the writers of the Constitution. They knew all along that it would be challenging to **ratify**, or pass, the new document.

The writers did two things to make ratification easier. First, only 9 states

This angered the farmers. One farmer, Daniel Shays, led an armed rebellion. Although it was crushed by the state militia, it scared many people. The national government, which had no army, just stood on the sidelines. It was so weak that it couldn't even deal with a small group of angry farmers.

The Constitutional Convention

People began to see a need to make the national government stronger. In May 1787 a group of delegates met in Philadelphia to strengthen the national government by fixing the Articles of Confederation. However, these men quickly saw that the Articles of Confederation couldn't do the job and a whole new government was needed.

 ratify To formally approve

had to ratify it, not all 13. Second, James Madison, Alexander Hamilton, and John Jay wrote a series of essays called *The Federalist* that tried to convince people to support the new Constitution.

The battle for ratification was fought from state to state. One problem was that the Constitution did not have a bill of rights. A bill of rights would clearly define people's rights. So the Constitution's supporters promised to add a bill of rights as soon as the Constitution was ratified.

This promise helped the process of ratification, but it still took a while. The map on this page shows what year each state approved the Constitution. It wasn't until June 21, 1788, that the ninth state, New Hampshire, voted yes. Virginia and New York soon followed. North Carolina held out until November 1789. Rhode Island didn't join the Union until May 1790. Finally, in 1791 the first ten amendments, known collectively as the **Bill of Rights**, were added to the Constitution.

You can read the Gallery of Presidents on pages 605–611.

Our First President

The Constitution provided for a President. But many Americans were concerned about the power of the President. Would the President really be a king with a different title? These fears were put to rest in 1789 when George Washington was unanimously elected President.

Washington was a great President. People watched his every move, knowing that he was setting the tone for future Presidents. Even the title Washington chose for himself, "Mr. President," is still used today. A Senate committee wanted to call him "His Highness, the President of the United States of America, and Protector of Liberties."

Washington chose a number of people to lead executive departments and advise him in important matters. He listened carefully to their advice. Today, certain advisors to the President are known as **Cabinet** members.

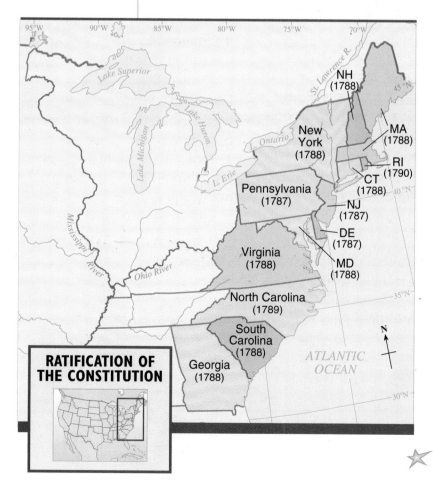

RATIFICATION OF THE CONSTITUTION

NH (1788)
New York (1788)
MA (1788)
RI (1790)
CT (1788)
Pennsylvania (1787)
NJ (1787)
DE (1787)
Virginia (1788)
MD (1788)
North Carolina (1789)
South Carolina (1788)
Georgia (1788)
ATLANTIC OCEAN

⭐ **Bill of Rights** The first ten amendments to the Constitution
Cabinet A group of advisors to the President

Washington on the way
to his inauguration as
President

Political Parties

Two of his best-known Cabinet officers were Alexander Hamilton, his secretary of the treasury, and Thomas Jefferson, his secretary of state. The two men disagreed on almost everything.

Hamilton wanted to encourage manufacturing. He hoped the United States would soon have many large cities. In addition, he wanted a large and powerful national government.

Jefferson hoped for a nation with some factories. But he wanted the United States to remain a mostly rural nation of small farms. He also wanted a small national government.

The disputes between these leaders led to the birth of **political parties**. In the 1790s, people who favored many of Hamilton's ideas were called *Federalists*. Jefferson's supporters were called *Democratic-Republicans*.

The government that governs best governs least.
—Thomas Jefferson

 political party A group of people who hold certain beliefs about how the government should be run

Whiskey Rebellion

Meanwhile, farmers in western Pennsylvania were angered by a tax on whiskey. Many of these farmers made whiskey out of their corn because it was cheaper to ship whiskey than corn. And corn sometimes spoiled before it was sold. These farmers felt that the tax was unfair, because they were being taxed on the only practical product they could sell.

The protesting farmers resorted to violent attacks against the government officers who enforced the tax. Would this be just like Shays's Rebellion? No. When George Washington sent 13,000 troops, the farmers put down their guns and fled. President Washington showed the new national government's strength.

The Second President

Washington served two terms, or eight years, as President. He was so popular that he would have been elected again if he had run for reelection. But in 1797 he stepped down and returned to his home at Mount Vernon.

John Adams, a Federalist who had been Washington's Vice President, was elected the nation's second President. During Adams's presidency, the United States was almost dragged into a war between Great Britain and France.

Adams knew that going to war might make him popular, but he also knew that war was not good for the country. While President Adams avoided war, his decision was not looked upon favorably.

The new nation survived, despite the lack of popularity of its new President. The Constitution had provided well for change as needed, even in its provision for presidential elections every four years.

◀ The Whiskey Rebellion

SHOW WHAT YOU KNOW!

REFOCUS
COMPREHENSION

1. How was the government's response to Shays's Rebellion different from the response to the Whiskey Rebellion?

2. How did political parties begin in the United States?

THINK ABOUT IT
CRITICAL THINKING

Do you think the delegates should have written a new Constitution when they were only supposed to revise the Articles of Confederation? Give reasons for your answer.

WRITE ABOUT IT
ACTIVITY

Make a flowchart that shows the steps that led to the ratification of the Constitution.

Dealing With Other Nations

FOCUS *Once the United States became independent, it had to deal with other nations in a new way. Between 1784 and 1800 there were threats of war, but American leaders tried to avoid military conflicts.*

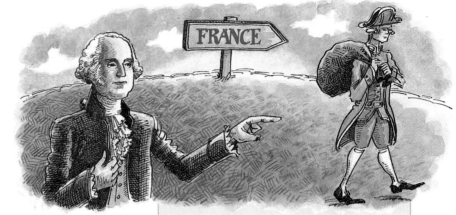

FIGHTING FOR THE LAND

America's independence didn't excite many Native Americans. They wanted to keep their land and protect their way of life. Americans moving west across the Appalachian Mountains wanted to push out the Native Americans. Between 1784 and 1786, Native Americans signed a series of treaties in which they gave up claims to some western lands.

Some Native Americans, however, wanted to fight for the land. As a result, several bloody battles were fought between Native Americans and white settlers throughout the late 1780s and early 1790s.

THE FRENCH REVOLUTION

It seemed as if the American ideals of freedom and equality had taken hold in France. In July 1789, the French people revolted against King Louis XVI. Later the French established a republic. Most Americans were overjoyed that the French, like themselves, had been successful in their revolution.

By 1793, however, the French Revolution had turned ugly. The king and queen were beheaded, and many others were killed in the "Reign of Terror."

This violence upset some Americans. Other Americans remembered how the French had helped America during its revolution and still supported the French in their revolution.

WAR AND GENÊT

In 1778 the United States had promised to help France in case of war. Then, in 1793, France went to war with Britain. Since the United States needed to continue trade with Britain, President Washington decided to remain *neutral*, or to stay out of the war completely.

Citizen Genêt (ZHUH ne), a Frenchman, came to America and pressured Americans into getting involved. Genêt tried to recruit Americans to fight the British.

Washington ordered Genêt to stop recruiting or be sent back to France. Genêt was afraid to return to Paris, because his political party had lost power. He obeyed Washington and stayed in the United States.

1784–1786
Treaties with
Native Americans

1789
French Revolution
begins

1793
France and
Britain at war

1793
British begin
impressment of
American sailors

1795
Spain and U.S. sign treaty
regarding Mississippi River

1784   1786   1788   1790   1792   1794   1796

SHOW WHAT YOU
KNOW!

TROUBLE WITH BRITAIN

The war between Great Britain and France affected the United States. According to the 1783 Treaty of Paris, British fur traders were to leave their forts in the Northwest Territory. Now, the British refused to leave. They did not recognize the right of a neutral United States to trade with France.

In 1793, British ships began stopping American ships at sea, forcing American sailors to serve in the British navy. Called *impressment*, this made some Americans angry enough to demand war. President Washington knew that America could not risk war so soon after its revolution. So the United States still remained neutral.

BETTER LUCK WITH SPAIN

Things went better with Spain than with France and Britain. Back in 1784, Spain had closed the port of New Orleans to American commerce. Later, in 1795, Spain feared Americans might attack Louisiana. So Spain signed a treaty allowing Americans to sail freely down the Mississippi River and to use the port of New Orleans. This treaty helped American farmers along the Mississippi River to ship their goods anywhere in the world.

REFOCUS
COMPREHENSION

1. How were Native Americans affected by America's independence?

2. How did the treaty between Spain and the United States benefit American farmers?

THINK ABOUT IT
CRITICAL THINKING

Do you think that the United States should have honored its promise to help France in case of war? Explain the reasons for your decision.

WRITE ABOUT IT
ACTIVITY

Suppose you are representing the United States in Great Britain. Write a speech that you would deliver to British leaders, protesting the impressment of American sailors.

The Constitutional Convention

FOCUS *Throughout the summer of 1787, delegates to the Constitutional Convention struggled to produce the Constitution of the United States.*

Philadelphia, 1787

You probably will arrive late. But so will almost everyone else. Except for James Madison and a few others, all the delegates to the 1787 Constitutional Convention in Philadelphia are late. Why? Well, eighteenth- century roads are awful. Buggies often get stuck in the muddy, rutted paths.

This is probably your first visit to Philadelphia. The city may seem noisy and dirty. Swarms of flies and other insects fill the air. Horses and wagons clog the streets. Smoke from wood-fired cooking stoves makes it hard to breathe.

You probably notice the heat the most. Philadelphia is having one of its hottest summers in 40 years. Everyone is sweating in the 90-degree heat.

Still, you feel a sense of excitement. There is so much to see and do. You can visit Peale's Museum. It's full of fossils, stuffed animal skins, and other "wonderful works of nature." You can

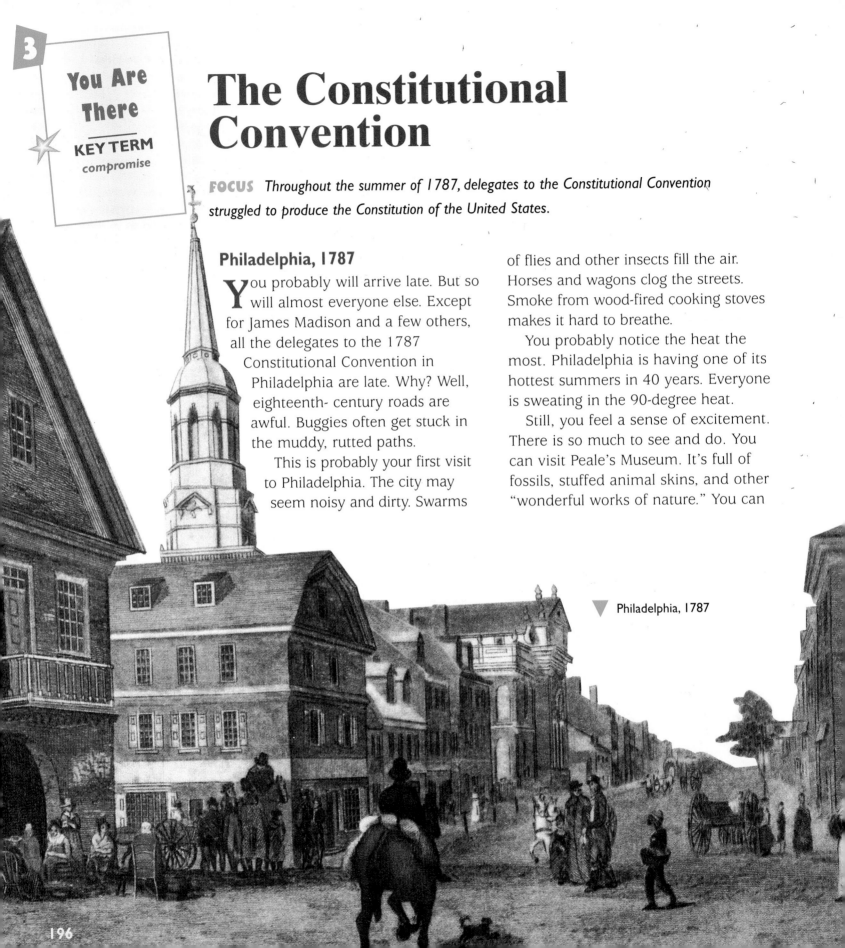

▼ Philadelphia, 1787

relax on the docks of the Delaware River and watch a demonstration of a new invention—the steam-powered boat. You might even visit a shop that's selling the latest fad from Europe—the toothbrush.

If you're hungry or thirsty, you can go to a tavern called the Indian Queen, where you'll see many other delegates. You all come here despite the huge open sewer being repaired across the street. And you never know which will be stronger—the smell of food cooking or the smell of the sewer. Despite the heat, you keep your windows closed at night to avoid the stinging flies while you sleep. You put up with these discomforts and remind yourself that you're here to do an important job.

Who's Here and Who's Not

The convention is scheduled to open on May 14, 1787, at the State House. It is May 25 before enough delegates reach the city to start the talks. Nineteen elected delegates never show up at all. Rhode Island doesn't want a strong national government, and doesn't send a delegate.

Looking at the other 54 delegates, you may notice that there are no

I was not absent a single day, nor more than a casual fraction of any hour in any day, so that I could not have lost a single speech, unless a very short one.
—James Madison

▲ Benjamin Franklin

It was a "convention of the well-bred, the well-fed, the well-read, and the well-wed."
—James MacGregor Burns

women, no Native Americans, and no African Americans. This meeting is for white men only—they are the only ones who can vote and hold office. Some well-known people are also missing. Patrick Henry, who had protested British taxes before the revolution, refuses to come, saying he "smelt a rat in Philadelphia." Others, such as Samuel Adams, are equally suspicious. Meanwhile, John Adams is in England and Thomas Jefferson is in France.

Still, many well-known people are here, including George Washington and the 81-year-old Benjamin Franklin. Franklin had spent a number of years in Europe, representing the interests of the colonies, and later, the new nation. And Alexander Hamilton has come to argue for the strongest possible national government.

Keeping a Secret

As the convention begins, you and the other delegates must decide if you should keep the windows open or closed in the sweltering heat. If you close the windows, you'll suffer even more from the heat, especially the New England delegates, in their heavy woolen suits and wigs. If you leave the windows open, you'll have to listen to the noise from the streets, your meetings won't be private, and more flies will get inside the building. Whatever you decide, it is important to keep the meetings secret. George Washington, as president of the convention, strictly bans the press and public from entering.

James Madison takes daily notes. Those notes will provide the greatest evidence of what goes on at these meetings in Philadelphia.

Each day, you see Benjamin Franklin being carried to the convention by prisoners from a local jail in a sedan chair with glass windows.

Not Everyone Agrees

Once the convention starts, you have hundreds of issues to consider. What powers will you give the President? Who will control commerce between the states? Should judges be elected or appointed? What, if anything, should be done about slavery? And so on. The big issue, however, is the new Congress—what will it look like?

Delegates from states with large populations prefer Madison's idea,

▲ The Constitution allowed slavery. Yet, in 1787 in Philadelphia, Absalom Jones and Richard Allen began an abolition, or antislavery, society. The picture above is a logo for an early abolition society.

known as the Virginia Plan. Since this plan suggests that representation be based on population, it gives large states more power. And delegates from small states like William Paterson's idea, known as the New Jersey Plan. It calls for equal representation for all states.

You and other delegates argue about this for seven weeks. At last, people begin to consider Roger Sherman's compromise. Known as the Great Compromise, it calls for Congress to have two houses. In the Senate, or upper house, every state gets two senators. This protects small states. The House of Representatives, or lower house, favors large states. In this house, representation is based on a state's population. Not everyone likes this idea, but after all this time they realize it is a workable solution.

Making Another Compromise

The Great Compromise brings about a new problem. How do you count population? Southern states want to count enslaved people. This will give southern states more representatives. Northern states only want free people counted.

Again, you and the other delegates reach a compromise. The Three-fifths

compromise An agreement in which each side gives in a little

Compromise says that 5 enslaved people will be counted as the equivalent of 3 free people. So for this purpose, 100 enslaved people count as 60 free people.

On July 16, the Great Compromise, suggested by Sherman, and the Three-fifths Compromise are passed. The issue of slavery is largely ignored. Gouverneur Morris of New York and George Mason of Virginia speak against it. Few delegates listen, and nothing is done to change the system of slavery.

Agreement at Last

It's been a long and trying four months. But on September 17 you and your fellow delegates sign the new Constitution. Will it work? Benjamin Franklin thinks so. He has been studying a carving on the back of Washington's chair. It shows the sun on the horizon. Franklin wonders whether it is a rising or a setting sun. At the end of the convention he says, "I have the happiness to know that it is a rising and not a setting sun."

On July 26, 1788, people celebrated as the Constitution became the law of the land.

Alexander Hamilton ▶

SHOW WHAT YOU KNOW!

REFOCUS
COMPREHENSION

1. List three issues that were discussed at the Constitutional Convention.

2. What groups were and were not represented at the convention?

THINK ABOUT IT
CRITICAL THINKING

Why is it sometimes necessary to make compromises in order to get things done?

WRITE ABOUT IT
ACTIVITY

It is September 1787. You and the other delegates have just signed the Constitution. Write a journal entry describing how you feel about what the convention has or has not accomplished.

4 Citizenship

KEY TERMS
executive branch
legislative branch
judicial branch
impeach
bill
federalism

How Our Government Works

FOCUS *Our government is limited because the people have freedoms that the government cannot take away and because no single person has all the political power.*

Basic Freedoms

In the Declaration of Independence, Thomas Jefferson wrote of "unalienable Rights." These are basic freedoms that Americans believe all people are born with. The Constitution's Bill of Rights is made up of ten amendments that provide many freedoms.

The five freedoms protected by the First Amendment are listed in the chart below. First is freedom of religion, which allows us to worship as we please. We can freely express our thoughts because we have freedom of speech. Freedom of the press enables us to freely express our ideas in writing. Freedom of assembly means that we can gather with other people to protest something. Last, we have freedom of petition, or the right to ask the government to change a law that we feel is wrong.

Freedoms Under the Constitution

Freedom of Religion	**Freedom of Speech**	**Freedom of the Press**	**Freedom of Assembly**	**Freedom of Petition**
The right to worship according to your own beliefs	The right to say what you believe	The right to publish newspapers, magazines, and books	The right to gather with other people and work for political action	The right to ask the government to right a wrong

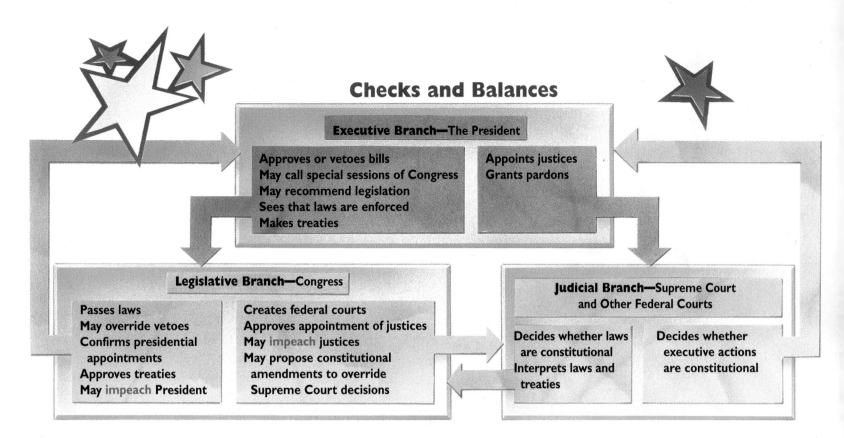

Checks and Balances

Executive Branch—The President

Approves or vetoes bills
May call special sessions of Congress
May recommend legislation
Sees that laws are enforced
Makes treaties

Appoints justices
Grants pardons

Legislative Branch—Congress

Passes laws
May override vetoes
Confirms presidential
  appointments
Approves treaties
May impeach President

Creates federal courts
Approves appointment of justices
May impeach justices
May propose constitutional
  amendments to override
  Supreme Court decisions

Judicial Branch—Supreme Court and Other Federal Courts

Decides whether laws
  are constitutional
Interprets laws and
  treaties

Decides whether
  executive actions
  are constitutional

Separation of Powers

The federal government is separated into three branches. The **executive branch,** headed by the President, is responsible for carrying out laws. The President is helped by departments that have special jobs.

The **legislative branch**, or Congress, is made up of the Senate and the House of Representatives. Congress is responsible for making the laws.

The **judicial branch**, or the federal court system, is responsible for deciding the meaning of the laws. The highest court is the Supreme Court. Federal courts also handle cases involving federal laws, and they settle disputes between the states.

The Constitution also has a system of checks and balances that prevents any of the three branches of government from becoming too powerful. Each branch can "check" or limit the power of the other two.

The chart above shows how this works. For example, the President can veto, or refuse to sign, bills passed by Congress. On the other hand, Congress can override a President's veto.

What is a check that the Supreme Court has on Congress? What is a check that Congress has on the Supreme Court? Can you find a check that the President has on Congress? Can you find a check on the President from Congress?

---

executive branch   The part of government that carries out laws
legislative branch   The part of government that makes laws
judicial branch   The part of government that decides the meaning of laws
impeach   To charge a public official with having done something illegal while in office

How a Bill Becomes a Law

This flowchart shows how a **bill** becomes a law.

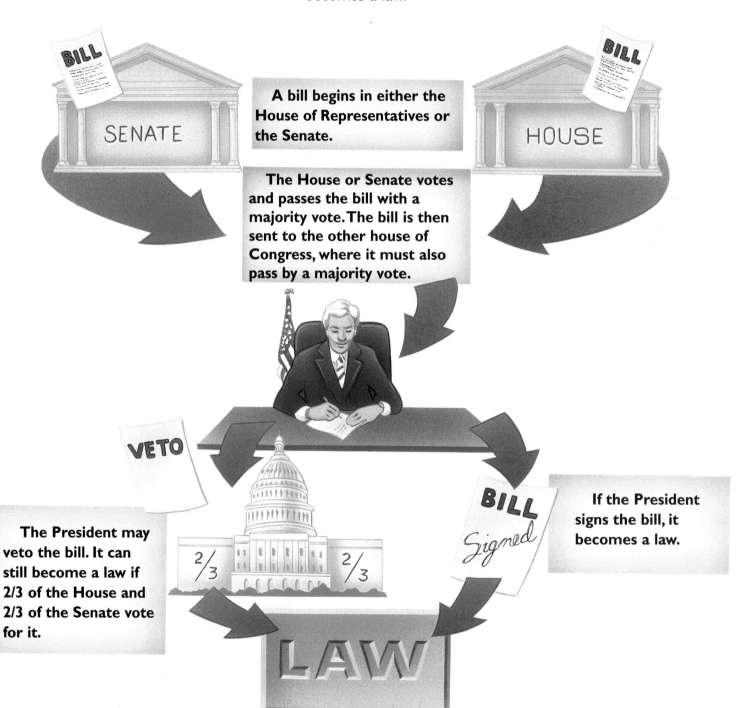

A bill begins in either the House of Representatives or the Senate.

The House or Senate votes and passes the bill with a majority vote. The bill is then sent to the other house of Congress, where it must also pass by a majority vote.

The President may veto the bill. It can still become a law if 2/3 of the House and 2/3 of the Senate vote for it.

If the President signs the bill, it becomes a law.

★ *bill* An officially suggested law

The Federal System

Powers of the National Government

Make laws about immigration and citizenship
Control trade between states and with foreign countries
Set standard weights and measures
Make copyright and patent laws
Establish a postal system
Print and coin money
Make foreign policy
Create armed forces
Declare war

Concurrent Powers

Collect taxes and borrow money
Create laws to maintain health, safety, and welfare
Set up court systems
Set minimum wage
Charter banks

Powers of the State Governments

Control trade within the state
Control education
Create local governments
Set requirements for elected officials
Create laws regulating marriage and divorce
Set standards for professional licenses

Federalism

The writers of the Constitution had to decide how much power to give the states and the national government. They decided on a system of shared power called **federalism**. The chart above shows how it works.

Only state governments can run schools. Only the federal government can declare war or print money. Other powers, called *concurrent powers*, are shared. For example, both the federal government and the state government can collect taxes.

---

federalism A system of government that divides powers between the national and state governments

Spotlight

KEY TERM
First Lady

Two First Ladies

FOCUS *As the first two First Ladies, Martha Washington and Abigail Adams influenced the nation in different ways.*

Martha Washington

Martha Washington's public life began long before her husband, George, became President. During the Revolutionary War, while George was serving in the military, Martha managed their household at Mount Vernon in Virginia. Yet Martha Washington left Mount Vernon to be with General Washington during the winters, even during the harsh winter at Valley Forge.

Martha Washington sometimes helped the general by performing clerical duties. At that time there were no copy machines. People hand copied important documents. When the general was short of staff, Mrs. Washington sometimes hand copied his letters so that he would have a copy.

Martha Washington also became involved in the "Association," an organization that raised money for the Continental troops to thank them for fighting. The money was spent on the troops as General Washington saw fit. It was not to be spent on clothing, food, or other basic provisions.

After the war Martha and George entertained many guests at Mount Vernon. Martha enjoyed spending time with her grandchildren and being back home. But that didn't last long. In 1789, George was elected President. They had to move to New York City, the nation's temporary capital.

Since George Washington had already gone to New York, Mrs. Washington traveled there without him. Along the way, crowds honored her with parades, fireworks, and bands. Being **First Lady** was an honor, but it brought duties, such as hosting formal dinners. If people came to see Martha Washington and she was not at home, she made sure to see them within the next three days.

At last, in 1797, George gave his farewell speech as President. The Washingtons returned to Mount Vernon, and in 1799, George Washington died. Martha was devastated. Two years later her health

---

⭐ **First Lady**   The President's wife

▲ Martha Washington and a quilt that she made

▲ Abigail Adams

States in France during the Revolutionary War, Abigail Adams managed the family farm in Massachusetts. She hired workers, collected rents, and did all that her husband normally did.

Abigail Adams wrote many letters about her ideas on public issues, even though she had never attended school. In letters to her husband, she argued for the rights of women. She wanted girls to be able to go to school. She wanted men to respect women and their work.

In one letter to her husband, Mrs. Adams argued for women's voting rights. She wrote, "Remember the Ladies . . . [We] will not hold ourselves bound by any laws in which we have no voice."

While First Lady, Mrs. Adams continued to write letters. Though most of her writings dealt with political issues of that time, she also wrote about life as First Lady.

Abigail and John Adams were the first family to live in the White House, even though it was not yet completed. There was no fence, no yard, no wood for the fireplace. The main staircase wasn't even built.

As First Ladies, Martha Washington and Abigail Adams had different personal interests. Even today, First Ladies have their own causes and particular interests.

failed. Wanting to protect her privacy, she burned all but two of the letters she and George had exchanged. In May 1802, Martha Washington died.

Abigail Adams

When John Adams became the second President, his wife, Abigail, became the second First Lady. Like Martha Washington's, Abigail Adams's story began long before she became First Lady. While John Adams was away serving in the Second Continental Congress or representing the United

SHOW WHAT YOU KNOW!

REFOCUS
COMPREHENSION

1. What are some jobs that Martha Washington did in her public life?

2. How do we know so much about Abigail Adams?

THINK ABOUT IT
CRITICAL THINKING

From reading about Martha Washington and Abigail Adams, what can you tell about what women could and could not do at this time?

WRITE ABOUT IT
ACTIVITY

Write a letter to the First Lady about an issue that is important to you.

SUMMING UP

1 DO YOU REMEMBER . . .
COMPREHENSION

1. Why did people want state governments to be stronger than the national government?

2. Why did Shays's Rebellion frighten people?

3. Why is the U.S. Constitution important?

4. What were the first two political parties?

5. How did Americans feel about the French Revolution?

6. What kept some leaders of the American Revolution from coming to the Constitutional Convention?

7. How did the New Jersey Plan and the Virginia Plan differ?

8. What was the Three-fifths Compromise?

9. What three branches of government did the Constitution create?

10. What were some goals Abigail Adams had for girls and women?

2 SKILL POWER
USING A FLOWCHART

In this chapter you learned how to use flowcharts. Using the flowchart on page 201, explain how the Constitution prevents any one branch of the government from becoming too powerful.

3 WHAT DO YOU THINK?
CRITICAL THINKING

1. Suppose the Constitution had never been written and the Articles of Confederation remained in effect. How might things be different today?

2. Support this statement with facts from this chapter: After the colonies became independent, the new nation had to learn to deal with other nations.

3. Why might some people have been disappointed by the results of the Constitutional Convention?

4. Why are the freedoms set forth in the Bill of Rights so important to Americans?

5. What do you think the American people expect of the First Lady?

4 SAY IT, WRITE IT, USE IT
VOCABULARY

Write a news story about the Constitutional Convention for a local newspaper. As you describe the delegates at work, use as many of the vocabulary words as possible.

bill	First Lady
Bill of Rights	impeach
Cabinet	judicial branch
compromise	legislative branch
constitution	political party
executive branch	ratify
federalism	republic

5 GEOGRAPHY AND YOU
MAP STUDY

Use the present-day map below and the maps on pages 188 and 191 to answer these questions.

1. What present-day states made up the land claimed by Georgia?

2. What river separated Spanish-held Louisiana and the United States?

3. What year did the first state ratify the Constitution? Name all the states that ratified the Constitution in that same year.

4. What bodies of water border on the Northwest Territory?

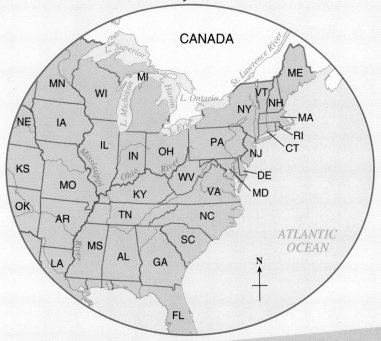

6 TAKE ACTION
CITIZENSHIP

The Constitution provides for the Senate and the House of Representatives. You have two senators and a representative in Washington, D.C. Do you know who they are? With a group of classmates, find out the names and addresses of your senators and representatives. Post this information on a classroom bulletin board. Then look for news articles that tell about their opinions and how they voted on issues. You may even wish to write to them explaining your ideas about an issue.

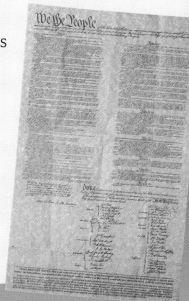

7 GET CREATIVE
ART CONNECTION

United States money honors many of the nation's founders and constitutional delegates. Design a new coin or bill that honors someone who you think has played an important part in the nation's heritage.

LOOKING AHEAD
In the next unit explore what the new nation goes through as it expands and changes.

Expansion AND Conflict

How Do People Deal With Conflict?

This is a time of growth, change, and conflict. Examine the differences that led to conflict and eventually to a war that pitted American against American.

209

GROWTH AND

Between 1800 and 1830 the United States grew rapidly and in many ways. There were growing pains, however, as sectional differences arose and threatened the Union.

How did young workers use bobbins and spindles in the early 1800s? Find out on page 232.

CONTENTS

CONFLICT

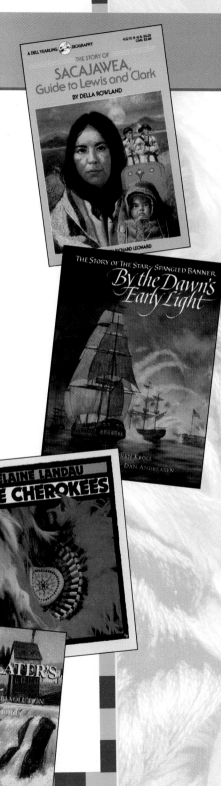

These books tell about how the United States grew and changed in the early 1800s. Read one that interests you and fill out a book-review form.

READ AND RESEARCH

The Story of Sacajawea, Guide to Lewis and Clark
by Della Rowland (Dell Publishing, 1989)
When she was 16, Sacajawea met Lewis and Clark. She helped guide their team of explorers through the western United States. Explore the land with the group and find out how Sacajawea contributed to their expedition. **(biography)**
•*You can read a selection from this story on page 222.*

By the Dawn's Early Light: The Story of the Star-Spangled Banner **by Steven Kroll** (Scholastic, 1994)
Travel back to the War of 1812 and meet Francis Scott Key, a Washington lawyer. Follow him as he tries to rescue a friend from British troops and ends up inspired to write what became our national anthem. **(nonfiction)**

The Cherokees **by Elaine Landau** (Franklin Watts, 1992)
Follow the story of the Cherokees from long ago to today. Learn about their daily life, festivals, religion, and history. Find out why their removal to Oklahoma was known as the Trail of Tears. **(nonfiction)**

Samuel Slater's Mill and the Industrial Revolution
by Christopher Simonds (Silver Burdett Press, 1990)
In 1789, Samuel Slater came to the United States from Great Britain. Learn how he inspired a revolution that changed the United States. **(nonfiction)**

Skill Power

Preparing for an Oral Report

Knowing how to give an oral report lets you share important information with others.

UNDERSTAND IT

You're the explorer Meriwether Lewis in 1806. You've just returned from an incredible two-and-a-half-year journey across the continent. You've discovered rivers, mountain ranges, native peoples, and hundreds of animals and plants that you've never seen before. You're bursting with information to share with the President and Congress. A good way to do it, you decide, is to give an oral report.

When you give an oral report, you share what you've learned with others. It's different from a written report because you have to face your audience. An oral report can be about things you've seen personally or things you've researched in books.

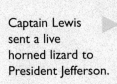

Captain Lewis sent a live horned lizard to President Jefferson.

EXPLORE IT

Here's how Meriwether Lewis might have prepared his oral report. Use these steps to prepare your own report.

1. **Narrow the topic.** Lewis couldn't talk about all of his discoveries in one brief report. So he might narrow the topic to "Animals We Saw for the First Time."

2. **Gather information.** Examining his journals, Lewis found details about the animals he saw on the expedition. (To write about something you didn't see, you'd use textbooks, encyclopedias, and other sources.)

3. **Take notes and make an outline on cards.** Note cards are easy to hold and look at when speaking aloud. Lewis might make an outline showing the main ideas and details he will cover.

4. **Write an introduction and conclusion.** Beginning with a dramatic fact or quotation catches the audience's attention. Lewis might begin by describing the vast herds of buffaloes. The conclusion should quickly sum up the main points of the report.

INDEX CARDS

5. **Use visual aids.** Lewis could show his sketches and stuffed animals. Photos, maps, and charts will make your report more interesting, too.

6. **Practice.** Try out your oral report for a friend or in front of a mirror. Find ways to use your voice, face, and hands to help express your ideas.

Follow the steps in Explore It to prepare notes for your own oral report. You might want to report on something you have seen or done personally, such as visiting a museum or historical site. Or you can look through this chapter and choose and narrow a topic that interests you.

When you listen to your classmates' reports, be a good listener. Here's how.

● Look at the speaker and pay attention.

● Listen for the main points.

● Form questions in your mind to ask the speaker later.

SKILL POWER SEARCH *What topics in this chapter would you like to know more about? Choose one for an oral report.*

Setting the Scene

KEY TERMS

Louisiana Purchase
territory
embargo
internal improvement
Industrial Revolution
Missouri Compromise

A CHANGING NATION

FOCUS *The United States grew in many ways in the early 1800s. Growth produced conflict and rising tensions with Great Britain as well as great expectations at home.*

Jefferson Arrives in Washington

On March 4, 1801, Thomas Jefferson walked slowly and confidently through the cheering crowded streets of Washington, D.C. He was on his way to be sworn in as the third President of the United States.

Jefferson wore a simple outfit—plain coat, plain pants. No powdered wig or fancy clothes for him. He wanted to show those who had voted for him that it was the ordinary American they had supported. The President, he felt, should get no special favors. But the crowds who lined his route knew exactly who he was—*their* President.

After taking the oath of office, Jefferson, a Democratic-Republican, spoke to the crowd. "Let us unite with one heart and one mind," he said.

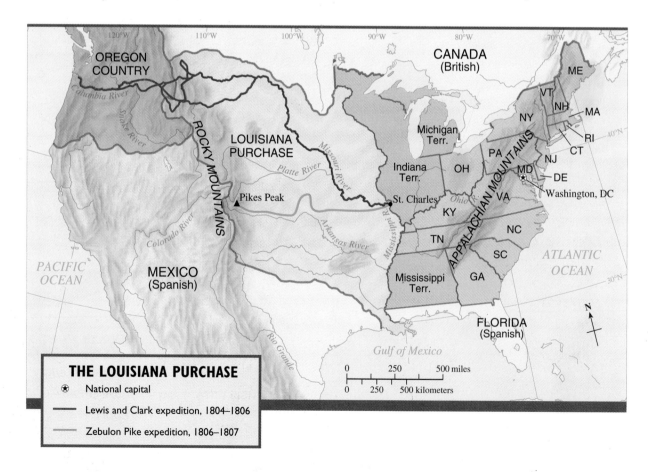

THE LOUISIANA PURCHASE

⊛   National capital

——   Lewis and Clark expedition, 1804–1806

——   Zebulon Pike expedition, 1806–1807

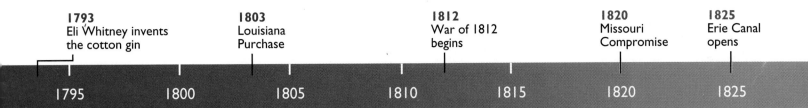

1793	1803	1812	1820	1825
Eli Whitney invents the cotton gin	Louisiana Purchase	War of 1812 begins	Missouri Compromise	Erie Canal opens

| 1795 | 1800 | 1805 | 1810 | 1815 | 1820 | 1825 |

"We are all Republicans—we are all Federalists." This meant that Jefferson wanted Americans to unite no matter which party they had voted for.

Thomas Jefferson and his fellow Democratic-Republicans undid many Federalist laws. They got rid of the hated whiskey tax. They cut government spending and reduced the size of the army and navy. But Jefferson's greatest accomplishment was to double the size of the country.

New Land Opportunities

By 1800, thousands of American hunters, trappers, and pioneers had crossed the Appalachian Mountains. The first settlers to cross the Appalachians were rewarded with fertile valleys and farmland. Word spread back east: The land west of the mountains was ripe for settlement. Native Americans, of course, had long been settled on the same land.

Spain had opened the port of New Orleans to American trade in 1795. But in 1802, Spain closed the port and then sold it to France. Americans wanted to gain control of New Orleans because it was the port through which all the goods from the Mississippi River valley were shipped.

The Louisiana Purchase

Jefferson wanted to purchase New Orleans from Napoleon, the French emperor. For years Napoleon had hoped to build an empire in America. But by 1800 he was preparing France for war with Great Britain. He knew he couldn't defend Louisiana against the British navy, and war was expensive. So he decided to sell it.

When the American representatives James Monroe and Robert Livingston offered $10 million for New Orleans, Napoleon's agents said no. But if the United States wanted to buy *all* of Louisiana, including New Orleans, for $15 million, a deal could be made.

Monroe and Livingston couldn't believe their ears. As you can see on the map on page 214, this area was huge. The **Louisiana Purchase** cost about three cents an acre. It was the greatest real estate bargain in history.

★ **Louisiana Purchase**   The purchase in 1803 of French lands in North America that doubled the size of the United States

215

Lewis and Clark drew pictures of animals they had never seen before. From top to bottom, they drew a white gull, a buzzard, and an American white-fronted goose.

The New Nation Expands

The Louisiana Purchase *doubled* the size of the United States. Americans had lots of questions about this new **territory**. Was it good for farming? How high were its mountains? In 1804, Jefferson sent Meriwether Lewis and William Clark off to find some answers. In May 1804, Lewis and Clark began to explore the Louisiana Territory by heading up the Missouri River by canoe. Some days they covered 15 miles. Other days they could travel only 3 or 4 miles. At last, in June 1805, they reached what is now Montana. Then they crossed the Rocky Mountains on horseback. From there they traveled down the Columbia River to the Pacific Ocean. On November 7, 1805, Clark wrote in his journal: "Ocean in view! O! the joy."

Soon after Lewis and Clark's successful expedition, the United States added parts of Florida to its territory. But Spain held on to the peninsula. Finally, in 1819 the United States bought the rest of Florida from Spain.

Britain–an Enemy Again

Meanwhile, the United States was once again having trouble with Great Britain. Even though Americans had won their revolution—or maybe *because* they had won their revolution—the British were provoking them. Britain still had claims to parts of North America. And the British encouraged Native Americans to fight Americans. The British also seized American ships and pressed American sailors into service, making them work on British ships.

President Jefferson persuaded Congress to pass an **embargo** against all foreign countries. This meant that the United States would no longer trade with any other nations. At the time, Britain was the main trading partner of the United States. Jefferson hoped the embargo would prove that the United States could survive without *any* European trade. But he was wrong. Americans needed to sell food, lumber, and other products to Europe. And they needed to purchase the finished goods that Europeans made from those raw materials.

The War of 1812

When the embargo failed and Great Britain resumed seizing America's ships, some Americans called for war. In June 1812 they got their way. President James Madison, who had been elected in 1808, asked Congress to declare war on Great Britain.

The War of 1812 started out on land but became known for its battles on water. It continued until January 1815. Commodore Oliver Perry's ships defeated a British force on Lake Erie and produced America's first victory in 1813. The British went on to capture

---

 territory   An area of land that has not yet become a state

 embargo   A government order that stops or slows trade with a particular nation

Washington, D.C., and to burn the White House. The map on the right shows several important battles. The battle of New Orleans was the largest. News traveled slowly in those days, so the battle was actually fought two weeks after both sides had signed a peace treaty.

The war itself didn't settle much. It wasn't a war over territories—no lands were won or lost. But Americans gained self-confidence. Twice now they had stood up to the mighty British Empire. Also, since Native Americans no longer had British support, it would now be easier for white settlers to move west.

During the war Francis Scott Key wrote a poem, "The Star-Spangled Banner." The words came to him as he watched Americans hold out against a British attack on Fort McHenry, in Maryland. Set to a familiar melody, his poem became so popular that it later became our national anthem.

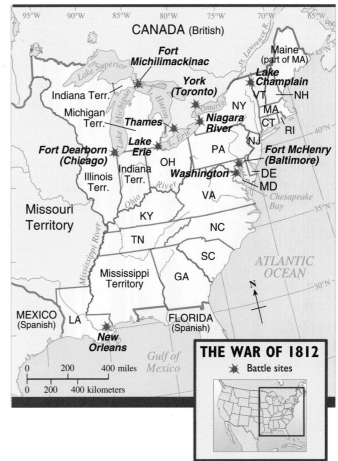

THE WAR OF 1812

* Battle sites

▼ The attack on Fort McHenry might have looked like this to Francis Scott Key.

Building a Nation

Since the United States was growing so much in the early 1800s, **internal improvements**, such as roads, canals, steamboats, and railroads, were built to link the new cities that sprang up. In 1807, Robert Fulton built the first successful steamboat, making it possible to sail *up* a river, against the current. The 363-mile-long Erie Canal opened in 1825. It linked the Great Lakes to New York City, so goods from Detroit and Buffalo could be carried by water instead of by more expensive overland routes. A great era of railroad building began during this time. Communications improved, too. In 1837, Samuel F. B. Morse demonstrated his telegraph, which carried messages quickly over long distances.

It wasn't just internal improvements that signaled a changing nation. Americans were used to weaving cloth by hand. But in Britain in the late 1700s, a new machine made it possible to spin cotton into thread. Another machine wove thread into cloth. These and other inventions were introduced to the United States and jump-started the **Industrial Revolution**. At first these machines ran on water power. Later they ran on steam.

---

internal improvement The building of transportation and communications systems to help a country's economy
Industrial Revolution The period of great change in how people lived and made products, brought about by power-driven machines

The Cotton Gin and the South

Southern planters had been growing cotton since the mid-1700s. But the kind of cotton that grew best in the South was filled with sticky seeds. It took a worker a whole day to clean one pound. That made cotton expensive to grow.

Eli Whitney's contribution to the Industrial Revolution changed that. In 1793 he invented the cotton gin. This little machine picked the seeds from cotton. It cleaned 50 pounds of cotton in one day. Thus, cotton became profitable to grow because it was easy to process.

Differences Arise

The United States was growing and changing. The North and the West

▼ An early artist's image of enslaved people and masters working at a cotton gin

MISSOURI COMPROMISE: 1820

- Free states and territories
- Free territory by Missouri Compromise
- Slave states and territories
- Slave territory by Missouri Compromise

SHOW WHAT YOU KNOW!

REFOCUS
COMPREHENSION

1. Why was the Louisiana Purchase important to the growth and development of the United States?

2. How did the Industrial Revolution affect the North and the South?

THINK ABOUT IT
CRITICAL THINKING

How might history have been different had the cotton gin not been invented?

WRITE ABOUT IT
ACTIVITY

If you were a non-slaveholding farmer in Missouri in 1820, how would you react to the news of the Missouri Compromise?

were changing one way, the South another. In the North and the West, mills that turned cotton into fashions sprang up. Canals were dug, and railroads were constructed.

In the South, on the other hand, the cotton that fed the Industrial Revolution in the North was king. It quickly became the most important crop grown in the South. The South grew more cotton more cheaply than any other place on earth. By 1820 the South grew 100 times more cotton than in 1790. The booming cotton business led to a new dependence on slavery, which had almost died out in the 1790s, when tobacco had declined in importance. Now that cotton made money, it was profitable to keep enslaved people. They grew the cotton and worked the gins that cleaned it.

Conflict and Compromise

Tensions arose between the South and the North. One issue was tariffs, or extra charges added to the cost of imported goods. The North wanted high tariffs to protect its new industries. The South wanted low tariffs to keep imports—goods brought from other countries—less costly. Another issue was slavery. Most northerners weren't ready to fight slavery in the South. But they did want to keep it out of new territories, because they worried that white workers would not be able to compete with slave labor. In 1820 the **Missouri Compromise** stated that Missouri could enter the Union as a slave state in exchange for Maine's entrance as a free state. The compromise forbade slavery in the rest of the Louisiana Territory, north of 36°30' north latitude. Find this line on the map above. But the time would soon come when such compromises would become more difficult.

⭐ *Missouri Compromise* The 1820 ruling that admitted Missouri as a slave state

2

Map Adventure

★ KEY TERMS
corps
interpreter

LITERATURE
The Story of Sacajawea

THE LEWIS AND CLARK EXPEDITION

FOCUS The expedition led by Meriwether Lewis and William Clark traveled over 7,000 miles, giving America much information about lands west of the Mississippi.

Pacific Ocean

Fort Mandan

Lewis's Route

Clark's Route

Mandan village

Columbia River

Clearwater River

Yellowstone River

Mississippi River

Missouri River

N
W — E
S

5
4
8
7
6
3
2
1

THE LEWIS AND CLARK EXPEDITION

Louisiana Territory

Westward journey

Return journey

0   100   200   300 miles

0   100   200   300 miles

Adventure in the Louisiana Territory

The "Corps of Discovery" began its two-year-long journey to explore the Louisiana Territory in May 1804. Over 40 men handled the large keelboat and two flat-bottomed dugout canoes, called pirogues (pih ROHGZ). The cargo included compasses, tents, medical supplies, and 193 pounds of "portable soup," a kind of food. Their mission: Find an all-water route to the Pacific, meet and observe Native American groups, and map out the new territory.

Map Legend

1 St. Louis In 1804 this city was little more than a few scattered buildings. Later, as thousands of settlers from the East passed through, it was called the "Gateway to the West."

2 Missouri River The Corps struggled against the Missouri River's strong current. Called the "Big Muddy" because of the soil it carries from the mountains, the river hid many dangers, including fallen trees and rocks.

3 Great Plains Passing through these grassy plains, Lewis and Clark took notes on everything they saw. Many animals looked strange to them, including prairie dogs, which Lewis called "barking squirrels."

4 Fort Mandan The Corps built this fort as a winter camp, near a Mandan Indian village. When spring came, they set out again with a Shoshoni guide, Sacajawea; Charbonneau, her French trapper husband; and their newborn son.

5 Great Falls The Corps reached these mighty waterfalls on June 13. Forced to carry their boats and supplies around the falls, they suffered through a month of rattlesnakes, floods, and grizzlies.

6 Three Forks Sacajawea recognized this area as her home and served as an interpreter when the Corps met the Shoshonis. The Shoshonis sold horses to Lewis and Clark and showed them a mountain pass.

⭐ **corps** A group of people who act together
interpreter A person who helps two people or groups understand the languages and customs of each other

7 Rocky Mountains The towering height of the Rockies convinced the Corps that there was no all-water route to the Pacific. Horses carried the supplies across, while most of the men walked.

8 Fort Clatsop The Corps finally reached the Pacific Ocean in November 1805 and camped here for the winter. Come spring, they faced a long journey home.

MAP IT

1. You are a member of the Corps. As you follow the Missouri River, you wonder whether it will take you directly to the Pacific Ocean. What do you discover?
2. The Corps finally ends its long westward journey and sets up Fort Clatsop. What ocean can you see from Fort Clatsop?
3. In the spring the Corps begins the return journey. When Lewis and Clark split up, you go with Clark. In what direction does your group head first? Have you seen any of this area before?
4. What river do you follow before you rejoin Lewis's group?

EXPLORE IT

Write a letter to a relative in which you describe some of the highlights of the Lewis and Clark expedition.

The Story of Sacajawea, Guide to Lewis and Clark

by Della Rowland

Sacajawea was a young Shoshoni who had been captured and raised by the Minnetaree people. When Lewis and Clark met her, they knew they had found the person who could help them meet the people and explore the land of the western United States. Here we join Sacajawea and the exploration Corps as they are about to explore the land in which she grew up.

A s they moved closer to the mountains, Captain Lewis worried that the river would become rocky. Sacajawea told him she knew this river and that it would not change or become dangerous. And she was right! Three days later, on July 28, 1805, they came safely to the Three Forks.

The Corps made camp right at the place where Sacajawea and her family had been camped when the Minnetarees captured her. With Charbonneau translating, she told the men how she and her people had been captured by the Minnetarees. She described to them how she had run for three miles up the widest of the three forks, hidden in the woods, and watched as many of her people were killed.

Sacajawea pointed out the spot where she had been grabbed up as she had tried to cross the river. That terrible moment had changed her whole life, but Sacajawea did not show her feelings about that fateful day. As a Shoshoni, she had been taught that it was weak and childish to act in an emotional way. . . .

The captains named the three forks of the rivers they had found the Jefferson, Madison, and Gallatin rivers, after three of the most important political leaders of the time. . . . Sacajawea had followed the Jefferson when she ran to escape the Minnetarees. Now the Corps followed it toward the mountains.

After they had traveled a few days along the river, Sacajawea looked up from her boat and pointed out a tall rock on a high plain. She said the Shoshoni called it Beaver's Head Rock because it looked like that familiar animal to them. To her, Beaver's Head Rock meant that they were near the pass where her people crossed the mountains each year in search of food. . . .

Sacajawea told the captains that to find her people, they should follow the Jefferson River until it divided. Then they should take the fork that went west. The Shoshoni would either be on the Jefferson River, or on the west fork. Then she showed them an Indian road beside the river. It was the road her people took back and forth from the mountains to the plains.

When Lewis heard this, he decided to cross the mountains immediately.

Find out more about how Sacajawea helped the expedition by checking the book out of your school or public library.

SHOW WHAT YOU KNOW!

REFOCUS
COMPREHENSION

1. What was the purpose of the Lewis and Clark expedition?

2. List some challenges and obstacles faced by the members of the expedition.

THINK ABOUT IT
CRITICAL THINKING

Describe how Sacajawea might have felt when the expedition reached the area where she had been captured.

WRITE ABOUT IT
ACTIVITY

Go to a local park or open space you've never been to before. Describe it as if you were Lewis or Clark, noting all that you see.

Spotlight

★ **KEY TERMS**

assimilate
Trail of Tears

NATIVE AMERICANS RESPOND

FOCUS *Native Americans responded in different ways as westward expansion resulted in the loss of more and more of their land.*

To Blend In or Fight?

Was it possible to trade land for peace? Some Native Americans in the early 1800s hoped so. They thought that if they sold *some* land to the settlers streaming into their lands from the east, they could hold on to the rest. Then they could live in peace. So Native Americans sold vast sections of their lands. But they could never sell enough. As settlements grew, Native Americans were forced to choose between two other options: fight, or **assimilate** into white society.

Given these choices, most Native Americans preferred to fight. From the late 1780s through the early 1800s, they fought several bitter wars against United States Army troops. One great Native American leader was Tecumseh (tih KUM-suh), a Shawnee warrior from the area of the Ohio and Indiana territories. He wanted Native Americans to unite against the settlers. Some agreed with him, but others did not.

In 1811, General William Henry Harrison was governor of the Indiana Territory. (Later he became

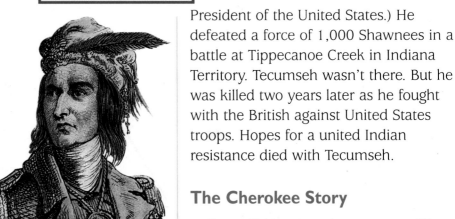

NATIVE AMERICAN REMOVAL: 1830–1840

- ← Cherokees
- ← Chickasaws
- ← Choctaws
- ← Creeks
- ← Seminoles

President of the United States.) He defeated a force of 1,000 Shawnees in a battle at Tippecanoe Creek in Indiana Territory. Tecumseh wasn't there. But he was killed two years later as he fought with the British against United States troops. Hopes for a united Indian resistance died with Tecumseh.

The Cherokee Story

Some Native Americans were willing to try to adapt to white culture. The

★ **assimilate** To become absorbed into another culture

Tecumseh

Cherokees, who lived in Georgia, Tennessee, and North Carolina, tried to combine white and Native American ways. They combined white laws with theirs. They gave up old ways of hunting and gardening and opened sawmills and blacksmith shops. Traditionally, the Cherokees shared property. Now they gave up shared property and moved to individual farms. Some stopped wearing buckskin shirts and dressed in cloth trousers. By adapting like this, they hoped they could keep their land.

But adaptation was *not* enough for many white Americans. They wanted Cherokee land. In 1828, Georgia's legislature declared Cherokee laws worthless. The Cherokees appealed to the Supreme Court. In 1832 the court ruled in their favor, saying that Georgia's laws did *not* apply to the Cherokee nation. The court's ruling should have been final, but President Andrew Jackson refused to enforce it.

Trail of Tears

In 1835, President Jackson told the Cherokees it would be "impossible" for them to live on their land any longer. Like other Native Americans, as you can see on the map on page 224, they were to move west of the Mississippi River.

The Cherokees refused to leave their land. But the United States Army, in the winter of 1838, forced 15,000 of them to give up their homes. They began a long, painful journey west. Many suffered from disease, hunger, and bitter cold. Four thousand died. The Cherokees remember this journey as the **Trail of Tears**.

▼ The Trail of Tears—sad, long, and brutal

⭐ **Trail of Tears** The removal of Cherokees from their homelands to what is now Oklahoma

SHOW WHAT YOU KNOW!

REFOCUS
COMPREHENSION

1. What were three ways in which Native Americans responded to westward expansion?

2. How did the Cherokees adapt their ways of living to become assimilated?

THINK ABOUT IT
CRITICAL THINKING

Describe what you would feel if your community was forced to move across the country.

WRITE ABOUT IT
ACTIVITY

Write a letter to President Jackson urging him to rethink his decision to move the Cherokees.

FASTER AND BETTER

FOCUS *As Americans spread out across the continent, the nation became linked by better and better systems of transportation and communication.*

A RIVER HIGHWAY

In 1807, Robert Fulton chugged *up* the Hudson River in his new steamboat, the *Clermont*. Just 32 hours after leaving New York City, Fulton reached Albany, 150 miles away. Fulton turned the Hudson—and other rivers, as well—into a two-way highway. In 1820 about 60 steamboats operated on the Mississippi River. By 1860 there were more than 1,000.

Faster and more powerful boats were developed. Some were able to travel in very shallow water. This was essential along western rivers, which were full of sandbars and rocks. In 1841 the *Orphan Boy* set a steamboat record. It carried 40 tons of freight as well as passengers through water only two feet deep.

THE "BIG DITCH"

In 1817 the New York State legislature approved $7 million to build a canal to help connect the Great Lakes to the Atlantic Ocean. It would never happen, said many critics. Some people laughed. They made fun of Governor DeWitt Clinton, who came up with the idea. They called the canal "Clinton's big ditch." After all, no existing canal was more than 28 miles long, and Clinton wanted to build one 363 miles long, from Albany to Buffalo.

But in 1825 the Erie Canal opened and became a huge success. Because it was now easier to move goods from Great Lakes cities to New York City, the freight charge dropped from $100 a ton to $10 a ton.

MIGHTY TOM THUMB

Peter Cooper's *Tom Thumb* was the first American-built steam locomotive. Cooper hoped to convince railroad owners to use locomotives, instead of horses, to pull their trains. In 1830 he showed that *Tom Thumb* could travel at 18 miles an hour for 13 miles.

The railroad industry grew quickly. By 1840 there were as many miles of railroad track as there were of canals. In the 1850s, the number of miles of railroad track increased from 8,879 miles to 30,626 miles. People stopped talking about canals. Railroads were the future.

1807
The *Clermont* sails up the Hudson River

1825
Erie Canal opens

1830
Tom Thumb runs in Baltimore

1844
S.F.B. Morse sends message in Morse Code

1848
Cunard's steamships sail from New York to Europe in 10 to 14 days

1805   1820   1830   1840   1850   1860

SINGING WIRES

On May 24, 1844, Samuel F. B. Morse sent a simple message. It said, "What hath God wrought?" Morse sent these words from Washington, D.C., to Baltimore. But the amazing thing was that he sent them over a piece of wire! His message traveled in the form of Morse Code. This is a system in which each letter in the alphabet has its own pattern of dots and dashes.

Morse demonstrated his telegraph in 1837, but he didn't have the money to string telegraph wire. By 1844, Morse had proved that his invention really worked, and Congress had spent $30,000 to build a telegraph line.

TIME TRAVEL

The world was changing faster and faster by the 1840s. Older Americans could still remember when everything moved at a snail's pace. It once took 74 days to sail to Europe and back. In 1848, Samuel Cunard's steamships made the trip in just 20 to 28 days.

The Erie Canal turned a four-week trip from Detroit to New York into a two-week jaunt. By 1857, Detroit was just an overnight train ride from New York City. In 1800, thanks to better roads, a horse and rider could go from New York to Philadelphia in two days. By 1820, that time was cut to one day. When George Washington died in 1799, the people in Boston didn't find out for 11 days. With the telegraph the sad news would have reached Boston within seconds.

SHOW WHAT YOU KNOW!

REFOCUS
COMPREHENSION

1. Why was the Erie Canal a success?

2. What were some ways in which transportation had improved by the 1850s?

THINK ABOUT IT
CRITICAL THINKING

The War of 1812 was over before the last battle was fought. What invention on this page could have brought the news of war's end sooner, and how?

WRITE ABOUT IT
ACTIVITY

Write about some forms of communication that are used today that were not available in the mid-1800s.

227

Connections

KEY TERMS

market
interchangeable
parts
mass production
literate

AMERICA ON THE MOVE

FOCUS *In the early 1800s, improvements in transportation and communication transformed the United States and changed the expectations of Americans.*

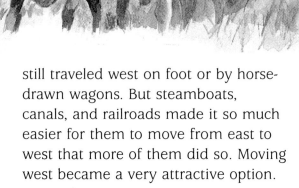

Getting Bigger—and Smaller

Between 1803 and 1853 what we know today as the continental United States was formed. The land area ruled by the United States had more than tripled. By 1853 the United States stretched from the potato fields of northern Maine to sunny California. It reached from the southern tip of Florida to beautiful Puget (PYOO jiht) Sound in what is now the state of Washington.

But at the same time, improvements in transportation and communication made the country *seem* smaller. Steamboats, canals, railroads, and the telegraph shrank distances. After all, for the traveler, the important measure of distance between point *A* and point *B* wasn't miles. It was time.

What did better transportation mean to the settlement of America's new territories? Well, many pioneers still traveled west on foot or by horse-drawn wagons. But steamboats, canals, and railroads made it so much easier for them to move from east to west that more of them did so. Moving west became a very attractive option.

Growing Markets

Equally important, steamboats, canals, and railroads opened up and linked new markets. Wheat and other grains that were grown in Ohio, Illinois, and Indiana were processed, and then shipped back to the East. From there they were shipped to markets around the world. New

 market A place where a buyer meets a seller to purchase a product or service

RAILROADS AND CANALS IN 1840

- ++++ Railroads
- ┬┬┬┬ Canals
- ──── National Road

industries, such as flour processing, sprang up. And new industries meant more jobs for people.

More and More Cities

As industries grew, so did the number of cities. Some of the cities are shown on the map above. Cities no longer had to be on the ocean to export their goods. With steamboats, canals, and railroads, they could be on lakes or rivers, as long as they had workers and the products that people wanted.

Chicago developed on Lake Michigan as a grain center. Cincinnati seemed to spring up overnight on the Ohio River. St. Louis, on the

▼ The *DeWitt Clinton*, a very early locomotive, chugged 16 miles in New York State in 1831.

 Occupations and opportunities for women began to increase by the early 1800s.

Mississippi, became a major trading center and the "Gateway to the West." These cities and many others helped to support the many smaller settlements in the West.

Industries Get a Boost

Americans in the early 1800s bubbled over with a "can-do" attitude. So much had been done since independence was won. The country had stood up to foreign powers, and the size of the country had doubled overnight in 1803. There seemed to be nothing Americans wouldn't tackle. They seemed to go out of their way to find a new problem. And, of course, every problem had a solution.

One great problem-solver was Eli Whitney. He developed the idea of **interchangeable parts**. This idea

called for a machine to make a part and then thousands of that part—all exactly alike.

Prior to 1800, for example, every gun was made by hand by a skilled worker called a gunsmith. But by 1800, Whitney showed that by mass producing each part, a gun could be assembled by anyone, even by an unskilled worker. Any barrel, any trigger, any firing pin for a particular kind of gun would fit. He built a gun factory in Connecticut to put his theory into practice.

The idea of interchangeable parts changed American industry drastically. It made **mass production** possible. Now factories could turn out vast quantities of identical goods.

Mass production was first used in gun factories. Later, it was used in making sewing machines and farm equipment. Even the machines that drove the factories were mass-produced, with interchangeable parts.

Women in the Workplace

New ways of doing things had a profound impact on women. Textile mills, for example, took some traditional work away from women. Clothes had been made at home by women who spun thread, wove cloth, and sewed shirts and dresses. By the early 1800s, fabrics of all sorts were being produced in mills.

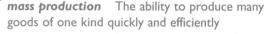

interchangeable parts Parts that can be used in place of each other

mass production The ability to produce many goods of one kind quickly and efficiently

On the other hand, textile mills gave women work. When mill owners couldn't get male farmers to work in the mills, they turned to women. In the end, women still made the clothes. But they did it in a factory instead of by the fireplace at home. Women also slowly became accepted as shop owners and merchants. This is the period in American history when people first got used to the idea of women working outside their homes.

Demand for Education

The inventiveness that American industry became known for helped lead to a demand for more public education. It was thought that people who were better educated would be better workers. The Erie Canal, for example, needed some highly educated and skilled workers in its construction. In Massachusetts, Horace Mann fought for higher teacher pay, more interesting classes, and better teacher training.

Mill owners also began to support public education. They saw the need for **literate** workers. Such workers were more reliable and better able to handle complex machinery. Public schools, by now including both boys and girls, did well. Private female academies were established and flourished. By 1840, a large percentage of white Americans were able to read and write.

▼ The Erie Canal was a symbol of American inventiveness and expansion.

⭐ *literate*　Having the ability to read and write

REFOCUS
COMPREHENSION

1. What factors helped the growth of cities in this period?

2. What effect did the growth of industry have on education in the United States?

THINK ABOUT IT
CRITICAL THINKING

Eli Whitney's theory of interchangeable parts changed the way that many people worked. How do you think a worker who was used to making a product by hand would feel about working in a factory?

WRITE ABOUT IT
ACTIVITY

Write a letter to your local paper asking for internal improvements that would make your neighborhood or community better.

THE "LOWELL GIRLS"

FOCUS *In the 1830s, owners of the Lowell mills hoped to create a new kind of working environment for young women.*

"With a Light Heart"

The factory bell is ringing. It's time to get up! You don't want to be late for your first day of work!

Getting ready for your new job in Lowell, Massachusetts, in 1831, you are so excited it's hard to believe you didn't awake at the crack of dawn. After all, the idea of working in a textile mill seems very glamorous. Perhaps you agree with Lucy Larcom, who wrote that she arrived for her first day of work "with a light heart."

There is good reason to have high hopes and few worries. The work isn't hard, even though the workdays are 12 hours long. As a new worker, your job is to change the bobbins on the spinning-frames every 45 minutes. That leaves time to laugh and tell stories with the friends you will make with other "Lowell girls." Most of the girls, like you, are in their teens or early twenties. You all enjoy being away from home, learning to be more independent and earning money.

You feel very lucky to be a Lowell girl in 1831. You can thank Francis Cabot Lowell for that. It was his idea

▲ Lowell girls carried lunch in tin boxes like this. They read the *Lowell Offering* in their spare time.

to create a good working environment for young women. He had seen dirty mill cities in Great Britain, and he wanted to build something much better for American workers.

Lowell died in 1817, but his grand plan was carried out by others. In the 1820s they built six mills along the Merrimack River in Massachusetts, in a city they named after Lowell. They planted trees and shrubs and built boarding houses. Visitors compared the town to a college campus.

The Good Life

Most Lowell girls are like you, from a small New England farm. According to Mr. Lowell's plan, you will work in the mills, save some money, and then move on to get married and raise a family.

These few years, however, are well spent. You live in a clean room, under the watchful eye of an older woman who makes sure you don't get into any trouble. Your new friends tell you that she will probably get on your nerves with her watchfulness. The pay is good—$3 a week. That's more than you

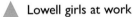
Lowell girls at work

might make teaching, cleaning house, or working on a farm. You also attend lectures, join a sewing circle, and go to church every Sunday. You even have time to read the magazine *Lowell Offering*, published for Lowell girls.

Time Brings Change

The Lowell plan works beautifully—for a few years. But the generous treatment of the Lowell girls comes with a price. The Lowell mills need to compete with other mills, so the owners have to cut costs. That means cutting wages. It also means getting more out of each worker. In the mid-1830s, you and other girls **strike** for better wages, but the strike is not very successful. By 1840 the mill owners

have turned up the speed of the machines. Workers like you have to change the bobbins more often and tend to more machines.

In a period of about 20 or 30 years, the Lowell mills go through a number of changes. The workday is harder and longer—for some, it is 14 hours. Lowell girls now have less free time for lectures and such. In time, many of them will quit. The mill owners will hire new workers to replace them. The replacements probably won't come from New England farms, as the early Lowell girls did. At about this time, many people were coming to America from Ireland. They had left their homeland because of a **famine**. Many of the jobs in the Lowell mills will be filled by young Irish workers.

 strike To refuse to work until certain demands, such as higher wages or better working conditions, are met

 famine A time when there is not enough food for everyone

SHOW WHAT YOU KNOW!

REFOCUS
COMPREHENSION

1. What was Francis Cabot Lowell's plan for his mills?

2. How did life change for the Lowell girls between the 1820s and 1840s?

THINK ABOUT IT
CRITICAL THINKING

About one in four Lowell workers were young men. Why, do you think, were there so few Lowell boys?

WRITE ABOUT IT
ACTIVITY

Write a story about a day in the life of a Lowell girl in the 1820s and 1830s.

SUMMING UP

COMPREHENSION

1. Why did Thomas Jefferson say, "We are all Republicans—we are all Federalists"?

2. How did the United States acquire the Louisiana Territory and Florida?

3. Why didn't Jefferson's embargo work?

4. Why did the North and the South feel differently about tariffs in the early 1800s?

5. What was the purpose of the Lewis and Clark expedition?

6. What was the Trail of Tears?

7. How did the inventions of Robert Fulton and Peter Cooper improve transportation in the United States?

8. How did the idea of interchangeable parts change American industry?

9. How did the rise of factories affect education in the United States?

10. What kind of working environment did Francis Cabot Lowell want to create?

2 SKILL POWER
PREPARING FOR AN ORAL REPORT

In this chapter you learned how to give an oral report. Use what you learned to report on any topic in the chapter that interests you. Some possible topics are

Louisiana Purchase	Erie Canal
Trail of Tears	telegraph
Missouri Compromise	War of 1812

Use details in the chapter as well as in other sources to prepare your report.

3 WHAT DO YOU THINK?
CRITICAL THINKING

1. Why did the British provoke the United States into war in 1812?

2. Why was Sacajawea so important to Lewis and Clark's Corps of Discovery?

3. What do you see in the painting on page 225 that shows how the Cherokees adapted to living like white Americans? What do you think the painting cannot show about the Trail of Tears?

4. Which do you think had a greater impact on most Americans' everyday lives—faster transportation, with canals and railroads, or faster communication, with the telegraph?

5. What do you think were some negative effects that the rise of mass production had on workers' lives?

4 SAY IT, WRITE IT, USE IT
VOCABULARY

The title of this chapter is "Growth and Conflict." Choose six of the vocabulary words below and tell what they mean. Explain how these terms show America's emergence as a major nation.

assimilate	literate
corps	Louisiana Purchase
embargo	market
famine	mass production
Industrial Revolution	Missouri Compromise
interchangeable parts	strike
internal improvement	territory
interpreter	Trail of Tears

5 GEOGRAPHY AND YOU
MAP STUDY

Use the map on page 214 to answer these questions.

1. What mountain range is located in the Louisiana Purchase?

2. What river did Lewis and Clark mainly travel on before they reached the Rocky Mountains?

3. What two territories did Lewis and Clark explore?

4. Name another expedition that explored the Louisiana Territory.

6 TAKE ACTION
CITIZENSHIP

The rise of mass production and mills in the 1840s created a need for better-educated workers. Today's workers require even more specialized skills. What type of education will you need to become a productive citizen and worker?

With a group of classmates, list some typical occupations in your community. Talk with adults or do library research to find out about the skills and education needed for each career. Show what you find out on a chart called "Getting Ready for a Career."

7 GET CREATIVE
SCIENCE CONNECTION

Find out more about one of the inventions or developments that helped America grow—the steamboat, the telegraph, the cotton gin, the canal, the locomotive. What scientific and technical problems did the inventor or builder have to solve to make the invention work? Draw a diagram or sketch that shows the main parts of the invention and how it worked.

LOOKING AHEAD In Chapter 11 learn about some of the differences between sections of the United States in the mid-1800s.

CHAPTER II

SECTIONALISM

With the acquisition of Mexican territory and the Oregon Country, the United States exhibited its "manifest destiny" by 1860. But the institution of slavery was raised as an issue every time the nation expanded.

CONTENTS

▼ What did settlers bring with them as they moved west? Find out on page 247.

AND EXPANSION

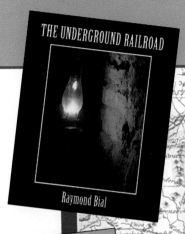

These books tell about people and places during the time that the United States expanded westward and had to address the issue of slavery. Read one that interests you and fill out a book-review form.

READ AND RESEARCH

The Underground Railroad by Raymond Bial
(Houghton Mifflin Co., 1995)
This book contains inspirational stories of men and women who risked their lives to help thousands of slaves find freedom. You will see photos of houses that were used to hide slaves on their dangerous journey. *(nonfiction)*

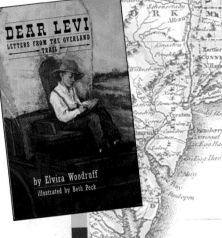

Dear Levi: Letters From the Overland Trail by Elvira Woodruff, illustrated by Beth Peck (Alfred A. Knopf, 1994)
Read the letters that 12-year-old Austin writes to his brother Levi as Austin travels west in his covered wagon to find his father's claim to gold in Oregon. *(historical fiction)*

Remember the Ladies: The First Women's Rights Convention by Norma Johnston (Scholastic, 1995)
Just one hundred years ago, women were without any political power. They could not even vote. Read about several women who were determined to find ways to change the laws that restricted their rights. *(nonfiction)*

Sojourner Truth: Ain't I a Woman? by Patricia and Fredrick McKissack (Scholastic, 1992)
Meet an amazing woman who was born into slavery but emerged as a strong and eloquent voice for the abolition movement and for women's rights. *(biography)*

Reading a Political Cartoon

Knowing how to interpret a political cartoon will help you understand different points of view on issues.

UNDERSTAND IT

Political cartoons have always been popular in the United States. In a clever, humorous way, a political cartoon presents one side, or point of view, of an issue.

For example, do you know that you have an Uncle Sam? Uncle Sam often shows up in political cartoons. He's a symbol of our country. If he is shown wearing worn-out clothes and with empty pockets, the person drawing the cartoon is probably saying our country has money problems. If Uncle Sam is polishing a gun, the cartoonist is showing readers that our country is preparing for war.

EXPLORE IT

To appreciate a political cartoon, you need to know something about the issue or subject. Back in 1832, for example, Andrew Jackson was reelected President in spite of differences in how Americans viewed him and the presidency. Was Jackson really a "man of the people," or was he more like a king, forcing his own views on America?

▲ A political cartoon of President Jackson

This cartoon poked fun at President Jackson, who is pictured here as a king who holds no regard for the Constitution or the interests of Americans. Notice how each part of the cartoon stands for something. His clothes are typical of clothes worn by kings of the day. (Note the throne in the background.) In one hand, he holds a paper marked "veto," the strongest power a United States President has. One of the papers he is standing on is the United States Constitution. The other papers under his feet mention the U.S. banking system and improvements to roads and canals.

The caption of a political cartoon sums up a cartoonist's point of view in words. Write a caption that expresses this cartoonist's point of view.

What is happening to Uncle Sam in this cartoon? ▶

TRY IT

In a newspaper or magazine, find a political cartoon about an issue that interests you. Discuss the cartoon with your parents, friends, or teacher to make sure you understand it. Then, in a paragraph, explain the issue and the cartoonist's point of view. Tape the cartoon and your explanation to chart paper. Draw arrows to the symbols in the cartoon and write what they stand for.

You may instead want to draw an original political cartoon. If so, pick a topic from current events, or choose a school situation or problem. Decide what symbols you will use to state your point of view. Remember: a good political cartoon makes its point without any extra explanation.

SKILL

POWER SEARCH *Look for another political cartoon in this chapter. Can you determine the issue being illustrated and the cartoonist's point of view?*

Setting the Scene

KEY TERMS

Tejano
Manifest Destiny
annex
abolitionist
Fugitive Slave Law
Republican party

THE ROAD TO WAR

FOCUS *America's expansion westward during the early and mid-1800s provided new and exciting opportunities for millions of Americans. It also emphasized slavery as the issue that divided Americans, no matter where they settled.*

New Frontiers

In the first half of the 1800s, as you learned in the last chapter, Americans could not be stopped from moving to western parts of the continent. As a result, 15 new states joined the Union between 1803 and 1850. Vast new territories came under American rule.

By 1850 the nation stretched from the Atlantic to the Pacific. The map on this page shows this growth. The wide-open areas between the two oceans lured many people. Some saw this new frontier as a place to start new businesses or to own farms of their own. Others saw the frontier as a place to set up new plantations with their slaves.

The United States grew in other ways as well. A steady flow of immigrants, mostly German and Irish, arrived on the nation's Atlantic shores. Between 1790 and 1860, over 5 million people immigrated from Europe. At first they settled in the cities of the East. Then they joined other Americans in the move west.

Americans in Texas

In 1821, Mexico won its independence from Spain. Texas was a Mexican territory. Since very few people lived in Texas, the Mexicans invited Americans to settle there. Mexico sold huge tracts of land for almost nothing. In return, an American had to adopt the Roman Catholic

CANADA

BRITISH CESSION 1818

OREGON COUNTRY 1846

LOUISIANA PURCHASE 1803

MEXICAN CESSION 1848

UNITED STATES IN 1783

GADSDEN PURCHASE 1853

TEXAS ANNEXATION 1845

PACIFIC OCEAN

1819

1810 1813 FLORIDA

ATLANTIC OCEAN

MEXICO

Gulf of Mexico

RUSSIA

ALASKA TERRITORY 1867

CANADA

HAWAII TERRITORY 1898

0   250   500 miles
0   250   500 kilometers

EXPANSION OF THE UNITED STATES

——— Present-day boundaries

1836
The Battle of
the Alamo

1850
Compromise
of 1850

1852
*Uncle Tom's
Cabin* published

1854
Kansas-
Nebraska Act

1857
Dred
Scott decision

1835   1840   1845   1850   1855   1860

religion, learn Spanish, and become a Mexican citizen. In the early 1820s, Stephen F. Austin led 300 American families to eastern Texas.

By 1835, over 35,000 Americans were living in Texas. But they hung on to their old customs. Most did not learn Spanish, and they did not adopt the Catholic religion. Although they did become Mexican citizens, most resented Mexican customs and laws.

Many of the settlers were from the American South and were slaveholders. In 1829, Mexico outlawed slavery, increasing tension on both the American and Mexican sides. In 1835, fighting broke out.

"Remember the Alamo!"

The Mexican dictator General Antonio López de Santa Anna thought that Texas settlers should be proud Mexican citizens. So he tried to crush the American presence in Texas. At the Battle of the Alamo, he and more than 4,000 men attacked some 180 Texans and **Tejanos** (te HAH nohz). The Texans and Tejanos held on to their fort, the Alamo, for 13 days. But on March 6, 1836, the

Mexicans scaled the fort's walls and killed its defenders, including Davy Crockett and Jim Bowie.

The Mexicans had won the battle, but the Texans had gained momentum. Under the leadership of Sam Houston, and with the rallying cry "Remember the Alamo!" more Americans in Texas moved against Santa Anna. On April 21, 1836, Houston's men crushed the Mexican army at the battle of San Jacinto (juh SIHN toh). Santa Anna was captured. He was forced to grant what the Texas settlers had come to want: the independent Republic of Texas, the "Lone Star Republic."

The Alamo today looks much as it did before it was attacked in 1836.

⭐ **Tejano**   A Texan of Mexican descent

STATES ENTERING THE UNION 1791-1859

State	Date
Vermont	1791
Kentucky	1792
Tennessee	1796
Ohio	1803
Louisiana	1812
Indiana	1816
Mississippi	1817
Illinois	1818
Alabama	1819
Maine	1820
Missouri	1821
Arkansas	1836
Michigan	1837
Florida	1845
Texas	1845
Iowa	1846
Wisconsin	1848
California	1850
Minnesota	1858
Oregon	1859

Oregon Country

During the early 1840s many Americans came down with a case of "Oregon fever." They had heard stories of the rich soil, the mild climate, and the natural beauty of what was known as Oregon Country. Oregon Country, as you can see on the map on this page, lay between the Rocky Mountains and the Pacific Ocean. Thousands wanted to load their wagons and follow the trail that missionaries and other early settlers had forged to Oregon.

There was one problem. Great Britain also had a claim to the Oregon Country. Americans wanted the entire area—from the northern California border to the southern tip of Alaska, at north latitude 54°40'. Some of them adopted the saying, "Fifty-four forty or fight." They felt that it was America's **Manifest Destiny** to expand as far as possible.

Clay and Polk

The issue of Oregon played a large role in the election of 1844. The Whig party nominated Henry Clay; the Democrats nominated James K. Polk.

Polk was not as well known to voters, but he was a man who knew

⭐ **Manifest Destiny** The belief that America should expand its territorial limits

just what he wanted. An avid expansionist, he wanted to **annex** the Lone Star Republic and take over the entire Oregon Country. Clay, on the other hand, opposed the annexation of Texas. He also feared war with Great Britain if the United States pushed its claims to Oregon too hard. Campaigning on the slogan "Fifty-four forty or fight," Polk won a close race.

President Polk got what he wanted. The United States annexed Texas in 1845. That led to a war with Mexico, which the United States won. In winning the war, the United States acquired a vast amount of land,

⭐ **annex** To add on or attach

THE OREGON COUNTRY

— Present-day boundaries

ALASKA (Russia)

CANADA (Great Britain)

Vancouver Island

OREGON

Fort Victoria

Line of 1846

Line of 1818

PACIFIC OCEAN

COUNTRY

Astoria

Portland

Fort Walla Walla

UNITED STATES

OREGON TRAIL

Fort Hall

MEXICO

including present-day California. Meanwhile, Polk avoided war with Great Britain. The two nations agreed to split the Oregon Country along the 49th parallel. Britain would control the area to the north; the United States would acquire the area to the south.

Expansion and Slavery

The issue of slavery had to be dealt with every time America moved to expand. As you have read, most Northerners opposed the spread of slavery into new territories. Southerners, on the other hand, supported the extension of slavery.

By the time Polk was elected, most Americans had an opinion about slavery. Americans took three basic positions on the issue. First, there were those, like John C. Calhoun of South Carolina, who strongly defended slavery. Second, there were those, like Daniel Webster of Massachusetts, who thought slavery was wrong but feared that any talk of abolishing it would divide the Union, another name for the United States. Webster didn't want to see slavery spread into new territories, though.

And third, there were **abolitionists**, who simply wanted to get rid of slavery, period. Two abolitionists were William Lloyd Garrison and Frederick Douglass. Many women were also outspoken supporters of abolition.

▲ A poster advertising a speech to be given by Frederick Douglass and a very early photograph of him

The Compromise of 1850

In 1849 there were 15 slave states and 15 free states in the Union, giving Southern and Northern states a balance of power in Congress. But that year, California asked to be admitted to the Union as a free state. This presented a problem, because the Missouri Compromise did not apply to California or other lands in the far western part of the country. The question that had to be answered was whether California was going to be allowed to enter the Union as a free state and upset the North-South balance of power.

Henry Clay, known as the Great Compromiser, suggested a plan to save the fragile balance. Eventually called the Compromise of 1850, his plan allowed California to be admitted as a free state. This pleased the North. The compromise also outlawed the slave trade (though not slavery itself) in Washington, D.C.

The South was pleased because the compromise called for a very tough **Fugitive Slave Law**. Now Northerners would *have to* return runaway slaves to their owners in the South. Also, the compromise created two new territories, called Utah and New Mexico. The Compromise of 1850 left

---

 abolitionist A person opposed to slavery and in favor of ending it

---

 Fugitive Slave Law A law that made it easier for slaveholders to get runaway slaves returned to them

An early copy of the book that brought attention to slavery

open the future of slavery in these territories, as you can see from the map on the left below.

Uncle Tom's Cabin and Slavery

The issue of slavery, however, didn't go away. The Fugitive Slave Law upset many Northerners. Many felt that it violated a "higher law" ensuring the freedom of all people.

In 1852, Harriet Beecher Stowe added fuel to the fire with her novel *Uncle Tom's Cabin*. It shocked Northern readers, and readers all around the world, by depicting the miserable lives of slaves. The impact of *Uncle Tom's Cabin* is hard to overstate. President Abraham Lincoln met Stowe during the war that would be fought between the North and the South in the 1860s. He supposedly greeted her by saying, "So you're the little woman who wrote the book that made this great war!"

A New Party Forms

Westward expansion also kept the issue of slavery alive. The Kansas-Nebraska Act of 1854 increased tensions. It repealed the Missouri Compromise by declaring that the citizens of the two new territories of Kansas and Nebraska could vote on whether to allow slavery or not. See the map on the right below. Under the Missouri Compromise there was to be *no* slavery in these territories. Now slavery in these lands was *possible*.

The Kansas-Nebraska Act set off firestorms of protest in the North. It led directly to the creation of the **Republican party**. The party's main goal was to fight the extension of slavery. One Republican was a lawyer

THE COMPROMISE OF 1850

- Free states and territories
- Slave states and territories
- Territorial voters to decide slavery issue

THE KANSAS-NEBRASKA ACT, 1854

- Free states and territories
- Slave states and territories
- Territorial voters to decide slavery issue

These photographs of Douglas and Lincoln, attached by a ribbon, were given away to people who attended their debates in 1858.

SHOW WHAT YOU KNOW!

REFOCUS
COMPREHENSION

1. Name two areas that became part of the United States as a result of the "Manifest Destiny" policy.

2. Explain how westward expansion and the slavery issue were connected.

THINK ABOUT IT
CRITICAL THINKING

Why do you think many people did not want to upset the balance of power between free states and slave states?

WRITE ABOUT IT
ACTIVITY

As a journalist for France, you have been asked to compare the three views on slavery common in America in the 1850s. Write a newspaper article comparing them.

from Illinois, Abraham Lincoln. In 1858 he ran for the United States Senate against Senator Stephen A. Douglas, the chief sponsor of the Kansas-Nebraska Act. In debates, Lincoln argued against the extension of slavery. Douglas felt that the issue should be decided by the people in the territories. Douglas won the election, but Lincoln—with his stance on slavery and his speaking skills—would be the Republican party presidential candidate in 1860.

No More Compromises

Southerners and Northerners rushed to settle Kansas, bringing with them supporters and opponents of slavery. But guns, not ballots, ruled the day. In 1856 a proslavery mob burned the town of Lawrence. John Brown, an abolitionist, led a raid on a proslavery settlement, killing five men. In 1857 the Supreme Court made its Dred Scott decision. Scott, a slave, had moved with his master from Missouri, a slave state, to Illinois, a free state. They later moved back to Missouri. Scott sued for his freedom when his master died because Scott had lived as a free man in the North. The Supreme Court ruled that Dred Scott was still a slave, and that slaves were not citizens. So they had no rights under the law. The decision meant that Congress could not really outlaw slavery anywhere. The Missouri Compromise was therefore meaningless. Any hope for further compromise on the issue of slavery was dead.

▲ Dred Scott

 Republican party A political party made up of people who wanted to keep the western territories free of slavery

LIFE ON THE OREGON TRAIL

FOCUS *Traveling the Oregon Trail was often hard and dangerous. But the hope for a better life at the end of the trail inspired people to face the challenge.*

Hopes and Fears

All kinds of thoughts are going through your mind as you get ready to leave all that you know behind. You and your family are headed for the green Willamette Valley in Oregon Country. To get there, you will be taking the Oregon Trail.

It is early spring. You and other families from your hometown have gathered at Independence, Missouri, and are meeting the many others who will start on the trail in about a month. You and your father have the chance to talk about your hopes and fears.

First of all, he tells you what to expect from the terrain of the trip. The first part, crossing the Great Plains, is relatively easy. You will be following the Platte River, and the land is fairly flat. But beyond the plains you must be ready to cross the Rocky Mountains at South Pass. On the other side of the mountains, the trail follows the Snake River and then the Columbia River, going through desert and scrub land before it takes you to your new home.

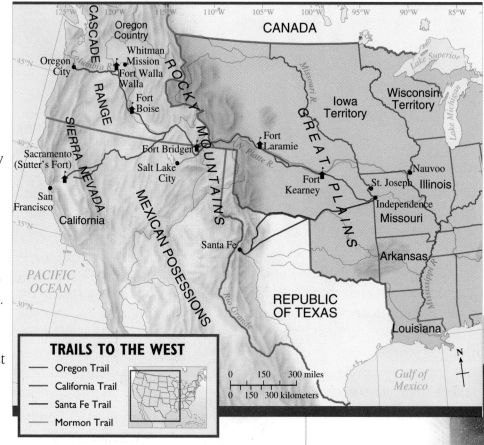

TRAILS TO THE WEST
- Oregon Trail
- California Trail
- Santa Fe Trail
- Mormon Trail

0   150   300 miles
0   150   300 kilometers

You feel sad about leaving your friends behind. On the other hand, you *are* pretty excited. You will see new parts of the country. And you will be going to a place where your family can make a better living. That is the reason your family is moving west.

Oregon Trail The trail blazed by pioneers who moved from Missouri to Oregon Country
terrain Land and landforms, including deserts, mountains, and valleys

246

Traveling the Trail

Packing for the trip hasn't been easy. You need to take almost everything you own. So into the covered wagon go the spinning wheel, the feather beds, and the iron stove. In goes your father's fiddle. You can't head west without cotton shirts, buckskin pants, sunbonnets, and boots. And of course you need guns, a kettle, and plenty of matches. Finally, you need hundreds of pounds of food. Most important are flour, salt, sugar, and bacon. By the time your wagon is fully loaded, it weighs 2,500 pounds!

Life on the trail is hard to get used to, especially in the beginning. Every day you must be up at sunrise. There is much to be done before the wagon train sets off. All day long, for the first month or so, you travel across endless prairie. The oxen move slowly under the heavy loads. On the best days you cover only 20 miles.

Sooner or later some travelers become sick. If your father and mother do, you will have to take over some of their duties. Your father cares for the animals, repairs the wagon, and hunts for food. Your mother cooks, washes, and takes care of the young children.

A New Home

The Rocky Mountain scenery is grand, but rainstorms make the ground soggy. Wagon wheels stick in the mud. Desperate to keep going, your parents drop the iron stove by the side of the trail to make the wagon lighter.

After the Rockies, just as your father said, comes the desert. The wagon train makes some of its slowest progress here. You are upset when you have to leave your bed by the side of the trail. It's hard, but you have to lighten your wagon even more. You begin to make out the green meadows of the Willamette Valley ahead. You're almost to your new home!

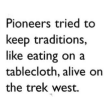
Pioneers tried to keep traditions, like eating on a tablecloth, alive on the trek west.

SHOW WHAT YOU KNOW!

REFOCUS
COMPREHENSION

1. What kinds of terrain did the Oregon Trail cover?

2. Why did pioneers need to pack so many items to travel west?

THINK ABOUT IT
CRITICAL THINKING

Why did people cross America on the Oregon Trail, in spite of all its hardships?

WRITE ABOUT IT
ACTIVITY

You are traveling on the Oregon Trail. Write a letter to a friend back home in which you describe life on the trail.

WESTWARD HO!

FOCUS *In the first half of the 1800s, the United States expanded its territory westward. This came largely at the expense of Mexico.*

AUSTIN BRINGS SETTLERS TO TEXAS

Thousands of Americans flocked to Texas beginning in 1821. Their leader, Stephen F. Austin, won a huge land grant from the Mexican government, allowing him to bring 300 American families to the Texas coast. Each family got an allotment of land and paid Austin just 12 1/2 cents per acre. That was quite a bargain, since land in the United States cost $1.25 an acre.

The fertile land of Texas allowed the settlers, mostly from the South, to plant cotton and other crops they already knew how to grow.

TEXAS INDEPENDENCE!

In 1836, Texas became an independent country. It called itself the Lone Star Republic. Texans wrote their own constitution, based on that of the United States. They elected Sam Houston their first president. They also made slavery legal to please settlers who had come from the southern United States.

WHAT ABOUT STATEHOOD?

Sam Houston wanted Texas to be one of the United States. He thought it was the only way to keep Texas protected from Mexico. Not everyone in Texas agreed with him. Some Texans wanted to keep their total independence.

One such person was Mirabeau Buonaparte Lamar (MIHR uh boh BOH-nuh pahrt luh MAHR), the second president of Texas. During his presidency Texans waged war on both Native Americans and Mexicans to expand Texas's influence. Houston, however, won back the presidency in 1841, and peace was restored. His likeness in the 1840s is captured in the painting below.

1821		1836		1841		1845
Stephen Austin settles Texas		Texas becomes an independent republic		Sam Houston wins back "Lone Star Republic" presidency		Texas joins the Union

1820   1822   1824   1836   1838   1840   1842   1844

"EXPANSION, EXPANSION, EXPANSION!"

James K. Polk's campaign message was simple: Expansion! Expansion! Expansion! He wanted to annex Texas. But that would cost him votes in the North. Maybe, he thought, he could get away with this position if he also favored the annexation of Oregon. That would win him support among northern voters.

Polk's plan worked. He won a narrow victory. But even before Polk took office, President John Tyler got Congress to pass a bill to annex Texas. On December 29, 1845, Texas joined the United States. And in 1846 the British backed down from their claim to the Oregon Country by signing the Oregon Treaty. In the treaty, Great Britain gave the United States all the territory west of the Rocky Mountains south of the 49th parallel. Cartoonists enjoyed portraying Britain as a looming bully and America as an underdog fighter.

WAR WITH MEXICO

The Mexicans claimed that the southern boundary of Texas was the Nueces (noo AY-says) River. The Americans said it was the Rio Grande, farther south. President Polk ordered troops to occupy the land between the two rivers. On April 26, 1846, angry Mexicans attacked the American troops and killed or wounded 16.

Congress declared war on Mexico. The Americans easily won the Mexican War (1846–1848). This was the first war in which some officers in the United States Army received medals, like the one on the left. In the Treaty of Guadalupe Hidalgo (GWAHD ul OOP hih-DAHL goh), the Mexicans gave up their claim to Texas. They also sold a vast area of land to the United States for just $15 million. Known as the Mexican Cession, it included California, Nevada, and Utah. It also included most of Arizona and parts of Wyoming, New Mexico, and Colorado.

1846
Oregon
Treaty
signed

1846–1848
Mexican
War

1847
Mormons
settle Utah

1853
Gadsden
Purchase

| 1846 | 1848 | 1850 | 1852 | 1854 | 1856 |

MORMONS IN UTAH

The Mormons had tried for years to find a place where they could live in peace. Other Americans often found their beliefs strange. Mormons, for example, believed in holding all property in common. They also believed in the right of a husband to have more than one wife.

In July 1847, Brigham Young led the Mormons to the Great Salt Lake in present-day Utah. As Young looked at the dry and empty valley, he said, "This is the place." The hard-working Mormons moved in large groups to Utah and turned the former wasteland into a prosperous community.

GADSDEN PURCHASE

In 1853 another piece of land was added to the United States. This was done with the Gadsden Purchase, named for the minister to Mexico at the time. The United States bought this land from Mexico for $10 million. It was located south of the Gila River and makes up the southern parts of present-day Arizona and New Mexico. The Gadsden Purchase—so named because James Gadsden negotiated the purchase—gave the United States a fairly flat tract of land as a possible route for a transcontinental railroad.

SHOW WHAT YOU KNOW!

REFOCUS
COMPREHENSION

1. Why was Texas so attractive to Stephen Austin and his settlers?

2. Why did the Mormons have difficulty finding a place to settle in?

THINK ABOUT IT
CRITICAL THINKING

How might the United States have been different if the Gadsden Purchase had not been made?

WRITE ABOUT IT
ACTIVITY

Write a report about President James K. Polk. Discuss Polk's contributions to the expansion of the United States.

REFORM AND REFORMERS

FOCUS *The spirit of reform spread across the nation, starting in the 1820s. This led to reform movements aimed at giving women more rights and ending the institution of slavery.*

The Rise of the Common Man

In the early days of the United States, only white men who owned property could vote. But in the early 1800s, attitudes changed. People wanted a democracy not just *for* the people but *by* the people. By the 1820s almost all adult white males had won the right to vote. These men wanted their voices to be heard on the issues of the day. Thus began "the rise of the common man."

Women, too, wanted to be involved in the issues of the day, even though they didn't have the right to vote. One of their targets was alcohol. Women believed men and teenagers drank too much. Those who opposed drinking felt that whiskey, rum, and hard cider made workers unreliable and kept people away from home and church. Women organized groups to promote temperance, or drinking less or not at all. These efforts paid off. By the mid-1830s more than a million men had signed pledges to cut down on drinking.

Women found that other issues could benefit from their involvement. In 1843, Dorothea Dix reported to the Massachusetts legislature on the condition of jails and poorhouses. Dix had found that mentally ill people were put "in cages, closets, cellars, stalls, pens!"

At first, people either didn't believe her or they didn't care enough. But Dix wouldn't quit. She got Massachusetts to build a larger state hospital. She spent the next 45 years working to get other states to build hospitals for the mentally ill.

Women's Rights

Women also fought for their own rights. In 1848, Lucretia Mott, Elizabeth Cady Stanton, and other women called for a meeting on women's rights. It was held in Seneca Falls, New York. Several hundred women attended. Stanton stirred the crowd when she read a declaration modeled on the Declaration of Independence. She announced, "We hold these truths to be self-evident: all men *and women* are created equal."

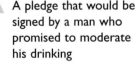

A pledge that would be signed by a man who promised to moderate his drinking

common man The "average" American citizen, whose concerns are represented in government

temperance Moderation in drinking alcohol or total abstinence from drinking alcohol

Elizabeth Cady Stanton addressing women at Seneca Falls ▶

For the rest of their lives, Stanton and Mott fought for women's rights. They were later joined by Susan B. Anthony, who fought to get women the right to vote. She and others saw some success in women's rights on the state level. But it would be a long time before women would win the rights they demanded.

The Abolitionists

Some Americans had always considered slavery wrong. As you have read, some settlers opposed it as far back as the 1600s. But for the most part, northerners hoped that slavery would just fade away—or they refused to think about it at all.

That started to change in the 1820s. Because of the cotton gin, it was clear that slavery wasn't going to just fade away. People who opposed slavery realized that they would have to speak out.

One leading abolitionist was William Lloyd Garrison. A deeply religious man, Garrison thought slavery was a sin in the eyes of God. Garrison started a newspaper called *The Liberator*. In article after article he pounded away at the cruelty of slavery.

Speaking Out Against Slavery

Garrison upset many people. They thought he was a troublemaker. But he was not a man to back down, even in the face of death threats. "I am in earnest," Garrison wrote. "I will not equivocate [compromise]—I will not excuse—I will not retreat a single inch—AND I WILL BE HEARD!" Garrison *was* heard. He caused many Americans to think for the first time about the true injustice of slavery.

Free African Americans had long spoken out against slavery. In 1827 the first black newspaper, *Freedom's Journal*,

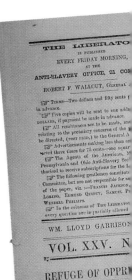

Susan B. Anthony ◀

took up the fight. But it was Frederick Douglass who really moved people. A fugitive slave from Maryland who lived in Rochester, New York, Douglass spoke and wrote eloquently about the evils of slavery. His first-hand knowledge made him one of the most popular speakers in the country. Like Garrison, Douglass published an antislavery newspaper. It was called *The North Star*.

The Movement Grows

As time went by, more and more people joined the abolition movement. Women joined in large numbers. More than half the members of Garrison's American Anti-Slavery Society were women.

Among them were two sisters named Sarah and Angelina Grimké, who had grown up on a South Carolina plantation. They had lived with slavery, and they hated it. They felt so strongly about it that they left the South. In the 1830s they began to give talks against slavery in northern cities and towns. The sisters angered many men, who booed and hissed when the sisters spoke. The men were not so much bothered that the Grimkés were speaking out against slavery. It was considered improper for women to speak out in public.

The Grimké sisters, however, kept lecturing and writing. In 1837, Sarah Grimké wrote that "men and women were created equal" and that "whatever is right for man to do, is *right* for woman."

Abby Kelly felt the same way. She traveled the nation, speaking out against slavery while her husband stayed home and cared for their daughter. In trying to free the slaves, Kelly said, women found out how much work they had to do to free themselves.

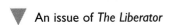

An issue of *The Liberator*

SHOW WHAT YOU KNOW!

REFOCUS
COMPREHENSION

1. What were the major reform movements of this period?

2. List some reformers and the causes they supported.

THINK ABOUT IT
CRITICAL THINKING

What kind of risks did the abolitionists face?

WRITE ABOUT IT
ACTIVITY

Lay out your own anti-slavery newspaper. What features would it include? Who would be its guest columnists?

Spotlight

KEY TERMS

discrimination
certificate of
freedom
Underground
Railroad
conductor

ENSLAVED AND FREE

FOCUS *The story of slavery was a sad chapter in American history. Yet, despite the cruel nature of this institution, enslaved people maintained their dignity as well as their desire to be free.*

The Work of Slaves

While white people debated what to do about slavery, 4 million African Americans were enslaved. For them, slavery was not just an issue to be debated by white Americans and freed black people; it was their life.

Enslaved African Americans had to do anything and everything their masters told them to do. They were made to work as lumberjacks in the Carolina forests. They were sent into the gold, coal, and salt mines of Virginia and Kentucky. They could be found working as wagon drivers in Georgia and Louisiana. From time to time, slaves were also given jobs as skilled laborers. They were carpenters, blacksmiths, and silversmiths.

Most slaves, however, worked on farms and plantations. They often spent 14 hours a day—or more—working in the fields. But it wasn't just the number of hours that made field work so brutal. It was the nature of the work.

Slaves labored in sun that was

▼ Enslaved brothers, in a photo taken in the 1850s

sweltering, in heat that was unbearable. In cotton fields, slaves had to stoop over to pick balls of cotton. It was just as bad on sugar plantations. Slaves there had to dig drainage ditches across snake-filled land. The sugar cane was hard to cut and heavy to carry. In some ways, rice workers had the worst conditions of all. Since rice grows in water, slaves spent long hours standing in water up to their knees.

A Grim Life for Slaves

Slaves who worked as house servants also suffered their share of misery. While both men and women were field hands, most of the indoor workers were women. They didn't suffer in the sun. Nor did they have to spend all day bending and lifting. But they faced different problems. They could be commanded to work at any time, day or night. Because they came into such close contact with white people, they endured constant criticism. They were sometimes insulted—or even beaten—by their masters.

Without question, a slave's life was grim. Yet every slave was expected to turn a cheerful face to his or her master, who did not want angry or sullen slaves. Any sign of unhappiness was taken as a sign of independence. And that was not allowed. Masters punished any slave who showed dissatisfaction. Slaves learned to approach their masters in a humble way. They learned to appear happy, even when they were miserable.

Free African Americans

Many free black people lived in both the North and the South. Some had been freed when Northern states passed laws against slavery. Some had escaped from plantations and had made their way to free states. Others had been freed by their owners. Still others had managed to buy their freedom. They had a different kind of struggle to face, yet they also suffered many of the same hardships as enslaved African Americans.

They might have been free, but their lives weren't easy. Wherever they went, they faced **discrimination**, or unfair

treatment because of their skin color. All across the North, they ran into limits on their freedom. In most states they did not enjoy the same voting rights as white people. In several states they were not allowed to own land. And

◀ Slaves as well as free African Americans did backbreaking work under the hot sun.

discrimination Action or policies against a minority group

AFRICAN AMERICANS IN THE SOUTH, 1820 AND 1860

	Enslaved African Americans		Free African Americans	
	1820	1860	1820	1860
Alabama	41,879	435,080	571	2,690
Arkansas	1,617	111,115	59	144
Delaware	4,509	1,798	12,958	19,829
Florida		61,745		932
Georgia	149,654	462,198	1,763	3,500
Kentucky	126,732	225,483	2,759	10,684
Louisiana	69,064	331,726	10,476	18,647
Maryland	107,397	87,189	39,730	83,942
Mississippi	32,814	436,631	458	773
Missouri	10,222	114,931	347	3,572
North Carolina	205,017	331,059	14,612	30,463
South Carolina	258,475	402,406	6,826	9,914
Tennessee	80,107	275,719	2,727	7,300
Texas		182,566		355
Virginia	425,153	490,865	36,889	58,042

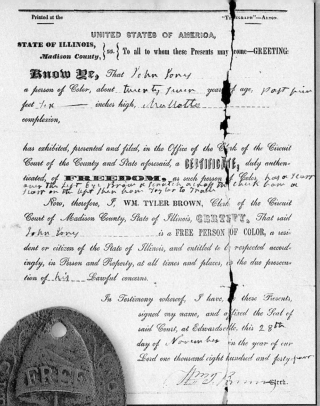

Two ways African Americans "proved" they were free: the certificate of freedom, and a badge, worn around the neck

wherever they went, free African Americans were banned from white hotels, theaters, and churches.

Finding work was not easy. New England mills wanted nothing to do with free African Americans. Factories and stores wouldn't hire black males, except as janitors and handymen. African American women could work as servants and cooks. But these jobs paid very little.

Sojourner Truth was an outspoken freed slave who traveled to cities in the North, speaking out for the rights of African Americans. She was also a supporter of women's rights. Although she could neither read nor write, she gave speeches that spellbound every member of her audience.

It was much worse in the South. Here African Americans who had been freed or who had bought their freedom lived almost like slaves. They were living in a society that suspected any "free" black person to be a runaway, so their **certificates of freedom** were very important. Only a few jobs were open to them. Laws prevented them from

⭐ **certificate of freedom** Paperwork that proved that a slave had been freed or had bought his or her freedom

being taught to read and write. Although many free black people lived in poverty, some became successful despite discrimination.

At the Mercy of the Owner

Slaves longed for freedom. They knew of and had heard stories of slaves who had escaped from their masters or bought their freedom. But for most slaves, freedom was a far-off dream.

Laws were designed to protect masters, not slaves. So owners were free to overwork their slaves. They could separate slave mothers and children by selling them to different plantations. They could feed slaves a diet lacking in meat, milk, and fresh vegetables. Finally, owners could punish their slaves almost any way they wanted to. Whippings, in front of family and friends,

This slave had to ▶ wear bells so that her master could track her movements.

Harriet Tubman ▶

were a humiliating but common form of punishment. In a system that upheld the right of masters to treat their slaves inhumanely, it is surprising that slaves survived at all.

Slaves Revolt

Some slaves did more than survive. They fought back. In the early 1800s some planned revolts. The most famous was Nat Turner's Rebellion in 1831. Turner and fellow slaves in Virginia killed about 60 slaveholders before being captured and killed. After that, slaves were watched closely. Although it was hard for them to organize revolts, individual slaves fought for better treatment by destroying crops, breaking tools, and setting fires. Their actions showed that many would risk death rather than continue living in slavery.

Other slaves tried to escape to the North. If they made it, they could start new lives as free persons. But if they were caught and returned to their masters, they faced terrible punishments. They might have bones in their feet broken or be severely whipped. Despite the risks, slaves kept escaping. The Underground Railroad was organized to help them escape.

The Underground Railroad

The Underground Railroad was run by free black people and abolitionists. They created a series of "stations," or places where runaway slaves could hide

on their way north. Called conductors, freed slaves led groups of runaways from one station to the next. It was risky. Yet they kept at it. One of the most remarkable Underground Railroad conductors was Harriet Tubman.

Tubman was born into slavery around 1820. In 1849 she escaped to freedom. In describing her decision, she later said, "There was one of two things I had a *right* to, liberty (freedom) or death; if I could not have one, I would have the other."

Tubman reached freedom by way of the Underground Railroad. After making it to safety, she became a conductor. Again and again, she risked her life, conducting at least 19 trips from the South. She helped more than 300 people escape from slavery. Not one of her "passengers" was ever caught.

⭐ **Underground Railroad** A system set up by opponents of slavery to help slaves flee from the South to the North

⭐ **conductor** A person who helped runaway slaves to hide and escape

SHOW WHAT YOU KNOW!

REFOCUS
COMPREHENSION

1. Which freed slave spoke out in the North against slavery?

2. What was Nat Turner's Rebellion?

THINK ABOUT IT
CRITICAL THINKING

How was the Underground Railroad like a real railroad? What made it different?

WRITE ABOUT IT
ACTIVITY

If you were a conductor on the Underground Railroad, how would you lead slaves to freedom?

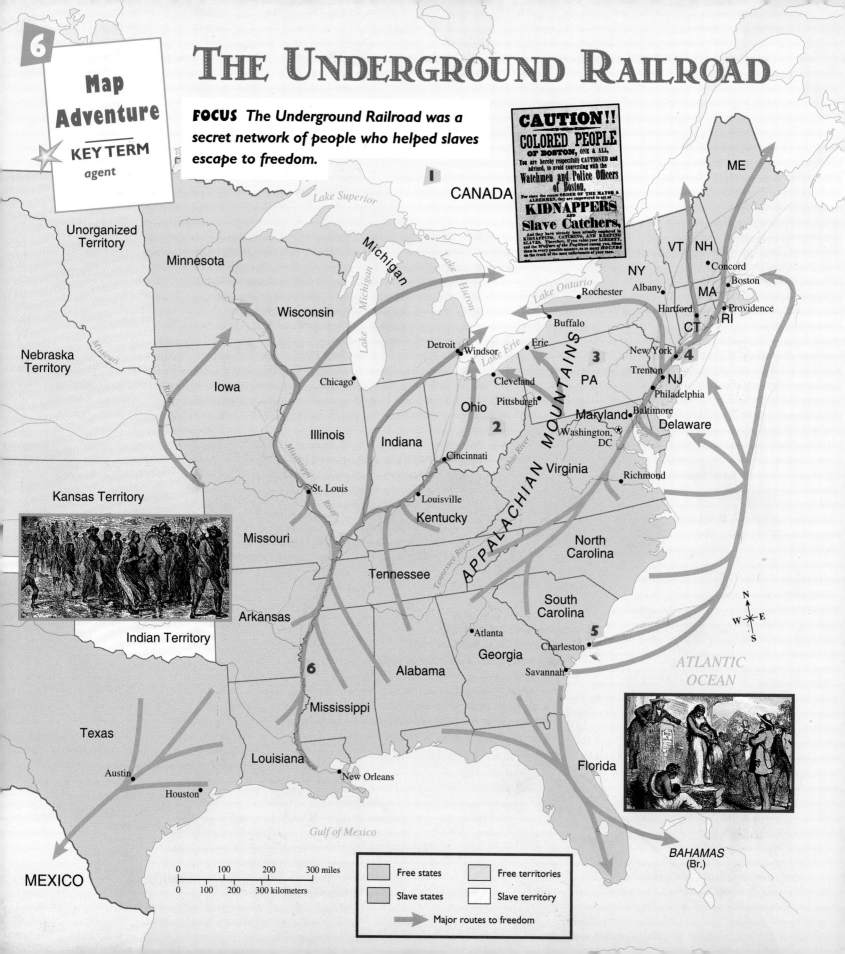

THE UNDERGROUND RAILROAD

FOCUS The Underground Railroad was a secret network of people who helped slaves escape to freedom.

CAUTION!!
COLORED PEOPLE
OF **BOSTON**, ONE & ALL,
You are hereby respectfully CAUTIONED and advised, to avoid conversing with the
Watchmen and Police Officers of Boston,
For since the recent ORDER OF THE MAYOR & ALDERMEN, they are empowered to act as
KIDNAPPERS
AND
Slave Catchers,
And they have already been actually employed in KIDNAPPING, CATCHING, AND KEEPING SLAVES. Therefore, if you value your LIBERTY, and the Welfare of the Fugitives among you, Shun them in every possible manner, as so many HOUNDS on the track of the most unfortunate of your race.

CANADA

1

Unorganized Territory

Minnesota

Lake Superior

ME

VT NH

Concord
Boston

NY

Albany

MA

Providence

Rochester

Hartford

RI

CT

Wisconsin

Lake Michigan

Lake Huron

Lake Ontario

Buffalo

Michigan

Nebraska Territory

Missouri River

Iowa

Chicago

Detroit

Windsor

Erie

Lake Erie

3

New York

4

Trenton

NJ

Cleveland

PA

Philadelphia

Illinois

Indiana

Ohio

Pittsburgh

APPALACHIAN MOUNTAINS

Maryland

Baltimore

Delaware

Washington, DC

Kansas Territory

Mississippi River

St. Louis

2

Cincinnati

Virginia

Richmond

Louisville

Kentucky

Missouri

Mississippi River

North Carolina

Tennessee

Tennessee River

Arkansas

South Carolina

5

Indian Territory

N W E S

Atlanta

Charleston

Georgia

6

Alabama

Savannah

ATLANTIC OCEAN

Texas

Mississippi

Louisiana

Florida

Austin

Houston

New Orleans

Gulf of Mexico

BAHAMAS (Br.)

MEXICO

| 0 | 100 | 200 | 300 miles |
| 0 | 100 | 200 | 300 kilometers |

Free states
Free territories
Slave states
Slave territory
→ Major routes to freedom

Adventure on the Run!

After 1850, slaves who had run away from their masters were no longer free in the North. Only Canada, Mexico, and the Bahamas were truly safe for escaped slaves. Thousands of people secretly hid runaways in attics, under floors, in haystacks, and even in secret rooms while slave hunters and agents combed the docks, streets, and woods of the North. Conductors risked their lives to hide and guide slaves along the way.

Map Legend

1 Canada Slavery was illegal in Canada, and runaways were free once they crossed the border. Here, former slaves could vote and own property.

2 Ohio Most escaping slaves passed through Ohio because it was close to the slave states and to freedom in Canada. Slaves followed the North Star to cross the Ohio River and headed north for Lake Erie and Canada. Many brave people in Ohio gave the runaways shelter, food, and clothes.

3 Pennsylvania Bordering three slave states, Pennsylvania had many conductors in its Quaker community. Quakers did not believe in slavery and began helping runaway slaves soon after the United States won its independence.

4 New York City Slave hunters searched the streets of this city while runaways were sheltered by New York's large free African American community. From here, most runaways continued north, but some outsmarted the slave hunters and became conductors in the city.

5 Charleston Slave hunters patrolled Charleston's piers looking for runaways. But many ship captains hid the runaways and sailed to Philadelphia, New York, and Boston. In these cities, runaways could find food, shelter, and help in reaching Canada.

6 Mississippi River For slaves in the deep South, the Mississippi was a main route of escape. Hiding on steamboats or rowing upriver in canoes, runaways would not leave a trail as they floated toward Illinois, Indiana, and Ohio.

---

 agent A person who acts for or represents another

MAP IT

You are a conductor on the Underground Railroad. You are planning routes to help slaves escape to freedom.

1. If you were to lead escaping slaves from Georgia to Canada by way of Buffalo, New York, what slave states would you pass through?
2. If you were headed from Arkansas to Windsor, Canada, by way of Indiana and Ohio, what cities would you pass through?
3. What river would you follow to get from Louisiana to Minnesota?
4. You plan to go from Charleston, South Carolina to New England by water. What city in Massachusetts is your destination?
5. You want to help some slaves in Florida escape to freedom. You decide the trip to Canada would take too long. What is the closest place that you could lead slaves to freedom?

EXPLORE IT

You have just escaped to freedom in Canada. Write a description of the route you took. Include some experiences you had on the Underground Railroad.

SUMMING UP

1 DO YOU REMEMBER . . .
COMPREHENSION

1. How was the issue of slavery related to the expansion of the United States?

2. Describe the three major positions on slavery taken by Americans in the 1800s.

3. What were some of the hardships faced by travelers along the Oregon Trail?

4. Why did the United States and Mexico go to war in the 1840s?

5. What land areas were added to the United States as a result of the Mexican Cession?

6. What were some of the issues that women reformers spoke out about?

7. Who was Frederick Douglass and why did so many people listen to him speak?

8. Describe some of the conditions that slaves on farms and plantations worked under.

9. What were some of the hardships faced by freed black Americans in the northern states?

10. Name three places outside the United States to which slaves escaped.

2 SKILL POWER
READING A POLITICAL CARTOON

In this chapter you saw that political cartoons can be used to express how people feel about issues. Look at political cartoons in your local paper or in a magazine. What do they tell you about the views of the cartoonist?

3 WHAT DO YOU THINK?
CRITICAL THINKING

1. How did the Dred Scott decision drive the nation further apart on the issue of slavery?

2. You and your family are moving to a part of the country you have never seen before. Write about how you feel.

3. Why did so many women become active abolitionists?

4. What effect do you think the abolitionists had on people's attitudes toward slavery?

5. How do you think slaveholders in America felt about Canada in the 1800s? Why?

CHAPTER 11

4 SAY IT, WRITE IT, USE IT
VOCABULARY

Suppose that you were with a group of fugitive slaves who risked their lives to reach freedom in the North. Write about your experience, describing the journey and the life you found in the North. Use as many vocabulary words as you can.

abolitionist

agent

annex

certificate of freedom

common man

conductor

discrimination

Fugitive Slave Law

Manifest Destiny

Oregon Trail

Republican party

Tejano

temperance

terrain

Underground Railroad

5 GEOGRAPHY AND YOU
MAP STUDY

Use the map on page 240 and the Atlas map on page 590 to answer these questions.

1. What present-day states made up the Mexican Cession?

2. What is the only territory shown on the map that does not touch a body of water?

3. What states besides Texas had land included in the Texas Annexation?

4. Which cessions or purchases touch the Pacific Ocean?

6 TAKE ACTION
CITIZENSHIP

Just like the reformers in the 1800s, there are people in your own community who think things should be changed. How do you think your community could be improved? Here are a few issues to think about: How well do different groups of people get along together? Are the parks and schools in good condition?

Is public transportation convenient and efficient? Choose an issue that you feel strongly about and talk to others about your ideas. By talking to people about community problems, you might figure out ways to do something about them.

7 GET CREATIVE
MATH CONNECTION

Portland, Oregon 500 miles

The journey along the Oregon Trail was long and hard. What would a trip from Missouri to the West Coast be like today? Using a road map, plan a car trip from Independence, Missouri, to Portland, Oregon. Choose the highways you would take. If you drove an average of 55 miles per hour, how many miles could you cover each day? How many days would the entire trip take?

LOOKING AHEAD — **In the next chapter, you will find out how the United States went from a divided country to Civil War.**

CHAPTER 12

The War Between

The North took up arms to preserve the Union; the South, to preserve its way of life. The War Between the States, or Civil War, was long and bloody, and Reconstruction did little to bring the nation back together.

CONTENTS

Who used the items this girl is holding? Turn to pages 274–275 to find out.

The States

These books tell about some people, places, and important events during the time of the Civil War. Read one that interests you and fill out a book-review form.

READ AND RESEARCH

Lincoln: A Photobiography by Russell Freedman
(Houghton Mifflin Co., 1987)
While reading the life of this great President, let the photographs help you picture the important events in our nation's history, especially the five years of the Civil War. *(biography)*
• *You can read a selection from this book on page 278.*

Clara Barton: Healing the Wounds
by Cathy East Dubowski (Silver Burdett Press, 1991)
Clara Barton, an army nurse during the Civil War, eased the suffering of many soldiers. Read about her courageous life both on and off the battlefield. *(biography)*

The Emancipation Proclamation: Why Lincoln Really Freed the Slaves by Robert Young (Silver Burdett Press, 1994)
Learn about the events leading up to Lincoln's famous Emancipation Proclamation. Then decide for yourself whether you think he issued the proclamation because of the evils of slavery or because he wanted the war to end and the Union to be preserved. *(nonfiction)*

Shades of Gray by Carolyn Reeder (Avon Books, 1991)
Will lost his entire family because of the Civil War. Now he must live with his Uncle Jed, a coward who refused to fight for the Confederacy. Can Will respect a man who would not defend his own Southern home? *(historical fiction)*

SKILL POWER

Analyzing a Document

Knowing how to analyze historical documents helps you understand the events of the past.

UNDERSTAND IT

The date is February 22, 1861. Newly-elected President Abraham Lincoln visits Independence Hall in Philadelphia. As he addresses the crowd, there is a question on everyone's mind. Will the nation soon be torn apart by a war?

Parts of Lincoln's speech are shown on this page. A speech is a kind of document. Documents take many forms. They can be speeches, letters, or even legal documents, like laws or treaties.

Documents provide firsthand accounts of events and show how people were thinking and feeling at a certain time.

EXPLORE IT

When you read the first part of a document, decide what the topic is. In this speech, for example, Lincoln stresses the importance of the Declaration of Independence.

As you continue to read, look for the main ideas of the document. In which part does Lincoln remind his listeners of the declaration's promise of equal freedom for all?

Each part of a document introduces new ideas. What idea does Lincoln express in part 3?

[1] . . . I have never had a feeling, politically, that did not spring from . . . the Declaration of Independence . . . I have often inquired of myself what great principle or idea it was that kept this Confederacy [the United States] so long together . . . .

[2] . . . the Declaration of Independence . . . gave promise that in due time the weights would be lifted from the shoulders of all men, and that all should have an equal chance . . . .

[3] . . . there is no need of bloodshed and war. There is no necessity for it. I am not in favor of such a course . . . .

Read the text of Lincoln's Gettysburg Address. As you analyze the document, list its topic or topics. Then list the main ideas of each part of the document. In a short talk with your classmates, sum up what you have learned.

THE GETTYSBURG ADDRESS

Four score and seven years ago our fathers brought forth, on this continent, a new nation, conceived in liberty, and dedicated to the proposition that "all men are created equal."

Now we are engaged in a great civil war, testing whether that nation, or any nation so conceived, and so dedicated, can long endure. We are met on a great battle field of that war. We have come to dedicate a portion of it, as a final resting place for those who died here that the nation might live. This we may in all propriety [proper behavior] do. But, in a larger sense, we can not dedicate— we can not consecrate—we can not hallow—this ground. The brave men, living and dead, who struggled here, have hallowed it far above our poor power to add or detract. The world will little note, nor long remember, what we say here, but it can never forget what they did here.

It is rather for us, the living, here to be dedicated to the great task remaining before us—that from these honored dead we take increased devotion to that cause for which they gave the last full measure of devotion—that we here highly resolve that these dead shall not have died in vain; that this nation, under God, shall have a new birth of freedom; and that government of the people, by the people, and for the people, shall not perish from the earth.

SKILL POWER SEARCH *Use what you know about analyzing documents to find out more about other historical events.*

Setting the Scene

KEY TERMS

secede
Confederacy
civil war
defensive war
blockade
Emancipation
Proclamation

The Nation Divides

FOCUS *All efforts at compromise between the North and the South ended in failure. The issue of slavery was finally settled on the battlefield in the bloodiest conflict in American history.*

Lincoln Is Elected

In November 1860, Abraham Lincoln was elected President. He had no plans to abolish slavery in the South. He had, however, promised that there would be "no slavery in the territories." This upset Southerners. They felt that, as Americans, they had as much right to the western territories as Northerners.

Southerners also believed that slavery in the territories was an issue for the

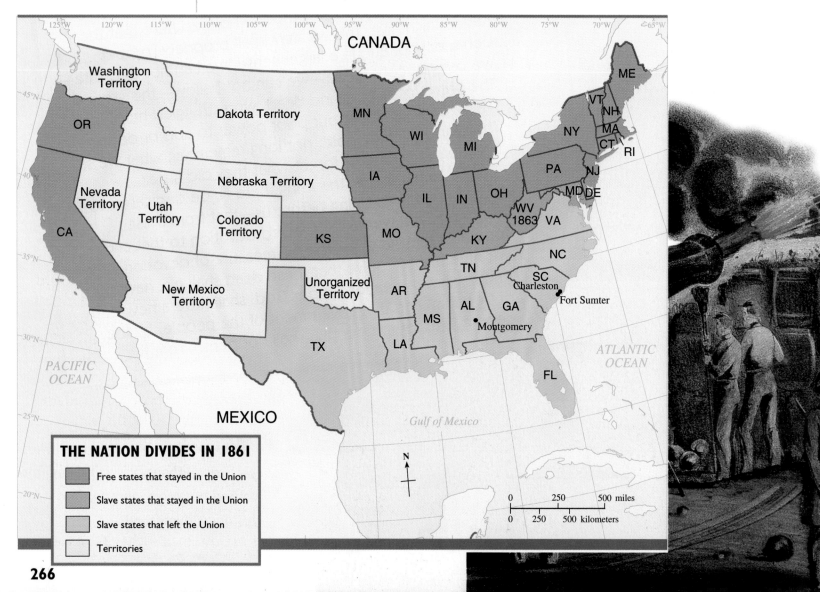

THE NATION DIVIDES IN 1861

- Free states that stayed in the Union
- Slave states that stayed in the Union
- Slave states that left the Union
- Territories

December 1860 South Carolina secedes	**February 1861** Confederate States of America formed	**April 1861** Confederates fire on Fort Sumter	**January 1863** Emancipation Proclamation	**November 1863** Gettysburg Address	**April 1865** Lee surrenders	

1860   1861   1862   1863   1864   1865

territories to decide, not the federal government. Lincoln argued that the federal government had the right to prohibit slavery in all the territories. Without new slave states, the Southerners would gradually lose their political power.

The Confederacy Is Born

To many Southerners, differences over slavery now seemed too great to resolve. In addition many Southerners believed in "states' rights." They thought that each state was independent and had the right to leave the Union if it wanted to. In December 1860, South Carolina **seceded** from the Union. Before Lincoln was inaugurated, six more states—Mississippi, Florida, Alabama,

Georgia, Louisiana, and Texas—also voted to leave. You can find these states on the map on the facing page. Together they formed a new nation, the **Confederacy**, or the Confederate States of America, on February 4, 1861. The capital was established in Montgomery, Alabama. Jefferson Davis was chosen president.

Firing on Fort Sumter

When Lincoln became President in March 1861, many still hoped that war could be avoided. Four slave states still remained in the Union. And even within the Confederacy some people still supported the Union.

Abraham Lincoln wanted to avoid **civil war**. But as President, he had a duty to preserve the Union. He said no state could decide on its own to leave the Union. He also told the South that he would hold on to all property owned by the United States government.

Although Lincoln had decided to fight if necessary, he didn't want to fire the first shot. And as things turned out, he didn't. On the morning of April 12, 1861, Confederate soldiers opened fire on Fort Sumter in the harbor of Charleston, South Carolina.

▼ The Confederate battery at Fort Moultrie firing on Fort Sumter in Charleston Harbor

 secede To withdraw from an organization or nation
Confederacy The nation formed by the states that seceded from the Union
civil war Armed fighting between groups within the same country

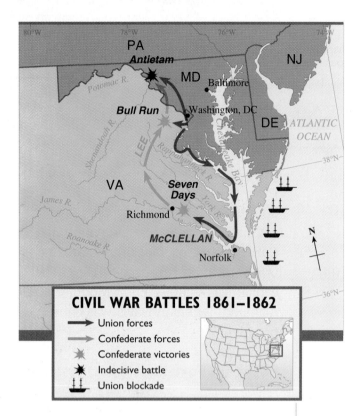

CIVIL WAR BATTLES 1861–1862

→ Union forces
→ Confederate forces
✹ Confederate victories
✸ Indecisive battle
⚓ Union blockade

Major Robert Anderson, the fort commander, had refused to hand the fort over to the Confederacy. Supplies at the fort were low, however, and Major Anderson told the President that he would have to give up the fort unless food arrived soon. Lincoln agreed to send supply ships to the fort. The President said the ships would not carry guns or troops, hoping that the Confederates would allow the ships to go through. But before the ships arrived, the Confederates demanded that Anderson surrender the fort. When he refused, Confederate cannons on shore opened fire. Major Anderson was forced to surrender.

Soon after, Lincoln called for Americans to join the army and help put down the rebellion. Even so, four more southern states—Virginia, North

▼ Union and Confederate soldiers at the battle of Bull Run

Carolina, Tennessee, and Arkansas—joined the Confederacy. The bloodiest war in America's history had begun.

Advantages and Disadvantages

Both the North and the South began the war in high spirits. The North had several advantages—a larger population, most of the industry, and many of the railroads. It also had more than 40 warships, while the South had none.

Even so, the South was hopeful. They had better-trained and more experienced generals, including Robert E. Lee. The South had another big advantage—fighting a **defensive war** on land they knew well. To win, the

 defensive war A war in which an army fights to defend its own territory

North would have to invade and conquer the South. Finally, the South didn't need long supply lines the way the North did. This gave the South the ability to move more quickly.

Battle of Bull Run

Only one soldier died at Fort Sumter. The real fighting started a few months later outside Manassas Junction, Virginia. Here 35,000 Union troops faced 25,000 Virginia soldiers. Many Union supporters traveled the 30 miles from Washington, D.C., to see this first battle of the war. They even brought picnic lunches.

The fighting began on July 21, 1861, near a small stream, Bull Run, shown on the map on page 268. The picnickers could hear the sound of cannon fire in the distance. "This should be quick," most of them thought. "We'll whip the Rebs [Rebels] here, and the war will be over."

At first the Union side was winning. Then fresh Confederate troops arrived, and the battle turned. The poorly trained Union soldiers began dropping their guns and retreating. Soon panicky picnickers and Union soldiers competed in dashing back to Washington. After the battle of Bull Run, both sides knew that the war would probably be long, bitter, and bloody.

War Strategies

The Union's plan for winning the war had several parts. First, Lincoln ordered a naval **blockade** of Southern ports so that the Confederacy could not get supplies from or sell its cotton to European countries. Second, the Union would try to invade the South and divide it into parts. And third, Union forces would attack Richmond, Virginia, the new capital of the Confederacy.

The Confederates had one basic plan—just hold on. Sooner or later the North would quit. Many thought that Northerners were too divided about the war to put up a good fight. Southerners also believed they were better fighters, boasting that one Rebel "could whip a half-dozen Yankees [Northerners] and not half try."

Fighting the War

In the early days of the war, the South looked strong. Under the leadership of General Robert E. Lee and General Thomas "Stonewall" Jackson, they beat the Union army again and again.

General George McClellan, leader of the Union troops, responded poorly. McClellan was a brilliant planner, but he hesitated to attack. Finally, Lincoln fired him. After trying several other generals, Lincoln found one that he felt could be

▲ President Abraham Lincoln with General George McClellan

 blockade A blocking of a port or region to prevent entering or leaving

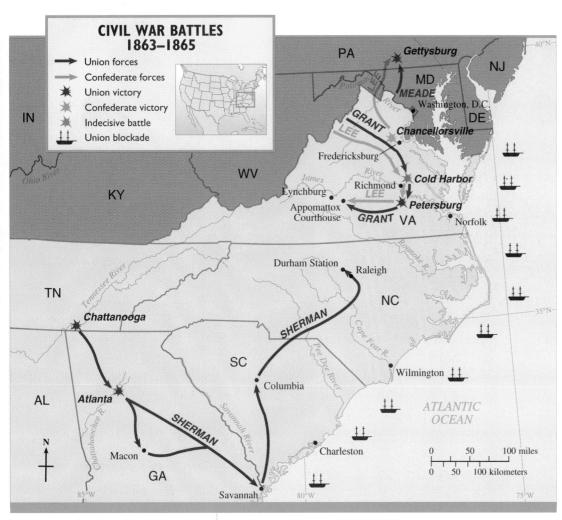

Union forces
Confederate forces
Union victory
Confederate victory
Indecisive battle
Union blockade

command of all Union armies.

Under Grant, the North continued trying to cut the South into thirds. General William Tecumseh Sherman led Union troops on a "march to the sea" through Georgia and then north through South Carolina. You can follow his route on the map at the left. Like Grant, Sherman believed in total war—destroying anything that might help the enemy. Crops, barns, bridges, and mills all became fair targets. Homes were ransacked and destroyed. Before General Sherman burned the city of Atlanta, he told the mayor, "War is cruelty."

Emancipation Proclamation

Guard detail of the 107th United States Colored Infantry

successful. That man, Ulysses S. Grant, had already won key victories. On March 9, 1864, Lincoln placed him in

In September 1862, President Lincoln announced that as of January 1, 1863, all slaves in the rebelling states

This painting shows the surrender at Appomattox Court House, April 9, 1865.

would be "forever free." The **Emancipation Proclamation** changed the focus of the war. It was no longer just a battle to preserve the Union. It now became a war to free the slaves.

Some freed African Americans now joined the Union army. At first many served as cooks, drivers, and workers—not as soldiers or sailors. But later they joined in large numbers and served as soldiers. Before the war was over, more than 185,000 African Americans had fought in the army. Many died, and 21 received the Congressional Medal of Honor, our country's highest award.

War Ends and Lincoln Dies

By the spring of 1865, the South was badly weakened. Its armies were running out of men and supplies. On April 9, 1865, Lee surrendered to Grant in a private home in the village of Appomattox Court House, Virginia.

The Civil War was over. The Union was saved, and slavery was abolished. But the cost of the war was huge. Over 600,000 people died. More soldiers died in the Civil War than in any other American war. Over 250,000 others were crippled for life.

Five days after the war ended, while Lincoln attended a play at Ford's Theater in Washington, D.C., John Wilkes Booth slipped into the President's box. Booth, a Confederate radical, shot Lincoln in the back of the head. Lincoln died a few hours later.

A nation mourned and wondered what to do about the Confederate states. Lincoln had wanted to treat the South firmly but "with malice [bad feelings] toward none, with charity for all." What would happen now that Lincoln was gone?

⭐ **Emancipation Proclamation** An order that declared freedom for the slaves in all the states that had left the Union

North Versus South

FOCUS *Most battles of the Civil War were bloody affairs. Just when people thought the fighting couldn't get any worse, it did.*

MONITOR AND MERRIMACK

In March 1862 a Confederate vessel covered with iron plates sailed out of Norfolk, Virginia. Called the *Merrimack* (later renamed the *Virginia*), its mission was to break the Union blockade so that needed Confederate supplies from abroad could arrive.

Soon *Merrimack* guns blasted the Union's wooden ships. Union cannon-balls just bounced off its sides. The next day the Union answered with its own ironclad ship, the *Monitor*. Neither ship could damage the other, and this historic battle ended in a draw. But it really was a Union victory because the blockade held. A few months later the Confederates sank the *Merrimack* to keep it from falling into enemy hands when Union forces captured Norfolk.

SHILOH
32 USA
1995

BATTLE OF SHILOH

On April 6, 1862, the South attacked Grant's army at Shiloh, Tennessee. Grant rallied his men and drove the Confederates back the next day. Although the battle had no clear winner, it showed just how bloody the war would be. At Bull Run, casualties were light, but Shiloh was a slaughter. Over 13,000 Union soldiers were killed, wounded, or captured. The South had almost 11,000 killed, wounded, or captured. More men died in this one battle than in America's three previous wars.

BATTLE OF ANTIETAM

In September 1862, General Robert E. Lee decided to invade the North. He hoped to win a quick victory and force the North to quit. On September 17 he came up against General George McClellan at Antietam Creek, near Sharpsburg, Maryland. McClellan almost surrounded Lee but moved too slowly. Fresh Confederate troops arrived in time to save Lee and his army. Antietam was not really the victory Lincoln was looking for, but Lee's advance into the North was stopped.

There were even more casualties at Antietam than at Shiloh. In just one awful day, the two armies had almost 23,000 killed, wounded, or captured. September 17, 1862, was the bloodiest day of the war.

32 USA
Robert E. Lee
1995

MONITOR★VIRGINIA
USA 32
1995

March 1862	April 1862	September 1862		July 1863	July 1863
Monitor and *Merrimack*	Battle of Shiloh	Battle of Antietam		Battle of Gettysburg	Battle of Vicksburg

JANUARY 1862   JULY   JANUARY 1863   JULY   JANUARY 1864

SHOW WHAT YOU KNOW!

BATTLE OF GETTYSBURG

On July 1, 1863, General Lee invaded the North for the last time. At Gettysburg, Pennsylvania, he clashed with a Union army led by General George Meade. The battle lasted three days and became the best-known battle of the war. Wave after wave of Southern soldiers attacked Union positions. On July 3, Lee ordered General George Pickett to make one final charge. The Union army drove the Confederates back. This battle was often looked on as the turning point in the war. After this, Lee ordered his army to retreat into Virginia.

Four months later President Lincoln dedicated a cemetery in Gettysburg in honor of the soldiers who had died there. His Gettysburg Address, which took less than five minutes to deliver, expressed the meaning of the horrible conflict for the whole world. He promised "that these dead shall not have died in vain; that this nation, under God, shall have a new birth of freedom; and that government of the people, by the people, and for the people, shall not perish from the earth."

BATTLE OF VICKSBURG

A day after the victory at Gettysburg, President Lincoln received more good news from the West. Union armies, led by General Grant, had captured the Confederate stronghold of Vicksburg, Mississippi. This was a critical victory for the Union. The North at last controlled the entire Mississippi River. Arkansas, Texas, and most of Louisiana were now cut off from the rest of the Confederacy. These states could no longer send troops and supplies across the Mississippi River to the main Confederate armies.

The victory also made General Grant a Northern war hero. Unlike some other Union generals, Grant showed a grim determination to do what had to be done. Lincoln now chose him to destroy Lee's army.

Ulysses S. Grant

REFOCUS
COMPREHENSION

1. Why can it be said that the battle of Antietam was not a victory for either side?

2. Why was it important for the Union to capture Vicksburg?

THINK ABOUT IT
CRITICAL THINKING

Why is a civil war especially tragic?

WRITE ABOUT IT
ACTIVITY

Read and analyze the quote from the Gettysburg Address. Then write in your journal, explaining the meaning of the words.

Life as a Soldier

FOCUS *Young soldiers on both sides in the Civil War believed in their cause, fought bravely, and suffered mightily.*

Hoping to Be a Hero

To young men looking for adventure, war sounds thrilling. How excited you must be if you are a 17- or 18-year-old farm boy in 1861. Until now your time has been spent plowing fields and milking cows. You might have dreamed of doing something heroic, but there aren't many chances to be a hero on the family farm.

Now, war is breaking out. If you join the army, you have a chance to put on a uniform, march into battle, and fight for a glorious cause. In the case of a New England farm boy, that means saving the Union. For a Southern farm boy, it is defending states' rights.

The Reality of Army Camps

If you are one of the tens of thousands of young boys and men who join the Confederate or Union army, you soon learn that war is not what you expected. Life in an army camp is hard. You become dirtier with each passing day; there is little time to wash clothes or take a bath. Soon your body is covered with lice.

As time passes, if you are lucky enough to have a uniform, it becomes ragged. Your boots wear out, but new ones are often impossible to get. You might find yourself marching through miles of sharp, tangled bushes in bare feet. The lack of tents means that you have to sleep on the ground, without regard to the weather. You and your fellow soldiers huddle under thin blankets—some so poorly made that they fall apart in the rain.

Food is another problem. It is usually scarce; even when you have some, it is often spoiled. A meal might consist of moldy bread and rotten meat. If there is no time to cook bacon, you have to eat it raw or go hungry.

▼ A Union cavalry trooper

Long, Lonely Days

As the weeks pass, your dreams of glory begin to slip away. Most of the time you aren't standing proudly on the battlefield but are marching through the rain or waiting around a campsite. You write long letters to your family back home, telling them of your loneliness. You try to keep up your spirits as this war drags on and on.

The Horrors of Battle

When fighting occurs, misery turns to horror. Most battles are chaotic. Smoke from guns and cannons fills the air. You hear the agonizing screams of wounded men. You might see friends shot or taken prisoner. As one Confederate soldier writes, "It is a sad sight to see the dead and if possible more sad to see the wounded—shot in every possible way you can imagine."

You yourself might end up among the dead or wounded. If you are wounded, you have to hope the injury isn't serious. Medical knowledge is very limited. Nurses can bandage wounds, and doctors can amputate shattered arms or legs. But beyond that, there isn't much anyone can do. Many soldiers die from infections and loss of blood. Also, there is the threat of dying from deadly **epidemic** diseases that are in the filthy, crowded army camps. In fact, for every Civil War soldier killed in battle, two die from disease.

⭐ **epidemic**   The spread of disease to a large number of people in a short period of time

▼A Confederate private

SHOW WHAT YOU KNOW!

REFOCUS
COMPREHENSION

1. Why did many young men volunteer for the army?

2. What were some of the problems that soldiers faced daily?

THINK ABOUT IT
CRITICAL THINKING

If you had lived during the time of the Civil War, would you have wanted to serve in the military? Give your reasons.

WRITE ABOUT IT
ACTIVITY

Suppose you are a Union or Confederate soldier. Write a letter home telling of life in your army camp.

Abraham Lincoln

FOCUS *Born in a log cabin, Abraham Lincoln rose to become President of the United States. His bold and courageous leadership helped the Union win the Civil War.*

Lincoln, "The Rail Splitter"

Humble Beginnings

When Abraham Lincoln was born in 1809, his future didn't look particularly bright. After all, his parents were poor farmers who had very little education. They lived in a log cabin in the woods of Kentucky.

As a child Lincoln spent much of his time helping his father scratch a living out of their small plot of land. When Lincoln was seven, the family moved to Indiana. Here he helped to farm and build a log cabin for the family. With all the chores to be done, little time was left for "book learning." In fact, in his entire childhood, Lincoln only spent about a year in school.

Yet he loved books. He read whenever and wherever he got the chance. He would walk miles to borrow a book. Often he tucked one into his pocket before heading out to split wood or plow a field.

Lawyer and Family Man

When Lincoln was a young adult, he moved to Illinois. After studying law books on his own and earning a license to practice, he became a successful lawyer. At the age of 25, he was elected to the Illinois state legislature and became a leader of the Republican party.

In 1842, Lincoln married Mary Todd of Lexington, Kentucky. The two were almost opposite in background. Mary was from a well-known, well-to-do family. By the time Lincoln ran for President, the couple had had four sons. Abraham Lincoln and Mary Todd were devoted to their family. They shared the tragedy of the deaths from disease of two of their four children.

Abraham Lincoln was often seen wearing his top hat.

President Lincoln

When the Civil War broke out, no one knew what kind of President Lincoln would be. He had been in office a little more than a month when the fighting started. At times over the next four years, many people had their doubts about President Lincoln. In the end, however, he proved to be a brilliant politician and an inspiring leader.

Lincoln possessed several great qualities. He was intelligent, shrewd, and courageous. His goal was to preserve the Union, and he was ready to do whatever it took to accomplish this goal. Again and again he angered Congress by acting without their consent. He used his power as President to do what he believed was necessary. Sometimes this meant spending more money than Congress had planned. Sometimes it meant throwing troublemakers in jail. In 1863 he announced that slaves in the rebelling states would be freed. Each of these actions met with criticism. But once Lincoln settled on a course of

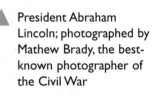

President Abraham Lincoln; photographed by Mathew Brady, the best-known photographer of the Civil War

Mary Todd Lincoln in formal dress; photographed by Brady in 1864

action, he rarely backed down.

One of Lincoln's talents was his ability to express himself. Speaking out in his high-pitched voice, he could state his ideas in ways that kept people spellbound. Two of the greatest speeches in American history were written by this self-taught man from the frontier—the Gettysburg Address and Lincoln's second **inaugural address**

 inaugural address The speech made at the start of a term of office

LITERATURE

Lincoln: A Photobiography

by Russell Freedman

Abraham Lincoln rose from humble beginnings to greatness. Through photographs and text, you will come to know the real Mr. Lincoln.

Abraham Lincoln wasn't the sort of man who could lose himself in a crowd. After all, he stood six feet four inches tall, and to top it off, he wore a high silk hat.

His height was mostly in his long bony legs. When he sat in a chair, he seemed no taller than anyone else. It was only when he stood up that he towered above other men.

At first glance, most people thought he was homely. Lincoln thought so too, referring once to his "poor, lean, lank face." As a young man he was sensitive about his gawky looks, but in time, he learned to laugh at himself. When a rival called him "two-faced" during a political debate, Lincoln replied: "I leave it to my audience. If I had another face, do you think I'd wear this one?"

According to those who knew him, Lincoln was a man of many faces. In repose, he often seemed sad and gloomy. But when he began to speak, his expression changed. "The dull, listless features dropped like a mask," said a Chicago newspaperman. "The eyes began to sparkle, the mouth to smile, the whole countenance was wreathed in animation, so that a stranger would have said, 'Why, this man, so angular and solemn a moment ago, is really handsome!'"

Lincoln may have seemed like a common man, but he wasn't. His friends agreed that he was one of the most ambitious people they had ever known. Lincoln struggled hard to rise above his log-cabin origins, and he was proud of his achievements. By the time he ran for president he was a wealthy man, earning a large income from his law practice and his many investments. As for the nickname Abe, he hated it. No one who knew him well ever called him Abe to his face. They addressed him as Lincoln or Mr. Lincoln.

It's true that Lincoln had little formal "eddication," as he would have pronounced it. Almost everything he "larned" he taught himself. All his life he said "thar" for *there,* "git" for *get,* "kin" for *can.* Even so, he became an eloquent public speaker who could hold a vast audience spellbound, and a great writer whose finest phrases still ring in our ears. He was known to sit up late into the night, discussing Shakespeare's plays with White House visitors.

Lincoln is best known as the Great Emancipator, the man who freed the slaves. Yet he did not enter the war with that idea in mind. "My paramount object in this struggle *is* to save the Union," he said in 1862, "and is *not* either to save or destroy slavery." As the war continued, Lincoln's attitude changed. Eventually he came to regard the conflict as a moral crusade to wipe out the sin of slavery.

Want to read more? You can by checking the book out of your school or public library.

SHOW WHAT YOU KNOW!

REFOCUS
COMPREHENSION

1. Describe Lincoln's early life.

2. What were some of Lincoln's accomplishments as a young man?

THINK ABOUT IT
CRITICAL THINKING

Why is Lincoln considered to have been a great President?

WRITE ABOUT IT
ACTIVITY

Based on your reading of the literature selection, write a description of Abraham Lincoln.

Women and the War Effort

FOCUS *Although few actually fought, women in the North and the South aided the Civil War effort in many important ways.*

Raising Money and Running Farms

While men faced each other on the battlefield, women had struggles of their own. Most women did not take up arms, but they found other ways to serve.

▼ Civil War nurses

In both the North and the South, women raised money to aid injured troops. Over 10,000 soldiers' aid societies were organized. Women rolled bandages, made tents, and sewed clothing to send to the troops. In addition, they took on much of the work that men ordinarily did, such as plowing fields, planting crops, and gathering harvests.

Helping the Wounded and Aiding the Fighting

Some women traveled to the battlefields to help the sick and wounded. In 1861, Dorothea Dix became the superintendent of nurses for the Union army. Under her direction, thousands of Northern women waded through blood and dirt to nurse soldiers in pain. One, Clara Barton, many years later used the skills she gained during the war to found the American branch of the **Red Cross**. Southern women also became nurses, cleaning wounds and comforting dying men. Sally Tompkins ran a private hospital in Richmond, Virginia, where she cared for both Confederate and Union soldiers.

Other women, eager to help the war cause, became spies. One of the North's spies was Harriet Tubman, the famed "conductor" on the Underground Railroad. Still others carried mail for the armies. Some women even went so far as to disguise themselves as men so that they could reach the battlefield.

Coping in the South

As the war dragged on, Southern women faced additional burdens. Many lost food supplies when the

 Red Cross An international society for the relief of suffering in times of war or disaster

Clara Barton, Civil War nurse and founder of the American Red Cross

War and Death

In addition to all else, both Northern and Southern women lived every day with the knowledge that war meant death. They knew that the men who marched off to battle might never return. To keep track of Union soldiers, Northerners started the United States Sanitary Commission. Many women worked for this organization. But news traveled slowly, and sometimes messages didn't get through at all.

One Southern woman wrote in her journal: "I have no heart to keep this journal or tell of the dreadful, fatal battles in Virginia. My heart is too heavy. I am entirely miserable. Many whom I know are killed and wounded."

Union army marched through. The army simply confiscated, or took, their crops. Some saw their farms burned and their fields destroyed.

Even women who lived far from the battle sites faced huge problems. They had to manage slaves who were becoming more and more restless. They also had to cope with the breakdown of wagons and plows. Since no one could get spare parts from the North, many farm implements just lay rusting in the fields.

Pauline Cushman (left) was a Union spy. Rose O'Neal Greenhow and her daughter (right) were spies for the Confederate cause.

SHOW WHAT YOU KNOW!

REFOCUS
COMPREHENSION

1. What organization did Clara Barton found after the Civil War?

2. Name two women who helped their side's cause. Tell what each did.

THINK ABOUT IT
CRITICAL THINKING

What do you think would have happened had women not aided the Civil War effort?

WRITE ABOUT IT
ACTIVITY

Write a paragraph describing several ways in which women helped the war effort during the Civil War.

Spotlight

KEY TERMS

Reconstruction
Radical Republican
black codes
carpetbagger
sharecropper
Jim Crow laws

Reconstruction

FOCUS President Andrew Johnson and Congress often clashed over how the defeated South should be treated. Meanwhile, newly freed slaves faced many challenges and difficulties.

▼ The ruins of Richmond after the Civil War

READMISSION OF STATES TO THE UNION

Mar. 30, 1870 Date of readmission

VA *Jan. 26, 1870*
TN *July 24, 1866*
NC *June 25, 1868*
AR *June 22, 1868*
SC *June 25, 1868*
MS *Feb. 23, 1870*
TX *Mar. 30, 1870*
AL *June 25, 1868*
GA *July 15, 1870*
LA *June 25, 1868*
FL *June 25, 1868*

0   150   300 miles
0   150   300 kilometers

The South in Ruins

By the end of the Civil War, the South was a wasteland. Cities such as Richmond and Atlanta lay in ruins. Railroad tracks were ripped up. Blackened chimneys were all that remained of burned factories. Fields, once filled with crops, had been reclaimed by weeds. Clearly, the people of the South—black and white— needed help. The plan to rebuild the South became known as Reconstruction.

Presidential Plan

With Lincoln's death, Vice President Andrew Johnson became President. Johnson presented a plan, known as the presidential plan, for bringing the South back into the Union. First, 10 percent of voters in each state had to take an oath of loyalty to the Union. Second, each state had to form a new government, with a new constitution. Third, the states had to ratify, or formally approve, the Thirteenth Amendment to the Constitution, which outlawed slavery.

When Johnson became President, he began pardoning many of the Confederate leaders. Some of these leaders were even elected to Congress. This upset many members of Congress, especially a group known as Radical

▲ Andrew Johnson

Republicans. This group was also angered to hear that the new Southern governments were passing black codes—laws that limited the rights of black citizens. The codes declared, for example, that African Americans couldn't travel without passes, couldn't change jobs, and couldn't vote.

Congressional Plan

Radical Republicans and Johnson fought bitterly over Reconstruction. Under Republican leadership, Congress passed a plan for reconstruction. This plan called for the Union army to occupy the South. It got rid of the all-white state governments that were being formed in the South. New state constitutions were to be written by conventions made up of black Americans as well as white Americans. Also, former Confederate leaders could not vote or hold office.

Congress's plan also required all Southern states to ratify the Fourteenth Amendment to the Constitution. This amendment made African Americans citizens and promised them "equal protection of the laws." When a state did these things, it could rejoin the Union. Only then would the United States army leave that state.

Later, in 1870, Congress passed the Fifteenth Amendment. This said

---

 Reconstruction · The name given to the plan to rebuild the South following the Civil War, 1865–1877

Radical Republican A member of the Republican party who wanted to punish the South and give land to black citizens

black codes Southern laws passed after the Civil War, aimed at limiting the rights and opportunities of African Americans

that no state could keep a person from voting because of his race or color. However, at this time neither black nor white women were allowed to vote.

Reconstruction Brings Change

By 1870 all states in the South had rejoined the Union. African Americans held public office for the first time, although most officeholders were still white. Some African Americans served in state governments and in the United States Congress. Three were elected lieutenant governors. About half had been free blacks before the war, but the other half had been slaves just a few years earlier.

To help needy black citizens and white citizens in the South, Congress created the Freedmen's Bureau. Freedmen were former slaves. The bureau provided food, medical care, and legal advice. It set up schools and hospitals. Many Northern women who were once abolitionists went south to teach in bureau schools. They taught thousands of African Americans,

young and old, to read and write.

Unlike the teachers who came to the South to help, others came hoping to make money from the South's misery. Most Southerners didn't like these people and called them **carpetbaggers**. A carpetbag is a cheap suitcase made out of pieces of carpet. Southerners said these people hoped to fill their carpetbags with riches.

Anger in the South

Many Southerners disliked Reconstruction. They were opposed to having their former slaves take part in government, to giving equal rights to African Americans, and to sending black children to school. Some white Southerners formed secret societies, such as the Ku Klux Klan. These groups tried to frighten freed African Americans and their white supporters. Wearing white sheets, the Klan usually struck at night. They beat or killed people and burned down homes as well as black schools and churches.

▲ "The Carpet Bagger": song sheet music cover of 1869

☆ **carpetbagger** The name given to a Northern white person who moved to the South after the Civil War

◀ The first African American senators and representatives in the 41st and 42nd Congresses of the United States

The Newly Freed

Southern agriculture was in shambles after the war. Some freed black citizens left the plantations to find work elsewhere. Some went searching for relatives separated during the days of slavery. Many stayed on the plantations to work the fields.

Their former owners, however, couldn't pay them wages. The newly freed citizens had no money to pay rent, so each agreed to share at harvest time. The **sharecropper** would get some of the crop, and the landowner would get the rest.

This sounded fair, but it wasn't. African Americans had to go into debt to buy seeds and other materials. Their half of the crop was just enough to pay off this debt and provide food for their families. Without money the only way they could survive was to stay in their current arrangement. To them, sharecropping seemed like slavery, only with a different name.

The End of Reconstruction

Newly freed African Americans worked hard to improve their lives. Family and church were the foundations of community life. Churches provided help to the poor and others in need and also helped people learn to

▲ Primary school for Freedmen

read. Black churches did even more teaching than the Freedmen's schools. Much of the money used for education came from within the African American community itself.

In 1877 the last United States troops left the South. White citizens who wanted to return to the old ways now controlled the Southern states. Reconstruction was over. So, too, was the progress black citizens had made. Over the next 20 years, African Americans lost nearly every right they had won during Reconstruction. **Jim Crow laws** segregated, or separated, black citizens and white citizens in restaurants and other public places. New laws made it nearly impossible for black citizens to vote or hold office. It would be many years before African Americans would regain the rights they had lost.

 sharecropper   A person who farms land owned by another and gives part of the crop in return for seeds, tools, and other supplies

 Jim Crow laws   Laws that segregated and discriminated against African Americans

SUMMING UP

1 DO YOU REMEMBER . . .
COMPREHENSION

1. How did the battle of Bull Run change the North's attitude toward the war?

2. How did the Emancipation Proclamation change the focus of the war?

3. What similar attitude toward war did General Grant and General Sherman share?

4. Why was the draw between the *Monitor* and the *Merrimack* really a victory for the Union?

5. What causes were most Union and Confederate soldiers fighting for?

6. What was the cause of death for most Civil War soldiers?

7. Give examples of how Lincoln used his powers as President to do what he thought was right despite Congress's objections.

8. How did the Civil War place greater burdens on the South than on the North?

9. What were the purposes of the Thirteenth and Fourteenth Amendments?

10. Why did many white Southerners dislike Reconstruction?

2 SKILL POWER
ANALYZING A DOCUMENT

Analyzing the Gettysburg Address helped you understand how President Lincoln felt about the war and the United States. Find other documents, such as speeches, letters, or even legal documents. Analyze each document by asking what is the topic and what are the main ideas. Share your findings.

3 WHAT DO YOU THINK?
CRITICAL THINKING

1. Which of the North's three strategies for winning the war was most important? Explain.

2. Why was the battle of Gettysburg seen as the turning point in the Civil War?

3. Suppose you were a typical Civil War soldier. Tell how your attitudes toward the war probably changed over time.

4. Would you agree that the Emancipation Proclamation was only a start in the direction of freeing slaves? Explain.

5. Do you think Reconstruction would have been a success if the presidential plan had been followed?

4 SAY IT, WRITE IT, USE IT
VOCABULARY

Write five questions that you might have asked President Lincoln about the Civil War. Write the answers that Lincoln might have given. Use one or more of the vocabulary words in each question and answer.

black codes	inaugural address
blockade	Jim Crow laws
carpetbagger	Radical Republican
civil war	Reconstruction
Confederacy	Red Cross
defensive war	secede
Emancipation Proclamation	sharecropper
epidemic	

5 GEOGRAPHY AND YOU
MAP STUDY

Use the maps in this chapter to answer the following questions.

1. What slave states remained in the Union in 1861?

2. List the free states that stayed in the Union and the slave states that left the Union.

3. Make a list of the sites where battles were fought between the Union and Confederate forces.

4. In what states were the battles of Antietam and Gettysburg fought?

6 TAKE ACTION
CITIZENSHIP

During the Civil War, Northerners and Southerners alike raised money to aid injured troops. Today, citizens also raise money for worthwhile causes. Find out about an organization in your community that raises money to achieve its goals. Talk to a member of the group to find out more about this work. Then share what you learn with the class.

7 GET CREATIVE
MUSIC CONNECTION

"Battle Cry of Freedom" was written during the Civil War. It was a popular rallying song of the North. Soldiers sang it in battle, in camps, and on long marches. The Confederates also liked this spirited tune and had a version of their own. With a group of classmates, find the words, music, and a recording of this song as well as other songs that came out of the Civil War. After reading about and listening to the songs, choose a few and share them with your class.

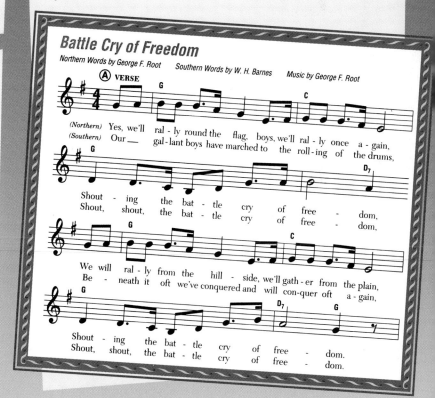

In the next chapter discover how people traveled westward and found new frontiers.

How Does Change Affect People's Lives?

How do changes that happened over 100 years ago still affect us? Identify ways in which industrialization changed people's lives. Learn how the nation expanded westward and far beyond its borders.

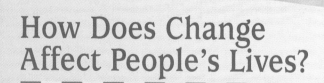

FRONTIERS OF

In the late 1800s, thousands of people journeyed westward and found new frontiers. Some went to find gold and strike it rich; others longed for the freedom of the open range or the opportunity to work a farm.

CONTENTS

▼ Do you know what this tool is used for? Read page 297 to find out.

THE WEST

These books tell about some people, places, and events of interest during the late 1800s. Read one that interests you and fill out a book-review form.

READ AND RESEARCH

A Boy Becomes a Man at Wounded Knee by Ted Wood with Wanbli Numpa Afraid of Hawk (Walker & Co., 1992)
Do you ever wonder about your ancestors of long ago? Follow Wanbli Numpa Afraid of Hawk, a Plains Indian boy, who takes a journey in memory of his ancestors. **(nonfiction)**
•*You can read a selection from this book on page 306.*

Cowboys of the Wild West
by Russell Freedman (Houghton Mifflin Co., 1985)
As you look at the photographs and read from the journals of real cowboys, try to experience what it was like to drive a herd of cattle from Texas to Montana over 100 years ago. **(nonfiction)**

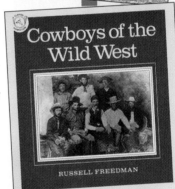

Ten Mile Day and the Building of the Transcontinental Railroad by Mary Ann Fraser (Henry Holt & Co., 1993)
Throughout the construction of the first transcontinental railroad, the Central Pacific workers boasted to the Union Pacific workers that they could lay ten miles of track in one day. Will they achieve their goal? **(nonfiction)**

Between Two Worlds by Candice F. Ransom (Scholastic, 1994)
Read how Sarah Winnemucca, granddaughter of a Native American chief, lived and traveled with a white family. Find out how she used her understanding of two cultures to work for peace "between two worlds." **(fiction)**

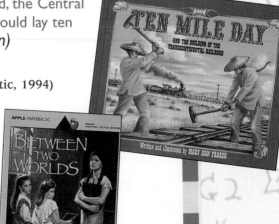

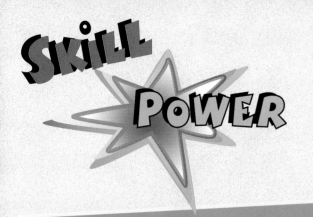

Using a Special-Purpose Map

Knowing how to use special-purpose maps helps you learn important facts about places.

UNDERSTAND IT

Have you eaten any bread today? What about pizza, or cookies, or cake? Did you know that the main ingredient in these foods is wheat, the grain that is milled into flour?

Before 1860 most Americans ate wheat that was grown close to home. That changed as more and more farmers began moving onto the Great Plains. The flat prairie land was ideal for wheat growing. As you can see from the special-purpose map on page 293, the Great Plains became America's "breadbasket."

EXPLORE IT

Special-purpose maps are full of useful information. They're easy to use, too. The first thing to do is read the map's title because it will tell you the purpose of the map. What is the purpose of the map on page 293?

Next, check the map key to see what the map symbols stand for. Does the map key on page 293 use drawings, colors, or shapes as symbols?

To answer these questions, study the map and its key together.

• How many bushels of wheat does Oklahoma produce each year?

• Which state produces the most wheat?

• How many states produce more than 100 million bushels of wheat a year?

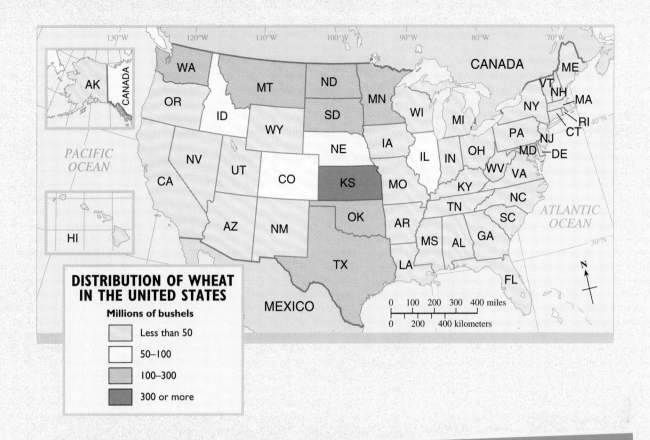

DISTRIBUTION OF WHEAT IN THE UNITED STATES

Millions of bushels

- Less than 50
- 50–100
- 100–300
- 300 or more

TRY IT

With a group of classmates, make a special-purpose map. Show something that interests you and your group. You might show the best recreation areas in your community or county, or you might show the best places to eat. On a map of the United States, you could show natural wonders, the cities of professional sports teams, or places where endangered animals live.

When you have agreed on an idea, find information for your map in reference books or at the library. Then create symbols for your map key. For example, if your map shows professional baseball teams, you could use one color for the American League and a second color for the National League. Or your symbols could be a bat for one league and a ball for the other.

SKILL POWER SEARCH Look through this chapter. How many special-purpose maps can you find? What does each one show?

Setting the Scene

KEY TERMS
forty-niner
Great Plains
vaquero
treaty
reservation

NEW FRONTIERS

FOCUS *People in the middle and late 1800s found new frontiers to conquer in the West. Their achievements, however, came at great cost to the Native Americans and Mexicans already living there.*

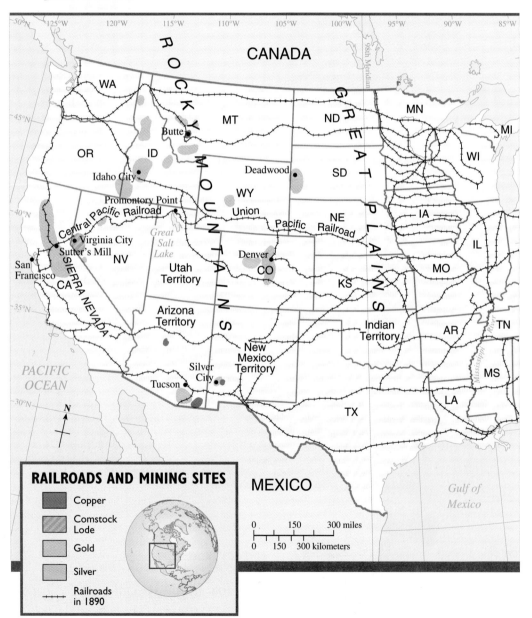

RAILROADS AND MINING SITES

- Copper
- Comstock Lode
- Gold
- Silver
- +++ Railroads in 1890

0   150   300 miles
0   150   300 kilometers

The West Expands

What exactly was the "West"? For many Americans it was the frontier. Life in the West meant danger and hard work. But it also meant excitement, discovery, and a new beginning.

In the mid-1800s the West began at the 98th meridian. As you can see on the map, this line of longitude ran from eastern North Dakota down through Texas. Over the next 50 years, however, there would be many frontiers. Read on to learn about three of them.

The Mining Frontier

Early in 1848, James Marshall stumbled on gold in a California stream at a place called Sutter's Mill. John Sutter, the owner of the land, and Marshall, whom Sutter had hired to build a sawmill, wanted to keep their discovery a secret. But by the middle of 1848, word had spread to the eastern United States, Europe, and the rest of

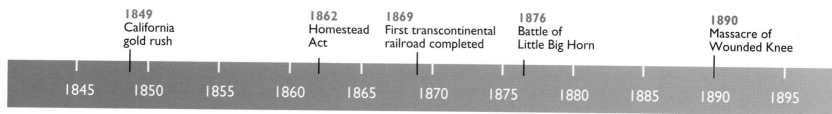

1849
California
gold rush

1862
Homestead
Act

1869
First transcontinental
railroad completed

1876
Battle of
Little Big Horn

1890
Massacre of
Wounded Knee

1845   1850   1855   1860   1865   1870   1875   1880   1885   1890   1895

the world. People dashed to California, hoping to make their fortunes. The great gold rush was on!

Getting to California

There was no easy way to get to California. Some gold-seekers traveled overland by wagon. While this was cheap, the trip took up to eight months. Others went by clipper ship, a fast ship that "clipped" travel time, around the tip of South America. This was more expensive and still took up to eight months. Some sailed to the east coast of Panama and then crossed the 40 miles of hot, mosquito-filled jungles by mule to the west coast, on the Pacific Ocean. From there they took a ship to California. People came by the thousands. In 1849 alone, more than 80,000 "gold rushers" arrived. They became known as the **forty-niners**.

People also went to California to sell things that miners wanted. A Boston woman made a small fortune baking and selling pies. A German immigrant, Levi Strauss, made work pants, later called Levis, for miners.

 forty-niner A person who went to California in 1849 to find gold

Boom Towns and Ghost Towns

Miners hoped to "strike it rich." A few did, but most failed. Only a little of the gold could be panned from riverbeds. The rest was deeply embedded in rock. Getting it out required costly equipment—the kind of equipment that only mining companies could afford. Miners often ended up working for hourly wages at mining companies.

Others decided to give up mining and stayed in California. As a result, some Mexicans who had lived there for generations were forced off their land. Mexicans fought back or went to court to save their land. These attempts were often unsuccessful.

Gold-seekers shoveled silt or dirt into strainers to sift out the gold.

295

When someone did find gold, a boom town popped up almost overnight. This happened in California, Colorado, and Nevada. For a while everything boomed. Stores, hotels, and other businesses opened. Some towns, like Denver, Colorado, survived the gold rush. Others didn't. When the gold ran out, people packed up and left, leaving a ghost town in their wake.

The Ranching Frontier

The farming and ranching frontiers could not have been opened without railroads. Railroads linked the resources of the West to the markets in the East. The first transcontinental railroad was completed in 1869. Before long, a web of railroad lines crisscrossed the nation, as shown on the map on page 294. Over 100,000 miles of track were built between 1877 and 1893. The golden

age of the railroad had arrived.

When the mining frontier opened, Americans played a kind of leapfrog. They had already settled between the Atlantic coast and the Mississippi River. They now leaped over the **Great Plains** to settle in Oregon and California.

The section they leaped over was sometimes called the Great American Desert. With little rain and few trees, this grassy land *did* seem like a desert. But in the late 1860s, Americans took a second look, and they saw a land of opportunity.

Ranchers first saw the possibilities of the Great Plains. Because of the growth of the railroads, ranchers no longer had to graze their cattle in Texas and then risk them on long cattle drives to the railroads in Missouri. Routes for some cattle

---

★ *Great Plains*   A region west of the Mississippi River that stretches westward to the Rocky Mountains

▼ Covered wagons and the first transcontinental steam train were at Promontory Point, Utah, on May 10, 1869.

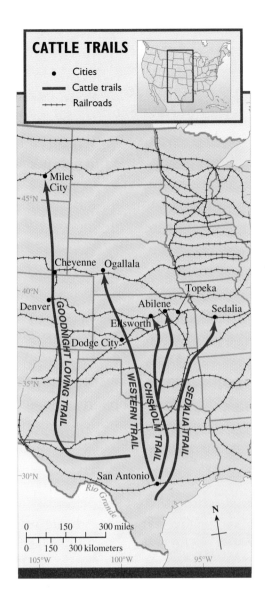

CATTLE TRAILS

- Cities
— Cattle trails
++ Railroads

0 150 300 miles
0 150 300 kilometers

The Western Cowboy

Ranching had created a new kind of American—the cowboy. In the days of cattle drives, cowboys rounded up the cattle and drove them to railroad centers. This dangerous work attracted young men looking for adventure.

The origins of the American cowboy were very diverse—a mixture of Spanish, Mexican, Native American, African American, and European American cultures. The western cowboy adopted the dress and many of the Spanish words and skills of the Mexican cowboy, or **vaquero** (vah KER-oh). American cowboys wore *sombreros (*sahm BRER ohz*)*, or wide-brimmed hats, to shield themselves from the sun. To protect their legs from the brush, they wore *chaparejos* (chap uh RAY hohs), or simply *chaps*. They also roped cattle with *lassos* or *lariats*.

The Farming Frontier

In the 1860s, farmers also began settling the Great Plains. They came because the Homestead Act of 1862 promised 160 acres *free* to qualified persons who would live on the land and farm it for five years.

Life was harsh in this treeless land, and the weather ranged from brutal cold to extreme heat. However, free land was

drives are shown on the map above. Prairie grass would support cattle, and by the 1860s, ranchers were turning the Great Plains into a "cattle kingdom." Their cattle roamed freely across the open range. Ranchers kept track of their animals by branding them with unique designs. (The girl pictured on page 290 is holding a branding iron.)

⭐ **vaquero** A Mexican cattle herder

▼ One famous cowboy was Nat Love, known as Deadwood Dick. Born into slavery, he became a legend for his roping and shooting talents.

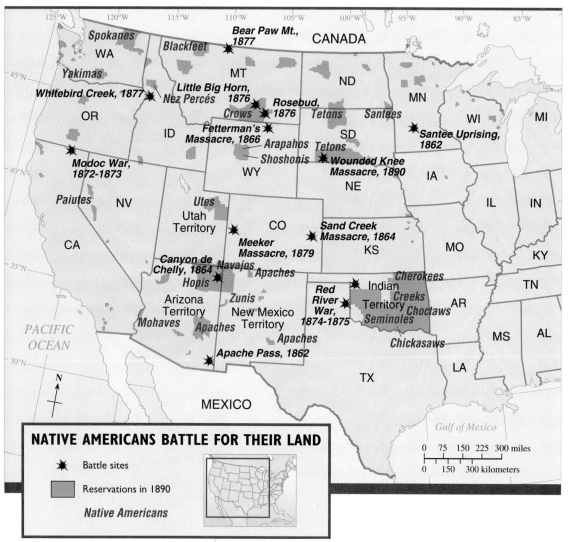

NATIVE AMERICANS BATTLE FOR THEIR LAND

* Battle sites

Reservations in 1890

Native Americans

Native Americans Are Forced From Their Lands

To many Americans the West seemed to be full of great open fields just waiting for them. To Native Americans it looked very different. In 1867 there were nearly 250,000 Native Americans living on the Great Plains. It was only natural that the Plains Indians would try to fight off the pioneers. Settlers had treated the Native Americans poorly, taking their land and killing the animals they depended on for their livelihood.

Treaties were set up by the United States government to prevent war. The government promised not to disturb Native American hunting and sacred grounds, and Native Americans promised not to bother incoming settlers. Unfortunately, individual settlers and Native Americans either did not know or did not care about the promises made by their leaders. White Americans who were eager to own land or to find gold began moving onto Native American land and claiming it as their own. Angrily, Native Americans fought back.

hard to turn down. By the 1870s, thousands had staked their claims. Most homesteaders were Swedes, Germans, Danes, other Europeans, and African Americans.

Within a few decades these pioneers turned the Great American Desert into the Great American Breadbasket—a productive grain-growing region.

 treaty A formal agreement between two nations

Putting Up a Fight

In the late 1860s the United States government forced many Native Americans to live on **reservations**. Army soldiers were sent west to make sure they settled where they were supposed to. For Native Americans this was a disaster. The reservations were set up on dry, barren lands. Besides, some Native Americans didn't want to give up lands where they had lived, hunted, and buried their dead.

Many decided to fight. Between 1868 and 1875, Native Americans and army soldiers fought 200 battles. Some of the battles are shown on the map on page 298. In 1876, General George Custer tried to push the Tetons out of South Dakota. On June 25, Chiefs Sitting Bull and Crazy Horse fought Custer at the Little Bighorn River. Custer and all of his men were killed.

A Way of Life Ends

The battle of Little Bighorn was the last great victory for Native Americans. White hunters were killing buffaloes at an unbelievable rate, and Native Americans were losing their food supply. Some Native Americans died in battle; others starved to death.

---

reservation A piece of public land set aside by the government for the use of a particular group of people

By 1877 more and more Native Americans were giving up. That year the great Nez Percé leader Chief Joseph laid down his weapons.

By 1885 almost every Native American had been forced onto a reservation. In 1886 the Apache leader Geronimo was captured.

Finally, in 1890 came the Massacre of Wounded Knee in South Dakota. Here army soldiers killed hundreds of Teton men, women, and children. It was the last time the Plains Indians would fight. From then on they either lived on the reservations or tried to adapt to white society. Either way, most lived in poverty. Their old way of life would never be the same.

I am tired of fighting. . . . My heart is sick and sad. From where the sun now stands, I will fight no more forever.—**Chief Joseph**

▲ Chief Joseph was leader of the Nez Percé Indians.

SHOW WHAT YOU KNOW!

REFOCUS
COMPREHENSION

1. What were three important frontiers in the settlement of the West?

2. In what ways did the Great Plains provide opportunities for both farmers and ranchers?

THINK ABOUT IT
CRITICAL THINKING

Why was it so important to build a transcontinental railroad?

WRITE ABOUT IT
ACTIVITY

Write a paragraph about how the lives of Native Americans changed as miners and white settlers moved westward.

You Are There

KEY TERMS

prairie
sod
homesteader
drought

GROWING UP ON THE FRONTIER

FOCUS *It's one thing to hear wonderful stories and read attractive posters about the western prairie. But what was life really like from one day to the next?*

▼ Advertisements for land, such as this one from 1875, helped lure people to the Great Plains.

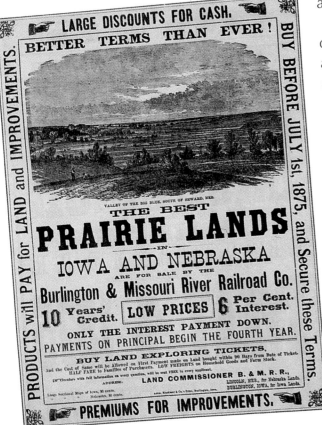

Moving West

"Oh give me a home, where the buffalo roam. . . ." According to the songwriter, a "Home on the Range" would be wonderful. Deer would frolic, and the sky would always be blue. Compare this image with the life you would *really* lead as a child on the frontier. How accurate is the song?

Whether you came because of advertisements or stories of others, here you are, surrounded by nothing but dry, wind-swept **prairie** grass.

A Roof Over Your Head

The first thing your family needs is shelter. With few trees on the Great Plains, how will you build a home? You might live in a dugout—a hole dug into a hillside.

Your family builds it using the only tools they have—an ax, a shovel, and a pick. The inside of the dugout is damp and dark, but at least it protects you from the sun and wind.

Later perhaps your family builds a more comfortable home made from chunks of **sod**, or grass-covered dirt. This home is called a "soddie," and you are a "sod-buster." Like the dugout, the soddie stays cool in summer and warm in winter, and it is fireproof.

But a soddie is so dirty! Bits of earth fall from the ceiling. Dirt gets in your hair, your eyes, your food. Eventually your mother tacks up cheesecloth to catch the crumbling dirt. Still, you have to watch out for field mice and snakes that tunnel right through the earth into your home.

You also have to worry about rain. Although good for the crops, rain turns the floor of your soddie to mud and makes everything you own wet and musty.

Work, Work, Work

Your family now turns its attention to farming. Boys help their fathers with outdoor chores—plowing fields,

---

★ **prairie** A large area of level or rolling grassland

★ **sod** A layer of turf containing grass plants and matted roots

A family poses outside their sod house.

digging wells, and putting up barbed wire fences. Girls help churn butter, wash clothes, prepare meals, and preserve all the food needed for the long winter. In addition, your mother makes clothing, quilts, soap, candles, and other goods. Women also collect cattle and buffalo droppings. Since there is no wood to burn, families use these dried "cow chips" for fuel.

Sometimes, when you look around your new homestead, you can hardly believe it is yours. You have acres and acres to call your own. Here, far from the crowded cities, you enjoy the clean air and star-filled skies.

At times, though, your new life seems lonely.

Quilts, such as this one for a baby, were often made by women as they traveled westward.

Your nearest neighbor might be a mile or more away. Your only playmates are your brothers and sisters. How excited you are when your family gets together with other **homesteaders** for special occasions or to work together on tasks such as quilting, sewing, and house building.

Changes and Challenges

As time goes on, life changes. More people arrive, and towns spring up. A school might be within a few miles of your home.

You go to school in a one-room building with a dirt floor. Students of all ages are in the same room with one teacher. The youngest are three or four years old, and the oldest are

---

★ **homesteader** A person who received land under the Homestead Act of 1862

sometimes older than the teacher. You don't start school until November, because you work on the harvest. Books and materials are very scarce, and you have to share with other children. There is usually no paper available, so your writing is done on a slate. You might even practice tracing your letters on the dirt floor of your schoolhouse or on the ground outside.

In time, railroad tracks might pass near your land, and telegraph wires might bring you messages from people back east. Your family may even have built a wooden house out of lumber carried in on trains. Still, life remains challenging. You never know when a tornado will blow across your land or when a swarm of grasshoppers will wipe out your crops. **Drought** is almost always a problem. Homesteaders may love their way of life, but is it really like that old song "Home on the Range"?

▼ Shop owners stand in front of their shops in 1894.

 drought A long period of extremely dry weather

SHOW WHAT YOU KNOW!

REFOCUS
COMPREHENSION

1. What were some advantages and disadvantages of a sod house?

2. List some ways you think frontier settlers dealt with loneliness.

THINK ABOUT IT
CRITICAL THINKING

Analyze how your everyday life is different from that of a child growing up on the Great Plains in the late 1800s.

WRITE ABOUT IT
ACTIVITY

Suppose that you have moved to the Great Plains in the late 1800s. Write a short description of your new home and new life. Include what your hopes and fears in this new place are.

3 Connections

⭐ **KEY TERMS**

barbed wire
dry farming
Bessemer process

📖 **LITERATURE**

A Boy Becomes a Man at Wounded Knee

FARMING, INVENTIONS, AND RAILROADS

FOCUS *The development of new frontiers posed many problems. Americans came up with creative solutions to these problems and also created new opportunities.*

A Tough People

The homesteaders who settled the Great Plains were a tough and resourceful lot. After all, these were the people who made homes out of dirt and burned cow and buffalo chips for fuel. As they struggled to survive on the Great Plains, they began to find solutions for the problems they faced.

Farmers needed to fence in their land. If they didn't, the cattle that wandered freely across the range would destroy their crops. But without wood, how could they build fences? They tried growing hedges and putting up plain wire. But neither worked well.

Then, in 1874, Joseph Glidden introduced **barbed wire**, which had sharp points every few inches. After a few scrapes, cattle learned to stay away from barbed wire fences.

By 1883 the Barb Fence Company was producing 600 miles of barbed

⭐ **barbed wire** A type of wire that has barbs, or sharp points, every few inches

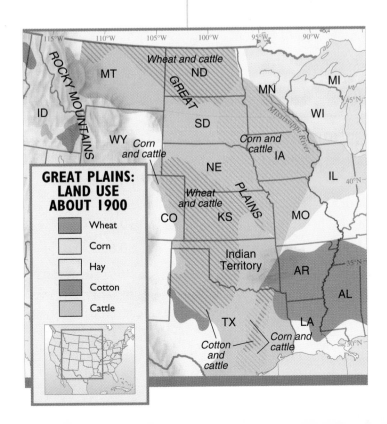

GREAT PLAINS: LAND USE ABOUT 1900

- Wheat
- Corn
- Hay
- Cotton
- Cattle

Wheat and cattle — ND
Corn and cattle — WY
Wheat and cattle — CO, KS
Corn and cattle — IA
Cotton and cattle — TX
Corn and cattle — LA

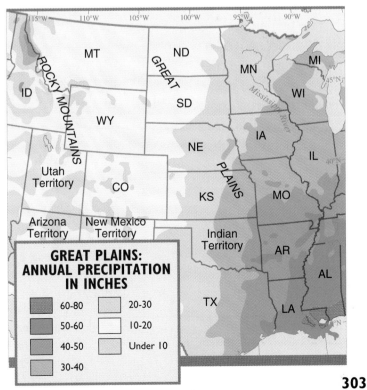

GREAT PLAINS: ANNUAL PRECIPITATION IN INCHES

- 60-80
- 50-60
- 40-50
- 30-40
- 20-30
- 10-20
- Under 10

Utah Territory
Arizona Territory
New Mexico Territory
Indian Territory

FARMERS FRIEND STEEL GRAIN DRILL.

FARMERS FRIEND.

◀ This is an 1893 advertisement for a steel grain drill, a machine used to make holes in the soil for seeds.

wire a day. The fencing needs of farmers had created a whole new industry.

Water Needs

The map on the right on page 303 shows that water was scarce on the Great Plains. With constant prairie winds a windmill could pump water for drinking, cooking, and washing.

For irrigating their fields, farmers adopted a method known as **dry farming**. Furrows, or small ditches, about a foot deep were dug on each side of a row of plants to collect rain. After a rainfall, the farmer quickly turned over the soil to move the wet soil closer to the roots of the plants. Farmers also switched to kinds of wheat and other crops that needed less water.

Machines and Steel

Homesteaders faced another problem—the rock-hard soil. Old wooden plows

couldn't make a dent in the thick matted roots of the prairie grass. John Deere's steel-bladed plow solved that problem. Other inventions, such as the mechanized grain drill, the reaper, and the thresher, made planting and harvesting easier. Producing farm machinery soon became a major industry.

Steel made the rapid growth of the West possible. Stronger than iron, it was needed for farm machinery and strong railroad tracks. To make steel quickly and cheaply, William "Pig Iron" Kelly of Kentucky and Henry Bessemer of England, working separately, came up with the same method. Although Kelly discovered it first, the new method became known as the **Bessemer process**. Steel factories in the East soon produced vast amounts of steel at low prices.

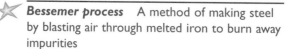

Harvesting: By Hand and By Machine

| | Time Worked | | Labor Cost | |
Crop	By Hand	By Machine	By Hand	By Machine
Corn	39 hours	15 hours	$3.62	$1.51
Hay	21 hours	4 hours	$1.75	$0.42
Wheat	61 hours	3 hours	$3.55	$0.66

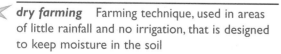

★ **dry farming** Farming technique, used in areas of little rainfall and no irrigation, that is designed to keep moisture in the soil

★ **Bessemer process** A method of making steel by blasting air through melted iron to burn away impurities

A Cheyenne family prepares to move.

Tying the Nation Together

The building of railroads didn't end with Promontory Point (see caption on page 296). By 1893 five transcontinental railroads had been completed.

Railroads were important to the economic development of the West. Many towns and cities had train stations. The railroads helped lure so many people to the West that nine new states joined the United States between 1867 and 1896.

Railroad building also created many jobs. Tens of thousands of workers were needed to lay the tracks. Thousands more worked in mills, producing the steel needed for farm machinery, tracks, and railroad cars.

The completed railroads opened up markets for products. Lumber from Oregon, minerals from California, and cattle from the Great Plains headed east. Eastern products such as stoves, clothing, and furniture headed west. Railroads were an economic boom for the East as well as the West.

Winners and Losers

Not everyone, however, was a winner. As you read on pages 298 and 299, Native Americans fought many battles and lost much land. Also, during the 1870s, millions of buffaloes were killed. These animals had provided Plains Indians with meat for food, bones for tools, and hides for clothing and shelter.

Ways of life and industries were also affected. New industries often killed old ones. Barbed wire put an end to the open range and the cowboy's way of life. Who wanted a wooden plow after trying a steel-bladed one? The railroad meant the end of the stagecoach and the overland wagon. Why take the Oregon Trail when you could just hop on the Northern Pacific Railroad?

Spikes such as this were used in laying railroad tracks.

A Boy Becomes a Man at Wounded Knee

Ted Wood with Wanbli Numpa Afraid of Hawk

This story is about a boy who travels to Wounded Knee with his father. Read about why his father decides to trace the steps of his ancestors.

My name is Wanbli Numpa Afraid of Hawk. I am an Oglala Lakota and in the old language my name means Two Eagles. I live with my family on the Cheyenne River Reservation in South Dakota, near Cherry Creek. Our house is only a few miles from the Cheyenne River, where Big Foot and his people lived.

My dad, Rocke, and my lala (grandfather) started telling me about Big Foot and his walk to Wounded Knee five years ago, when I was four years old. They told me that my great-lala was with Big Foot at Wounded Knee. He was only ten years old, almost my age. When the soldiers started shooting, he hid in a creek gully, my dad said. Bullets were flying everywhere, but he didn't get shot. Then he ran up the creek and escaped into the hills.

. . . even after all these years our people were still in pain from Wounded Knee, my dad said, and he wanted to do something to help. So five years ago, he went with my uncles, Alex White Plume and Birgil Kills Straight, to see a medicine man named Curtis Kills Ree. They asked Curtis what could be done to end the Lakota's sadness.

The medicine man told them that the massacre had broken the sacred hoop of the world. The hoop is the unity of all life for the Lakota. When our people were killed at Wounded Knee, there was such sadness that the Lakota people lost their way for one hundred years. They forgot how to be strong together as a tribe. To mend the sacred hoop, he said, my dad and uncles had to take horses and wagons on the same path Big Foot and his people traveled. They had to leave at the same time Big Foot left, travel the same way his people did, sleep in the same places, and feel the same cold. They had to do this five times for five years. The last year would be the one hundredth anniversary of the massacre, and then the hoop would be mended. The journeys would wipe away the tears of sadness so that Lakota children, like me, could lead the Lakota as one tribe into the future.

The first four winters, I watched my dad leave with our horses for the ride. I wanted to go so much, but I was too young. It was a hard and dangerous ride. But in the winter of 1990, I was eight years old and I was strong enough to go. For four years I had prepared for this and now it was time to become a man.

You can find out about the journey of Wanbli Numpa Afraid of Hawk by checking the book out of your school or public library.

SHOW WHAT YOU KNOW!

REFOCUS
COMPREHENSION

1. How did farmers solve the problem of scarce water?

2. How did steel making and railroads contribute to the development of the West?

THINK ABOUT IT
CRITICAL THINKING

How, do you think, would the settlement of the West have been different if there had not been railroads?

WRITE ABOUT IT
ACTIVITY

Write a paragraph describing how you might have felt as you started out on the journey of the boy in the story.

OPENING THE WEST

FOCUS *Miners came in search of precious metals, homesteaders took the offer of free land, railroads streamed across the land, and new industries expanded rapidly.*

SILVER DISCOVERED

In 1859 two miners named Pete O'Reilly and Pat McLaughlin headed for Nevada looking for gold. There, a man named Henry Comstock became their partner. One day O'Reilly and McLaughlin dug up some heavy blue-colored rock. They showed it to a couple of Californians, who saw that the rock was filled with silver. These men didn't share the news. Instead, they offered to buy the land for a few thousand dollars.

O'Reilly, McLaughlin, and Comstock were delighted. They thought it was a terrific deal. It wasn't! Over the next 20 years, the land, now known as the Comstock Lode, would produce $300 million worth of silver.

FREE LAND

Pay a ten-dollar filing fee, agree to live on the land for five consecutive years, and you can have 160 free acres of land. The Homestead Act of 1862 made this offer to American citizens and immigrants alike. Immigrants had to plan to become citizens.

If you were a married woman, you couldn't file a claim. However, if you were a single woman or a widow, this offer was for you!

"COW TOWN" SPRINGS UP

Joseph McCoy wanted to build a cow town. He hoped to ship cattle, driven up the Chisholm Trail from Texas, to cities in the East by railroad. In early 1867 he bought the tiny town of Abilene, Kansas, for a very low price. In just 60 days he built a stockyard, a barn, and a hotel. That September, McCoy sent 20 carloads of cattle to Chicago. Soon, Abilene was booming.

1857	1859	1861	1863	1865	1867	1869	1871	1873

1859
Silver discovered at Comstock Lode

1862
Homestead Act

1867
Joseph McCoy buys Abilene, Kansas

1869
Transcontinental railroad completed

1873
Levi Strauss patents denim pants

ONE TOUGH PAIR OF PANTS

When German immigrant Levi Strauss arrived in San Francisco in 1853, he had some canvas with him. He hoped to use it to make tents. But it turned out to be the wrong kind of canvas. Then one day a gold miner told him that good rugged pants were impossible to find. Strauss got an idea. Why not use his canvas to make some pants?

The miner loved the thick, stiff pants. Soon other miners wanted "those pants of Levi's." Strauss was in business. He began to use a blue-colored cloth—and the famous American "blue jean" was born. Finally, in 1873, Levi Strauss received a patent for his blue denim pants with the copper rivets.

EAST MEETS WEST

On May 10, 1869, the Union Pacific and the Central Pacific railroads finally met at Promontory Point in Utah. To symbolize the linkup, Leland Stanford, the governor of California, tried to drive in a golden spike. On his first attempt he missed the spike. But his second swing was right on target. The workers, mostly Irish, Mexican, and Chinese, cheered and waved their hats. People could now ride all the way across the country on "the iron horse."

SHOW WHAT YOU KNOW!

REFOCUS
COMPREHENSION

1. How did homesteaders get free land?

2. Why was Levi Strauss so successful in selling jeans?

THINK ABOUT IT
CRITICAL THINKING

Why, do you think, did the builders use a golden spike to link the two tracks at Promontory Point in 1869?

WRITE ABOUT IT
ACTIVITY

Write a paragraph stating why you would or would not go west to look for gold or silver.

309

SUMMING UP

1 DO YOU REMEMBER . . .
COMPREHENSION

1. Why was California settled so rapidly in the late 1840s?

2. What was the Great American Desert?

3. Why did so many farmers begin settling the Great Plains in the late 1860s?

4. Why didn't Native Americans want to live on reservations?

5. What did American cowboys borrow from Mexican *vaqueros*?

6. What happened at the battle of Little Bighorn?

7. How did the invention of barbed wire affect the cowboys' way of life?

8. How did railroads help open the frontier?

9. What was the Comstock Lode?

10. What happened at Promontory Point in Utah?

2 SKILL POWER
USING A SPECIAL-PURPOSE MAP

In this chapter, special-purpose maps helped provide you with information. Can you find more examples of special-purpose maps? Team up with a partner, visit your school or public library, and start your search. Share what you find with the rest of your class.

3 WHAT DO YOU THINK?
CRITICAL THINKING

1. Why, do you think, was the work of cowboys described as "dangerous"?

2. Why, do you think, did the United States government pass the Homestead Act?

3. What might settlers have done to treat Native Americans in the West more fairly?

4. Would you rather be a miner in the West in the 1870s or a homesteader on the Great Plains? Explain.

5. Would you agree that "the West was built with steel"? Explain why.

4 SAY IT, WRITE IT, USE IT
VOCABULARY

Write a conversation between two travelers heading westward on the new transcontinental railroad. Describe what they see and talk about as they travel. Use as many vocabulary words as possible in your conversation.

barbed wire	homesteader
Bessemer process	prairie
drought	reservation
dry farming	sod
forty-niner	treaty
Great Plains	*vaquero*

CHAPTER 13

5 GEOGRAPHY AND YOU
MAP STUDY

Use the map below to answer the following questions.

1. What lake is located in the Utah Territory?

2. What are the southernmost territories shown on the map?

3. What is the name of the mountain range in California?

4. What towns, states, and territories would you pass through traveling on the railroad from Denver to San Francisco?

6 TAKE ACTION
CITIZENSHIP

Unfortunately, the land-hungry settlers in the West often ignored or didn't know about the treaties their government had made with Native Americans. Are people in your community ever unaware or unsure of certain laws? Talk to a police officer or other official about laws that people most often misunderstand. Then make posters to describe these laws and explain why they're important. Try to find a public place to hang your posters.

7 GET CREATIVE
COMPUTER CONNECTION

New inventions—like barbed wire, farm equipment, and cheap steel—revolutionized the lives of farmers on the plains. Similarly, the invention of the computer is revolutionizing many areas of our life today. Choose one area of life—business, education, communications, entertainment—and list several ways in which computers have changed it.

LOOKING AHEAD In the next chapter you can explore some of the many inventions that changed the world.

THE MACHINE

Have you ever been disappointed when the power was out and you couldn't turn on a lamp, or when the phone lines were down and you couldn't use the phone? This chapter is about many of the amazing inventions of the late nineteenth century.

CONTENTS

Does this early telephone look like the first phone? Look on page 327 to see the first phone.

AGE

These books tell about some people, places, and events of interest during the Machine Age. Read one that interests you and fill out a book-review form.

READ AND RESEARCH

The Real McCoy: The Life of an African American Inventor by Wendy Towle (Scholastic, 1993)

Have you ever heard the expression "the real McCoy"? Learn about Elijah McCoy, an African American inventor, and find out why his name means "perfection." *(biography)*

Thomas Edison and Electricity by Steve Parker (Chelsea House, 1995)

Can you picture your life without electric lights and movies? Read about these and many other uses for electricity that Thomas Edison found. *(biography)*

Click! A Story About George Eastman by Barbara Mitchell (Carolrhoda Books, 1986)

When George Eastman was young, it took 50 pounds of equipment just to take a picture! Later, his Kodak camera made taking a picture as simple as pushing a button. *(biography)*

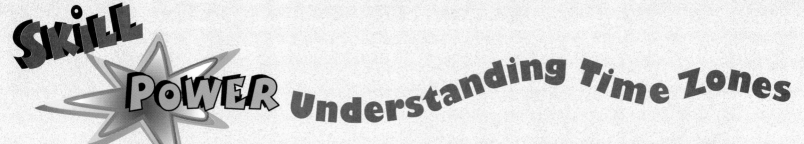

SKILL POWER Understanding Time Zones

When you understand time zones, you can figure out what time it is anywhere in the world.

UNDERSTAND IT

Our planet spins on an axis, so when it's morning on one side of Earth it's evening on the other side. Long ago, people used the sun to tell time. But as communication and travel increased, people wanted more exact ways of telling time.

So in 1884 the world was divided into 24 standard time zones. To help keep track of these 24 time zones, there are two special longitude lines—the prime meridian and the international date line. The prime meridian passes through Greenwich, England. By international agreement, time around the world is measured against Greenwich time. The international date line is where the date changes. The date east of this line is one day earlier than the date west of it. When it is Tuesday, May 12, on the east side of the line, it is Wednesday, May 13, on the west side.

A sundial

EXPLORE IT

When people travel east, they set their watches ahead one hour for each time zone they enter. When they travel west, they set their watches back one hour for each time zone. A traveler going from Los Angeles to Miami enters three time zones and sets his or her watch ahead three hours.

When it is 3:00 P.M. in Nairobi, Kenya, what time is it in Lima, Peru? Locate both places on the map. Begin at Nairobi and subtract one hour for each time zone to the west. When it's 3:00 P.M. in Nairobi, it's 2:00 P.M. in Johannesburg, 1:00 P.M. in Oslo, noon in London, and so on. It's 7:00 A.M. in Lima, Peru.

The arrow shows the direction in which Earth spins.

If you leave Mexico City at 3:00 P.M. for a five-hour flight to Miami, what time will it be when you arrive? Begin by adding five hours of flight time to the present time. It will be 8:00 P.M. in Mexico City when you arrive in Miami. Now look at the map to see what time it will be in Miami.

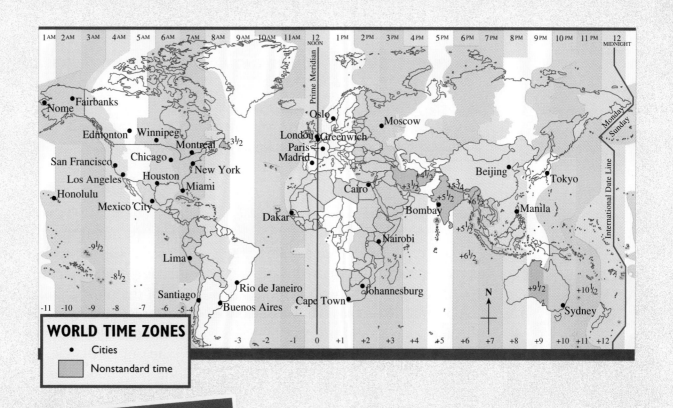

WORLD TIME ZONES

- • Cities
- Nonstandard time

Map labels: Nome, Fairbanks, Edmonton, Winnipeg, Montreal, San Francisco, Chicago, Houston, New York, Los Angeles, Honolulu, Miami, Mexico City, Lima, Santiago, Rio de Janeiro, Buenos Aires, Cape Town, Oslo, London, Greenwich, Paris, Madrid, Moscow, Cairo, Dakar, Nairobi, Johannesburg, Bombay, Beijing, Tokyo, Manila, Sydney

Time headings: 1 AM, 2 AM, 3 AM, 4 AM, 5 AM, 6 AM, 7 AM, 8 AM, 9 AM, 10 AM, 11 AM, 12 NOON, Prime Meridian, 1 PM, 2 PM, 3 PM, 4 PM, 5 PM, 6 PM, 7 PM, 8 PM, 9 PM, 10 PM, 11 PM, 12 MIDNIGHT

Offsets: -11, -10, -9, -8, -7, -6, -5, -4, -3, -2, -1, 0, +1, +2, +3, +4, +5, +6, +7, +8, +9, +10, +11, +12

Nonstandard: $-9\frac{1}{2}$, $-8\frac{1}{2}$, $-3\frac{1}{2}$, $+3\frac{1}{2}$, $+4\frac{1}{2}$, $+5\frac{1}{2}$, $+5\frac{3}{4}$, $+6\frac{1}{2}$, $+9\frac{1}{2}$, $+10\frac{1}{2}$

International Date Line — Monday / Sunday

N

TRY IT

You need to call someone in another city—a museum director in Winnipeg, Canada; an artist in Tokyo, Japan; or a movie star in Buenos Aires, Argentina. What is a good time of day to call? Remember, people may be grouchy in the middle of the night! Find your time zone on the map and decide when to call.

Write down the place that you are calling, and the time of your call in both locations. Take turns with your classmates telling about your calls.

Houston Cairo Manila Sydney

SKILL

POWER SEARCH
Look in this chapter to find out why time zones were created.

The Nation Industrializes

FOCUS *Before the Civil War the United States had few factories. By about 1900 the United States had become the world's leading industrial nation.*

Celebrating the Centennial

In 1876 the United States celebrated its *centennial*, or hundredth birthday, by having the Centennial Exposition. The exposition was held in Philadelphia. It ran from May to November and was a huge success. On some days over 200,000 people attended. Before it ended, one out of every five Americans had visited it.

These visitors saw hundreds of amazing new machines and gadgets. Two of the most popular exhibits were the Corliss steam engine and the telephone invented by Americans.

The Corliss engine, built by George Corliss of Rhode Island, provided

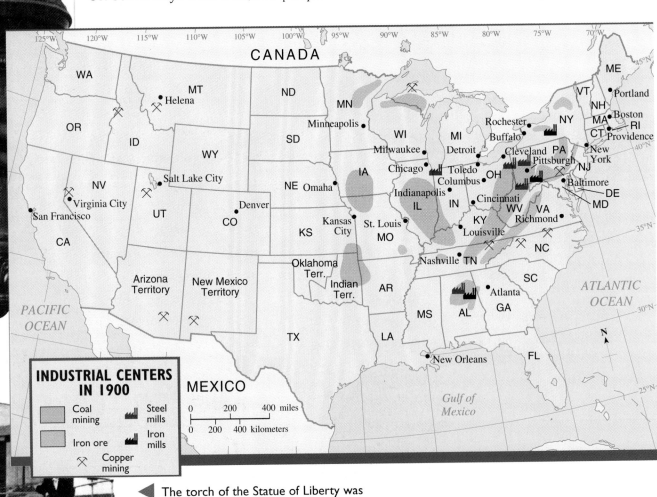

INDUSTRIAL CENTERS IN 1900

- Coal mining
- Iron ore
- Copper mining
- Steel mills
- Iron mills

The torch of the Statue of Liberty was displayed at the Centennial Exposition.

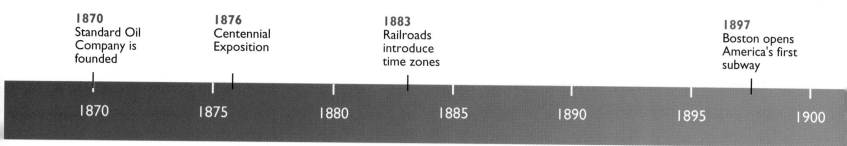

1870
Standard Oil
Company is
founded

1876
Centennial
Exposition

1883
Railroads
introduce
time zones

1897
Boston opens
America's first
subway

1870   1875   1880   1885   1890   1895   1900

power for all the machines at the fair. People looked up in awe at this nearly 40-foot-tall, 680-ton machine. The Corliss engine was a symbol of America's growing industrial strength.

The telephone, invented by Alexander Graham Bell, was even more amazing. It forever changed the way people communicated.

Improving Past Inventions

The 1870s did not mark the beginning of America's scientific triumphs. Before the Civil War, Americans had invented all kinds of fantastic things. Robert Fulton built a steamboat. Cyrus McCormick invented a mechanical reaper.

Now inventors improved earlier inventions and created new ones. Every day, it seemed, wizards like Thomas Alva Edison and Alexander Graham Bell came up with more unusual inventions to improve the lives of many Americans. It is no wonder that the end of the 1800s became known as the Machine Age.

The Corliss steam engine ▶

Electricity Is Needed

Many of these machines and gadgets required electricity. In fact, hundreds of Edison's inventions used electricity, including the copy machine, the phonograph, and the moving picture machine. Edison's masterpiece was the incandescent light bulb. It is hard for us today to understand how wondrous this

GEORGE H. CORLISS   PROVIDENCE, R.I.

This original model of the typewriter used children's blocks for the placement of the keys.

was. Edison had banished darkness!

Electric lights meant that factories, stores, and mills, such as those shown on the map on page 316, could stay open at night. Suddenly more workers were needed to cover these extra hours. More workers, in turn, cranked out more products.

Other Resources Needed

Many people wanted electricity, but how could they get it? Electric power plants needed to be built. Companies located on waterways could use water to turn the electric generators. Other companies needed coal. People had to find and develop new coal mines.

Copper wiring was needed to carry the electricity. Thus, people had to find and mine the copper. Additional people were needed to make wires, to string power lines, to build electric motors, and so on. As you can see, the demand for electricity created hundreds of new industries.

Resources by Rail

In Chapter 13 you read about how railroads linked the western frontiers to eastern cities. These railroads carried the resources that new industries needed. Copper mined in Arizona, lumber cut in Oregon, and iron ore mined in Minnesota all traveled by train to other locations in the nation.

The railroads were not perfect, however. One problem was that the train lines did not all have the same time on their clocks. Each city would base its time on the sun's position. That meant that different cities had different times, and it was hard to figure out what time it would be in each town before you got there. Think about how difficult it was to use a train schedule without knowing what time it would be when you arrived in that city—especially if you had to change trains a few times. In Illinois there were 27 different time zones.

In 1872, railroad companies met in St. Louis, Missouri, to solve this problem. However, it took them 11 years to finally approve and use the four time zones shown on page 319.

An electric power plant ▶

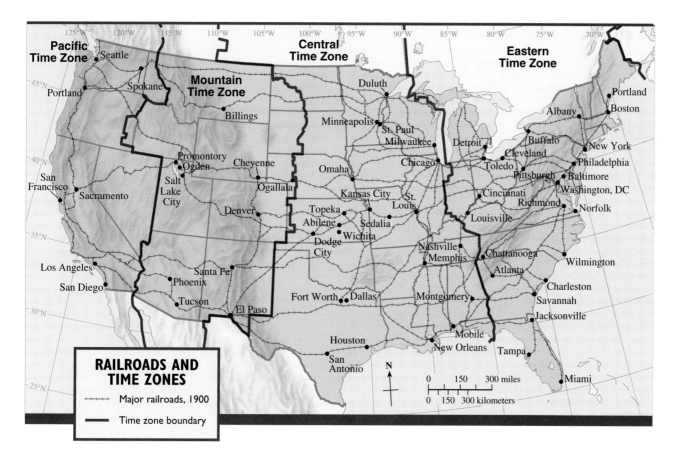

RAILROADS AND TIME ZONES

├┼┤ Major railroads, 1900

─── Time zone boundary

Pacific Time Zone
Mountain Time Zone
Central Time Zone
Eastern Time Zone

The map above shows how much simpler the time zones made things.

Railroads had other problems. Most railroads were not transcontinental—they didn't link the East to the West. All across America, hundreds of tiny train lines connected one town to another, but they didn't necessarily connect two major cities without many stops in between.

In addition, local train lines used different *gauges*, or distances between tracks. This meant that each company's trains were built with different widths between their wheels. And each company's trains could run only on its own tracks. Therefore, no passenger or product could travel far without changing trains several times.

Railroad Improvements

In the late 1800s, railroads became larger, faster, and safer. One way this happened was by consolidation. Larger railroad companies bought up smaller ones. The larger company then changed all of its newly bought tracks so that the gauges were all the same. By the end of the century, all trains used the same gauges. Thus, passengers and goods didn't have to change trains as often.

Other railroad improvements, such as air brakes and stronger

 consolidation The combining of many small companies into fewer large companies

▼ Refrigerated train cars shipped fresh fruits and vegetables around the country.

319

steel rails, made travel safer. And dining cars, where people were served restaurant-style meals, made travel more comfortable.

Railroads Impact Other Industries

The need for railroad tracks created a need for steel. Steel was stronger and easier to work with than iron. But it was very expensive to make until Henry Bessemer invented a new process of making steel.

One person who saw this as an opportunity to make a great profit was Andrew Carnegie. He sold everything he owned to build a steel company.

Once Carnegie got involved in this industry, he kept ahead of other steel companies by constantly updating his methods of steelmaking and by hiring some of the industry's best people. By the 1890s, Carnegie's steel mills made almost as much steel as all the other companies put together.

While railroads did not need oil, they did impact the oil industry. When John D. Rockefeller consolidated the oil industry, he needed help from the railroad companies that transported his products. Rockefeller made secret deals with railroad companies so that it cost him less to use the trains than it cost other oil companies. This, along with running an efficient company, helped Rockefeller develop a **monopoly** in the oil industry. In fact, by 1900 he controlled more than 90 percent of the nation's oil business. You will read more about how this monopoly was created on pages 322–323.

▲ Breaker boys sorted coal in the mines.

Progress Isn't for Everyone

The nation grew wealthier, and people had things in 1900 that they never would have imagined in 1867.

But not everyone prospered. Farmers and skilled workers used to be able to take great pride in their work. Now agricultural machinery replaced hand labor on farms. Other machinery replaced skilled labor. Whereas it might have taken years to learn to make shoes, for example, it now took a factory worker little time to learn how to nail heels on shoes with a machine. Men who had been farmers and skilled workers now often worked at boring repetitive jobs. People who used to take great pride in their work now rarely got the satisfaction of making an entire product, such as a pair of shoes.

Women who worked in factories often were given dirty, dangerous jobs. They were paid poorly—almost always less than men. Most of the women looking for work were young or poor or both. Often they took whatever job they could find.

monopoly   The complete control of an industry

In addition, many children worked long hours in filthy, unsafe coal mines and mills. They worked 10 to 12 hours a day, six days a week. They didn't go to school. For their work these children often earned less than a dollar a week.

The Rural South

Most of the industrialization took place in the northern United States. Although some steel and textile mills were built in the South, for the most part the South remained agricultural. Cotton mills did increase in number after the Civil War, but as other parts of the country grew more urban, the South remained rural.

After the Civil War, northern **speculators** moved to the South and bought up large tracts of southern timberland. They established saw mills and shipped the lumber north. In doing so, the speculators hoped both to make money and to prevent southerners from competing with their industries in the North.

In this way the northern industries did not have as much competition. And the South remained dependent on the North and the East for money and goods.

★ *speculator* Someone who takes great financial risks, hoping to make a huge profit

Many women worked difficult jobs in filthy, unsafe factories. Others became telephone operators. ▼

SHOW WHAT YOU KNOW!

REFOCUS
COMPREHENSION

1. Why are the late 1800s called the Machine Age?

2. How did electricity affect railroads and other industries?

THINK ABOUT IT
CRITICAL THINKING

How do you think time zones help us today?

WRITE ABOUT IT
ACTIVITY

It is July 1876 and you have just been to the Centennial Exposition. Write a journal entry describing all that you have seen.

Standard Oil's Monopoly

FOCUS *When the oil industry began, there were many companies in the field. Find out how John D. Rockefeller created a monopoly in this industry.*

1 Rockefeller ran a more efficient and profitable refinery than his **competitors**.

2 Standard Oil bought some smaller oil companies and soon became a giant in the oil industry.

3 Rockefeller made a secret deal with the railroads. He gave them lots of business. They returned half of what he paid them for shipping his oil.

4 Standard Oil could now charge less than the competition. Thus, Rockefeller forced the competition out of business. Many owners sold their refineries to Rockefeller. Others decided to fight, but they could not win. Standard Oil could afford to lower its prices even more than the competition could. Eventually the competition would go out of business.

★ **competitor** A company in the same industry that wants the same customer's business

5 There were still some other large oil companies. These competitors and Rockefeller agreed to control the price of oil.

6 Standard Oil now had a monopoly and could charge as much as it wanted for its products.

7 Rockefeller built oil pipelines and tried to control all the steps in the oil industry. He also made and sold his own oil products. Soon Rockefeller controlled refining as well as transportation.

In 1902, Ida M. Tarbell wrote about how Rockefeller gained his monopoly. People began to see the negative side of a monopoly—mainly that they had to pay whatever price Standard Oil charged.

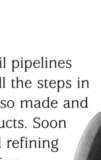

It is doubtful if. . . [Mr. Rockefeller ever] has run a race with a competitor and started fair. Business played in this way loses all its sportsmanlike qualities. It is fit only for tricksters.
Ida Tarbell

SHOW WHAT YOU KNOW!

REFOCUS
COMPREHENSION

1. In the early years of Standard Oil, how was Rockefeller able to purchase more oil companies?

2. In what two ways did Rockefeller get rid of the competition?

THINK ABOUT IT
CRITICAL THINKING

How do you think people reacted to Ida Tarbell's writings?

WRITE ABOUT IT
ACTIVITY

What do you think about Rockefeller's secret deal with the railroads? Explain your opinion in a letter to Ida Tarbell.

The Growing Consumer Market

FOCUS *The inventions of the late 1800s led to the production of many new goods. These, in turn, produced a new kind of American—the consumer.*

A National Market Develops

You don't have to look beyond the dinner table to see how the Machine Age changed daily life in America. In 1867, everything was grown close to home. Meat, flour, and fruit came from local butchers, mills, and gardens. Markets were local, meaning the buyer and the seller were neighbors.

By 1900, however, markets had become national. Most meat, flour, and fruit came to town in railroad cars from faraway states. This change

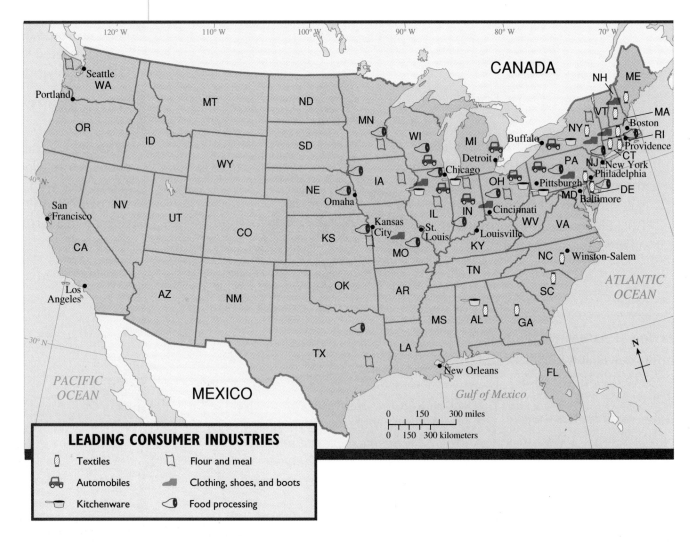

LEADING CONSUMER INDUSTRIES

Textiles		Flour and meal	
Automobiles		Clothing, shoes, and boots	
Kitchenware		Food processing	

This ad uses a slogan to create a need.

meant that there might be a thousand miles between the buyer, now called a **consumer**, and the seller. New consumer industries sprang up all across the country. Some of these are shown on the map on page 324.

Sellers of new products used **advertising** to persuade consumers to buy the new products. Other sellers used advertising to create brand loyalty. They wanted to convince consumers that their brand of soup, for example, was better than a competitor's brand.

Borden Creates a Need

Gail Borden had to create a need or want for his product. In the 1800s, it was risky to drink milk. Milk spoiled quickly and often caused people to become ill.

Borden invented condensed milk and put it in a can. It was safer and healthier for people to drink than fresh milk. But Borden had to get people to buy it. So he used advertising to convince people that his product was healthful. His advertising worked—Borden's condensed milk is still sold today.

Swift Develops Brand Loyalty

Gustavus Swift, a cattle dealer, didn't have to convince people to eat beef. They were already doing that. Swift, however, wanted to convince people to buy meat from him instead of their local butcher.

In the 1870s, cattle were shipped by train to eastern cities, where they were slaughtered by local butchers and sold to local consumers. Often the cattle got sick and lost weight while traveling, thus lowering their value. Also, butchers' slaughterhouses were small and wasted many parts of the animal. Labor costs were high, too.

Swift found a better way. He built a huge slaughterhouse in Chicago and shipped sides of beef on refrigerated railroad cars. But people preferred locally slaughtered meat.

Swift advertised to convince people that his meat was as safe as the local butcher's. He also sold his meat at a much lower price than local butchers did. As more and more people bought Swift's meat, the days of the local slaughterhouse butcher were numbered.

Other companies used newspaper and magazine advertising to find consumers.

A Swift ad

consumer Someone who buys or uses a product
advertising The art of getting someone to like or want a product

325

NEW ORLEANS IN 1900

- Built up by 1841
- Built up by 1878
- Built up by 1900
- Streetcar lines by 1900

Brand names, slogans, and labels became even more important in reaching customers and winning customer loyalty. Many of these products and brand names still exist.

Shopping Days

Before shopping malls there were department stores. These stores offered a wide variety of products, allowing people to get many things in one place.

Some stores, such as Montgomery Ward, developed mail order catalogs for people who did not live in the city. By 1900, shopping became a national pastime.

In 1897, Boston opened the nation's first subway train. Many other cities built trolley systems. The map above shows streetcar lines in New Orleans.

It was now possible for people to live miles from work or the nearest store. People no longer had to shop locally. They could order from a catalog. Or, if they lived near a city, they could hop on an electric trolley car to reach a nearby department store.

The first Macy's in New York City

SHOW WHAT YOU KNOW!

REFOCUS
COMPREHENSION

1. How did Gail Borden and Gustavus Swift create markets for their products?

2. How did the trolley car change people's daily lives?

THINK ABOUT IT
CRITICAL THINKING

What factors led to the growth of national markets by 1900?

WRITE ABOUT IT
ACTIVITY

You are developing a new product. You can create a desire for an entirely new product or just convince people that your product is better than another. Write an advertisement for your product.

Inventions! Inventions!

FOCUS *The period from 1868 to 1896 was a boom time for inventors. As a result of their work, the economic power of the United States grew rapidly.*

THE KEYBOARD

Latham Sholes didn't make the first typewriter. About 50 models came before his. But he did build on the work of others.

Finally he got it right. In 1868, Sholes received a patent for the "Type-Writer." The patent meant that no one else could make or sell a keyboard like Sholes's for a certain number of years. His keyboard design is still used today. The next time you type something into a computer, say a quick "thanks!" to Latham Sholes.

THE REAL McCOY

Elijah McCoy was the son of enslaved persons who escaped and ran away to Canada. In 1872, McCoy invented the lubricating cup, which allowed machines to be oiled while still running. Before this invention, machines had to be turned off to be oiled. And many machines had to be oiled several times a day. McCoy's oil cup saved time and helped machines run smoother.

People liked his product so much that they wanted to be sure they were getting McCoy's oil cup. So they insisted on "the real McCoy." The saying is still used today. It means "the real thing, not something fake or second-rate."

IT TALKS!

On June 25, 1876, Dom Pedro II, the emperor of Brazil, was at the Centennial Exposition. He wanted to see Alexander Graham Bell's exhibit because he had met Bell earlier in Boston and was very impressed with his work.

Bell demonstrated his new telephone to Pedro. "Do you understand what I say?" asked Bell, over a long wire.

Amazed, Dom Pedro shouted, "It talks!" Only 25 years later there were 1 million telephones in America.

1868
Latham Sholes patents the Type-Writer

1872
Elijah McCoy invents the lubricating cup

1872
George Westinghouse invents the automatic air brake

1876
Alexander Graham Bell displays the telephone

1879
Thomas Edison invents the incandescent light bulb

1870   1875   1880

STOP THE TRAIN

One day George Westinghouse was on a train that had to stop quickly because of an accident on the track ahead. From then on, Westinghouse invented ways to make trains safer.

One unsafe thing about trains was that they were very difficult to stop. Each railroad car had its own brake system. A brakeman was needed for each car.

What if an engineer could use one brake switch to stop all the cars on a train? In 1869, Westinghouse invented an air brake that could do just that.

In 1872, Westinghouse invented the automatic air brake. This was even safer than his earlier air brake. He continued to develop other braking systems and automatic signaling devices, or automatic traffic lights, for trains.

LIGHTING THE WORLD

Thomas Edison worked to invent the incandescent light bulb. It would end the need for gas lamps, which were smelly and dangerous.

Edison looked for something to carry electricity inside the bulb. He tried everything—bark, hair, copper, even lemon peel. Nothing worked. Then in 1879, he tried a special kind of carbonized cotton thread. It worked! The thread glowed without burning up.

Working around the clock with Edison was Lewis H. Latimer, the son of a former slave. Latimer helped Edison improve the light bulb. Later, Latimer guided the installation of city lights in New York City, Philadelphia, Montreal, and London.

PRESS THE BUTTON

The Kodak was the first easy-to-use camera. George Eastman invented it in 1888. He made up the word *Kodak*, thinking it was easy to spell and to pronounce. Eastman's camera ads read "You press the button, we do the rest."

The camera cost $25 and took 100 pictures. Once the pictures were taken, the camera and the film had to be sent to the factory with $10. The film was developed, and the camera was reloaded with new film and returned to the sender.

1888
George Eastman
invents the Kodak

1889
Thomas Edison
invents the
kinetograph

1896
Henry Ford
completes his
"horseless carriage"

1885   1890   1895

MOVIES

In 1888, Thomas Edison began working on a moving picture machine. With his assistant, William Dickson, and George Eastman's film, Thomas Edison succeeded in 1889. He called this new machine a kinetograph.

This wasn't the first movie machine. And it wouldn't be the last. The production of moving pictures, or movies, changed dramatically over the next century. Yet, Eastman and Edison's combined efforts and creativity contributed greatly to the growth of the movie industry.

THE HORSELESS CARRIAGE

In the 1880s, Henry Ford earned his living repairing and operating steam engines. When he was not at his job, he was working on his "horseless carriage."

In June 1896, Ford began riding around in his first horseless carriage. At the same time, the Duryea brothers and several other people were doing the same thing.

Ford was not the first or only one to think of making a horseless carriage. However, he was one of the first to make this invention available to the average American. And in part it was because of Henry Ford that there were soon automobiles everywhere in America.

329

SUMMING UP

1 DO YOU REMEMBER . . .
COMPREHENSION

1. What did the Corliss engine symbolize?

2. How did the demand for electricity create whole new industries?

3. Who was hurt by the new inventions of the Machine Age?

4. How did consolidation help the railroads?

5. Why didn't the South industrialize as fast as the North?

6. How did Standard Oil force its competitors out of business?

7. What did Ida Tarbell think of Rockefeller?

8. How did food markets change between 1867 and 1900?

9. How was Gustavus Swift's meat delivery an improvement?

10. What are two of Thomas Edison's important inventions?

2 SKILL POWER
UNDERSTANDING TIME ZONES

Use the railroad map showing time zones, on page 319, to answer these questions.

1. How many time zones are in the 48 contiguous, or adjoining, United States?

2. If you fly from Salt Lake City to Chattanooga, how many time zones do you pass through?

3. In what time zone is Santa Fe, New Mexico?

4. At 1:00 P.M. in Billings, Montana, what time is it in Abilene, Kansas?

3 WHAT DO YOU THINK?
CRITICAL THINKING

1. Which invention of the Machine Age do you think was most important? Give three reasons.

2. What drawbacks of industrialization might not have been obvious to Americans at first?

3. How do you think John D. Rockefeller might have justified his oil monopoly?

4. What effects do you think the national market had on farmers?

5. What products and services might future inventors develop? Why would these be a valuable contribution?

4 SAY IT, WRITE IT, USE IT
VOCABULARY

Write a newspaper editorial. Tell whether you think it was right for John D. Rockefeller to control the oil business. Use as many of the vocabulary words as possible.

advertising   consumer

competitor   monopoly

consolidation   speculator

5 GEOGRAPHY AND YOU
MAP STUDY

Use the maps on pages 319 and 324 to answer these questions.

1. In what states were textiles among the leading consumer industries?

2. What were the leading consumer industries in your state?

3. What important role did the railroads play during the Machine Age?

4. In what states do there seem to be the most major railroads?

6 TAKE ACTION
CITIZENSHIP

In 1876 the Corliss engine stood for American economic and industrial strength. Over time the Statue of Liberty became a symbol of American freedom. Today Lady Liberty still stands for freedom, but our nation needs a new symbol for economic strength. What do you think it should be? Brainstorm ideas with some classmates. Then create a poster that shows your symbol. Write a catchy phrase that sums up your feelings and ideas about the symbol.

7 GET CREATIVE
SCIENCE CONNECTION

In an encyclopedia or library book, read more about one of the inventions described in this chapter. Then write about one problem or difficulty that the inventor had to overcome to make the invention work. Draw a diagram that shows the problem and its solution.

LOOKING AHEAD   In the next chapter find out how the growth of cities and increased immigration changed the nation.

UNDERSTAND

CHAPTER 15

URBAN LIFE AND

Between 1870 and 1920, cities grew rapidly as native-born Americans and immigrants alike were attracted by the opportunities and excitement that cities offered.

CONTENTS

◀ How did kids and others have fun in cities around 1900? Find out on page 339.

IMMIGRATION

These books tell about some people, places, and events of interest during the late 1800s and early 1900s. Read one that interests you and fill out a book-review form.

READ AND RESEARCH

The Story of the Statue of Liberty by Betsy and Giulio Maestro
(William Morrow & Co., 1989)
The Statue of Liberty stands in New York Harbor, symbolizing hope and freedom. Follow the story of "Lady Liberty" from the beginning, when she was just an idea in the mind of a French sculptor, to her unveiling as a statue and her role as an American symbol. (nonfiction)

Ellis Island: New Hope in a New Land by William Jay Jacobs
(Simon & Schuster Children's Publishing, 1990)
Imagine that you and your family have traveled from Europe to America to begin a new life. Learn all about the experience of landing at Ellis Island in the late 1800s and about the dream that many had of finding a "new hope in a new land." (nonfiction)

The Great Ancestor Hunt: The Fun of Finding Out Who You Are by Lila Perl (Houghton Mifflin Co., 1989)
Did you ever come across an old family photo and wonder about the people in it? Now you can find out how to go on an ancestor hunt and answer your questions! You will learn about your family, American history, and yourself in the process. (nonfiction)

Mother Jones: One Woman's Fight for Labor by Betsy Harvey Kraft (Houghton Mifflin Co., 1995)
Meet Mother Jones, a crusader for the rights of American laborers. Read how her courage to speak out made people listen and improved the conditions under which many worked. (biography)

SKILL POWER Reading Graphs

When facts are organized in graphs, it is easy to understand the facts and the relationships between them.

UNDERSTAND IT

Some people have called the latter part of the 1900s "The Information Age." The name comes from the idea that advances in computers, communications, and technology are making millions of facts and ideas available to many of the world's people. There is so much information that it is hard to keep track of it all. Bar graphs and line graphs help to make it easier to understand large amounts of information.

EXPLORE IT

Graphs show a lot of information in a small space. There are many kinds of graphs.

A bar graph lets you compare information easily. The bar graph on the left shows the population of America's ten largest cities in 1900. Find Philadelphia at the bottom of the graph. Look at the figures on the left. You will see that Philadelphia's population was over 1 million.

- Which city on the graph had the largest population? Which city had the smallest population?

A line graph shows change over time. The one below shows the population of Detroit between 1870 and 1910.

- What was Detroit's population in 1880 and in 1910?

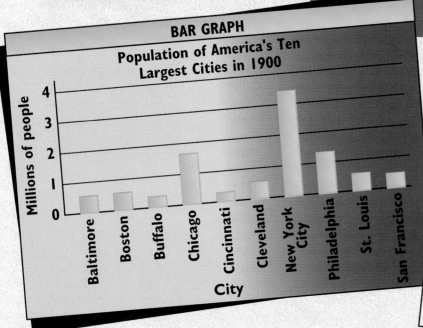

BAR GRAPH
Population of America's Ten Largest Cities in 1900

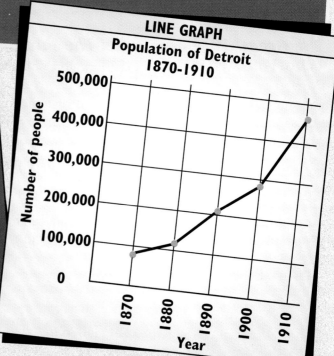

LINE GRAPH
Population of Detroit 1870-1910

Work with two or three of your classmates to think of ideas for a bar graph and a line graph. For example, you might make a bar graph that compares the all-time top-ten point scorers in basketball or the favorite videos of everyone in the class.

Complete the line graph below. First, copy it into your notebook and add dots for the years we've left out: 300 students at Center School in 1990 and 400 in 1995. Then draw a line connecting the dots.

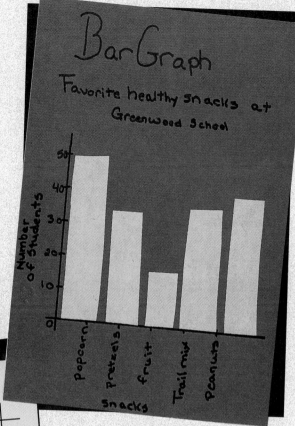

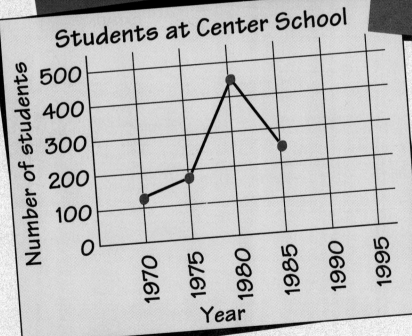

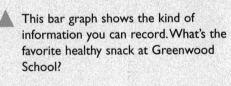

This bar graph shows the kind of information you can record. What's the favorite healthy snack at Greenwood School?

SKILL POWER SEARCH In this chapter compare how information is shown on two kinds of graphs.

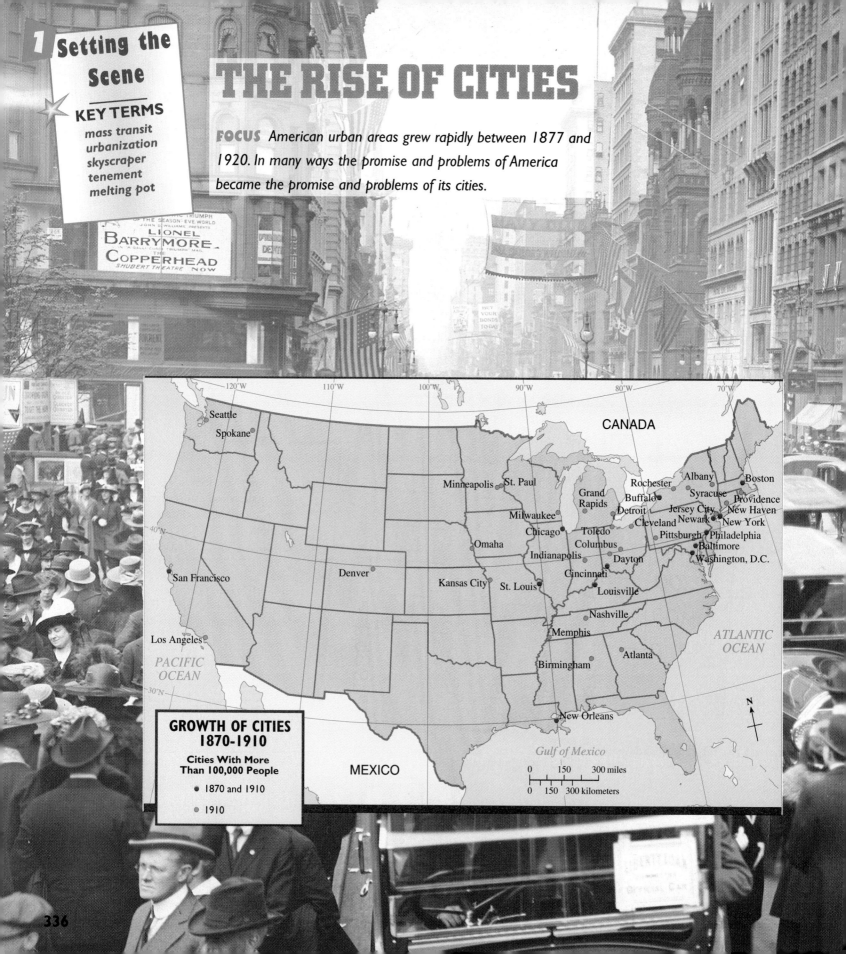

KEY TERMS

mass transit
urbanization
skyscraper
tenement
melting pot

THE RISE OF CITIES

FOCUS American urban areas grew rapidly between 1877 and 1920. In many ways the promise and problems of America became the promise and problems of its cities.

GROWTH OF CITIES 1870–1910

Cities With More Than 100,000 People

- 1870 and 1910
- 1910

CANADA

Seattle
Spokane
Minneapolis   St. Paul
Grand Rapids
Rochester   Albany   Boston
Buffalo   Syracuse   Providence
Milwaukee   Detroit   Jersey City   New Haven
Chicago   Toledo   Cleveland   Newark   New York
Omaha   Columbus   Pittsburgh   Philadelphia
Indianapolis   Dayton   Baltimore
Denver   Cincinnati   Washington, D.C.
Kansas City   St. Louis   Louisville
San Francisco
Nashville
Los Angeles   Memphis
PACIFIC OCEAN
Birmingham   Atlanta
ATLANTIC OCEAN
New Orleans
MEXICO
Gulf of Mexico

0   150   300 miles
0   150   300 kilometers

N

1890
Jacob Riis reveals poor
tenement conditions

1904
Broadway subway
opens in New York

1907
Peak year of immigration
into the United States

1913
Woolworth Building
erected

1890   1895   1900   1905   1910   1915

The Growth of Cities

Cities sprouted across the United States like mushrooms in the latter part of the 1800s. In just 20 years—from 1880 to 1900—the number of people living in cities more than doubled. In 1870 the United States had 13 cities with over 100,000 people. Find them on the map on the facing page. As you can see on the map, by 1910 the number of cities with over 100,000 people had increased dramatically.

Why did cities grow during this time? Where did they come from? They grew out of small towns and villages that were located in the right place—close to resources, transportation, and markets. Such new cities included Atlanta, Los Angeles, and Seattle.

The expansion of older cities was also quite startling. Between 1880 and 1900 the population of New York City grew from 1.9 million to 3.4 million. Put another way, the city grew by about 75,000 people every year! During the same period Chicago's population increased from 500,000 to 1.7 million.

The Promise of Cities

Why were cities such an attraction to so many people? To many people the city was an exciting place to be. For immigrants the city offered a place to make a fresh start in America. For poorer rural Americans it promised better jobs. For young people it promised glamour and entertainment, with its concerts, museums, amusement parks, and restaurants. A big city held all sorts of promises and offered people the chance to pursue every imaginable opportunity.

So cities, like magnets, attracted people. They also attracted raw materials and money. That's what it took to bring industry to America's cities. By 1900 about 90 percent of all manufacturing took place in cities.

Most cities came to specialize in certain industries. Pittsburgh, for example, had steel mills. Cleveland had oil refineries. New York City had banks and a stock market. Chicago and Omaha had meatpacking companies.

Making Cities Bigger and Better

But you couldn't pack a larger population into the same city limits without finding some new ways of doing things. Inventions made cities click and work and hum. Consider the problem of getting people from place to place. Just how many horse-drawn wagons could a city's streets hold?

Something new was needed. That something was public transportation, or **mass transit**. Underground trains, or subways, moved people in cities such as Boston and New York. In San Francisco, above-ground trains—known as cable cars—came to the rescue. Pulled by underground cables, cable cars moved thousands of people up and down the city's steep hills every day. Richmond, Virginia, used electric trolley cars. These were run by overhead power lines. By 1900 the electric trolley car was the most popular form of mass transit in the country.

With mass transit, people could live farther away from the center of the city, where work and shopping were found. This led to **urbanization**, or the expansion of cities outward from their central areas. New city neighborhoods developed, along with neighborhoods in suburbs, the areas surrounding cities. The map on the right shows you how Chicago grew during this time. These developments gave people more choices about where they could live.

Other inventions also helped cities grow. Steel frames let engineers build taller buildings with elevators. And so **skyscrapers** were born. These saved space and made it possible for a city to build *up* as well as *out*.

The first skyscraper was completed in 1885. It was the Home Insurance Building in Chicago. In 1913 the 60-story Woolworth Building was built in New York City. It remained the world's tallest building until 1930.

No Place to Live

In the 1800s, no one planned the growth of American cities. Rural people and immigrants streamed into cities faster than housing could be built. Not surprisingly, cities faced severe housing shortages.

Families often had to move in with other families. Many people who couldn't afford to live in the new urban or suburban neighborhoods had no choice but to live in dirty, dark, rat-infested **tenements** in the inner city. *Tenement* originally meant any "apartment house for three or more

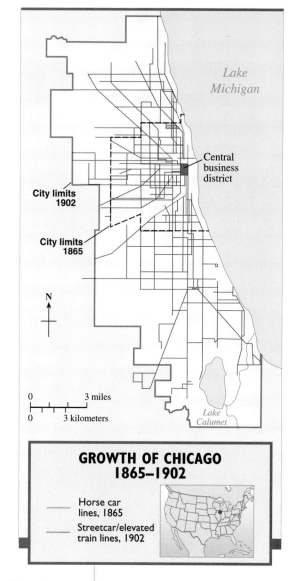

GROWTH OF CHICAGO 1865–1902

Horse car lines, 1865

Streetcar/elevated train lines, 1902

---

 mass transit   Public transportation, including trains, trolleys, buses, subways, and streetcars
urbanization   The process through which cities expand their boundaries

 skyscraper   A very tall, many-storied building with elevators and a steel frame
tenement   An apartment building shared by several families

families." Later it became associated with the worst of city life—the slum.

Life in a tenement was not easy. Noise, disease, raw sewage, and grime were all around. Things on the outside of tenements weren't much better. Most streets were not paved. In Chicago, for example, only 629 miles out of 2,048 miles of road were paved in 1890. Streets, the only playground for poor kids, often had the odor of rotting garbage and horse manure. Worse, raw sewage was dumped into nearby lakes and rivers. Polluted water caused many people to get sick and some to die. When it rained, dirt roads turned into muddy rivers. When the weather was dry, traffic on these roads kicked up terrible clouds of dust.

If the mud and dust didn't get you, maybe a trolley car would. Brooklyn had so many trolleys that people had

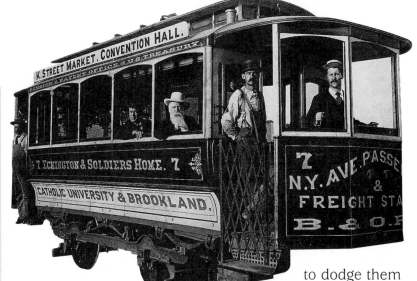

▲ A Washington, D.C., trolley car

to dodge them whenever they crossed the street. That's why the city's major league baseball team was originally named the Trolley Dodgers. (The team kept part of its name even when it moved to Los Angeles.)

Work: A Risky Business

Life in the city was especially tough for poor families. Fathers worked long hours for low pay. They often did dangerous work in factories, risking disease, injury, and death. If a father was hurt on the job, that meant he might not be able to work. If he couldn't work, he didn't get paid. Also, there were many other workers available to take his job. Women and children had a rough time, too. In factories they often did the same work as men but for even lower pay. African Americans and immigrants were the lowest

▲ The boy on the right worked for a tailor. He lived in a tenement, like this one, and played stickball, a city version of baseball, in his free time.

This African American family arrived in Chicago from the South about 1910.

paid workers on the wage scale.

Black Americans faced one special problem. Even when they were willing to work for low wages, some factory owners wouldn't hire them.

In 1910, for example, only 18 of 152 southern cotton mills employed any black Americans. The other mills wanted nothing to do with black workers. This was evidence of racism, or the belief that one race is superior to another. Racism was common in all cities.

Leaving Home

All these problems didn't keep people away from America's cities. African Americans from the rural South came to cities in the North and Midwest in large numbers after 1917. They, like many other people, hoped to escape poverty and find better jobs. Other rural Americans also flocked to cities. While some inventions pulled farmers to the cities, other inventions were pushing them off the farm. One farmer with new machines could now do the work of 50 people. By the early 1900s, millions of farmers and farm workers had fled to the city looking for work.

People from other countries, too, were lured by the promise of America. They arrived by the boatload. Between 1877 and 1910 over 18 million immigrants entered the United States. Many came from eastern and southern Europe. But some immigrants also came from Asia, Mexico, the Caribbean, and Latin America.

Everyone had his or her own reasons for coming. Some came in hopes of finding a better job. Others came to escape cruelty in their homelands. Some came for religious freedom. Still others came for the pure thrill of an adventure.

A Patchwork of Cultures

America has often been called a **melting pot**. But in reality, American cities were more like a salad bowl, in which different groups kept their own identities. Immigrants tended to settle with people from the same "old country." That's why most major cities had a Little Italy, a Polish neighborhood, a Swedish section, or a Chinatown. These immigrants didn't forget their culture. They printed newspapers in their own language. They had their own places of worship, such as churches and synagogues. They had their own food stores, holidays, and social customs.

 melting pot The concept that characteristics of different peoples could meld together and form an "American" identity

Immigration to the United States

Millions of immigrants

9
8
7
6
5
4
3
2
1
0

1861-1870 1871-1880 1881-1890 1891-1900 1901-1910 1911-1920

Years

willing to work for less than native-born workers. Also, some earlier immigrants resented new immigrants and often thought they were competing for the same jobs.

Many Americans wanted to close the door to immigrants. In 1882 and 1907, laws that limited the immigration of Asians were passed. In 1921 and 1924, laws were passed restricting the number of people who could come from parts of Europe and other continents. As a result, only a few Europeans and still fewer Asians were allowed to move to America.

Closing the Door

The huge variety of languages, religions, and customs made the city a cultural wonderland. Immigrants brought new life to America's cities. But not everyone thought that was a good thing. Some native-born Americans felt threatened by immigrants who spoke different languages, worshiped in different ways, and ate different foods. Some people blamed the newcomers for the ills of the city—poverty, crime, overcrowding, and violence. They also argued that immigrants *lowered* wages because they were

This Japanese woman and child have just arrived at the port of San Francisco. ▶

SHOW WHAT YOU
KNOW!

REFOCUS
COMPREHENSION

1. Why did many Americans and immigrants move to cities?

2. How did mass transit and skyscrapers help cities grow?

THINK ABOUT IT
CRITICAL THINKING

How do you think life in a city differed from life on a farm?

WRITE ABOUT IT
ACTIVITY

Write a newspaper article about what life was like for an immigrant.

Spotlight

KEY TERMS

labor union
reformer
suffrage

REFORM MOVEMENTS

FOCUS *As cities grew, it became clear that some people were treated unjustly. Reformers fought for fair treatment of children, African Americans, women, and other workers.*

Power for Workers?

The average worker in the late 1800s had little power. Few laws gave him or her the right to ask for a raise or to complain about poor working conditions. The mere request for a raise could get a worker fired on the spot. The supervisor could always hire someone else. After all, immigrants and other people were coming to manufacturing cities every day, looking for any job at all.

Some workers wondered whether things would be different if they joined together. If enough workers did this, employers might listen to what they had to say. Some workers formed **labor unions**. These organizations tried to help their members by seeking higher pay and better working conditions. One early union was the Knights of Labor. The Knights fought for the rights of many groups of workers—men, women, immigrants, and African Americans. By 1893, however, its membership had dropped to 75,000 from a high of 700,000 in 1886. By 1900 the union no longer existed. But it had set the stage. Later unions were successful in helping workers get higher pay and better working conditions.

The union members in this photo are from several different countries. How can you tell?

★ *labor union* An organization of workers that tries to help its members

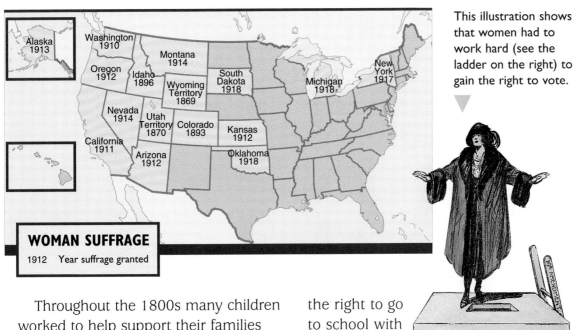

Alaska 1913
Washington 1910
Oregon 1912
Idaho 1896
Montana 1914
Wyoming Territory 1869
South Dakota 1918
Michigan 1918
New York 1917
Nevada 1914
Utah Territory 1870
Colorado 1893
Kansas 1912
California 1911
Arizona 1912
Oklahoma 1918

WOMAN SUFFRAGE

1912   Year suffrage granted

This illustration shows that women had to work hard (see the ladder on the right) to gain the right to vote.

BALLOT BOX

SHOW WHAT YOU KNOW!

REFOCUS
COMPREHENSION

1. What were some ways in which people tried to improve life for children and young workers?

2. How did Jim Crow laws affect African Americans?

THINK ABOUT IT
CRITICAL THINKING

Why was it difficult to pass laws limiting child labor?

WRITE ABOUT IT
ACTIVITY

Write a play in which you and your classmates are workers in a factory. Address the issues you face.

Throughout the 1800s many children worked to help support their families instead of going to school. Often the conditions under which these children worked were unsafe and unhealthy.

Reformers fought to improve conditions for workers. Jane Addams worked to get factories inspected and to shorten the workday for women. Mother Jones worked to help coal miners and to end child labor. Many factory owners opposed change. They didn't want to lose cheap young workers. As a result, Congress didn't pass a child labor law until 1916. It didn't prohibit child labor until 1938.

Equality for Some

Although life improved for some Americans, it didn't for many black Americans. During Reconstruction, Jim Crow laws were passed. These laws made life worse for African Americans long after Reconstruction. They could not eat or sleep in the same places as white Americans. Black children lost the right to go to school with white children. Leading African American reformers Frederick Douglass, W.E.B. DuBois, and Ida B. Wells wanted these and other rights restored. Sadly, they were voices that few people heard. African Americans did not win many of their rights back until the 1960s.

Women fared better. They won the right to get a better education. By 1900 there were 7,000 female doctors and 1,000 female lawyers in the United States. State governments limited the number of hours women could work in factories. The map above shows in which states and territories women could vote before 1920. The biggest victory for women came in 1920, when the Nineteenth Amendment was added to the Constitution. The Nineteenth Amendment granted all American women **suffrage**, or the right to vote.

 reformer   A person who works for a cause such as improved conditions for workers

 suffrage   The right to vote

343

LIVING IN THE CITY

FOCUS *Immigrants came to America with great hopes and dreams. But what was life really like after they arrived on our shores?*

Hopes and Fears

Picture your excitement as your ship from Italy nears New York City in 1903. You see the new Statue of Liberty in New York Harbor! At last you are starting a new life in America. You have been dreaming of this day for months. Chances are some relatives—in your case, your father—came to New York ahead of you. In his letters he described the jobs and freedom he hoped to find in America.

Of course, you are probably a little scared, too. Will you learn to speak English? Will you make new friends? Will people laugh at your clothes or hairstyle?

▲ An immigrant woman and children arrive at Ellis Island.

As it turns out, you aren't going directly into New York City. Your first stop is at Ellis Island. (If you came to the United States from Asia, you would cross the Pacific Ocean and head for San Francisco. Your first stop would be Angel Island, not Ellis Island.) Your mother has told you to put on your best clothes before you get off the boat. Everyone in your family is dressing up, hoping to make a good impression on the immigration officers. After all, everyone knew that Giovanni, from your hometown, had come all this way last year, only to be turned back by an immigration officer who thought he was sick because he was dressed in dirty clothes and had a cough.

Like the other 20 million immigrants who eventually pass through Ellis Island, you are going to have to answer lots of questions. Is someone waiting for you to arrive? Do you have any skills? Have you been sick recently? If your name is long or difficult to pronounce, the officer may simply change it! Suddenly you might no longer be the Tuccini (too CHEE nee) family. You might be the Tuckers.

A Poor Start

If you are poor—and many immigrants are—you might end up living in a couple of tiny tenement rooms. Or you might share an apartment with another family.

If you are Jewish, you will probably go to the Lower East Side of New York City. As an Italian, Little Italy is your destination. Your father has found a place for you to live on Grand Street. You feel comfortable living near those who share your customs and speak your language. You will see other children who look and talk like you. America isn't so different after all!

Life in a tenement house is quite an experience. It is crowded living in two rooms with your mother, father, and six brothers and sisters. There is only one window in the whole place. The dark rooms are dreary. And you quickly tire of tripping over other people.

On the other hand, you enjoy living in a place with three or four other

families right on the same floor. The father of one of the families and your father became friends on board the ship when they came over. You have made friends with his children and many others who live on your floor. After dark you meet your new friends in the hallway of the tenement to talk and play.

▲ Hester Street in New York City was full of tenements.

Families such as this one did piecework in their tenements.

A Saturday Night Bath

Good news—sort of. You probably take only one bath a week. It's simply too much work to bathe any more often than that.

Remember, your tenement has no indoor plumbing or water heater. Bath water is taken from rain barrels outside. And you're the one to haul it. You have to lug heavy buckets of water up the stairs. Sometimes you and your friend race each other to see who can carry the water the fastest. You also have to heat the water on the coal stove. By the time your mother finishes getting the bath ready, you're sweaty enough to need it. But sometimes there is not enough water, so you have to bathe in the same water as your sisters, Maria and Sylvia. Sharing water is not healthy and is an easy way to pass and spread diseases.

Lack of indoor plumbing creates another problem. There are no toilets

Dolls that Russian immigrants brought to America about 1900

in the tenement. Like most tenements, yours has an outdoor toilet, or outhouse. This is a simple wooden building with a hole in the ground. You discovered on the first night in your new home that getting up in the middle of a cold rainy night for a trip to the outhouse is no fun.

All in a Day's Work

After six months in school, you stop going. You are now 12 years old, and it is time to help support your family. You find a job in what people call a **sweatshop**. You work in a factory that makes collars for men's shirts. Lots of workers are crowded into each of the factory's stuffy, smelly, and dirty rooms.

You are paid for **piecework**. That means you earn a certain amount of money for each piece you produce. Other friends of yours sew shirts, make artificial flowers, and roll cigars. Whatever you do, you have to hurry. The slower you work, the less money you make.

Hurrying can be dangerous, though. It sometimes leads to accidents. Your uncle, who worked in a factory that makes men's pants, caught his finger in a sewing machine, and the needle went right through it!

If you don't work in a sweatshop, you might work in a meat-processing

sweatshop A place where workers work long hours at low wages under poor conditions
piecework Work done and paid for by the piece

plant. Or you might be a ragpicker. That means you dig through other people's garbage, trying to find things you can sell to a second-hand store. People in your tenement have worked as ragpickers when they haven't had other work.

Whatever you do, your job is tiring. Your back aches from long hours bent over a worktable. But you feel proud to be helping your family make it in America. Without your earnings your family might not eat at night.

The Bright Side

Parts of your new life are pretty grim. But you know you also have opportunities that you didn't have in the "old country." On Sundays you and your friends can go to the beach, an amusement park, or a baseball game. You might visit a museum or take in a play with your father. Or you might just sit on the front steps and chat with your friends.

Perhaps the best thing about life in America, you realize, is that most people have a chance to change their lives. You may have started out in a tenement, but in time you might move up to a big bright apartment with electricity and running water. With enough hard work and a little luck, you might even get rich! It was the promise of opportunity that drew you and your family to America in the first place.

The beach attracted many city-dwellers on Sundays. This beach is in Minneapolis. ▼

SHOW WHAT YOU KNOW!

REFOCUS
COMPREHENSION

1. What were some challenges that new immigrants faced?

2. Why were Sunday amusements so popular with city people?

THINK ABOUT IT
CRITICAL THINKING

How was America a land of opportunity for many immigrants?

WRITE ABOUT IT
ACTIVITY

Write a journal entry about a week in the life of an immigrant city kid.

March of Time

1893 TO 1903

TIME FOR LEISURE

FOCUS *The years 1877 to 1920 saw the average American grow richer. This increasing wealth led to more free time and a desire to have some fun.*

BICYCLES, BICYCLES

In the late 1800s a new fad swept the country. Everyone, it seemed, could be seen riding a bicycle through the city park or down a country lane. People called it "the most spectacular craze of all." By 1893 more than 1 million Americans were cycling. Many were women. One reason that many women loved biking was that they could wear clothes that were not as bulky as those they usually wore. Many women cyclists had an excuse to wear simple clothing. They liked the freedom this gave them. Women kept the clothes, even when the bicycling fad declined after 1900.

FUN IN THE SUN

Coney Island in New York City became more popular by the day. New Yorkers poured into its amusement park by the thousands to escape the city's summer heat. Trolleys and trains made getting to the beach cheap and easy. City folks from all walks of life enjoyed the roller coaster and other rides. In 1894, Coney Island got its first Ferris wheel.

1893
1 million
Americans bicycling

1894
First Ferris wheel
at Coney Island

1899
Scott Joplin writes
"Maple Leaf Rag"

1903
Baseball has two
major leagues

1903
*The Great Train
Robbery* is released

1890   1895   1900   1905

THAT'S ENTERTAINMENT

In 1899, Scott Joplin's "Maple Leaf Rag" was the first piece of sheet music to sell more than 1 million copies. People loved his ragtime music because it was fun. (Ragtime is a jazzy offbeat music played on a piano.) But Joplin wanted his songs to be taken seriously. Unfortunately, that didn't happen in his lifetime.

A MOVING PICTURE?

The Great Train Robbery, made in 1903, was the first "moving picture" that many Americans saw. People flocked to see it, even though it was only about 10 minutes long. The movie cost about $100 to make. (These days, movies cost millions of dollars to make.) America's first "big" movie, it made movie-watching an American pastime. By the 1920s, movies were all the rage the world over.

PLAY BALL!

The first professional baseball club was organized in Cincinnati in 1869. By 1903, baseball had two major leagues, the National and the American. That year they settled the question of who was best by playing a World Series. The Boston Red Sox, the American League champs, beat the Pittsburgh Pirates, the National League winners. From then on, the World Series has been played every year but two—in 1904 and 1994.

This is the great picture upon which the famous comedian has worked a whole year.

6 reels of Joy.

Charles Chaplin
IN
"THE KID"

Written and directed by Charles Chaplin
A First National Attraction

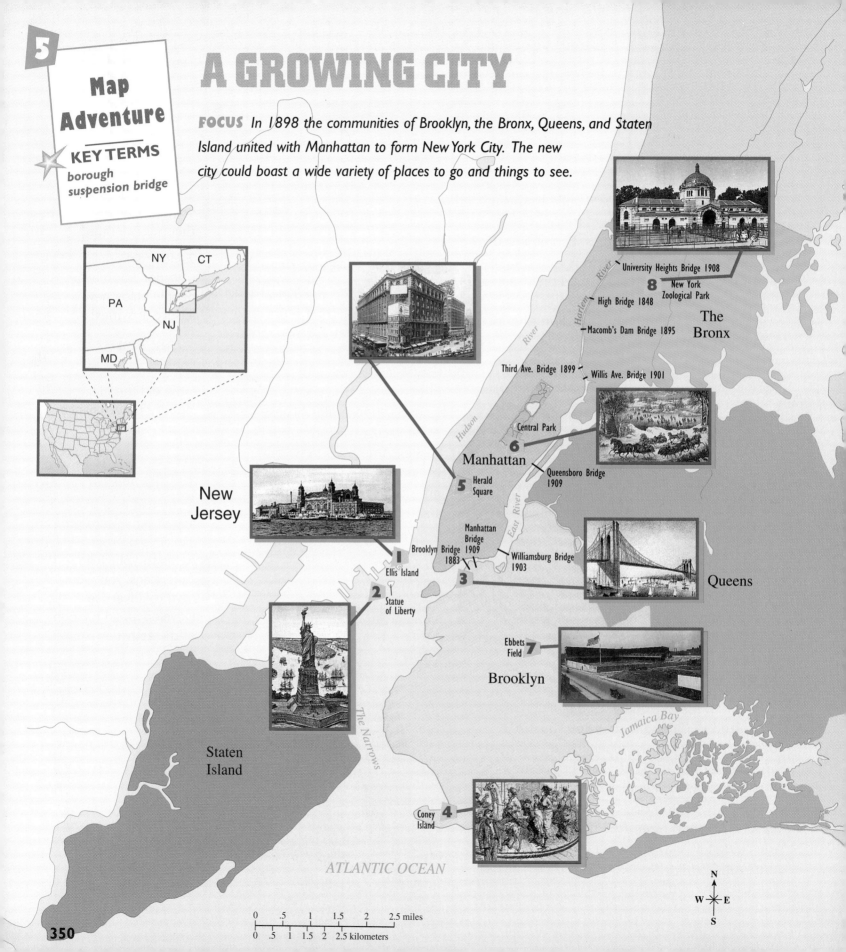

Map Adventure

★ **KEY TERMS**

borough
suspension bridge

A GROWING CITY

FOCUS In 1898 the communities of Brooklyn, the Bronx, Queens, and Staten Island united with Manhattan to form New York City. The new city could boast a wide variety of places to go and things to see.

NY   CT

PA

NJ

MD

The Bronx

University Heights Bridge 1908

8 New York Zoological Park

High Bridge 1848

Macomb's Dam Bridge 1895

Third Ave. Bridge 1899

Willis Ave. Bridge 1901

Hudson River

Harlem River

Central Park

6

Manhattan

Queensboro Bridge 1909

5 Herald Square

East River

Manhattan Bridge 1909

Brooklyn Bridge 1883

Williamsburg Bridge 1903

3

Queens

New Jersey

1 Ellis Island

2 Statue of Liberty

Ebbets Field **7**

Brooklyn

Jamaica Bay

The Narrows

Staten Island

4 Coney Island

ATLANTIC OCEAN

N
W   E
S

0   .5   1   1.5   2   2.5 miles

0   .5   1   1.5   2   2.5 kilometers

Adventure in New York City

After the five communities joined together, they kept their identities as **boroughs** of New York City. Over 3 million people called New York City home in 1898. Manhattan alone swelled with about 2 million people. With thousands of immigrants arriving every day, the city was changing quickly. New York was an exciting place to be, and there was much for its inhabitants—new and old—to do and explore.

Map Legend

1 Ellis Island This tiny island was the first stop for immigrants on their way to New York and other cities from 1892 to 1943.

2 Statue of Liberty This statue, on Bedloe's Island, was a gift from France in 1886.

3 Brooklyn Bridge When this bridge opened in 1883, it was the world's longest suspension bridge.

4 Coney Island Hot, humid summers drove thousands to the beach at Coney Island. A carousel, a Ferris wheel, and a roller coaster were inexpensive fun for city folks.

5 Herald Square After Macy's Emporium opened in 1902, this square became a bustling shopping district. The stores were beautiful and well-stocked.

6 Central Park Over 800 acres were set aside for the park in 1853. People came to it to stroll, play, and listen to concerts. A carousel was added later.

7 Ebbets Field Charles Ebbets, owner of the Brooklyn Dodgers, built this 22,000-seat ballpark in 1912. Brooklyn's open grassy parks were perfect for playing baseball.

8 New York Zoological Park On November 8, 1899, this zoo opened its doors. It boasted 843 animals from 137 species.

---

borough A distinct self-governing area that is part of a larger city
suspension bridge A bridge whose roadway is suspended by steel cables supported by two high towers

MAP IT

You are an immigrant from Poland, and your family lives in lower Manhattan.

1. What island was the first stop for your family when it arrived in the United States? What famous monument stands nearby?

2. A friend tells you he saw a bear in New York City. When you don't believe him, he says he also saw an alligator. Where in New York City could these animals be found?

3. On a sweltering July morning, your parents tell you you're going to Coney Island. In which borough is it located? What river must you cross to get there? If you wanted to cross the world's longest suspension bridge, which bridge would you use? What other point of interest is located in the same borough as Coney Island?

EXPLORE IT

Write a letter to a friend in Poland. Describe your new life in New York City. Include things to see and do around the city.

SUMMING UP

1 DO YOU REMEMBER . . .
COMPREHENSION

1. Why did American cities attract so many people in the late 1800s?

2. In what ways was life in cities unhealthy?

3. Why were so many Americans forced to leave their farms at the turn of the century?

4. What special problems did African Americans face in cities?

5. Were American cities really a melting pot? Explain.

6. How did reformers try to improve the lives of children in the late 1800s?

7. What did the Nineteenth Amendment do?

8. Why did immigrants on the East Coast first stop at Ellis Island?

9. What new forms of entertainment became popular in cities at the turn of the century?

10. What five boroughs made up New York City?

2 SKILL POWER
READING GRAPHS

Use the bar graph on the right to answer these questions.

1. What does this graph tell you?

2. About how many immigrants came to the United States between 1881 and 1890?

3. In what years did the most immigrants come? In what years did the fewest come?

3 WHAT DO YOU THINK?
CRITICAL THINKING

1. How has city life improved since 1900?

2. Why did women want the right to vote?

3. How did America's "patchwork of cultures" help new immigrants adjust?

4. Why did leisure time activities develop?

5. Why was New York so exciting for immigrants?

4 SAY IT, WRITE IT, USE IT
VOCABULARY

Write a short paragraph describing American cities around 1900. Try to use six or more of the vocabulary words.

borough	skyscraper
labor union	suffrage
mass transit	suspension bridge
melting pot	sweatshop
piecework	tenement
reformer	urbanization

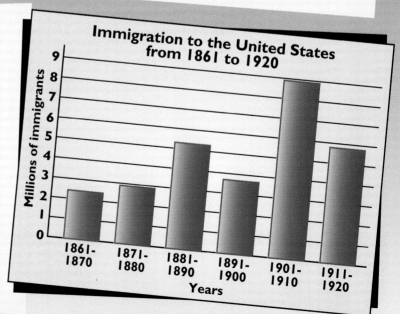

Immigration to the United States from 1861 to 1920

5 GEOGRAPHY AND YOU
MAP STUDY

Use the maps on pages 336 and 343 to help you answer these questions.

1. What part(s) of the United States had the most states that allowed women to vote before 1920?

2. What part(s) of the United States had the fewest states that allowed women's suffrage before 1920?

3. In 1910, could women in Boston vote?

4. In 1910, could women in Denver vote?

6 TAKE ACTION
CITIZENSHIP

Find out more about the major groups of immigrants who settled in your city or region between 1877 and 1920. Where did they come from and why? What are some of the contributions they made? With a group of classmates, prepare a bulletin-board display about the diversity these immigrants brought to your area.

7 GET CREATIVE
HEALTH CONNECTION

City residents faced serious health problems in 1900. Noise, raw sewage, dust, and dangerous working conditions all took their toll. Research one of these problems to find out about its negative effects on health. Then learn what you can about how modern communities deal with the problem. Show your findings on a chart.

LOOKING AHEAD In the next chapter, find out how America was also growing *outside* its boundaries during this time.

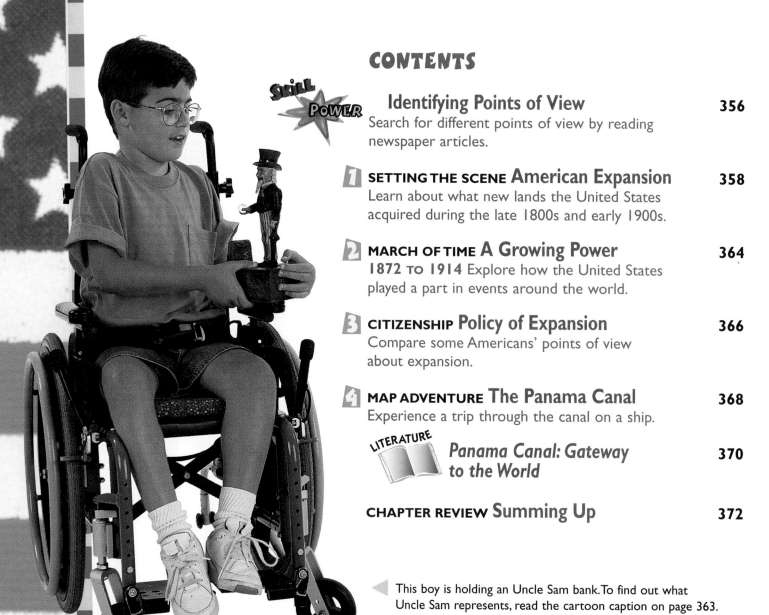

LEARN ABOUT

CHAPTER 16

AMERICA'S

Between 1865 and 1917 the United States extended its control and influence beyond its borders. As the nation became a world power, new and controversial issues were raised.

CONTENTS

◀ This boy is holding an Uncle Sam bank. To find out what Uncle Sam represents, read the cartoon caption on page 363.

EMPIRE

These books tell about some people, places, and events of interest during the late 1800s and early 1900s. Read one that interests you and fill out a book-review form.

READ AND RESEARCH

Panama Canal: Gateway to the World
by Judith St. George (G. P. Putnam's Sons, 1989)
The building of the Panama Canal solved the centuries-old problem of connecting the Atlantic and Pacific oceans. From construction to controversy, read all about the history of the Panama Canal. *(nonfiction)*
•*You can read a selection from this book on page 370.*

Bully for You, Teddy Roosevelt!
by Jean Fritz (G. P. Putnam's Sons, 1991)
Did you know that people referred to Theodore Roosevelt as "a cyclone" and an "express locomotive"? Learn all about the life of Teddy—his family, his politics, his love for the outdoors, and the energy that allowed him to accomplish his goals. *(biography)*

The Last Princess: The Story of Princess Ka'iulani of Hawaii
by Fay Stanley (Simon & Schuster Children's Publishing, 1991)
Princess Ka'iulani is the only person who can save Hawaii, an ancient island kingdom, from trouble. Can she keep the United States from claiming the kingdom or will she be too late? *(biography)*

Skill Power

Identifying Points of View

Identifying the different points of view of historical figures will help you understand why certain events occurred the way they did.

UNDERSTAND IT

Did you ever argue with a friend or relative over an issue affecting your school, town, or country? If so, you probably had different points of view. Your point of view is where you stand on an issue, and it affects what you say and do.

Throughout history, people have had different viewpoints on major events. Recall how the Loyalists and Patriots disagreed over American independence. Recall, too, how different points of view in the North and the South caused tension to mount before the Civil War.

Union soldier

Confederate soldier

EXPLORE IT

One night in 1898 the American battleship *Maine* blew up without warning in the harbor of Havana, Cuba. What happened?

Spanish officials, who ruled Cuba at that time, denied having anything to do with the explosion. From their point of view, ammunition on the *Maine* exploded by accident. Some American officers saw it the same way.

Newspapers in the United States reflected a different point of view about the explosion. How did that point of view differ from the Spanish point of view?

When the *Maine* went down, Spain was trying hard to hold on to its last colonies—Cuba, Puerto Rico, and the Philippines. The United States, however, was rapidly expanding. How might these facts explain each nation's point of view about the *Maine*?

$50,000 REWARD.—WHO DESTROYED THE MAINE!—$50,000 REWARD

NEW YORK JOURNAL
AND ADVERTISER. FIRST EDITION.

NEW YORK, THURSDAY, FEBRUARY 17, 1898.—16 PAGES. PRICE ONE CENT

DESTRUCTION OF THE WAR SHIP MAINE WAS THE WORK OF AN ENEMY

$50,000!
$50,000 REWARD!
For the Detection of the Perpetrator of the Maine Outrage!

Assistant Secretary Roosevelt Convinced the Explosion of the War Ship Was Not an Accident.

$50,000!
$50,000 REWARD!
For the Detection of the Perpetrator of the Maine Outrage!

TRY IT

Looking through local newspapers, find some issues in your community about which people have different points of view. (You'll often find people's points of view on the editorial page or in the letters to the editor.) Cut out the articles, editorials, or letters that interest you most. For each clipping, sum up the main issue in a sentence or two. Then list two different points of view on the issue.

With a partner, debate some of the issues that you have chosen. Each partner should take a different point of view on the issue. Then prepare a brief presentation to help convince your partner to agree with your point of view.

ISSUE: The Fairmount Town Board proposes closing Main Street to traffic, making it a pedestrian mall.

Viewpoint 1: Eliminating traffic would make the downtown business district quieter, safer, and more pleasant for shopping.

Viewpoint 2: Eliminating cars from downtown would make shopping less convenient for some, and receiving deliveries would be more difficult.

SKILL
POWER SEARCH

As you read this chapter, look for other issues on which Americans had different points of view. How did their points of view affect their actions?

AMERICAN EXPANSION

FOCUS *Between 1865 and 1917, Americans began to see the United States as a growing world power. This led to a demand to extend our influence in the world and to obtain colonies.*

Needs at Home

"Who cares about the rest of the world?" That was the attitude of many Americans before 1865. Troubles in Europe or Asia did not seem to be our concern. After all, no foreign country was going to invade the United States. This country was protected by vast oceans.

During this time Europeans were acquiring colonies around the world as sources of raw materials and new markets. They could pressure people in their colonies to buy goods from the home country.

Americans, however, had no interest in acquiring colonies or expanding. They had things to do at home, such as to build cities, factories, and railroads. Besides, the United States was a huge country, and there was still plenty of land in the West.

Another reason the United States didn't seek colonies was that ruling over others seemed un-American. Our nation had been born in a bitter struggle against colonial control. Many Americans did not want to do to others what the British had done to them.

Thinking of Expansion

After the Civil War, however, a few bold thinkers peeked into the future and saw

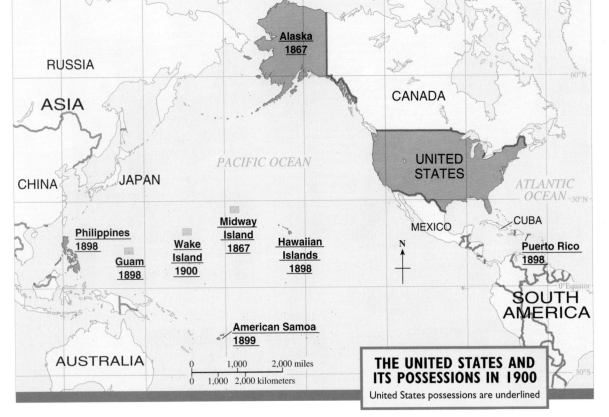

THE UNITED STATES AND ITS POSSESSIONS IN 1900
United States possessions are underlined

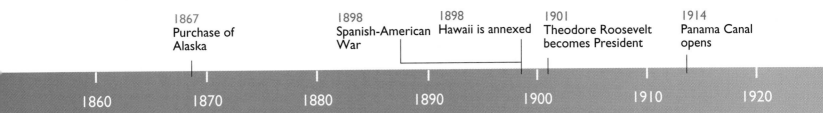

1867
Purchase of
Alaska

1898
Spanish-American
War

1898
Hawaii is annexed

1901
Theodore Roosevelt
becomes President

1914
Panama Canal
opens

1860   1870   1880   1890   1900   1910   1920

that the United States would not always be so isolated from the rest of the world. Change would come.

One person who realized this was William Seward, who was secretary of state. Seward believed that the United States could become a world power. First, the country had to be linked east to west, so Seward supported the transcontinental railroad. He argued for an expanded telegraph system. He even proposed a canal across Central America, which would link America to markets in Asia. This became a reality in 1914.

Buying Alaska

Seward also wanted the United States to expand. In 1867 he steered the United States into buying Alaska from Russia for $7.2 million. Find Alaska on the map on page 358. Many people poked fun at Seward's purchase, calling it "Seward's Folly" and "Seward's Ice Box." One newspaper wrote that Alaskan cows gave ice cream instead of milk!

Seward knew better. Alaska turned out to be one of the great bargains in history. It gave the United States an

▲ An 1867 American cartoon shows a politician trying to find voters in newly acquired Alaska, where few people lived.

enormous new territory that was rich with minerals and oil, was a key location in the North Pacific, and ended Russia's presence in North America.

Looking for an Empire

Slowly, attitudes toward expansion changed. By the late 1890s the United States was a mighty industrial nation. But was it a world power? All the world powers—Great Britain, France, Germany, and Japan—had colonies. Many Americans felt that it was time for their nation to have its own empire, or territories under its control.

Why this new attitude? First, many Americans believed in an idea called Manifest Destiny, or the right to expand. For years Americans believed it was their right to expand in North America. Now, some people thought it was their right to expand over the globe.

Second, Americans loved to conquer new frontiers. According to one historian, Frederick Jackson Turner, and the 1890 census, the frontier had closed. That meant that there were no new lands to settle in the American West. To some it was time to seek new frontiers beyond the borders of the United States.

Third, Americans liked to make money. By the late 1890s more goods were produced than could be consumed at home. Americans needed new places to sell their products. Business leaders were excited thinking about the huge markets in Asia and Latin America.

Annexing Hawaii

In 1898, Hawaii became the first American colony. Over the years American missionaries, sugar planters, and merchants had gone to Hawaii. In fact, American sugar planters had controlled much of the land since the 1840s. They wanted the United States to annex Hawaii. Native Hawaiians, led by Queen Liliuokalani (lih lee oo oh-kah LAH nee), did not.

The Americans, however, were powerful. Backed by its navy, the United States forced the queen to step down in 1893. Hawaii became a **protectorate**. The United States would "protect" Hawaii from other foreign powers.

Some Americans thought a protectorate went too far and said that Hawaiians

Queen Liliuokalani was queen of Hawaii from 1891 to 1893.

should be free. Others thought a protectorate didn't go far enough. They said it was good business to make Hawaii a colony. After arguing for five years over what to do, the people who wanted to take over the islands won. In 1898, Congress annexed Hawaii.

Trouble in the Caribbean

Meanwhile, trouble arose in the Caribbean. Puerto Rico and Cuba were still Spanish colonies. The Cubans were not happy with their foreign rulers, and in 1895 they rebelled under the leadership of José Martí. Spain struck back by waging a brutal war against the Cubans.

Should the United States help the Cubans win their freedom? Many Americans thought so. War fever began to sweep the United States. Two newspaper publishers, Joseph Pulitzer and William Randolph Hearst, fanned the flames. They printed stories about Spanish war crimes, whipping up sympathy for the Cubans. Their sensational style of writing was called yellow journalism.

"Remember the *Maine*"

The war in Cuba threatened Americans living there. The United States sent the battleship *Maine* to Havana, Cuba, to protect Americans there. On February 15, 1898, the *Maine* blew up, killing 260 Americans.

★ **protectorate** A place or country under the protection of another country

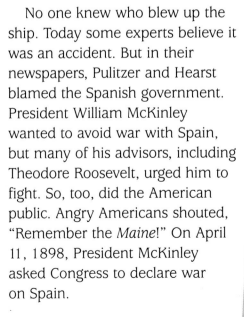

Spanish-American War

Americans went to war in Cuba, and many things went wrong. Their food rotted in the hot Caribbean sun. Their wool clothing was too warm for the climate. They lacked medical supplies and ammunition. Still, they managed to defeat a much larger Spanish army in less than two months.

In the battle of San Juan Hill, shown on the map on the left, the tide turned in favor of the Cubans and Americans. The future President, Theodore Roosevelt, led the charge of his **Rough Riders**. He and his troops quickly became heroes. Members of the 10th

★ **Rough Riders** Volunteer soldiers in the Spanish-American War, led by Theodore Roosevelt

▼ The sinking of the *Maine* was one of the causes of the Spanish-American War.

No one knew who blew up the ship. Today some experts believe it was an accident. But in their newspapers, Pulitzer and Hearst blamed the Spanish government. President William McKinley wanted to avoid war with Spain, but many of his advisors, including Theodore Roosevelt, urged him to fight. So, too, did the American public. Angry Americans shouted, "Remember the *Maine*!" On April 11, 1898, President McKinley asked Congress to declare war on Spain.

Negro Cavalry had helped ensure their victory by attacking on the right side of the Spanish line.

War in the Philippines

The Spanish-American War wasn't fought only in Cuba. More fighting took place halfway around the world. Since Spain ruled the Philippines (FIHL uh-peenz), the United States attacked the Spanish forces there as well. On May 1, 1898, Admiral George Dewey destroyed the Spanish fleet in Manila Bay. Find where the fleet was destroyed on the map on the left.

The days of Spain as a world power were over. In the peace treaty of 1898, Spain gave Cuba its freedom. Spain also gave Puerto Rico, the Philippines,

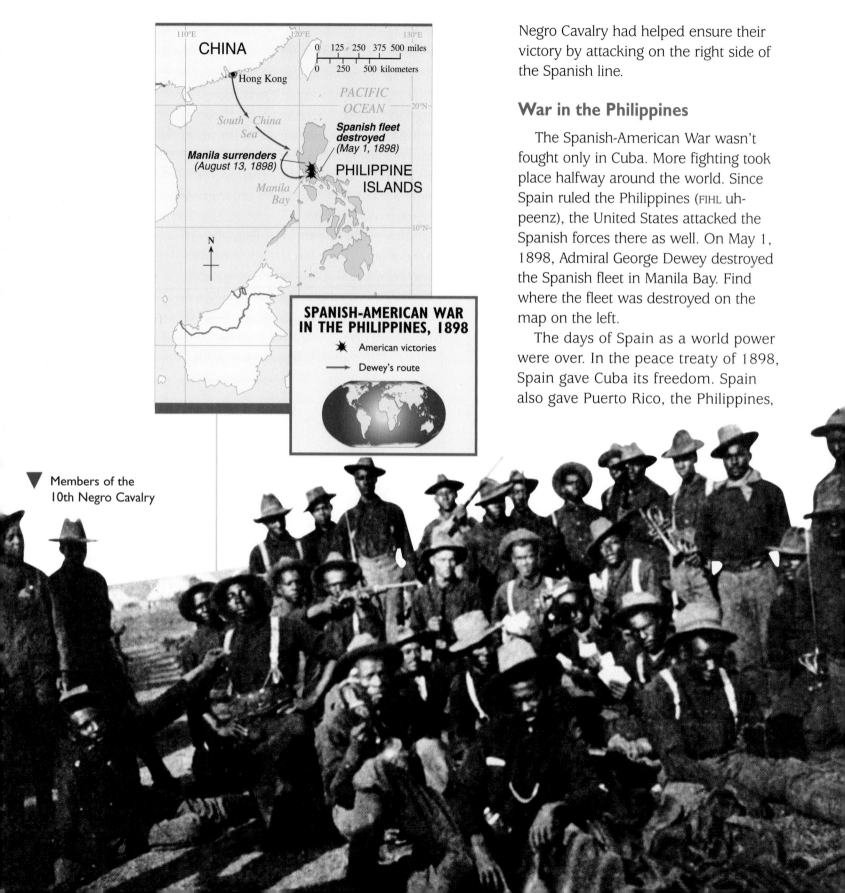

SPANISH-AMERICAN WAR IN THE PHILIPPINES, 1898
✴ American victories
→ Dewey's route

▼ Members of the 10th Negro Cavalry

A towering Uncle Sam, a symbol of the United States, holds the key to the open doors of China. Around him other nations wait to get in.

and the Pacific island of Guam to the United States. The American empire now stretched from the Caribbean Sea across to the Pacific Ocean.

What were Americans going to do with the Philippines? Many thought it should be set free. The Filipinos had fought hard against their Spanish rulers.

Others disagreed. They said that as a world power, America needed a place in the Pacific to act as a staging ground for their trade with Asian countries. If America didn't rule the Philippines, another country might. Also, these people claimed, Filipinos needed America to teach them about democracy, even to Christianize them.

The Filipinos had their own ideas. They wanted their freedom, and they were willing to fight for it. A bloody war broke out in 1899. The Filipinos gave up only after the Americans captured their leader, Emilio Aguinaldo (ahg ee NAHL doh). The United States ruled the Philippines until 1946, when the islands gained their independence.

Open-Door Policy in China

In the late 1800s, China's government was weak. Five European nations moved in and divided China into **spheres of influence**.

The United States didn't have a sphere, and Americans worried about being shut out of China's markets. So in 1899 and again in 1900, Secretary of State John Hay proposed an open-door policy. First, the policy said that all nations should be free to trade with China. Second, the spheres of influence should not be turned into colonies. After some negotiation, the European powers agreed to accept the American proposal.

The Great White Fleet

In 1907, President Roosevelt wanted to convince the world that the United States was a military power. He sent the Great White Fleet—16 white battleships—on a 14-month world tour. The ships returned to the United States shortly before Roosevelt's second presidential term ended. The tour had succeeded in displaying American military power.

 sphere of influence Area or country where another nation has gained special privileges and rights for itself

SHOW WHAT YOU KNOW!

REFOCUS
COMPREHENSION

1. What new lands did the United States acquire during the late 1800s?

2. How did "Seward's Folly" turn out to be "Seward's Bargain"?

THINK ABOUT IT
CRITICAL THINKING

Based on Hawaii's location, why was the United States interested in annexing it in 1898?

WRITE ABOUT IT
ACTIVITY

Write a newspaper account explaining why the United States built an empire.

A GROWING POWER

FOCUS *The United States gained power and influence around the world in the late 1800s and early 1900s.*

FUELING UP

Goodbye, wind; hello, coal! The elegant clipper ships of the old days were being replaced by faster steamships. But that created a problem. Steamships used coal to power their engines. The United States needed coaling stations around the world to refuel its steamships. This was particularly important in the vast Pacific Ocean.

In 1872 the United States obtained the right to set up a coaling station in the harbor of Pago Pago in the Samoa Islands. This move showed many Americans the importance of gaining overseas territories.

BOXER REBELLION

Many Chinese didn't want their country divided into spheres by Europeans. They also didn't like business people and missionaries bringing their foreign ways into China. Thousands joined secret societies to drive out the foreigners. Europeans called these Chinese "Boxers," because their symbol was a fist.

In June 1900 the Boxers entered Peking (Beijing), burning churches and killing Chinese Christians on sight. On June 20 they trapped almost 900 people inside some British buildings and a cathedral. Eight foreign nations, including the United States, quickly formed a special army. On August 14 this force defeated the Boxers and saved the trapped people.

Some Europeans thought this was the time to take more control of China, but the United States did not agree. Americans feared the loss of trading rights in China. At this point the Europeans accepted Secretary of State John Hay's open-door policy.

1872
Coaling station set
up in Samoa Islands

1900
Boxer
Rebellion

1909
William Howard Taft
becomes President

1914
Panama Canal
opens

1870   1880   1890   1900   1910   1920

SHOW WHAT YOU
KNOW!

REFOCUS
COMPREHENSION

1. What were some
ways in which the
United States
expanded its influence?

2. What was the goal
of the Boxer Rebellion?
What were the results?

THINK ABOUT IT
CRITICAL THINKING

What are some
advantages and
disadvantages of dollar
diplomacy?

WRITE ABOUT IT
ACTIVITY

Write a letter to a
friend about the
working and living
conditions during
the building of the
Panama Canal.

DOLLAR DIPLOMACY

William Howard Taft, who became President in 1909, favored a strong United States role in Latin America. The United States had key markets there that it wanted to protect. It could protect these markets in two ways. It could threaten the use of force, called gunboat diplomacy, or it could use money, called dollar diplomacy. Taft wanted to "substitute dollars for bullets." He urged bankers and business leaders from the United States to invest in Latin America. It was better to use trade instead of warships to expand American influence.

Investors responded and helped to build roads, railroads, and harbors in Latin America. These improvements increased trade, helping both investors in the United States and local Latin American governments.

PANAMA CANAL OPENED

The Panama Canal opened at last! In 1914 the first ship sailed through it. The Atlantic Ocean was now linked to the Pacific. President Theodore Roosevelt called it "the greatest task of its own kind that has ever been performed in the world."

Building the canal took three years of planning and seven years of digging through hills, swamps, and jungles. The work began in 1904. But it slowed down the next year because malaria and yellow fever were killing too many workers. Luckily an army medical officer, Colonel William Gorgas, stepped in. He wiped out mosquitoes. Still, the cost of building the canal was frightful. Almost 6,000 men died from disease, landslides, and accidents.

Citizenship

KEY TERM

imperialism

POLICY OF EXPANSION

FOCUS *As the power of the United States grew, one burning issue that split the American people was the role the United States should play on the world stage.*

In this chapter you have been learning about America's policy of expansion, or **imperialism**. Americans at this time had different views of imperialism. Some favored the policy, others didn't. Also, people had different reasons for either supporting or opposing imperialism. The following quotations are from well-known Americans of the late 1800s and early 1900s.

★ **imperialism** The policy of extending the rule of one country over other countries or lands

---

The quotations below are from people who *supported* imperialism. As you read, ask yourself why each person supported this policy.

—**President William McKinley**, explaining why he decided to annex the Philippine Islands. Earlier, McKinley had traveled the United States testing public opinion. He found that most Americans supported annexation.

[I believed] that we could not leave them [the Filipinos] to themselves—they were unfit for self-government—and they would soon have anarchy [a total breakdown of law and order] and misrule over there worse than Spain's was; and that there was nothing left for us to do but to take them all, and to educate the Filipinos, and uplift and civilize them.

—**Senator Albert Beveridge** of Indiana during the debate over whether the United States should keep the Philippines or let them govern themselves.

The Philippines are ours forever. . . . We will not renounce our part in the mission of our race . . . . [Give thanks] to Almighty God that He has marked us as His chosen people.

—**President Woodrow Wilson**, who believed America should teach democracy to the rest of the world.

Every nation needs [to be] taught the habit of law and obedience. . . . We are chosen, and prominently chosen, to show the way to the nations of the world how they shall walk in the paths of liberty.

The following quotations are from people who were *opposed* to imperialism. Identify their reasons for thinking the policy was wrong.

—From a statement by **Queen Liliuokalani,** who had assumed the throne in 1891 and believed that foreign elements, like the Americans, exercised too much control over Hawaii.

Hawaii for the Hawaiians

—From a statement by the American Anti-Imperialist League. **Jane Addams** was a member. Other members included such famous Americans as former President Grover Cleveland, author Mark Twain, and Andrew Carnegie.

Imperialism is hostile to liberty. . . . We earnestly condemn the policy of the [President] in the Philippines. It seeks to extinguish the spirit of 1776.

—**Booker T. Washington**, African American educator, who demanded that the United States take care of its own problems at home first before going out to save the world.

Until our nation has settled the Negro and Indian problems, I do not believe that we have a right to assume more social problems.

If you had lived during this time period, would you have *supported* or *opposed* imperialism? Give your reasons.

REFOCUS
COMPREHENSION

1. Why did President McKinley think it was important for the United States to control the Philippines?

2. What were Booker T. Washington's reasons for opposing control of foreign nations?

THINK ABOUT IT
CRITICAL THINKING

The United States was formed when 13 colonies gained their independence from Great Britain. Should the United States have acquired colonies of its own? Why or why not?

WRITE ABOUT IT
ACTIVITY

Investigate an issue in your school or community about which there are different opinions. Write about the various points of view.

367

THE PANAMA CANAL

4

Map Adventure

★ **KEY TERM**
isthmus

📖 **LITERATURE**
Panama Canal

FOCUS The Panama Canal was completed in 1914. It cut across the *Isthmus* of Panama, linking the Atlantic Ocean to the Pacific Ocean. Ships could now travel from one ocean to the other without going around South America.

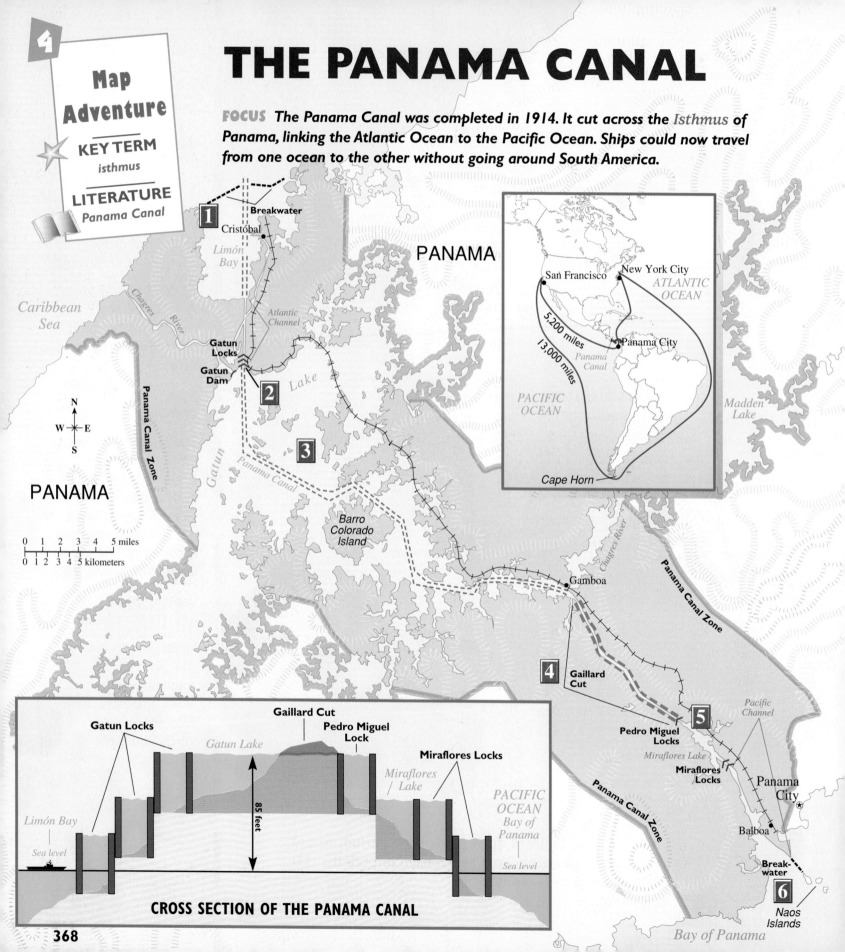

1
Breakwater
Cristóbal
Limón Bay
Chagres River
Caribbean Sea
Atlantic Channel
Gatun Locks
Gatun Dam
2
Gatun Lake
Panama Canal Zone
PANAMA
3
Panama Canal
Barro Colorado Island

PANAMA

San Francisco — New York City — ATLANTIC OCEAN
5,200 miles
13,000 miles
Panama City
Panama Canal
PACIFIC OCEAN
Cape Horn
Madden Lake

Gamboa
Chagres River
Panama Canal Zone
4 Gaillard Cut
5
Pedro Miguel Locks
Pacific Channel
Miraflores Lake
Miraflores Locks
Panama City
Panama Canal Zone
Balboa
Breakwater
6
Naos Islands
Bay of Panama

N W E S

0 1 2 3 4 5 miles
0 1 2 3 4 5 kilometers

CROSS SECTION OF THE PANAMA CANAL

Gatun Locks
Gaillard Cut
Pedro Miguel Lock
Gatun Lake
Miraflores Locks
Miraflores Lake
PACIFIC OCEAN Bay of Panama
Limón Bay
Sea level
85 feet
Sea level

Adventure in the Panama Canal

Until 1914, ships sailing from New York to San Francisco had to travel 13,000 miles around the continents of North and South America. The United States began digging the canal in 1904. By 1914, over 45,000 workers had moved more than 232 million cubic yards of earth, built a huge dam, and constructed three sets of locks. Ships could now sail through the canal, cutting almost 8,000 miles off their voyage.

Map Key

1 Limón Bay Ships coming from the Atlantic Ocean enter the canal at Limón Bay. A breakwater, or barrier, protects the bay from the Atlantic's high waves. After passing through Limón Bay, ships enter the seven-mile Atlantic Channel leading to the Gatun Locks.

2 Gatun Locks These are a series of three chambers that raise and lower ships to and from the Atlantic Channel and Gatun Lake. Electric locomotives called mules pull a ship into the locks. Large steel doors close behind the ship. Water is pumped into or out of the chamber until the water level is even with the next chamber. Then the doors to the next lock open, the ship enters, and the process is repeated.

3 Gatun Lake This 164-square-mile lake was created when Gatun Dam was built. One of the largest dams in the world, Gatun Dam is 105 feet high and made of sand, stones, and concrete.

4 Gaillard Cut This cut, or channel, was dug between two hills. It is eight miles long and 500 feet wide. Despite heavy rain and landslides, workers removed over 147 million cubic yards of earth to build this part of the canal.

5 Pedro Miguel and Miraflores Locks These locks are separated by Miraflores Lake. Ships are raised and lowered as much as 52 feet depending upon the height of the Pacific Ocean. Tides in the Pacific rise and fall 12 1/2 feet a day.

6 The Bay of Panama This is the Pacific entrance to the canal. To protect the canal from the Pacific Ocean's high tides, a breakwater was built from Balboa to the Naos Islands, using rock and soil excavated from the Gaillard Cut.

MAP IT

1. It is 1915 and you are the navigator of a ship in the Atlantic Ocean traveling from New York to San Francisco. Where do you enter the Panama Canal?
2. As you go from the Atlantic Channel to Gatun Lake, what locks do you pass through?
3. How high above sea level is the ship raised to get to Gatun Lake?
4. You go through the Gaillard Cut on your way to the Pedro Miguel and Miraflores Locks. What happens to your ship as it passes through these locks?
5. What bay do you sail into on your way to the Pacific Ocean?

EXPLORE IT

You must now bring the ship from San Francisco to New York. Record in your journal the route of your return voyage through the canal.

⭐ *isthmus*   A narrow strip of land joining two larger bodies of land

Panama Canal
Gateway to the World

by Judith St. George

This is the story of the Panama Canal, from its beginnings in 1904 until it opened in 1914. It was a ten-year struggle transforming Panama's jungle, swamp, and mountain ranges into a 50-mile-long canal that connected the Atlantic and Pacific oceans. Read also about the people behind the construction—equally as fascinating as the construction itself.

It didn't seem possible that President Theodore Roosevelt was actually going to Panama. After all, no president serving in office had ever left the United States before and yet here was the president planning to travel all the way to Central America to check on how work was going on his Panama Canal. Still, it had been two years since construction had begun and everyone knew that Roosevelt considered the canal a top priority of his presidency. . . .

It was typical of Roosevelt that he had chosen to visit Panama in the middle of the rainy season. He wanted to see work on the canal under the most difficult conditions and his wish was granted. He later wrote to his son Kermit, "For two days there [were] uninterrupted tropic rains without a glimpse of the sun . . . so that we saw the climate at its worst. It was just what I desired to do."

On the second day of his visit, three inches of rain fell in two hours, the worst downpour in fifteen years. The rain didn't bother Roosevelt a bit. While traveling along the canal route by train, he spotted several steam shovels excavating for the channel. He ordered the train to stop, got out, slogged through the mud, climbed up onto the driver's seat of one of the mammoth steam shovels and asked the driver to show him how it worked. An obviously delighted president was at the controls for about twenty minutes while the torrential rains soaked everyone, including Roosevelt, who was dressed all in white.

By the time the president and his party sailed from Panama after their three-day visit, the canal staff was exhausted and waterlogged. "I have blisters on both my feet and am worn out," complained the chief engineer.

On shipboard, Roosevelt wrote to Kermit describing work on the canal: ". . . the huge shovels are hard at it; scooping huge masses of rock and gravel and dirt. . . . They are eating steadily into the mountain, cutting it down and down." He added, "It [Panama] is a real tropic forest, palms and bananas, breadfruit trees, bamboos and gorgeous butterflies and brilliant colored birds fluttering among the orchids. There are beautiful flowers, too."

Read more about the building of the Panama Canal by checking the book out of your school or public library.

SHOW WHAT YOU KNOW!

REFOCUS
COMPREHENSION

1. What bodies of water does the Panama Canal connect?

2. Name the different locks in the Panama Canal.

THINK ABOUT IT
CRITICAL THINKING

Why was the building of the Panama Canal a top priority for President Theodore Roosevelt?

WRITE ABOUT IT
ACTIVITY

You are traveling with President Roosevelt on his visit to the Panama Canal. Write a letter home giving details about the weather, the sights, and the building of the canal.

SUMMING UP

1 DO YOU REMEMBER...
COMPREHENSION

1. Why didn't Americans want an empire during most of the 1800s?

2. Why did the United States begin to expand beyond North America in the 1890s?

3. Why did the United States want an open-door policy in China?

4. What is yellow journalism and how did it affect American feelings about Cuba?

5. On which islands were the major battles of the Spanish-American War fought?

6. How did the new steamships change American attitudes toward overseas territories?

7. How did dollar diplomacy expand the influence of the United States?

8. What did President Woodrow Wilson hope the example of the United States could teach other nations?

9. Why did Queen Liliuokalani say, "Hawaii for the Hawaiians"?

10. Name the Atlantic and Pacific entrances to the Panama Canal.

2 SKILL POWER
IDENTIFYING POINTS OF VIEW

With a group of classmates, look back through the chapters of this book that you've already read. Choose three chapters and in each one try to find an example of individuals or groups who had different points of view. Sum up these different points of view and tell how or if they were resolved.

3 WHAT DO YOU THINK?
CRITICAL THINKING

1. Think about the role some newspapers played in the Spanish-American War. What does this suggest about the responsibilities of journalists?

2. Do you think the United States still practices dollar diplomacy? How do American businesses and banks expand American influence around the world?

3. How do you think the Chinese felt about the spheres of influence and the open-door policy?

4. What do you think the Anti-Imperialist League meant when it said that the United States policy in the Philippines would "extinguish the spirit of 1776"?

5. Do you think the Panama Canal is as important today as it was in 1914? Explain.

4 SAY IT, WRITE IT, USE IT
VOCABULARY

Suppose you are living at the turn of the century. Write a letter to a newspaper telling how you feel about the efforts of the United States to gain new lands and markets overseas. In your letter include as many of the vocabulary words as you can.

imperialism
isthmus
protectorate

Rough Riders
sphere of influence

5 GEOGRAPHY AND YOU
MAP STUDY

Use the maps on pages 358, 361, and 362 to answer the following questions.

1. On what island is the city of Havana located?

2. What state in the United States is located between Russia and Canada?

3. What sea lies between China and the Philippine Islands?

4. In what direction would you travel to go from Cuba to Florida?

6 TAKE ACTION
CITIZENSHIP

The role of the United States on the world stage was a burning question that split the American people in 1900. In today's fast-changing world, Americans still debate this question. With a group of classmates, discuss what you think the role of the United States should be. Should we intervene to stop wars and aggression in other countries? What are our responsibilities in times of disaster? How can we best promote democracy? After the discussion, write a group statement that expresses the views of the group.

7 GET CREATIVE
SCIENCE CONNECTION

"The Land Divided, the World United" is the slogan of the Panama Canal. Find out more about how the canal was built and how it operates. Draw a sketch to show how the canal locks raise and lower water levels so that ships can cross the isthmus.

LOOKING AHEAD In the next chapter learn about the United States in World War I and changes the war brought at home.

UNIT 6

Into THE Twentieth Century

CHAPTER 17
World War I

CHAPTER 18
The 1920s

CHAPTER 19
The Great Depression

CHAPTER 20
World War II

What Does It Mean to Be a World Power?

How did the United States become a world power in the early twentieth century? Examine the events that propelled the country into two world wars, and learn how the nation experienced both prosperity and economic depression.

WORLD WAR I

Submarines, machine guns, and trenches were all part of a new kind of warfare in World War I. Have you wondered what this war was about and how it affected the United States? This chapter tells how the United States changed the war and was changed by it.

CONTENTS

▲ What does knitting socks have to do with World War I? Look on page 391 to find out.

These books tell about some people, places, and events of interest during the time of the First World War. Read one that interests you and fill out a book-review form.

READ AND RESEARCH

The Great Migration: An American Story
Paintings by Jacob Lawrence (HarperCollins Publishers, 1993)

Jacob Lawrence painted pictures that tell the story of why so many African Americans moved from the South to northern cities around the time of World War I. His paintings reflect his personal experiences as the child of parents who were part of this Great Migration. *(nonfiction)*

- *You can read a selection from this story on page 398.*

Hero Over Here: A Story of World War I
by Kathleen V. Kudlinski (Penguin USA, 1990)

When his father and older brother go off to war, ten-year-old Theodore becomes the man of the house. Read how he becomes a hero when the flu epidemic comes to his town. *(historical fiction)*

World War I by Tom McGowen (Franklin Watts, 1993)

Track the United States' involvement in the First World War. Discover more about the major battles through powerful photographs and detailed maps. Notice the destruction that was caused by this war. *(nonfiction)*

Edith Wilson: The Woman Who Ran the United States
by James Cross Giblin (Penguin USA, 1993)

When President Woodrow Wilson suffered a stroke in 1919, the First Lady helped him with his presidential responsibilities. Consider why Edith Wilson is sometimes called America's first woman President. *(biography)*

SKILL POWER

Understanding Generalizations

Knowing how to make and recognize generalizations can help you pull together ideas so that you understand them.

UNDERSTAND IT

Do you think you'd agree with a neighbor who made these statements?

"Things always used to be terrific in this town."

"Now everything's going downhill."

Chances are you wouldn't agree with such sweeping generalizations. After all, you know that lots of good things are going on in your community. What's more, history tells you that everything wasn't always so terrific in the past.

A generalization is a statement that applies to many different people or events. Before you make or agree with a generalization, think about whether there are enough facts and examples to support it.

EXPLORE IT

When writers make generalizations, they often use clue words and phrases—*in general, as a rule, usually, often, most, many, generally, tend to.* These clues tell the reader that the statement applies to a large group, but not all, of the people and events being described. Careful writers also support their generalizations with facts and examples. That way a reader can better judge whether the generalization is accurate.

There are two generalizations in the following paragraph. What clue words help you find them? What facts or examples support each generalization?

Historians generally agree that World War I was unlike any previous European war. In earlier wars, hired soldiers did the fighting. World War I was fought by ordinary men drafted into their country's army. World War I also saw the first use of airplanes, trucks, tanks, and submarines in warfare. The fighting tended to be more destructive, too. In one battle in 1916, for example, 700,000 men were killed or wounded.

As a rule, I am usually right.

In general, you tend to be wrong.

TRY IT

Choose something familiar about your school or community—cafeteria food, a nearby park, a local ball team, the school library. Think of a generalization you could make about this topic.

Write your generalization on a piece of paper. Then list some facts and examples that support it. You can draw pictures to illustrate your generalization, too.

Read your generalization to your classmates or post it on a bulletin board. Does your generalization fit in with what your classmates know about the subject? Do you agree with your classmates' generalizations?

From news headlines like these, you could make a positive generalization about the environment in your community.

Find some generalizations about World War I in this chapter.

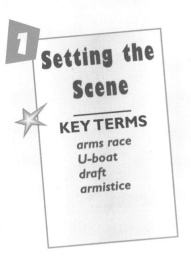

1 Setting the Scene

★

KEY TERMS

arms race
U-boat
draft
armistice

THE GREAT WAR

FOCUS *In 1914, war broke out in Europe. The United States stayed out of the war until 1917. Then the American troops greatly impacted the course of the war.*

Causes for War in Europe

In 1914, war broke out in Europe. This war had many causes. First, European nations wanted to grow economically. They competed for world markets and colonies because colonies provided natural resources and consumers of products.

Second, European nations didn't trust each other. So they built *alliances* with other nations. In this way, if one nation was attacked, its allies would join in the fight to defend it. Since these alliances still allowed for the possibility of war, an **arms race** began. Many nations, especially Germany, built up their military strength.

The War Begins

Bosnia was a territory of the Austro-Hungarian Empire. Find Bosnia on the map. Most of Bosnia's people were Serbs. Austria-Hungary was a large empire, with people from many different backgrounds, including Austrians, Hungarians, Slovaks, and Serbs. Some of these people wanted independent nations. For example, the Serbs in Bosnia wanted their territory to be joined with the bordering nation of Serbia.

On June 28, 1914, the archduke Ferdinand was assassinated in Sarajevo, Bosnia. Ferdinand was next in line to be emperor of Austria-Hungary. The Austrians were upset. Blaming the Serbs for Ferdinand's death, they declared war on Serbia. To help

EUROPE IN 1914

- ▢ Allies
- ▢ Central Powers
- ▢ Neutral countries

★ ***arms race*** When countries compete to have more firepower than one another

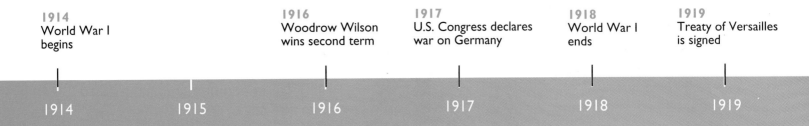

1914
World War I begins

1916
Woodrow Wilson wins second term

1917
U.S. Congress declares war on Germany

1918
World War I ends

1919
Treaty of Versailles is signed

1914 1915 1916 1917 1918 1919

Serbia, Russia got involved. Before long many of Europe's nations declared war on each other.

Great Britain, France, Belgium, and Russia were the most powerful nations on one side. They were known as the Allied Powers, or the Allies. The largest nations on the other side were Germany, Austria-Hungary, and the Ottoman Empire. They were known as the Central Powers. Even the colonies of the warring nations were drawn into the war. Europe's war would be known as the Great War (it would later be called World War I). Find the Allies and the Central Powers on the map on page 380.

The United States Is Neutral

President Wilson announced that the United States would be neutral, or not take a side in the war. Most Americans agreed with this policy.

And some Americans profited from the war. American businesses sold Europeans many important goods, such as cotton. Shipping to warring nations was dangerous. Nations tried to stop ships from carrying goods to their enemies. But profits were large, so some

The *Lusitania* and note found in the wreckage

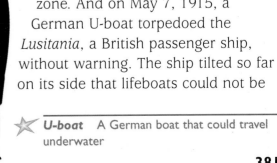

▼ President Woodrow Wilson and Edith Wilson

Americans found it worth the risk.

One great risk was the German **U-boat**, or submarine. A U-boat could sink a larger ship with a single torpedo, fired from under the water. Germans used submarines to sink the Allies' ships. Sometimes U-boat torpedoes hit passenger ships and killed many innocent people.

In late April 1915, Germans warned Americans not to sail on Great Britain's ships in the war zone. And on May 7, 1915, a German U-boat torpedoed the *Lusitania*, a British passenger ship, without warning. The ship tilted so far on its side that lifeboats could not be

⭐ **U-boat** A German boat that could travel underwater

launched. In about 18 minutes, the ship sank. Nearly 1,200 people died, 128 of whom were Americans. Many Americans were outraged by this attack. After this, President Wilson pressured the Germans to promise to warn ships before torpedoing them, giving the people on board a chance to escape in lifeboats.

In 1916, with the United States still remaining neutral, Wilson won a second term as President. His campaign slogan was "He kept us out of war!" For a while it appeared that President Wilson would continue to do so.

Declaring War

In early 1917, Germany decided to make an all-out effort to win the war. Germans declared that their U-boats

I WANT YOU FOR U.S. ARMY
NEAREST RECRUITING STATION

▲ Army recruiting poster

▼ National Guardsmen before they received their uniforms

A U.S. draft card

REGISTRATION CERTIFICATE

would no longer give warnings. In addition to sinking Allied ships, German submarines would now also sink the ships of neutral countries. And in one day, March 18, Germans attacked three American ships.

On April 2, 1917, in response to these attacks, President Wilson asked Congress to declare war against Germany. Many members of Congress applauded the President's speech. After the speech, Wilson told his secretary, "My message today was a message of death for our young men. How strange it seems . . . to applaud that."

Thinking of American boys dying on the battlefields of Europe caused some people to oppose the war. Women, in particular, campaigned to keep the United States neutral. Still, four days after President Wilson's speech, Congress approved his request to declare war.

Building an Army

Now the United States needed soldiers. Only a small army stood prepared, and this war would call for a large one. Some men quickly volunteered for the army. However, the United States still needed a **draft** to get enough soldiers. All young men between the ages of 21 and 30 had to register for the draft. There

---

draft A process of randomly choosing young men for military service

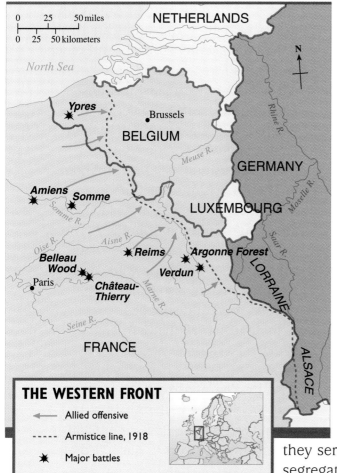

THE WESTERN FRONT

← Allied offensive

---- Armistice line, 1918

✳ Major battles

were about 24 million men in that age group, with close to 4 million of them eventually serving in the armed services during the war.

African Americans were among the many young men who were drafted to fight in World War I. In addition, many others served in the armed forces as volunteers. The total African American force numbered about 400,000. But they served only in segregated units.

Men from other ethnic groups also fought. Puerto Rican soldiers numbered about 20,000, and a large number of Mexican Americans served. In addition, Native Americans, who were not citizens and could not be drafted, still volunteered to fight.

Women were not drafted, but about 130,000 voluntarily joined the military. They worked behind the battle lines doing office work. For the first time in America's history, women could hold official military rank in the navy and in the marines. But that was not the case in the army. In fact, the 18,000 women who served in the Army Nurse Corps didn't even get paid for their tireless efforts during the war.

The War on the Western Front

The war itself was fought on two major fronts: the eastern front and the western front. The map on the left shows the western front. To the east, Germans continually defeated the Russians. As the war progressed, conditions in Russia grew terrible, and many Russians wanted a revolution. In March 1917, Russian revolutionaries overthrew the czar (zahr), or emperor, and set up a temporary government that called for democratic freedoms.

▲ Allied soldiers in a trench in France

Eight months later, however, another revolution took place. Russia adopted *communism*, an economic system in which the government owns all the land and businesses. (This is different from the free enterprise system in the United States. In this economic system, businesses are owned by individuals and companies rather than by the government.) Russia's new government signed a peace treaty with Germany.

Now Germany could devote all its energy to fight the British and French on the western front. Here both sides dug hundreds of miles of trenches to protect their troops. Soon neither side had a clear advantage. It was here that American soldiers fought.

American Troops Arrive

When American troops first went to Europe, they fought as part of the French and British armies. Then, in the spring of 1918, large numbers of American soldiers arrived. General John J. Pershing, commander of the American Expeditionary Forces in Europe, wanted American troops to fight as an American army, not as replacements for fallen French and British troops. The European Allies did not agree with Pershing. Yet Pershing did eventually get what he wanted. On August 10, 1918, the U.S. First Army was organized, with General Pershing as its commander.

The American troops made a difference in the war, and slowly the advantage shifted to the Allies. The U.S. Navy began sinking German submarines. And along with sending troops, America also sent much needed food and supplies.

In August 1918 the Germans launched a massive attack. But by then enough Americans had arrived to help push the Germans back. The last great battle took place in the Argonne (AHR-gahn) Forest. More than 1.2 million Americans took part in this Allied effort.

The War Ends

At last, in the fall of 1918, the Germans saw that they couldn't win the war, and they asked for an **armistice**. On November 11, 1918, at 11:00 A.M., the guns fell silent. World War I was over.

Early in 1919 the Allies gathered at the Palace of Versailles (vur SYE)

⭐ **armistice**   A halt to fighting by agreement between warring nations

U.S. Marines arriving in France

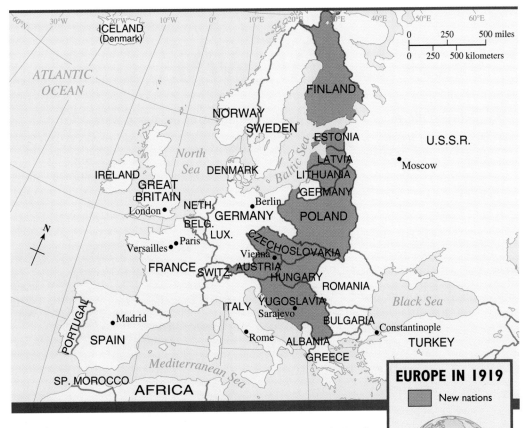

EUROPE IN 1919

■ New nations

outside Paris, France. They met to write a peace treaty and to find a way to make Germany pay for its role in the war. The Allies decided that Germany should pay the Allies for war damages, give up its colonies, and give up some land. Many Germans resented this treatment. In time, their anger would erupt in an even bigger war—World War II. The map above shows Europe after the end of World War I.

The League of Nations

The peace treaty ending the war included President Wilson's plan for a League of Nations. This new world organization was supposed to help nations peacefully deal with any disputes.

In the fall of 1919, Wilson traveled around the United States, trying to get Americans to support his idea. But Americans didn't want the United States involved in any international peacekeeping organizations. The United States Senate agreed. The Senate must ratify all treaties, but it voted against this treaty and the League of Nations.

Most of the other countries did join the League of Nations. But without the support of the United States, now the most powerful country in the world, the League of Nations had little power.

SHOW WHAT YOU KNOW!

REFOCUS
COMPREHENSION

1. What nations made up the Allied Powers? What nations made up the Central Powers?

2. List some events that led to the United States' declaration of war on Germany.

THINK ABOUT IT
CRITICAL THINKING

Why do you think women worked in the army, even though they weren't given official titles or pay?

WRITE ABOUT IT
ACTIVITY

Make a chart listing the causes of World War I.

A WORLD AT WAR

FOCUS *Between the years 1914 and 1918, the nations of the world were fighting World War I battles, a revolution, and the flu.*

ASSASSINATION IN BOSNIA

On June 28, 1914, Archduke Francis Ferdinand and his wife, Sophie, visited Bosnia. Ferdinand was the heir to the throne of Austria-Hungary. A crowd gathered on the streets of Sarajevo to watch the royal couple pass.

In a nearby cafe sat Gavrilo Princip, a young Serb who didn't want the Austrians ruling his people. When Ferdinand's car stopped in front of the cafe, Princip leapt up and shot the archduke and his wife. This assassination plunged Europe into the Great War.

THE RUSSIAN REVOLUTION

World War I was very expensive for Russia. Its government had to provide soldiers with clothing, food, and ammunition. And the government had to support its citizens at home.

Soon the war affected civilian life. Railroads no longer transported people and resources throughout the country. Instead the trains transported military supplies.

As people struggled with the lack of food, fuel, and housing that resulted from the war, they lost confidence in their government.

The people revolted against the government. Within eight months, a second revolution brought another change in the leadership of Russia.

DECLARING WAR

By April 6, 1917, President Wilson and Congress had agreed to declare war on Germany. The vote in the Senate was 82 to 6. The vote in the House was 373 to 50.

Jeanette Rankin of Montana, a member of the House of Representatives, was the first woman ever to serve in Congress. She voted against the war. Rankin, a pacifist, was opposed to all wars. "I want to stand by my country," she said, "but I cannot vote for war."

June 1914
Archduke Ferdinand
is assassinated

March 1917
Russian
Revolution
begins

April 1917
Congress
declares war
on Germany

March 1918
Flu first strikes
in the United
States

November 1918
World War I ends

1914   1915   1916   1917   1918   1919

THE FLU PANDEMIC

In March 1918 the flu struck Fort Riley, Kansas. Within a month 8,000 people in Fort Riley had gotten the flu. Soon this flu became a *pandemic*, or an illness that spread in many countries.

The flu struck so many people at once that doctors and hospitals couldn't handle all the patients. And few medicines were available to help people with symptoms.

Many towns passed laws to help prevent the spread of the flu. Some towns required people to wear gauze masks. But the disease continued to spread.

The pandemic lasted about nine months. It struck around 130 million people, killing 20 million. More people died from the flu than from fighting in the war.

PEACE RETURNS

It was near the end of the year 1918. On the eleventh hour of the eleventh day of the eleventh month, peace returned to Europe. All over the world, church bells rang out. People danced in the streets. Total strangers hugged each other.

One year later, Americans celebrated Armistice Day on November 11. At 11:00 A.M., people stopped everything they were doing for two minutes of silence. And in schools throughout the country, children thought about family members who had fought in the war.

REFOCUS
COMPREHENSION

1. How did World War I affect Russia?

2. Why did United States cities pass laws requiring people to wear masks?

THINK ABOUT IT
CRITICAL THINKING

What might be some reasons that pacifists are against *all* kinds of war?

WRITE ABOUT IT
ACTIVITY

November 11 is now the date that Veteran's Day is celebrated. Do some research to find out about a veteran from your family or neighborhood. Write a paragraph about that person.

THE HOME FRONT

FOCUS *During World War I most Americans got involved in the war effort. Government agencies were created, people volunteered their services, and even children got involved.*

Mobilizing the Economy

After declaring war, the United States had a lot to do in preparation for war. The nation needed more fuel, tanks, warships, and food. This required a total **mobilization** of the nation's economy. Everyone had to pitch in and help. The federal govern-

ment set up more than 500 agencies to direct the war effort. Under the direction of these agencies, more military supplies and ships were produced. The map below shows the location of some war industries.

The Fuel Administration had to get fuel to the military. Headed by Harry Garfield, the Administration stepped

⭐ **mobilization** The organization of people and resources to help a cause

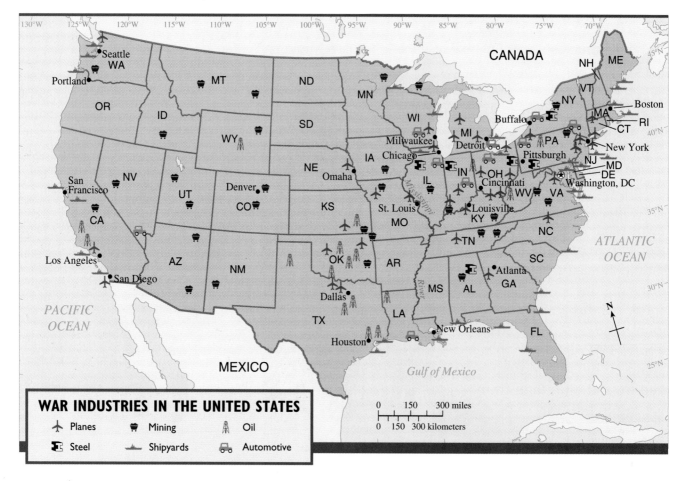

WAR INDUSTRIES IN THE UNITED STATES

| ✈ Planes | ⛏ Mining | 🛢 Oil |
| 🏭 Steel | ⚓ Shipyards | 🚗 Automotive |

0   150   300 miles

0   150   300 kilometers

up the mining of coal and encouraged **civilians** to cut back on their use of fuel. Garfield asked people to have "lightless nights" and "heatless Mondays." And he asked motorists not to drive on Sundays. In another attempt to conserve fuel, Garfield introduced daylight saving time.

Saving Food

The Food Administration was also involved in the war effort. Herbert Hoover, a future President, headed this agency. Hoover didn't want to **ration** food. Instead, he urged farmers to grow more food, and he asked American families to voluntarily save food. Many Americans limited the amount of food they bought by planting "victory gardens" in their backyards. Or they didn't eat certain foods on certain days. Soon, people were having "wheatless Mondays," "meatless Tuesdays," and "porkless Thursdays."

These were small sacrifices, but they were important. In

Food *is* Ammunition—
Don't waste it.
UNITED STATES FOOD ADMINISTRATION

this way, even small children could feel that they too were part of helping the war effort.

Selecting Soldiers

In addition to needing extra fuel and food for the war, the nation needed soldiers. And in May 1917, Congress passed the Selective Service Act. This act required all men between the ages of 21 and 30 to register for the draft. (Later, in 1918, in an effort to get more soldiers, the age range became 18 to 45.)

On the first day that the act went into effect—June 5, 1917—more than 9.5 million men registered for the

▼ American soldiers

civilian A person who is not a member of the armed forces
ration To limit the amount of something that each person can get

draft. Most of these men did so gladly because they thought of military service as their duty as citizens. Other men, however, tried to evade, or avoid, the draft. These men were scorned and were called "slackers."

Raising Public Support

Another great need for the war was money. The United States raised this money through increased taxes and war bonds. The extra tax money came in the form of increased income tax and increased taxes on goods such as tobacco and movie tickets.

However, most of the money was raised with Liberty and Victory bonds. This meant that American people were lending the United States government their money. Children even got

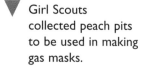

Girl Scouts collected peach pits to be used in making gas masks.

You Save Peach Seeds — They Will Save Soldiers Lives

involved by buying Thrift Stamps for just 25 cents. By the end of the war, the American people had loaned the government over $21 billion.

Many people supported the war by saving food, growing vegetables, and buying war bonds. But not

everyone favored the war. People who opposed it came from many different backgrounds.

A Show of Patriotism

For the most part, Americans thought that supporting the war was a way to display their patriotism. Many American children participated in patriotic events. They fought play-battles between the Yanks and the Germans. Children went to parades to see soldiers march off to war. And children collected rubber and other things needed for the war effort. They also helped their mothers plant victory gardens. In school, they wrote letters to soldiers in Europe and essays on being a patriot.

Patriotism was important, but sometimes people took it too far. Some Americans rejected Germans and *anything* German. Many public schools stopped teaching the German language. In Oklahoma, books about Germany were burned in school-yards. The great music of German composers, such as Mozart and Beethoven, was banned. Even everyday German words such as *hamburger* and *sauerkraut* were changed to *Salisbury steak* and *liberty cabbage* during the war.

Voluntary Service

People also served the war effort by volunteering their services in practical ways. Some American women volunteered as nurses or worked with the Red Cross in Europe. Other women taught French classes for nurses that were going overseas.

Many other people worked toward a World War I victory in the United States. Some women and children sewed uniforms and knitted socks and sweaters for soldiers. Other people collected items needed in the war effort, such as books for soldiers to read and peach stones to be used in making gas masks.

In many ways American civilians, both young and old, helped in the war effort, even though they were not on the battle front.

A woman, standing on a pile of books, shouts for people to donate more books for soldiers.

Knitting scarves and sweaters for soldiers

SHOW WHAT YOU KNOW!

REFOCUS
COMPREHENSION

1. How did the government mobilize the economy to get the supplies needed for the war?

2. What were some ways that Americans at home supported the war effort?

THINK ABOUT IT
CRITICAL THINKING

How do you think volunteerism affected the way Americans felt about their country?

WRITE ABOUT IT
ACTIVITY

Make a list of some statements from this lesson that are generalizations. Then find the facts to support the generalizations.

TECHNOLOGY CHANGES WAR

FOCUS *Technology greatly affected the way that World War I battles were fought. New weapons created a need for new fighting tactics.*

A New Kind of War

▼ A gas mask

World War I introduced many weapons that had never been used before, such as machine guns, armored tanks, and poison gas. These weapons forever changed the ways that wars were fought.

One machine gun could shoot down dozens of men in a few seconds. Since this meant that many more soldiers would be killed by one gunman, man-to-man combat became much less frequent than it had been in the Civil War.

Misery of the Trenches

The use of machine guns made trench warfare much more necessary. Since soldiers couldn't confront the enemy at ground level, they dug huge trenches into the ground.

Trenches were used mainly on the western front. In fact, hundreds of miles of these ditches zigzagged across the countryside. They stretched from the coast of Belgium across France to the border of Switzerland.

Trench warfare was awful. Soldiers had to endure cold, snow, and drenching rain. They slept on the ground in oozing mud. Rats the size of small dogs dashed around them in the trenches.

In between the trenches of the Allies and the Central Powers lay a treacherous land known as "**no man's land.**" It was a dark and eerie place filled with barbed wire, charred tree trunks, and dead soldiers.

Any assault in this

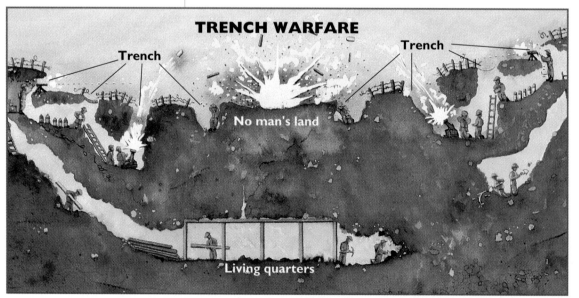

TRENCH WARFARE

Trench

Trench

No man's land

Living quarters

no man's land The land separating opposing armies

wasteland would mean facing the enemy's machine guns. If that was not bad enough, both sides now had poison gas. The effect of poison gas was so horrible that its use was outlawed after World War I.

An American World War I airplane

Under the Sea and Overhead

Two other inventions that forever changed war were the submarine and the airplane. Before the submarine was invented, ships at sea had battled each other in the open. Now the enemy remained unseen beneath the waves. Submarines soon became a weapon used by every warring naval power.

A tank

Before the airplane, enemy troops could not spy on each other from the skies, let alone fight in the skies. Now all that changed.

Early in World War I, planes were only used to observe the enemy's movements. But then, as the technology improved, each side put machine guns into their planes. Now the planes would shoot each other down. Soon the plane became another weapon. The average pilot lived about three weeks, because most pilots were poorly trained and flew in flimsy planes.

Still, the best pilots captured the thoughts of people on both sides. Like brave knights from earlier wars, they fought one on one. In such an aerial **dogfight**, it was the skill of the pilot, not his plane, that counted most. Two of the most famous pilots were Germany's "Red Baron" and America's Eddie Rickenbacker.

Because of these changes in warfare, World War I is known as the first modern war. Today, wars are fought using a number of these technological advances and others.

dogfight   A battle between two or more planes within close range of each other in the air

SHOW WHAT YOU KNOW!

REFOCUS
COMPREHENSION

1. List some ways in which new technology created new battle tactics.

2. How did submarines change naval warfare?

THINK ABOUT IT
CRITICAL THINKING

Why do you think some pilots became heroes to many people?

WRITE ABOUT IT
ACTIVITY

Draw a picture or write a paragraph describing what a pilot who was spying on enemy troops might have seen.

A submarine

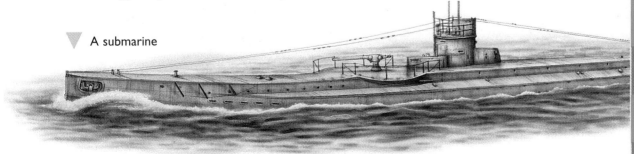

Spotlight

★ **KEY TERMS**
migrant worker
prohibition

📖 **LITERATURE**
The Great Migration

WAR CHANGES A NATION

FOCUS *During and after Europe's Great War, the United States changed dramatically. Compare people's hopes for change with what actually took place.*

A Changing Work Force

American involvement in World War I led to many changes in the United States. The war effort created a dramatic change in the factory work force. More jobs became available because men had left their jobs for the battlefield. And there were fewer workers available because immigration had decreased during the war. But war industries needed workers, and many new job opportunities existed in northern cities.

Black Americans wanted those jobs, so they moved to northern cities by the thousands, in what came to be known as the Great Migration. Before the war began, 90 percent of black citizens lived in the South, mostly in rural areas. Between 1914 and 1920 about 500,000 moved north.

African Americans also moved north to escape segregation and discrimination in the South. But, while they found jobs in the North, they did not find an integrated culture. Even though northern cities did not have laws protecting segregation as the South did, racial segregation and discrimination were still practiced in the North. Black Americans lived in separate areas. They went to separate schools. And they worshiped in separate churches.

Sometimes racial tensions turned violent. In 1917 a riot broke out in East St. Louis. The fighting left 39 black Americans dead. In addition, fires destroyed the homes of more than 6,000 people.

Women Work and Vote

During this time, many women worked at northern factories. For many women this was the first time they had worked at jobs outside their homes. Women from the South and from rural areas flocked to northern cities to work in factories. In all, about 1.5 million women got factory jobs making military supplies. When the war ended, however, nearly all these women lost their jobs.

Still, working in factories during the war helped women gain suffrage. As women

These women took over men's jobs at the Northern Pacific Railway

worked at factory jobs and volunteered in the war effort, they gained experience in organizing and campaigning for their rights. They marched in front of the White House. They staged hunger strikes. Some women were even arrested.

Finally, in 1917, President Wilson asked Congress to vote for the Nineteenth Amendment. Also known as the Susan B. Anthony Amendment, it provided for woman suffrage. At last, in 1920, the amendment was approved by 36 states, and women in the United States could vote.

Workers for the Farms

Since farm workers had moved to the city, a labor shortage developed on farms. The United States filled this need with Mexican **migrant workers**. During harvest time, Mexican workers came into the United States. The people who hired Mexican workers were responsible for paying their transportation costs to and from the United States

Mexican migrant workers in a Texas cotton field

and for providing housing. Other Mexicans worked on the railroads. As a result, many Mexican American communities expanded.

Black Americans Join the Army

Fighting in the war led many black Americans to become hopeful about ways that their country might change. They expected to have more influence in the democratic process of the United States.

When men began signing up for the draft and serving voluntarily, many African American leaders encouraged black people to become involved in the war effort. They saw the war as an opportunity to show their patriotism. And black soldiers hoped that fighting for

Close our ranks shoulder to shoulder with our own white fellow citizens.

– W.E.B. DuBois

migrant worker A worker who travels from place to place to harvest crops

democracy in Europe would help them to be treated more fairly at home.

During World War I, the army was completely segregated. Black soldiers were separated from white soldiers and were often given low-skill jobs. However, some black Americans did serve in combat, many of them with great honor.

The 369th Infantry Regiment served for the longest time of any of the American troops. They lived and fought in the trenches for 191 days. The French awarded the entire unit the *Croix de Guerre* (krwahd GER), or

▼ These men were part of the 369th Infantry.

"Cross of War," their highest wartime medal. In addition, the French specifically noted 171 individual black soldiers for their bravery.

When the war ended, African Americans were optimistic. Yet the hopes of W.E.B. DuBois and other black leaders were not realized. African Americans did not gain greater equality at home. Despite their bravery and service, they still faced racial discrimination.

A New Amendment

The war also changed certain American values. The spirit of temperance filled the air. During the war, grain was needed to feed the troops. Little was left over to make beer or whiskey, so people learned to live without alcohol.

Many rural states already had passed laws against the sale of alcohol. But now temperance leaders pushed for a **prohibition** amendment to eliminate alcohol from the entire country. Those who supported prohibition were called "drys." Those who opposed it were called "wets." The drys won. In 1917, Congress approved the Eighteenth Amendment, which made it

★ **prohibition** A law making it illegal to make or sell alcoholic beverages

illegal for anyone to sell alcoholic beverages. In 1919 the states ratified, or approved, the amendment.

The Troops Come Home

In 1917, America had mobilized for war. In late 1918, when the troops came home at the end of the war, the country had to readjust for peace. The United States didn't need as many tanks and airplanes as it did before. The government stopped ordering military supplies. So factories produced less and many people lost their jobs.

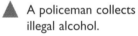
A policeman collects illegal alcohol.

Meanwhile, the army began to discharge soldiers. These men also needed jobs. By 1919, millions of people were unemployed. It would take nearly five years for the economy to create enough jobs for most American workers.

World War I brought many changes to the United States. Some changes created new problems. Other changes were positive. But Americans would not easily give up on those areas that needed to be improved. In this way the American experience has always been changing.

An unemployed man sleeps on a park bench.

LITERATURE

The Great Migration

Paintings by Jacob Lawrence

Jacob Lawrence's parents moved to the North as part of the Great Migration. When he was 22 years old, Lawrence decided to paint pictures that would tell the story of the Great Migration.

Railroad stations were so crowded with migrants that guards were called in to keep order.

The flood of migrants northward left crops back home to dry and spoil.

Want to see more paintings of the Great Migration? You can find out more about this time in America's history by checking the book out of your school or public library.

REFOCUS
COMPREHENSION

1. How did the work force in U.S. factories and on farms change when men went to fight in World War I?

2. What did the Eighteenth and Nineteenth Amendments provide for?

THINK ABOUT IT
CRITICAL THINKING

Summarize the experience of African Americans during World War I and immediately after it.

WRITE ABOUT IT
ACTIVITY

Lawrence's pictures say much more than the words alone. Choose one of the pictures shown here and write about what you learned from the picture.

SUMMING UP

1 DO YOU REMEMBER...
COMPREHENSION

1. What led to the outbreak of World War I?

2. Why did the United States become involved in the war?

3. How did the peace treaty that Germany signed with Russia affect the war?

4. Why couldn't doctors help flu patients during the pandemic of 1918?

5. How did the United States raise money for the war?

6. How were American children involved in the war effort?

7. What was trench warfare?

8. What made World War I a modern war?

9. How did the United States solve the problem of the labor shortage on farms?

10. Why was unemployment so high in the years immediately following the war?

2 SKILL POWER
UNDERSTANDING GENERALIZATIONS

Using the information in the chapter, make a generalization about each of these topics.

- how Americans felt about United States involvement in the war
- how the war affected African Americans
- how the war effort was supported at home

3 WHAT DO YOU THINK?
CRITICAL THINKING

1. Some people said that President Wilson initially kept the United States out of the war in order to get reelected. Is this accusation fair? Give reasons for your answer.

2. In what ways might the war have been different if Germany and Russia hadn't signed a peace treaty?

3. Even though Americans made sacrifices during the war, many of them looked back on these years with positive feelings. Why was this so?

4. How did World War I change the way people felt about war in general?

5. How did the lives of women change after the war? Why?

4 SAY IT, WRITE IT, USE IT
VOCABULARY

It is 1918 and you are going to ask the U.S. Congress to declare war on Germany. Write the first paragraph of your speech, using as many of the vocabulary words as you can.

armistice	mobilization
arms race	no man's land
civilian	prohibition
dogfight	ration
draft	U-boat
migrant worker	

5 GEOGRAPHY AND YOU
MAP STUDY

Use the maps throughout the chapter to answer these questions.

1. The western front was fought along the borders of what countries?

2. Name four states that had shipyards during the war.

3. What new nations were formed at the end of World War I?

4. Name the bodies of water that surround Great Britain.

6 GET CREATIVE
LANGUAGE ARTS CONNECTION

Write a patriotic speech about the United States today. With a group of your classmates, take turns presenting your speeches. Your speech should clearly express your ideas and point of view.

7 TAKE ACTION
CITIZENSHIP

Unfortunately, the nations of the world can't always solve their disputes peacefully. Neither can individuals. The next time you get into an argument, see if you can settle it peacefully. Here are some strategies to try.

Consider the other person's point of view.

Agree to take a few minutes so that you and the other person can calm down.

Try to reach a compromise.

Your class might set up a "peer court," or a court of your fellow students. When students can't settle a disagreement, they can take their dispute to court.

LOOKING AHEAD Discover in the next chapter how the nation changed as more people had cars and other consumer products.

The 1920s

The 1920s saw the beginnings of modern America. The city and the automobile became important parts of life in the United States. Some Americans enjoyed the highest standard of living in the world.

▼ What is he listening to? Turn to page 423 to find out.

CONTENTS

These books tell about people, places, and important events during the decade of the 1920s. Read one that interests you and fill out a book-review form.

READ AND RESEARCH

Flight by **Robert Burleigh** (Putnam Publishing Group, 1991)
Your grandparents or great-grandparents can describe how exciting it was to hear about Charles Lindbergh's nonstop flight across the Atlantic in 1927. Reading this book will help you capture some of that excitement. *(historical fiction)*

• *You can read a selection from this book on page 414.*

Ticket to the Twenties: A Time Traveler's Guide by **Mary Blocksma** (Little, Brown & Co., 1993)
Travel back in time to the days of Babe Ruth and Amelia Earhart. Read about women in the United States voting for the first time, and people seeing a Saturday afternoon movie for only a dime. *(nonfiction)*

Radio by **Bill Balcziak** (Rourke Enterprises, 1989)
The Walkman you listen to today got its start back in the 1920s. That's when radio station KDKA, Pittsburgh, went on the air. Find out more about the early days of radio. *(nonfiction)*

Shadow Ball: The History of the Negro Leagues by **Geoffrey C. Ward and Ken Burns, with Jim O'Connor** (Alfred A. Knopf, 1994)
Eight teams of black players formed the Negro National League in 1920. Follow the hardships and triumphs of these African American ballplayers as they excelled in America's favorite game. *(nonfiction)*

SKILL POWER

Classifying Information

Knowing how to classify information makes it easier to remember and learn the material you read.

UNDERSTAND IT

Suppose your school wasn't divided into classes. There would be noise and confusion. No one would know what to do or where to go.

Schools are organized by grouping students into classes by age or subject matter. In a similar way you can organize information. It's called classifying. When you classify, you group together words and ideas that are alike. By fitting new information into categories you have a better chance of learning and remembering it.

EXPLORE IT

One way to classify information is by placing it in a word web. The word web below organizes some information about the 1920s, a decade called the Roaring Twenties.

As you can see, this information about the Roaring Twenties is classified according to topics, or categories: the automobile, advances by women, and popular heroes.

What Made the Roaring Twenties Roar?

The Automobile

Car making and related industries made the economy boom.

1 in 5 Americans had a car.

People traveled faster and farther.

Advances by Women

Women got the right to vote.

More women went to college.

Flappers were women who enjoyed new freedoms.

Popular Heroes

Babe Ruth—baseball
Josh Gibson—baseball
Mildred "Babe" Didrikson—golf

Charles Lindbergh—flew across the Atlantic in 1927

TRY IT

Take a look back at Chapter 17 to see what you learned about World War I. Then make a word web to help you classify the most important information. Begin with the title of your word web— "World War I." Then, as you review the chapter, think of four or five categories that will help you classify the major facts and ideas. One category might be *Causes of the War*; another might be *America's Role in the War*.

SKILL
POWER SEARCH As you read this chapter, look for more information that you could add to each category in the word web for the Roaring Twenties.

KEY TERMS
prosperity
quota
disarmament

Prosperity and Change

FOCUS *During the 1920s many people moved from the country to the city. New technology made life easier and more exciting. For some Americans, however, the decade was marked by increasing discrimination.*

Return to Normal Times

By 1920, Americans had just come out of the horrors of World War I. They were weary of the problems and demands created by the war. In addition, there had been a worldwide outbreak of influenza in 1918, a disease that killed more than 500,000 Americans.

Now, some people wanted to return to a more normal, or usual, time, when life was more simple. Of course those days had never really existed for many people, especially African Americans.

Americans also looked for Presidents who fit their image of traditional, old-fashioned men. In 1920 they elected Warren Harding from Ohio, a jovial example of small-town America. Harding said that Americans wanted "not heroism, but healing, not nostrums [remedies], but normalcy."

Calvin Coolidge, a thrifty Vermonter, became President in 1923 when Harding died. Known as "Silent Cal," Coolidge spoke little in public. Honest and thrifty, he had the Puritan values that many Americans admired.

Coolidge announced that he did not choose to run for reelection in 1928. The presidency was won by the popular but somber Herbert C. Hoover, by an overwhelming majority. A wealthy self-made man, Hoover predicted "two cars in each garage and a chicken in every pot."

▲ Presidential campaign buttons

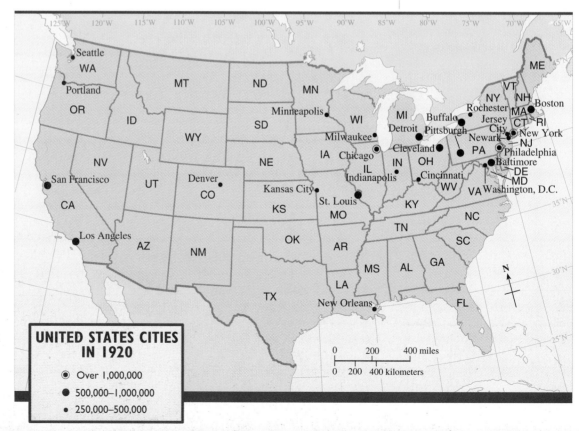

UNITED STATES CITIES IN 1920

◉ Over 1,000,000
● 500,000–1,000,000
• 250,000–500,000

Prosperity and Problems

Few doubted Hoover's words. At the time, many Americans were enjoying the highest standard of living in the world. Many believed that there would be no end to this **prosperity**.

Between 1900 and 1920, electricity replaced steam power as a form of energy. Powered by electricity, American industries could now turn out many more goods than ten years earlier. By 1929, two thirds of U.S. homes were supplied with electricity. Electricity meant new labor-saving products for the home, such as vacuum cleaners, washing machines, and electric sewing machines. And the automobile created millions of new jobs, not only in car factories but also in industries that produced the materials needed to make cars.

Not everyone, however, enjoyed this prosperity. For example, only about 10 percent of rural families in the United States had electricity at this time.

Farmers had their own set of problems. For a time after World War I, American farmers were feeding hungry Europeans. But once European farmers recovered from the war, they were able to grow their own food. There were record harvests in the United States, but farmers couldn't sell all the food, causing prices to drop sharply. The price of wheat fell from more than $2.00 a bushel just after World War I to $1.00 a bushel in the 1920s.

Growth of Cities

The automobile, as well as trains, enabled American cities to expand into the countryside. Suburbs were created in the late nineteenth century, but they grew immensely in the 1920s. Because

▼ A 1920s vacuum cleaner

▼ Skyline of New York City in 1929

★ **prosperity** A time of economic well-being

▲ Diego Rivera's mural: "The Detroit Industry" represents industry in Detroit and celebrates its workers.

of the automobile, industries could also move to the suburbs.

In 1920, for the first time in United States history, more Americans lived in urban rather than in rural areas. More than 5 million people moved to cities in the 1920s. Immigrants from southern and eastern Europe came to north-eastern cities. People from nearby farmlands came to such cities as Cincinnati, Kansas City, and Denver.

Cities offered better jobs at higher pay. They were especially appealing to young people who preferred the excitement of city life to the lonely and sometimes harsh life of the farm.

Every city was changed by the automobile, but the greatest growth occurred in Detroit and Los Angeles. Detroit grew from 300,000 in 1900 to almost 2 million in 1930. Los Angeles became the city of the future, with its shopping and housing centers connected by a network of roads.

Cities grew not only outward but also upward. New skylines were created with

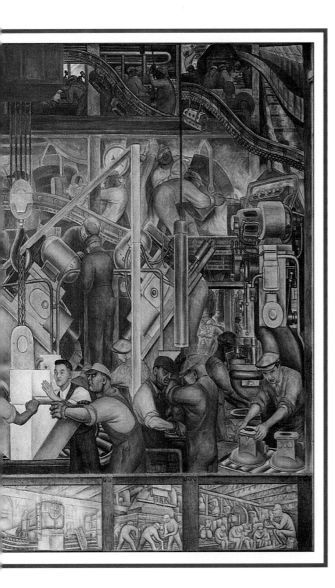

discriminated against Asians and people from eastern and southern Europe.

The laws did not, however, put quotas on immigrants from the Western Hemisphere, so Mexicans still came to the United States in large numbers. Many worked on farms in the West and Southwest. Others moved to the Midwest, taking jobs in industries such as meatpacking and steelmaking.

Like some other ethnic groups, Mexicans and Mexican Americans faced discrimination. Discrimination came not only from white Americans but also from black Americans. African Americans saw Mexican Americans and other Hispanics as rivals for jobs, housing, and better pay.

Mexican Americans faced other problems, too. They had difficulty finding housing and jobs and also

the building of skyscrapers. By 1929 there were 377 buildings of 20 stories or more in American cities.

A Change in Immigration

During this decade new laws were passed that affected those wanting to immigrate to America. In 1921 and 1924, Congress enacted strict new immigration **quotas** that permitted more people from northern and western Europe to enter the country than people from other areas. The laws

⭐ **quota** The number of people that are allowed to enter a country

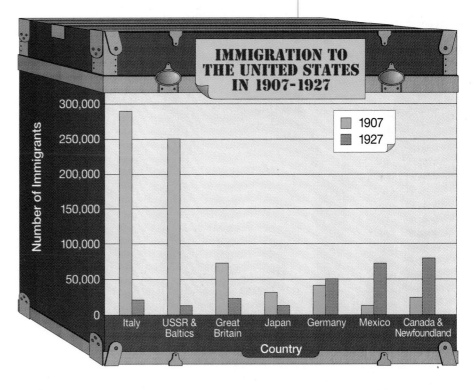

IMMIGRATION TO THE UNITED STATES IN 1907–1927

Number of Immigrants: 0, 50,000, 100,000, 150,000, 200,000, 250,000, 300,000

Country: Italy, USSR & Baltics, Great Britain, Japan, Germany, Mexico, Canada & Newfoundland

Legend: 1907, 1927

schools for their children. To support their new communities, Hispanics formed *mutualistas*, or mutual aid societies. These worked to end discrimination against Mexicans, helped children learn some English before they entered school, and pointed out economic, social, and cultural contributions made by Mexican Americans to the United States. Mutualistas published newspapers to inform people of Mexican descent about events in their communities and in Mexico. They also sponsored plays, dances, musicals, symphonies, and public lectures.

Native Americans Make Gains

The growth of American cities, interest in consumer goods, and a rising divorce rate left some people dissatisfied.

They admired the traditional communities and close-knit families that native peoples often had, and so new attention was given to Native Americans. Reformers began trying to do away with government policies that forced Native Americans to give up their lands and their cultures.

The American Indian Defense Association called for better health and education services on reservations and a recognition of Indian tribal government and culture. This prompted Congress to extend citizenship to all Native Americans in 1924. About one third of all Native Americans were not yet citizens at this time because they feared losing their tribal rights. The new law guaranteed those rights.

Some American Indians were citizens before 1924. Here, American Horse becomes a citizen in 1907.

▲ Frank B. Kellogg is shown signing the Kellogg-Briand Pact in Paris, 1928. The signatures of Kellogg and Briand are shown above the photograph.

The United States and the World

In the 1920s many Americans did not want to be involved with the rest of the world. They preferred isolation. But the United States was a world power, which made isolation impossible. Businesses needed international markets to sell their products. So the government worked to protect the interests of U.S. businesses abroad.

The United States also promoted **disarmament**. In 1922 the United States hosted the Washington Naval Conference. One of its goals was to prevent the kind of costly arms race that had helped trigger World War I. At this conference the United States, Great Britain, Japan, France, and Italy agreed to limit the number of warships they

would build. In 1923 the Naval Conference was acclaimed as the very first attempt of the major nations of the world to disarm.

In 1928 the United States and France signed the Kellogg-Briand Pact. The treaty was negotiated by Aristide Briand (air ihs TEED bree AHN), the French foreign minister, and Frank B. Kellogg, Coolidge's secretary of state. In the pact the two nations renounced war between themselves forever. Then Kellogg suggested that other nations sign it as well.

Eventually, 64 nations signed the pact. People thought that all disputes could be settled peacefully. However, this didn't happen because there was no way to enforce the agreement.

★ **disarmament** Cutting back or totally eliminating the weapons a nation has

SHOW WHAT YOU KNOW!

REFOCUS
COMPREHENSION

1. Give examples to show that the 1920s were a time of prosperity for some Americans, but not for all.

2. What effect did immigration quotas have on people wanting to come to the United States?

THINK ABOUT IT
CRITICAL THINKING

Why is discrimination harmful?

WRITE ABOUT IT
ACTIVITY

Make a word web that shows why cities grew in this period.

The Roaring Twenties

FOCUS *The decade of the 1920s was a time of prosperity, cultural change, and personal independence. The high hopes of these years, however, ended with the stock market crash of 1929.*

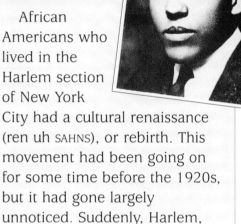

WOMEN CAN VOTE

In 1920, women won the right to vote with the ratification of the Nineteenth Amendment. Some women felt that getting the vote was only a first step. They supported an equal rights amendment. This, they insisted, was necessary if women were to enjoy the same rights as men in the workplace.

Other women disagreed. They didn't support an equal rights amendment because they feared that women would lose more than they gained. For two decades, women had fought for—and won—laws to protect themselves and their children from working more than 10 hours a day. Some worried that an equal rights amendment, in which the same laws applied to men and women, might wipe out these gains.

THE JAZZ AGE

The 1920s were called the Jazz Age. Jazz, an American form of music, originated with southern African Americans in the mid-1800s. Among top jazz musicians of the 1920s was trumpeter and singer Louis Armstrong (shown below). One of his most famous recordings, *St. Louis Blues* (1925), featured the great jazz singer Bessie Smith. Duke Ellington is generally regarded as the most important composer in jazz history. He also was a band leader and pianist. Most of the pieces he recorded were his own, and many of his works are often performed today.

HARLEM RENAISSANCE

African Americans who lived in the Harlem section of New York City had a cultural renaissance (ren uh SAHNS), or rebirth. This movement had been going on for some time before the 1920s, but it had gone largely unnoticed. Suddenly, Harlem, the largest black community in the United States, became known for its wealth of performers, artists, and writers.

The renaissance was fueled by talented writers such as Langston Hughes (shown above), Countee Cullen, Zora Neale Hurston, and Alain Locke. Their influence extended well beyond Harlem. These writers and performers explored the cultural roots of their African and African American experience.

1920	1925	1926	1927	1929
Nineteenth Amendment	Louis Armstrong performs *St. Louis Blues*	Langston Hughes publishes first poetry	Lindbergh's flight	Stock market crash

1920   1922   1924   1926   1928   1930

LUCKY LINDY

On May 20, 1927, Charles Lindbergh climbed into his plane, the *Spirit of St. Louis*. His goal was to fly from New York to Paris, France. He would be the first person to make a solo nonstop flight across the Atlantic Ocean. Navigating by the stars, he touched down at Le Bourget (luh boor ZHAY) airport near Paris 33 hours later.

"The Lone Eagle," as people called him, instantly became an international hero. Everywhere Lindbergh went, people recognized him and cheered. He even had a dance, the Lindy, named after him. His flight made him one of the most famous Americans of the 1920s.

STOCK MARKET CRASHES

"Wall Street Lays an Egg" read one famous newspaper headline. On October 29, 1929, the New York Stock Market crashed. (A stock market is a place where people trade stocks, or shares of ownership in companies.) Prices of stocks fell sharply. Many people panicked and tried to sell their stocks all at once, before prices fell even further. But their actions only drove prices lower still.

By the next morning the total value of stocks had dropped by more than $30 billion. As a result of the crash, the days of prosperity came to an end for many Americans.

Flight

by Robert Burleigh

illustrated by Mike Wimmer

What lies ahead for Charles Lindbergh as he begins his solo flight across the Atlantic?

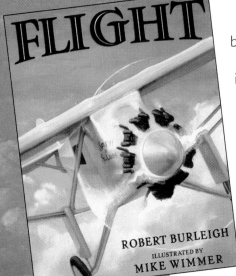

I t is 1927, and his name is Charles Lindbergh.

Later they will call him the Lone Eagle.

Later they will call him Lucky Lindy.

But not now.

Now it is May 20, 1927, and he is standing in the still-dark dawn.

He watches rain drizzle down on the airfield. And on his small airplane.

The airplane has a name painted on its side: *Spirit of St. Louis.*

Lindbergh is nearly as tall as the plane itself.

And yet—he is about to attempt what no one has done before:

To fly—without a stop—from New York to Paris, France.

Over 3,600 miles away.

Across the Atlantic Ocean.

Alone.

He climbs into the boxlike cockpit that will be his only home for many, many hours.

He clicks on the engine. He listens as it catches, gurgles, and roars.

A few friends are here to say good-bye.

They are only a few feet away, and yet to Lindbergh how far off they seem.

They look up at him and wave. "Good luck! Keep safe!" . . .

Will the *Spirit of St. Louis*, with its over 5,000 pounds, rise into the air?

To keep the plane lighter, Lindbergh is leaving behind his radio and parachute.

Will that be enough? . . .

Lindbergh lowers his goggles and nods his head: "Go!"

Men on each side push to help the plane roll over the soggy ground.

The little plane bumps forward, gaining speed. . . .

The plane seems to hop, taking its "last bow to earth."

On the third try it stays aloft. . . .

The *Spirit of St. Louis* rises in the air. . . .

Lindbergh points his plane toward the Atlantic and beyond, toward Paris.

Want to read more? You can by checking the book out of your school or public library.

SHOW WHAT YOU KNOW!

REFOCUS
COMPREHENSION

1. Identify the following people: Louis Armstrong, Langston Hughes, and Charles Lindbergh.

2. What was the Harlem Renaissance?

THINK ABOUT IT
CRITICAL THINKING

Why were people so anxious to sell their stocks when prices started to drop?

WRITE ABOUT IT
ACTIVITY

Write a paragraph explaining why Charles Lindbergh was called the Lone Eagle and Lucky Lindy.

Fads and Flappers

FOCUS *In the 1920s, people wanted to leave the troubles of war and disease behind them. They often dressed and behaved as if they didn't have a care in the world.*

Time for Fun

The war was over, things were getting back to normal, and it was time to have some fun. From Maine to California many people threw themselves into a whole variety of crazy activities. They wanted to enjoy life.

People held contests to see how long they could sit on top of flagpoles. They had rocking chair competitions, talking contests, and long-distance races. Some became daredevils, plunging over Niagara Falls in barrels and walking on the wings of airplanes. The best of these "wing walkers" could play tennis in the air or even jump from one moving plane to another. Some of the best wing walkers were women.

Many of these activities were fads, things that were popular for only a short time. In 1923, for instance, "Tutmania" swept the country. Scientists in Egypt had just uncovered the ancient tomb of King Tutankhamen (toot-ahngk AH mun).

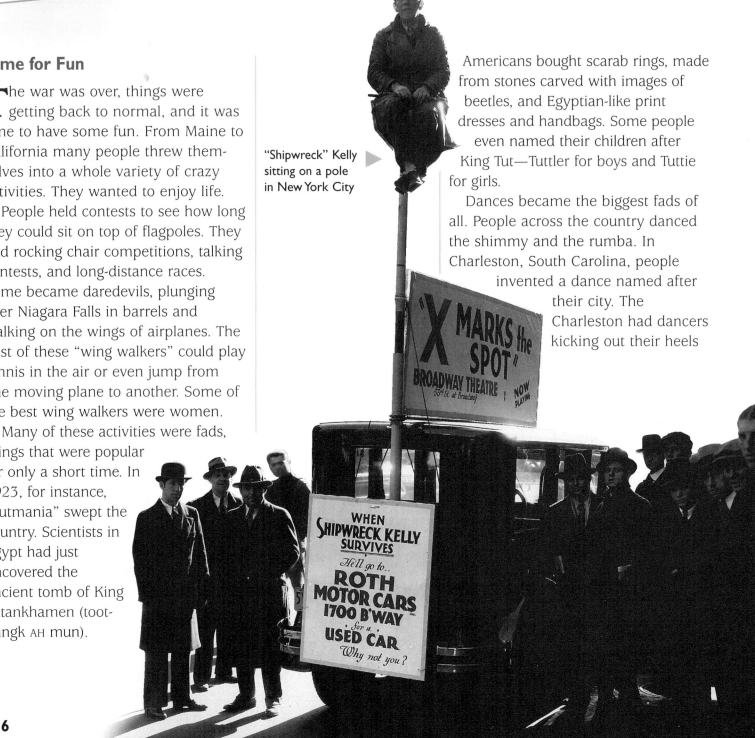

"Shipwreck" Kelly sitting on a pole in New York City

WHEN SHIPWRECK KELLY SURVIVES
He'll go to..
ROTH MOTOR CARS 1700 B'WAY Inc.
for a
USED CAR
Why not you?

"X MARKS the SPOT"
BROADWAY THEATRE
53rd St. at Broadway
NOW PLAYING

Americans bought scarab rings, made from stones carved with images of beetles, and Egyptian-like print dresses and handbags. Some people even named their children after King Tut—Tuttler for boys and Tuttie for girls.

Dances became the biggest fads of all. People across the country danced the shimmy and the rumba. In Charleston, South Carolina, people invented a dance named after their city. The Charleston had dancers kicking out their heels and waving their arms. It was a wild dance, and it fit perfectly with the wild pace of life in the 1920s.

More Independence for Women

As people's idea of fun became more creative, so too did fashions. No longer did women confine themselves to long, heavy clothing. Now they wore skirts that ended above the knee, or slacks. They put on lipstick, cut their hair in short bobs, and wore unbuckled rain boots. When they walked down the street, their boots made a flapping sound. These women became known as flappers.

It wasn't just women's clothes that changed. Women became more independent in many ways. They drove around in Model T Fords, nicknamed Tin Lizzies. Women could vote now, and some even ran for public office. In 1924, Wyoming's Nellie Tayloe Ross was elected governor. In Texas, Miriam A. Ferguson also became governor. More women went to college, and more worked outside the home. Although many women lost their factory jobs at the end of the war, they became secretaries, salesclerks, and telephone operators.

Consumer Demand

One way that people enjoyed themselves was by buying new things. The 1920s was an age of increased **consumerism**. If something was new,

different, or made life easier, people wanted it. They wanted electric lights and indoor plumbing. They hurried to buy refrigerators, telephones, washing machines, radios, irons, and vacuum cleaners. They also bought more processed foods and ready-to-wear clothes.

Some consumers didn't have the money to buy everything they wanted. So they paid for items, using **installment plans**. Department stores offered charge accounts, and finance companies grew. In the past many Americans had put off purchases until they could pay for them. But now the motto became Buy now, pay later.

▲ Official portrait of Miriam Amanda Ferguson, governor of Texas, 1925–1927

Winners of a Charleston dance contest in the 1920s ▶

★ **consumerism**   The buying of goods and services
installment plan   A credit system where purchased items are paid for at regular intervals

Radio store in New York City in the 1920s

Magazine advertisement from 1919

Advertising

Newspapers, magazines, and billboards advertised products to encourage the new spending habits. Every product promised to make people happier, healthier, prettier, smarter. In 1920 the first radio station went on the air. Two years later, radio broadcasts were being used to sell products.

Movies, too, supported consumerism. During this time, millions of Americans went to the movies every week. In the early 1920s they watched silent movies. Beginning in 1927 they could also buy tickets to talking motion pictures, or "talkies." People did more than buy tickets, however. They tried to imitate the lifestyles they saw on the big screen. They wanted the same clothes, home furnishings, and cars that movie stars had. In this way movies helped set trends for the entire nation.

A magazine cover of December 1928

SHOW WHAT YOU KNOW!

REFOCUS
COMPREHENSION

1. Name some fads from the 1920s.

2. Describe ways in which women of the 1920s were independent.

THINK ABOUT IT
CRITICAL THINKING

What effects of the installment plan do we see today?

WRITE ABOUT IT
ACTIVITY

Make a chart listing products or items that became available in the 1920s. Next to each item list at least one way it changed people's lives.

Impact of the Automobile

FOCUS *The automobile industry fueled the great prosperity of the 1920s. The automobile also gave many people a sense of freedom they had never known before.*

Growth of the Auto Industry

At the turn of the century, automobile ownership was limited to the rich. But in 1908, Henry Ford produced the first Model T—a practical car that could travel over poor roads and run for years. When it did break down, it was easy to repair. Its low price tag put it within the reach of many Americans. By 1920, Ford had sold over a million of these Tin Lizzies.

As his business grew, Ford looked for better ways to build cars. In 1914 he introduced the moving **assembly line**. By the time cars reached the end of the assembly line, they were built, polished, and ready for sale.

Ford's assembly line allowed him to build cars faster and cheaper than before. By the 1920s, Ford factories were turning out a Model T every 10 seconds, and the price dropped from $825 to about $300.

Henry Ford with one of his Model T automobiles, about 1920

Other car companies quickly copied Ford's methods. Soon automobile manufacturing was the largest industry in the nation. From 1920 to 1930 the number of cars on the road surged from 9.2 million to 26.7 million.

The Economy Booms

The growing auto industry sparked new growth in many other industries. Cars needed gasoline, so the oil industry boomed. Hundreds of oil wells were drilled in Oklahoma, Texas, and California. As workers poured into these states, demand rose for more stores, restaurants, and other businesses. New businesses meant new construction, which meant even more new jobs.

It was the same in other industries. Find where some of these industries were located on the map on page 420. Cars were made of rubber, paint, steel, glass, and leather. These industries experienced a huge boost in sales. Cars also needed roads, so highway construction expanded. Cars even created new industries, such as gas stations, motels, and car repair shops.

assembly line A process in which each worker in a factory performs a different step or job in putting together the product

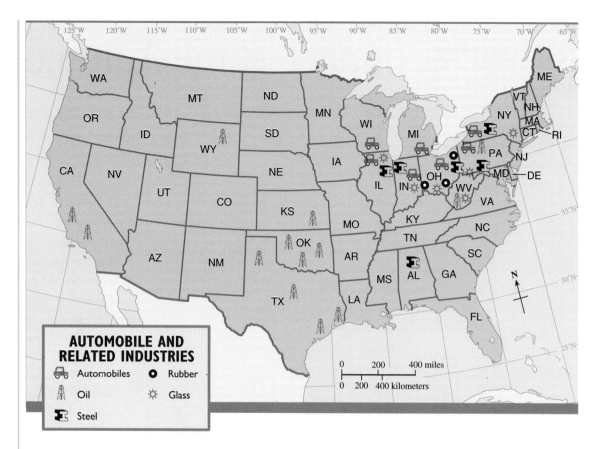

AUTOMOBILE AND RELATED INDUSTRIES

🚗 Automobiles   ⊙ Rubber

🗼 Oil   ☼ Glass

🏭 Steel

A Changing Way of Life

The automobile changed the way Americans lived, giving them more freedom than they had ever dreamed of. No longer did people need to live near public transportation so that they could get to work. Now they could move to the country and drive to work each day. As a result suburbs—communities outside a city—were created.

With cars, people could take vacations. They could—and did—drive far from home. This led Congress to create more and more national parks.

A guidebook for Yellowstone National Park (*below*) and a postcard (*right*)

Y. P. 62 THE GARDINER ENTRANCE ARCH. YELLOWSTONE PARK

The national parks helped people experience nature.

Cars also allowed women to leave the house more easily during the day, and allowed people in rural areas to make more frequent visits to the city. One farm woman was asked why her family had bought a car instead of indoor plumbing. "Why," she said, "you can't go to town in a bathtub."

Beyond their everyday usefulness, cars became status symbols. Advertisers encouraged this idea by linking their products with images of "the good life." Car advertisements told consumers that cars meant fun, freedom, and status. Many people believed this. As with other purchases, Americans turned to installment plans to buy their cars. By the late 1920s, about two thirds of all American cars were being bought on credit.

Automobiles Brought Problems

The automobile did have negative impacts. Working in car factories was tiring and tedious. Assembly-line workers repeated the same tasks all day long. Although they were well paid, the workers became bored.

On the roads the problem wasn't boredom, it was chaos (KAY ahs)—much confusion. Traffic clogged city streets, cars sank into mud on country roads, and traffic accidents claimed lives.

Billboards began to clutter roadsides. Junkyards became home to millions of rusting cars. Pollution poured from car exhaust pipes, and the noise of auto engines made people's ears ring. Some suggested that it was this noise that gave the decade its nickname, the Roaring Twenties.

▲ Auto traffic jam and billboards in the 1920s

▼ A Yellowstone National Park sticker

5

You Are There

☆ **KEY TERM**

broadcast

Growing Up in the 1920s

FOCUS *Children in the 1920s had many traditional chores to do. But there were new ways of doing things, too—including new ways to spend leisure time.*

The Old and the New

If you were a child in the 1920s, your life would be a mixture of the old and the new. On the one hand, you can choose from new packaged breakfast cereals. On the other hand, the milk you pour on those cereals is not homogenized, or blended to break up the fat. You can see the cream rise to the top, and the only cover for the milk bottle is a paper cap.

Your home might have electricity—about half the homes do. But your family probably uses it only for lighting. It is too expensive to use for much else. Your parents might be among the many people who bought plugs for their outlets so the electricity would not "leak out." You probably don't have a telephone yet. But even if you do, you use it for serious business only, not for chatting with friends.

Perhaps you have a radio. You and your entire family gather around to listen to news **broadcasts**. You might also tune in for music concerts, serial stories, and sporting events.

▲ Beanies were popular hats in the 1920s.

▼ Marbles championship in the 1920s

☆ **broadcast** A program sent to a large audience

422

Taking Care of Chores

Perhaps your family splurges on an electric refrigerator. But more likely, you still use an icebox. Food is kept cool by placing a large block of ice in the top compartment. Every few days the iceman comes in his truck to deliver a new block of ice. Putting ice in the top part of the icebox keeps food in the bottom part cool. As the ice melts, water collects in a tray below the icebox. This water needs to be emptied daily—a chore that you most likely do.

Another of your chores might be chopping wood for the stove—unless your family is fortunate enough to have a gas or electric one. You also have to clean the ashes out of the furnace and fill the furnace with more coal. Most of the time you are completely covered with ashes and soot by the time you complete this chore.

Having Fun

You also have some time for fun. Boys especially like to play baseball

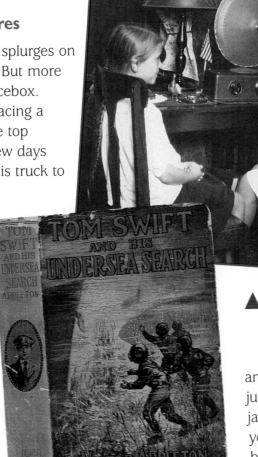

Front jacket cover of a favorite 1920s book

Listening to the radio in the 1920s

and marbles. Girls jump rope and play jacks—a game where you throw a rubber ball into the air and then try to scoop up little pronged metal jacks before catching the ball.

On weekends you might go to the movies. There you can watch popular stars, such as Rudolph Valentino or Clara Bow, on the big screen. Or you might curl up with a book. Boys often read about Tom Swift, a genius boy inventor. Girls like Ruth Fielding books by Alice B. Emerson. Some people enjoy Zane Grey's western novels, and almost everyone, it seems, enjoys stories about Tarzan by Edgar Rice Burroughs.

SHOW WHAT YOU KNOW!

REFOCUS
COMPREHENSION

1. Name some activities children of the 1920s participated in.

2. What were some "modern" conveniences of the 1920s?

THINK ABOUT IT
CRITICAL THINKING

How is the way you spend your leisure time alike and different from that of a child in the 1920s?

WRITE ABOUT IT
ACTIVITY

Make a "time travel" account of the last 12 months in your life. Using pictures and words, describe events that were important to you.

Sports and Leisure

FOCUS *In the 1920s, spectator sports gave America new national heroes. With more free time the American people also participated more in sports themselves.*

The National Pastime

George Herman "Babe" Ruth changed baseball. In 1920, Ruth hit 54 home runs, playing for the New York Yankees. That was more than any other player hit that year. In fact, it was more than any other team hit that year.

Ruth made baseball a hitter's game. Soon other sluggers, such as teammate Lou Gehrig, began hitting lots of home runs. But nobody could match the Babe. In 1927 he hit 60 home runs, a record that stood until 1961.

Other spectator sports, or sports that people watch, also became more popular. They, too, produced their share of heroes. Among them were Red Grange in football, Jack Dempsey in boxing, Gertrude Ederle in swimming, Helen Wills in tennis, Bobby Jones in golf, and Mildred "Babe" Didrikson, who excelled at many sports, including golf and track and field.

Black and Hispanic Leagues

Babe Ruth only played against other white players. Unfortunately the same **prejudice** that barred African Americans from restaurants, hotels, schools, and public transportation also kept them off major league ball fields. Black

Helen Wills, tennis star of the 1920s

Sports Card

---

prejudice Dislike or distrust of people just because they are of another race, religion, or country

424

Gertrude Ederle at the time she swam the English Channel in 1926

players had to form their own leagues. Some of the greatest players in the history of the game played in these leagues, including Josh Gibson, Satchel Paige, James "Cool Papa" Bell, and Buck Leonard.

Many of these black teams toured the country, sometimes playing several games a day. But despite their skill and their love of the game, African Americans would not break baseball's color barrier— discrimination based on race—until 1947, when Jackie Robinson played for the Brooklyn Dodgers.

Hispanics also loved baseball. They, too, formed their own teams. Sometimes they made up all-star teams to play against teams from either the major leagues or the black leagues.

Americans Become Active

During the 1920s many Americans had more leisure time than ever before. They used their free time not only to turn out in record numbers for such spectator sports as horse racing, baseball, and football but also to participate in more sports themselves. Young people made up their own teams, playing baseball and football in parks and fields. Older people played tennis, went bowling, or golfed. People of all ages had more time to enjoy the outdoors. Hiking, camping, and biking all became popular leisure-time activities.

Cool Papa Bell (*seated, center*), Satchel Paige (*standing, far right*), and other members of an American Negro league all-star team, who played in a Caribbean tournament

Babe Ruth and fan in the 1920s

SHOW WHAT YOU KNOW!

REFOCUS
COMPREHENSION

1. Who were Babe Ruth, Gertrude Ederle, and Helen Wills?

2. Why did African Americans form their own baseball leagues?

THINK ABOUT IT
CRITICAL THINKING

What was the significance of separate black and Hispanic baseball leagues?

WRITE ABOUT IT
ACTIVITY

Identify a sport or activity that you enjoy in your leisure time and explain why you enjoy it.

SUMMING UP

1 DO YOU REMEMBER . . .
COMPREHENSION

1. What were some effects of the immigration laws of the 1920s?

2. What was the purpose of the Kellogg-Briand Pact?

3. What was the Nineteenth Amendment?

4. What event marked the end of prosperity in the 1920s? When did it happen?

5. How did the popularity of movies affect consumerism in the 1920s?

6. In what important ways did automobiles change the way Americans lived?

7. What new problems did automobiles cause?

8. What common chores of the 1920s rarely have to be done today?

9. What did Gertrude Ederle achieve in 1926?

10. Why did many Americans begin to enjoy sports more in the 1920s?

2 SKILL POWER
CLASSIFYING INFORMATION

Make a word web like the ones on pages 404–405. Add new details from this chapter to each category. Also add a new category based on information in the chapter.

3 WHAT DO YOU THINK?
CRITICAL THINKING

1. Do you think the United States did return to normalcy during the 1920s? Explain.

2. Do you think the Roaring Twenties was a good name for the decade of the 1920s? Use examples to explain why.

3. Are the same factors that caused consumerism in the 1920s at work today? Explain.

4. Did the benefits of automobiles outweigh the problems they caused?

5. What traits do you think are most important in a sports hero?

4 SAY IT, WRITE IT, USE IT
VOCABULARY

Suppose you are running for office in the 1920s. Prepare a short speech on four of the topics listed below. Try to include as many vocabulary terms as possible.

assembly line	installment plan
broadcast	prejudice
consumerism	prosperity
disarmament	quota

5 GEOGRAPHY AND YOU
MAP STUDY

Grand Teton was designated a national park in 1929. Use the map below to answer these questions.

1. What roads lead into the entrance on the north side of the park?

2. List the mountain peaks shown on the map.

3. What river flows through the park?

4. What is the largest lake in the park?

GRAND TETON NATIONAL PARK

■ Visitor centers
▲ Mountain peaks
— Major roads
— Minor roads

6 TAKE ACTION
CITIZENSHIP

World War I, the influenza outbreak—by 1920, Americans were weary of bad news. Today, many Americans also tire of the bad news they read in newspapers and see on TV. You can help raise their spirits with a "Good News Only" bulletin board. Look for items of good news in newspapers and magazines. Or summarize positive stories you've heard on radio or TV. You can also write your own news stories about good things happening in your community.

7 GET CREATIVE
MUSIC CONNECTION

The 1920s was the golden age of jazz. Americans listened to the music of Fats Waller, Louis Armstrong, Jelly Roll Morton, and other jazz greats. With a partner, research one or two jazz musicians of the twenties. Find out what made his or her work special. Then share what you learned with the class, playing a CD or tape to illustrate the musical style.

The Roaring Twenties were also a time of new social dances, such as the Charleston and the shimmy. If you prefer, you might perform one of these dances for the class.

LOOKING AHEAD In the next chapter you will find out about the **Great Depression of the 1930s.**

The Great

During the Great Depression many Americans could not find jobs. Some lost their homes. And they waited on long lines for bread. Find out how Americans survived this desperate time.

How did WPA workers use puppets like these? Find out on page 440.

CONTENTS

Depression

These books tell about people, places, and events of importance during the Great Depression. Read one that interests you and fill out a book-review form.

READ AND RESEARCH

Grandpa's Mountain by Carolyn Reeder (Avon Books, 1993)
During the Great Depression even young people feel the weight of shattered dreams. Carrie's grandparents might lose their home when the government creates a national park in the Blue Ridge Mountains. *(historical fiction)*

- *You can read a selection from this story on page 442.*

The Dust Bowl: Disaster on the Plains
by Tricia Andryszewski (The Millbrook Press, 1993)
The tragic dust storms that hit the Great Plains in the 1930s had both human and natural causes. Find out what life was like during this devastating period. *(nonfiction)*

Eleanor Roosevelt: A Life of Discovery
by Russell Freedman (Houghton Mifflin Co., 1992)
Eleanor Roosevelt was loved and admired by much of the world. Learn how she used her role as First Lady to help people during the Great Depression. *(biography)*

Dorothea Lange by Robyn Montana Turner
(Little, Brown & Co., 1994)
Dorothea Lange's photographs of the poor during the depression were so powerful that they influenced the government to develop even more relief projects. *(biography)*

Problem Solving

Defining a problem clearly and examining different possible solutions are important problem-solving skills.

UNDERSTAND IT

The fifth graders at Springfield School have a problem.

For social studies, they have planned a bus trip to Washington, D.C. However, the bus fare, admission fees, meals, and other costs come to over $50.00 a student. Most of the students feel that $50.00 is too expensive. What should the fifth graders do?

EXPLORE IT

These four steps can help you solve problems.

1. Define the problem as clearly as possible. In this case, the fifth graders should find out how many students would be willing to pay $50.00. They should also calculate how much the other students can pay.

2. List possible solutions. There are usually several ways to solve a problem. The fifth graders thought of these possible solutions.
   - Cancel the trip.
   - Let the fifth graders who can spend $50.00 per student take the trip. The others will stay home.
   - Have a class fundraiser to help pay some of the costs of the trip.

3. Explore each solution. Most solutions have good points and bad points. If students cancel the trip, they won't get to visit our nation's capital. If only those students with $50.00 go, other students may resent them. If they have a fundraiser, everyone can go, but they'll have to work hard to raise the money.

4. Decide on the one solution that seems best. The fifth graders decide to have a "Schoolyard Sale." They will sell old books, toys, and CDs. They will also hold a car wash, a spaghetti supper, and a bake sale. In the end, each student will have to pay $20.00, and everyone can go on the trip.

TRY IT

Make a list of some problems in your school or community. Talking to classmates, teachers, and the principal should give you plenty of ideas. Choose one problem that interests you and list two or more possible solutions. For each solution, list the advantages and disadvantages. Then decide which solution you think is best. Make a poster that shows how you arrived at your solution.

SKILL POWER SEARCH As you read this chapter, think about how people tried to solve the problems caused by the Great Depression.

Setting the Scene

Hard Times

FOCUS *The Great Depression of the 1930s brought hunger, homelessness, and joblessness to many Americans. It lasted over ten years and dominated almost every aspect of American life.*

The Stock Market Crash

The **stock market** is the place where stocks, or business shares, are bought and sold. When someone buys stocks in a business, he or she becomes a part owner of that business. If the business succeeds, the stocks increase in value, which means that they are worth more than the person originally paid for them.

In the late 1920s, companies were doing very well and people who bought stocks could make a lot of money. As more people bought stocks, the prices went up. Then even more people bought stocks. Stock prices continued to rise, and a lot of people got very rich. People wanted to make even more money, so they borrowed money to buy more stocks.

Eventually, in the autumn of 1929, stock prices began to fall. Once the prices started to drop, people wanted to sell their stocks quickly to avoid losing too much money. Since so many people sold their stocks at the same time, the prices dropped even more. On October 29, 1929, stock prices suddenly plunged. Many people lost all they owned.

Individual people weren't the only ones who bought stocks. Bankers also did, sometimes using their customers' savings to pay for the stocks. When the stock market crashed, these bankers lost their customers' money. The 1929 stock market crash marked the beginning of hard times, known as the **Great Depression**.

Unsold Goods and Bank Failures

The stock market crash wasn't the only cause of the Great Depression. Another reason was that Americans couldn't buy all the goods that were produced. In the 1920s, companies

UNEMPLOYMENT IN 1934

5–10%	21–25%
11–15%	26–30%
16–20%	30% and over

---

stock market   The place where business shares are bought and sold

Great Depression   Economic hard times in the United States, 1929–1941

| 1928 | 1929 | | 1932 | 1933 | 1933 | | | | | | | 1939 |
| Hoover elected President | Stock market crash | | FDR elected President | Dust Bowl begins | Unemployment peaks | | | | | | | Dust Bowl ends |

1928 · 1929 · 1930 · 1931 · 1932 · 1933 · 1934 · 1935 · 1936 · 1937 · 1938 · 1939

sold so much that they kept increasing the number of products they made. By the early 1930s many companies produced more than Americans could consume.

As unsold goods piled up, some factories made fewer things. Then they needed fewer workers, so they laid off some of their employees. Without income these people couldn't buy much. The companies sold even fewer goods and needed even fewer workers. This spiral of unsold goods and lost jobs continued. By 1932, one out of every four Americans was unemployed. Look at the map on page 432 to see the unemployment percentages for each state in 1934.

People who lost their jobs couldn't repay their loans to the banks. This, combined with the bank losses from the stock market crash, caused hundreds of banks to go out of business. Many bank customers lost their life's savings.

Herbert Hoover

Since Herbert Hoover was President when the depression began, many Americans blamed him for the hard times. They wanted President Hoover and the government to help them through these hard times and to end the depression.

Of course Hoover wanted to end the crisis. But he thought local and private groups, not the government, should help needy people. He thought that government aid would destroy people's freedom and self-reliance.

Hoover asked union leaders to have their members work fewer hours so that more people could work. And he asked business leaders not to lay off workers or lower their wages. But union and business leaders didn't cooperate.

As the depression got worse, Hoover tried to do more. But it was too late. People soon grew bitter. Some families

▼ A man tries to sell his car to make money.

ran out of money and lost their homes. Some of them then had to live in flimsy cardboard shacks. There were "towns" made up of these shacks, called Hoovervilles, all over the country.

President Hoover wasn't popular among soldiers, either. All World War I veterans were supposed to get a cash bonus in 1945. But soldiers who had no money wanted the bonuses early. In 1932 they marched on Washington, D.C., and demanded that their bonuses be given to them right away. Hoover refused to even talk with the marchers.

Many people saw this as final proof that President Hoover didn't care about their problems.

A New President

Franklin Delano Roosevelt (FDR) easily defeated Hoover for the presidency in 1932. Compare the results of the 1928 and 1932 elections on the maps below. FDR promised people a **New Deal**. He planned to use the government to help Americans survive the depression. He believed it was important to do something. If one idea didn't work, he would just try something else.

Roosevelt knew that Americans needed confidence. He used radio broadcasts to reassure Americans that better

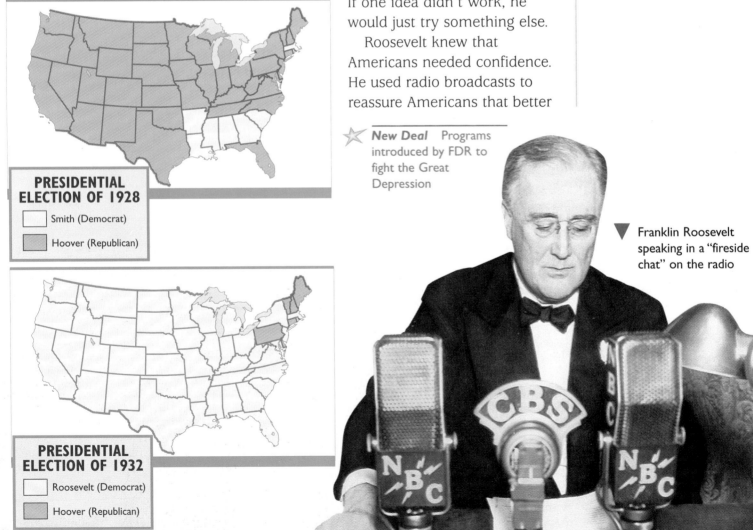

PRESIDENTIAL ELECTION OF 1928

☐ Smith (Democrat)

▦ Hoover (Republican)

PRESIDENTIAL ELECTION OF 1932

☐ Roosevelt (Democrat)

▦ Hoover (Republican)

★ **New Deal** Programs introduced by FDR to fight the Great Depression

▼ Franklin Roosevelt speaking in a "fireside chat" on the radio

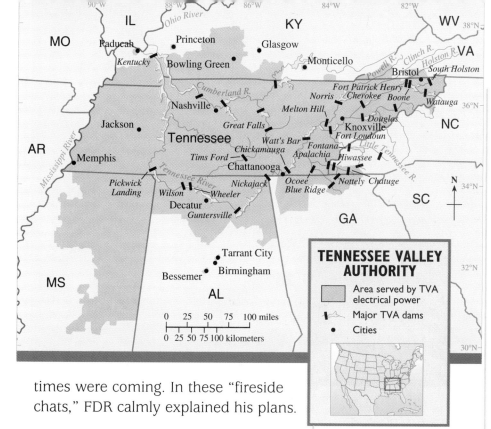

TENNESSEE VALLEY AUTHORITY

Area served by TVA electrical power

Major TVA dams

Cities

times were coming. In these "fireside chats," FDR calmly explained his plans.

The New Deal

The first problem FDR dealt with was the banks. On March 6, 1933, he declared a "bank holiday" and closed all the banks for four days. All the banks were then examined, and only the ones that were following good business practices could reopen.

Many of FDR's New Deal programs gave people jobs. FDR believed that giving people jobs would enable them to buy goods with the money they earned. Then factories could hire more people to produce more goods.

The Tennessee Valley Authority (TVA) was one New Deal program. TVA workers built dams on the Tennessee River and its branches. These dams controlled flooding that had caused great damage in the past. The dams also produced electricity for the region,

giving many people electricity for the first time. The map on this page shows the area that the TVA served. Later the government also built several dams in the western United States.

Another New Deal program helped farmers. Just as manufacturing companies produced more than people could buy, farmers also produced more food than they could sell. The abundance of crops lowered prices. Some farmers burned their crops rather than sell them at low prices. With the 1933 Agricultural Adjustment Act (AAA), the government paid farmers *not* to plant crops on some of their land. After all, if there were fewer crops for sale, farmers could get better prices for them.

The Dust Bowl

Meanwhile, nature made the depression even worse for farmers. In the early 1930s there was a drought (drout) on the Great Plains. The hot sun

▼ Leaving the Dust Bowl

A 1934 dust storm in Lamar, Colorado

Mexican Americans living in a Hooverville

baked the topsoil into a dry powder. Then gusty winds began sweeping across the plains, kicking up dust. Huge clouds reaching as high as 8,000 feet blackened the afternoon sky. By the mid-1930s the Great Plains became one great **Dust Bowl**

Many farm families couldn't take it anymore. Thousands of these farmers left the Dust Bowl and looked for work elsewhere. Many became migrant workers in California.

The Depression Affects Everyone

The depression affected minorities in different ways than it affected white Americans. During these hard times some white Americans blamed Mexican migrant workers for taking their jobs and accepting lower wages. Sometimes employers laid off Mexican workers so that they could hire unemployed white workers. In addition, many Mexicans were forced to go back to Mexico.

Native Americans suffered from poverty and unemployment to the same extent that they had before the depression. But some things did change. FDR named John Collier as commissioner of Indian affairs. Collier got Congress to return some tribal lands to Native Americans. He also

Dust Bowl   An area in the Great Plains that had large dust storms in the 1930s

continued the work begun in the 1920s to preserve Native American customs, religions, and languages.

Unions Gain Strength

Under the New Deal, workers won the right to organize and bargain with their employers. And in the 1930s, unions gained members and power. For the first time, unions organized workers in industries such as automobile, steel, and rubber.

By 1938, union membership reached 8 million. The unions were supposed to fight for working people. Yet some unions would not let African Americans or Mexican Americans join. And some unions thought it was fair to pay women less than men for doing the same work.

Giving Americans Hope

Despite all the programs, the New Deal *did not* end the Great Depression. It was World War II that turned the economy around. The demand for tanks, planes, ships, and guns finally put Americans back to work.

Still, FDR's programs helped many people. Bankers, farmers, unemployed workers, and others gained from New Deal programs. But perhaps FDR's greatest contribution was that he gave Americans hope.

Another American, Jesse Owens, also inspired the nation. Owens was a young track star from Ohio State University. In 1935, after spending several days in bed with the flu, he tied or broke four world records in one day.

Then, at the 1936 Olympic Games in Berlin, Germany, he won four gold medals. Owens made Americans very proud. People like Franklin Delano Roosevelt and Jesse Owens helped Americans to hope for a better future.

And America survived these very hard times.

▼ Jesse Owens

A 1936 Olympic gold medal ▶

The Dust Bowl

FOCUS During the 1930s terrible dust storms swept through the Great Plains. Crops were ruined, and farms were buried. Many families who lost their land traveled to California to begin again.

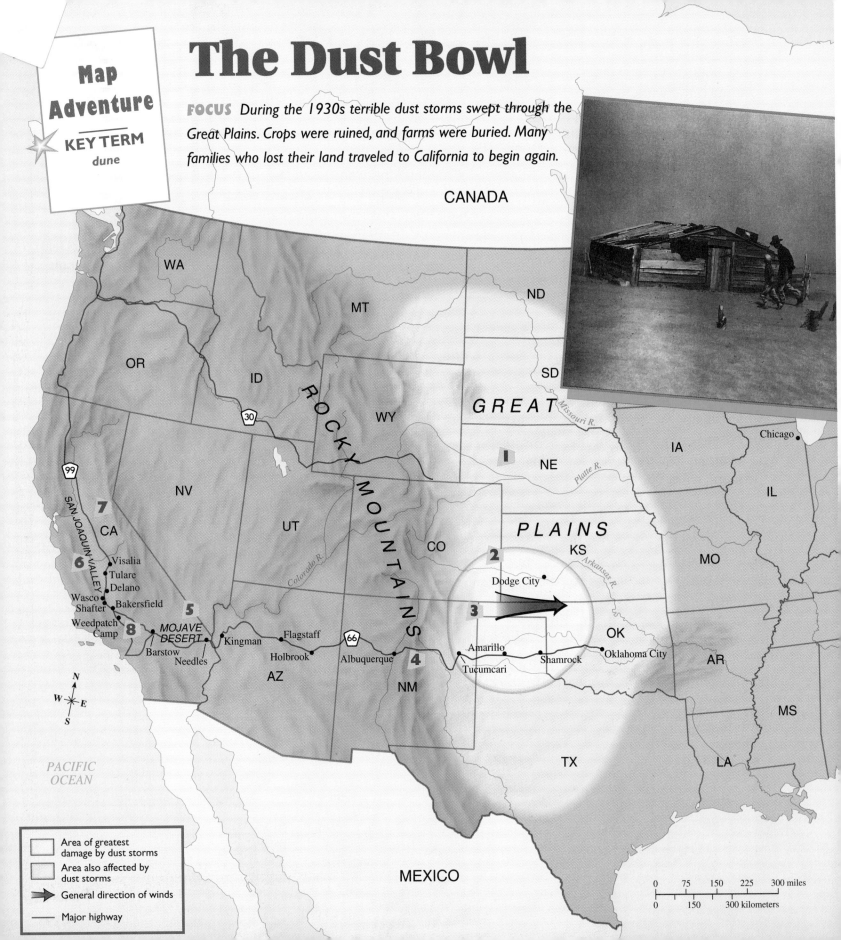

CANADA

WA

OR

ID

MT

ND

SD

WY

ROCKY MOUNTAINS

30

NV

UT

CO

99

CA

7

SAN JOAQUIN VALLEY

Visalia
Tulare
Delano
Wasco
Shafter
Bakersfield
Weedpatch
Camp

6

5

8

MOJAVE
DESERT

Barstow
Needles

Kingman

Flagstaff

Holbrook

66

Albuquerque

AZ

NM

4

Colorado R.

Chicago

IA

IL

GREAT

Missouri R.

Platte R.

NE

1

PLAINS

KS

2

Dodge City

Arkansas R.

3

Amarillo
Tucumcari

Shamrock

Oklahoma City

OK

MO

AR

MS

TX

LA

PACIFIC
OCEAN

N
W · E
S

MEXICO

Legend:
- ☐ Area of greatest damage by dust storms
- ☐ Area also affected by dust storms
- ➤ General direction of winds
- — Major highway

0   75   150   225   300 miles

0   150   300 kilometers

Adventure From the Great Plains to California

From many miles away, farmers could see black clouds of dust moving swiftly across the Great Plains, blocking the sunlight. Each year the storms dumped dust on towns, houses, livestock, fields—everything. The crops were choked by the dust and sand **dunes**. One place offered hope: California. Posters told of rich soil, many jobs, and food for the hungry. Faced with starvation, these farmers migrated to the West, where they would be known as Okies.

Map Legend

1 Great Plains Overplanting and overgrazing made the drought worse. Crops were ruined, and farmers couldn't repay their loans, so they lost their land to the banks.

2 Prairie winds Strong winds carried tons of soil over the Great Plains and the eastern United States. Twelve million tons of dust fell like snow in Chicago. Dust even fell on ships 500 miles out on the Atlantic Ocean.

3 Oklahoma Panhandle This region was hardest hit by the dust storms. Fierce winds buried animals in sand, tore seeds and crops from the fields, and left behind only hard red clay and sand dunes.

4 Route 66 Desperate to reach California, Okies braved the floods, mudslides, potholes, steep hills, and hairpin turns of Route 66.

5 Mojave Desert Daytime temperatures often reached 120°F. Okies traveled the 143 miles across the desert at night so their cars wouldn't overheat.

6 San Joaquin Valley Here farmers needed helpers to pick their crops, such as grapes and beans. The Okies saw endless fields and orchards.

7 California A fruitful land of rich soil, it should have been paradise for Okies. But there were fewer jobs than Okies. Many found no work at all.

⭐ *dune* A hill of sand formed by winds

8 Weedpatch Camp One of the camps built for homeless Okies in California. Here Okies were given meals and basic health care, and their children were able to go to school.

MAP IT

1. *In 1935 your family loses its farm in the Oklahoma Panhandle. Your parents discuss moving north to Nebraska to avoid the dust storms. Would this be a good idea? Explain.*

2. *Your father hears of work in Bakersfield, California. What road will take you there? In which direction are you headed?*

3. *After leaving Needles, your car's engine overheats. What state are you in? Describe what you see around you. How many more miles must you go to reach Bakersfield?*

4. *When your father cannot find work in Bakersfield, your family decides to head north and try another town. What road will take you north? What towns are near this road?*

EXPLORE IT

Your family finally settles in Visalia. Write a letter to a friend back in Oklahoma, describing your experiences since you left home. Be sure to mention the route you took and the towns you passed through.

The New Deal

FOCUS *The New Deal started several government programs that created jobs for people and helped them through the depression. Many of these programs continue to help people today.*

SAFE BANKS

In the early 1930s, millions of people lost their life's savings because of bank failures. To correct this, the U.S. Congress created the Federal Deposit Insurance Corporation (FDIC) in June 1933.

The FDIC prevents bank customers from losing their money when banks are robbed or go bankrupt. The FDIC guarantees bank deposits up to a certain amount. This means the FDIC would give customers their money if the bank couldn't. The FDIC helped restore people's confidence in banks.

WPA

In 1935, at FDR's request, Congress created the Works Progress Administration (WPA). The WPA provided nearly 2 million jobs.

WPA workers built schools, bridges, post offices, and hospitals. They went to schools and used puppets to teach children about nutrition. They worked on flood control and brought electricity to rural areas.

The WPA also paid artists, musicians, writers, and actors to decorate public buildings, give free concerts, write guidebooks, and stage plays in parks. African American writers used WPA money to write a history of slavery.

SOCIAL SECURITY

In 1935, Congress passed the Social Security Act. Social Security is a kind of insurance for workers who retire. During their years on the job, workers and their employers both pay a tax into a special fund. When workers retire, they receive monthly payments from this fund.

This act also provides assistance for people who need it for other reasons. For example, a widow with children receives financial assistance until her children are 18. Also, people who lose their jobs receive monthly income, known as unemployment insurance.

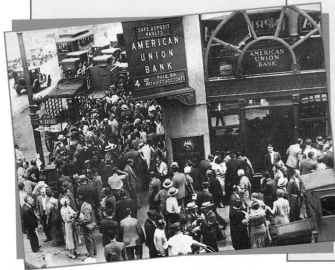

1933
FDIC begins insuring
bank funds

1935
WPA is
created

1935
Congress passes
Social Security Act

1936
Rural Electrification
Act is passed

1937
CCC helps flood victims
in Ohio and Mississippi

1939
FAS gives painting
to post office

1933   1934   1935   1936   1937   1938   1939

RURAL ELECTRIFICATION

Before 1936 many Americans living in rural areas did not have electricity. And few electric companies planned to bring electricity to these widely scattered homes. There was too much labor and cost involved. After all, these customers wouldn't spend enough on electricity for the utility companies to make a profit.

Then, in 1936, Congress passed the Rural Electrification Act. This Act provided government funds to finally bring electricity to the rural areas that had been ignored by private utility companies. Now farmers, too, could enjoy the luxury of modern appliances and electric lights.

CCC

The Civilian Conservation Corps (CCC) was a New Deal program that gave work to over 250,000 jobless men between the ages of 18 and 25. These men, who became known as soil soldiers, helped to conserve the nation's natural resources. They planted trees, cleaned up beaches and camping areas, stocked fish in lakes, and built hiking trails.

They also helped put out forest fires and helped people during natural disasters. In 1937, when the Ohio and Mississippi River valleys flooded, soil soldiers helped. They rescued many people and saved a lot of property that would have been ravaged by the floods.

POST OFFICE MURALS

Artists were hired by the Fine Arts Section (FAS) of the Treasury Department to create paintings in federal buildings throughout the country. The FAS hired many artists to create about 1,400 pieces of art, most of which would be in post offices.

One post office, in Pleasant Hill, Missouri, received an FAS painting in 1939. Entitled *Back Home: April 1865*, the painting showed people at the end of the Civil War. Pleasant Hill residents now could enjoy the artwork every day as well as be reminded that Americans had survived other hard times.

Grandpa's Mountain

by Carolyn Reeder

Carrie, a girl about your age, spends the summers with her grandparents in Virginia's Blue Ridge Mountains. This summer, which is during the depression, Carrie learns that the government plans to build a national park where they live. Her grandparents may be forced to leave their home.

It was just the way Carrie always thought of it when she lost herself in summer memories. . . . She loved the way summers with her grandparents were always the same— carefree days divided between helping Grandma and visiting with Kate and Luanne, her friends who lived up the road. And Sunday afternoons spent with her cousin Amanda. She could hardly wait to see Amanda again!

"I wish I could live here in the country all year," Carrie said, buttering one of Grandma's freshly baked biscuits.

"Oh, now, Carrie! Think how much you'd miss your Mama and Daddy!" Grandma said. Her gray eyes looked shocked.

But Grandpa agreed. "Right here on this mountain is the best possible place to live," he said emphatically. "I was born here and I intend to die here," he continued, accepting a second serving of fried chicken. "We work hard, and we don't owe anything. No matter what happens in this Depression, we'll be fine."

"Now, Claude, I'm sure Carrie doesn't want to talk about the Depression," Grandma said.

Carrie stared down at her plate. She didn't even want to *think* about it. She wanted to forget the months and months her father had been out of work, and how quickly the hopeful look left Mama's face each evening when he came home and sank listlessly into his chair, mumbling, "Nothing today, either." She wanted to forget how they'd had to move to an even smaller apartment, and how hard it had been to change schools in the middle of the year and to make friends in the new neighborhood. She even wanted to forget what life at home was like now that Daddy finally had found a job. He worked at night and needed to sleep during the day, so she had to remember to tiptoe and whisper, and her friends couldn't visit anymore. Worst of all, she saw Daddy only at suppertime, and the evenings alone with Mama seemed so long and dreary. . . .

Grandpa's voice brought her back to the present. "No, Sarah, I think it's important for Carrie to know that we're safe from the Depression here. We can't lose our house or the store, because there's no mortgage on either one of them. And we'll always have plenty to eat because of the garden and your flock of chickens. The future looks pretty good to me."

"To me, too," Carrie said, thinking of the long, peaceful summer stretching before her.

The next morning Carrie woke to the sound of Grandma's roosters crowing and the smell of bacon frying. She rolled out of bed, slipped into her clothes, and ran a comb through her short curls before hurrying down to the kitchen.

"Good morning, Sunshine!" Grandma said, flipping a pancake. "And what are you going to do today?"

"Everything!" Carrie said, beaming with pleasure at the sound of the pet name her grandparents had given her years before. "I'm going to do everything I always do here. First, I'll help you bake pies for the lunchroom, and then I'll walk up the road and see Kate and Luanne. . . .

Carrie flattened herself against the front of the store as Grandpa burst out the door and hurried down the steps and around the house toward the car shed. Grandma came out of the lunchroom to see what was happening. Carrie joined her, and they watched Grandpa drive around the house, pull onto the road and head toward town. . . .

It was mid-afternoon before the old Dodge turned off the road and disappeared around the side of the house. And it was several minutes before Grandpa appeared. Carrie slipped out of the lunchroom and ran over to the store to join her grandmother. Together, they stood just inside the screen door, waiting to see what would happen.

The men on the porch grew silent when they saw Grandpa striding toward them. At the foot of the steps, he stopped and surveyed them grimly. . . .

Grandpa looked from man to man. When he was sure he had everyone's attention, he began, "The government in Washington wants to have a new national park—and they're going to put it right along these mountains. Right along the Blue Ridge. They want it to be a place where city people from all over the East can come and enjoy nature. Where they can see trees and wild animals." . . .

"They want to take the farm of every man here, and they want to take this place, too!" His voice shook with anger. . . .

"When I was in town just now I saw the map," Grandpa said. "All the houses from the old road to the mill on across the mountains are on land they want to take for the new park. For Shenandoah National Park." His voice was scornful.

The men on the porch stirred uneasily, and Grandma slipped a comforting arm around Carrie's waist.

"You can sit here and take this if you want to," Grandpa said, "but I'm going to fight it. I'm a Virginian and an American, and I've got the Declaration of Independence and the U.S. Constitution behind me." He glared at the silent men for a moment before he turned and headed toward the house.

Will Grandpa keep his home in the Blue Ridge Mountains? You can read more about Carrie's summer by checking the book out of your school or public library.

SHOW WHAT YOU KNOW!

REFOCUS
COMPREHENSION

1. How did the FDIC help to make banks safe again?

2. List some ways in which the CCC helped preserve natural resources.

THINK ABOUT IT
CRITICAL THINKING

What might Grandpa do to try to save his land?

WRITE ABOUT IT
ACTIVITY

The FDIC and Social Security are two New Deal programs that still exist. Write an essay, explaining why they are both important.

445

Eleanor Roosevelt

FOCUS *Eleanor Roosevelt struggled with shyness and a lack of self-confidence. Yet she did not let this stop her from becoming an active First Lady and a model citizen.*

Helping Others

Eleanor Roosevelt was born into a wealthy New York family in 1884. She was not a happy child. Eleanor was never comfortable with her appearance and was terribly shy. For most of her childhood, Eleanor lived with her stern grandmother.

It wasn't until she went to school in England at age 15 that Eleanor began to enjoy life. She gained confidence and even took on a leadership role at school. She helped her classmates to do their best. And Eleanor discovered that helping others made her happy.

She finished school and later, in 1905, she married her distant cousin Franklin Delano Roosevelt. Together the Roosevelts had six children, one of whom died as an infant.

Entering Politics

In 1910, Franklin Roosevelt entered politics. Then in 1921, he came down with polio, a disease that left his legs paralyzed. His political career seemed over. But Eleanor Roosevelt convinced him to return to public life. She knew that FDR enjoyed politics, and she believed he could help people. Her husband's happiness was important to her. So was helping others.

When FDR became President in 1932, Mrs. Roosevelt found new ways to help people. Her husband had many duties in Washington, and his paralysis

Eleanor Roosevelt visiting a coal mine

made it hard for him to travel. The First Lady helped him keep in touch with the American public. She traveled around the country, visiting hospitals, schools, and many other places, and found out what people were thinking and talking about. She reported what she learned to the President.

Fighting for Civil Rights

Eleanor Roosevelt also worked to correct many of America's social and economic problems. She pushed to get women the same wages as men. She fought for better health and education programs on Indian reservations.

Mrs. Roosevelt also fought racism. In 1938 she went to a meeting in Alabama with a black friend, named Mary McLeod Bethune. The First Lady refused to obey the law that prevented her from sitting with her friend. When confronted by the police, Eleanor Roosevelt moved her chair and sat *between* the black section and the white section.

Later that year, one of the nation's leading singers, Marian Anderson, wanted to give a concert in Washington, D.C. But because Anderson was African American, she was denied the use of a hall owned by the Daughters of the American Revolution (DAR). This was the only auditorium in Washington, D.C., that was large enough for the audience Anderson would draw. Not only did Mrs. Roosevelt resign from the DAR, but she also arranged to have Marian Anderson sing in front of the Lincoln Memorial. There Anderson had an audience of 75,000 people, including Eleanor Roosevelt.

Mrs. Roosevelt continued to help people throughout her life. After World War II, she became a delegate to the United Nations. And for the rest of her life, she continued to fight for the civil rights of all Americans.

⭐ **civil rights** Personal freedoms of citizens

The First Lady working ▶ in a soup kitchen

Life in the Depression

FOCUS *The Great Depression brought hard times, but Americans found ways to survive. People worked together, and many families even grew closer.*

This unemployed man sells apples to support his family.

A Lack of Jobs

Americans had seen hard times before, but nothing like the Great Depression. It was now difficult for people to find any work at all.

For middle-class white men, it had generally been easy to find work. They grew up believing that all it took to support a family was a good work ethic. Now all of that changed. Some of these men clung to the idea that if they tried hard enough, they would get jobs. Day after day they searched for work. Night after night they came home with nothing. In time their shoes wore out. Holes appeared in the soles, and the little nails around the edges dug into their heels.

Other men tried to keep up the appearance of success. They put on their good business clothes every morning as if dressing for work. As soon as they were out of sight of neighbors and friends, they changed into old clothes. After carefully folding up their business clothes and placing them in a bag, they looked for a way to pass the hours until nightfall. Some begged for money on the streets. Some searched for odd jobs. Some simply sat, defeated, on park benches. At the end of the day, they put their business clothes back on and walked home.

Women Go to Work

The depression affected not only men but also entire families. Sometimes there was not enough food to eat, and often there was no coal for the furnace. And if children got sick, parents couldn't afford a doctor.

Many women would have to work outside the home. In general, women did not compete with men for jobs. The jobs that women took—typing, nursing, working in

A WPA poster advertises jobs for women.

textile factories—were thought of as "women's work." They were usually low-paying jobs.

Some women, however, did find real opportunities during the depression. For example, in 1933, Frances Perkins became the first woman to serve in the President's Cabinet. Also a few other women got important government jobs through the New Deal.

Children Are Affected

For some children the depression abruptly ended their childhood. Lack of money caused their schools to close. They saw their fathers humiliated by the experience of being unable to provide for them. Some of these children took low-paying jobs to help support their families.

Other children even lost the comfort of family life. When parents ran out of money, they sometimes sent their children off to live with relatives. Alma Meyer was ten years old when this happened to her. Meyer later spoke of this experience saying, "I cried the night I left. I told my parents that if they kept me, I'd eat only one meal a day so they could save money. . . . It broke my child's heart, I can tell you that."

Still, many children worked together with their families. And many children and parents found that their families had grown much closer by the time the depression had ended.

Americans Work Together

Middle-class white families weren't the only ones who struggled during the Great Depression. In fact, black Americans suffered from the effects of the depression much sooner than most white Americans. Black workers

Percentages of People Unemployed

Children show their prizes after watching the movie.

were the first to lose their jobs. By 1932 the **jobless rate** among African Americans was 50 percent—double the national average.

African Americans in the South had an especially tough time. Falling crop prices left sharecroppers in worse shape than ever. Some lost their land. Some moved to the North in an unsuccessful search for jobs.

A few survived in the South. They joined with poor white farmers to start the Southern Tenant Farmers Union. The union wasn't very powerful, but black Americans and white Americans worked together for a common cause.

During this time many black Americans turned to their communities for help. African American churches set up soup kitchens. Groups such as the National Urban League offered people clothing and medical care. And some families held "house rent parties." At these

▼ A 1933 movie poster

parties all the guests paid a small fee to help the host raise enough cash to pay the rent.

Movies and Radio

As bad as the Great Depression was, most Americans survived. They even found ways to have fun. They flocked to theaters to see *King Kong* and *The Wizard of Oz*.

In fact, the movie industry really grew during this time. The theaters began to develop special nights, when they would give away prizes such as dishes or board games. Often the dishes that were given away were glass, now known as *depression glass*.

People did go to movies for more than the prizes. The entertainment took people away from their problems. In the theater, people were escorted to their seats and treated as if they were special, regardless of their economic status.

⭐ *jobless rate* The percentage of workers who are unemployed

A depression glass vase

Radios also entertained people. Americans listened to such radio shows as soap operas, quiz shows, and variety shows. *The Shadow*, *The Lone Ranger*, *Dick Tracy*, and *Superman* were the most popular adventure programs. The radio also provided people with the news. On October 30, 1938, Orson Welles combined a news broadcast with entertainment in *The War of the Worlds*. It was a drama of the world being invaded by Martians.

The show began at 8:00 P.M., but many people tuned in late and thought the story was real. They didn't believe the several announcements during the show, saying that the invasion wasn't real. Some people rushed off to find and save loved ones or ran for their lives. It took several days before everyone realized the "invasion" was a radio program.

Surviving Difficult Times

Family members did more than gather together in front of their radios. They talked and read together. They followed their favorite sports heroes, such as Mildred "Babe" Didrikson and Jesse Owens. They played board games and worked together in their backyard gardens.

Many families actually grew closer as they struggled through this hard time. Americans clung to the hope that the hard times would end. Although it took more than ten years, they were right—prosperity did eventually return to the United States.

Orson Welles ▶

REFOCUS
COMPREHENSION

1. Why were women able to find jobs when men could not?

2. How did African Americans cope with the depression?

THINK ABOUT IT
CRITICAL THINKING

Why did some men try to keep up the appearance of success?

WRITE ABOUT IT
ACTIVITY

Make a chart that shows the positive things and negative things families experienced during the depression.

451

SUMMING UP

1 DO YOU REMEMBER . . .
COMPREHENSION

1. What were the major problems that people faced during the Great Depression?

2. Why wouldn't people in rural areas have gotten electricity without the help of the Rural Electrification Act?

3. How did the Great Depression finally end?

4. How did the Social Security Act provide security to Americans?

5. What was the Works Progress Administration?

6. How did the Dust Bowl affect farmers on the Great Plains?

7. How did Eleanor Roosevelt work to improve the lives of women and Native Americans?

8. What typical hardships did people face during the Great Depression?

9. Why did the movie industry grow more popular during the depression?

10. Why did black Americans suffer more than white Americans during the depression?

2 SKILL POWER
PROBLEM SOLVING

Both President Hoover and President Roosevelt tried to solve the problem of the Great Depression. Make a chart that shows the ideas that each leader tried. Tell which ideas seemed most effective.

3 WHAT DO YOU THINK?
CRITICAL THINKING

1. Why did Herbert Hoover believe that government aid would destroy people's freedom and self-reliance? Explain.

2. Why were people leaving the Dust Bowl willing to risk the dangers of the Mojave Desert?

3. What types of problems might a modern-day New Deal try to solve?

4. How was Eleanor Roosevelt a role model for future First Ladies?

5. Why did some families draw closer together during the hard times of the depression?

4 SAY IT, WRITE IT, USE IT
VOCABULARY

Write a conversation that two farmers on the Great Plains might have had in the mid-1930s. Using the terms below, describe how economic and natural events affected their everyday lives.

civil rights	jobless rate
dune	New Deal
Dust Bowl	stock market
Great Depression	

5 GEOGRAPHY AND YOU
MAP STUDY

Use the map below and the map on page 435 to answer these questions.

1. Which state had the highest unemployment percentage in 1934?

2. What was the unemployment percentage in your state? Make a list of all the states that had the same level of unemployment.

3. Which states had the lowest unemployment percentage in 1934?

4. List the states that were affected by the Tennessee Valley Authority. Beside each state, write its 1934 unemployment percentage.

6 TAKE ACTION
CITIZENSHIP

In the 1930s, Civilian Conservation Corps workers, or soil soldiers, helped conserve the nation's natural resources. With a group of classmates and an adult advisor, organize a similar project that you can do in your local community. For example, you and your fellow soil soldiers might clean an area along a riverbank or beach, plant trees, or help maintain a hiking trail.

7 GET CREATIVE
ART CONNECTION

During the depression, WPA artists created murals for post offices and public buildings. The murals showed the historical and cultural heritage of a town or region. Create a mural for your school. Work with a group of classmates to plan figures and events that highlight your area's unique heritage. Once you agree on a design, create the mural on a large sheet of poster paper.

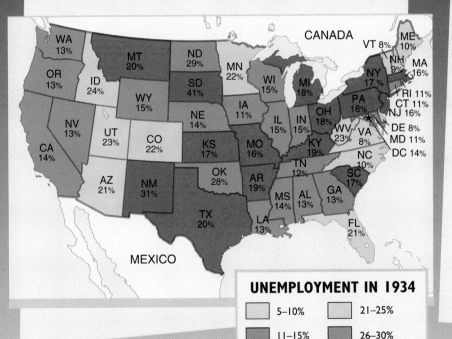

UNEMPLOYMENT IN 1934

5–10%	21–25%
11–15%	26–30%
16–20%	30% and over

LOOKING AHEAD Find out in the next chapter how economic depressions throughout the world led to a second world war.

REFLECT ON

CHAPTER 20

WORLD WAR II

Americans tried to forget about world affairs during the depression. But they could no longer put them out of mind when events in Asia and Europe brought war to the world again.

▼ How did canning food help the war effort? Find out on page 469.

CONTENTS

These books tell about people and places of the Second World War. Read one that interests you and fill out a book-review form.

READ AND RESEARCH

Journey to Topaz by Yoshiko Uchida
(Creative Arts Book Co., 1985)
Yuki Sakane's world turns upside down in December 1941. Her father is taken away, and her family, because they are Japanese American, must go to an internment camp. *(historical fiction)*
• *You can read a selection from this story on page 472.*

World War II by Tom McGowen (Franklin Watts, 1993)
This book will help you follow the main events of the war. Maps show you how the countries of Europe and Asia were occupied by their enemies. *(nonfiction)*

I Am a Star: Child of the Holocaust by Inge Auerbacher
(Penguin USA, 1993)
As the only Jewish child to survive from the German state of Württemberg, Inge's remembrances are an important testimony to the horrors of war. *(biography)*

Rosie the Riveter: Women Working on the Home Front in World War II by Penny Colman (Random House, 1995)
When American men went to war, women went to work in factories to keep up the production of military supplies. Find out how women's careers began to change as a result of the war. *(nonfiction)*

SKILL POWER

Distinguishing Between Fact and Opinion

Being able to recognize facts and opinions will help you decide whether information is true.

UNDERSTAND IT

When the United States entered World War II, millions of people were needed for the war effort. The poster below persuaded women to join the Navy. Notice the message on it.

"Don't miss your great opportunity. . . The Navy needs you in the WAVES (Women Accepted for Volunteer Service)."

If you were a woman in 1941, how could you be sure the statement was true? Would you want to know some facts about the war before you believed the poster's message?

EXPLORE IT

A fact is true information that can be checked. This statement, for example, is a fact: *Over 300,000 American women joined the armed forces during World War II.* You could check it in reference books or by going through official records.

An opinion is what someone *thinks* is true. There's no sure way to prove an opinion. Since opinions express feelings and thoughts, they often contain clue words, such as *think, need, believe, like, dislike, good,* and *bad.* Usually, people use facts to show how they arrived at an opinion. For example, the fact that 300,000 women served in World War II helps support the opinion that it was a woman's war, too.

Can you find an opinion in the following paragraph? What facts help support the opinion?

Women played a very important role in America's war effort. During the first five months of the war, 750,000 women volunteered to work in arms plants. By 1944, about 3.5 million women worked on assembly lines turning out tanks, ships, and guns. In the aviation industry alone, women made up two thirds of the work force.

Don't miss your great opportunity..

THE NAVY NEEDS YOU IN THE **WAVES**

This recruiting poster was used to get women to support World War II.

TRY IT

Read the statements on the right about women in World War II. Think about how you could find out whether each statement is true. Then decide whether it is a fact or an opinion.

Now look for statements of opinion in an earlier chapter of this book. On a sheet of paper, list the opinions you find. Beneath each opinion, list any facts that support the opinion.

Fact **Opinion**

☐ ☐ **1** During World War II, American women were very patriotic.

☐ ☐ **2** By 1944, 37 percent of all adult American women were working outside the home.

☐ ☐ **3** Women in the Air Force flew tracking missions and conducted engineering tests on planes.

☐ ☐ **4** About 140,000 women enlisted in the Army.

☐ ☐ **5** Most women loved working in defense plants.

SKILL POWER SEARCH *Look for examples of opinions in this chapter. For each opinion you find, look for facts to support it.*

A WORLD AT WAR AGAIN

FOCUS *After World War I the United States tried to stay out of European affairs. But soon the country was again drawn into a global conflict.*

"Losing the Peace"

It is one thing to win a war. It is another thing, however, to "win the peace." The Allies, including the United States, had won the Great War in 1918. But they "lost the peace." In other words, they were not able to make the peace last.

One way they lost the peace was by imposing the harsh Treaty of Versailles on Germany. The treaty made sense to the Allies at the time. The Allies wanted to make sure that Germany would never be able to wage a war again. But the treaty's demand that Germany pay for all war damages was particularly harsh. The demand guaranteed that the German economy would face great difficulties as Germany struggled to pay those damages.

Staying Neutral

During the 1920s, Germany slipped into economic chaos. Its government tried to cope with the problems, but it failed. So did an appeal for international sympathy. Because of their experiences in World War I, France and Britain were not concerned that Germany was struggling.

Most Americans wanted nothing to do with Europe after

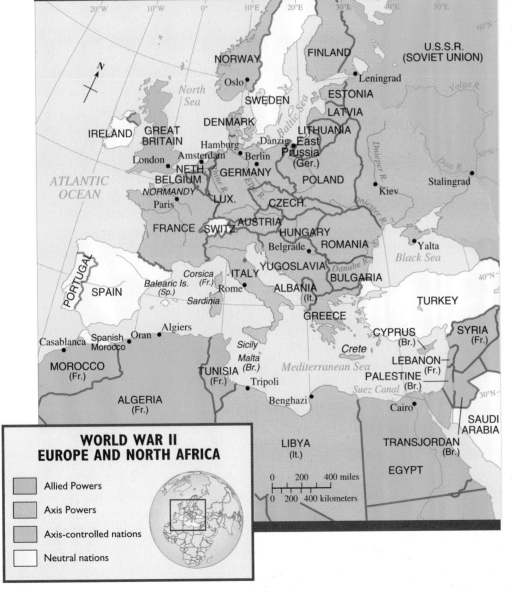

**WORLD WAR II
EUROPE AND NORTH AFRICA**

- Allied Powers
- Axis Powers
- Axis-controlled nations
- Neutral nations

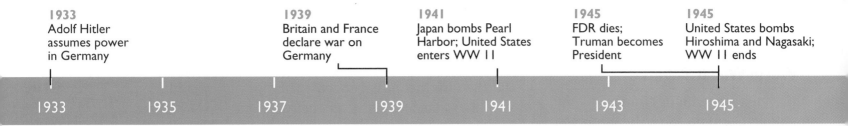

1933
Adolf Hitler assumes power in Germany

1939
Britain and France declare war on Germany

1941
Japan bombs Pearl Harbor; United States enters WW II

1945
FDR dies; Truman becomes President

1945
United States bombs Hiroshima and Nagasaki; WW II ends

1933   1935   1937   1939   1941   1943   1945

the Great War. One European war, they felt, had been enough for the United States. The country had problems of its own dealing with the Great Depression. So the United States adopted a policy of **isolationism** toward Europe by the 1930s. That meant staying out of world affairs that had no direct effect on the United States.

The Rise of Dictators

Many countries hit hard by the economics of the Treaty of Versailles and the depression turned to all-powerful leaders, called **dictators**, who had no use

⭐ **isolationism** The policy of staying out of international affairs

dictator A ruler with absolute power in a country

▼ Adolf Hitler won support with his message that Germany had suffered because of the Treaty of Versailles.

for democracy. They promised that they would free their nations from the postwar restrictions other countries had placed on them. The dictators also promised that they could restore their countries to the power and glory they once had, even if that meant war.

In Italy, Benito Mussolini (be NEE toh moos soh LEE nee) came to power in 1922. Joseph Stalin (JOH zuf STAH lihn) took over as ruler of the Soviet Union several years later. In Japan a group of army generals took power in the late 1930s. In Germany, Adolf Hitler set up his dictatorship in 1933. Hitler ruled the **Nazi** political party. He and the Nazis blamed Jews, whom they did not see as true Germans, for Germany's defeat in World War I. Hitler claimed that the German people were a "master race" who should rule over all of Europe, much as they had wanted to in centuries past.

In 1936, Italy, Germany, and Japan agreed to work together. The dictatorships called themselves the **Axis Powers**. Find the Allied Powers and the Axis Powers on the map on page 458.

⭐ **Nazi** The political party that came to power in Germany in the 1930s

Axis Powers The countries that fought against the Allies in World War II

World War II Begins

Hitler wasted little time trying to rebuild Germany. First, he improved Germany's military. Then he began to occupy lands bordering Germany. In 1938 he took over Austria. In 1939, Germany stormed into Czechoslovakia (chek uh sloh VAH kee uh). All of these actions violated the Treaty of Versailles but the Allies did not stop Hitler.

Hitler at last went too far for the Allies. France and Great Britain had warned him not to invade Poland. But on September 1, 1939, he sent his invading armies into Poland anyway. France and Britain immediately declared war on Germany. In 1941, the Soviet Union entered the war after being invaded by Germany. Europe was in flames again. Barely 20 years after World War I ended, World War II began.

For a while the United States stayed out of this conflict. President Franklin Roosevelt tried to alert Americans to the dangers of dictatorships. But most Americans remained isolationists. One poll found that 67 percent of Americans wanted the nation to stay out of the war.

America Gets Involved

Japan had invaded China in 1937. The Allies and the United States protested but did nothing. At last, in 1940, Roosevelt cut off trade with Japan. Japan would no longer get the fuel and scrap metal it needed for its war activities. This greatly angered the Japanese generals. They saw the United States as an enemy.

On December 7, 1941, the Japanese launched a surprise attack on the United States. Their target was the Navy base at Pearl Harbor in Hawaii. This attack killed thousands of soldiers and civilians and nearly destroyed the U.S. Navy. In a flash the policy of isolationism was dead, and the United States declared war on Japan. Because Japan was allied with Germany and Italy, those nations declared war on the United States.

Allied War Plans

Unlike World War I, World War II forced the United States to fight on two fronts. America had to fight Germany and Italy in Europe and in Africa, where both the Allies and Axis Powers had territories. The United States also had to fight Japan in Asia.

▲ Posters like this encouraged Americans to work together and support the war effort.

▼ Winston Churchill (left), Britain's leader; Roosevelt (center); and Stalin (right) met to discuss Allied strategy.

The Americans, along with their allies, decided to fight the Axis Powers in Europe first. Germany seemed a greater military threat than Japan.

By 1941 the Germans had overtaken most of Europe, including France. They had invaded and conquered part of the Soviet Union. But in 1942 the tide of war began to turn. In brutal fighting, the Soviets managed to stop Germany's advance.

In late 1942, American and British soldiers scored major victories over the Germans in North Africa. The next year the Allies knocked Italy out of the war. Then, on June 6, 1944, Allied troops sailed from Britain and landed on the beaches of Normandy, France. By summer's end, the Allies had driven Germany out of most of France.

The Americans and British closed in on Germany from the west. The Soviets closed in from the east. Hitler finally realized that Germany was beaten. On May 7, 1945, Germany surrendered. The Nazis were forced out of power. Many were later put on trial for **war crimes**.

The Holocaust

Allied victory revealed the true nature of Hitler's rule. As Allied soldiers advanced into Germany and German-controlled areas, they were horrified. They came upon one death camp after another. Most were in secret locations deep inside Poland.

All during the war the Nazis had sent people to these camps. There prisoners were made to work like slaves. Most of them were Jews. But they also included people with physical or mental defects, Gypsies and other minorities, and enemies of the Nazi party.

Those who couldn't work—the very old, the very sick, and the very young—were slaughtered right away. The Nazis forced stronger, healthier prisoners to work until they became ill or injured. Then the Nazis killed them, too. Most died in gas chambers. More than 6 million Jews and several million other people perished in these death camps and elsewhere. This mass murder is now known as the **Holocaust**.

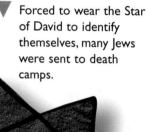

Forced to wear the Star of David to identify themselves, many Jews were sent to death camps.

 war crime   A crime that violates accepted laws of war or norms of humane behavior

 Holocaust   The mass murder of millions of Jews and other people by the Nazis

Americans were shocked when they discovered what had happened. They had heard rumors about a holocaust during the war. But the nature of such mass murder was too monstrous for them to believe. The gas chambers and the testimony of survivors showed everyone the horrible truth.

Moving Against Japan

As the Allies struggled against the Nazis in Europe, the United States made steady headway against Japan. In tough fighting, Americans took back islands in the Pacific Ocean that Japan had conquered. By early 1945 the Americans had destroyed most of Japan's navy and air force. Meanwhile, American planes rained bombs on Japan almost daily. Major Pacific battles are shown on the map on the right.

Still, Japan didn't surrender. To end the war, Allied leaders thought it would be necessary to invade Japan. They calculated that perhaps as many as several million soldiers would be killed or wounded in such an invasion.

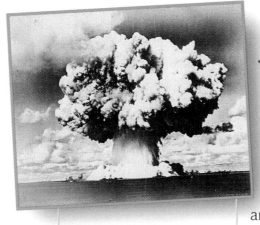

▲ The test of the atomic bomb

The Atomic Bomb

The United States government knew there was a way to end the war without further loss of American life. Scientists had been working, in secret, since the beginning of the war to develop a powerful new weapon— an atomic bomb, capable of immediate and massive destruction. In July 1945 they successfully tested the bomb in the New Mexican desert.

The timing of the test was crucial.

WORLD WAR II IN EAST ASIA AND THE PACIFIC

Areas under Japanese control, 1942

✳ Major battles

Atomic bombings, 1945

PEACE!

THE INDIANAPOLIS STAR EXTRA

WAR IS ENDED—TRUMAN

American newspapers communicated information about U.S. troops in action.

Since the bomb's strength was proved, it became an alternative to sending one million American soldiers to Japan. The decision on when and how to use such a powerful bomb was solely in the President's hands. President Roosevelt had died in the spring, so the new President, Harry S Truman, had to decide whether to use the bomb.

It was an incredibly difficult decision to make. Truman was advised by a panel of scientists and top officials. They told him the bomb would kill many people and release a long-lasting kind of poison called radiation. So some of Truman's advisors opposed using the bomb. Others, however, believed it was the way to end a long and brutal war.

The End of the War

At last President Truman made the decision. On August 6, 1945, an American plane dropped an atomic bomb on the Japanese city of Hiroshima (hihr uh SHEE-muh). When the bomb exploded, an enormous light flashed as bright as the sun. Over 60,000

people died instantly. At least 40,000 more died in the days that followed. Radiation caused 100,000 more deaths in the next few years.

Three days later the United States dropped an atomic bomb on the city of Nagasaki (nah guh SAH kee). The loss of life and destruction from the bombings prompted Japan to surrender on August 14, 1945. World War II was over at last. Americans at home and abroad were relieved that the long war was over. For days they celebrated, hoping that the world had been forever changed because of the war.

Ticker tape parades in cities like New York greeted returning soldiers.

SHOW WHAT YOU KNOW!

REFOCUS
COMPREHENSION

1. How did the attack on Pearl Harbor change Americans' attitude about entering the war?

2. Why was June 6, 1944, an important day in the course of the war?

THINK ABOUT IT
CRITICAL THINKING

Contrast the Allied victory over Germany with the United States' victory over Japan. How were the victories similar and different? Why?

WRITE ABOUT IT
ACTIVITY

You are a German citizen who has immigrated to the United States in the late 1930s. You have been asked to give a speech about how life in Germany has changed under Nazi rule. Outline your speech.

HOW WE FOUGHT

FOCUS *Forced to abandon its policy of neutrality, the United States and its allies waged a tough and aggressive war against the Axis Powers.*

LEND-LEASE

In March 1941, Congress passed the Lend-Lease Act after a heated debate. "Lend-lease" was President Roosevelt's idea. He wanted to help Britain and other nations under attack from Germany.

Under this law the United States would "lend" or "lease" whatever goods and materials the Allies needed. Roosevelt compared lend-lease to lending a garden hose to a neighbor whose house was on fire. As a result of this law, FDR referred to the United States as an "arsenal of democracy." (An *arsenal* is a storehouse of weapons.) Lend-lease showed that the United States clearly supported Britain in this European war.

PEARL HARBOR

The Japanese attacked the United States on a Sunday morning just before 8 o'clock, December 7, 1941. It caught the nation completely by surprise. One wave of planes after another attacked the U.S. naval base at Pearl Harbor, Hawaii. The attack damaged or sank 19 ships and 150 planes. It killed 2,335 soldiers and sailors, as well as 68 civilians.

The next day, President Roosevelt went before Congress and asked for a declaration of war. He said that December 7, 1941, was a date that would "live in infamy [disgrace]." Congress voted for war with only one representative, Jeannette Rankin, voting against it.

THE BATTLES OF MIDWAY AND GUADALCANAL

On June 4, 1942, the Japanese attacked the American-held island of Midway in the Pacific Ocean. The Americans, however, had broken Japan's secret code and were ready for the attack. The battle was fought between aircraft carriers. American planes sank four Japanese carriers, while the Japanese sank only one American carrier, the *Yorktown*. This was a major American victory and a turning point in the Pacific war. It paved the way for the long battle of Guadalcanal, America's first successful land battle against the Japanese. In victory the United States gained possession of the Solomon Islands, a key stepping stone to Japan itself.

March 11, 1941	December 7, 1941	June 6, 1942	November 8, 1942
Lend-Lease Act passed	Pearl Harbor attacked	Battle of Midway won	Allied troops land in North Africa

1941　　　　　　　　　　　　　　　　1942　　　　　　　　　　　　　　　　1943

THREE AMERICAN GENERALS

During World War II, American forces fought in North Africa, the Pacific, and Europe. George Patton, Douglas MacArthur, and Dwight Eisenhower were three leaders in charge of U.S. forces in these areas.

In November 1942, General George S. Patton, Jr., led forces in the Allied invasion of North Africa. In 1943 his troops invaded the island of Sicily. Later, Patton led troops in other parts of Europe.

General Douglas MacArthur led the defense of the Philippines when the Japanese began their conquest of the islands. After being ordered by President Franklin Roosevelt to leave the Philippines in 1942, MacArthur pledged "I shall return." He carried out that pledge when his forces landed on the island of Leyte on October 20, 1944.

In 1943, President Franklin D. Roosevelt put General Dwight Eisenhower in charge of the Allied forces in Europe. Eisenhower's huge task was to plan an Allied invasion of France. That plan was put into action on D-Day.

D-DAY

June 6, 1944, was D-Day. (*D-Day* was short for "designated day.") Early in the morning the Allies launched the greatest invasion force in history. A force of 600 warships and 4,000 other boats carried 176,000 soldiers from Britain to the coast of Normandy, France. Despite tough fighting, the landing was a success. Within a week the Allies were able to land 100,000 tons of supplies, 50,000 vehicles, and more than 325,000 soldiers in France.

One reason the invasion worked was that the Allies had managed to trick Hitler. They had sent false signals that the invasion was going to be at Calais (ka LAY), a city farther up the French coast. So Hitler had sent many of his best units to Calais.

465

June 6, 1944	February 19, 1945	May 8, 1945	August 15, 1945
D-Day invasion	U.S. invades Iwo Jima	V-E Day	V-J Day

1944   1945   1946

IWO JIMA

On February 19, 1945, the United States Marines landed on the tiny island of Iwo Jima (EE woh JEE-muh), about 750 miles from Tokyo. For the next four weeks, the Marines and the Japanese soldiers fought in bloody combat. This fighting was typical of Pacific island warfare. The Japanese had built strong fortifications in the mountains. The Marines had to find and destroy these positions. The Marines lost about 4,000 men in the desperate fight. On February 23 they climbed Mount Suribachi (soor uh BAH chee) and planted the American flag. Victory over Japan was in sight.

VICTORY

The United States celebrated victory in World War II *twice*. By April 1945, Germany did not have enough soldiers to face the Allied armies that were marching toward Berlin. Germany surrendered to the Allied forces on May 7 at Reims, France. The next day was declared V-E (Victory in Europe) Day. But President Truman warned Americans not to celebrate just yet. Victory over Japan came on August 14, when the Japanese, stunned by the devastation of the atomic bombs, finally surrendered. V-J Day was celebrated the following day.

SHOW WHAT YOU KNOW!

REFOCUS
COMPREHENSION

1. What battle marked the turning point in the war in the Pacific?

2. Why was D-Day important?

THINK ABOUT IT
CRITICAL THINKING

Why did the Lend-Lease Act signal the end of United States neutrality in World War II?

WRITE ABOUT IT
ACTIVITY

Many of the turning points in World War II were photographed. If you were a photographer, you would have to write captions describing what you photographed. Do so for the photos on these pages.

"WE CAN DO IT" LIFE AT HOME

FOCUS *Americans not on the battlefield found many ways to contribute to the war effort on the home front.*

The Need for Workers

As soon as America entered World War II, Americans sensed it was going to be a long, bloody war. They realized it would take a heroic effort to defeat enemy forces in Europe and in Asia. People who did not fight on the battlefields felt it was their duty to support the war. They pledged to do whatever they could to help the cause.

As workers went off to fight, more and more Help Wanted signs appeared on businesses across the country. Who filled those jobs is a fascinating chapter in America's history.

Women in the Work Force

Women stepped forward in large numbers to fill job openings. Many positions were in industries that had never been open to women before. Suddenly there were female meatpackers and railroad workers. Women built aircraft, sawed lumber, and drove buses. Americans were struck by the image of women fastening rivets,

Posters like this encouraged women to work during World War II. ▼

▼ These women worked at a factory that made bombers during the war.

We Can Do It!

467

War ration books were first handed out to families in May 1942. Their coupons allowed Americans to buy rationed sugar and gas.

or steel bolts, into the sides of ships. In fact, "Rosie the Riveter" became a popular symbol for the more than 6 million women who joined the work force during these years.

Women didn't have an easy time in their new jobs. They were paid much less than men for the same work. Often they faced complaints from their male co-workers. These men may have supported the *idea* of women pitching in to help win the war, but in reality, they didn't like to see women taking over "men's work." Despite such problems, women stuck with it. By 1943 they made up one third of the work force in the United States.

Saving Resources

At the same time, women whose husbands were at war were expected to run the household, manage the finances, do the cooking, and fix broken appliances. These women were greatly affected by rationing, which made people at home save basic materials for the war effort. The war

effort demanded a tremendous amount of America's resources. Early in the war, sugar and gasoline were rationed. A family of four was limited to four pounds of sugar every two weeks, and 25 to 30 gallons of gas per month. By the end of 1943, butter, cheese, coffee, flour, and meat were rationed. Each American was allotted three pairs of leather shoes a year.

People back home worked hard to free up these resources. Gas was rationed because it was needed for tanks, trucks, and military jeeps. Nylon was rationed because it was used to make parachutes. So car owners cut down on their driving, and women stopped wearing nylon stockings. As one ad said, "Every time you decide *not* to buy something you help win the war." Americans also held **scrap drives**. They collected old tires, cans, papers—anything that could be recycled into war material.

Everyone Helps the War Effort

Men who were too young or too old for the armed forces and those who had disabilities also filled job vacancies. Some had never worked before, and some were retired. Thousands of older Americans volunteered for the Red Cross. They knitted sweaters and socks for the troops. They donated blood and planted **victory gardens**.

Meanwhile, on farms, Mexican workers were brought in to harvest

---

 scrap drive A call for discarded material to be used to support the war effort

victory garden A garden planted by people to show that they could be self-sufficient

crops. These workers were called **braceros** (bruh SER-ohz), which means "helping arms" in Spanish. Without their assistance many American crops would have been left rotting in the fields during the war, while farmers were serving on the battlefields.

Children, too, did their part. They collected Christmas presents for soldiers without families. They sent books and magazines to wounded men in veterans' hospitals. With most factories building war materials, fewer toys were on the market. Children learned to be happy

"We'll have lots to eat this winter, won't we Mother?"

Grow your own
Can your own

▶ Posters encouraged Americans to can fruits and other foods.

with gifts of fruit or clothing instead of sleds, games, bikes, or puzzles. Many children used their allowance to buy War Stamps. Like Liberty bonds in World War I, these helped raise money for war. War Stamps helped pay for machine guns, helmets, and even airplanes.

In schools, children followed the movement of troops on classroom maps. They studied world geography. They learned the names of world leaders. They sang patriotic songs. They and their families learned what it meant to be Americans.

⭐ *bracero* One of a group of Mexican farm workers who took the place of American farm workers during World War II

◀ These New York City schoolchildren were happy to collect metal for a scrap drive.

SHOW WHAT YOU
KNOW!

REFOCUS
COMPREHENSION

1. How did Americans on the home front help the war effort?

2. Who were the braceros?

THINK ABOUT IT
CRITICAL THINKING

How did America pull together on the home front in support of the war?

WRITE ABOUT IT
ACTIVITY

List three facts about American life on the home front. Then list three opinions you have about how people lived at home during World War II.

Spotlight

KEY TERMS

nisei
internment camp

LITERATURE

Journey to Topaz

INTERNMENT CAMPS

FOCUS *During World War II, Japanese Americans were unfairly accused of helping Japan. As a result, many Japanese Americans endured years in internment camps.*

The Media Fans Suspicion

Immediately after Pearl Harbor, fear and anger swept across the United States. Americans were outraged at Japan and many believed that some Japanese Americans might be spies for Japan. Newspapers and radio spread false reports that Japanese Americans were more loyal to Japan than to the United States. It didn't matter that most of them were **nisei** (NEE-say), second-generation American citizens of Japanese descent.

Japanese Americans had been struggling against discrimination since the 1800s. Laws were passed to restrict immigration from Japan. Also, some people tried to keep Japanese immigrants who were already here from becoming citizens.

After Pearl Harbor, Japanese Americans felt they had to prove that they were loyal citizens. They hung American flags. They bought war bonds. Many got rid of all traces of their Japanese heritage. They burned family photos and smashed treasured Japanese vases. The Japanese American Citizens League sent a telegram to President Roosevelt. It said, "We pledge our fullest cooperation to you, Mr. President, and to our country. There can not be any question. . . . We in our hearts know we are Americans, loyal to America."

Internment Camps

Camp	State	Number of people interned
Gila River	Arizona	13,348
Granada	Colorado	7,318
Heart Mountain	Wyoming	10,767
Jerome	Arkansas	8,497
Manzanar	California	10,046
Minidoka	Idaho	9,397
Poston	Arizona	17,814
Rohwer	Arkansas	8,475
Topaz	Utah	8,130
Tule Lake	California	18,789

nisei A United States citizen born in America to parents of Japanese descent

Life in Internment Camps

Despite the efforts of Japanese Americans to prove their loyalty, in 1942 President Roosevelt ordered the removal of all persons of Japanese ancestry from western Washington, Oregon, California, and parts of Arizona. Over 100,000 Japanese Americans were rounded up from their homes and sent to **internment camps**. The internment camps were little more than prisons. Barbed wire surrounded the camps. Armed guards stood at the entrances. Searchlights followed the movements of prisoners at night. The living quarters were cramped tar-paper huts with very little privacy. The Japanese Americans living in them had been forced to leave most of their belongings behind, except for clothes and a few utensils.

Japanese Americans lived in these camps for four years. They tried to make the best of their situation. They planted gardens and started churches. They organized schools where their children faithfully recited the Pledge of Allegiance.

Loyal Americans

Japanese Americans continued to fight for their rights as American citizens. They convinced the United States government to let them volunteer for the army. Many joined the 442nd Combat Team, a unit of Japanese Americans. The 442nd was the most highly decorated unit, for its size and service, in World War II.

Not a single Japanese American was ever found to have worked against the United States during the war. For years Japanese Americans fought to prove that they had been treated unfairly. In 1988 the American government apologized to Japanese Americans. It paid $20,000 to each survivor of the internment camps.

internment camp A prisonlike place in which people are held during a war

▲ These nisei children are identified as being of Japanese descent by the tags they wear.

▼ An internment camp in California

Journey to Topaz

by Yoshiko Uchida

Illustrated by Donald Carrick

Yuki and Ken's father has been taken from his family by the FBI during the early days of the war. But the family does not know where he is or how he is being treated. They eagerly await word from him to learn what to expect next.

On the sixth day after he was taken away, a postcard finally arrived from Father. He told them that he was being held at the Immigration Detention Headquarters in San Francisco and asked for his shaving kit and some clean clothing.

"Am safe and well," he wrote, "and pray that you are too."

"Thank goodness," Mother sighed as she read it. It was not knowing where or how he was that had been the worst part of the long wait.

In a few more days, Father wrote that they could come to San Francisco to visit him and he hoped to see them soon. The very next day, Ken and Yuki stayed home from school and Ken drove them in the family car to San Francisco. . . . He drove silently over the Bay Bridge and scarcely spoke until they reached the Immigration Headquarters.

Yuki didn't like the looks of the building. Somehow all government buildings seemed austere and unfriendly, smelling of stale cigar smoke and cleaning fluids. She disliked this one more than most and hated the thought of Father being held there like a prisoner.

They waited for him in a small dark room, and when he came in followed by a guard, he looked tired and worn. Father, who never left the house without a neat crease in his trousers and a black bow tie at his neck, was tieless and rumpled, still wearing the gardening clothes in which he had been taken. He tried to be cheerful, however, and told them that everything was fine. . . .

It was only when their short visit was coming to an end that Father told them that he was among a group of ninety men being sent to an Army Internment Camp in Missoula, Montana.

"Montana!" Mother gasped.

"When do you leave?" Ken asked, trying to keep his voice steady.

"In a few hours," Father said. "I'm glad we had this chance to say goodbye."

Yuki was too stunned to say much. "But Montana is miles away," she said, her voice rising. "We won't be able to visit you."

Father nodded. "Not for a while, Yuki Chan, but I'll be back soon. . . . Be careful in every way."

Find out what happens to Yuki and Ken's family. Check this book out of your school or public library.

SHOW WHAT YOU KNOW!

REFOCUS
COMPREHENSION

1. Why were Japanese Americans sent to internment camps?

2. What did Japanese Americans do to show that they were loyal Americans?

THINK ABOUT IT
CRITICAL THINKING

Why did Father act cheerful when his family visited him?

WRITE ABOUT IT
ACTIVITY

Write a letter to a newspaper describing life in an internment camp.

BATTLING DISCRIMINATION

FOCUS *Not only did African Americans battle the enemy during World War II, but they also battled discrimination at home and in the military.*

Armed Forces Discrimination

One million African Americans served in World War II. Like most Americans, they wanted to support and defend their country. But they faced a problem: some Americans didn't *want* their help. Discrimination was such a part of American life that some white soldiers wanted nothing to do with black soldiers.

African Americans did serve, as they had in World War I. But the military refused to let black soldiers live in the same barracks as white soldiers. It would not let them command white troops, either. For the most part, black Americans were given the lowest possible positions in the armed forces. They peeled potatoes and cleaned toilets. A few were given combat posts, but they were put in separate all-black units, away from white troops. That meant that **integration** of troops was forbidden.

It was not just the lowly positions that made military life hard for black soldiers. It was the way the men were treated. They were treated with even less respect than white **prisoners of war**.

The Distinguished Flying Cross, presented to many members of the 99th

On trains, black American soldiers were kicked out of "white seats" to make room for German war prisoners.

The Tuskegee Airmen

Discrimination was certainly not new to African Americans. All their lives, they had dealt with discrimination—even hatred—shown by some white Americans. At the start of World War II, for example, black workers were kept out of many jobs. They did not have equal access to housing or medical care. Still, discrimination became especially clear during the war. Black Americans were ready to die in the service of their country, yet their country was treating them poorly.

A few brave Americans spoke out on this issue. A. Philip Randolph, an African American labor leader, was one. Eleanor Roosevelt was another. By 1941 the U.S. Army reluctantly agreed to set up a flight-training school for black pilots. Located in Tuskegee

Benjamin O. Davis, Jr., the first black American major general, who led the 99th Pursuit Squadron

integration Bringing together people of different racial or ethnic groups

prisoner of war One who is captured and held by an enemy during a war

(tus KEE gee), Alabama, it eventually trained over 900 African Americans.

These pilots were superbly qualified. Many scored higher on military tests than their white counterparts. But these Tuskegee airmen still faced discrimination. They had to deal with the fact that few people had any confidence in them. Again and again, their elite group, the 99th Pursuit Squadron, was passed over for missions. Meanwhile, black pilots were not allowed into white officers' clubs.

The Black Eagles

By January 1944 the 99th was flying low-risk missions over Axis-controlled territory. One day the squadron ran into trouble. It came upon a group of enemy planes. Within minutes the pilots shot down five of these planes. To many people this proved that the 99th Squadron was ready for bigger jobs.

Soon the 99th was handling much more dangerous missions. They began accompanying bombers on flights. Their duty was to protect these bombers from enemy planes. Now called the Black Eagles, they never failed to get their bombers back safely. They were so good, in fact, that other bomber pilots began requesting them for every possible mission.

Members of the Black Eagles pose ▶ in front of one of their planes.

In time the 99th joined with a larger black unit called the 332nd. Altogether this unit flew 1,578 missions during World War II. Its members won close to 800 medals, including the Distinguished Flying Cross, presented by the President for "heroism or extraordinary achievement in flight." Yet when the war ended, none of the Black Eagles were able to get jobs with civilian airlines. Many became successful in other fields. One became mayor of Detroit. Others became teachers and businessmen. Discrimination was still a part of American life, but the success of the Black Eagles reminded all Americans of the contributions African Americans made to society.

SHOW WHAT YOU KNOW!

REFOCUS
COMPREHENSION

1. What were some ways in which African Americans were discriminated against in the armed forces?

2. What were some accomplishments of the Tuskegee Airmen?

THINK ABOUT IT
CRITICAL THINKING

How did the accomplishments of the Black Eagles help change how white Americans felt about black Americans?

WRITE ABOUT IT
ACTIVITY

Write an editorial in which you urge Americans to support black soldiers and fighter pilots.

Connections

KEY TERMS
GI Bill of Rights
United Nations
Marshall Plan

COMING HOME

FOCUS *American soldiers finally returned home from war. Meanwhile, the United States wanted to avoid the mistakes it had made after World War I.*

The Soldiers Come Home

World War II officially ended on September 2, 1945. That was the day the Japanese signed a document of surrender aboard the U.S.S. *Missouri* in Tokyo Bay. Within a few months, millions of American veterans left the military and returned home.

Cheering crowds greeted the ships that brought these heroes home. Many towns held special parades for the veterans. More importantly, families were brought together again. Wives were reunited with their husbands. Some soldiers, who had been away from home for over three years, saw their own young son or daughter for the first time.

A Peacetime Economy

By 1945 the Great Depression was but a memory. Factories had been humming at full capacity for several years. But they no longer needed to crank out war materials. Many businesses converted to the production of consumer goods. And there was plenty of built-up demand from eager American consumers. People had done without many things throughout the war. Now they were ready to buy.

Before the war, people had purchased refrigerators, bicycles, and washing machines. Some of these had broken down during the war, but they could not be replaced. The machines that made consumer goods had been used by war-related industries. Now, people could buy new cars and radios and by 1948, a new invention—black and white television.

Returning soldiers didn't have much trouble finding jobs. Many women workers gave up their positions to make way for veterans. But the concept that a married woman could work outside the home was here to stay.

Norman Rockwell's magazine cover showed what coming home was like.

Replacement bicycles were available only after the war ended.

With the GI Bill, the Army promised college to its recruits. ▶

The GI Bill

The country had done little to help veterans after World War I. So even before World War II ended, Congress passed the **GI Bill of Rights**. (*GI* stands for "government issue." It means an American soldier.) The GI Bill of Rights provided care for sick and wounded soldiers. It set aside money for veterans who wanted to start their own businesses. It gave them money to go to college or get job training. It lent them money to buy a house. Over 8 million veterans took advantage of the GI Bill.

America as a World Power

The United States did not repeat the mistakes it and its allies had made after World War I. It was now a world power, and it planned to behave like one. First, the United States immediately helped establish an organization of countries that were dedicated to promoting world peace—the **United Nations** (UN). The United States not only joined the UN but it also allowed UN headquarters to be built in New York City.

Under the **Marshall Plan**, the United States gave billions of dollars to help Europe recover from World War II. More than half the money went to Britain, France, and West Germany. (At the end of the war, Germany was divided into East Germany and West Germany.) A healthy, prosperous Europe provided a huge market for American goods, which kept the economy booming. It also provided some security against the growing threat of the Soviet Union. The United States was suddenly a very different place in a whole new world.

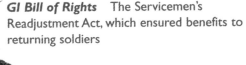 **GI Bill of Rights**   The Servicemen's Readjustment Act, which ensured benefits to returning soldiers

United Nations   An organization of world nations pledged to promote peace and security
Marshall Plan   A plan of economic assistance from the U.S. to European nations after WW II

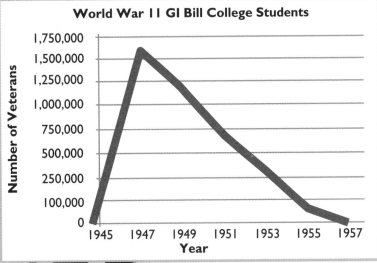

World War II GI Bill College Students

Number of Veterans

(y-axis: 0, 100,000, 250,000, 500,000, 750,000, 1,000,000, 1,250,000, 1,500,000, 1,750,000)

(x-axis: 1945, 1947, 1949, 1951, 1953, 1955, 1957)

Year

SHOW WHAT YOU KNOW!

REFOCUS
COMPREHENSION

1. How did the American economy and work force change after the end of World War II?

2. Explain ways in which the United States tried to avoid the mistakes the Allies had made after World War I.

THINK ABOUT IT
CRITICAL THINKING

How did the GI Bill change the American economy and the lives of many soldiers?

WRITE ABOUT IT
ACTIVITY

You are an American who has lived in another country for ten years. On returning to your home in 1948, describe how the United States has changed during that time.

SUMMING UP

1 DO YOU REMEMBER . . .
COMPREHENSION

1. Why were so many Americans isolationists in the 1930s?

2. What caused the United States to enter World War II?

3. What events in August 1945 led the Japanese to surrender?

4. Who were the main victims of the Nazis in the death camps?

5. What were V-E Day and V-J Day?

6. Why was rationing necessary during the war?

7. Why did American women work outside the home in record numbers during the war?

8. Why were Japanese Americans interned in camps during World War II?

9. How were African Americans discriminated against in the armed forces during World War II?

10. How did the type of goods produced in American factories change after the end of the war?

2 SKILL POWER
DISTINGUISHING BETWEEN FACT AND OPINION

Choose one of the following opinions. Then write facts from this chapter that support the opinion.

- America waged a tough and aggressive war against the Axis Powers.

- Americans at home played a major role in the war effort.

- For some civilians the war meant suffering and sacrifice.

- After the war the United States found useful ways to improve people's lives and chances for peace.

3 WHAT DO YOU THINK?
CRITICAL THINKING

1. Did the treaty ending World War I set the scene for World War II? Explain.

2. Do you think dictators can ever be good for a country? Why or why not?

3. Could the Allies have won World War II without the sacrifices of Americans on the home front? Explain.

4. Why do you think Japanese Americans remained loyal to the United States during their internment?

5. Why was the Marshall Plan in the interest of the United States?

478

4 SAY IT, WRITE IT, USE IT
VOCABULARY

Suppose you worked for a magazine. Write a short description that would explain five of the terms below.

Axis Powers	Marshall Plan
bracero	Nazi
dictator	nisei
GI Bill of Rights	prisoner of war
Holocaust	scrap drive
integration	United Nations
internment camp	victory garden
isolationism	war crime

5 GEOGRAPHY AND YOU
MAP STUDY

Use the maps on pages 458 and 462 to help you answer the following questions:

1. Name the Allied Powers you see on the map. Name five Axis or Axis-controlled countries.

2. Make a list of the countries that were neutral. Given that they were neither Allied nor Axis, what do you think neutral means in war?

3. Name a battle site in the Philippine Islands and in the Solomon Islands.

4. Name the two Japanese cities on which atomic bombs were dropped.

6 TAKE ACTION
CITIZENSHIP

During World War II, Americans at home made many sacrifices to contribute to victory. Think of some struggles that the United States is involved in today. These include the war on drugs, the fight against pollution, and the struggle for better schools and safer neighborhoods. Choose one of these struggles. Then list five things that you, your family, and neighbors could do to help win the struggle.

7 GET CREATIVE
LANGUAGE ARTS CONNECTION

During World War II most Americans got their news about the war from radio. Write a radio news report that describes an event from the war. You could describe a battle, tell about a political development, or give news from the home front. You and your classmates can deliver your newscasts in time order, from the attack on Pearl Harbor to V-J Day.

LOOKING AHEAD
In the next chapter you'll see that the war had made the United States a very different place.

UNIT 7

Modern TIMES

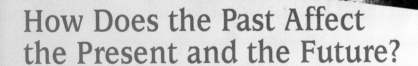

How Does the Past Affect the Present and the Future?

Do you ever think about how life in the past was different from life today? Do you wonder what life will be like in the future? Examine some ways in which the past affects the present and provides a glimpse into the future.

480

481

CHAPTER 21

THE 1950s

After the Second World War, the United States felt renewed. It grew by leaps and bounds, and its economy boomed. There were new frontiers to conquer, but it became apparent that there were also old wounds to heal.

▼ What is this toy? Turn to page 504 to find out about this and other fads of the 1950s.

CONTENTS

These books tell about some people, places, and important events following World War II and continuing through the 1950s. Read one that interests you and fill out a book-review form.

READ AND RESEARCH

The Year They Walked by Beatrice Siegel
(Macmillan Publishing, 1992)
Find out how the arrest of a courageous woman named Rosa Parks led to the year-long Montgomery bus boycott and a renewed struggle for civil rights. *(biography)*

Close to Home: A Story of the Polio Epidemic
by Lydia Weaver (Penguin USA, 1993)
Betsy's friend, Leticia, becomes ill with polio, a crippling disease. Will Betsy's mother and the scientists and doctors she is working with find a cure for this dreaded disease? *(historical fiction)*

The Korean War by Tom McGowen (Franklin Watts, 1992)
The author uses his interest in military history to vividly describe this war of the fifties. He also shows how America's attitudes about war and its military strength began to change after this conflict. *(nonfiction)*

SKILL POWER

Identifying the Main Idea

Being able to identify the main idea will help you understand what is most important about what you read.

UNDERSTAND IT

What idea or information about the 1950s does the photograph below express?

Here's a paragraph about Hula-Hoops. Which sentence do you think states the most important idea?

The Hula-Hoop fad took America by storm in the late 1950s. Two California toy makers invented the plastic hoops in 1958. Within six months over 20 million hoops spun into action. In all, 40 companies were soon producing the two-dollar toys.

EXPLORE IT

The main idea of a paragraph is often stated in a single sentence called the topic sentence. In the paragraph you read about Hula-Hoops, for example, the topic sentence comes first. The other sentences are detail sentences. They tell about and develop the main idea.

Topic Sentence: The Hula-Hoop fad took America by storm in the late 1950s.

Detail 1: Two California toy makers invented the plastic hoops in 1958.

Detail 2: Within six months over 30 million hoops spun into action.

Detail 3: In all, 40 companies were soon producing the two-dollar toys.

Some paragraphs don't have topic sentences. Then it's up to you to figure out the main idea. All you have to do is think about the topic— what the sentences are about.

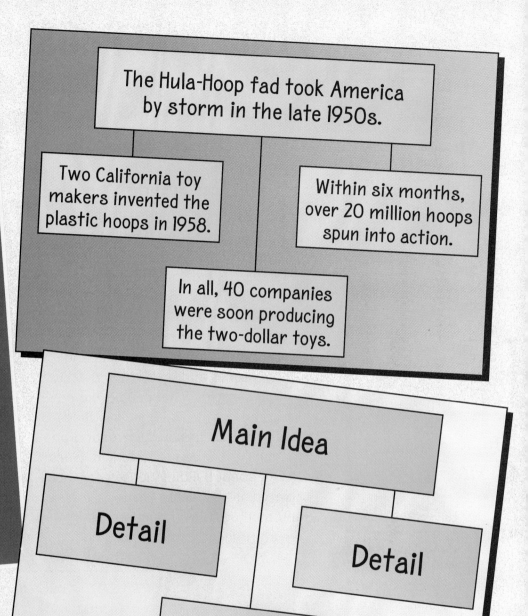

TRY IT

On a separate sheet of paper, draw a graphic organizer like the one on the right. Then look back through the chapters of this book to find a paragraph with a topic sentence and several detail sentences. Write the sentences in the appropriate boxes of the organizer.

Next, draw another copy of the organizer. This time, though, look for a paragraph that has no topic sentence. Write the detail sentences in their boxes. Think about the main idea they describe. Then write a topic sentence that could be used with the paragraph.

The Hula-Hoop fad took America by storm in the late 1950s.

Two California toy makers invented the plastic hoops in 1958.

Within six months, over 20 million hoops spun into action.

In all, 40 companies were soon producing the two-dollar toys.

Main Idea

Detail

Detail

Detail

SKILL POWER SEARCH As you read this chapter, think about the main ideas and details that are used in paragraphs.

Setting the Scene

⭐ **KEY TERMS**

inflation
closed shop
union shop
minimum wage
satellite

PEACE AND PROSPERITY

FOCUS   *After World War II the nation's economy boomed, and many Americans enjoyed prosperity. But inflation and labor strikes concerned many people.*

The American Suburbs

By 1948 most American troops had come home from World War II. The return of more than 10 million veterans created some immediate problems. One was housing. There were not enough homes for all the veterans and their new families. The solution was simple—build lots and lots of homes and build them quickly.

That's exactly what people like William J. Levitt did. Since city land was costly, Levitt bought farmland on the outskirts of major American cities. He set about building houses the way Henry Ford built cars. Using assembly line methods, Levitt built homes in record time. In just four years he

turned potato farms outside New York City into a new community, called Levittown, with 17,000 homes. Similar towns were developed outside other urban centers throughout the 1950s. Millions of Americans moved into these tidy and affordable homes.

The housing boom created new kinds of jobs. Suburbanites, people who lived in the suburbs, needed schools and roads. They wanted dishwashers and air conditioners. They needed diapers and toys for their children. All this demand meant jobs for anyone who wanted to work.

▼ Housing developments such as this one changed how Americans lived after World War II.

1948 Truman wins second term	1952 Dwight D. Eisenhower elected President	1956 Interstate Highway Act	1958 National Defense Education Act	1959 Alaska and Hawaii become states

1948	1952	1953	1954	1955	1956	1957	1958	1959

Inflation and Strikes

America's postwar economy appeared to be booming. But problems resulted from this growth. No matter how explosive the growth was, it just couldn't keep up with the demands of so many new consumers. As demand for items grew faster than supply, prices rose. This meant **inflation**, or a rise in the average level of prices. In the late 1940s the price of nearly everything—especially food and clothing—skyrocketed.

★ *inflation* An increase in price, causing a decline in purchasing power

Rising prices led workers to call for wage increases. When their requests were denied, they often went on strike. In 1946, for example, more than 4.5 million men and women went on strike. Some of these strikes hit key industries, such as railroads and mining. They hurt the economy as a whole. Many Americans became angry and demanded that something be done to reduce the power of labor unions that had called the strikes.

Taft-Hartley Act

In 1947, Congress responded by passing the Taft-Hartley Act. This reduced the power of unions in several ways. It outlawed the **closed shop**, a requirement that all workers must be union members *before* they could be hired. The act did not outlaw the **union shop**, but it allowed states to do so if they wanted to. The union shop required workers to join a union *after* they were hired. The Taft-Hartley Act also gave the President

★ *closed shop* A business or factory that agrees to hire only union members
union shop A business or factory that requires workers to join a union after being hired

THE UNITED STATES INTERSTATE HIGHWAY SYSTEM

- • Cities
- -35- Interstate highways

(No interstate highways)

0 100 200 miles
0 200 kilometers

An empty Grand Central Station during the 1946 railroad strike ▶

power to force striking union members in a vital industry to go back to work for 80 days. During these 80 days, union and management had to talk. It was hoped that this would force them to reach an agreement and save the country from the effects of the strike.

The unions fought vigorously against the Taft-Hartley Act. President Truman even vetoed the bill. But Congress ignored the unions and overrode the veto.

Truman as President

Harry S Truman was a President who was popular and unpopular at the same time. People found reason to back him one minute and be angered by his actions the next. For example, Americans supported him in the final months of World War II. But by 1946 they blamed him for high inflation as well as all the strikes. Republicans campaigned in 1946 on the slogan "Had enough?" They won control of both houses in Congress for the first time since 1928.

Few people gave Truman, a Democrat, much of a chance to win the 1948 presidential election. But he

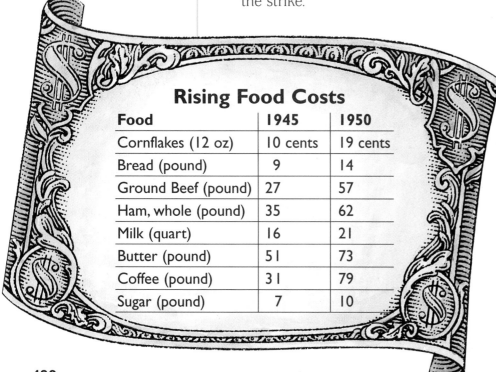

Rising Food Costs

Food	1945	1950
Cornflakes (12 oz)	10 cents	19 cents
Bread (pound)	9	14
Ground Beef (pound)	27	57
Ham, whole (pound)	35	62
Milk (quart)	16	21
Butter (pound)	51	73
Coffee (pound)	31	79
Sugar (pound)	7	10

was a tough fighter. He flooded Congress with lots of bills. The Republicans voted down every one. Truman then blamed Congress, calling it a do-nothing Congress. People responded to this, and Truman's popularity swung back up again. He beat Thomas E. Dewey, the Republican candidate, in a very close election.

During his second term Truman promised the American people a "fair deal." The Fair Deal extended many of the New Deal's ideas. For example, social security benefits were raised. So, too, was the **minimum wage**,

---

minimum wage A wage established by law as the lowest that may be paid to an employee

which had been signed into law in 1938. President Truman also started the construction of nearly 1 million low-income-housing units. Such federal spending programs helped to keep the economy in high gear.

The 1952 Election

In 1952, Truman decided not to run for President again. His popularity was falling once more. One poll showed that only 23 percent of the people supported him. Americans blamed him for an economy that was slipping and for failing in some areas of international relations.

So the Democrats turned to Governor Adlai E. Stevenson of Illinois. The Republicans chose Dwight D. Eisenhower, a popular World War II general who had directed the Normandy invasion.

Eisenhower, or "Ike" as Americans liked to call him, won in a landslide—an overwhelming majority. Ike's personal charm and warm smile appealed to people. In addition, the voters longed for change.

A Chicago newspaper reported that Truman had lost the close 1948 election. Truman enjoyed proving that early predictions can be wrong.

489

his eight years in office, he expanded many federal programs, such as social security benefits. Like Truman, he provided low-income housing for many Americans. Ike also raised the minimum wage.

Eisenhower spent federal funds to improve transportation. He approved construction of the St. Lawrence Seaway. When it was completed, ships could travel from Lake Superior to the Atlantic Ocean—a distance of 2,342 miles.

Eisenhower also sponsored the Interstate Highway Act, which Congress passed into law in 1956. In time this law created a 41,000-mile system of expressways. It soon became possible to drive across the country and not have to stop for a single traffic light. You can see on the map on page 487 the web of highways that resulted. Expressways encouraged

After all, the Democrats had controlled the White House since 1933.

Eisenhower as President

Many Americans had struggled through the Great Depression and World War II. They felt that they had endured enough hardship for one lifetime. Ike, steady and calm, was just the kind of President many of these people wanted. His brother and advisor, Milton Eisenhower, put it this way: "We should keep what we have [and] catch our breath for a while."

Ike was a popular President. In 1956 he was reelected in another landslide, again defeating Adlai Stevenson. Although Eisenhower believed in limited government, he did not believe in a do-nothing government. During

America in the 1950s relied on the automobile. Roadside stands, like this ice-cream stand, competed for weary travelers. ▶

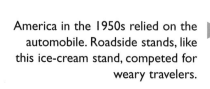

the growth of still more suburbs. They also made more and more people dependent on the automobile.

Sputnik and American Schools

On October 4, 1957, the Soviets sent into orbit the first **satellite** made by people. It was called *Sputnik*. The next month they sent up another larger satellite with a dog on board. The Russians' success at conquering the frontier of space shocked many Americans. They had assumed the United States was the world leader in science and technology. Now they wondered how the Soviets managed to be first in space.

Many blamed the schools for doing a poor job of teaching math and science. In response, Congress passed the National Defense Education Act of 1958. This law provided $1 billion to produce more science teachers and to train more scientists.

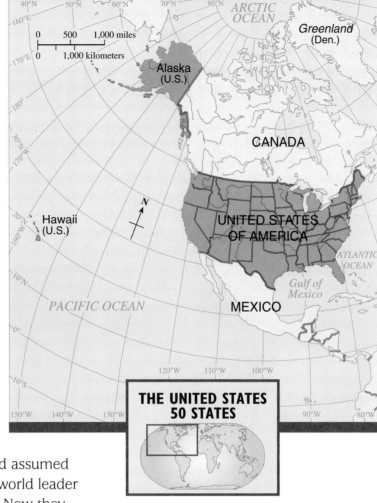

THE UNITED STATES 50 STATES

Alaska and Hawaii

In 1959 two more states entered the Union. On January 3, Alaska became the forty-ninth state. The largest state, Alaska offered rich resources including fish, timber, and oil. On August 21, Hawaii became the fiftieth state. After World War II many vacationers discovered the islands. Alaska and Hawaii are the only two states not connected to the other 48 states.

◀ After the launching of *Sputnik*, American boys and girls became interested in the solar system, as this game pack shows.

 satellite An object rocketed into orbit around the earth, moon, or other planets

SHOW WHAT YOU KNOW!

REFOCUS
COMPREHENSION

1. List some accomplishments of Presidents Truman and Eisenhower.

2. How did the Interstate Highway Act connect the continental United States?

THINK ABOUT IT
CRITICAL THINKING

How did Milton Eisenhower's quote on page 490 describe the United States in the 1950s?

WRITE ABOUT IT
ACTIVITY

Write a letter to the President urging him to support the National Defense Education Act.

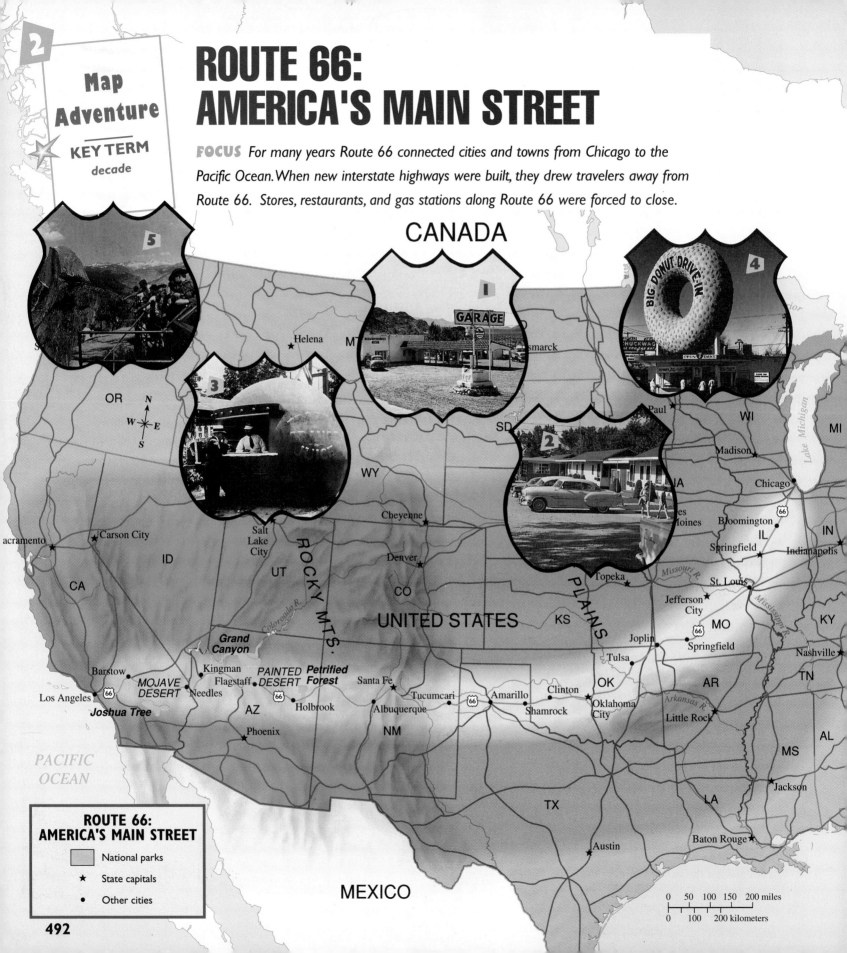

Map Adventure

KEY TERM
decade

ROUTE 66: AMERICA'S MAIN STREET

FOCUS For many years Route 66 connected cities and towns from Chicago to the Pacific Ocean. When new interstate highways were built, they drew travelers away from Route 66. Stores, restaurants, and gas stations along Route 66 were forced to close.

CANADA

GARAGE

BIG DONUT DRIVE-IN

CANADA

Helena

bismarck

Paul

OR

N
W E
S

WI

MI

Lake Michigan

Madison

Chicago

SD

Cheyenne

IA

es Moines

Bloomington

IN

Carson City

Salt Lake City

ROCKY MTS.

WY

Springfield

IL

Indianapolis

acramento

ID

UT

Denver

CO

UNITED STATES

KS

Topeka

Missouri R.

St. Louis

Mississippi R.

KY

CA

Grand Canyon

Colorado R.

Jefferson City

MO

Springfield

Nashville

TN

Barstow

Kingman

Flagstaff

PAINTED DESERT

Petrified Forest

Santa Fe

Joplin

Tulsa

OK

AR

Los Angeles

MOJAVE DESERT

Needles

Tucumcari

Amarillo

Clinton

Oklahoma City

Arkansas R.

Little Rock

Joshua Tree

AZ

Holbrook

Albuquerque

Shamrock

NM

Phoenix

PLAINS

AL

MS

PACIFIC OCEAN

TX

LA

Jackson

Austin

Baton Rouge

MEXICO

ROUTE 66: AMERICA'S MAIN STREET

National parks

★ State capitals

• Other cities

0   50   100   150   200 miles

0   100   200 kilometers

Adventure on Route 66

In the 1950s it seemed that everyone wanted to drive somewhere. Thousands of tourists, migrant workers, and truckers had used twisty, narrow Route 66 for **decades**. Roadside shops, gas stations, and tourist attractions provided jobs for people in small towns along the route. All that changed when interstate highways were built. The new highways bypassed many towns, cutting off local shops from passing travelers. Though the interstate highways took decades to complete, the glory days of Route 66, the "Main Street of America," were over.

Map Legend

1 **Gas stations** Travelers had no trouble getting gas along Route 66. Small family-owned gas stations offered low prices and friendly service. Many stations were forced to close or relocate when the interstates came through.

2 **Motels** As more Americans took road trips for their vacations, motels appeared along the highways. Motels on Route 66 were small and family-owned. Some used western themes to attract customers.

3 **Stores** Tourists could stop at Route 66's many souvenir shops. There they could find everything from postcards and bubble gum to toy statues, local crafts, and baked goods. To attract customers' attention, stores often used neon signs or were located in funny-shaped buildings.

4 **Restaurants** Hungry travelers crowded the local diners and small stands on Route 66. Many of these restaurants struggled for survival as large fast-food restaurants appeared with the interstates.

5 **Natural scenery** Route 66 and connecting roads brought millions of people to see some of the country's most beautiful scenery. It ranged from majestic mountains to the Grand Canyon.

⭐ *decade* A period of ten years

MAP IT

1. You leave Chicago on a trip to Los Angeles along Route 66. In what direction are you headed? About how many miles will you travel?

2. You cross the Mississippi River and enter the city of St. Louis. What state did you just leave? What state are you now in?

3. When you arrive in Amarillo, the cook at the diner tells you to head south out of the city to reach Los Angeles. Look at your map. Do you believe him? Explain.

4. After leaving Texas, you drive to California. What national parks and other tourist attractions are near Route 66?

5. You finally reach Los Angeles. Look back at the route you traveled. Through what states did you pass?

EXPLORE IT

Use a current road atlas to plan a trip from Chicago to Los Angeles on the interstate highways. What highways will you use? What cities, towns, and states will you pass through?

Spotlight

KEY TERMS

cold war
communism
iron curtain
containment
Truman Doctrine
Berlin airlift

THE IRON CURTAIN YEARS

FOCUS   *Soon after World War II, a fear of communism gripped many Americans. Americans not only feared the Communists in Russia and China but also feared communism at home.*

▼ Joseph Stalin

The Cold War

By the end of 1946, the United States and the Soviet Union were at odds. People referred to this relationship as a **cold war**. The word *cold* was used because the two countries weren't actually fighting each other. The cold war was fought mostly with angry words, threats, and money. The fear that the cold war might turn hot caused anxiety among many Americans. This fear only grew worse when the Soviets developed their own atomic bomb in 1949.

Why were the United States and the Soviet Union enemies? First, the Soviet Union had occupied Eastern Europe after World War II. Between 1945 and 1947 the Soviets installed Communist governments in several of those countries. That made the Soviet Union a powerful empire and a powerful opponent of the United States. And some people suspected that the Soviet Union wanted to set up Communist governments in other countries. You can see

the Communist countries on the map below.

The second reason Americans feared the Soviets was the *idea* of **communism**. The Soviet Union was a Communist country and had been since Russia's revolution of 1917. The Soviets believed that all sources of wealth—mines, factories, mills, farms, and railroads—belonged to the

⭐ **communism**   The common ownership of lands and industries by people as a group

⭐ **cold war**   Sharp conflict between countries without actual war

EUROPE IN 1945

☐ Communist countries
— Iron Curtain

ICELAND
ATLANTIC OCEAN
NORWAY
SWEDEN
FINLAND
North Sea
IRELAND GREAT BRITAIN DENMARK
NETH. EAST GERMANY POLAND
BELG. WEST GERMANY CZECH.
LUX.
FRANCE
SWITZ. AUSTRIA HUNGARY
ROMANIA
YUGOSLAVIA
PORTUGAL
SPAIN ITALY BULGARIA
ALB. GREECE TURKEY
UNION OF SOVIET SOCIALIST REPUBLICS
Baltic Sea
Black Sea
Caspian Sea
Mediterranean Sea

0   300   600 miles
0   300   600 kilometers

workers or "the people." In this sense communism is an economic system.

But communism is also a *political* system. The Soviet leadership believed in an all-powerful state with only one political party—the Communist party. The Soviets talked about democratic elections, but they never held them. Also, the Soviet people had no personal democratic freedoms. They couldn't speak openly or write freely.

Americans, on the other hand, were capitalists. Capitalists believe that all sources of wealth should be owned by individuals or companies. In addition, Americans—Democrats as well as Republicans—believed in a democratic form of government. On the political side, Americans believed that people should be free to vote in real elections with a choice of candidates.

The Iron Curtain

Allies of the United States agreed that the Soviet Union was a fearsome force after World War II. In a speech on March 5, 1946, Prime Minister Winston S. Churchill of Great Britain declared that an iron curtain had descended across Eastern Europe. On one side of the curtain were the free nations of Western Europe. On the other side were the Communist nations of Eastern Europe, ruled directly by the Soviet Union.

In time both sides formed their own military alliances. The United States,

▲ Workers in a Moscow factory in 1947 are reading *Pravda*, the official government newspaper.

Canada, and the nations of Western Europe created the North Atlantic Treaty Organization (NATO). The Soviet Union answered by creating the Warsaw Pact with the Communist nations of Eastern Europe.

Containment Policy

President Truman responded quickly to the perceived Communist menace. Americans worried that the Soviets would move to conquer the world with their economic and political beliefs. So, Truman adopted a policy of containment. That meant that the United States would "contain" communism. America would not allow it to spread to any more countries.

When Greece was threatened by a Communist takeover in 1947, the United States sent military aid to the Greek forces fighting against communism. This idea of supporting anti-Communist governments was known as the Truman Doctrine. It

iron curtain A barrier of secrecy isolating the Soviet Union and other countries in its sphere of influence

containment The policy of limiting the expansion of communism
Truman Doctrine A program by the government to aid any nation threatened by communism

Korean citizens fleeing as American soldiers march into South Korea ▶

became the foundation for the United States' cold-war policy, which would last for a long time.

The Soviets and Communism

After World War II, Germany was split into two nations. East Germany was Communist, and its affairs were controlled quite closely by the Soviet Union. West Germany was capitalist and democratic and looked to the United States as an ally. The German city of Berlin was also divided into East Berlin and West Berlin. Both sides of Berlin, however, were located entirely *inside* East Germany.

In 1948, Stalin decided that East Germany should take over West Berlin. So he blocked all roads and railroad tracks leading into West Berlin. The United States beat the blockade by flying in supplies. This **Berlin airlift** saved the city. After several months Stalin gave up and lifted his blockade.

The United States, however, did not actively try to overthrow communism in Soviet-dominated areas of Europe. In 1953, East Germans rallied against the Soviets, but the United States did not aid them. In 1956, Hungarians rose up against the Soviet Union's domination of their country. But Eisenhower knew that if the United States or NATO intervened, a third world war might be a real possibility. And in 1959, the United States could

do little but watch as the Soviets installed the Communist-led government of Fidel Castro in Cuba.

Korea

The United States *did* move to stop the spread of communism in Korea. Like Germany, this Asian nation was divided following World War II. North Korea was Communist, and South Korea was not.

 Berlin airlift   The program undertaken by the United States to deliver supplies to West Berlin in 1948 and 1949

In June 1950 the Communist North Koreans attacked South Korea. The United Nations (UN) sent troops to help South Korea. Most of these UN troops were American. The UN armies drove the North Koreans out of South Korea, and for a time it looked as though the Communists would lose. Then in November 1950, China, which had become a Communist country in 1949, sent a huge army to help the North Koreans. The war ended in 1953 in a stalemate—an unresolved situation. There are still two Koreas—North Korea and South Korea.

Communism at Home

The fear of communism was also felt at home. Many Americans wondered why communism was spreading so fast. China, for example, had always been an American ally, most recently during World War II. Now, suddenly, it seemed to be against everything America stood for, as it fell to the Communists during the 1949 revolution. People asked questions such as Who lost China? and How did the Soviets get the atomic bomb so quickly?

Some people thought that there were Communists in the United States helping the Soviets. This fear led to loyalty oaths. To keep a job with the government, a person had to swear loyalty to the United States. Those who didn't were fired for being disloyal, even though there was no proof of disloyalty.

The fear of being labeled a Communist had a chilling effect on free speech during the 1950s. Many Americans, especially government workers and teachers, worried about speaking their minds. They feared that their own words might be used against them. In a sense, then, the cold war was being fought at home as well as overseas.

▼ Senator Joseph R. McCarthy was the leading supporter of loyalty oaths. Here he shows where he thinks Communists have organized in the United States.

DESEGREGATION BEGINS

FOCUS *African Americans made some progress in the fight for civil rights during the 1950s. Many other battles, however, remained to be fought.*

COMMITTEE ON CIVIL RIGHTS

The unjust treatment of black Americans who served in World War II proved that black Americans and white Americans were not treated equally. President Harry Truman was troubled by this, and in 1946 he set up the President's Committee on Civil Rights. This committee called for an end to many laws that discriminated against black Americans.

Truman asked Congress to act on the committee's report. Congress refused. So in 1948, Truman acted on his own. He made it illegal for the government to discriminate when hiring new workers. He also ordered the desegregation of the armed forces. No longer could black soldiers legally be kept apart from white soldiers.

BROWN V. BOARD OF EDUCATION OF TOPEKA

Linda Brown lived near an elementary school in Topeka, Kansas. But because she was African American, she was not allowed to attend it. Instead, she had to go to a school for black students only, more than two miles away.

In 1951, Linda Brown's parents sued—brought legal action against—the Topeka school board to change its policy of segregation. The case made its way through the courts to the Supreme Court of the United States. On May 17, 1954, the Browns and their young lawyer, Thurgood Marshall (shown in the center, at right), won their case. The Supreme Court declared that public schools had to admit students of all races. Black Americans would have a chance to get the same education as white Americans.

1946	1954	1955		1957
President's Committee on Civil Rights	Supreme Court orders school desegregation	Montgomery bus boycott		Little Rock high school desegregated

1946 ⟋ 1954 1955 1956 1957

SHOW WHAT YOU KNOW!

REFOCUS
COMPREHENSION

1. What was the outcome of *Brown v. Board of Education of Topeka*?

2. Why did President Eisenhower send federal troops to Little Rock?

THINK ABOUT IT
CRITICAL THINKING

Why is Rosa Parks an important figure in the civil rights movement?

WRITE ABOUT IT
ACTIVITY

Write in your journal about what you can do to help people or groups that are being discriminated against.

ROSA PARKS SITS DOWN

In Montgomery, Alabama, African Americans were required to give up their seats on public buses if no seats remained for white passengers. On December 1, 1955, Rosa Parks was seated on the bus after working all day. When the bus driver ordered her to give up her seat to a white man, Parks refused. Within minutes she was arrested.

Mrs. Parks's treatment sparked anger throughout the black community. Four days later African Americans began to boycott, or refuse to ride, the city buses. This action continued for months. At last, on November 13, 1956, the Supreme Court ordered the city to desegregate its buses.

TROUBLE IN LITTLE ROCK, ARKANSAS

Three years after *Brown* v. *Board of Education,* many American schools remained segregated. Many Southern white leaders followed the court's desegregation order as slowly as they could. In Little Rock, Arkansas, a federal court ordered Central High School to admit black students. Nine African Americans got ready to attend classes there. But when they arrived at the school on September 4, 1957, Arkansas National Guardsmen, sent by Governor Orval E. Faubus, blocked their way.

President Eisenhower then sent 1,000 federal troops to Central High to help the African American students. The students attended Central High, but they had to be protected by armed guards.

499

PROGRESS FOR MANY

FOCUS *The 1950s were years of prosperity and confidence for many Americans. Others, however, struggled to keep pace.*

Good Times for Many

For many middle-class Americans, the 1950s were good times. People had more money than ever before. They splurged on modern kitchens, complete with electric stoves, freezers, and washing machines. They began cooling their homes with air conditioning. They found it easy to care for new suits made of polyester.

Another exciting element in people's lives was the television. In 1946 only a few thousand Americans owned a TV set. Four years later the number jumped to 5 million. And by the early 1960s, 90 percent of all American households had at least one TV.

Television brought a new level of entertainment into people's lives. Families no longer had to go to the movies to see famous actors and comedians. They no longer had to rely on radio for quiz shows and soap operas. Now people could sit in their living rooms and laugh their way through *I Love Lucy* or cheer for heroes such as The Lone Ranger or *Dragnet*'s Joe Friday.

Television Advertising

Television did something else, as well. It brought advertisements to life. Suddenly,

Television changed America in the 1950s, bringing antennas to the landscape and advertisements and entertainment into homes.

people weren't just reading about shiny new power lawn mowers or close-cutting electric shavers. They were seeing these modern marvels right in front of them by means of TV commercials. People found themselves wanting everything from refrigerators to chewing gum. In this way television encouraged the long buying spree that so many Americans undertook. Manufacturers were quick to note the power of TV advertising. In the ten years from 1950 to 1960, television advertising budgets were greatly increased.

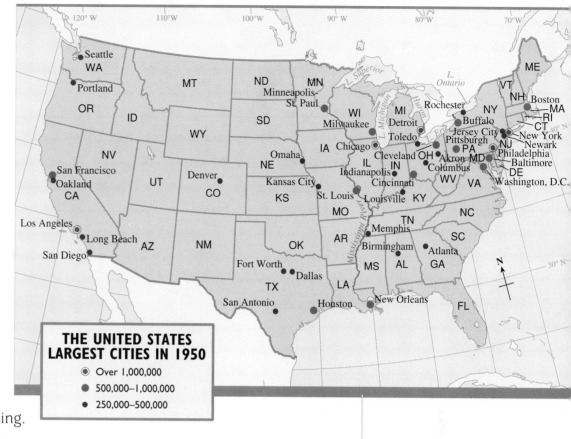

THE UNITED STATES LARGEST CITIES IN 1950
- Over 1,000,000
- 500,000–1,000,000
- 250,000–500,000

The Automobile

Cars were very heavily advertised on TV. People were told, "See the U.S.A. in your Chevrolet." They were urged, "Put a Ford in your future!" And, for the most part, people listened. Fifty-eight million cars were bought during the 1950s. These cars were bigger and flashier than ever before. They came in new colors. They had power brakes, power steering, and bigger engines.

As cars and roads became more reliable, many Americans moved to the suburbs.

They were attracted by the idea of new houses, big backyards, and lower crime rates. Some people, particularly older Americans, moved to the **Sunbelt**—the hot, sunny states of the South and Southwest. With air conditioning and specially designed wells, families could, for the first time,

---

Sunbelt Most of the states of the South and Southwest, where the climate is warm and sunny

The pink Cadillac: a great 1950s car

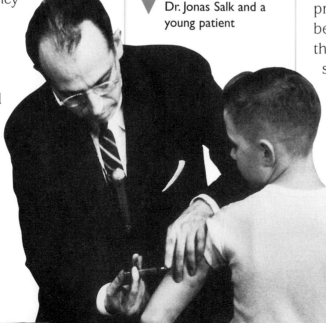

Many retired people moved to the Sunbelt and enjoyed recreation.

live in comfort away from the snow and cold temperatures of the North.

People also traveled more on vacations. They bought campers and other recreational vehicles. Many parks and landmarks became accessible by automobile in the 1950s.

A Growing Confidence

Not only did Americans now have lots of things—cars, appliances, TVs—but they also had hope for the future. If war didn't break out with the Soviets, life would just keep getting better and better.

Their confidence was pushed even higher on April 12, 1955. A doctor named Jonas E. Salk made a staggering

Dr. Jonas Salk and a young patient

announcement. Salk had found a way to protect people from polio. This was a much-feared contagious disease that often left patients with permanent disabilities. Now, polio no longer would cripple and kill America's children—Salk's polio **vaccine** brought much suffering to an end.

The confidence Americans felt about the future helped lead to a **baby boom**, or huge growth in the birth-rate. People felt sure they could provide for their children. They believed life would be even better for the next generation of Americans. And so people had babies, lots of babies. During the 1950s, the population of the United States climbed from 151 million to 180 million.

vaccine A preparation that prevents a disease from occurring in humans and animals

baby boom The period between 1946 and 1964, during which there was a great increase in the number of babies born

502

A migrant worker picking cherries

SHOW WHAT YOU KNOW!

REFOCUS
COMPREHENSION

1. Give some examples that show how many Americans enjoyed prosperity in the 1950s.

2. List some groups of people who did not share the good life of the 1950s.

THINK ABOUT IT
CRITICAL THINKING

How did advertising affect how Americans lived during the 1950s?

WRITE ABOUT IT
ACTIVITY

Write a news report announcing the Salk vaccine.

Problems in America

Not all Americans were so confident and pleased with the way life was going. Some people thought the nation was becoming too wrapped up in material goods. Some felt that television didn't require people to think. Others pointed to the pollution being dumped into the nation's water and air by new appliances and automobiles. And Americans knew that while some laws that discriminated against African Americans and others had been eliminated, many more remained. The voices of these critics were not loud in the 1950s. But they would grow. By the 1960s some of these issues would erupt into full-scale protest movements.

Meanwhile, poor Americans did not share in the good times enjoyed by the middle class. During this decade, one fifth of all Americans lived in pockets of poverty throughout the United States. These people included rural Americans, particularly those who lived in mountain regions. They included Mexican American migrant workers. They included African Americans and Puerto Ricans who had migrated to cities and had limited opportunities. And they included Native Americans who were still mostly confined to reservations, with few available jobs. The issues faced by poor Americans of all ethnic groups would become more apparent in the 1960s.

GROWING UP IN THE 1950s

FOCUS *The 1950s introduced wild fads, new fashions, and new possibilities for entertainment.*

New Ways to Have Fun

There are some very serious aspects to life in the 1950s. But growing up during this decade, you find new ways to have fun. For a while college students are trying to see how many people can fit into a phone booth. You might pick up a new toy called a Slinky or put on a coonskin cap and join the millions of kids who sing "The Ballad of Davy Crockett." For $1.98 you can buy a new toy called a Hula-Hoop (which you can see on pages 482 and 505). A few dollars more will get you a paint kit that lets you "paint by numbers."

Entertainment for Everyone

Everyone around you says that new toys, television, movies, music, and fads are examples of popular culture, or **pop culture**—entertainment for everybody. In fact, in the 1950s, average people are influencing entertainment. People love the movies, but movie attendance is dropping. Theaters respond because they want you to keep coming to the movies. Now you can see a movie in a drive-in

theater. Here you can watch the show on a giant screen as you sit parked in your own car. Traditional movie theaters offer a new twist, too. By putting on a special pair of glasses, you can watch a movie in three dimensions (a 3-D effect), where items appear to be flying off the screen directly toward you.

Television entertains you day and night with plenty of zany shows. The people in charge of TV stations want you to like their shows—after all, your eyes are on the advertisements as well as on the shows themselves. You might watch bus driver Ralph Cramden work his way into jams on *The Honeymooners*. You can also enjoy a lighthearted view of the army on *The Phil Silvers Show*. You also can

---

pop culture Entertainment, such as art, music, books, and television that is aimed at the general masses of people

view comedies such as *The Red Skelton Show* and *The Burns and Allen Show*. And you surely watch the very popular *Hopalong Cassidy*. Although color sets are available, most likely you're watching TV in black and white.

Rock 'n' Roll

Television helps keep you in touch with the world of music. Your parents might stick to shows that highlight opera, show tunes, or old ballads. But chances are you're drawn to a whole new kind of music. It's fast, loud, and exciting. It's rock 'n' roll!

Your parents may not understand the appeal of Jerry Lee Lewis, Fats Domino, or Little Richard. And they can't get excited about a Tennessee boy named Elvis Presley. But like most young people, you love Elvis, the undisputed king of rock 'n' roll.

Along with rock 'n' roll comes a whole new way of dancing. You learn the Bop, the Circle, and the Stroll. In any case, you're moving around the dance floor wildly. Dancing isn't just for ballrooms anymore.

Fashion Fads

Meanwhile, you like to keep up with the changing world of fashion. Guys sport crew cuts—hair cropped short—one year. The next they're combing longer hair into ducktails. Girls go from the short curly look of the poodle cut to longer ponytails.

Boys want shoes called "white bucks" and pants that are pegged, or narrowed, at the ankles. Girls like saddle shoes and poodle skirts. No matter what the style, pink is the hottest color of all. People wear everything from pink dresses to pink ties. Even though life has its problems, the 1950s are so full of choices that you know you will remember these years for the rest of your life.

SHOW WHAT YOU KNOW!

REFOCUS
COMPREHENSION

1. What impact did television have on the movie industry and on American life?

2. List some examples of fads and popular culture of the 1950s.

THINK ABOUT IT
CRITICAL THINKING

How was life in the 1950s different from life during World War II?

WRITE ABOUT IT
ACTIVITY

Think about some elements of the pop culture of the 1950s that are still part of our pop culture today. Write an essay about those elements.

SUMMING UP

1 DO YOU REMEMBER...
COMPREHENSION

1. In what ways did America's economy boom after World War II?

2. What problems resulted from this economic boom in the late 1940s?

3. What was President Truman's "fair deal"?

4. Why was Route 66 important in the 1950s and earlier? How did interstate highways put an end to "the Main Street of America"?

5. How do communism and capitalism differ?

6. Describe what the "iron curtain" was.

7. What role did the United States play in the Korean War? What was the result of the war?

8. What role did Rosa Parks play in furthering the progress of desegregation?

9. Why was the desegregation of the Little Rock high school in 1957 a memorable event?

10. How did television change America in the 1950s?

2 SKILL POWER
IDENTIFYING THE MAIN IDEA

Spend some time reading at least one newspaper article and one magazine article. If possible, cut them out and underline the main ideas. If the main idea is not stated in a topic sentence, use the details to help you write your own topic sentence. Share your findings with your classmates.

3 WHAT DO YOU THINK?
CRITICAL THINKING

1. In what way was the Cold War being fought at home as well as overseas?

2. Do you think that another title for this chapter might have been "The Iron Curtain Years"? Explain.

3. Why were people surprised that the Soviets sent the first satellite made by people into orbit?

4. How would people's lives in the 1950s have been different if television sets had not become so available and affordable?

5. Computers seem to have as great an impact on life in the 1990s as television had in the 1950s. How do you think computers will affect our lives in the next decade?

4 SAY IT, WRITE IT, USE IT
VOCABULARY

Prepare a series of questions to interview someone about the 1950s. Then work with a partner to answer the questions. Use as many vocabulary words as you can. You and your partner might tape record your interview and play it for the class, or present your interview in person.

baby boom	iron curtain
Berlin Airlift	minimum wage
closed shop	pop culture
cold war	satellite
communism	Sunbelt
containment	Truman Doctrine
decade	union shop
inflation	vaccine

CHAPTER 21

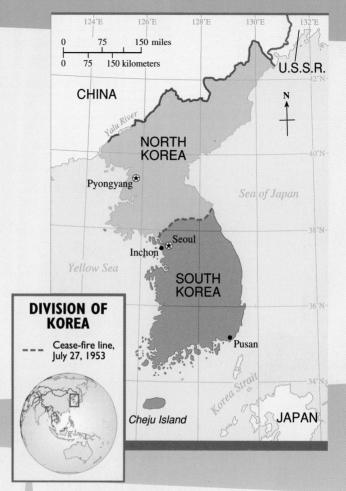

⑤ GEOGRAPHY AND YOU

MAP STUDY

Look at this map of Korea and the maps on pages 487 and 494 to answer the following questions.

1. What interstate highway would you take from Seattle to San Diego?

2. What countries were Communist in 1945?

3. What seas border North Korea and South Korea?

4. What line of latitude runs through the cease-fire line in Korea?

⑥ TAKE ACTION

CITIZENSHIP

In the 1950s many people focused on things that were American and perhaps didn't share much about their own cultures. Over the years people have realized how important all cultures are to our country. Set aside a day to share stories, food, and holidays from your heritage with your classmates. Getting to know more about others creates an atmosphere that respects the rights and views of all individuals.

⑦ GET CREATIVE

MUSIC CONNECTION

If you do not know some of the dances mentioned in the chapter, find an adult family member or someone in your neighborhood to teach you one or more. You can then, in turn, teach your classmates. Select some appropriate music to play and dance your way back to the 1950s!

LOOKING AHEAD In the next chapter find out how many Americans actively worked for social change.

CHAPTER 22

Conflict

Between 1960 and 1974, Americans became divided about issues such as the Vietnam War, discrimination and desegregation, and women's rights. This chapter is about how Americans worked toward change.

CONTENTS

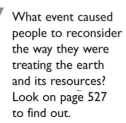

▼ What event caused
people to reconsider
the way they were
treating the earth
and its resources?
Look on page 527
to find out.

WE RECYCLE

and Change

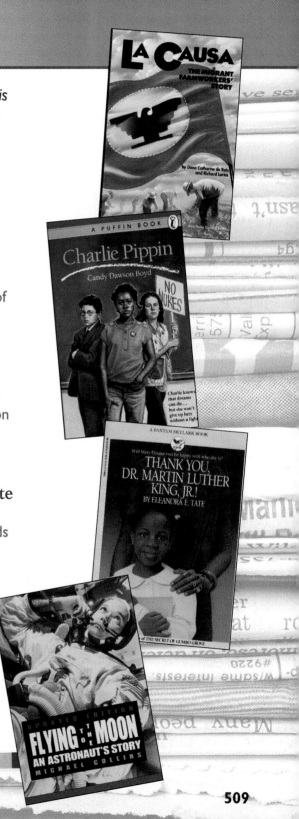

These books tell about some people, places, and events of interest during this time of intense change in America. Read one that interests you and fill out a book-review form.

READ AND RESEARCH

La Causa: The Migrant Farmworkers' Story
by Dana Catharine de Ruiz and Richard Larios
(Steck-Vaughn Co., 1993)
For years migrant workers were treated unfairly and received very little pay. Find out how Cesar Chavez used nonviolent methods to improve the lives of this important group of farmworkers. *(biography)*
• *You can read a selection from this story on page 528.*

Charlie Pippin **by Candy Dawson Boyd** (Penguin USA, 1988)
Charlie Pippin can't understand why her father won't talk about the Vietnam War. Then Charlie works on a class report about the Vietnam War. In addition to learning about the war itself, Charlie discovers some things about her father's experiences in the war. *(fiction)*

Thank You, Dr. Martin Luther King, Jr.! **by Eleanora E. Tate**
(Bantam Doubleday Dell Books for Young Readers, 1992)
Mary Elouise cannot see her own beauty and is not sure who her real friends are. She is not happy with her part in the school play until she listens to storytellers share wonderful tales of her African heritage. *(fiction)*

Flying to the Moon: An Astronaut's Story
by Michael Collins (Farrar, Straus, & Giroux, 1994)
Michael Collins writes about his life as an astronaut and vividly describes the Apollo 11 moon landing mission of 1969. He will challenge you to continue in the adventure of exploring space. *(autobiography)*

SKILL POWER Predicting Future Outcomes

Being able to predict outcomes will help you focus on what you are reading.

UNDERSTAND IT

This political cartoon from 1963 is about the African American struggle for equal rights. At that time Jim Crow laws stood in the way of equality.

What do you predict the American eagle in the cartoon will do next?

"I've decided I want my seat back."

If you said that the eagle would get rid of Jim Crow, you just predicted a probable outcome.

EXPLORE IT

Predicting outcomes, or thinking about what will happen next, helps you focus on what you're reading. Use the steps below to predict outcomes as you read.

1. Read the paragraph or section.

After 1960, black Americans developed new tactics to fight segregation and Jim Crow laws. Some black Americans sat in at whites-only lunch counters, refusing to move until they were served. Other people rode buses, sitting in sections that were set aside for white people. Unfortunately, these protests brought out the worst in some white southerners.

2. Predict what will happen next. Think about what has happened and how that might affect what will happen next.

3. Verify your prediction. Continue reading to find out the actual outcome.

In some southern cities, white people attacked protesters who sat in at lunch counters. Police used dogs against civil rights marchers, and firefighters turned hoses on them. TV cameras recorded all this violence, and people around the country watched in horror.

4. Make new predictions based on all that you've read so far. Then continue reading to verify the new prediction.

A Freedom Ride bus was bombed. After that, the National Guard protected Freedom Riders at the bus station.

TRY IT

Reread the paragraph under step 3. Then write a probable outcome of the events described there. Verify your prediction when you read the Citizenship lesson on pages 522–525.

What's going to happen in the news in the months and years ahead? Research a topic in newspapers and news magazines. Make some predictions based on what you read. With your classmates make a "News of the Future" bulletin board. Include the news items you read and the outcomes you predict.

SKILL POWER SEARCH *As you read this chapter, look for opportunities to predict future outcomes.*

Setting the Scene

KEY TERMS

activism
Peace Corps
Great Society

Reshaping America

FOCUS *Americans began the year 1960 with a sense of hope and commitment. The next 14 years were filled with conflict and change and ended with a President resigning from office.*

President Kennedy

John Fitzgerald Kennedy was just 43 years old when he became President in 1961. That made him the youngest elected President in America's history.

Kennedy brought much more than youth to the White House. He had goals for changing American ideas about the country and the world. These goals became known as the New Frontier, which Kennedy said, "sums up not what I intend to offer the American people, but what I intend to ask of them. It appeals to their pride, not their pocketbook." Kennedy asked Americans to become more actively involved in their government and the world.

Kennedy's presidency ushered in a time of American **activism**. Political activists took up many causes, including the civil rights movement. The map on this page shows some of the civil rights protests that people participated in. You will find out about other activist movements throughout this chapter.

The First Lady, Jacqueline Bouvier Kennedy, got involved in making changes of a different kind. She wanted to restore the White House to its original

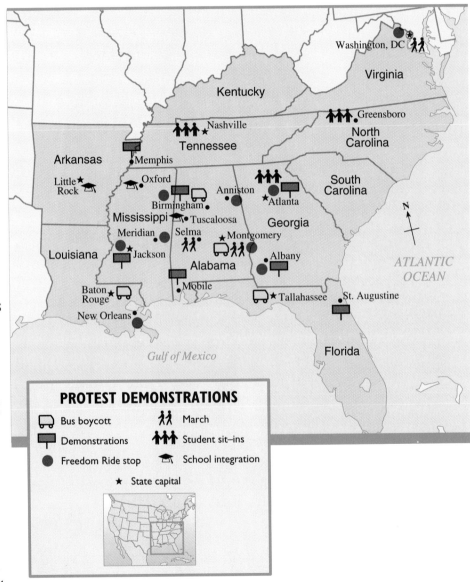

PROTEST DEMONSTRATIONS

🚌 Bus boycott   🚶 March

▬ Demonstrations   👫 Student sit-ins

● Freedom Ride stop   🎓 School integration

★ State capital

 activism Participation in working for change

| 1960 John Kennedy elected President | 1963 John Kennedy assassinated | 1963 Lyndon Johnson becomes President | 1968 Richard Nixon elected President | 1974 Richard Nixon resigns | 1974 Gerald Ford becomes President |

| 1960 | 1962 | 1964 | 1966 | 1968 | 1970 | 1972 | 1974 |

appearance so that Americans could better appreciate its history. She worked with a special committee to redecorate the mansion and to locate furnishings from the days of earlier Presidents. Mrs. Kennedy conducted a television tour of the redecorated White House in which she explained some of the changes that restoration had brought.

Kennedy's Vision

President Kennedy's New Frontier included many other plans. He wanted government to help improve all Americans' lives. He proposed laws to provide more money for schools. Kennedy asked Congress to provide funds to help cities solve transportation and housing problems. And he wanted to end racial discrimination. So he asked Congress to pass a civil rights law, making racial discrimination illegal in all public places. President Kennedy also supported the space program. Shortly after he took office, the Soviet Union put the first man into orbit around Earth. In May 1961, Kennedy announced Project Apollo. Its goal was to put a man on the moon before 1970.

THE SPACE RACE

DATE	EVENT
July 1958	NASA is created.
January 1961	Chimpanzee named Ham is put into space.
May 1962	Scott Carpenter orbits Earth 3 times in *Aurora 7*.
December 1965	Americans extend time in space to a 13-day flight.
December 1968	Three astronauts aboard *Apollo 8* are the first humans to orbit the moon.
July 1969	Neil Armstrong and Edwin E. Aldrin, Jr., walk on the moon.

◀ President Kennedy speaking at his inauguration

The Peace Corps

President Kennedy also wanted to help poorer nations of the world. Through the **Peace Corps**, the United States would send volunteers to those nations. Thousands of Peace Corps teachers, farmers, nurses, and others served around the world. They helped in various ways, including teaching people better farming techniques or better nutrition practices.

Many Peace Corps workers were college-aged people who had been moved by Kennedy's call for service. One volunteer said, "We had such faith in what Kennedy was doing, and we all wanted to be a part of it."

President Kennedy's Assassination

President John Kennedy motivated many people to work for change. He was a man of great vision. But he did not live to see many of his dreams become reality.

On November 22, 1963, Kennedy went to Dallas, Texas, to promote his New Frontier ideas. It was a sunny day, and he waved at the crowds as he rode in an open-air car. Suddenly, he was shot by Lee Harvey Oswald. Kennedy was

▲ A Peace Corps volunteer in Nigeria

▼ President Johnson with children on the day he introduced Project Head Start

quickly rushed to the hospital, but at 1:00 P.M., doctors announced that the President was dead.

The Johnson Presidency

Then Vice President Lyndon Baines Johnson became President. Like Kennedy, Johnson believed the government should make life better for all Americans. Johnson's ideas became known as the **Great Society**.

As a longtime leader in the United States Senate, Johnson knew how to get things done. As President, he used the same skills to get bills passed by Congress. Johnson was able to turn many of Kennedy's hopes into law, especially in the areas of civil rights and voting rights for African Americans.

Part of Johnson's goal for the Great Society was that the government would help people in need. In 1964 he declared war on poverty.

That same year, Lyndon Johnson ran for President and won. He had now been elected President on his own. Johnson continued fighting the war on poverty.

He introduced Head Start, which helped preschool children from low-income families learn the skills they

⭐ **Peace Corps** A program for volunteers to help people in developing countries

⭐ **Great Society** President Johnson's plan to improve life for all Americans

would need to succeed in elementary school. Upward Bound helped low-income high school students prepare for college. And Congress passed the Medicare and Medicaid programs to help elderly and poor people pay their medical bills. Many of these programs continue to help people today.

Johnson also called on Americans to become involved in fighting poverty. He started Volunteers in Service to America (VISTA), which is a domestic version of the Peace Corps. Instead of going to other countries, the volunteers help needy people in the United States.

The War in Vietnam

While President Johnson was fighting poverty in the United States, American soldiers were also fighting overseas—in Vietnam's civil war.

Vietnam had been one of France's colonies. Then in 1954, Vietnam won its independence. Shortly after that, the country was divided into North Vietnam and South Vietnam. North Vietnam was Communist. The two nations fought each other. Each wanted to make the other part of its country. The United States didn't want Communist North Vietnam to win, so it got involved in the war to help South Vietnam defeat North Vietnam.

Many Americans opposed U.S. involvement. As the war went on, war protests became very common, especially on college campuses. This opposition to the war made President Johnson much less popular than he had been earlier. And in 1968 Johnson decided not to run for reelection. Johnson's Vice President, Hubert H. Humphrey, became the Democratic candidate. Richard Milhous Nixon, who promised to end the Vietnam War, became the Republican candidate. It was a close election, but Nixon won.

▲ A Nixon campaign button

▼ Expressing antiwar feelings at the 1968 Democratic Convention

Police escort buses to an integrated school in South Boston, Massachusetts.

President Nixon

While Richard Nixon was President, many programs that Kennedy and Johnson had begun earlier were continued. For example, civil rights legislation and the space race lived on throughout Nixon's presidency.

Nixon worked on keeping his promise to end the Vietnam War. Slowly, he pulled American soldiers out of Vietnam, and the last troops came home in 1973.

Nixon also saw the achievement of President Kennedy's goal to put a man on the moon before 1970. On July 20, 1969, *Apollo 11* landed on the moon. Later that night 600 million people watched on TV as astronaut Neil Armstrong took his first step on the moon's surface. Armstrong said, "That's one small step for man, one giant leap for mankind."

Integrating Schools

During Nixon's presidency the civil rights movement continued. For example, many states had to find ways to integrate schools. Many children lived in all-white or all-black neighborhoods. Since they usually went to school in their own neighborhood, these children attended segregated schools.

To integrate schools, children were bused to schools outside their neighborhoods. But not everyone wanted the schools to be integrated. At times federal troops had to protect students who were riding on the buses.

Fighting Inflation

While Johnson was President, the federal government had spent billions of dollars on the Vietnam War and social welfare programs. All of this led to inflation during Nixon's presidency.

At first President Nixon did little about rising costs. Then, on August 15, 1971, he announced a 90-day wage-and-price freeze. That meant that salaries and prices for goods could not go up for 90 days. By 1972, inflation was under control for a while. That same year, Nixon was reelected to the presidency.

A button commemorating the first moon landing

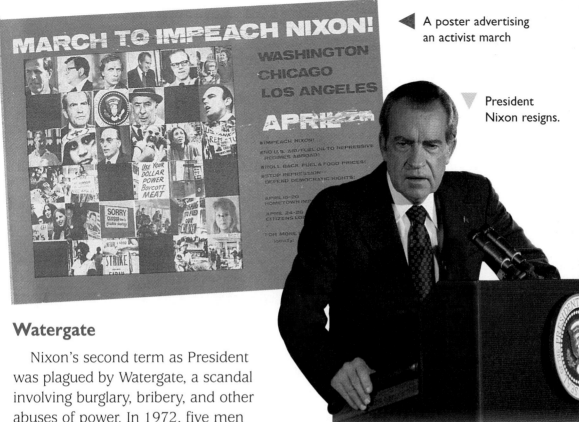

A poster advertising an activist march

President Nixon resigns.

Watergate

Nixon's second term as President was plagued by Watergate, a scandal involving burglary, bribery, and other abuses of power. In 1972, five men broke into the headquarters of the Democratic party at the Watergate Hotel in Washington, D.C. They wanted to steal information that could be used to help Nixon get reelected. But the burglars were caught at the hotel.

It became known that the burglars worked for Richard Nixon's reelection committee. An attempt was made to cover up the burglars' connection with Nixon's campaign, and Nixon claimed to know nothing about the break-in. Nixon then broke the law by trying to block investigations of the break-in.

At this time a scandal arose surrounding Vice President Spiro Agnew, who eventually resigned. Nixon had to choose a new Vice President and he selected Congressman Gerald R. Ford, Jr. Congress approved the selection, and Ford became Vice President.

As the Watergate investigations continued, Nixon was forced to release tape-recorded conversations he had held with his staff. The tapes revealed that Nixon had helped cover up the Watergate break-in.

It became clear that the House of Representatives would impeach Nixon, and that the Senate might remove him from office. To avoid that possibility, Nixon resigned, or gave up his position, on August 9, 1974. This was the first time that a U.S. President resigned.

Gerald R. Ford, Jr., became President. Nelson Rockefeller, a former governor of New York, became Vice President. This was the first time that the country had both a President and a Vice President who were not elected by the people.

SHOW WHAT YOU KNOW!

REFOCUS
COMPREHENSION

1. What were some major events of the 1960s and early 1970s?

2. How did the Watergate burglary lead to the resignation of Richard Nixon?

THINK ABOUT IT
CRITICAL THINKING

How has our country benefited from the programs of President Kennedy's New Frontier?

WRITE ABOUT IT
ACTIVITY

Write a journal entry describing President Johnson's Great Society programs. Be sure to write about how each program helped people.

Spotlight

KEY TERMS

Cuban missile crisis
Berlin Wall
escalation
Vietnamization

International Affairs

FOCUS *Americans greatly feared the spread of communism. And the United States confronted communism in several places around the world.*

Communism in Cuba

In 1959, Fidel Castro came to power in Cuba. At first most Americans supported Castro. They thought he would create a democratic government in Cuba. But when Castro turned out to be a Communist and a dictator, he lost American support.

Many Cubans who didn't support Castro fled to the United States. On April 17, 1961, some of these Cubans, assisted by Americans, tried to take their country back. About 1,500 people landed at the Bay of Pigs. The Cuban army crushed the invaders easily. The defeat deeply embarrassed President Kennedy, who supported the invasion.

Relations between the United States and Cuba continued to decline. And in 1962 the Soviet Union secretly built missile bases in Cuba. The map on this page shows where these missile sites were located. These bases would enable the Soviet Union to launch nuclear weapons that could hit the United States within minutes.

President Kennedy found out about the secret bases and demanded that the missiles be removed. The Soviets

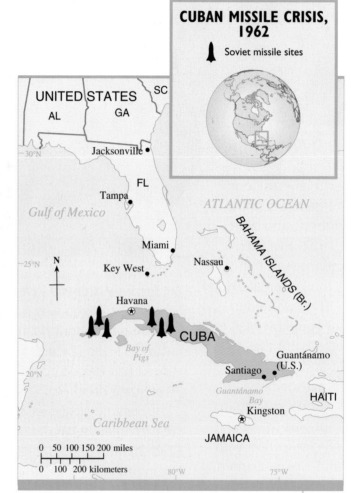

CUBAN MISSILE CRISIS, 1962

Soviet missile sites

refused. Kennedy then ordered the U.S. Navy to stop Soviet ships heading for Cuban ports to deliver the missiles.

After a few tense days the **Cuban missile crisis** ended. The Soviets agreed to remove their missiles, and the United States promised not to invade Cuba.

 Cuban missile crisis The conflict that occurred when the Soviet Union built missile bases in Cuba

▲ Building the Berlin Wall

East Berlin and West Berlin

There was still tension between the United States and the Soviet Union over Berlin. After World War II, the city of Berlin was divided into two sections. The United States and its European allies occupied West Berlin, and the Soviet Union occupied East Berlin. Many East Germans were moving to West Berlin. This angered the Soviets.

The Soviets wanted Americans and other Europeans to leave West Berlin. The Soviets also threatened to blockade the city, just as they had done in 1948. But President Kennedy refused to back down. He sent American troops to stop any blockade.

The Soviets were not willing to risk a war with the United States over Berlin. In 1961, instead of blockading the city, they built a wall separating East and West Berlin. The Berlin Wall, made of brick and topped with barbed wire and guard towers, prevented most East Germans from escaping to West Berlin.

▲ Standing near the Berlin Wall

The Vietnam War

In Vietnam the cold war led to actual fighting. In 1954, Vietnam had been split into two countries (see map on page 520). That same year a civil war broke out, as North Vietnam, which was Communist, and South Vietnam fought to form one country.

Americans didn't want the united Vietnam to be a Communist nation, so it got involved in the war. At first Americans sent mostly money and supplies. In the early 1960s, American military advisors were sent to train South Vietnam's soldiers. Finally, in 1965, President Lyndon Johnson sent American soldiers to fight. Some Americans supported Johnson's policy of escalation. They didn't want communism to spread.

⭐ **Berlin Wall** The wall built to separate East Berlin and West Berlin

escalation The act of becoming more involved

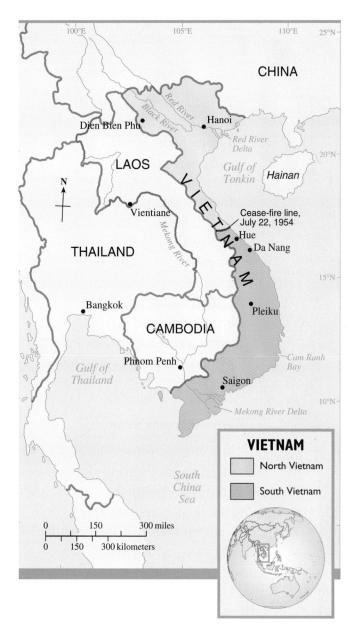

marches, sang antiwar songs, handed out leaflets, and wrote letters to politicians. Even some American soldiers didn't believe in the war. But they fought because they believed they should serve their country when called upon to do so. Other soldiers and civilians rallied in support of the war. But the war deeply divided Americans.

Leaving Vietnam

In 1969, Nixon introduced a plan of **Vietnamization**. Under this plan, U.S. troops would train South Vietnamese troops to take over the fighting. Four years later the last American troops left Vietnam. The North Vietnamese troops quickly destroyed the South Vietnamese army. North Vietnam won the war, so the united Vietnam became Communist.

The Vietnam War was the first war in United States history that it had not won. There were no victory parades for the returning soldiers. Many Americans couldn't separate their feelings about the war from their feelings about the American soldiers who had fought.

It wasn't until the 1980s that many Americans recognized the courage and

▲ This child is taking a rubbing of someone's name from the Vietnam Veterans Memorial.

People opposed the war for a variety of reasons. Some felt that it wasn't our war to fight, that the war was between the Vietnamese people. Others were pacifists, who didn't believe war was ever justified. Many of the people who objected to the war were college students.

As the war continued, the antiwar movement grew. People held antiwar

---

 Vietnamization The plan to turn the fighting over to South Vietnamese troops

◀ Visiting the Vietnam Veterans Memorial

sacrifice of the men and women who had fought. In 1982 the Vietnam Veterans Memorial was built in Washington, D.C. It was designed by a Chinese American woman named Maya Ying Lin. Here people can read the names of all the soldiers who were killed or missing in action. Many visitors to the memorial leave letters or other personal items at the wall.

China and the Soviet Union

While trying to get Americans out of Vietnam, President Richard Nixon also tried to improve the United States' relations with Communist China. The two countries had been in conflict since 1949. But the Chinese began to hint that they too would like better relations.

In 1971, China invited an American table tennis team to play. President Nixon agreed to let the team go to China. The next year Nixon visited China himself. The United States and China agreed to trade with one another and began friendly relations.

Nixon also improved relations with the Soviet Union. Three months after visiting China, he became the first American President to visit the Soviet Union. As a result of his efforts, the United States and the Soviet Union agreed to limit the number of new weapons they would build. They also increased trade and encouraged exchange visits between American and Soviet artists, teachers, and students.

▼ President Nixon and the prime minister of China, Chou En-lai

521

Moving Toward Equality

FOCUS *The civil rights movement involved a long, slow struggle to end discrimination. Protesters often faced violence, and the movement's greatest leader, Dr. Martin Luther King, Jr., was killed.*

Dr. Martin Luther King, Jr.

As late as 1960, discrimination against African Americans continued, especially in the South. African Americans couldn't eat at lunch counters, drink from water fountains, or get on elevators that were reserved for white people. And black people didn't have the same voting rights as white people. Some African Americans were determined to change this. They decided to fight for their civil rights. Dr. Martin Luther King, Jr., soon emerged as the leader of the civil rights movement.

Martin Luther King, Jr., was born in Atlanta, Georgia, in 1929. His father was a Baptist minister, and his mother was a teacher. King experienced discrimination early in his childhood. His two best friends were white boys who lived across the street from him. When King was six years old, his friends' mother would not allow them to play with him anymore. Now that her sons were going to school, they could only play with white friends.

Martin Luther King, Jr., grew up in a segregated

◀ Dr. Martin Luther King, Jr.

world. He attended a school for black children only. And at the age of 15, he attended a blacks-only college— Morehouse College in Atlanta. King then went on to earn his doctorate in religious studies. During this time he met many white people who didn't care about the color of his skin. He later said, "I began to see that they weren't the enemy. The evil was segregation itself."

Peaceful Demonstrations

By 1954, Dr. King was the pastor of a Baptist church in Montgomery, Alabama. He was also ready to fight a nonviolent battle for equality for African Americans. He felt that nonviolent protest was the right way to change the world.

In 1955, King organized the bus boycott after Rosa Parks was arrested. In 1960, he led a series of **sit-ins** across the South. At these protests African Americans entered whites-only restaurants, sat down, and refused to leave until they were served. Most of the time they weren't served. Instead, the demonstrators, including King, were beaten and arrested. But the sit-ins had a powerful effect. Like the bus

 sit-in A protest in which people sit down in a place and refuse to leave

A sit-in in Greensboro, North Carolina

Violent Responses

In 1962, James Meredith was the first African American to attend the University of Mississippi. The courts granted him the right to attend this all-white school. But when Meredith went to the school, a group of white people began to riot. President John F. Kennedy sent 5,000 federal troops to Mississippi to protect Meredith. Two people died, and hundreds were injured in the rioting. But Meredith continued to attend. He would be the first black person to graduate from the University of Mississippi.

The violent responses faced by civil rights protesters were horrifying. Still, Dr. King continued to call for nonviolent demonstrations. In the spring of 1963, King organized a march in Birmingham, Alabama. Thousands of African Americans—some as young as six years old—began walking through the streets of the city.

The police arrested many of the marchers, but the march continued. Then police dogs and fire hoses were used to attack the marchers. On television sets across the country, Americans were shocked to see the protesters being attacked. They saw the hateful nature of racism.

But the violence against civil rights activists had not ended. In June 1963, Medgar Evers, a civil rights leader, was murdered. And in September of that

boycott, the sit-ins showed that African Americans were peacefully going to demand their civil rights.

By 1961 the civil rights movement was gaining support throughout the country. A group of both black and white college students planned a **Freedom Ride**. They rode buses from Washington, D.C., to Alabama. By sitting together, they hoped to show that there were both black and white people who supported desegregation.

Unfortunately, some white people resented the civil rights movement and often responded to the protests violently. One bus was bombed, and several Freedom Riders were beaten. But the Freedom Rides continued. And hundreds of people began to take Freedom Rides of their own.

 Freedom Ride   A bus trip taken in order to integrate buses

year, an African American church in Birmingham was bombed, killing four teenage girls. Nevertheless, the peaceful fight for equality continued.

"I Have a Dream"

In August 1963, King planned a peaceful demonstration at the nation's capital. He hoped that 25,000 people would come. In fact, the march drew 250,000 people.

During the march Dr. King spoke about civil rights. "I have a dream," he told the crowd, "that my four little children will one day live in a nation where they will not be judged by the color of their skin but by the content of their character."

And he ended the speech saying, "When we let freedom ring, when we let it ring from every village and every hamlet, from every state and every city, we will be able to speed up that day when all of God's children, black men and white men, Jews and Gentiles, Protestants and Catholics, will be able to join hands and sing in the

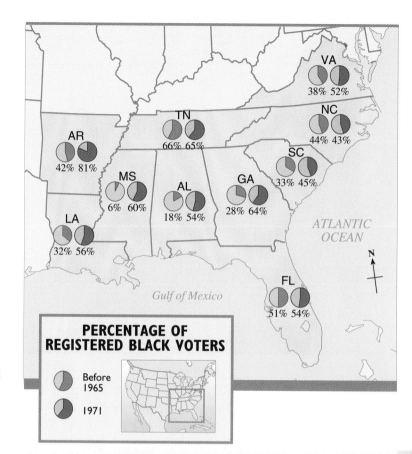

PERCENTAGE OF REGISTERED BLACK VOTERS

Before 1965

1971

VA 38% 52%
TN 66% 65%
NC 44% 43%
AR 42% 81%
SC 33% 45%
MS 6% 60%
AL 18% 54%
GA 28% 64%
LA 32% 56%
FL 51% 54%

ATLANTIC OCEAN

Gulf of Mexico

N

▼ March on Washington, 1963

▲ Registering to vote in Birmingham, Alabama

words of the old Negro spiritual, 'Free at last! Free at last! Thank God Almighty, we are free at last!'"

The following year Congress passed the Civil Rights Act, which outlawed segregation in all public places.

Voting Rights

One year later, in 1965, Congress passed the Voting Rights Act to outlaw discrimination in voter registration. As the map on page 524 shows, very few African Americans of voting age were actually registered to vote in the South. You can also see on the map that this had changed drastically by 1971.

Before the Voting Rights Act was passed, African Americans in the South often were not allowed to register to vote. But it was more than the new law that helped make possible the changes you see on the map. College students and other volunteers went to different cities in the South and helped African Americans register to vote.

Losing a Great Leader

After years of dealing with violence, some black people rejected Dr. King's ideas of peaceful demonstration. Malcolm X, for example, urged African Americans to take control of schools and government offices in their area. Malcolm X was shot and killed in February 1965.

And other black Americans formed a political party called the Black Panther party. In 1966 this party carried the theme of black pride. And the Black Panthers also declared that white violence should be met with black violence.

Through all of this, Martin Luther King, Jr., continued to call for nonviolent protest. On April 4, 1968, King was shot and killed in Tennessee. After King's assassination, the struggle for racial equality continued. But the movement had lost its greatest hero, and the nation had lost a man of great vision and courage.

Working for Change

FOCUS *Just as John F. Kennedy urged in his inaugural speech, Americans became involved in changing their country. They worked to get better wages for migrant workers, to achieve equal rights for women and minorities, and to protect the environment.*

ORGANIZING MIGRANT WORKERS

Cesar Chavez was a Mexican American who had spent many years working as a migrant farm worker. In 1962 he began the National Farm Workers Association (NFWA), a union for migrant farm workers. Within two years, NFWA had 1,000 members and was becoming a powerful voice for migrant workers.

In 1965 some California grape-pickers went on strike to get better wages. Over the next few years, NFWA struck against different California grape growers.

Then Cesar Chavez and the NFWA started a national boycott of California grapes. NFWA members went to cities around the country and spoke to local organizations, such as labor unions and school groups. They asked volunteers to picket and encouraged people to boycott California grapes.

The boycott worked. Nationwide many people didn't buy California grapes. Eventually California grape-pickers won the wages they wanted.

VISTA

VISTA began in 1964. It is similar to the Peace Corps, except that it is for Americans at home. VISTA volunteers try to improve the lives of poor Americans by helping them gain greater control over their communities and rise out of poverty.

VISTA volunteers sign up for one year of service. They work throughout the country in low-income rural and urban communities. They work as teachers, nurses, architects, and community organizers.

Within the first year about 2,500 VISTA volunteers had been trained and were serving. Most of these were college graduates who didn't come from low-income families. They wanted to help others.

1962	1964	1965			1970	1972
National Farm Workers Association is founded	VISTA is established	National Council on Indian Opportunity established			Earth Day	Congress presents the ERA to the states

| 1962 | 1964 | 1966 | 1968 | 1970 | 1972 |

NATIVE AMERICAN CIVIL RIGHTS

In 1964, hundreds of Native Americans marched in Washington. They wanted to be included in the war on poverty.

The next year President Lyndon Johnson established the National Council on Indian Opportunity. Under President Richard Nixon the government continued to respond to Native American concerns.

Nixon wanted Native Americans to have true political freedom, especially to govern reservations. Throughout the 1970s many laws were passed regarding Native American education, housing, and religious freedom.

The changes were not just legal. Sometimes the U.S. government returned lands to Native Americans. For example, in 1970 the U.S. government returned Blue Lake and the area surrounding it to the Taos Pueblo Indians of New Mexico. This ended a dispute over the land that had begun more than 60 years earlier.

EARTH DAY

Americans were concerned about the environment. They worried about polluting land, water, and air.

Denis Hayes organized Earth Day, hoping that Americans would take one day to show their support for protecting the earth. On April 22, 1970—Earth Day—about 20 million people rallied to the cause. Some picked up trash along roadsides. Others refused to use their cars. In Florida an old car was even put on "trial" and found guilty of pollution.

WOMEN'S RIGHTS

In the 1970s some women wanted equal pay in the workplace. And they didn't want women to be kept from holding certain jobs. In 1972 an Equal Rights Amendment (ERA) was presented to the states by Congress. The ERA, which had first been introduced to Congress in 1923, would guarantee equal treatment for men and women.

ERA didn't get enough state votes to be ratified. But the women's movement greatly impacted the lives of American women. New career opportunities became available to women. And women's pay came closer to men's.

La Causa: The Migrant Farmworkers' Story

by Dana Catharine de Ruiz and Richard Larios

Cesar Chavez worked very hard to change the working situation for migrant workers in America. He organized protest demonstrations, but migrant workers were still treated poorly. They earned wages that were too low to support them, and sometimes land owners didn't even pay them at all. In March 1962, Chavez, along with help from others such as Dolores Huerta, organized a labor union for migrant workers. Attend this union's first meeting.

Some who came into the hall had worked with Cesar and Dolores to help organize tonight's meeting. They nodded or exchanged smiles with Dolores as they passed. Some had tried and failed earlier to start a union of migrant farmworkers. They had been beaten or arrested or both. Tonight they wondered whether this effort would be any more successful than those of the past.

Dolores wondered, too. Would this idea of a union work, or was it too much of a dream? She walked through the growing crowd, working her way through the streams of people. Cesar had arrived and was on stage.

It was Cesar who believed that the time was right to build a union. Others disagreed. Even Dolores wasn't sure, but Cesar had said to her, "The *only* way farmworkers will be helped is to start a union."

. . . Without a union, farmworkers couldn't get a fair wage from the growers. They couldn't get better working conditions or be protected from crooked labor contractors. They needed a union. . . .

There were many obstacles. For one thing, it was against the law to organize a union of farmworkers. For another, farmworkers were always on the move. They didn't work in the same place day in and day out, week in and week out, like factory workers. Most of them didn't even have home addresses to which union information could be mailed. But the greatest obstacle was simply that the workers were so poor. Where would they find the money for union dues? How could the union go on strike if it had no dues money saved up to buy food or medicine for its striking workers?

But Cesar knew all this. He didn't say a union was the easiest way; he said it was the only way. So what was the point in waiting? Why not get started now? Cesar could make the impossible seem practical. A union would work, he said, if the workers believed in it. Tonight they would learn whether the workers believed or not.

Dolores mounted the metal stairs to the stage. To the left was a sign that said, in Spanish and in English, "National Farm Workers Association." Using *Association* instead of *Union* was Cesar's idea. A farmworkers' union was against the law. An association—well, the law didn't say anything about that!

Cesar was standing on stage. He was very happy as he looked out over the growing crowd. He saw the hope and determination in their faces. These people believed. Cesar felt sure of that. He and Dolores greeted each other and settled in chairs on the stage with the other leaders.

Then a strong voice rang out over the crowded hall. It was the voice of the singer Rosa Gloria. She was singing a *corrido*—a folk song—that she had written. . . .

This was the signal to begin the meeting. As the applause following Rosa's song died down, Cesar stood. Nearly covering the theater screen behind him was an enormous flag wrapped in brown paper. Cesar's cousin Manuel had made the flag for the new union. He and Cesar had planned it together.

As Manuel walked to the wrapped flag, a rustle of excitement moved through the hall. Some pointed. *¿Qué es eso?* they asked each other. What is that? Then Manuel pulled a cord, releasing the brown paper wrapping. People gasped. Cesar could see pride brightening their faces.

Cesar turned to look at the flag. In a white circle at the flag's center flew a black eagle, a symbol of strength and courage. Surrounding the white circle was a field of red. Red meant courage and union.

Most of the farmworkers were of Mexican descent. In the center of the Mexican flag is an eagle. And red and white are two of the colors in Mexico's flag. Cesar turned back to address the crowd. He described the flag as "a strong and beautiful sign of hope." He then introduced Manuel.

Manuel stepped forward. He explained that the black eagle stood for the strength that the farmworkers needed to face their problems. The white circle meant hope. The red background showed the workers' determination and unity in the struggle to achieve their goals.

Amid the cries of *¡Viva! ¡Viva La Causa!*—Long live the cause!— came foot-stomping, whistling, and applause. Into this roar of approval, Manuel cried out, "When the eagle flies, the problems of the farmworker will be solved."

Dolores and many others made speeches that night. All were received with great applause. It soon became clear what the workers would decide. Sure enough, by the meeting's end, they voted Cesar Chavez president of the new union and Dolores Huerta vice president.

The union had begun. Now it was up to the eagle to fly.

Want to learn more about the accomplishments of Cesar Chavez and the National Farm Workers Association? You can check the book out of your school or public library.

SHOW WHAT YOU KNOW!

REFOCUS
COMPREHENSION

1. How did the 1970s women's movement affect women?

2. What things did the U.S. government do in response to Native Americans' concerns?

THINK ABOUT IT
CRITICAL THINKING

Why did Chavez think that only a union could help the farmworkers?

WRITE ABOUT IT
ACTIVITY

Write a speech or an essay predicting the benefits that could result from people working together to protect the environment.

SUMMING UP

1. What were three of President Kennedy's goals for the nation?

2. What programs were part of President Johnson's war on poverty?

3. Why was President Nixon forced to resign in 1974?

4. How was the Cuban missile crisis settled?

5. How did the United States become involved in the Vietnam War?

6. Why were some people opposed to U.S. involvement in the Vietnam War?

7. What were some nonviolent ways that black Americans demanded their civil rights?

8. What does the Civil Rights Act of 1964 outlaw?

9. What would the Equal Rights Amendment have guaranteed?

10. How was VISTA different from the Peace Corps?

2 SKILL POWER
PREDICTING OUTCOMES

Read a news article about a conflict or change that is affecting people in your community or state today. Predict a probable outcome of the situation.

3 WHAT DO YOU THINK?
CRITICAL THINKING

1. What do you think was the most important change that occurred in the United States during the 1960s and 1970s?

2. Are people today less likely to protest social and economic conditions than they were in the 1960s? Explain your answer.

3. Why did the United States and the Soviet Union avoid fighting each other directly during the cold war?

4. Why was registering black voters an important accomplishment in the South?

5. Do you think men and women have equal rights today in the United States? Explain.

4 SAY IT, WRITE IT, USE IT
VOCABULARY

You are a newspaper editor during the 1960s and 1970s. Write headlines that use the terms below. Then write a short news story to go with one of the headlines.

activism	Great Society
Berlin Wall	Peace Corps
Cuban missile crisis	sit-in
escalation	Vietnamization
Freedom Ride	

5 GEOGRAPHY AND YOU

MAP STUDY

Use the maps throughout the chapter to answer the following questions.

1. In what cities were there bus boycotts?

2. What U.S. state is closest to Cuba?

3. Name the countries that were on the western borders of North Vietnam and South Vietnam.

4. Which southern state had the greatest increase in voter registration from 1965 to 1971?

7 TAKE ACTION

CITIZENSHIP

In 1963, Dr. Martin Luther King, Jr., gave his famous "I Have a Dream" speech. In it, he described his vision for America. What dreams do you have for your community or country? How would you like citizens and government officials to act? Write a short speech in which you set forth the changes that you would most like. Present your speech to your class.

6 GET CREATIVE

LANGUAGE ARTS CONNECTION

Look at the Earth Day poster on page 527. As you can see, it shows the artist's feelings about the environment. Think about this and other issues that affected our nation in the 1960s and 1970s and issues that affect us today. Design a poster to express your feelings about one of these issues. Use words and art to present the message clearly.

LOOKING AHEAD

In the next chapter, read about the development of the present-day world role of the United States.

AMERICA'S PLACE

Between the mid-1970s and the mid-1990s, the United States and the world went through a period of great change.

What did yellow ribbons symbolize in the United States? Find out on pages 556–557.

CONTENTS

IN A NEW WORLD

These books tell about some people and events of interest during a time of change in the United States and the world. Read one that interests you and fill out a book-review form.

READ AND RESEARCH

Ronald Reagan by George Sullivan (Silver Burdett Press, 1991)
Americans express their hopes, fears, and goals when they vote for their President. When they elected Ronald Reagan in 1980, they were hoping for lower prices and more security in their lives. Find out whether Reagan fulfilled the expectations of the people. *(biography)*

To Space and Back by Sally Ride, with Susan Okie
(William Morrow & Co., 1991) Join space shuttle astronaut Sally Ride on her spectacular flight into space. It's a grand scientific exploration made possible by the support of hundreds of scientists and technicians at the space centers in Houston, Texas, and Cape Canaveral, Florida. *(nonfiction)*

The Gulf War by Dr. John King (Silver Burdett Press, 1991)
Read about the complex political and economic pressures that brought about the United States' involvement in the dispute between Iraq and Kuwait. Photos show some of the destruction that modern warfare produces. *(nonfiction)*

The Big Book for Peace edited by Ann Durell and Marilyn Sachs (Dutton Children's Books, 1990)
Through the pictures and words of some of your favorite authors and illustrators, you will see the beauty of a friendly world in which people try to understand and get along with one another. *(fiction)*

SKILL POWER

Reading a Population Density Map

Knowing how to read a population density map will let you see where people live.

UNDERSTAND IT

It's a good thing land surfaces aren't like seesaws, because in most countries, populations are not evenly spread out or balanced. Instead, people tend to live in groups in certain areas. These areas are said to have high population density.

Population density is the measure of the number of people who live in one square mile. (A square mile is a square area with sides 1 mile long.) The more people per square mile, the higher the population density.

EXPLORE IT

Look at the squares shown below. Each one represents a square mile. Which square has the highest density of dots? Which has the lowest density of dots? If each dot stands for a certain number of people, the square with the most dots would have the highest population density.

Look at the population density map on page 537. It shows where people lived in the United States around 1900. In which areas was the population denser? In which areas did fewer people live?

Each of these squares represents one square mile. ▶

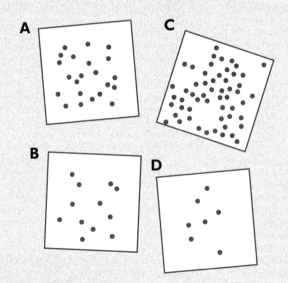

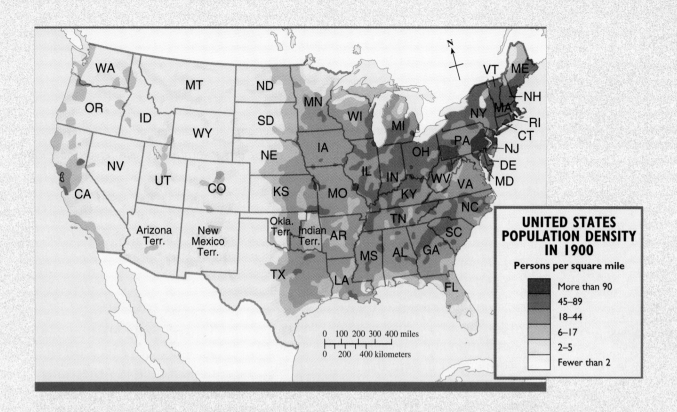

UNITED STATES
POPULATION DENSITY
IN 1900

Persons per square mile

More than 90
45–89
18–44
6–17
2–5
Fewer than 2

0 100 200 300 400 miles

0   200   400 kilometers

TRY IT

Working together, make a population density map of the students in your class. First, get or make a large map of your town or community. Then, using one color only, have each student place a dot on the map where he or she lives.

Display the map and discuss which areas of your community are most densely populated by students in your class. Which areas have the lowest population density?

You may wish to invite one or more classes in your school to add their populations to your map.

SKILL POWER SEARCH *In this chapter look for a map that shows population density in the United States today.*

Setting the Scene

★ KEY TERMS

pardon
Camp David Accords
deficit
national debt
service job
Contract With America

YEARS OF CHANGE

FOCUS *Questions about jobs and the economy have challenged all recent American Presidents. In many ways, people's ideas about the government's role have also changed.*

A Changing Nation

The Watergate scandal was a turning point for the United States. As a result of the scandal, many Americans lost confidence in their government. After this crisis, Presidents as well as other men and women in politics had to work harder to earn the people's trust.

Problems with the economy made this job harder. So did events in the rest of the world. Many people were worried about their jobs and fearful of the future. For a time, many Americans lost some of their spirit of hope and optimism.

Ford as President

When Gerald Ford took over the presidency after Richard Nixon resigned, he told Americans, "Our long national nightmare is over." People wanted very much to believe him. In 1974 many Americans saw Ford as a President who could give them a little time to recover from Watergate and other events.

Ford also knew this was what people wanted. It was one reason he **pardoned** former President Nixon, who could have been put on trial for crimes related to Watergate. Ford said he wanted to "write an end" to Watergate.

With a presidential election just two years away, people wondered just

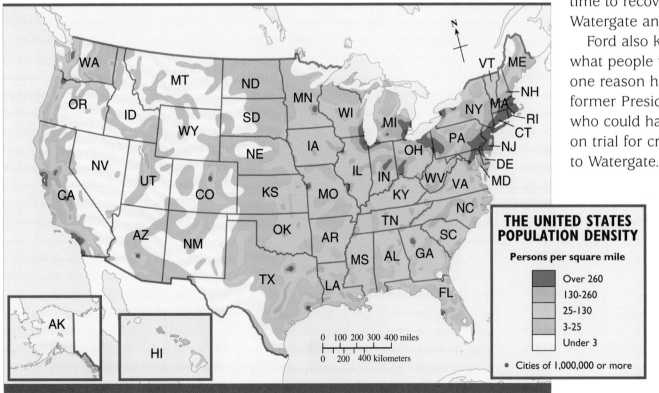

THE UNITED STATES POPULATION DENSITY

Persons per square mile

- Over 260
- 130–260
- 25–130
- 3–25
- Under 3

● Cities of 1,000,000 or more

0 100 200 300 400 miles
0 200 400 kilometers

★ *pardon* To forgive for a crime

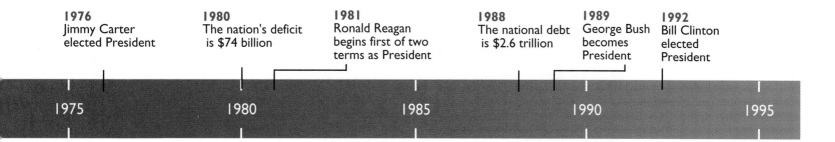

1976
Jimmy Carter
elected President

1980
The nation's deficit
is $74 billion

1981
Ronald Reagan
begins first of two
terms as President

1988
The national debt
is $2.6 trillion

1989
George Bush
becomes
President

1992
Bill Clinton
elected
President

1975   1980   1985   1990   1995

what Ford would be able to do. President Ford's most pressing problem was the economy. It was in terrible shape—the worst since the Great Depression. Inflation was high, and many people were out of work. Ford did what he could to encourage people to "Whip Inflation Now." But that did little good, and when Ford ran for President in 1976, voters turned instead to Jimmy Carter, a Democrat.

The Election of Jimmy Carter

James Earl "Jimmy" Carter, Jr., was a former governor of Georgia who was also a successful farmer. Many people had not heard of him before 1976. They asked, "Jimmy who?" Carter played up the idea that he was an outsider, new to Washington politics. A deeply religious man with a broad smile, he was perceived as honest and trustworthy. Carter promised never to lie to the American people. Americans liked that.

It seemed that many Americans, two years after Watergate, were still disillusioned with politics. Only about 54 percent of Americans voted in the 1976 election. Carter was elected over Ford by a narrow margin.

While people liked the idea that

Carter was an outsider in Washington, this made it harder for him to get things done. He and his staff had little experience in working with Congress.

President Carter faced many challenges. At home, inflation continued to worsen. It reached 13 percent in 1979 and climbed even higher in 1980. High prices meant that people couldn't afford to buy new goods. That, in turn, hurt industry and put more people out of work.

In foreign policy, Carter tried to put his belief in human rights into action. This helped him take a big step toward peace in the Middle East. Ever since the state of Israel was formed in 1948, its Arab neighbors had been hostile to it. In over 30 years, Arabs and Israelis had fought four bloody wars.

In 1978, Carter invited Anwar el-Sadat (AHN wahr el sah DAHT), the president of Egypt, an Arab nation,

▲ Jimmy Carter offered a relaxed, down-to-earth approach to the presidency.

and Menachem Begin (muh NAHKH um BAY-gihn), the prime minister of Israel, to the United States. For 13 days, Carter worked with these men to help them settle differences between their countries. At last, Sadat and Begin agreed to sign a peace treaty. This agreement became known as the **Camp David Accords**. The leaders had met at Camp David, Maryland, a country retreat of American Presidents.

▲ Sadat (left), Carter (center), and Begin (right) sign the Camp David Accords.

Reagan Runs for President

In 1980, President Carter ran for a second term. Although he was a successful peacemaker, Carter had not solved the economic crisis at home. The country had changed over the years. People were frustrated by soaring inflation, and they wanted a President who could offer fresh solutions for fixing the economy. They also wanted someone who would restore pride in the nation, which had not been strong since the Vietnam War and Watergate. The candidate who seemed to promise this was Ronald Reagan, a former movie and television actor who had been governor of California.

Reagan ran a "feel good" campaign and promised to bring back the

▼ Ronald Reagan

nation's greatness. He won the election by more than 8 million votes. Again, slightly more than half of the registered voters voted.

Reagan's First Year

At age 70, Reagan was the oldest President ever elected. Yet he acted like a much younger man. He rode horses and chopped wood on his California ranch.

But on March 30, 1981, he almost lost his life. On that day, he was shot in the chest by a would-be assassin. Seriously wounded, Reagan never lost his sense of humor. When his wife, Nancy, visited him in the hospital, he joked, "Honey, I forgot to duck." Reagan did recover and served eight years as President.

The "Reagan Revolution"

Reagan promised people a new approach to the country's problems. It was the beginning of major changes in American government. Reagan and many new members of Congress were more conservative than previous politicians.

The center of Reagan's plan was the idea of limited government. For years, government programs had been growing. Reagan wanted to reduce the number of government programs. "Government," he said, "is not the solution to our problems. Government is the problem."

Camp David Accords The treaty signed by Israel and Egypt that brought peace between the two countries for the first time in 30 years

Reagan also wanted to help businesses, because a growing economy would mean more jobs and better wages. Reaganomics—as this plan was known—was a mix of fewer government regulations on businesses, tax cuts, and reductions in government spending.

Spending cuts were supposed to reduce how much money the government spent. But President Reagan believed the country should spend *more* on national defense. Most spending cuts came in social programs, such as food stamps, loans to students, and welfare benefits.

The Economy in the 1980s

Reaganomics worked in some ways and for some people. After 1982 the economy began to boom. Many people had never been so successful. About 100,000 Americans became millionaires every year. The nation's economic output doubled during the 1980s.

For many others the 1980s was a time of failure. The gap between the rich and the poor grew larger. As a result of the combination of tax cuts and increased spending in some areas, the federal **deficit** increased. The federal deficit is the amount of money the government spends that is not covered by the taxes it collects. In 1980 the deficit

 deficit The amount of spending that exceeds income

was $74 billion. The deficit grew larger through the decade. By 1988, the **national debt** (all those annual deficits added up) was more than $2.6 trillion!

To make things worse, many more people lost jobs during the 1980s. One way for companies to make profits was to merge, or join together. Sometimes this meant that several people were doing the same job for the new company. The new and larger companies then laid off workers they no longer needed. Other people lost jobs because the American economy was changing. There were fewer jobs in factories that made goods. More

national debt The total of monies owed by the government of a nation

THE NATIONAL DEBT

(in trillions of dollars)

Year: 1940, 1945, 1950, 1955, 1960, 1965, 1970, 1975, 1980, 1985, 1990, 1995 (est.)

Lines like this were common in the 1980s, as out-of-work people applied for jobs.

people held **service jobs**. Instead of making cars or refrigerators, they provided medical care or sold insurance. They worked in offices. They repaired and serviced cars or TVs or plumbing. Many factory jobs simply disappeared or were done by people in other countries.

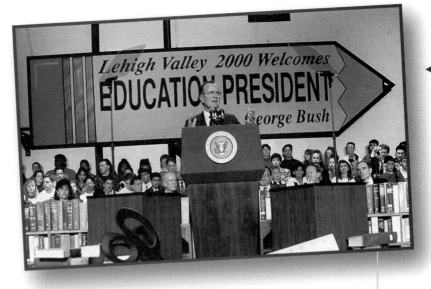

President Bush speaking to a group of students and teachers

George Bush Succeeds Reagan

After two terms as President, Ronald Reagan could not run again in 1988, even though he was still very popular. His Vice President, George Bush, ran and won. Like Reagan, President Bush wanted people to look to each other for help, instead of to the federal government. He spoke about "a thousand points of light," meaning that Americans should help each other. Each person could add a "point of light" by reaching out to someone in need. George Bush's wife, Barbara, was a popular First Lady. She advocated literacy and urged adults and children to read together.

Bush did believe that the federal government had to solve certain problems, such as the drug problem, which was a major concern for Americans in the 1980s. Most illegal drugs were smuggled into the United States from countries such as Colombia and Panama.

Americans Lose Confidence

Like Presidents before him, George Bush ran into trouble with the economy. The budget deficit kept increasing. Foreign trade was also a problem. Americans were buying more imported goods than they were selling as exports. Many Americans continued to lose jobs as international companies made goods overseas, where workers were paid less. American workers and politicians urged people to spend more money on goods—from clothes to cars—made in this country than on imports.

Americans lost confidence in Bush's ability to solve such problems. In 1992 he lost the presidential election to a young Democrat, William Jefferson "Bill" Clinton.

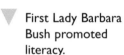

First Lady Barbara Bush promoted literacy.

---

 service job A job that provides a service instead of producing goods

President Clinton's Plans

Clinton, who had been governor of Arkansas, promised to be a "new kind of Democrat." He didn't offer a huge spending program like the New Deal of the 1930s. The large national debt made that impossible. But Clinton did have big plans, including reforming health care, reducing crime, and improving the economy. His wife, Hillary Rodham Clinton, a lawyer, played a role in creating a plan to provide more Americans with health care. Though the plan was not passed into law, it did bring the issue of health care coverage to the attention of many Americans.

Clinton and his Vice President, Al Gore, also offered plans to make government smaller. To Clinton's disappointment, many of his plans for change met opposition in Congress and from some of the public.

A New Vision

Still, American voters were not happy. In 1994 they elected many Republicans to Congress. For the first time in nearly 50 years, Republicans had control of both houses of Congress. Most wanted to carry on the kind of policies started under President Reagan—cutting government programs and spending.

During the 1994 campaign the Republicans, led by Representative Newt Gingrich of Georgia, offered a **Contract With America**. It called for tax cuts, a balanced budget, reductions in welfare programs for the poor and disabled, and limits on how long a person could serve in Congress.

These plans reflected a great change in thinking. After being out of power for so long, the new Republican lawmakers wanted to undo some programs that had been put in place over the years. They wanted the federal government to do less for people, and the state and local governments to do more. This meant major changes in programs such as Medicare, the health plan for older people; Social Security, a program for retirement income; and welfare plans that help poor people.

 Contract With America A pledge signed by Republican members of Congress to seek a balanced budget

SHOW WHAT YOU KNOW!

REFOCUS
COMPREHENSION

1. Describe Ronald Reagan's goals as President.

2. What did the Camp David Accords achieve?

THINK ABOUT IT
CRITICAL THINKING

Do you think the federal government should be more involved or less involved in solving problems? Give reasons for your answer.

WRITE ABOUT IT
ACTIVITY

Study the map on page 538. Write a paragraph on what you learned about the population density of your state.

Spotlight

KEY TERMS

Sandinista
Contra
hostage
Operation Desert
Storm

THE INTERNATIONAL SCENE

FOCUS *Many changes after the 1970s affected the United States' role in the world. The cold war came to an end, and the United States became the only superpower.*

The Cold War

For many decades it seemed that the cold war between the United States and the Soviet Union might never end. Both sides kept their weapons and armies ready. Sometimes, events relaxed the mood. But other events made the cold war more threatening.

Tensions increased in 1979, when the Soviet Union invaded its neighbor Afghanistan. In response, President Jimmy Carter cut off the sale of American grain to the Soviet Union. And he asked American athletes to boycott the 1980 Summer Olympic Games in Moscow, the Soviet Union's capital.

President Ronald Reagan, Carter's successor, was a strong anti-Communist. He called the Soviet Union an "evil empire." Still, Reagan developed a friendly relationship with Mikhail Gorbachev (mee khah EEL GOR buh chawf), the new Soviet leader. Starting in 1985, Gorbachev made changes in the Soviet Union. He gave the Soviet people more economic, political, and religious freedom. For the first time in nearly 70 years, the Soviet people could write and say what they thought.

The Soviet Union Breaks Up

The idea of change spread from the Soviet Union throughout Communist Eastern Europe. At first the changes occurred slowly, but then they became more drastic and happened much more rapidly. In November 1989 the East German government opened the gates of the Berlin Wall, between East Berlin and West Berlin. Joyful Germans soon tore down the hated wall. Eleven months later, East Germany and West Germany reunited to become one democratic nation. Other Communist governments in Europe, such as those of Poland and Czechoslovakia, also collapsed.

Soon the Soviet Union itself fell apart. Gorbachev had given the Soviet people a taste of freedom, but by 1991 they wanted more. The republics that once made up the Soviet Union became independent nations. The largest of

▼ People cheered wildly and tried to tear down the Berlin Wall themselves.

RUSSIA AND NEIGHBORING COUNTRIES

these new nations was Russia, as you can see on the map above.

This meant that the cold war between the Soviet Union and the United States was over. So Russia, along with other new nations in Eastern Europe, and the United States looked for new ways to work together.

Challenges in China

China's government has been Communist since 1949. After President Nixon's visit in 1972, relations between China and the United States slowly improved. The two countries began trading goods with each other.

But a problem remained. Chinese officials often denied their people basic human rights. The government controlled people's personal lives. People could not criticize their leaders without being arrested or harmed.

China's government began to grant its people freedom to run their own farms and businesses. But many Chinese people wanted political freedom as well. In May 1989 hundreds of thousands of Chinese students and workers crowded into Tiananmen (tyahn-ahn men) Square in Beijing, the capital. They wanted their leaders to listen to their demands for democracy.

The government crushed the protest. Soldiers killed, wounded, and arrested

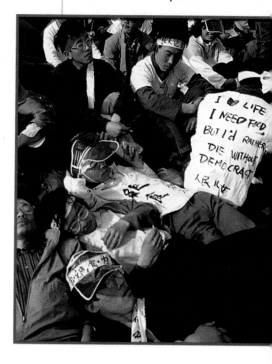

Many students were among those who protested at Tiananmen Square.

thousands of protesters. This assault horrified Americans, chilling relations between China and the United States.

Relations in the Americas

Closer to home, countries in Central America have long had special importance to the United States. Since 1904 the United States controlled the Panama Canal, connecting the Atlantic and Pacific oceans. Many Latin Americans objected to this control. In 1978, Carter signed a treaty returning the Canal to Panama by 1999.

Later, President Ronald Reagan became concerned that some countries in Central America might become Communist. In Nicaragua the Sandinistas (san duh NEES tuz), a Communist revolutionary group, overthrew a dictator in 1979. Reagan feared that the Sandinista government would spread communism in the region. He supported the Contras, who opposed the Sandinistas.

War in Nicaragua brought misery to the people and heated debate in the United States. Congress voted against sending money to support the Contras. However, some officials raised funds to support the Contras by selling weapons to Iran, an enemy of the United States. This illegal act became known as the Iran-Contra Affair. Meanwhile, war in Nicaragua ended. In 1990, Nicaraguans voted for a new, moderate government.

Reagan also intervened when a pro-Communist group gained power in Grenada, an island in the Caribbean. In October 1983, troops from the United States and several Caribbean countries invaded Grenada. In just a few days, they defeated troops from Grenada and Cuba.

Middle East Crises

There was also trouble in the Middle East. In Iran in 1979, students opposed to American support of Middle East peace efforts seized U.S. embassy workers as **hostages**. The American

Iranian students posing for a photo with one of their hostages

---

 Sandinista A member of the Communist group that took power in Nicaragua in 1979
Contra A member of a group seeking to overthrow the Sandinistas

 hostage A person taken and held prisoner by an enemy until certain conditions are met

General Colin Powell conducts a press conference during Operation Desert Storm.

government worked to negotiate the hostages' freedom, but it was not until 444 days later that they were released.

In 1990, Saddam Hussein (sah DAHM hoo SAYN), Iraq's dictator, invaded Kuwait, a small, oil-rich country. President George Bush and other world leaders demanded that Saddam leave Kuwait. When he refused, an international army drove him out in Operation Desert Storm—the Persian Gulf War.

International "Hot Spots"

The end of the cold war brought what President Bush called a "new world order." Relations between the United States and the Soviet Union no longer dominated the news. With the breakup of the Soviet Union and the downfall of communism in Eastern Europe came civil wars. Attention was focused on these wars, and the United States struggled with the role it should play in them.

Different groups of people in Yugoslavia had lived together in relative peace under a Communist government. In the 1990s, Yugoslavia broke apart. The peoples of the region—Serbs, Bosnian Muslims, and Croats—began fighting a brutal war.

Civil wars also broke out in parts of Africa. In some conflicts, American forces cooperated with European and United Nations troops to try to bring peace. President Bill Clinton also continued the policy of negotiating peace between Arabs and Israelis. In 1994 he brought together Yasir Arafat, leader of the Palestine Liberation Organization, and Yitzhak Rabin (yihts-KHAHK rah BEEN), president of Israel. Sadly, Rabin was assassinated by an opponent of the peace plan in 1995.

President Clinton watched as two enemies, Arafat (right) and Rabin (left), shook hands for the first time.

⭐ **Operation Desert Storm**
The common name for the Persian Gulf War

RESOURCES AND THE ENVIRONMENT

FOCUS *Over the last few decades, Americans have become aware of environmental problems. They have begun to look for ways to protect and use natural resources wisely.*

The Energy Crisis

For a long time, the United States produced all the energy it needed. By the late 1940s though, Americans were using much more energy than they could produce. The United States began to import oil from the Middle East because it was cheap and plentiful.

By the 1970s over 90 percent of the American economy depended on energy from burning fossil fuels: coal, oil, and natural gas. Oil and gasoline provided fuel for running cars, trucks, machines, and factories, and for heating homes and offices.

In 1973 many of the Arab nations in the Middle East were angry at the United States for supporting Israel during an Arab-Israeli war. As a form of protest, Saudi Arabia and other Arab nations in the Middle East cut off oil shipments to the United States. These nations were members of OPEC, the Organization of Petroleum Exporting Countries, shown on the map on this page. This embargo, or ban, decreased the American supply of oil tremendously. It created an energy crisis in the United States.

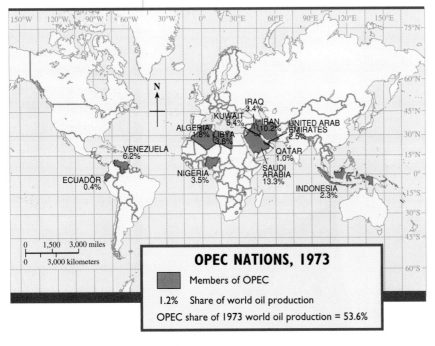

OPEC NATIONS, 1973

Members of OPEC

1.2% Share of world oil production

OPEC share of 1973 world oil production = 53.6%

Closed gas pumps were common during the energy crisis. ▶

Americans felt the oil shortage in many ways. They could only buy gas for their cars on certain days.

Sometimes there was no gas at all. Prices of products and services skyrocketed. It cost more to travel by car, bus, and airplane. It became more expensive to produce and ship food and other products. So the prices of food and other products went up, too. A loaf of bread that had cost 28 cents a few years earlier now cost 90 cents. As prices increased, inflation grew worse. America's economy suffered.

Even after the end of the embargo in March 1974, oil prices remained high. In 1979, oil-producing countries raised their prices steeply. Between 1978 and 1980 the price of a barrel of imported oil shot up from $13 a barrel to $31 a barrel. The energy crisis continued.

Seeking Solutions

Many Americans saw the energy crisis as a warning. They saw two basic solutions. First, Americans could simply use less oil. (In 1975, Americans made up 5 percent of the world's population but used 33 percent of the world's energy.) Second, they could supply more of their own energy. President Jimmy Carter encouraged both solutions.

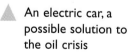

An electric car, a possible solution to the oil crisis

Americans worked hard to make important changes. To use less oil, they practiced **energy conservation**. People turned down the heat at home. They walked to work or formed car pools. They insulated their homes and made factories more efficient. They also demanded smaller cars that used less gasoline.

Energy Alternatives

Americans also explored new ways to produce and use energy. They tried to use the power of the sun, the wind, and ocean tides. They tried to build cars that would run on electricity or batteries. But these ideas were not practical for most Americans. Some thought that nuclear energy—made by a controlled atomic reaction—would be a good solution. But the dangers of nuclear power worried many people. In 1979 an accident at the Three Mile Island nuclear plant in Pennsylvania released many gallons of radioactive water. No one was killed, but the accident frightened Americans away from nuclear power. Today nuclear plants generate less than 10 percent of the nation's energy.

 energy conservation Using energy wisely or preventing it from being wasted

Pollution

The energy crisis convinced people to protect other resources. **Pollution**, for example, threatened the environment. So in recent years, Congress has passed laws to protect clean air and water and to stop further pollution.

Still, problems continue. One source of pollution is **acid rain**. Certain industrial chemicals combine with water high in the atmosphere. When the water falls as rain, it is very acidic—sometimes as acidic as vinegar. Acid rain kills trees and fish. It eats away at stone and bricks on buildings.

Accidental oil spills are a major cause of pollution in ocean waters. The worst spill in American history happened in 1989. The oil tanker *Exxon Valdez* ripped open when it hit underwater rocks. More than 10 million barrels of oil spilled into the clean water of Prince William Sound on the coast of Alaska. The oil coated the rocks, animals, and plants along 1,000 miles of shoreline. It also hurt the area's fishing industry.

Recycling

Another cause of pollution is garbage. Newspapers and plastics pile up in dumps or are buried in the ground. One way to fight pollution is by recycling.

Efforts at recycling have caught on. Many companies use recycled materials. A jacket's insulation can be made from recycled plastic bottles. Today most paper products contain some recycled paper. Every year, Americans of all ages recycle millions of tons of newspapers, plastic milk jugs, glass bottles, tin cans, and aluminum foil.

 pollution Environmental damage from harmful materials
acid rain Rain with a high concentration of acid produced by burning fossil fuels

These volunteers helped clean up a beach in California.

SHOW WHAT YOU KNOW!

REFOCUS
COMPREHENSION

1. What caused the energy crisis in the 1970s?

2. What were the effects of the *Exxon Valdez* oil spill?

THINK ABOUT IT
CRITICAL THINKING

Why is it important to protect the environment?

WRITE ABOUT IT
ACTIVITY

Make a plan for ways that you and your family can help to conserve energy and reduce pollution.

CHANGING FORTUNES

FOCUS *During the 1980s the economy prospered, but not everyone shared in the good times. Still, some groups made great strides toward taking an equal place in American society.*

The Nation Gets Richer

Like the 1920s, the 1980s was a good time to make money. Business executives earned huge salaries. People enjoyed spending money on luxuries. This spending helped fuel the economy. In the 1980s some Americans saw being rich and having power as important goals. Even those who weren't rich and powerful spent time finding out about those who were. Popular TV shows featured wealthy, glamorous people. Best-selling books promised to help people become successful quickly.

Many people with well-paying jobs used their money to buy and fix up houses or apartment buildings in older parts of cities. These new landlords helped bring life back to city neighborhoods. New shops and restaurants opened up.

The Nation Gets Poorer

There was another side to the story. Not all Americans did well during the 1980s. Twenty percent of American families earned less money at the end of the 1980s than at the beginning. The number of people living in poverty rose from 26 million to 32 million.

Joblessness and homelessness became major problems. This was especially true in cities. Many workers lost their jobs as industries had work done in other countries with less expensive labor costs. Wages for other jobs remained low, which meant that people had to struggle to pay their bills. Costs of renting or buying a place to live went up everywhere. As a result, more people ended up living on the streets than at any time since the Great Depression. By 1985, hundreds of thousands of Americans were homeless.

Homelessness came to the attention of the public during the 1980s. ▶

Equal Opportunities

Despite these problems the 1980s was a time of opportunity for many. Movements for equal rights had been strong in the 1960s. Now women, African Americans, and immigrants could see the results. Most of the laws that had kept them out of schools, jobs, and housing were gone. New professions and new fields were open to them.

Programs of **affirmative action** helped many groups of people get ahead. An affirmative action law known as Title IX forced public schools to provide equal opportunities for girls and boys. That meant sports teams for girls, as well as opportunities to take wood and metal shop and other classes previously open only to boys. In addition, businesses were required to make an effort to hire women, African Americans, Hispanic Americans, and others who had not had equal chances before. The Americans with Disabilities Act of 1990 protected disabled people from discrimination by private employers and required that public buildings and mass transit be accessible to all. Not everyone supported affirmative action. Its opponents claimed that it was just another form of discrimination.

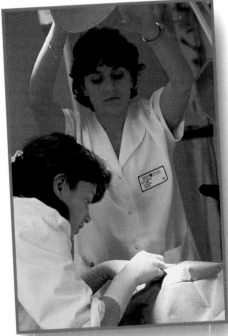

▲ Women became physicians in increasing numbers.

▲ Sandra Day O'Connor

New Roles for Women

Throughout the 1980s, women streamed into the work force. By the end of the decade, nearly 60 percent of women held jobs outside the home. They made up more than 45 percent of all American workers.

Some women worked in fields that had previously barred women. In 1976, women entered the U.S. Air Force Academy. In 1983, astronaut Sally Ride became the first American woman in space. Women pilots flew helicopters in the Gulf War. Women also took jobs on construction crews, as truck drivers, and as members of police and fire departments. With the Equal Credit Opportunity Act of 1975, women could no longer be barred from obtaining bank loans or credit simply because they were women.

Women in Politics

Many more women reached positions of leadership. In 1981, President Reagan named Sandra Day O'Connor as the first woman justice on the Supreme Court. In 1993 she was joined by Justice Ruth Bader Ginsburg. In 1984 the Democratic party nominated Geraldine Ferraro for Vice President of the United States. She was the first woman on a major party ticket. By the 1990s the number of women elected to Congress had increased greatly.

 affirmative action A policy or program for correcting the effects of discrimination

Alex Haley, with copies of many of the foreign-language editions of his bestseller, *Roots*

African Americans Make Gains

African Americans were another group that made gains. They, too, saw many old barriers fall away. Good jobs in many businesses opened up. Americans could no longer refuse to hire a qualified person because of his or her skin color. Black Americans could now attend any college and live in any neighborhood.

Black political leaders stepped forward, and by the mid-1990s they held 38 seats in Congress. Thousands more held local and state offices. Thirty cities had black mayors.

Jesse Jackson

In 1989, Douglas Wilder of Virginia became the first African American to be elected state governor. In the 1980s, black leader Jesse Jackson was able to make two runs for the presidency. General Colin Powell, the son of immigrants from Jamaica, became head of the Joint Chiefs of Staff, the nation's top military post.

The Media's Role

TV and movies began to pay more attention to African Americans. In 1977, *Roots*, a TV miniseries, captured the nation's attention. It told the story of an enslaved African, who was brought to the United States, and his descendants up through the 1900s. Writer Alex Haley based the story on his own family's history. By highlighting the struggles of African Americans, *Roots* gave pride to black communities. People of all races learned about African American history.

In the 1980s, entertainer Bill Cosby created a hit TV show featuring a successful African American family. By the 1990s a number of popular TV shows were about black American life. The casts of many other shows included black actors as well as Hispanics and Asian Americans.

Map Adventure

⭐ **KEY TERM**
downtown

THE NEW DOWNTOWN

FOCUS *Since the 1960s, Americans have turned to shopping malls to buy goods, meet friends, watch a movie, and enjoy other leisure-time activities that were once found only* **downtown**.

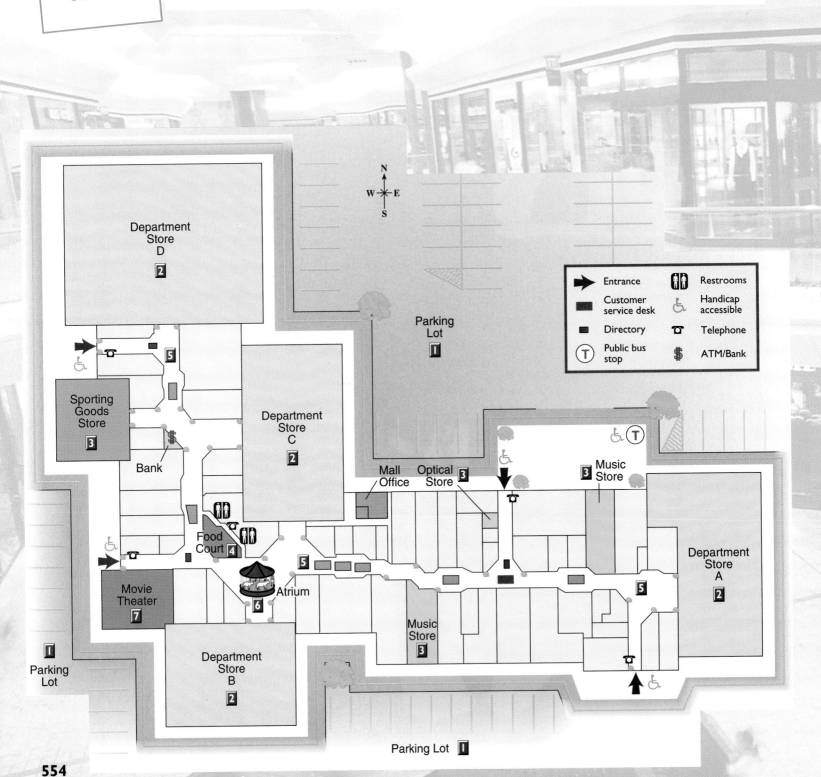

Department
Store
D
2

N
W ✦ E
S

Parking
Lot
1

	Entrance	👫	Restrooms
▬	Customer service desk	♿	Handicap accessible
■	Directory	☎	Telephone
ⓣ	Public bus stop	$	ATM/Bank

Sporting
Goods
Store
3

Bank

Department
Store
C
2

5

♿ ⓣ

Mall
Office

Optical
Store
3

☎

3 Music
Store

👫

👫

Food
Court
4

5

♿
☎

Movie
Theater
7

Atrium
6

Music
Store
3

Department
Store
A
2

5

☎ ♿

1
Parking
Lot

Department
Store
B
2

⬆ ♿

Parking Lot 1

Adventure in a Shopping Mall

People scurry through a vast parking lot toward a large building. Inside, neat rows of stores line wide halls filled with plants, trees, and benches. Pedestrians stroll down clean hallways kept cool in the summer and warm in the winter. Crowds gather in the food court for a quick meal, while others flock to the atrium to enjoy entertainment. Welcome to the new downtown.

Map Legend

1 Parking lots Huge parking lots surround the shopping mall and provide access to stores from every direction. This is different from downtown shopping, where people park behind a store or on the street in front of a store.

2 Department stores These large stores are located at the ends of the mall. They offer customers everything from designer clothing to furniture and power tools.

3 Specialty stores Once found downtown, these small stores line the corridors of the mall. They usually sell only one type of product, such as clothing, art, or pet supplies.

4 Food court The food court offers fast food and ample seating for hungry shoppers. Food courts are usually centrally located for the customer's convenience.

5 Hallways Bright, clean, and wide hallways provide access to stores and shelter from the cold and rain. In the early morning hours, many walking clubs use the corridors for year-round exercise.

6 Atrium Here shoppers are entertained by carousel rides, concerts, and demonstrations. Most atriums are centrally located near the food court.

7 Movie theater Once found only downtown, some movie theaters are now at the mall. People can eat dinner, shop, and see a movie all in one trip.

⭐ **downtown** The main business section of a town or city

MAP IT

1. You decide to see a movie at the mall. You find a parking space in the lot near Department Store A. How many other department stores are there in the mall?

2. After the movie you decide to go shopping. But you realize that you need money. In which direction will you go to find a bank? What area do you pass on the way to the bank?

3. Leaving the bank, you decide to buy a new music CD. Where is the closest music store? Describe what you will pass on the way.

4. As you search the racks for that new CD, you break your glasses. Where can you have them fixed? Which way will you walk?

EXPLORE IT

Design an ideal mall on a separate sheet of paper. Remember to include department stores, a food court, parking lots, and an atrium. Then describe what services your mall offers to its customers. Be sure to include services that you wish the mall closest to you had.

COMING TOGETHER

FOCUS *During the years 1976 to 1991, a number of events helped bring Americans together. Whether happy or sad, these events made people feel like one nation.*

THE BICENTENNIAL CELEBRATION

On July 4, 1976, America celebrated its bicentennial—the 200th anniversary of the Declaration of Independence. In cities and towns all across the country, people proudly displayed their American spirit. They decorated their homes with red, white, and blue. They marched in parades and set off dazzling fireworks.

The bicentennial was a national birthday party. Americans remembered the ideal of equality and the desire for liberty on which the country was founded.

A GOLD MEDAL FOR AMERICA!

No one expected the United States ice hockey team to do very well in the 1980 Olympics. As usual, the team was made up of college and other nonprofessional athletes. The team didn't seem to stand a chance against teams from Canada, Europe, and the Soviet Union. Soviet teams had won every hockey gold medal since 1964.

The Americans surprised everyone! They beat the Soviets, 4–3. Two days later they defeated Finland and won the gold medal.

A wave of pride swept across America. People had tears in their eyes as "The Star-Spangled Banner" was played for the winning team. They cheered wildly and waved American flags in the streets.

THE HOSTAGES COME HOME

In 1979, a revolution in Iran set up a new government. Its leaders were opposed to the United States and its way of life. On November 4, 1979, angry Iranians seized 52 Americans from the American Embassy in Teheran, Iran's capital. They were held hostage for 444 days.

In the United States, people watched television clips released by Iran and hoped for the safety of the hostages. President Jimmy Carter worked for the hostages' freedom, but it was not easy. Americans grew angry and frustrated. Many displayed yellow ribbons to show support for the hostages and their families.

At last, on January 20, 1981, the hostages were released. Americans responded with joy. They wrapped yellow ribbons around every tree and lamppost in sight, and cheered at parades held for their heroes.

July 4, 1976	February 24, 1980	January 20, 1981	January 28, 1986	February 28, 1991
U.S. celebrates its bicentennial	U.S. hockey team wins Olympic gold medal	American hostages are freed in Iran	Space shuttle *Challenger* explodes	Operation Desert Storm ends in victory

| 1975 | 1980 | 1985 | 1990 | 1995 |

THE PERSIAN GULF WAR

Americans were tense as Operation Desert Storm began on January 16, 1991. Not since Vietnam had so many American lives been at risk in a foreign war. Now our troops headed an international force determined to push Saddam Hussein out of Kuwait.

American planes pounded the Iraqi army and its supply centers. Then ground troops attacked. Within a few weeks Kuwait was free and Iraq's army was damaged. By February 28 the Gulf War was over. Americans cheered their heroic and victorious troops who marched in ticker-tape parades. Yellow ribbons reappeared, this time showing support for the war.

One of the heroes was the commanding general, Norman Schwarzkopf. Another was the country's chief military officer, Colin Powell, chairman of the Joint Chiefs of Staff.

TRAGEDY IN SPACE

On January 28, 1986, the space shuttle *Challenger* rocketed into the sky over Florida. *Challenger* and other shuttles had made many flights before.

For the first time a civilian was aboard a shuttle—Christa McAuliffe, a schoolteacher from New Hampshire. McAuliffe promised to share the excitement of space travel with America's youth.

Just 73 seconds after liftoff, disaster struck. *Challenger* exploded, killing all seven crew members. Americans watching the explosion on TV screens across the country clung to each other in sorrow and disbelief.

In September 1988, Americans sighed with relief when the space shuttle *Discovery* returned from a safe and successful mission.

SUMMING UP

❶ DO YOU REMEMBER...
COMPREHENSION

1. What economic problems affected the United States during the late 1970s?

2. What was President Reagan's plan for government?

3. What economic problems caused trouble for President Bush?

4. Why wasn't the Tiananmen Square protest for democracy in China successful?

5. What event led the U.S. into the Persian Gulf War in 1991?

6. Why did some Arab nations cut off oil shipments to the United States in 1973?

7. What two basic solutions did Americans see to the energy crisis of the 1970s?

8. What group(s) of people did not do well in the prospering economy of the 1980s?

9. What is America's "new downtown"?

10. Why did Iranians seize 52 Americans as hostages in 1979?

❷ SKILL POWER
READING A POPULATION DENSITY MAP

Population densities change over time. Go to the library and ask the librarian to help you find population density maps of your area that show change over time. Identify some changes that have occurred.

❸ WHAT DO YOU THINK?
CRITICAL THINKING

1. How was the Contract With America similar to the Reagan Revolution?

2. What are three different ways that the United States responded to conflicts and "hot spots" around the world in the 1980s and 1990s?

3. What do you think is the best solution to America's dependence on imported oil?

4. How does affirmative action help people who have been discriminated against?

5. Can you think of any similarities between the taking of American hostages in Iran and the invasion of Kuwait by Iraq?

4 SAY IT, WRITE IT, USE IT
VOCABULARY

Think about the meaning of each vocabulary word below. Then classify the words into these four groups: the economy, the environment, U.S. politics, and foreign affairs. Compare your categories with those of a partner. If you have classified some of the words differently, discuss why.

acid rain	hostage
affirmative action	national debt
Camp David Accords	Operation Desert Storm
Contra	pardon
Contract With America	pollution
deficit	Sandinista
downtown	service job
energy conservation	

6 TAKE ACTION
CITIZENSHIP

The Energy Crisis of 1973 made Americans realize how much they depended on foreign oil. Today we're in danger of forgetting that lesson since foreign oil seems plentiful again. With a group of classmates, research energy conservation and create a list called The Top Ten Oil Savers. List in order the ten best steps people can take to save oil. Show your findings on a chart, but also make copies of it as a handout for students to post in their homes.

5 GEOGRAPHY AND YOU
MAP STUDY

Use the maps on pages 545 and 548 to answer the following questions.

1. Name six countries that border on Russia.

2. What area forms part of the northern border of Russia?

3. List the OPEC member nations in 1973.

4. What percentage of world oil did Saudi Arabia and Iran produce in 1973?

7 GET CREATIVE
LANGUAGE ARTS CONNECTION

By the 1990s, a number of popular TV shows in America featured African American, Hispanic, and Asian casts. Think of an idea for an original TV sitcom that captures the American scene as you know and live it. With a group of classmates, write a short script that features some typical Americans of your community dealing with everyday situations in a humorous way. Practice and present your script to the whole class.

LOOKING AHEAD In the next chapter, find out how the United States has built on its past to enter the next century.

CHAPTER 24

LOOKING BACK,

The history of the United States has many recurring themes, some of which you will read about in this chapter. Find out how they have affected our nation's past and present and will probably affect our future.

▼ What has greatly affected the way you record information? Look on page 569 to find out.

CONTENTS

LOOKING AHEAD

These books tell about issues and concerns that are similar to those that many Americans have faced throughout history. Read one that interests you and fill out a book-review form.

READ AND RESEARCH

Celebrate America in Poetry and Art **edited by Nora Panzer** (Hyperion Books for Children, 1994)
Culture and traditions have shaped people's different feelings about America. In this collection, writers and artists use their pens and brushes to express their own ideas about our nation. *(poetry)*
•*You can read a selection from this book on page 580.*

I'm New Here **by Bud Howlett** (Houghton Mifflin Co., 1993)
Jazmin Escalante has just emigrated from El Salvador. She is about to begin school in America, and she only speaks Spanish. How do you think she will feel on her first day? Read to find out what happens to Jazmin at school. *(biography)*

My Fellow Americans: A Family Album **by Alice Provensen** (Harcourt Brace & Co., 1995)
The author grew up learning to love America and the people who make up its history. Using her talents as an artist and a writer, she shares her remembrances of these famous Americans. *(nonfiction)*

L5: Behind the Moon **by Steve Tracy** (Silver Burdett Press, 1995)
The year is 2060, and Amelia is headed for Space Station Colony L5, where she will be reunited with her dad. What seems to be worrying him all the time? *(science fiction)*

SKILL POWER — Drawing Conclusions

Knowing how to draw conclusions can help you understand the events, characters, and reasons things happen in history.

UNDERSTAND IT

Did you ever walk into a situation and see two people ignoring each other? If you know that the two people have been friends for years, you might draw the conclusion that they had had a disagreement. You took what you saw, combined it with what you already knew, and drew a conclusion.

When you read something, you also must draw conclusions. Writers cannot supply every bit of information. They must depend on the reader to fill in some of the missing pieces.

EXPLORE IT

First, read what the writer has written. This is called the *selection information*. Next, add facts and ideas that you already know. This is called *known information*. Then add the two kinds of information together and draw a *conclusion*.

selection information
+
known information
=
conclusion

Read the following selection. Use a diagram like the one above to reach a conclusion.

The 363-mile Erie Canal connected Albany to Buffalo, New York. Locks opened or closed to change the water level for boats. Mules walked beside the canal and pulled boats between the locks. The mules' top speed was four miles an hour. So the entire trip took about one week. When the canal was first built, it cut travel time to less than half of what it had been.
But by the early 1900s, traffic decreased due to the increased use of railroads. Today, the Erie Canal is used mostly for recreation and flood control.

Selection Information

The trip took about a week. Freight traffic decreased.

+

Known Information

Trucks, trains, and planes can go faster than mules and boats.

=

Conclusion

A canal is not as useful when faster transportation is available.

TRY IT

Work with a partner. Find a paragraph you have read in this book or in another nonfiction book that requires you to add known information to draw a conclusion.

Then make a diagram of the paragraph you choose. Don't forget to include selection information, known information, and your conclusion.

SKILL POWER SEARCH *While reading this chapter, diagram one paragraph that requires you to draw a conclusion.*

SETTLEMENT PATTERNS

FOCUS *The United States is a vast nation. Throughout its history, people have moved and settled in different areas. The patterns of that settlement have changed over time.*

The Earliest Americans

Americans have always been on the move. Thousands of years ago the first Americans migrated across the Bering Strait from Asia. These Native Americans were hunters who wandered across the land bridge in search of food.

Over time, Native Americans fanned out across the vast American continent. Some of them migrated farther south. Eventually, Native Americans inhabited areas of both North and South America. Some wanderers settled down and began to farm. Thanks to a stable food supply, they now had more time to devote to other skills. They could spend more time weaving materials, making pottery, and creating works of art. Some Native Americans, such as the Maya, the Incas, and the Aztecs, built impressive cities, with large buildings.

Europeans Arrive

Native Americans had North and South America all to themselves until a little over 500 years ago. Then European explorers and settlers began to arrive. At first, most of these Europeans were Spaniards looking for gold and converts to Christianity. Spaniards settled in the Caribbean, Mexico,

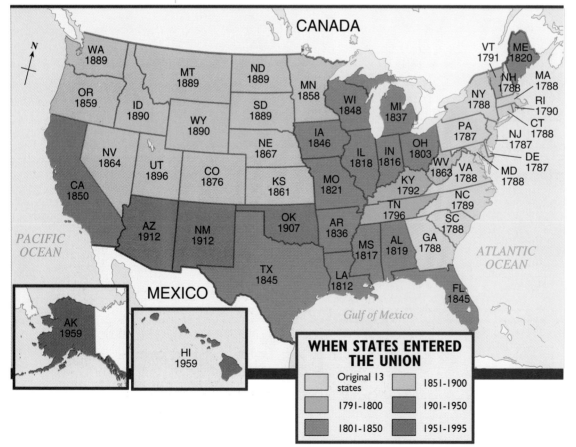

WHEN STATES ENTERED THE UNION

Original 13 states	1851-1900
1791-1800	1901-1950
1801-1850	1951-1995

Central America, and South America.

Later, other Europeans from France, the Netherlands, Sweden, and elsewhere also came. However, it was the English who sank the deepest roots in North America. They came here to stay, building stable settlements along the Atlantic coast.

The Westward Movement

A powerful thirst for land drove many American settlers west. They moved away from coastal settlements to search for better farmland. They found it in places such as the valleys of the Ohio River, the Mississippi River, and the South.

The notion of what was "the West" changed with time. In colonial days it was that vast unexplored region beyond the next hill. By the late 1700s and early 1800s, it meant any place on the other side of the Appalachian Mountains. By the mid-1800s "the West" meant Oregon and California. Settlers pushed westward in wagon trains to Oregon to start new lives in the fertile Willamette Valley. In 1849, gold prospectors rushed to California to seek their fortune.

Americans then began to fill in the middle of the United States. The Homestead Act of 1862 led to a dramatic increase in this westward movement. Farmers and ranchers moved on to the Great Plains and turned the Great American Desert into the Great American Breadbasket.

From the beginning, Native Americans were affected by the arrival of Europeans. Slowly, they were pushed off their ancestral homelands, and many died in wars with the Europeans or of European diseases.

As settlers continued to move farther west, Native Americans were forced to give up their way of life and more and more of their land. The

Before Americans moved westward, they sent explorers, such as Lewis and Clark.

The horse, brought to America by Europeans, dramatically affected the settlement patterns of the Native Americans.

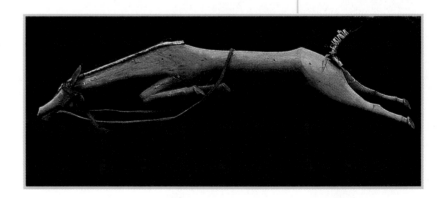

removal of the Cherokees in the Trail of Tears is only one example of this forced migration. The steady **displacement** of Native American peoples continued until the end of the 1800s.

The Growth of Cities

Not all Americans were farmers moving west for more land. In colonial days many Americans stayed in coastal cities to work in such industries as fishing, shipping, and banking and at various trades.

Then, in the early 1800s the Industrial Revolution brought about more changes in settlement patterns. Old cities grew bigger. New cities were born. The growth of industry drew more people to cities. Among them were many rural people who moved to the cities to find better-paying jobs.

At this time many southern and eastern Europeans, seeking economic opportunity and personal freedom, immigrated to the United States. This growing tide of immigration continued into the twentieth century. Immigrants, too, helped cities to grow.

The attraction of jobs in the city also triggered the Great Migration. This movement of African Americans from the South to northern cities lasted from 1910–1930. It changed the face and culture of many northern cities. Also, many Mexicans and people from the Caribbean and from Latin America moved into the cities.

Cities and Suburbs

Cities offered many advantages, but they were also plagued with pollution, congestion, and high prices for property. Over time people began to move into the suburbs so that they could enjoy the city and still be able to own their own homes.

As the combined population of the city and its suburbs grew enormously, a new type of city developed—the **megalopolis**. The map on the next page shows the different megalopolis areas in the United States today.

Migration Today and Tomorrow

In the most recent past, American settlement patterns have changed once again. Older Americans, seeking clear skies and warm weather, are moving to Florida and the Sunbelt of Arizona and New Mexico. With the end of legal

▼ Today, many people live in the suburbs and commute into cities to work.

---

discrimination and the increase in industrialization of the South, many African Americans are moving to what people now call the New South.

Settlement patterns have also changed as a result of technology. In the future, technology may soon enable many people to live wherever they want. More and more people will be able to work out of their own homes. An "office" may become any place where there is a computer and a fax machine.

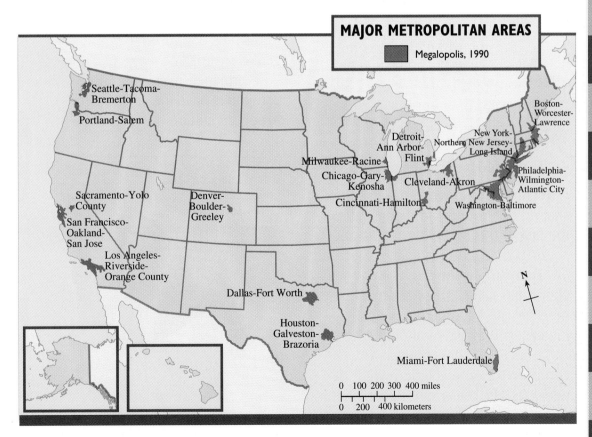

The airplane has made our society even more mobile.

People may even live and work in space colonies or in colonies under the ocean. As long as there is some place interesting to go, it's a safe bet that Americans will be there.

MAJOR METROPOLITAN AREAS

Megalopolis, 1990

Seattle-Tacoma-Bremerton
Portland-Salem
Sacramento-Yolo County
San Francisco-Oakland-San Jose
Los Angeles-Riverside-Orange County
Denver-Boulder-Greeley
Dallas-Fort Worth
Houston-Galveston-Brazoria
Milwaukee-Racine
Chicago-Gary-Kenosha
Cincinnati-Hamilton
Detroit-Ann Arbor-Flint
Cleveland-Akron
New York-Northern New Jersey-Long Island
Boston-Worcester-Lawrence
Philadelphia-Wilmington-Atlantic City
Washington-Baltimore
Miami-Fort Lauderdale

0 100 200 300 400 miles
0   200   400 kilometers

N

SHOW WHAT YOU KNOW!

REFOCUS
COMPREHENSION

1. What were some of the reasons that settlers moved westward?

2. How did settlement patterns change after the growth of cities?

THINK ABOUT IT
CRITICAL THINKING

In what ways might settlement patterns change if more people start to work out of their homes?

WRITE ABOUT IT
ACTIVITY

Review the skill on pages 562–563. Then choose a paragraph in this lesson. List the selection information, known information, and your conclusion.

TECHNOLOGY AND INNOVATION

FOCUS *Americans have a long history of solving problems creatively, from the revolutionary ideas that our founders had about government to the many American inventions. All of these innovations have changed the way people live.*

A History of Innovation

Americans have always been willing to look at old problems in new ways. Creative problem solving has played a central role in the nation's history.

One of the most impressive American **innovations** is the United States government. The framers of the Constitution demonstrated great insight when writing this document. They took a bold step by not having a monarch. And they were the first modern people to create a democratic government.

Technology Shapes a Country

Technological inventions also have shaped this country in many ways. In the late 1700s and early 1800s, the country changed drastically as a result of American inventions. Eli Whitney's cotton gin and Cyrus McCormick's mechanical reaper led to huge increases in agricultural output.

Samuel F. B. Morse began a communication revolution when he perfected the telegraph. Robert Fulton introduced the steamboat, turning rivers into two-way water highways. Other Americans designed canals and constructed railroads.

The late 1800s saw even more spectacular advances. From Thomas Edison's incandescent light bulb to Alexander Graham Bell's telephone, new technology continued to shape people's lives.

This trend has continued throughout the 1900s. In the past hundred years, Americans have used their creative genius in amazing ways. Just think of how airplanes, televisions, and computers have forever changed American culture.

▲ Today, CDs provide music for entertainment.

Before television the radio was a major source of entertainment and news. ▶

⭐ *innovation* A newly introduced product, idea, or custom

Adapting to New Situations

Americans have been known to adapt, or change, existing technology to new situations. When early settlers came to North America, they faced a host of unfamiliar conditions. So they adapted many survival techniques used by Native Americans. These enabled them not only to survive but eventually to thrive on the rugged new land.

Early colonists also learned from Africans. Many southern landowners benefited from the farming techniques used by their slaves. By adopting African methods, southern farmers increased their productivity.

Other examples of American ingenuity can be seen in everything from national parks to fast-food restaurants. Over the years, American jazz musicians and rock 'n' roll stars have drawn new sounds from traditional instruments. And using little more than a ball, a glove, and a piece of wood, Americans created the game of baseball.

Sometimes American innovations have brought new challenges. For example, mass production meant more products at lower costs, but it also meant the loss of jobs for many **artisans** and other skilled laborers.

The game of baseball is an American innovation.

Future Innovations

Technology has affected people's lifestyles in many ways. Today, many people spend less time cooking by using microwave ovens. People can do their banking during nonbusiness hours by going to an automated teller machine (ATM). And people are able to gather information by using computers, without seeing books or other people.

More advances are just around the corner. It was only about 30 years ago that the first American set foot on the moon. Today, space travel by astronauts is much more common, and even a few civilians have traveled in space. How will future inventions change space travel? How will that affect American culture? In the future, Americans will continue to adapt as they have throughout history.

Today, people use computers to research and record information.

---

artisan A worker in a skilled trade

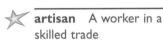

SHOW WHAT YOU KNOW!

REFOCUS
COMPREHENSION

1. What makes the Constitution one of the nation's greatest innovations?

2. What were some technological innovations of the 1700s and 1800s?

THINK ABOUT IT
CRITICAL THINKING

In the future, space travel will likely be much more common. What challenges might this bring?

WRITE ABOUT IT
ACTIVITY

Think of a recent invention or think of something that you would like to see invented. Write about how the invention has changed or will change your way of life.

Theme

REVOLUTION AND CHANGE

FOCUS *Revolution and change have been a continuous theme in American history. Change has occurred in many ways and for many reasons.*

A Nation of Revolution

The history of the United States is full of revolutions. They take different forms. Revolutions can be political, recreating the form of government, its powers, and the way people participate in that government. Revolutions can be technological, transforming the nature of people's jobs and society itself. And they can be social, altering the way people relate to their fellow citizens.

Sometimes revolutions are drastic and sudden, such as the American Revolution.

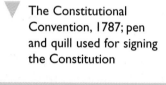

The Constitutional Convention, 1787; pen and quill used for signing the Constitution

Other revolutions take place over a long period of time, slowly rearranging things. One example of this is the revolution in communications, which began with the telegraph and continues today with the cordless telephone and the computer modem.

Tobacco Changes the South

It may not have seemed like a revolution when John Rolfe discovered that tobacco grown in Virginia could be a cash crop. Tobacco would forever change the course of the colony of Virginia and the other Southern Colonies.

To begin with, the economies of Virginia and the other Southern Colonies blossomed as tobacco sales increased. Tobacco also brought about other changes. The colonists needed workers, so they brought enslaved Africans to the country. The colonists also wanted much more land, so they forced Native Americans to move west. Truly, John Rolfe's discovery drastically changed the lives of many people from all over the world.

Detail, *Washington Addressing the Constitutional Convention*, J.B. Stearns
The Virginia Museum of Fine Arts

The American Revolution

The American Revolution was a major historical event around the world. Americans became the first modern colonists to successfully break away from their colonial rulers. They fought for their freedom and won it. And the American rebels inspired other people, such as the French, to fight for their rights.

The American Revolution began in 1775 and brought many changes in a short period of time. Yet the scene was set long before the first shot was fired. Colonists had begun to think of themselves as more "American" than English or European. It was the small changes in ideas that led to the larger political revolution.

The actual fighting was only part of the American Revolution. Another part was the writing of the Constitution. The Constitution, with its Bill of Rights, established American freedoms. And the Constitution determined the form of the national government and how much power it would have.

Of course, the political system didn't stop changing after the Constitution was written. In fact, the Constitution actually encouraged adaptations by providing a way for amendments to be added. Including the Bill of Rights, 27 amendments have been added to the Constitution.

Industrial Revolution

Another great revolution in the history of the United States was the Industrial Revolution, which began at the end of the 1700s and continues today. This technological revolution changed the nature of work. It also changed society by creating wealth that was undreamed of by earlier generations. Today, an average American has a lifestyle that is drastically different from the American lifestyle of 100 years ago.

The Industrial Revolution led to the growth of cities. The promise of jobs in the city drew millions of workers from the nation's farms and from Europe. In cities the population density is much greater than it is in rural areas. So people adapted to this change in living conditions, and society was altered.

People's work habits have also changed. In the past, on farms, the demands of the changing seasons set work schedules. Today, work schedules are determined by many factors.

Revolutions in industry continue to change the way that goods are produced.

The Machine Age

Later, during the Machine Age, technological advances made other types of changes possible. For example, refrigerated railroad cars enabled food markets to become national. A person in Iowa could now buy oranges from Florida.

At the same time, trolley cars and subways enabled people to live farther away from their jobs and from stores. Today, the nation continues to adapt to new inventions and the technological revolutions they cause.

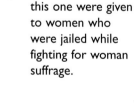

In 1917, pins like this one were given to women who were jailed while fighting for woman suffrage.

Women's Rights

Americans have also undergone several social revolutions. Many groups of people are treated differently from the way they were treated when the country was founded.

Women, for example, now have equal rights with men. They can vote, hold political office, and work as doctors and lawyers. None of these

National Percentage of Graduates by Area of Study

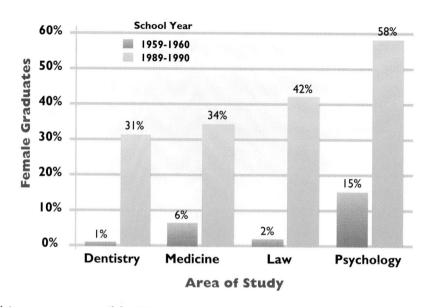

things were possible 200 years ago. This revolution continues to change the country even today. The chart above shows the increase in women graduates in dentistry, medicine, law, and psychology by 1990.

Civil Rights for Black Americans

The social revolution has been even greater for black Americans. For hundreds of years many black Americans were enslaved. It took a civil war to end their slavery. Black Americans have won the right to vote, hold political office, and work in every kind of job.

While complete social equality has not been achieved, the gains

▼ Douglas Wilder, the nation's first elected black governor

As more women work outside the home, day-care centers have become important.

have been enormous. By the late 1900s, black Americans held many positions of power. These range from corporate executive to army general to United States senator. It took a long time, but the changes in race relations since the Civil War have been truly revolutionary.

Changing Roles for Children

Children's social roles have also changed. Children are no longer viewed as miniature adults. They are no longer forced to work in dirty, unhealthy factories. And their future is no longer determined solely by the financial status of their parents. Today, hundreds of laws protect the well-being of American children.

Change and revolution have always been part of American life. And they always will be. Americans are still trying to fulfill the great promise of the American Revolution. When the fighting stopped, Dr. Benjamin Rush, a signer of the Declaration of Independence, put it this way: "The American war is over, but this is far from being the case with the American Revolution. Nothing but the first act of the drama is closed."

Today, Americans from all backgrounds can go to school together.

SHOW WHAT YOU KNOW!

REFOCUS
COMPREHENSION

1. Describe some different kinds of revolutions that are part of United States history.

2. How did the Machine Age change American culture?

THINK ABOUT IT
CRITICAL THINKING

Do you think that Dr. Benjamin Rush's words could describe the United States today? Explain your answer.

WRITE ABOUT IT
ACTIVITY

Write a journal entry explaining how different life is for children today than it was in the past.

RIGHTS AND RESPONSIBILITIES

FOCUS *All American citizens are guaranteed certain rights. But with rights come responsibilities. Throughout the history of the United States, many Americans have lived up to the challenge of balancing rights and responsibilities.*

Gaining Equality

While writing the Declaration of Independence in 1776, Thomas Jefferson included the phrase "all men are created equal." Yet the United States did not actually practice this ideal for many years. In 1776 only white men who owned property were considered "equal" and could vote. In addition, many people at that time were enslaved and treated like property.

Still, people used Jefferson's phrase from the Declaration of Independence to defend their right to change the situation. Slowly, other people won the right to vote. First, non-property-owning white men were given the right to vote.

Then, in 1870, the Fifteenth Amendment allowed black men to vote. However, in some parts of the country, black men wouldn't be able to exercise this legal right for many years. After the amendment was passed, it still took almost 100 years before many black citizens could vote in the South.

Women also couldn't vote for a long time. In 1920 the Nineteenth Amendment granted women the right to vote.

And in 1924, Native Americans, the first immigrants, were granted full citizenship and voting rights. Finally, in 1971, all legal adult citizens could vote. In that year the Twenty-sixth Amendment lowered the voting age from 21 to 18. It had taken a long time, but Jefferson's ideal had at last become a legal reality.

Voting—How and Why

Throughout the history of the United States, Americans have voted in a number of ways. Early on, people voted on paper ballots, which they placed in a box. Someone then counted the votes by hand. Later, voting machines were used. Today, people often vote on computerized voting machines, which tally the votes.

While the methods of voting have changed, the importance of voting

▼ Oseola McCarty, a retired washerwoman, donates money for scholarships for black college students.

▲ This ballot box was used in the late 1800s.

has not. Good citizens know that they must vote responsibly. That means more than simply marking an X on a piece of paper. In order to vote responsibly, the voter must take time to study the issues and the candidates.

Being Responsible Citizens

Citizenship brings other responsibilities as well. People should obey the laws. If Americans believe a law is wrong, they can work to change it. Throughout the country's history, American citizens have often exercised this responsibility. The civil rights movement is one example of how citizens worked to change laws.

Another example is the movement for the Equal Rights Amendment. People were working to change the Constitution. And while the amendment itself was not passed, the people who worked in this movement did change many other laws regarding equality for women.

Another responsibility of citizenship is to help others in the community. During the history of the United States, **community action** has taken many forms, including victory gardens, protests, and volunteering for VISTA. Today, even schoolchildren find ways to help others. They might tutor a younger child or volunteer to serve meals to homeless people.

One responsibility has not always been so obvious to Americans—caring for the environment. For many years, Americans assumed that the country's natural resources were limitless.

People hunted the American buffaloes until the animals almost were extinct. But then some other

Doing volunteer work in a hospital is a form of community service.

⭐ **community action** The act of supporting the needs of the neighborhood, state, or nation

Demonstrating for the Equal Rights Amendment

people stepped in and protected the buffaloes. The same can be said for other animal species and for wilderness areas. Today, many Americans understand the need to take care of the environment.

Balancing Freedoms

Americans have always taken great pride in the freedom they have. But no freedom is absolute. Every American must balance his or her rights against the rights of others. For example, one person's freedom of speech cannot be used as a way of denying another person's freedom. Americans should protect the privacy of individuals. And they should show respect for both private and public property. Throughout the nation's history, American citizens have sought to protect their freedoms and rights. But they have also recognized that freedom has limits.

This points out an essential element in any democracy—the need to compromise. No one can always have his or her own way. In a democracy, people must listen to other points of view. The candidate who receives the most votes in an election wins. The same is true when an issue is voted on. In a democracy, though, the rights of the minority should be respected by the majority.

American history is full of compromises, such as the compromise regarding representation in Congress. The small states benefit from the representation by state in the Senate. The large states benefit from the representation by population in the House of Representatives. Today most bills that Congress passes are as a result of compromise.

The United States will face new problems in the future. People will still need to compromise. They must always respect the freedoms and rights of each other and take their own responsibilities as citizens seriously.

Recycling is another way of being a responsible citizen.

SHOW WHAT YOU KNOW!

REFOCUS
COMPREHENSION

1. Trace the history of the expansion of voting rights in the United States.

2. Why is compromise an essential element of democracy?

THINK ABOUT IT
CRITICAL THINKING

Why do you think people believed that the nation's natural resources were limitless?

WRITE ABOUT IT
ACTIVITY

What types of community service interest you? Write a plan describing how you will become active in your community.

5

Theme

KEY TERMS
descendant
emigrate

LITERATURE
Celebrate America
in Poetry and Art

DIVERSITY AND UNITY

FOCUS *America is a nation of great diversity. Although this diversity sometimes leads to conflict, it has also offered great benefits to all Americans.*

American music has been influenced by many cultures. Shown below, left to right, a South American charango, a European saxophone, a Native American drum

A Land of Many People

Every American is an immigrant or a **descendant** of immigrants. As you have read, by crossing the land bridge from Asia in search of food, Native Americans became America's first immigrants.

Thousands of years later, other immigrants arrived on America's shores. Spanish settlers sailed to America, looking for gold. Other Europeans came with dreams of a better life. Sometimes the settlers were also fleeing from religious or political persecution. Other immigrants were driven by a desire to own land. Most of America's early immigrants came from England, but many came from the Netherlands, Germany, France, and other countries.

Beginning in 1619, colonists also brought Africans to America. These Africans were brought here against their will. Although they came here under the most dismal conditions, these Africans adapted to their new surroundings and contributed to the building of a nation.

From the very beginning, all of America's people influenced each other, blending their cultures. Eventually, an American culture was born. Throughout the history of the United States, as different immigrants came, the American culture continued to change and develop.

Immigration Continues

The 1800s saw the arrival of more new people. People **emigrated** from Ireland, Germany, Switzerland, Norway, and China. Near the end of that century, immigrants from Poland, Greece, and Italy filled ships and sailed to the United States. Most of these immigrants hoped to find new economic opportunities. And sometimes they also hoped to escape poor treatment in their homelands.

descendant   A person descending, or coming from, a certain ancestor
emigrate   To leave one's country

577

Immigrants on the wharf in Boston, 1880s

The banjo is based on an instrument that was played in Africa.

Immigration continued in the 1900s. And recently, other immigrants have come. Mexicans have come in search of jobs. Koreans, Cambodians, and Vietnamese have come as war refugees. Others, such as Cubans and Hungarians, have been attracted by the political freedom that America offers. Like most earlier immigrants, these people have shared the hope of a better life in America.

Differences Lead to Conflict

Life is sometimes difficult for America's newcomers. Often they don't know the language, and the culture is very different. But more than these problems, immigrants often have to deal with the tension and conflict that come from bringing different groups of people together.

America's first immigrants—Native Americans—sometimes fought with each other. Then, when European settlers moved in, conflicts over land arose between Native Americans and Europeans. European settlers wanted to own the land that Native Americans were living on. For many years these groups fought. Unfortunately, many Native American nations were destroyed by these wars.

For hundreds of years, there were conflicts between white Americans and black Americans. Many of the disputes continued until black people were finally granted rights as full citizens.

Other immigrant groups also had trouble. In the mid-1800s, Chinese immigrants faced terrible discrimination and isolation. So did the Irish and, later, the eastern Europeans. In the early 1900s, anti-immigrant feelings ran particularly high. And laws were passed limiting immigration to America.

In part, hostility toward immigrants often came from economic fears. Sometimes Americans have been afraid that the newcomers would steal their jobs.

Sometimes the anger has come from a lack of

understanding. Different groups have brought different languages, clothing, traditions, and values to America. People are often afraid of what they do not understand. And this fear can lead to hostility.

The Benefits of Diversity

And yet it is the differences between people that has shaped America. The country benefits greatly from the rich variety of ideas, skills, insights, and customs that immigrants have brought with them. Contributions are seen in all areas of life, including food, clothing, sports, art, farming, and medicine. To appreciate these contributions, consider an America without pizza, blue jeans, or soccer. These aspects of our culture all came from immigrants.

Diversity also teaches Americans that there is more than one way of looking at the world.

The Statue of Liberty and the flag are both symbols of America.

People can find happiness in the countryside, the city, or the suburbs. People can worship in churches, temples, meetinghouses, or mosques. Being diverse reminds Americans that each culture has its own special qualities.

A Unique American Culture

The United States has a distinct culture, which has been created over time with the influence of all Americans. Despite the various backgrounds, Americans are unified by many common experiences. Americans watch the same television shows, sports events, and movies. They listen to the same music and are led by the same leaders.

Exposure to common experiences helps soften the ethnic, racial, and religious differences between Americans. And it helps unite Americans of all backgrounds. In addition to cultural ties, they also share certain ideals. Americans are committed to the principles on which the nation was founded.

Celebrate America in Poetry and Art

edited by Nora Panzer

This book has a collection of poems, drawings, paintings, and other pieces of art that celebrate what makes America unique. Each piece tells about a different part of America's history or a different idea about the people, government, or ideas of America. The following two pieces are examples from this collection.

We are not afraid to entrust the American people with unpleasant facts, foreign ideas, alien philosophies, and competitive values. For a nation that is afraid to let its people judge the truth and falsehood in an open market is a nation that is afraid of its people.

—John F. Kennedy

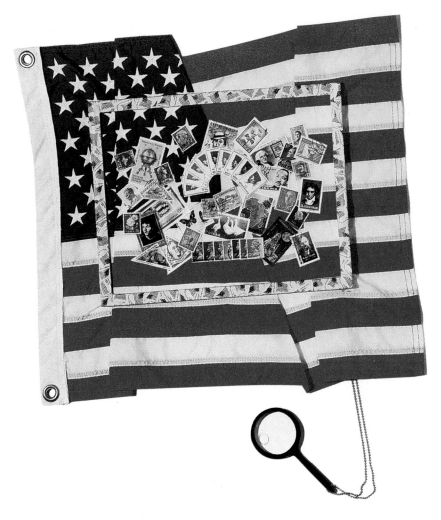

"We Are Not Afraid. . . ."

by Kenneth Josephson

Want to look at other people's ideas about America? You can see more pieces of art and read more poems by checking the book out of your school or public library.

REFOCUS
COMPREHENSION

1. What are some of the reasons that people have immigrated to the United States?

2. Why did conflicts arise between different groups?

THINK ABOUT IT
CRITICAL THINKING

What are some factors and experiences that help unite Americans?

WRITE ABOUT IT
ACTIVITY

Write a poem or create a drawing that illustrates how having a diverse society has contributed to American life.

SUMMING UP

582

1 DO YOU REMEMBER . . .
COMPREHENSION

1. How did the notion of the West change throughout the history of the United States?

2. List an example of a political revolution, a technological revolution, and a social revolution.

3. Why did people leave cities and move to suburbs?

4. What inventions of the late 1700s and early 1800s led to huge increases in agricultural output in the United States?

5. List a positive result and a negative result of mass production.

6. What are some social revolutions that have impacted American society?

7. When did black men first get the vote? When did women and Native Americans get the vote?

8. Why do all our freedoms as American citizens have limits?

9. What are some reasons that people immigrated to the United States?

10. What are some experiences that unify Americans of all backgrounds?

2 SKILL POWER
DRAWING CONCLUSIONS

Select an article from your local newspaper that requires you to draw conclusions. Make a diagram showing the steps you took to draw those conclusions.

3 WHAT DO YOU THINK?
CRITICAL THINKING

1. Give examples from history to show how Americans are always on the move.

2. What special problems or challenges might result from the widespread use of computers in our society?

3. What changes or new laws might be needed to further improve the lives of American children?

4. Although voting is a responsibility of citizenship, too few eligible voters go to the polls. What do you think can be done to change this?

5. In what ways do you think the growth of the megalopolis changed American culture?

4 SAY IT, WRITE IT, USE IT
VOCABULARY

Suppose an immigrant who arrived in the United States today could speak with an immigrant who came hundreds of years ago. Write what they might say to each other about their experiences. Use as many of the vocabulary terms as you can.

artisan	emigrate
community action	innovation
descendant	megalopolis
displacement	social revolution

582

5 GEOGRAPHY AND YOU
MAP STUDY

Use the maps on pages 564 and 567 to answer the following questions.

1. In what 50-year period did the most states join the Union?

2. What were the last two territories to become states before Alaska and Hawaii?

3. List the megalopolis areas in California and Texas.

4. What cities are part of the megalopolis area around Boston?

6 TAKE ACTION
CITIZENSHIP

Obeying laws, caring for the environment, community service—citizenship brings many responsibilities with it. Make a list of the top seven responsibilities of citizenship in your opinion. For each responsibility, list ways in which fifth graders can fulfill it. You may want to take photographs of people meeting some of these responsibilities and use the photos in a photo essay.

Citizenship Responsibilities	
Responsibility	Ways to fulfill
1.	
2.	
3.	
4.	

DUTCH FAMILY, ELLIS ISLAND   5 202-1

7 GET CREATIVE
MATH CONNECTION

Over the last 150 years, immigrants have come to our country in successive waves. Make a line graph that charts the flow of newcomers to our shores over a certain period of years. Or, if you prefer, create circle graphs that show the major countries of origin for immigrants in 1890 and 1990. You can use encyclopedias, almanacs, and other reference books to find the data for your graphs.

EXPLORE

REFERENCE

CONTENTS

Atlas

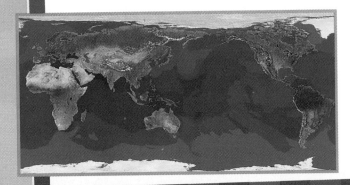

SECTION

RESEARCH AND REFERENCE

While studying the history of our United States, you can use these books to locate where an event took place, to learn more about the people and places involved, and to discover the role that each of our Presidents played in the growth of our country.

The Kingfisher Young People's Encyclopedia of the United States edited by William E. Shapiro
(Kingfisher, 1994)
Colorful illustrations and photographs will help you get to know the people, places, and events that contribute to the uniqueness of the United States.

Encyclopedia of the Presidents and Their Times by David Rubel (Scholastic, 1994)
Fun-filled facts and illustrations will introduce you to America's 42 Presidents of the past and present. Find out where they were born, their nicknames, and what they have done to help our country.

The Reader's Digest Children's World Atlas edited by Nicola Barber and Nicholas Harris
(The Reader's Digest Association, 1995)
Maps, photographs, and illustrations will enrich your study of our country's history. You will realize how important the United States is to the rest of the world.

ATLAS

ARCTIC OCEAN

Arctic Circle

Alaska (U.S.)

ALEUTIAN IS. (U.S.)

CANADA

NORTH

AMERICA

UNITED STATES

See inset below

Greenland
(Den.)

Bermuda (U.K.)

AZORES
(Port.)

ATLANTIC OCEAN

Midway I. (U.S.)

Tropic of Cancer

HAWAII (U.S.)

MEXICO

Caribbean Sea

CAPE VERDE

VENEZUELA
COLOMBIA

GUYANA
SURINAME
French Guiana
(Fr.)

GALÁPAGOS IS.
(Ecuador)

ECUADOR

SOUTH

AMERICA
BRAZIL

0° Equator

PERU

PACIFIC OCEAN

WESTERN
SAMOA

AMERICAN
SAMOA (U.S.)

FRENCH POLYNESIA
(Fr.)

BOLIVIA

TONGA

20°S

Pitcairn I. (U.K.)

Tropic of Capricorn

PARAGUAY

COOK IS. (N.Z.)

Easter I.
(Chile)

CHILE

URUGUAY

N
W   E
S

ARGENTINA

International Date Line

40°S

FALKLAND IS.
(U.K.)

60°S

Antarctic Circle

80°S

80°N 160°W 140°W 120°W 100°W 80°W 60°W 40°W
60°N
40°N
20°N

**WEST INDIES AND
CENTRAL AMERICA**

0   150   300 miles
0   150   300 kilometers

UNITED STATES

30°N

N
W   E
S

Gulf of Mexico

ATLANTIC OCEAN

25°N
Tropic of Cancer

BAHAMAS

CUBA

TURKS AND
CAICOS IS. (U.K.)

BR. VIRGIN IS.
(U.K.)

ANTIGUA
AND BARBUDA

20°N

MEXICO

CAYMAN
ISLANDS
(U.K.)

GREATER ANTILLES

Hispaniola

HAITI

DOMINICAN
REPUBLIC

Puerto Rico
(U.S.)

Guadeloupe (Fr.)

BELIZE

JAMAICA

VIRGIN ISLANDS (U.S.)

ST. KITTS AND NEVIS

DOMINICA

Martinique (Fr.)

GUATEMALA

15°N

Caribbean Sea

ST. LUCIA

HONDURAS

NETH. ANTILLES (Neth.)

ST. VINCENT AND
THE GRENADINES

BARBADOS

EL SALVADOR

NICARAGUA

ARUBA

GRENADA

LESSER ANTILLES

COSTA
RICA

10°N

TRINIDAD
AND
TOBAGO

PANAMA

COLOMBIA

VENEZUELA

90°W 85°W 80°W 75°W 70°W 65°W 60°W

586

North Pole

SVALBARD
(Nor.)

See inset below

ICELAND

EUROPE

RUSSIA

ASIA

KAZAKSTAN

MONGOLIA

GEORGIA
ARMENIA
TURKEY
MALTA CYPRUS
SYRIA
AZERBAIJAN
TUNISIA
LEBANON
ISRAEL
West Bank
and Gaza Strip
MOROCCO
ALGERIA
LIBYA
EGYPT

KYRGYZSTAN

TAJIKISTAN

CHINA

N. KOREA
S. KOREA   JAPAN

IRAQ
JORDAN
KUWAIT
QATAR
BAHRAIN
SAUDI
ARABIA
U.A.E.

IRAN

AFGHANISTAN

PAKISTAN

NEPAL

BHUTAN

TAIWAN

PACIFIC OCEAN

Western
Sahara
(Mor.)

INDIA

MYANMAR
(BURMA)

Hong Kong
Macao (Port.)

NORTHERN
MARIANA IS. (U.S.)   Wake I. (U.S.)

AFRICA

MAURITANIA
SENEGAL   MALI
GAMBIA
GUINEA-BISSAU   BURKINA
GUINEA   FASO
SIERRA
LEONE
LIBERIA
EQUATORIAL
GUINEA
SAÕ TOMÉ
AND PRÍNCIPE

NIGER

CHAD

ERITREA

YEMEN   OMAN

DJIBOUTI

BANGLA-
DESH

THAILAND

LAOS

VIETNAM

Guam
(U.S.)

MARSHALL IS.

NIGERIA

CÔTE
D'IVOIRE
GHANA
TOGO
BENIN
CAMEROON
GABON

SUDAN

ETHIOPIA

CENTRAL
AFRICAN
REP.

UGANDA

SRI
LANKA

MALDIVES

CAMBODIA
BRUNEI
MALAYSIA

PALAU

FEDERATED STATES
OF MICRONESIA

NAURU

Cabinda
(Angola)

ZAIRE
RWANDA
BURUNDI

KENYA

SINGAPORE

SEYCHELLES

INDONESIA

PAPUA
NEW GUINEA

KIRIBATI

TUVALU

SOLOMON IS.

ANGOLA   MALAWI
ZAMBIA
ZIMBABWE

TANZANIA

COMOROS

Réunion (Fr.)

VANUATU

FIJI

NAMIBIA
BOTSWANA

MADAGASCAR

MAURITIUS

New Caledonia (Fr.)

INDIAN OCEAN

AUSTRALIA

SOUTH
AFRICA

SWAZILAND

LESOTHO

WORLD POLITICAL

0   1,000   2,000 miles

0   1,000   2,000 kilometers

NEW
ZEALAND

ANTARCTICA

South Pole

EUROPE

0   200   400 miles

0   400 kilometers

20°E   30°E   40°E

10°E

Arctic Circle

N

W   E

S

60°N

NORWAY

FINLAND

10°W

SWEDEN

ESTONIA

RUSSIA

North Sea

Baltic Sea

LATVIA

UNITED
KINGDOM

DENMARK

LITHUANIA
RUSSIA

IRELAND

NETHERLANDS

BELARUS

POLAND

50°N

ATLANTIC
OCEAN

GERMANY

BELGIUM
LUX.

CZECH
REP.
SLOVAKIA

UKRAINE

FRANCE

LIECH.

AUSTRIA

HUNGARY

ROMANIA

MOLDOVA

SWITZ.
SLOVENIA

MONACO

SAN
MARINO

CROATIA

BOSNIA-
HERZ.

YUGO.

BULGARIA

PORTUGAL

ANDORRA

Corsica (Fr.)

ITALY

MACEDONIA

Black Sea

40°N

SPAIN

Sardinia (It.)

ALBANIA

GREECE

TURKEY

BALEARIC IS. (Sp.)

Gibraltar (U.K.)

Sicily (It.)

Mediterranean Sea

WORLD PHYSICAL

Land Elevation

Feet	Meters
Over 9,841	Over 3,001
6,581-9,840	2,001-3,000
3,281-6,580	1,001-2,000
661-3,280	201-1,000
0-660	0-200
Below sea level	Below sea level

☐ Ice-covered land

▲ Mountain peak

0   500   1,000   1,500   2,000 miles

0   1,000   2,000 kilometers

SVALBARD

Barents Sea

ARCTIC OCEAN

Novaya
Zemlya

SIBERIA

Lena R.

Ob R.

Yenisey R.

Irtysh R.

Sea of Okhotsk

KAMCHATKA
PENINSULA

URAL MTS.

*Baltic
Sea*

Volga R.

Ural R.

Sakhalin

North
Sea

EUROPE

ALTAI MTS.

ASIA

L.
Baikal

Amur R.

Hokkaido

CARPATHIANS

Danube R.

ALPS

Mt. Blanc

CAUCASUS
MTS.

*Aral
Sea*

GOBI

*Sea of
Japan*

Honshu

BALKAN
PEN.

Black Sea

Mt. Ararat

Caspian Sea

Mt.
Damavand

TIBETAN
PLATEAU

Huang He

Shikoku
Kyushu

*Mediterranean
Sea*

Chang Jiang/Yangzi R.

East
China
Sea

SAHARA

ARABIAN
PENINSULA

THAR
DESERT

Mt.
Everest

Red Sea

Ganges R.

Taiwan

NUBIAN
DESERT

*Persian
Gulf*

DECCAN
PLATEAU

Hainan

Nile R.

SUDAN

*Arabian
Sea*

*Bay of
Bengal*

South
China
Sea

PHILIPPINE
ISLANDS

AFRICA

MICRONESIA

GREAT RIFT VALLEY

Sri
Lanka

PACIFIC OCEAN

Congo (Zaire) R.

L. Victoria

Mt. Kenya

MALAY
PEN.

ZAIRE
BASIN

Mt. Kilimanjaro

Sumatra

Borneo

INDONESIA

Zambezi R.

SEYCHELLES

Celebes

New Guinea

Java

Timor

MELANESIA

INDIAN
OCEAN

Madagascar

KALAHARI
DESERT

Orange R.

GREAT SANDY
DESERT

Cape of
Good Hope

AUSTRALIA

North
Island

NULLARBOR
PLAIN

Darling R.

Tasmania

South
Island

NEW ZEALAND

ANTARCTICA

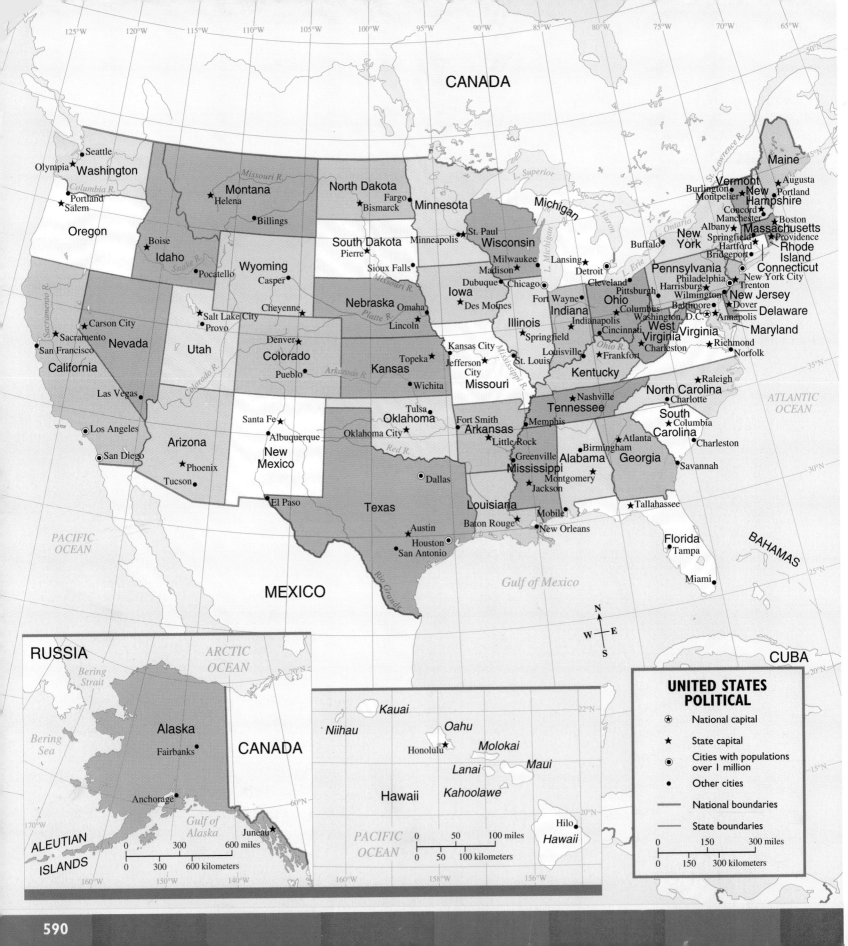

UNITED STATES POLITICAL

National capital
State capital
Cities with populations over 1 million
Other cities
National boundaries
State boundaries

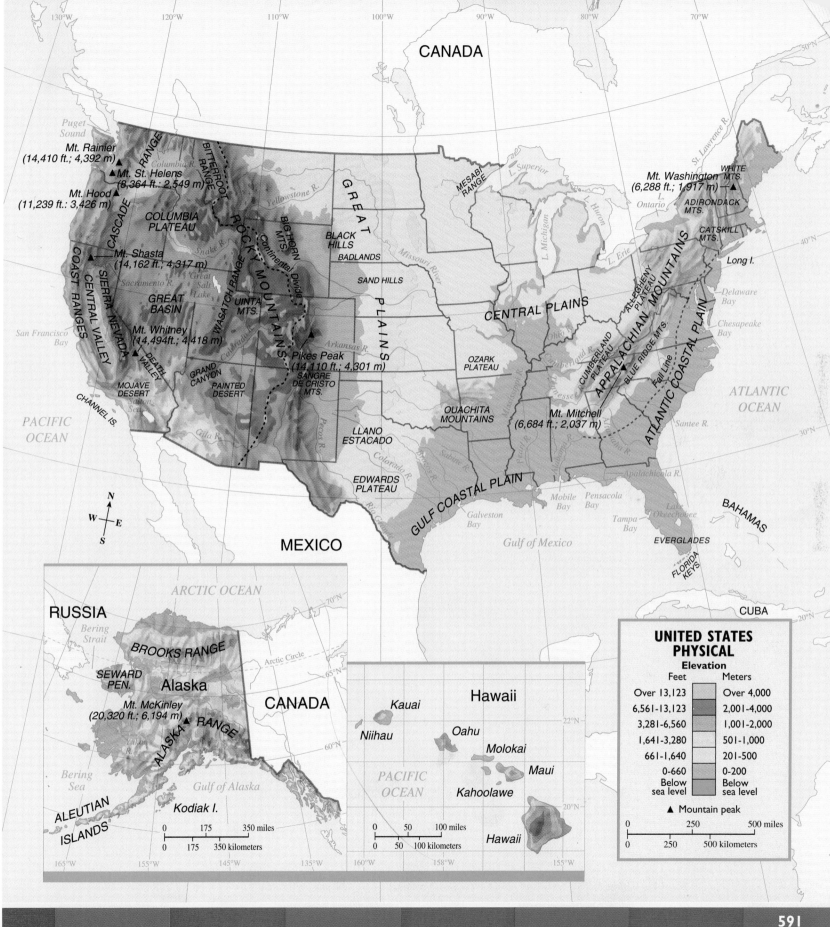

CANADA

Mt. Rainier
(14,410 ft.; 4,392 m) ▲

▲ Mt. St. Helens
(8,364 ft.; 2,549 m)

Mt. Hood
(11,239 ft.; 3,426 m)

CASCADE RANGE

BITTERROOT RANGE

COLUMBIA
PLATEAU

Columbia R.

Yellowstone R.

Snake R.

GREAT

Mt. Shasta
(14,162 ft.; 4,317 m) ▲

COAST RANGES

SIERRA NEVADA

CENTRAL VALLEY

Sacramento R.

ROCKY MOUNTAINS

BIG HORN MTS.

Continental Divide

WASATCH RANGE

Great Salt Lake

UINTA MTS.

GREAT
BASIN

PLAINS

BLACK
HILLS

BADLANDS

SAND HILLS

Missouri River

MESABI RANGE

L. Superior

L. Michigan

L. Huron

L. Ontario

L. Erie

Mt. Washington
(6,288 ft.; 1,917 m) ▲

WHITE
MTS.

ADIRONDACK
MTS.

CATSKILL
MTS.

St. Lawrence R.

Long I.

Mt. Whitney
(14,494 ft.; 4,418 m) ▲

Mt. Whitney
(14,494ft.; 4,418 m)

DEATH VALLEY ▲

Colorado R.

GRAND
CANYON

PAINTED
DESERT

Arkansas R.

Pikes Peak
(14,110 ft.; 4,301 m)

SANGRE
DE CRISTO
MTS.

CENTRAL PLAINS

OZARK
PLATEAU

Ohio R.

Cumberland R.

Tennessee R.

CUMBERLAND
PLATEAU

ALLEGHENY
PLATEAU

APPALACHIAN MOUNTAINS

BLUE RIDGE MTS.

Fall Line

ATLANTIC COASTAL PLAIN

Delaware
Bay

Chesapeake
Bay

San Francisco
Bay

MOJAVE
DESERT

Salton
Sea

CHANNEL IS.

Gila R.

LLANO
ESTACADO

Pecos R.

OUACHITA
MOUNTAINS

Mississippi R.

Red R.

Sabine R.

Mt. Mitchell
(6,684 ft.; 2,037 m)

Arkansas R.

Alabama R.

Santee R.

ATLANTIC
OCEAN

PACIFIC
OCEAN

EDWARDS
PLATEAU

Colorado R.

Brazos R.

Platte R.

GULF COASTAL PLAIN

Apalachicola R.

EVERGLADES

BAHAMAS

Rio Grande

Galveston
Bay

Mobile
Bay

Pensacola
Bay

Tampa
Bay

Lake
Okeechobee

FLORIDA
KEYS

MEXICO

Gulf of Mexico

CUBA

N
W E
S

RUSSIA

ARCTIC OCEAN

Bering
Strait

BROOKS RANGE

Arctic Circle

SEWARD
PEN.

Alaska

CANADA

Mt. McKinley
(20,320 ft.; 6,194 m) ▲

ALASKA RANGE

Yukon R.

Bering
Sea

Gulf of Alaska

ALEUTIAN
ISLANDS

Kodiak I.

| 0 | 175 | 350 miles |
| 0 | 175 | 350 kilometers |

Hawaii

Kauai

Niihau

Oahu

Molokai

Maui

PACIFIC
OCEAN

Kahoolawe

Hawaii

| 0 | 50 | 100 miles |
| 0 | 50 | 100 kilometers |

UNITED STATES
PHYSICAL
Elevation

Feet	Meters
Over 13,123	Over 4,000
6,561–13,123	2,001–4,000
3,281–6,560	1,001–2,000
1,641–3,280	501–1,000
661–1,640	201–500
0–660	0–200
Below sea level	Below sea level

▲ Mountain peak

| 0 | 250 | 500 miles |
| 0 | 250 | 500 kilometers |

ASIA

EUROPE

ARCTIC OCEAN

Bering Sea

Bering Strait

•Barrow

Beaufort Sea

Alaska
(U.S.)

•Anchorage

Gulf of Alaska

•Whitehorse

Juneau•

•Yellowknife

Great Bear Lake

Great Slave Lake

•Qaanaaq

Greenland
(Kalaalit Nunaat)
(Den.)

Baffin Bay

•Nuuk

•Iqaluit

Labrador Sea

•Churchill

Hudson Bay

CANADA

•Edmonton

Vancouver•

Victoria•

Seattle•

Portland•

Spokane•

•Calgary

•Saskatoon

•Regina

Lake Winnipeg

•Winnipeg

•Goose Bay

Sept-Îles•

•Gander
St. John's•

PACIFIC OCEAN

Columbia R.

Missouri R.

San Francisco•

Great Salt Lake

•Salt Lake City

•Denver

Colorado R.

Minneapolis•

•St. Paul

•Omaha

Milwaukee•

•Quebec

ST. PIERRE-
MIQUELON (Fr.)

•St. John

Montreal★
Ottawa★

•Halifax

Los Angeles◉

San Diego◉

Phoenix•

Kansas
City•

UNITED STATES

Arkansas R.

Chicago•

St. Louis•

Great Lakes

Toronto★
Detroit◉

Cincinnati•

Cleveland•

Buffalo•

Pittsburgh•

Boston◉

New York◉

Philadelphia◉

Washington, D.C.★

ATLANTIC OCEAN

El Paso•

Dallas◉

Rio Grande

Memphis•

Mississippi R.

Ohio R.

Norfolk•

Atlanta•

Bermuda
(U.K.)

San Antonio•

Monterrey◉

MEXICO

Houston◉

New Orleans•

Gulf of Mexico

Miami•

BAHAMAS

Nassau★

N
W   E
S

Guadalajara◉

Mexico City◉

•Orizaba

Havana★

CUBA

Santiago•

HAITI
Port-au-Prince★

DOMINICAN
REPUBLIC

Santo
Domingo★

Puerto
Rico
(U.S.)

VIRGIN IS. (U.S.-U.K.)

ANTIGUA AND
BARBUDA

CAYMAN
ISLANDS
(U.K.)

Belmopan★

BELIZE

JAMAICA

Kingston★

ST. KITTS
AND NEVIS

Guadeloupe
(Fr.)

*Clipperton Island
(Fr.)*

GUATEMALA

Guatemala★

San Salvador★

EL SALVADOR

HONDURAS

•Tegucigalpa

NICARAGUA

Managua★

San José★

COSTA
RICA

PANAMA

Panama Canal

Panama★

Caribbean Sea

NETH.
ANTILLES
(Neth.)

ARUBA

DOMINICA
ST. LUCIA

MARTINIQUE (Fr.)

BARBADOS

ST. VINCENT AND THE
GRENADINES

GRENADA

TRINIDAD
AND TOBAGO

SOUTH AMERICA

NORTH AMERICA
POLITICAL

★ National capitals

◉ Cities with populations
over 1 million

• Major cities

— National boundaries

— State boundaries

0   300   600 miles

0   300   600 kilometers

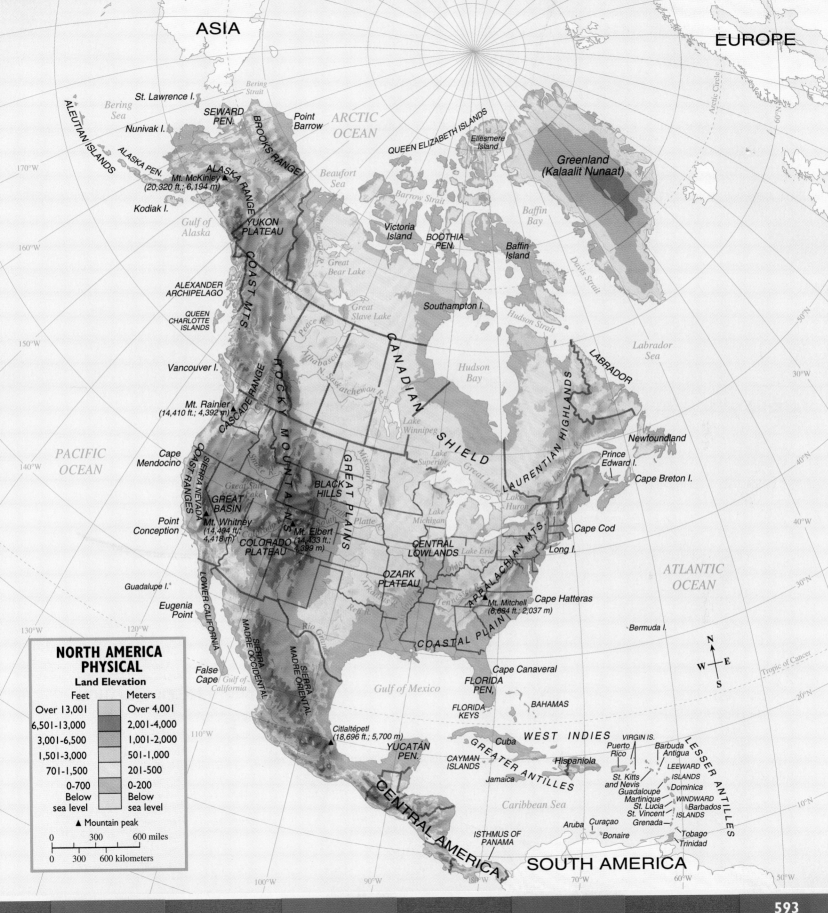

ASIA

EUROPE

ARCTIC OCEAN

Bering Strait

St. Lawrence I.

Bering Sea

SEWARD PEN.

Point Barrow

BROOKS RANGE

QUEEN ELIZABETH ISLANDS

Ellesmere Island

Greenland (Kalaalit Nunaat)

Nunivak I.

ALASKA PEN.

ALEUTIAN ISLANDS

ALASKA RANGE

Mt. McKinley (20,320 ft.; 6,194 m)

Yukon R.

Beaufort Sea

Barrow Strait

Victoria Island

BOOTHIA PEN.

Baffin Bay

Baffin Island

Kodiak I.

Gulf of Alaska

YUKON PLATEAU

Mackenzie R.

Great Bear Lake

Southampton I.

Davis Strait

Hudson Strait

ALEXANDER ARCHIPELAGO

COAST MTS.

Peace R.

Great Slave Lake

Athabasca R.

N. Saskatchewan R.

CANADIAN SHIELD

Hudson Bay

Labrador Sea

QUEEN CHARLOTTE ISLANDS

Vancouver I.

ROCKY MOUNTAINS

CASCADE RANGE

Mt. Rainier (14,410 ft.; 4,392 m)

Lake Winnipeg

LABRADOR

LAURENTIAN HIGHLANDS

Newfoundland

Prince Edward I.

Cape Breton I.

PACIFIC OCEAN

Cape Mendocino

COAST RANGES

SIERRA NEVADA

Snake R.

Great Salt Lake

GREAT BASIN

BLACK HILLS

GREAT PLAINS

Missouri R.

Lake Superior

Great Lakes

Lake Michigan

Lake Huron

Cape Cod

Long I.

Point Conception

Mt. Whitney (14,494 ft.; 4,418 m)

COLORADO PLATEAU

Mt. Elbert (14,433 ft.; 4,399 m)

Platte R.

CENTRAL LOWLANDS

Lake Erie

APPALACHIAN MTS.

ATLANTIC OCEAN

Guadalupe I.

LOWER CALIFORNIA

OZARK PLATEAU

Arkansas R.

Cape Hatteras

Eugenia Point

Red R.

Tennessee R.

Mt. Mitchell (6,684 ft.; 2,037 m)

Bermuda I.

SIERRA MADRE OCCIDENTAL

SIERRA MADRE ORIENTAL

Rio Grande

COASTAL PLAIN

N
W   E
S

Tropic of Cancer

False Cape

Gulf of California

Cape Canaveral

FLORIDA PEN.

Gulf of Mexico

FLORIDA KEYS

BAHAMAS

WEST INDIES

VIRGIN IS.

Barbuda

Citlaltépetl (18,696 ft.; 5,700 m)

YUCATÁN PEN.

Cuba

CAYMAN ISLANDS

GREATER ANTILLES

Hispaniola

Puerto Rico

Antigua

LEEWARD ISLANDS

Dominica

WINDWARD ISLANDS

Barbados

LESSER ANTILLES

Jamaica

St. Kitts and Nevis

Guadaloupe

Martinique

St. Lucia

St. Vincent

Grenada

Caribbean Sea

Aruba

Curaçao

Bonaire

Tobago

Trinidad

CENTRAL AMERICA

ISTHMUS OF PANAMA

SOUTH AMERICA

NORTH AMERICA PHYSICAL

Land Elevation

Feet		Meters
Over 13,001		Over 4,001
6,501–13,000		2,001–4,000
3,001–6,500		1,001–2,000
1,501–3,000		501–1,000
701–1,500		201–500
0–700		0–200
Below sea level		Below sea level

▲ Mountain peak

0   300   600 miles
0   300   600 kilometers

Caribbean Sea

Barranquilla
Cartagena
Cúcuta
Maracaibo
Valencia • Caracas
Barquisimeto
San Cristóbal
Bucaramanga
Medellín • Bogotá
Cali

GUYANA   **SURINAME**

Georgetown   **French Guiana (Fr.)**
Paramaribo
Cayenne

VENEZUELA

Orinoco R.

ATLANTIC OCEAN

COLOMBIA

Mapelo I. (Colombia)

Equator

Quito

ECUADOR

GALÁPAGOS IS. (Ecuador)

Guayaquil

Iquitos

Belém

Manaus   *Amazon R.*   São Luís

Fortaleza

Madeira R.

B R A Z I L

Xingu R.

Recife

Trujillo

PERU

Maceió

Araguaia R.   *Tocantins R.*

Lima
Callao   Cuzco

L. Titicaca

Salvador

Arequipa

La Paz

BOLIVIA

Sucre

Brasília

São Francisco R.

Belo Horizonte

Chuquicamata

Paraguay R.

PARAGUAY

Paraná R.

Tropic of Capricorn

Antofagasta

Asunción

Rio de Janeiro
São Paulo   Niterói
Santos

San Felix I. (Chile)   San Ambrosio I. (Chile)

Tucumán

Curitiba

Uruguay R.

Pôrto Alegre

Córdoba

CHILE

Santa Fe
Paraná
Rosario

URUGUAY

Valparaíso

Juan Fernández Is. (Chile)

Santiago

Buenos Aires
La Plata   Montevideo

Concepción

ARGENTINA

Mar del Plata

Bahía Blanca

PACIFIC OCEAN

ATLANTIC OCEAN

N
W **E**
S

Strait of Magellan

FALKLAND IS. (U.K.) (MALVINAS IS.)

Punta Arenas

SOUTH AMERICA POLITICAL

✪   National capitals

◉   Cities with populations over one million

•   Other cities

──   International boundaries

| 0 | 400 | 800 miles |
| 0 | 400 | 800 kilometers |

10°N

Equator

10°S

20°S

30°S

40°S

50°S

100°W   90°W   80°W   70°W   60°W   50°W   40°W   30°W   20°W   10°W

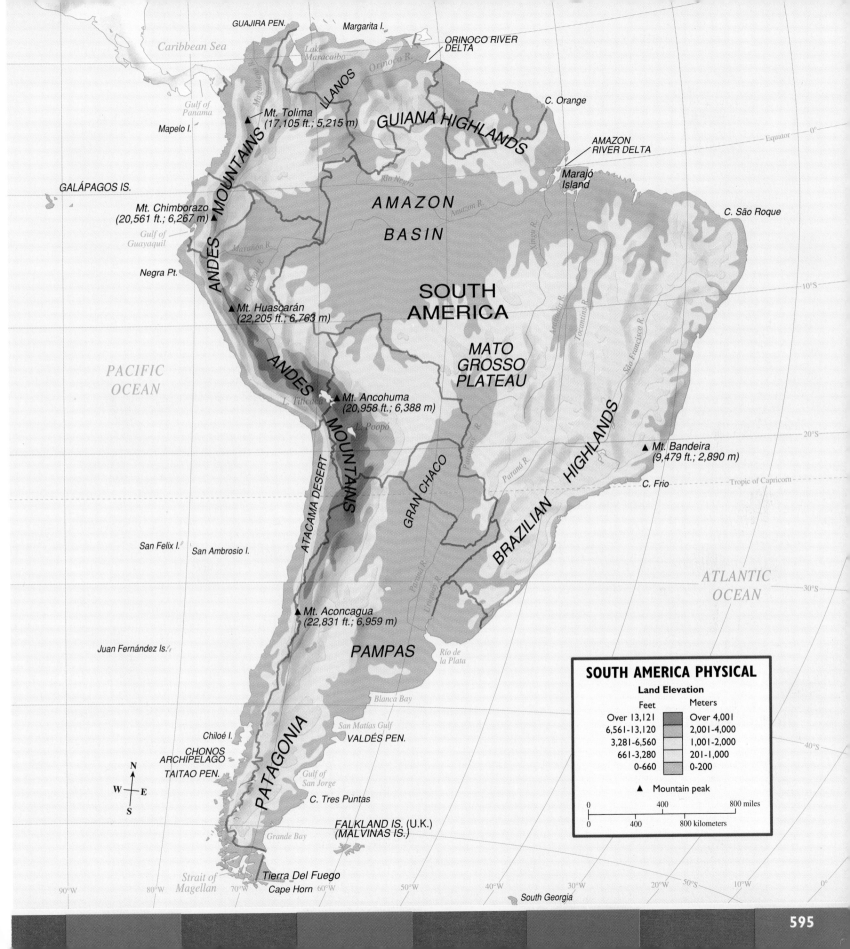

GUAJIRA PEN.
Margarita I.
Caribbean Sea
ORINOCO RIVER DELTA
Gulf of Panama
LLANOS
Orinoco R.
C. Orange
Mt. Tolima
(17,105 ft.; 5,215 m)
GUIANA HIGHLANDS
Mapelo I.
Lake Maracaibo
Magdalena R.

GALÁPAGOS IS.
Equator 0°
Río Negro
AMAZON RIVER DELTA
Marajó Island

Mt. Chimborazo
(20,561 ft.; 6,267 m)
AMAZON
Amazon R.
C. São Roque
Gulf of Guayaquil
Marañón R.
BASIN

ANDES MOUNTAINS
Ucayali R.
SOUTH
10°S
Negra Pt.
AMERICA

Mt. Huascarán
(22,205 ft.; 6,763 m)
MATO GROSSO PLATEAU
Xingu R.
Araguaia R.
Tocantins R.
São Francisco R.

PACIFIC OCEAN
ANDES MOUNTAINS
Mt. Ancohuma
(20,958 ft.; 6,388 m)
L. Titicaca
L. Poopó
Mt. Bandeira
(9,479 ft.; 2,890 m)
20°S

San Felix I.
San Ambrosio I.
ATACAMA DESERT
GRAN CHACO
Paraguay R.
Paraná R.
BRAZILIAN HIGHLANDS
C. Frio
Tropic of Capricorn

Juan Fernández Is.
Paraná R.
Uruguay R.
ATLANTIC OCEAN
30°S

Mt. Aconcagua
(22,831 ft.; 6,959 m)
Río de la Plata
PAMPAS

Blanca Bay
San Matías Gulf
VALDÉS PEN.
40°S

Chiloé I.
CHONOS ARCHIPELAGO
TAITAO PEN.
PATAGONIA
Gulf of San Jorge
C. Tres Puntas

N
W E
S

FALKLAND IS. (U.K.)
(MALVINAS IS.)
Grande Bay
50°S

Strait of Magellan
Tierra Del Fuego
Cape Horn
South Georgia

SOUTH AMERICA PHYSICAL
Land Elevation

Feet		Meters
Over 13,121		Over 4,001
6,561–13,120		2,001–4,000
3,281–6,560		1,001–2,000
661–3,280		201–1,000
0–660		0–200

▲ Mountain peak

0   400   800 miles
0   400   800 kilometers

90°W   80°W   70°W   60°W   50°W   40°W   30°W   20°W   10°W   0°

EUROPE

ASIA

N
W E
S

Mediterranean Sea

MADEIRA IS. (Port.)

15°W

Tangier ●
Rabat ⊛
Casablanca ⊙
MOROCCO
Marrakech ●

Algiers ⊛
Oran ●

Tunis ⊛
TUNISIA
Tripoli ⊛

Benghazi ●

Suez Canal
Alexandria ⊙
Cairo ⊙
EGYPT

30°N
CANARY IS. (Sp.)

El Aaiún ●

ALGERIA

LIBYA

Nile R.

Tropic of Cancer

Western Sahara (Morocco)

L. Nasser

Red Sea

Port Sudan ●

MAURITANIA
Nouakchott ⊛

MALI
Timbuktu ●

NIGER

CHAD

Khartoum ⊛

SUDAN

Blue Nile R.

ERITREA
Asmara ⊛

DJIBOUTI
Djibouti ⊛

Gulf of Aden

Dakar ⊛
15°N
SENEGAL
GAMBIA ⊛ Banjul
Bissau ⊛
GUINEA-BISSAU
GUINEA
Conakry ⊛
Freetown ⊛
SIERRA LEONE
Monrovia ⊛
LIBERIA

Bamako ⊛
BURKINA FASO
Ouagadougou ⊛
Niamey ⊛
L. Chad
N'Djamena ⊛
NIGERIA
Abuja ⊛

Niger R.

CÔTE D'IVOIRE
Yamoussoukro ⊛
Accra ⊛
GHANA
TOGO
BENIN
Lomé ⊛
Porto-Novo ⊛
Lagos ⊙

White Nile R.

ETHIOPIA
Addis Ababa ⊛

SOMALIA

0° Equator

CAMEROON
Bangui ⊛
Yaounde ⊛
Malabo ⊛
EQUATORIAL GUINEA
SÃO TOMÉ AND PRÍNCIPE
São Tomé ⊛
Libreville ⊛
GABON
CONGO
Brazzaville ⊛
Kinshasa ⊙
Cabinda (Angola)

CENTRAL AFRICAN REPUBLIC

Zaire (Congo) River

ZAIRE

Kampala ⊛
UGANDA
Kigali ⊛
RWANDA
Bujumbura ⊛
BURUNDI
L. Victoria
L. Turkana
KENYA
Nairobi ⊛
Mogadishu ●

Mombasa ●

SEYCHELLES
Victoria ⊛

INDIAN OCEAN

Ascension (Br.)

Luanda ⊛

TANZANIA
Dar es Salaam ●
L. Tanganyika

ATLANTIC OCEAN

ANGOLA

St. Helena (Br.)

L. Nyasa

COMOROS
Moroni ⊛

15°S

ZAMBIA
Lusaka ⊛
L. Kariba

MALAWI
Lilongwe ⊛

Zambezi R.

MOZAMBIQUE

NAMIBIA
Windhoek ⊛

Harare ⊛
ZIMBABWE

Antananarivo ⊛

MADAGASCAR

MAURITIUS
Réunion (Fr.)
Port-Louis ⊛

Tropic of Capricorn

BOTSWANA
Gaborone ⊛
Pretoria ⊛
Johannesburg ⊙
Maputo ⊛
Mbabane ⊛
SWAZILAND

LEGEND — AFRICA POLITICAL

⊛ National capitals
⊙ Cities with populations over one million
● Other cities
— International boundaries
--- Disputed boundaries

0 — 500 — 1,000 miles
0 — 500 — 1,000 kilometers

30°S

Maseru ⊛
Durban ●
LESOTHO
SOUTH AFRICA
Umtata ●

Cape Town ⊛
Port Elizabeth ●

0° · 15°E · 30°E · 45°E

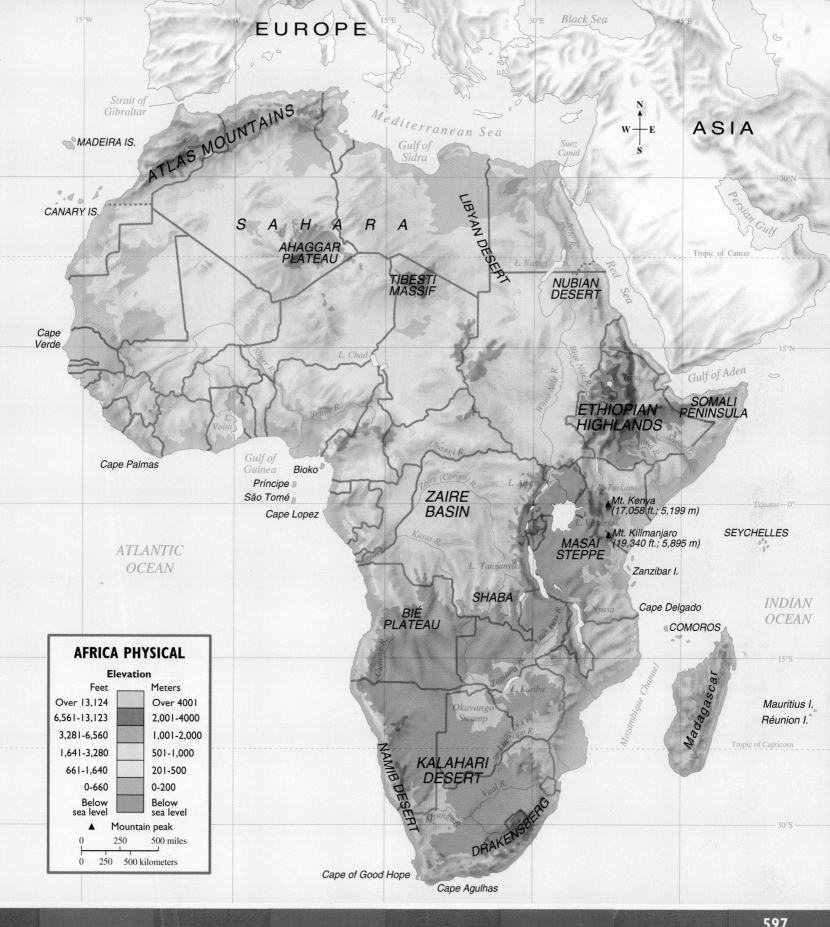

EUROPE

ASIA

Strait of Gibraltar

Mediterranean Sea

Black Sea

Gulf of Sidra

Suez Canal

Persian Gulf

MADEIRA IS.

ATLAS MOUNTAINS

CANARY IS.

S A H A R A

AHAGGAR PLATEAU

TIBESTI MASSIF

LIBYAN DESERT

L. Nasser

NUBIAN DESERT

Nile R.

Red Sea

Tropic of Cancer

30°N

Cape Verde

Senegal R.

Niger R.

L. Chad

Benue R.

White Nile R.

Blue Nile R.

L. Tana

Gulf of Aden

15°N

ETHIOPIAN HIGHLANDS

SOMALI PENINSULA

Shebelle

Juba R.

Cape Palmas

Gulf of Guinea

Bioko

Príncipe

São Tomé

Cape Lopez

L. Volta

Ubangi R.

Zaire (Congo) R.

ZAIRE BASIN

Kasai R.

L. Albert

L. Turkana

▲ Mt. Kenya (17,058 ft.; 5,199 m)

L. Victoria

▲ Mt. Kilimanjaro (19,340 ft.; 5,895 m)

MASAI STEPPE

Equator — 0°

SEYCHELLES

ATLANTIC OCEAN

L. Tanganyika

Zanzibar I.

SHABA

Nyasa

Cape Delgado

INDIAN OCEAN

BIÉ PLATEAU

Cunene R.

Zambezi R.

L. Kariba

Luangwa R.

COMOROS

15°S

Mozambique Channel

Madagascar

Mauritius I.

Réunion I.

Okavango Swamp

AFRICA PHYSICAL

Elevation

Feet		Meters
Over 13,124		Over 4001
6,561-13,123		2,001-4000
3,281-6,560		1,001-2,000
1,641-3,280		501-1,000
661-1,640		201-500
0-660		0-200
Below sea level		Below sea level

▲ Mountain peak

0   250   500 miles

0   250   500 kilometers

NAMIB DESERT

KALAHARI DESERT

Limpopo R.

Vaal R.

Orange R.

DRAKENSBERG

Tropic of Capricorn

30°S

Cape of Good Hope

Cape Agulhas

ATLANTIC OCEAN

MADEIRA IS. (Port.)

AFRICA

IRELAND
Dublin ⊛ · Glasgow

UNITED KINGDOM
London ⊛

PORTUGAL
Lisbon ⊛
Madrid ⊛
SPAIN
Valencia ·
Barcelona ·
BALEARIC IS. (Sp.)
Corsica (Fr.)
Sardinia
ITALY
Rome ⊛
Naples ·
Palermo ·
Sicily

FRANCE
Bordeaux ·
Paris ⊛
Bern ⊛
Nice ·
Marseille ·
Brussels ⊛
Amsterdam ⊛
2
3
5
The Hague
6
8 Prague
Munich 22
Milan ·
7
9
10
11
12
13 Zagreb
14
Ljubljana
20
21

NORWAY
Oslo ⊛
Narvik ·

SWEDEN
Copenhagen ⊛
4
Stockholm ⊛

FINLAND
Helsinki ⊛
Murmansk ·

Barents Sea

Novaya Zemlya

SVALBARD (Nor.)

ARCTIC OCEAN

NORTH LAND (SEVERNAYA ZEMLYA)

Berlin ⊛
RUSSIA
Kaliningrad
23 Warsaw ⊛
Vienna ⊛
Bratislava ⊛
Budapest ⊛
24
Riga ⊛
Tallinn ⊛
26
25
Vilnius ⊛
Minsk ⊛
27
28
Kiev ⊛
29

St. Petersburg ·
Arkhangel'sk ·

Moscow ⊛

Kazan ·
Perm ·
Yekaterinburg ·

RUSSIA

Tomsk ·

Sarajevo ·
Tiranë ⊛
Belgrade ⊛
19
Bucharest ⊛
15
16
17
18
Skopje ⊛
Sofia ⊛
GREECE
Athens ⊛
30
Valletta ·
Crete (Gr.)

Mediterranean Sea

Tropic of Cancer

Istanbul ·
Izmir ·
Ankara ⊛
TURKEY

Chisinau ⊛
Odesa ·
Kharkiv ·

Black Sea

Krasnodar ·
Volgograd ·
Saratov ·
Volga R.
Samara ·
Magnitogorsk ·
Ufa ·
Chelyabinsk ·

Omsk ·
Novosibirsk ·
Krasnoyarsk ·

Irtysh R.
Ob River

GEORGIA
Tbilisi ⊛

Caspian Sea

Aral Sea

L. Balgash

KAZAKSTAN

CYPRUS
Nicosia ⊛
LEBANON
Beirut ⊛
ISRAEL
Jerusalem ⊛
31
SYRIA
Damascus ⊛
Amman ⊛
JORDAN
IRAQ

ARMENIA
Yerevan ⊛
AZERBAIJAN
Baku ⊛
Baghdad ·

TURKMENISTAN
Ashgabat ⊛
Tehran ⊛

UZBEKISTAN
Tashkent ⊛

Almaty ·

Bishkek ⊛
Dushanbe ⊛

KYRGYZSTAN

TAJIKISTAN

1-Andorra
2-Belgium
3-Netherlands
4-Denmark
5-Luxembourg
6-Germany
7-Switzerland
8-Liechtenstein
9-Monaco
10-San Marino
11-Austria
12-Slovenia
13-Croatia
14-Bosnia and Herzegovina
15-Yugoslavia

16-Albania
17-Macedonia
18-Bulgaria
19-Romania
20-Hungary
21-Slovakia
22-Czech Republic
23-Poland
24-Lithuania
25-Latvia
26-Estonia
27-Belarus
28-Ukraine
29-Moldova
30-Malta
31-West Bank and Gaza Strip

KUWAIT
Kuwait ⊛
SAUDI ARABIA
Riyadh ⊛
QATAR
Doha ⊛
U.A.E.
Abu Dhabi ⊛
Manama ⊛
BAHRAIN

Persian Gulf

Tigris R.
Euphrates R.

IRAN

Kabul ⊛
AFGHANISTAN
Islamabad ⊛
Jammu and Kashmir
Lahore ·
PAKISTAN

Red Sea

San'a ⊛
YEMEN
Aden ·

Muscat ⊛
OMAN

Gulf of Aden

Socotra (Yemen)

Arabian Sea

Karachi ·
Hyderabad ·

Delhi ·
New Delhi ⊛
Tibet
Kathmandu ⊛
NEPAL
Thimphu ⊛
BHUTAN
Lhasa ·

Ahmadabad ·
Bombay ·
Hyderabad ·
INDIA
Madras ·

Ganges R.
Brahmaputra R.
Dhaka ⊛
BANGLADESH
Mandalay ·
MYANMAR (BURMA)
Yangon (Rangoon) ⊛

Indus R.

INDIAN OCEAN

SRI LANKA
Colombo ⊛

Male ·
MALDIVES

Bay of Bengal

ANDAMAN IS. (India)

NICOBAR IS. (India)

EURASIA POLITICAL

⊛ National capitals
○ Cities with populations over one million
• Other cities

0   500   1,000 miles
0   500   1,000 kilometers

Bering Sea

NEW SIBERIAN IS.

ALEUTIAN IS. (U.S.)

Magadan

Sea of Okhotsk

Yakutsk

Lena R.

Sakhalin Is.

KURIL IS. (Russia)

Lake Baikal

Khabarovsk

Sapporo

Irkutsk

Manchuria

Harbin

Vladivostok

JAPAN

Sea of Japan

Ulaanbaatar

MONGOLIA

Shenyang

Fushun

NORTH KOREA

Tokyo
Yokohama
Nagoya

P'yongyang

Seoul

Kobe
Kyoto
Osaka

Great Wall

Beijing

Tianjin

Dalian

SOUTH KOREA

Kitakyushu

MARSHALL ISLANDS

Majuro

Taiyuan

Qingdao

Lanzhou

Huang He

Nanjing

Shanghai

East China Sea

CHINA

Wuhan

Chengdu

Chongqing

Changjiang

PACIFIC OCEAN

Bairiki

KIRIBATI

Taipei

RYUKYU IS. (Japan)

Kunming

Guangzhou

TAIWAN

N

NORTHERN MARIANA ISLANDS (U.S.)

Palikir

Macao (Port.)

Hong Kong

PHILIPPINES

FEDERATED STATES OF MICRONESIA

Hanoi

LAOS

South China Sea

Manila

Guam (U.S.)

THAILAND

Vientiane

Hue

Da Nang

Koror

SOLOMON ISLANDS

Bangkok

CAMBODIA

VIETNAM

Davao

PALAU

Honiara

Phnom Penh

Ho Chi Minh City (Saigon)

VANUATU

BRUNEI

Bandar Seri Begawan

Manado

Jayapura

New Guinea

Lae

Port-Vila

Kuala Lumpur

MALAYSIA

Borneo

Samarinda

Celebes

Irian Jaya

Port Moresby

SINGAPORE

Singapore

Pontianak

PAPUA NEW GUINEA

New Caledonia (Fr.)

Banjarmasin

Ujung Pandang

East Timor (Indo.)

Sumatra

Arafura Sea

Coral Sea

INDONESIA

Java

Timor

Jakarta

Bandung

Surabaya

AUSTRALIA

ATLANTIC
OCEAN

Ireland

BRITISH ISLES

Great Britain

MADEIRA IS.

North
Sea

SVALBARD

ARCTIC
OCEAN

NORTH
LAND

SCANDINAVIAN
PENINSULA
LAPLAND

Novaya
Zemlya

Kara
Sea

TAYMYR
PEN.

Strait of
Gibraltar

IBERIAN
PENINSULA

PYRENEES

KOLA
PEN.

Barents
Sea

Baltic Sea

YAMAL
PEN.

CENTRAL
SIBERIAN
PLATEAU

BALEARIC IS.

Corsica

Sardinia

Tyrrhenian
Sea

NORTH EUROPEAN PLAIN

URAL MOUNTAINS

WEST
SIBERIAN
PLAIN

SIBERIA

ALPS

CARPATHIAN MTS.

Lower Tunguska R.

Sicily

Malta

Ionian
Sea

Aegean Sea

BALKAN
PENINSULA

Adriatic Sea

Black Sea

Volga R.

Kama R.

Angara R.

Crete

ANATOLIAN
PLATEAU

CAUCASUS
MOUNTAINS

Caspian Sea

Aral
Sea

KIRGIZ
STEPPE

KAZAK
UPLANDS

ALTAI MTS.

Cyprus

Dnieper R.

Mediterranean Sea

TURAN LOWLAND

L. Balqash

Suez
Canal

SINAI
PENINSULA

SYRIAN
DESERT

ELBURZ MTS.

Syr Darya R.

TIAN SHAN

TARIM
BASIN

AFRICA

Euphrates R.

Tigris R.

ZAGROS MTS.

PLATEAU
OF
IRAN

PAMIRS

HINDU KUSH

KUNLUN SHAN

Red Sea

Persian Gulf

ARABIAN
PENINSULA

TIBETAN PLATEAU

Gulf of Oman

RUB AL' KHALI
DESERT

GREAT
INDIAN
DESERT

HIMALAYAS

Mt. Everest
(29,028 ft.
8,848 m)

Salween R.

Gulf of Aden

Arabian
Sea

Indus R.

Sutlej R.

Ganges R.

Brahmaputra R.

GANGES PLAIN

DECCAN
PLATEAU

Godavari R.

Bay of
Bengal

LAKSHADWEEP

WESTERN GHATS

EASTERN GHATS

ANDAMAN
IS.

N

W   E

S

MALDIVE IS.

Sri
Lanka

NICOBAR
IS.

INDIAN
OCEAN

Tropic of Cancer

Equator

10°N

0°

10°S

20°S

30°S

20°N

30°N

40°N

50°N

60°N

70°N

80°N

Arctic Circle

40°E

60°E

80°E

100°E

120°E

EURASIA PHYSICAL

Elevation

Feet		Meters
Over 13,120		Over 4,000
6,561–13,120		2,001–4,000
3,281–6,560		1,001–2,000
1,641–3,280		501–1,000
661–1,640		201–500
0–660		0–200
Below sea level		Below sea level

0   500   1,000 miles

0   500   1,000 kilometers

NEW SIBERIAN ISLANDS

East Siberian Sea

Laptev Sea

Bering Sea

CHERSKI RANGE

VERKHOYANSK RANGE

KOLYMA RANGE

CENTRAL RANGE

KAMCHATKA PENINSULA

SIBERIA

Sea of Okhotsk

L. Baikal

GREATER KHINGAN RANGE

Sakhalin

KURIL ISLANDS

MONGOLIAN PLATEAU

MANCHURIAN PLAIN

Hokkaido

Sea of Japan

Honshu

GOBI

Great Wall

KOREAN PEN.

NAN SHAN

Korea Strait

Mt. Fuji
(12,389 ft.; 3,776 m)

Yellow Sea

Shikoku

Kyushu

JAPANESE ARCHIPELAGO

MARSHALL IS.

NORTH CHINA PLAIN

East China Sea

RYUKYU IS.

PACIFIC OCEAN

GILBERT IS.

BOHEA HILLS

Okinawa

Taiwan

MARIANA IS.

Guam

Luzon Strait

Philippine Sea

Hainan

South China Sea

Luzon

Samar

CAROLINE IS.

Mindoro

PHILIPPINE ISLANDS

PALAU IS.

New Ireland

SOLOMON IS.

INDOCHINA PENINSULA

Panay

Negros

Palawan

Mindanao

ADMIRALTY IS.

New Britain

VANUATU (NEW HEBRIDES)

Gulf of Thailand

Halmahera

MOLUCCAS

Celebes Sea

Ceram

MAOKE MTS.

New Guinea

MALAY PENINSULA

Buru

ARU IS.

New Caledonia

Strait of Malacca

Celebes

Java Sea

Coral Sea

Sumatra

Borneo

Bangka

EAST INDIES

Arafura Sea

MENTAWAI IS.

GREATER SUNDA ISLANDS

Sumbawa

Lombok

Flores

Timor

Bali

Sumba

AUSTRALIA

Java

LESSER SUNDA ISLANDS

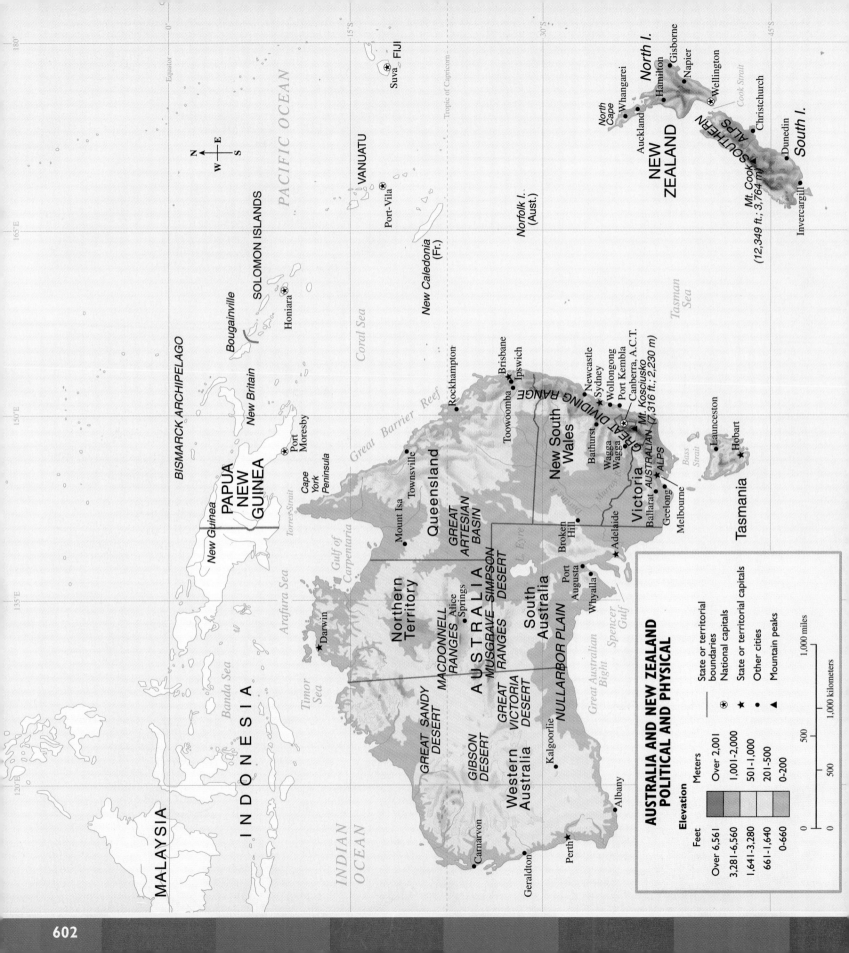

MALAYSIA

INDONESIA

PACIFIC OCEAN

Equator

180

165°E

150°E

135°E

120°E

15°S

Tropic of Capricorn

30°S

45°S

BISMARCK ARCHIPELAGO

Bougainville

New Britain

SOLOMON ISLANDS

Honiara ⊛

New Guinea

PAPUA
NEW
GUINEA

Port
Moresby

VANUATU

Port-Vila ⊛

New Caledonia
(Fr.)

FIJI
Suva ⊛

Norfolk I.
(Aust.)

*Tasman
Sea*

Coral Sea

Banda Sea

Arafura Sea

*Timor
Sea*

Torres Strait

*Gulf of
Carpentaria*

Cape
York
Peninsula

Great Barrier Reef

Rockhampton ●

Brisbane ★
Ipswich ●

Townsville ●

Mount Isa ●

Queensland

*GREAT
ARTESIAN
BASIN*

Darwin ★

Northern
Territory

*MACDONNELL
RANGES* Alice
Springs ●

*MUSGRAVE
RANGES*

*SIMPSON
DESERT*

AUSTRALIA

*GREAT SANDY
DESERT*

*GIBSON
DESERT*

*GREAT
VICTORIA
DESERT*

Western
Australia

Kalgoorlie ●

NULLARBOR PLAIN

South
Australia

L. Eyre

Broken
Hill ●

Port
Augusta ●
Whyalla ●

Adelaide ★

*Spencer
Gulf*

*Great Australian
Bight*

Carnarvon ●

Geraldton ●

Perth ★

Albany ●

*INDIAN
OCEAN*

Toowoomba ●

New South
Wales

Bathurst ●
Wagga
Wagga ●

Newcastle ●
Sydney ●
Wollongong ●
Port Kembla ●
Canberra, A.C.T. ★

GREAT DIVIDING RANGE

Mt. Kosciusko
(7,316 ft.; 2,230 m)

*AUSTRALIAN
ALPS*

Victoria

Ballarat ●
Geelong ●
Melbourne ●

*Bass
Strait*

Launceston ●
Hobart ★

Tasmania

NEW
ZEALAND

North I.

North
Cape

Whangarei ●
Auckland ●
Hamilton ●
Gisborne ●
Napier ●
Wellington ⊛

Christchurch ●

South I.

*SOUTHERN
ALPS*

Mt. Cook
(12,349 ft.; 3,764 m)

Dunedin ●

Invercargill ●

Cook Strait

AUSTRALIA AND NEW ZEALAND
POLITICAL AND PHYSICAL

State or territorial
boundaries

⊛ National capitals

★ State or territorial capitals

● Other cities

▲ Mountain peaks

Elevation

Feet	Meters
Over 6,561	Over 2,001
3,281–6,560	1,001–2,000
1,641–3,280	501–1,000
661–1,640	201–500
0–660	0–200

0   500   1,000 miles

0   500   1,000 kilometers

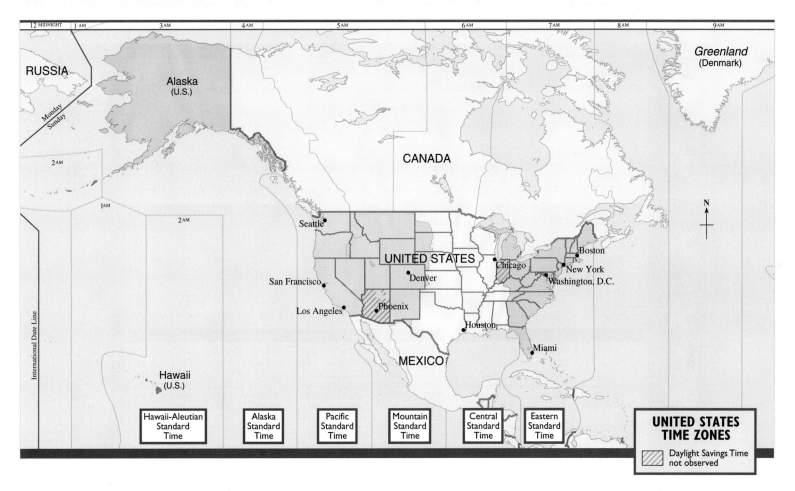

UNITED STATES TIME ZONES

12 MIDNIGHT | 1 AM | 3 AM | 4 AM | 5 AM | 6 AM | 7 AM | 8 AM | 9 AM

RUSSIA

Monday
Sunday

Alaska
(U.S.)

2 AM

1 AM

2 AM

International Date Line

CANADA

Seattle

UNITED STATES

San Francisco

Denver

Chicago

Boston

New York
Washington, D.C.

Los Angeles

Phoenix

Houston

Miami

Hawaii
(U.S.)

MEXICO

Greenland
(Denmark)

N

| Hawaii-Aleutian Standard Time | Alaska Standard Time | Pacific Standard Time | Mountain Standard Time | Central Standard Time | Eastern Standard Time |

UNITED STATES TIME ZONES

Daylight Savings Time not observed

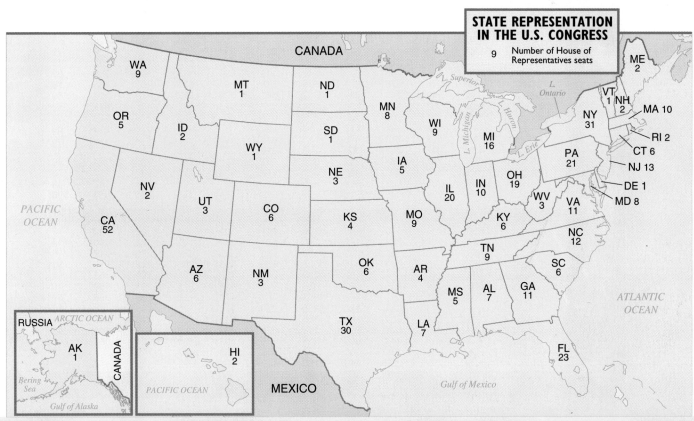

STATE REPRESENTATION IN THE U.S. CONGRESS

9   Number of House of Representatives seats

CANADA

WA 9
MT 1
ND 1
MN 8
ME 2
OR 5
ID 2
SD 1
WI 9
MI 16
VT 1
NH 2
MA 10
NY 31
RI 2
WY 1
IA 5
PA 21
CT 6
NJ 13
NV 2
UT 3
CO 6
NE 3
IL 20
IN 10
OH 19
WV 3
VA 11
DE 1
MD 8
CA 52
KS 4
MO 9
KY 6
NC 12
PACIFIC OCEAN
AZ 6
NM 3
OK 6
AR 4
TN 9
SC 6
MS 5
AL 7
GA 11
ATLANTIC OCEAN
TX 30
LA 7
FL 23

L. Superior
L. Ontario
L. Michigan
L. Huron
L. Erie

RUSSIA   ARCTIC OCEAN
PACIFIC OCEAN
AK 1
CANADA
Bering Sea
Gulf of Alaska

HI 2
PACIFIC OCEAN

MEXICO

Gulf of Mexico

STATE POPULATION BY AGE

(In thousands; as of July 1, 1994)

REGION AND STATE	Total	Under 5 years	5 to 17 years	18 to 24 years	25 to 34 years	35 to 44 years	45 to 54 years	55 to 64 years	65 to 74 years	75 to 84 years	85 years and over
U.S.	260,341	19,727	48,291	25,263	41,354	41,659	29,871	21,018	18,712	10,925	3,522
Northeast	**51,396**	**3,681**	**8,853**	**4,711**	**8,224**	**8,265**	**6,077**	**4,347**	**4,037**	**2,411**	**790**
ME	1,240	78	228	115	183	210	150	104	95	57	20
NH	1,137	80	212	100	190	203	134	83	76	44	16
VT	580	38	108	57	88	102	72	45	39	23	8
MA	6,041	423	1,001	566	1,058	972	699	473	460	288	101
RI	997	71	169	97	161	157	109	77	84	53	18
CT	3,275	231	557	281	531	538	401	271	253	159	53
NY	18,169	1,382	3,129	1,702	2,987	2,875	2,147	1,552	1,341	784	268
NJ	7,904	579	1,352	688	1,264	1,301	966	676	612	356	109
PA	12,052	799	2,099	1,105	1,760	1,906	1,399	1,066	1,077	644	197
Midwest	**61,394**	**4,444**	**11,699**	**5,940**	**9,370**	**9,796**	**6,992**	**5,046**	**4,456**	**2,716**	**935**
OH	11,102	784	2,070	1,079	1,673	1,773	1,287	945	850	486	155
IN	5,752	407	1,066	591	878	919	674	483	413	241	80
IL	11,752	915	2,168	1,128	1,886	1,878	1,341	955	818	499	164
MI	9,496	701	1,824	932	1,457	1,539	1,101	762	673	385	121
WI	5,082	350	997	483	771	817	570	412	364	236	84
MN	4,567	327	914	416	723	757	511	348	300	198	75
IA	2,829	188	541	274	393	434	316	246	226	152	59
MO	5,278	376	1,003	498	792	816	600	448	405	249	91
ND	638	43	129	66	90	99	66	52	47	34	13
SD	721	54	154	70	97	108	73	58	55	36	14
NE	1,623	116	326	158	232	253	176	133	119	79	32
KS	2,554	184	506	247	378	403	278	203	187	120	47
South	**90,692**	**6,786**	**16,824**	**9,076**	**14,283**	**14,285**	**10,440**	**7,468**	**6,614**	**3,749**	**1,167**
DE	706	51	124	68	120	114	81	58	54	27	8
MD	5,006	379	884	441	876	861	616	391	330	175	55
DC	570	43	76	58	114	91	65	46	43	25	9
VA	6,552	469	1,134	670	1,135	1,098	804	517	426	229	70
WV	1,822	108	321	190	235	286	225	176	160	92	28
NC	7,070	510	1,246	733	1,143	1,119	834	599	521	280	83
SC	3,664	274	678	394	576	576	430	301	262	135	38
GA	7,055	549	1,344	729	1,207	1,161	830	527	413	228	69
FL	13,953	962	2,300	1,174	2,069	2,077	1,543	1,256	1,441	873	257
KY	3,827	261	709	400	577	604	455	333	278	159	52
TN	5,175	366	931	518	799	822	630	452	375	215	69
AL	4,219	302	778	446	631	648	491	371	317	179	56
MS	2,669	207	549	304	382	390	287	219	187	109	36
AR	2,453	172	468	247	343	357	284	219	199	124	40
LA	4,315	337	898	458	642	663	476	347	287	157	50
OK	3,258	237	643	328	459	489	374	285	244	147	52
TX	18,378	1,559	3,742	1,919	2,975	2,929	2,014	1,371	1,078	594	196
West	**56,859**	**4,816**	**10,915**	**5,536**	**9,478**	**9,313**	**6,362**	**4,157**	**3,604**	**2,049**	**629**
MT	856	59	179	80	106	141	104	74	62	40	12
ID	1,133	87	252	120	149	177	127	89	72	46	14
WY	476	33	104	49	60	82	57	39	30	17	5
CO	3,656	270	700	344	575	660	453	286	212	117	39
NM	1,654	140	358	162	238	261	183	131	106	58	17
AZ	4,075	344	795	392	633	612	436	317	317	180	49
UT	1,908	181	491	232	283	261	173	118	96	56	17
NV	1,457	115	261	124	250	238	179	126	106	48	10
WA	5,343	394	1,014	492	845	929	649	402	345	208	65
OR	3,086	209	574	278	440	528	386	249	232	145	45
CA	31,431	2,833	5,844	3,085	5,615	5,109	3,403	2,195	1,921	1,084	342
AK	606	56	136	61	98	118	73	37	19	7	2
HI	1,179	95	209	116	186	199	138	94	86	43	12

Source: Statistical Abstracts of the United States, 1995

PRESIDENTS

George Washington (1789–1797)

BORN Feb. 22, 1732 **DIED** Dec. 14, 1799
EARLY CAREER Surveyor; head of Virginia militia; plantation owner
MARRIED Martha Dandridge Custis; one stepdaughter, one stepson
POLITICAL PARTY Federalist
VICE PRESIDENT John Adams
HOBBIES Fox hunting; raising mules; daily walks
ADMINISTRATION Departments of Foreign Affairs, Treasury, and War created; Attorney General established; Post Office continued
ANECDOTES Disapproved of swearing; commander in chief of Continental Army; lived at No. 1 Cherry Street, New York City, the first presidential mansion

John Adams (1797–1801)

BORN Oct. 30, 1735 **DIED** July 4, 1826
EARLY CAREER Schoolteacher; lawyer
MARRIED Abigail Smith; three sons, two daughters
POLITICAL PARTY Federalist
VICE PRESIDENT Thomas Jefferson
HOBBIES Reading; keeping diaries; walking five miles a day; fishing; playing whist
ADMINISTRATION Library of Congress, Marine Corps, Navy, and Public Health Services established
ANECDOTES Read seven languages; was married more than 54 years, longer than any other President; lived more than 90 years, longer than any other President; died on fiftieth anniversary of the signing of the Declaration of Independence

Thomas Jefferson (1801–1809)

BORN April 13, 1743 **DIED** July 4, 1826
EARLY CAREER Lawyer; plantation owner; writer
MARRIED Martha Wayles Skelton; one son, five daughters
POLITICAL PARTY Democratic-Republican
VICE PRESIDENT Aaron Burr; George Clinton
HOBBIES Playing the violin; cooking (introduced ice cream, waffles, and macaroni to the U.S.); inventing; designing Monticello, his home; scientist; book collecting
ADMINISTRATION Made the Louisiana Purchase; authorized Lewis and Clark Expedition; African slave import ended
ANECDOTES Ranked writing the Declaration of Independence as his finest achievement; died on the same day as John Adams; his personal library became part of the Library of Congress

James Madison (1809–1817)

BORN March 16, 1751 **DIED** June 28, 1836
EARLY CAREER Farmer; lawyer
MARRIED Dolley Payne Todd; one stepson
POLITICAL PARTY Democratic-Republican
VICE PRESIDENT George Clinton, Elbridge Gerry
HOBBIES Horseback riding; playing chess; reading Latin and Greek texts
ADMINISTRATION First war bonds issued; U.S. defeated England in the War of 1812
ANECDOTES The shortest President, 5' 4"; wrote nine of the ten amendments that are the Bill of Rights; Dolley, his wife, packed a valuable portrait of George Washington before the British burned the White House; his portrait is on the $5,000 bill

James Monroe (1817–1825)

BORN April 28, 1758 **DIED** July 4, 1831
EARLY CAREER Lawyer; farmer; writer; soldier
MARRIED Elizabeth Kortright; two daughters, one son
POLITICAL PARTY Democratic-Republican
VICE PRESIDENT Daniel D. Tompkins
HOBBIES Horseback riding; hunting
ADMINISTRATION Purchased Florida; issued Monroe Doctrine; Missouri Compromise; Era of Good Feeling
ANECDOTES Wounded as a soldier in Continental Army by a bullet that remained in his shoulder; the only President to have a foreign capital city named after him: Monrovia, in Liberia

John Quincy Adams (1825–1829)

BORN July 11, 1767 **DIED** February 23, 1848
EARLY CAREER Lawyer; private secretary
MARRIED Louise Catherine Johnson; three sons, one daughter
POLITICAL PARTY Democratic-Republican
VICE PRESIDENT John C. Calhoun
HOBBIES Swimming daily in Potomac River; playing billiards; growing mulberry trees; raising silkworms
ADMINISTRATION Smithsonian Institution established
ANECDOTES Read Shakespeare at age 10; attended schools in France and Holland; at 14, served as private secretary to first U.S. diplomat in Russia; only son of a President to become President; received fewer electoral and popular votes than his opponent

Andrew Jackson (1829–1837)

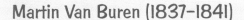

BORN March 15, 1767 **DIED** June 8, 1845
EARLY CAREER Lawyer; soldier; landowner; saddler
MARRIED Rachel Donelson Robards; one stepson
POLITICAL PARTY Democratic
VICE PRESIDENTS John C. Calhoun; Martin Van Buren
HOBBIES Owning racehorses; playing practical jokes; collecting pipes from all over the world; reading newspapers
ADMINISTRATION Introduced spoils system so that friends could get government jobs
ANECDOTES A poor orphan, at 13 he joined Continental Army; was quick tempered; dressed fashionably in Washington; 20,000 supporters jammed his inaugural reception at the White House

Martin Van Buren (1837–1841)

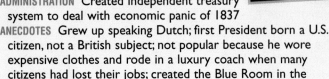

BORN Dec. 5, 1782 **DIED** July 24, 1862
EARLY CAREER Lawyer
MARRIED Hannah Hoes; four sons
POLITICAL PARTY Democratic
VICE PRESIDENT Richard M. Johnson
HOBBIES Attending theater and opera; fishing
ADMINISTRATION Created independent treasury system to deal with economic panic of 1837
ANECDOTES Grew up speaking Dutch; first President born a U.S. citizen, not a British subject; not popular because he wore expensive clothes and rode in a luxury coach when many citizens had lost their jobs; created the Blue Room in the White House

William Henry Harrison (1841)

BORN Feb. 9, 1773 **DIED** April 4, 1841
EARLY CAREER Army officer
MARRIED Anna Symmes; six sons, four daughters
POLITICAL PARTY Whig
VICE PRESIDENT John Tyler
HOBBIES Brisk walks; horseback riding; reading the Bible
ADMINISTRATION Did not make one major decision during his 35 days in office; hoped to end the spoils system
ANECDOTES Quit premedical studies and became a soldier when his father died; during a storm, while making longest inaugural speech (1 hour 45 minutes), he caught a cold and died one month later

John Tyler (1841–1845)

BORN March 29, 1790 **DIED** Jan. 18, 1862
EARLY CAREER Lawyer; militia captain
MARRIED Letitia Christian; three sons, five daughters. Julia Gardiner; five sons, two daughters
POLITICAL PARTY Whig
VICE PRESIDENT None
HOBBIES Playing the violin; fox hunting; caring for pets
ADMINISTRATION Annexation of Texas; signed trade treaty with China
ANECDOTES First Vice President to become President through death of a President; enjoyed giving parties for his 15 children; youngest child was born when Tyler was 70 years old

James K. Polk (1845–1849)

BORN Nov. 2, 1795 **DIED** June 15, 1849
EARLY CAREER Store clerk; lawyer
MARRIED Sarah Childress; no children
POLITICAL PARTY Democratic
VICE PRESIDENT George M. Dallas
HOBBIES None, he worked 14 hours a day
ADMINISTRATION Manifest Destiny; Mexican-American War of 1846; Department of Interior established; laid cornerstone of Washington Monument
ANECDOTES At 10, moved 500 miles from North Carolina to Tennessee in a covered wagon; first President whose inaugural address was reported by telegraph, as Samuel F. B. Morse sent the speech by wire to Baltimore, MD

Zachary Taylor (1849–1850)

BORN Nov. 24, 1784 **DIED** July 9, 1850
EARLY CAREER Farmer; army officer
MARRIED Margaret Sackall Smith; five daughters, one son
POLITICAL PARTY Whig
VICE PRESIDENT Millard Fillmore
HOBBIES Riding; being with friends
ADMINISTRATION Compromise of 1850; signed treaty with Hawaiian Islands
ANECDOTES The only President who never voted in an election, he first voted when he was 62 years old; allowed his favorite war horse, Whitey, to graze on the White House lawn; was second cousin of James Madison

Millard Fillmore (1850–1853)

BORN Jan. 7, 1800 **DIED** March 8, 1874
EARLY CAREER Apprenticed to clothmaker; teacher; lawyer
MARRIED Abigail Powers; one son, one daughter. Caroline Carmichael McIntosh; no children
POLITICAL PARTY Whig
VICE PRESIDENT None
HOBBIES Collecting books; civic volunteer
ADMINISTRATION Sent Commodore Perry to Japan to open up trade; Fugitive Slave Act became law; California admitted to Union
ANECDOTES His first wife had been his teacher; did not attend college; created first permanent library in the White House; the last Whig President; installed first bathtub in the White House

Franklin Pierce (1853–1857)

BORN Nov. 23, 1804 **DIED** Oct. 8, 1869
EARLY CAREER Lawyer
MARRIED Jane Means Appleton; three sons
POLITICAL PARTY Democratic
VICE PRESIDENT William R. King
HOBBIES Fishing
ADMINISTRATION Signed trade treaty with Japan; Gadsden Purchase of Mexican borderland; Kansas-Nebraska Act
ANECDOTES Nicknamed Handsome Frank; made no speeches during campaign; the only President elected to office who was not renominated by his political party for a second term; kept same Cabinet for four years

James Buchanan (1857–1861)

BORN April 23, 1791 **DIED** June 1, 1868
EARLY CAREER Lawyer
MARRIED The only bachelor President
POLITICAL PARTY Democratic
VICE PRESIDENT John Breckinridge
HOBBIES Reading; entertaining friends; playing cards
ADMINISTRATION Dred Scott decision enacted; Pony Express begun
ANECDOTES Tilted his head when he spoke because one eye was nearsighted and the other eye was farsighted; gave all presidential gifts to the Patent Office; raised his orphaned niece, Harriet Lane, who later served as White House hostess

Abraham Lincoln (1861–1865)

BORN Feb. 12, 1809 **DIED** April 15, 1865
EARLY CAREER Rail-splitter; ferryboat captain; store clerk; postmaster; lawyer
MARRIED Mary Todd; four sons
POLITICAL PARTY Republican
VICE PRESIDENTS Hannibal Hamlin; Andrew Johnson
HOBBIES Reading; memorizing poetry; swapping jokes; attending theater; wrestling; walking
ADMINISTRATION Civil War fought; Emancipation Proclamation; Department of Agriculture established; signed Homestead Act
ANECDOTES The tallest President, 6' 4"; did not attend college; first President assassinated

Andrew Johnson (1865–1869)

BORN Dec. 29, 1808 **DIED** July 31, 1875
EARLY CAREER Tailor
MARRIED Eliza McCardle; three sons, two daughters
POLITICAL PARTY Union
VICE PRESIDENT None
HOBBIES Playing checkers; tending own vegetable garden; attending circus and minstrel shows
ADMINISTRATION 13th Amendment abolished slavery; 14th Amendment passed; purchased Alaska
ANECDOTES Never attended school and was illiterate at 17 when he opened a tailor shop; married at 18, his wife taught him to read, write, and figure math; the only President who was impeached

Ulysses Simpson Grant (1869–1877)

BORN April 27, 1822 **DIED** July 23, 1885
EARLY CAREER Farmer; store clerk; commanding general of the Union army at the end of the Civil War
MARRIED Julia Dent; three sons, one daughter
POLITICAL PARTY Republican
VICE PRESIDENTS Schuyler Colfax; Henry Wilson
HOBBIES Drawing; painting; riding horses
ADMINISTRATION Department of Justice created; first national park, Yellowstone, established
ANECDOTES Changed his name from Hiram, because his initials, HUG, bothered him; died penniless, four days after completing his autobiography, which earned his family nearly half a million dollars

Rutherford B. Hayes (1877-1881)

BORN Oct. 4, 1822 DIED Jan. 17, 1893
EARLY CAREER Lawyer; major general
MARRIED Lucy Ware Webb; seven sons, one
daughter
POLITICAL PARTY Republican
VICE PRESIDENT William A. Wheeler
HOBBIES Morning exercise; hunting; fishing;
shooting; playing chess and croquet; landscaping; reading
ADMINISTRATION Women permitted to practice law before U.S.
Supreme Court; last federal troops removed from South
ANECDOTES Distinguished himself in the Civil War (wounded four
times); his wife was the first First Lady to graduate from college;
first President to install a telephone in the White House; first
President to visit the West Coast (in 1880)

James A. Garfield (1881)

BORN Nov. 19, 1831 DIED Sept. 19, 1881
EARLY CAREER Farmer; carpenter; college professor
and president; lawyer; Civil War general
MARRIED Lucretia Rudolph; five sons, two
daughters
POLITICAL PARTY Republican
VICE PRESIDENT Chester A. Arthur
HOBBIES Reading, especially to Molly, his daughter; hunting; fishing;
playing chess and billiards
ADMINISTRATION American Red Cross established
ANECDOTES One of youngest Civil War generals; could write Greek
with one hand and Latin with the other at the same time; died 80
days after he was shot, the second of four Presidents assassinated

Chester A. Arthur (1881-1885)

BORN Oct. 5, 1829 DIED Nov. 18, 1886
EARLY CAREER Teacher; lawyer
MARRIED Ellen Lewis Herndon; two sons, one
daughter
POLITICAL PARTY Republican
VICE PRESIDENT none
HOBBIES Fishing, once catching an 80-pound
bass
ADMINISTRATION Civil Service Commission organized; Washington
Monument dedicated; standard time adopted
ANECDOTES Enjoyed fine clothes and fashionable surroundings;
moved into the White House only after the old furniture was
removed and the rooms were redecorated

Grover Cleveland (1885-1889 and 1893-1897)

BORN March 18, 1837 DIED June 24, 1908
EARLY CAREER Store clerk; teacher at school
for the blind; book editor; lawyer; sheriff
MARRIED Frances Folsom; three daughters,
two sons
POLITICAL PARTY Democratic
VICE PRESIDENT Thomas A. Hendricks
HOBBIES Fishing; morning walks; playing poker
ADMINISTRATION Interstate Commerce Commission established;
gold standard maintained; homesteaders settled the West
ANECDOTES Did not attend college; the only President married in the
White House; the only President to serve two nonconsecutive
terms; the candy bar Baby Ruth was named after his daughter

Benjamin Harrison (1889-1893)

BORN Aug. 20, 1833 DIED March 13, 1901
EARLY CAREER Lawyer
MARRIED Caroline Lavinia Scott; one son, one
daughter. Mary Lord Dimmick; one daughter
POLITICAL PARTY Republican
VICE PRESIDENT Levi P. Morton
HOBBIES Daily walks; duck hunting; playing billiards
ADMINISTRATION Pan-American Conference held; Sherman Antitrust
Act passed; six states entered the Union
ANECDOTES The only grandson of a President to become a
President; had the first billion dollar national budget; loved pets
and kept a goat named Old Whiskers for his grandchildren

William McKinley (1897-1901)

BORN Jan. 29, 1843 DIED Sept. 14, 1901
EARLY CAREER Teacher; post office clerk;
Civil War captain; lawyer
MARRIED Ida Saxton; two daughters
POLITICAL PARTY Republican
VICE PRESIDENTS Garret A. Hobart; Theodore
Roosevelt
HOBBIES Attending opera and theater;
playing cribbage
ADMINISTRATION Spanish-American War won, U.S. acquired the
Philippines, Puerto Rico, Guam, Samoa; Hawaii became U.S. territory
ANECDOTES Always wore a red carnation in his lapel for good luck;
was devoted to his invalid wife; campaigned from his front porch
in Canton, Ohio, where 750,000 people came to hear him; at an
exposition in Buffalo, NY, he was shot; died 8 days later, the third
of four Presidents assassinated

Theodore Roosevelt (1901–1909)

BORN Oct. 27, 1858 **DIED** Jan. 6, 1919
EARLY CAREER Cowboy; deputy sheriff; Rough Riders colonel
MARRIED Alice Hathaway Lee; one daughter. Edith Kermit Carow; four sons, one daughter
POLITICAL PARTY Republican
VICE PRESIDENT Charles W. Fairbanks
HOBBIES Horseback riding; hiking; swimming; hunting; boxing; reading
ADMINISTRATION Departments of Commerce and Labor created; Panama Canal Zone leased
ANECDOTES The youngest President; first American to win Nobel Peace Prize; was shot, but finished delivering speech before going to hospital to remove bullet; the original teddy bear was named after him because he refused to shoot a bear cub while hunting

William H. Taft (1909–1913)

BORN Sept. 15, 1859 **DIED** March 8, 1930
EARLY CAREER Reporter; lawyer; judge; professor and dean of law school
MARRIED Helen Herron; two sons, one daughter
POLITICAL PARTY Republican
VICE PRESIDENT James S. Sherman
HOBBIES Attending theater, playing golf
ADMINISTRATION Established parcel post; income tax established
ANECDOTES The heaviest President, weighing more than 330 pounds; once became stuck in bathtub; first President to throw out ball on opening day of baseball season; kept a cow named Pauline Wayne on the White House grounds; first President to become Chief Justice of U.S. Supreme Court, a job he enjoyed more than being President

Woodrow Wilson (1913–1921)

BORN Dec. 28, 1856 **DIED** Feb. 3, 1924
EARLY CAREER Lawyer; professor; president of Princeton University
MARRIED Ellen L. Axson; three daughters. Edith Bolling Galt; no children
POLITICAL PARTY Democratic
VICE PRESIDENT Thomas R. Marshall
HOBBIES Playing golf (painted golf balls black to see them in snow); horseback riding; attending musical comedies
ADMINISTRATION Purchased Virgin Islands; Federal Reserve Act passed; 19th Amendment guaranteed women's right to vote
ANECDOTES First President to earn a doctoral (PhD) degree and to hold a news conference; kept sheep to trim the White House lawn; because of a stroke, his wife Edith helped him complete his second term

Warren G. Harding (1921–1923)

BORN Nov. 2, 1865 **DIED** Aug. 2, 1923
EARLY CAREER Teacher; newspaper editor and publisher
MARRIED Florence Kling DeWolfe; one stepson
VICE PRESIDENT Calvin Coolidge
POLITICAL PARTY Republican
HOBBIES Playing golf; attending baseball games; boxing
ADMINISTRATION Teapot Dome scandal
ANECDOTES First President to give a speech over radio; first President to visit Alaska and Canada; interrupted a game of golf to sign peace treaty ending World War I and then resumed playing; loved his dog, Laddie Boy, an Airedale; complained his "friends. . . [are] the ones that keep me walking the floors nights"

Calvin Coolidge (1923–1929)

BORN July 4, 1872 **DIED** Jan. 5, 1933
EARLY CAREER Lawyer
MARRIED Grace Anna Goodhue; two sons
POLITICAL PARTY Republican
VICE PRESIDENT Charles G. Dawes
HOBBIES Playing the harmonica; fishing; playing golf; exercising with Indian clubs and mechanical horse
ADMINISTRATION U.S. Foreign Service created; U.S. citizenship granted to Native Americans
ANECDOTES Coolidge was sworn in by his father, a notary, by the light of a kerosene lamp, at 2:45 A.M., at his Vermont farm; first President born of Indian ancestry; walked his pet raccoon on a leash; had reputation for never wasting a penny or a word

Herbert C. Hoover (1929–1933)

BORN Aug. 10, 1874 **DIED** Oct. 20, 1964
EARLY CAREER Newsboy; mining engineer; supervisor of refugee relief in Europe during World War I
MARRIED Lou Henry; two sons
POLITICAL PARTY Republican
VICE PRESIDENT Charles Curtis
HOBBIES Fly-fishing; tossing medicine ball with Cabinet members
ADMINISTRATION Veterans Administration created; Great Depression occurred; "Star-Spangled Banner" adopted as national anthem
ANECDOTES Born poor, he was an orphan at nine; became a successful engineer and was worth $4 million by the age of 40; China's chief mining engineer; spoke Chinese with his wife in the White House for privacy; son had two alligators that sometimes wandered loose around the White House

Franklin D. Roosevelt (1933–1945)

BORN Jan. 30, 1882 **DIED** April 12, 1945
EARLY CAREER Lawyer
MARRIED Anna Eleanor Roosevelt, a distant cousin; five sons, one daughter
POLITICAL PARTY Democratic
VICE PRESIDENTS John N. Garner; Henry A. Wallace; Harry S Truman
HOBBIES Collecting stamps; sailing; swimming; playing poker
ADMINISTRATION New Deal of government relief and work programs; World War II
ANECDOTES Elected to four terms, more than any other President; appointed first woman Cabinet officer, Frances Perkins, Secretary of Labor; paralyzed from the waist down by polio; spoke to the people by radio in "fireside chats"

Harry S Truman (1945–1953)

BORN May 8, 1884 **DIED** Dec. 26, 1972
EARLY CAREER Railroad timekeeper; farmer; haberdasher; judge
MARRIED Bess Wallace; one daughter
POLITICAL PARTY Democratic
VICE PRESIDENT Alben W. Barkley
HOBBIES Playing the piano; early morning walks; architecture; playing poker; swimming
ADMINISTRATION Atomic bomb dropped, ending World War II; Truman Doctrine; NATO organized; ratified 22nd Amendment
ANECDOTES The only President of the 20th century who did not attend college; his middle initial, S, did not stand for anything; sign on his desk read "The Buck Stops Here," meaning he took responsibility for decisions

Dwight D. Eisenhower (1953–1961)

BORN Oct. 14, 1890 **DIED** March 28, 1969
EARLY CAREER West Point cadet; supreme Allied commander in Europe during World War II; President, Columbia University; organized NATO
MARRIED Marie "Mamie" G. Doud; two sons
POLITICAL PARTY Republican
VICE PRESIDENT Richard M. Nixon
HOBBIES Playing golf, cooking, landscape painting; reading westerns
ADMINISTRATION NASA established; Alaska and Hawaii became states; 1st U.S. satellite launched
ANECDOTES The third of six sons, all nicknamed "Ike"; superstitious, he carried three lucky coins: a silver dollar, five-guinea gold piece, and a French franc; lived in 28 different homes before his retirement; first President to be a licensed airplane pilot

John F. Kennedy (1961–1963)

BORN May 29, 1917 **DIED** Nov. 22, 1963
EARLY CAREER Navy lieutenant; journalist
MARRIED Jacqueline Lee Bouvier; one daughter, two sons
POLITICAL PARTY Democratic
VICE PRESIDENT Lyndon B. Johnson
HOBBIES Playing touch football and golf; sailing; swimming
ADMINISTRATION Peace Corps created; Nuclear Test Ban Treaty; Civil Rights March; first U.S. astronaut in space
ANECDOTES First President born in 20th century; was a Boy Scout as a youth; could read 2,000 words per minute and understand most of it; only President to win a Pulitzer Prize, for *Profiles in Courage,* a biography; fourth of four Presidents assassinated

Lyndon B. Johnson (1963–1969)

BORN Aug. 27, 1908 **DIED** Jan. 22, 1973
EARLY CAREER Teacher; rancher
MARRIED Claudia "Lady Bird" Taylor; two daughters
POLITICAL PARTY Democratic
VICE PRESIDENT Hubert H. Humphrey
HOBBIES Enjoying life on his ranch; horseback riding; fishing; hunting
ADMINISTRATION Signed Civil Rights Act; proposed Great Society; Department of Housing and Urban Development created; increased number of troops sent to Vietnam; appointed first African American justice of the U.S. Supreme Court, Thurgood Marshall
ANECDOTES Took oath of office on jet airplane after the assassination of President Kennedy; first President sworn in by a woman

Richard M. Nixon (1969–1974)

BORN Jan 9, 1913 **DIED** April 22, 1994
EARLY CAREER Naval officer; lawyer; owned frozen-orange-juice company
MARRIED Thelma Catherine "Pat" Ryan; two daughters
POLITICAL PARTY Republican
VICE PRESIDENT Spiro T. Agnew; Gerald R. Ford
HOBBIES Playing the piano; bowling; playing golf; swimming; reading history
ADMINISTRATION Established relations with China; withdrew troops from Vietnam; first U.S. astronauts walk on moon; voting age lowered from 21 to 18
ANECDOTES First President to visit Communist China; only President to resign from office, which he did on Aug. 9, 1974, to avoid impeachment for his part in Watergate scandal

Gerald R. Ford (1974–1977)

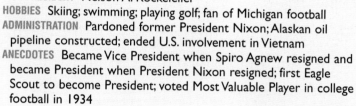

BORN July 14, 1913
EARLY CAREER National Park ranger; college football coach; naval officer; lawyer
MARRIED Elizabeth (Betty) Bloomer Warren; three sons, one daughter
POLITICAL PARTY Republican
VICE PRESIDENT Nelson A. Rockefeller
HOBBIES Skiing; swimming; playing golf; fan of Michigan football
ADMINISTRATION Pardoned former President Nixon; Alaskan oil pipeline constructed; ended U.S. involvement in Vietnam
ANECDOTES Became Vice President when Spiro Agnew resigned and became President when President Nixon resigned; first Eagle Scout to become President; voted Most Valuable Player in college football in 1934

James Earl "Jimmy" Carter (1977–1981)

BORN Oct. 1, 1924
EARLY CAREER Naval officer; owned peanut farm
MARRIED Rosalynn Smith; one daughter, three sons
POLITICAL PARTY Democratic
VICE PRESIDENT Walter F. Mondale
HOBBIES Jogging; fishing; playing tennis; reading
ADMINISTRATION Human rights in foreign policy; Camp David accords; recognized China; Department of Energy created
ANECDOTES First President born in a hospital; graduated with honors from U.S. Naval Academy; helped develop first nuclear-powered submarine; at first presidential phone-in, more than 9 million people tried to speak to Carter, and 42 actually got through

Ronald Reagan (1981–1989)

BORN Feb. 6, 1911
EARLY CAREER Radio announcer; actor; union president; corporate spokesman
MARRIED Jane Wyman; one son, one daughter. Anne "Nancy" Davis; one son, one daughter
POLITICAL PARTY Republican
VICE PRESIDENT George H.W. Bush
HOBBIES Horseback riding; ranching; exercising
ADMINISTRATION Reaganomics; appointed first woman justice of U.S. Supreme Court; Iran-Contra scandal; invasion of Grenada; Strategic Defense Initiative (Star Wars)
ANECDOTES Oldest man elected President; as a lifeguard in Illinois (1927–1932), he saved 77 people from drowning, and the town put up a plaque in his honor; kept jar of jelly beans for Cabinet meetings; after assassination attempt and before doctors removed a bullet from his lung, he said, "Please assure me you are all Republicans."

George H.W. Bush (1989–1993)

BORN June 12, 1924
EARLY CAREER Navy pilot; founded oil companies
MARRIED Barbara Pierce; four sons, two daughters
POLITICAL PARTY Republican
VICE PRESIDENT J. Danforth Quayle
HOBBIES Boating; fishing; hunting; playing horseshoes and tennis
ADMINISTRATION Concluded North American Free Trade Agreement; Persian Gulf War; first U.S.-Russia summit; savings and loan crisis; Americans With Disabilities Act
ANECDOTES Awarded the Distinguished Flying Cross for heroism in World War II; was ambassador to the United Nations and CIA director; headed U.S. Liaison Office in Beijing, China

William J. "Bill" Clinton (1993–

BORN August 19, 1946
EARLY CAREER Law professor
MARRIED Hillary Rodham; one daughter
POLITICAL PARTY Democratic
VICE PRESIDENT Albert Gore, Jr.
HOBBIES Jogging; playing golf; reading; playing tenor saxophone
ADMINISTRATION Anticrime law passed; joint space effort with Russia; appointed first female U.S. Attorney General, Janet Reno; troops sent to Haiti and Bosnia
ANECDOTES First President born after World War II; named after his father, he was adopted by his stepfather; at 17, as delegate to American Legion Boys Nation, he went to White House and shook hands with President Kennedy; first President who had been a Rhodes scholar

The Declaration of Independence

In Congress, July 4, 1776

Why the Declaration of Independence Was Issued
This paragraph states that it has become necessary for the American colonists to break their political ties with Great Britain, and that it is only proper to explain why they are taking this step. (One reason was that the colonists hoped to get help from other nations.)

When, in the course of human events, it becomes necessary for one people to dissolve the political bands which have connected them with another, and to assume, among the powers of the earth, the separate and equal station to which the laws of nature and nature's God entitle them, a decent respect to the opinions of mankind requires that they should declare the causes which impel them to the separation.

The Purposes of Government
This paragraph is the very heart of the Declaration of Independence. It states that all men are born with equal claims to "life, liberty, and the pursuit of happiness." These rights, given by the Creator, are "unalienable," that is, they cannot be given away, nor can a government take them away.

The paragraph goes on to state that governments were created to protect these human rights. Whenever a government interferes with them, its citizens have the right as well as the duty to change or do away with the government. A government must be based on the consent of the governed. Changing or doing away with a government will be carried out, however, only after events have proved that the government has abused its powers.

We hold these truths to be self-evident; that all men are created equal, that they are endowed by their Creator with certain unalienable rights, that among these are life, liberty, and the pursuit of happiness. That to secure these rights, governments are instituted among men, deriving their just powers from the consent of the governed; that whenever any form of government becomes destructive of these ends, it is the right of the people to alter or to abolish it, and to institute new government, laying its foundation on such principles, and organizing its powers in such form, as to them shall seem most likely to effect their safety and happiness. Prudence, indeed, will dictate that governments long established should not be changed for light and transient causes; and accordingly all experience hath shown that mankind are more disposed to suffer, while evils are sufferable, than to right themselves by abolishing the forms to which they are accustomed. But when a long train of abuses and usurpations, pursuing invariably the same object, evinces a design to reduce them under absolute despotism, it is their right, it is their duty, to throw off such government, and to provide new guards for their future security.

The Charges Against the British King
Here the Declaration of Independence reviews the years between 1763 and 1776, stating that the colonists believed the king's government had many times denied their basic human rights. King George III and his government are charged with committing a long list of misdeeds. Because of these acts, the declaration states that the king is no longer entitled to rule the American colonies. He no longer has the consent of the governed.

Such has been the patient sufferance of these colonies; and such is now the necessity which constrains them to alter their former systems of government. The history of the present king of Great Britain is a history of repeated injuries and usurpations, all having in direct object the establishment of an absolute tyranny over these states. To prove this, let facts be submitted to a candid world.

He has refused his assent to laws the most wholesome and necessary for the public good.

He has forbidden his governors to pass laws of immediate and pressing importance, unless suspended in their operation till his assent should be obtained; and when so suspended, he has utterly neglected to attend to them.

He has refused to pass other laws for the accommodation of large districts of people, unless those people would relinquish the right of representation in the legislature, a right inestimable to them, and formidable to tyrants only.

He has called together legislative bodies at places unusual, uncomfortable, and distant from the depository of their public records, for the sole purpose of fatiguing them into compliance with his measures.

He has dissolved representative houses repeatedly, for opposing, with manly firmness, his invasions on the rights of the people.

He has refused, for a long time after such dissolutions, to cause others to be elected; whereby the legislative powers, incapable of annihilation, have returned to the people at large for their exercise; the state remaining, in the meantime, exposed to all the dangers of invasion from without and convulsions within.

He has endeavored to prevent the population of these states; for that purpose obstructing the laws for the naturalization of foreigners, refusing to pass others to encourage their migrations hither, and raising the conditions of new appropriations of lands.

He has obstructed the administration of justice, by refusing his assent to laws for establishing judiciary powers.

He has made judges dependent on his will alone for the tenure of their offices, and the amount and payment of their salaries.

He has erected a multitude of new offices, and sent hither swarms of officers to harass our people and eat out their substance.

He has kept among us, in times of peace, standing armies, without the consent of our legislatures.

He has affected to render the military independent of, and superior to, the civil power.

He has combined with others to subject us to a jurisdiction foreign to our constitution and unacknowledged by our laws, giving his assent to their acts of pretended legislation:

For quartering large bodies of armed troops among us;

For protecting them, by a mock trial, from punishment for any murders which they should commit on the inhabitants of these states;

For cutting off our trade with all parts of the world;

For imposing taxes on us without our consent;

For depriving us, in many cases, of the benefits of trial by jury;

For transporting us beyond seas, to be tried for pretended offenses;

For abolishing the free system of English laws in a neighboring province, establishing therein an arbitrary government, and enlarging its boundaries, so as to render it at once an example and fit instrument for introducing the same absolute rule into these colonies;

For taking away our charters, abolishing our most valuable laws, and altering fundamentally the forms of our governments;

For suspending our own legislatures, and declaring themselves invested with power to legislate for us in all cases whatsoever.

He has abdicated government here, by declaring us out of his protection and waging war against us.

He has plundered our seas, ravaged our coasts, burned our towns, and destroyed the lives of our people.

He is at this time transporting large armies of foreign mercenaries to complete the works of death, desolation, and tyranny already begun with circumstances of cruelty and perfidy scarcely paralleled in the most barbarous ages, and totally unworthy the head of a civilized nation.

He has constrained our fellow-citizens, taken captive on the high seas, to bear arms against their country, to become the executioners of their friends and brethren, or to fall themselves by their hands.

He has excited domestic insurrection among us, and has endeavored to bring on the inhabitants of our frontiers, the merciless Indian savages, whose known rule of warfare is an undistinguished destruction of all ages, sexes, and conditions.

In every stage of these oppressions we have petitioned for redress in the most humble terms; our repeated petitions have been answered only by repeated injury. A prince whose character is thus marked by every act which may define a tyrant is unfit to be the ruler of a free people.

Nor have we been wanting in attentions to our British brethren. We have warned them, from time to time, of attempts by their legislature to extend an unwarrantable jurisdiction over us. We have reminded them of the circumstances of our emigration and settlement here. We have appealed to their native justice and magnanimity; and we have conjured them, by the ties of our common kindred, to disavow these usurpations, which would inevitably interrupt our connections and correspondence. They, too, have been deaf to the voice of justice and consanguinity. We must, therefore, acquiesce in the necessity which denounces our separation, and hold them, as we hold the rest of mankind, enemies in war; in peace, friends.

We, therefore, the representatives of the United States of America, in General Congress assembled, appealing to the Supreme Judge of the world for the rectitude of our intentions, do, in the name and by the authority of the good people of these colonies, solemnly publish and declare that these United Colonies are, and of right ought to be, free and independent states; that they are absolved from all allegiance to the British crown, and that all political connection between them and the state of Great Britain is, and ought to be, totally dissolved; and that, as free and independent states, they have full power to levy war, conclude peace, contract alliances, establish commerce, and do all other acts and things which independent states may of right do. And, for the support of this declaration, with a firm reliance on the protection of Divine Providence, we mutually pledge to each other our lives, our fortunes, and our sacred honor.

The Attempts to Obtain Justice
These two paragraphs state that the American colonists have asked the British king for justice. They have also appealed to the British people. Yet neither the king nor the British people have responded to the colonists' pleas.

The Colonies Declare Their Independence
This final paragraph actually proclaims independence. It also lists those things that the new United States of America may do as an independent country.

In the last sentence the signers pledge their lives and all they own to support the cause of independence. This was a serious matter, for as Benjamin Franklin said, "Now we must all hang together, or we will all hang separately." Still, they took the risk and signed the document that proclaimed to the world the independence of the United States of America.

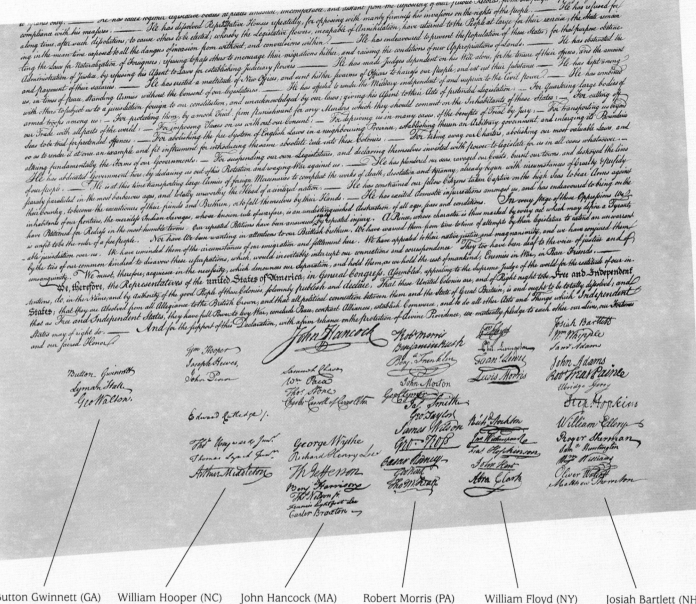

Button Gwinnett (GA)
Lymann Hall (GA)
George Walton (GA)

William Hooper (NC)
Joseph Hewes (NC)
John Penn (NC)

Edward Rutledge (SC)

Thomas Heyward, Jr. (SC)

Thomas Lynch, Jr. (SC)
Arthur Middleton (SC)

John Hancock (MA)

Samuel Chase (MD)
William Paca (MD)
Thomas Stone (MD)
Charles Carroll of Carrollton (MD)

George Wythe (VA)
Richard Henry Lee (VA)
Thomas Jefferson (VA)
Benjamin Harrison (VA)
Thomas Nelson, Jr. (VA)
Francis Lightfoot Lee (VA)
Carter Braxton (VA)

Robert Morris (PA)
Benjamin Rush (PA)
Benjamin Franklin (PA)
John Morton (PA)
George Clymer (PA)
James Smith (PA)
George Taylor (PA)
James Wilson (PA)
George Ross (PA)
Caesar Rodney (DE)
George Read (DE)
Thomas McKean (DE)

William Floyd (NY)
Philip Livingston (NY)
Francis Lewis (NY)
Lewis Morris (NY)

Richard Stockton (NJ)
John Witherspoon (NJ)
Francis Hopkinson (NJ)
John Hart (NJ)
Abraham Clark (NJ)

Josiah Bartlett (NH)
William Whipple (NH)
Samuel Adams (MA)

John Adams (MA)
Robert Treat Paine (MA)
Elbridge Gerry (MA)
Stephen Hopkins (RI)
William Ellery (RI)
Roger Sherman (CT)
Samuel Huntington (CT)
William Williams (CT)
Oliver Wolcott (CT)
Matthew Thornton (NH)

The Constitution of the United States of America

We the people of the United States, in order to form a more perfect union, establish justice, insure domestic tranquility, provide for the common defense, promote the general welfare, and secure the blessings of liberty to ourselves and our posterity, do ordain and establish this Constitution for the United States of America.

ARTICLE I

SECTION 1.

All legislative powers herein granted shall be vested in a Congress of the United States, which shall consist of a Senate and House of Representatives.

SECTION 2.

The House of Representatives shall be composed of members chosen every second year by the people of the several States, and the electors in each State shall have the qualifications requisite for electors of the most numerous branch of the State legislature.

No person shall be a representative who shall not have attained to the age of twenty-five years, and been seven years a citizen of the United States, and who shall not, when elected, be an inhabitant of that State in which he shall be chosen.

Representatives and direct taxes shall be apportioned among the several States which may be included within this Union, according to their respective numbers, which shall be determined by adding to the whole numbers of free persons, including those bound to service for a term of years, and excluding Indians not taxed, three fifths of all other persons.* The actual enumeration shall be made within three years after the first meeting of the Congress of the United States, and within every subsequent term of ten years, in such manner as they shall by law direct. The number of representatives shall not exceed one for every thirty thousand, but each State shall have at least one representative; and until such enumeration shall be made, the State of New Hampshire shall be entitled to choose three, Massachusetts eight, Rhode Island and Providence Plantations one, Connecticut five, New York six, New Jersey four, Pennsylvania eight, Delaware one, Maryland six, Virginia ten, North Carolina five, South Carolina five, and Georgia

---

The Preamble

This Constitution has been written and put into practice for the following reasons:
- To have a better government than that under the Articles of Confederation
- To see that everyone is treated fairly
- To keep peace within the country
- To defend the country from enemies
- To see that people live comfortably and well
- To keep people free both now and in the future.

Article I
The Legislative Branch
Section 1

All legislative, or law making, powers are given to the Congress. It has two parts, or houses: the Senate and the House of Representatives.

Section 2

Members of the House of Representatives serve a 2-year term. A term is a length of time. A representative must have been a citizen of the United States for at least 7 years, must be at least 25 years old, and must live in the state he or she will represent when elected.

The number of representatives from each state depends on that state's population. Each state has at least one representative. The total membership of the House of Representatives is limited to 435 voting members.

To decide the number of representatives from each state, the national government must count the number of people every 10 years. This count of population is called a census.

three. (*Changed by the Fourteenth Amendment*)

When vacancies happen in the representation from any State, the executive authority thereof shall issue writs of election to fill such vacancies.

The House of Representatives shall choose their speaker and other officers, and shall have the sole power of impeachment.

SECTION 3.

The Senate of the United States shall be composed of two senators from each State, chosen by the legislature thereof,* for six years; and each senator shall have one vote. (*Changed by the Seventeenth Amendment*)

Immediately after they shall be assembled in consequence of the first election, they shall be divided as equally as may be into three classes. The seats of the senators of the first class shall be vacated at the expiration of the second year, of the second class at the expiration of the fourth year, and of the third class at the expiration of the sixth year, so that one third may be chosen every second year; and if vacancies happen by resignation, or otherwise, during the recess of the legislature of any State, the executive thereof may make temporary appointments until the next meeting of the legislature, which shall then fill such vacancies.* (*Changed by the Seventeenth Amendment*)

No person shall be a senator who shall not have attained to the age of thirty years, and been nine years a citizen of the United States, and who shall not, when elected, be an inhabitant of that State for which he shall be chosen.

The Vice President of the United States shall be president of the Senate, but shall have no vote, unless they be equally divided.

The Senate shall choose their other officers, and also a president pro tempore, in the absence of the Vice President, or when he shall exercise the office of President of the United States.

The Senate shall have the sole power to try all impeachments. When sitting for that purpose, they shall be an oath or affirmation. When the President of the United States is tried, the Chief Justice shall preside: and no person shall be convicted without the concurrence of two thirds of the members present.

Judgment in cases of impeachment shall not extend further than to removal from office, and disqualification to hold any office of honor, trust or profit under the United States: but the party convicted shall nevertheless be liable and subject to indictment, trial, judgment and punishment, according to law.

SECTION 4.

The times, places, and manner of holding elections for senators and representatives shall be prescribed in each State by the legislature thereof; but the Congress may at any time by law make or alter such regulations, except as to the places of choosing senators.

The Congress shall assemble at least once in every year, and such

Section 3
The Senate is made up of two senators from each state. A senator serves a 6-year term. One third of the total membership of the Senate is elected every 2 years.

A senator must have been a citizen of the United States for at least 9 years, must be at least 30 years old, and must live in the state he or she will represent.

The Vice President of the United States is in charge of the Senate but may vote only to break a tie vote.

Both the House and the Senate have roles in the process known as impeachment. It is the House of Representatives that charges a government official with misconduct. The Senate then acts as a court to decide if the official is guilty. If two thirds of the senators agree that the official is guilty, he or she is removed from office. If the official is the President, then the Chief Justice of the United States acts as the judge.

Sections 4–7
Rules for running the House and the Senate are described here. Each house must keep a daily record of its actions. This is published so that people can find out how their representatives voted on bills. Members of Congress are paid by the government.

meeting shall be on the first Monday in December,* unless they shall by law appoint a different day. (*Changed by the Twentieth Amendment)

SECTION 5.

Each house shall be the judge of the elections, returns and qualifications of its own members, and a majority of each shall constitute a quorum to do business; but a smaller number may adjourn from day to day, and may be authorized to compel the attendance of absent members, in such manner, and under such penalties as each house may provide.

Each house may determine the rules of its proceedings, punish its members for disorderly behavior, and, with the concurrence of two thirds, expel a member.

Each house shall keep a journal of its proceedings, and from time to time publish the same, excepting such parts as may in their judgment require secrecy; and the yeas and nays of the members of either house on any question shall, at the desire of one fifth of those present, be entered on the journal.

Neither house, during the session of Congress, shall, without the consent of the other, adjourn for more than three days, nor to any other place than that in which the two houses shall be sitting.

SECTION 6.

The senators and representatives shall receive a compensation for their services, to be ascertained by law, and paid out of the Treasury of the United States. They shall in all cases, except treason, felony and breach of the peace, be privileged from arrest during their attendance at the session of their respective houses, and in going to and returning from the same; and for any speech or debate in either house, they shall not be questioned in any other place.

No senator or representative shall, during the time for which he was elected, be appointed to any civil office under the authority of the United States, which shall have been created, or the emoluments thereof shall have been increased during such time; and no person holding any office under the United States shall be a member of either house during his continuance in office.

SECTION 7.

All bills for raising revenue shall originate in the House of Representatives; but the Senate may propose or concur with amendments as on other bills.

Every bill which shall have passed the House of Representatives and the Senate, shall, before it become a law, be presented to the President of the United States; if he approve he shall sign it, but if not he shall return it, with his objections to that house in which it shall have originated, who shall enter the objections at large on their journal, and proceed to reconsider it. If after such reconsideration two thirds of that house shall agree to pass the bill, it shall be sent, together with the objections, to the other house, by which it shall likewise be reconsidered, and if approved by two thirds of that house, it shall become a law. But in all such cases the votes of both houses shall be determined by yeas and nays, and the names of the persons voting for and against the bill shall be entered on the journal of each house respectively. If any bill shall not be returned by the President within ten days (Sundays excepted) after it shall have been presented to him, the same shall be a law, in like manner as if he had signed it, unless the Congress by their adjournment prevent its return, in which case it shall not be a law.

Every order, resolution, or vote to which the concurrence of the Senate and House of Representatives may be necessary (except on a question of adjournment) shall be presented to the President of the United States; and before the same shall take effect, shall be approved by him, or being disapproved by him, shall be repassed by two thirds of the Senate and House of Representatives, according to the rules and limitations prescribed in the case of a bill.

SECTION 8.

The Congress shall have power to lay and collect taxes, duties, imposts and excises, to pay the debts and provide for the common defense and general welfare of the United States; but all duties, imposts and excises shall be uniform throughout the United States;

To borrow money on the credit of the United States;

To regulate commerce with foreign nations, and among the several States, and with the Indian tribes;

To establish a uniform rule of naturalization, and uniform laws on the subject of bankruptcies through the United States;

To coin money, regulate the value thereof, and of foreign coin, and fix the standard of weights and measures;

To provide for the punishment of counterfeiting the securities and current coin of the United States;

To establish post offices and post roads;

To promote the progress of science and useful arts by securing for limited times to authors and inventors the exclusive right to their respective writings and discoveries;

To constitute tribunals inferior to the Supreme Court;

To define and punish piracies and felonies committed on the high seas, and offenses against the law of nations;

To declare war, grant letters of marque and reprisal, and make rules concerning captures on land and water;

To raise and support armies, but no appropriation of money to that use shall be for a longer term than two years;

To provide and maintain a navy;

To make rules for the government and regulations of the land and naval forces;

To provide for calling forth the militia to execute the laws of the Union, suppress insurrections and repel invasions;

Section 8
The powers and duties of Congress are listed here. Congress makes all laws concerning money and trade. Congress decides how people become citizens of the United States. It has the power to declare war.

The last paragraph of Section 8 is the "elastic clause." It gives Congress the power to make whatever laws it thinks necessary to carry out the powers listed in Section 8.

To provide for organizing, arming, and disciplining the militia, and for governing such part of them as may be employed in the service of the United States, reserving to the States respectively the appointment of the officers, and the authority of training the militia according to the discipline prescribed by Congress;

To exercise exclusive legislation in all cases whatsoever, over such district (not exceeding ten miles square) as may, by cession of particular States and the acceptance of Congress, become the seat of the government of the United States, and to exercise like authority over all places purchased by the consent of the legislature of the State in which the same shall be, for the erection of forts, magazines, arsenals, dockyards, and other needful buildings; and

To make all laws which shall be necessary and proper for carrying into execution the foregoing powers, and all other powers vested by this Constitution in the government of the United States, or in any department or officer thereof.

SECTION 9.

Section 9
There are actions that Congress may not take. This section protects the people of the United States against injustice.

The migration or importation of such persons as any of the States now existing shall think proper to admit, shall not be prohibited by the Congress prior to the year one thousand eight hundred and eight, but a tax or duty may be imposed on such importation, not exceeding ten dollars for each person.

The privilege of the writ of habeas corpus shall not be suspended, unless when in cases of rebellion or invasion the public safety may require it.

No bill of attainder or ex post facto law shall be passed.

No capitation, or other direct,* tax shall be laid, unless in proportion to the census or enumeration herein before directed to be taken. (*Changed by the Sixteenth Amendment)

No tax or duty shall be laid on articles exported from any State.

No preference shall be given by any regulation of commerce or revenue to the ports of one State over those of another; nor shall vessels bound to, or from, one State be obliged to enter, clear, or pay duties in another.

No money shall be drawn from the Treasury, but in consequence of appropriations made by law; and a regular statement and account of the receipts and expenditures of all public money shall be published from time to time.

No title of nobility shall be granted by the United States: and no person holding any office of profit or trust under them, shall, without the consent of the Congress, accept of any present, emolument, office, or title of any kind whatever, from any king, prince, or foreign State.

SECTION 10.

Section 10
The states may not assume any of the powers that are specifically given to Congress. The states also may not do certain things that the national government cannot do.

No State shall enter into any treaty, alliance, or confederation; grant letters of marque and reprisal; coin money; emit bills of credit; make anything but gold and silver coin a tender in payment of debts;

pass any bill of attainder, ex post facto law, or law impairing the obligation of contracts, or grant any title of nobility.

No State shall, without the consent of the Congress, lay any imposts or duties on imports or exports, except what may be absolutely necessary for executing its inspection laws: and the net produce of all duties and imposts laid by any State on imports or exports, shall be for the use of the Treasury of the United States; and all such laws shall be subject to the revision and control of the Congress.

No State shall, without the consent of Congress, lay any duty of tonnage, keep troops, or ships of war in time of peace, enter into any agreement or compact with another State, or with a foreign power, or engage in war, unless actually invaded, or in such imminent danger as will not admit of delay.

ARTICLE II

SECTION 1.

The executive power shall be vested in a President of the United States of America. He shall hold his office during the term of four years, and, together with the Vice President chosen for the same term, be elected as follows:

Each State shall appoint, in such manner as the legislature thereof may direct, a number of electors, equal to the whole number of senators and representatives to which the State may be entitled in the Congress: but no senator or representative, or person holding an office of trust or profit under the United States, shall be appointed an elector.

The electors shall meet in their respective States, and vote by ballot for two persons, of whom one at least shall not be an inhabitant of the same State with themselves. And they shall make a list of all the persons voted for, and of the number of votes for each; which they shall sign and certify, and transmit sealed to the seat of the government of the United States, directed to the president of the Senate. The president of the Senate shall, in the presence of the Senate and House of Representatives, open all the certificates, and the votes shall then be counted. The person having the greatest number of votes shall be the President, if such number be a majority of the whole number of electors appointed; and if there be more than one who have such majority, and have an equal number of votes, then the House of Representatives shall immediately choose by ballot one of them for President; and if no person have a majority, then from the five highest on the list the said house shall in like manner choose the President. But in choosing the President, the votes shall be taken by States, the representation from each State having one vote; a quorum for this purpose shall consist of a member or members from two thirds of the States, and a majority of all the States shall be necessary to a choice.

Article II
The Executive Branch
Section I
The executive branch is the President, Vice President, and those who help carry out the laws passed by Congress. The President manages the government. The President and Vice President are elected to a 4-year term. The Vice President takes office if the President dies or resigns.
A President must have been born in the United States, must be at least 35 years old, and must have lived in the United States for at least 14 years.

In every case, after the choice of the President, the person having the greatest number of votes of the electors shall be the Vice President. But if there should remain two or more who have equal votes, the Senate shall choose from them by ballot the Vice President.*
(*Changed by the Twelfth Amendment)

The Congress may determine the time of choosing the electors, and the day on which they shall give their votes; which day shall be the same throughout the United States.

No person except a natural-born citizen, or a citizen of the United States, at the time of the adoption of this Constitution, shall be eligible to the office of President; neither shall any person be eligible to that office who shall not have attained to the age of thirty-five years, and been fourteen years a resident within the United States.

In case of the removal of the President from office, or of his death, resignation, or inability to discharge the powers and duties of the said office, the same shall devolve on the Vice President, and the Congress may by law provide for the case of removal, death, resignation, or inability, both of the President and Vice President, declaring what officer shall then act as President, and such officer shall act accordingly, until the disability be removed, or a President shall be elected.

The President shall, at stated times, receive for his services a compensation, which shall neither be increased nor diminished during the period for which he shall have been elected, and he shall not receive within that period any other emolument from the United States, or any of them.

Before he enter on the execution of his office, he shall take the following oath or affirmation:—"I do solemnly swear (or affirm) that I will faithfully execute the office of President of the United States, and will to the best of my ability, preserve, protect and defend the Constitution of the United States."

SECTION 2.

The President shall be commander in chief of the army and navy of the United States, and of the militia of the several States, when called into the actual service of the United States; he may require the opinion, in writing, of the principal officer in each of the executive departments, upon any subject relating to the duties of their respective offices, and he shall have power to grant reprieves and pardons for offenses against the United States, except in cases of impeachment.

He shall have power, by and with the advice and consent of the Senate, to make treaties, provided two thirds of the senators present concur; and he shall nominate, and by and with the advice and consent of the Senate, shall appoint ambassadors, other public ministers and consuls, judges of the Supreme Court, and all other officers of the United States, whose appointments are not herein otherwise provided for, and which shall be established by law: but the Congress may by law vest the appointment of such inferior officers, as they think proper, in the President alone, in the courts of law, or in the heads of

Sections 2–4
Some of the President's duties include carrying out the laws made by Congress, commanding all the armed forces, pardoning crimes, and reporting to Congress at least once a year on the overall condition of the nation. The President makes treaties and appoints government leaders with the approval of the Senate.

departments.

The President shall have power to fill up all vacancies that may happen during the recess of the Senate, by granting commissions which shall expire at the end of their next session.

SECTION 3.

He shall from time to time give to the Congress information of the state of the Union, and recommend to their consideration such measures as he shall judge necessary and expedient; he may, on extraordinary occasions, convene both houses, or either of them, and in case of disagreement between them with respect to the time of adjournment, he may adjourn them to such time as he shall think proper; he shall receive ambassadors and other public ministers; he shall take care that the laws be faithfully executed, and shall commission all the officers of the United States.

SECTION 4.

The President, Vice President, and all civil officers of the United States, shall be removed from office on impeachment for, and conviction of, treason, bribery, or other high crimes and misdemeanors.

ARTICLE III

SECTION 1.

The judicial power of the United States shall be vested in one Supreme Court, and in such inferior courts as the Congress may from time to time ordain and establish. The judges, both of the Supreme and inferior courts, shall hold their offices during good behavior, and shall, at stated times, receive for their services, a compensation which shall not be diminished during their continuance in office.

SECTION 2.

The judicial power shall extend to all cases, in law and equity, arising under this Constitution, the laws of the United States, and treaties made, or which shall be made, under their authority;—to all cases affecting ambassadors, other public ministers and consuls;—to all cases of admiralty and maritime jurisdiction;—to controversies to which the United States shall be a party;—to controversies between two or more States;—between a State and citizens of another State;—between citizens of different States;—between citizens of the same State claiming lands under grants of different States, and between a State, or the citizens thereof, and foreign States, citizens or subjects.

In all cases affecting ambassadors, other public ministers and consuls, and those in which a State shall be party, the Supreme Court shall have original jurisdiction. In all the other cases before mentioned, the Supreme Court shall have appellate jurisdiction, both as to law and

Article III
The Judicial Branch
Section 1
The federal court system is the judicial branch of government. The Supreme Court is the nation's highest court. It makes the final decisions in all matters of law. Federal judges are not elected. They are the only officials of the national government who may hold office for life.

Section 2
Federal courts handle certain kinds of cases. Only a few are handled directly by the Supreme Court. The judgment of the Supreme Court is final.

One of the great powers of our federal courts is their right to declare an act of Congress or a state legislature unconstitutional. This right is not mentioned specifically in any part of the Constitution.

fact, with such exceptions, and under such regulations as the Congress shall make.

The trial of all crimes, except in cases of impeachment, shall be by jury; and such trial shall be held in the State where the said crimes shall have been committed; but when not committed within any State, the trial shall be at such place or places as the Congress may by law have directed.

SECTION 3.

Treason against the United States shall consist only in levying war against them, or in adhering to their enemies, giving them aid and comfort. No person shall be convicted of treason unless on the testimony of two witnesses to the same overt act, or on confession in open court.

The Congress shall have power to declare the punishment of treason, but no attainder of treason shall work corruption of blood, or forfeiture except during the life of the person attained.

ARTICLE IV

SECTION 1.

Full faith and credit shall be given in each State to the public acts, records, and judicial proceedings of every other State. And the Congress may by general laws prescribe the manner in which such acts, records, and proceedings shall be proved, and the effect thereof.

SECTION 2.

The citizens of each State shall be entitled to all privileges and immunities of citizens in the several States.

A person charged in any State with treason, felony, or other crime, who shall flee from justice, and be found in another State, shall on demand of the executive authority of the State from which he fled, be delivered up to be removed to the State having jurisdiction of the crime.

No person held to service or labor in the State, under the laws thereof, escaping into another, shall, in consequence of any law or regulation therein, be discharged from such service or labor, but shall be delivered up on claim of the party to whom such service or labor may be due.* (*Changed by the Thirteenth Amendment)

SECTION 3.

New States may be admitted by the Congress into this Union; but no new State shall be formed or erected within the jurisdiction of any other State; nor any State be formed by the junction of two or more States, or parts of States, without the consent of the legislatures of the

Section 3
The crime of treason—that is, of trying to overthrow the government—is explained.

Article IV
The States
Sections 1–2
All states must accept acts, records, and laws of other states. A citizen of one state must be given the same rights as a citizen of another state when visiting that other state. The governor of one state has the power to send someone accused of a crime in another state back to that state for trial.

Sections 3–4
New states may be added to the United States. The United States government will protect all states from enemies.

States concerned as well as of the Congress.

The Congress shall have power to dispose of and make all needful rules and regulations respecting the territory or other property belonging to the United States; and nothing in this Constitution shall be so construed as to prejudice any claims of the United States, or of any particular State.

SECTION 4.

The United States shall guarantee to every State in this Union a republican form of government, and shall protect each of them against invasion; and on application of the legislature, or of the executive (when the legislature cannot be convened) against domestic violence.

ARTICLE V

The Congress, whenever two thirds of both houses shall deem it necessary, shall propose amendments to this Constitution, or, on the application of the legislatures of two thirds of the several States, shall call a convention for proposing amendments, which, in either case, shall be valid to all intents and purposes, as part of this Constitution, when ratified by the legislatures of three fourths of the several States, or by conventions in three fourths thereof, as the one or the other mode of ratification may be proposed by the Congress; provided [that no amendment which may be made prior to the year one thousand eight hundred and eight shall in any manner affect the first and fourth clauses in the ninth section of the first article, and] that no State, without its consent, shall be deprived of its equal suffrage in the Senate.

Article V
Making Changes
The Constitution may be amended, or changed. The ways of amending the Constitution are explained. Only 26 amendments have been made since the Constitution was adopted.

ARTICLE VI

All debts contracted and engagements entered into, before the adoption of this Constitution, shall be as valid against the United States under this Constitution, as under the Confederation.

This Constitution, and the laws of the United States which shall be made in pursuance thereof; and all treaties made, or which shall be made, under the authority of the United States, shall be the supreme law of the land; and the judges in every State shall be bound thereby, anything in the Constitution or laws of any State to the contrary notwithstanding.

The senators and representatives before mentioned, and the members of the several State legislatures, and all executive and judicial officers, both of the United States, and of the several States, shall be bound by oath or affirmation to support this Constitution; but no religious test shall ever be required as a qualification to any office or public trust under the United States.

Article VI
The Highest Law
The Constitution of the United States is the highest law of the land. State laws must be in agreement with the laws of the Constitution. All national and state lawmakers must support the Constitution.

The last article says that the Constitution was to become law when 9 of 13 states ratified, or approved, it. The members of the Constitutional Convention present on September 17, 1787, witnessed and signed the Constitution.

ARTICLE VII

The ratification of the conventions of nine States shall be sufficient for the establishment of this Constitution between the States so ratifying the same.

Done in Convention by the unanimous consent of the States present the seventeenth day of September in the year of our Lord one thousand seven hundred and eighty-seven, and of the independence of the United States of America the twelfth. In witness whereof we have hereunto subscribed our names.

GEORGE WASHINGTON, PRESIDENT   (VIRGINIA)

Massachusetts
Nathaniel Gorham
Rufus King

New York
Alexander Hamilton

Georgia
William Few
Abraham Baldwin

Delaware
George Read
Gunning Bedford
John Dickinson
Richard Bassett
Jacob Broom

Virginia
John Blair
James Madison

Pennsylvania
Benjamin Franklin
Thomas Mifflin
Robert Morris
George Clymer
Thomas FitzSimons
Jared Ingersoll
James Wilson
Gouvernor Morris

New Hampshire
John Langdon
Nicholas Gilman

New Jersey
William Livingston
David Brearley
William Paterson
Jonathan Dayton

Connecticut
William Samuel
   Johnson
Roger Sherman

North Carolina
William Blount
Richard Dobbs
   Spaight
Hugh Williamson

South Carolina
John Rutledge
Charles Cotesworth
   Pinckney
Charles Pinckney
Pierce Butler

Maryland
James McHenry
Daniel of St. Thomas
   Jenifer
Daniel Carroll

FIRST AMENDMENT — 1791

Congress shall make no law respecting an establishment of religion, or prohibiting the free exercise thereof; or abridging the freedom of speech, or of the press; or the right of the people peaceably to assemble, and to petition the government for a redress of grievances.

SECOND AMENDMENT — 1791

A well-regulated militia, being necessary to the security of a free State, the right of the people to keep and bear arms, shall not be infringed.

THIRD AMENDMENT — 1791

No soldier shall, in time of peace, be quartered in any house, without the consent of the owner, nor in time of war, but in a manner to be prescribed by law.

FOURTH AMENDMENT — 1791

The right of the people to be secure in their persons, houses, papers, and effects, against unreasonable searches and seizures, shall not be violated, and no warrants shall issue, but upon probable cause, supported by oath or affirmation, and particularly describing the place to be searched, and the persons or things to be seized.

FIFTH AMENDMENT — 1791

No person shall be held to answer for a capital or otherwise infamous crime, unless on a presentment or indictment of a grand jury, except in cases arising in the land or naval forces, or in the militia, when in actual service in time of war or public danger; nor shall any person be subject for the same offense to be twice put in jeopardy of life or limb; nor shall be compelled in any criminal case to be a witness against himself, nor be deprived of life, liberty, or property, without due process of law; nor shall private property be taken for public use without just compensation.

SIXTH AMENDMENT — 1791

In all criminal prosecutions, the accused shall enjoy the right to a speedy and public trial, by an impartial jury of the State and district wherein the crime shall have been committed, which district shall have been previously ascertained by law, and to be informed of the nature and cause of the accusation; to be confronted with the witnesses against him; to have compulsory process for obtaining witnesses in his favor, and to have the assistance of counsel for his defense.

The Bill of Rights
The first ten amendments are known as the Bill of Rights. They protect the basic freedoms of the American people.

First Amendment (1791)
Congress may not make rules to take away freedom of religion, freedom of speech, freedom of the press, or the right of people to come together in a peaceful way or to send petitions to their government.

Second Amendment (1791)
In order to have a prepared military, the people have the right to keep and bear arms.

Third Amendment (1791)
During peacetime the government cannot make citizens feed and house soldiers in their homes.

Fourth Amendment (1791)
People or their homes may not be searched without a good reason.

Fifth Amendment (1791)
Only a grand jury can accuse people of serious crimes. People cannot be forced to give evidence against themselves. If one is found not guilty of a crime, he or she cannot be tried again for the same crime. People's lives, freedom, and property may not be taken from them unfairly. The government must pay the owner for any property taken for public use.

Sixth Amendment (1791)
Persons accused of serious crimes have the right to a speedy and public trial. They must be told what they are accused of. They have the right to have a lawyer and to see and question those who accuse them.

Seventh Amendment (1791)
In most cases, people have the right to a jury trial.

Eighth Amendment (1791)
Punishment may not be cruel or unusual.

Ninth Amendment (1791)
The people may have rights that have not been listed in the Constitution.

Tenth Amendment (1791)
If the Constitution does not give a certain right to the United States government and also does not forbid a state government to have that right, then the states and the people have that right.

Eleventh Amendment (1795)
The power of the judicial branch is limited to certain kinds of cases.

Twelfth Amendment (1804)
Electors vote for President and Vice President separately. An elector is a person chosen by the state legislature to elect the President.

SEVENTH AMENDMENT — 1791
In suits at common law, where the value in controversy shall exceed twenty dollars, the right of trial by jury shall be preserved, and no fact tried by a jury shall be otherwise reexamined in any court of the United States, than according to the rules of the common law.

EIGHTH AMENDMENT — 1791
Excessive bail shall not be required, nor excessive fines imposed, nor cruel and unusual punishments inflicted.

NINTH AMENDMENT — 1791
The enumeration in the Constitution of certain rights shall not be construed to deny or disparage others retained by the people.

TENTH AMENDMENT — 1791
The powers not delegated to the United States by the Constitution, nor prohibited by it to the States are reserved to the States respectively, or to the people.

ELEVENTH AMENDMENT — 1795
The judicial power of the United States shall not be construed to extend to any suit in law or equity, commenced or prosecuted against one of the United States, by citizens of another State, or by citizens or subjects of any foreign State.

TWELFTH AMENDMENT — 1804
The electors shall meet in their respective States, and vote by ballot for President and Vice President, one of whom, at least, shall not be an inhabitant of the same State with themselves; they shall name in their ballots the person voted for as Vice President, and they shall make distinct lists of all persons voted for as President and of all persons voted for as Vice President, and of the number of votes for each, which lists they shall sign and certify, and transmit sealed to the seat of government of the United States, directed to the president of the Senate;—The president of the Senate shall, in the presence of the Senate and House of Representatives, open all the certificates and the votes shall then be counted;—The person having the greatest number of votes for President shall be the President, if such number be a majority of the whole number of electors appointed; and if no person have such majority, then from the persons having the highest numbers not exceeding three on the list of those voted for as President, the House of Representatives shall choose immediately, by ballot, the

President. But in choosing the President, the votes shall be taken by States, the representation from each State having one vote; a quorum for this purpose shall consist of a member or members from two thirds of the States, and a majority of all the States shall be necessary to a choice. And if the House of Representatives shall not choose a President whenever the right of choice shall devolve upon them, before the fourth day of March next following,* then the Vice President shall act as President, as in the case of the death or other constitutional disability of the President. The person having the greatest number of votes as Vice President shall be the Vice President, if such number be a majority of the whole number of electors appointed, and if no person have a majority, then from the two highest numbers on the list, the Senate shall choose the Vice President; a quorum for the purpose shall consist of two thirds of the whole number of senators and a majority of the whole number shall be necessary to a choice. But no person constitutionally ineligible to the office of President shall be eligible to that of Vice President of the United States. (*Changed by the Twentieth Amendment)

THIRTEENTH AMENDMENT — 1865

SECTION 1.

Neither slavery nor involuntary servitude, except as a punishment for crime whereof the party shall have been duly convicted, shall exist within the United States, or any place subject to their jurisdiction.

SECTION 2.

Congress shall have power to enforce this article by appropriate legislation.

Thirteenth Amendment (1865)
Slavery is forbidden in the United States. Congress has the power to make laws to do away with slavery.

FOURTEENTH AMENDMENT — 1868

SECTION 1.

All persons born or naturalized in the United States, and subject to the jurisdiction thereof, are citizens of the United States and of the State wherein they reside. No State shall make or enforce any law which shall abridge the privileges or immunities of citizens of the United States; nor shall any State deprive any person of life, liberty, or property, without due process of law; nor deny to any person within its jurisdiction the equal protection of the laws.

SECTION 2.

Representatives shall be apportioned among the several States according to their respective numbers, counting the whole number of persons in each State, excluding Indians not taxed. But when the right to vote at any election for the choice of electors for President and Vice

Fourteenth Amendment (1868)
People who are born in the United States or who are granted citizenship are United States citizens. They are also citizens of the states they live in.
States may not make laws that limit the rights of citizens of the United States. They may not take away a person's life, freedom, or property unfairly. They must treat all people equally under the law.

President of the United States, representatives in Congress, the executive and judicial officers of a State, or the members of the legislature thereof, is denied to any of the male inhabitants of such State, being twenty-one years of age, and citizens of the United States, or in any way abridged, except for participation in rebellion, or other crime, the basis of representation therein shall be reduced in the proportion which the number of such male citizens shall bear to the whole number of male citizens twenty-one years of age in such State.

SECTION 3.

No person shall be a senator or representative in Congress, or elector of President and Vice President, or hold any office, civil or military, under the United States, or under any State, who, having previously taken an oath, as a member of Congress, or as an officer of the United States, or as a member of any State legislature, or as an executive or judicial officer of any State, to support the Constitution of the United States, shall have engaged in insurrection or rebellion against the same, or given aid or comfort to the enemies thereof. But Congress may by a vote of two thirds of each house, remove such disability.

SECTION 4.

The validity of the public debt of the United States, authorized by law, including debts incurred for payment of pensions and bounties for services in suppressing insurrection or rebellion, shall not be questioned. But neither the United States nor any State shall assume or pay any debt or obligation incurred in aid of insurrection or rebellion against the United States, or any claim for the loss or emancipation of any slave; but all such debts, obligations and claims shall be held illegal and void.

SECTION 5.

The Congress shall have power to enforce, by appropriate legislation, the provisions of this article.

FIFTEENTH AMENDMENT — 1870

Fifteenth Amendment (1870)
No citizen may be denied the right to vote because of race or color.

SECTION 1.

The right of citizens of the United States to vote shall not be denied or abridged by the United States or by any State on account of race, color, or previous condition of servitude.

SECTION 2.

The Congress shall have power to enforce this article by appropriate legislation.

SIXTEENTH AMENDMENT — 1913

The Congress shall have power to lay and collect taxes on incomes, from whatever source derived, without apportionment among the several States, and without regard to any census or enumeration.

Sixteenth Amendment (1913)
Congress is allowed to pass a tax on income.

SEVENTEENTH AMENDMENT — 1913

The Senate of the United States shall be composed of two senators from each State, elected by the people thereof, for six years; and each senator shall have one vote. The electors in each State shall have the qualifications requisite for electors of the most numerous branch of the State legislatures.

When vacancies happen in the representation of any State in the Senate, the executive authority of such State shall issue writs of election to fill such vacancies: Provided, that the legislature of any State may empower the executive thereof to make temporary appointments until the people fill the vacancies by election as the legislature may direct.

Seventeenth Amendment (1913)
United States senators are to be elected directly by the people.

EIGHTEENTH AMENDMENT* — 1919 (*REPEALED BY THE TWENTY-FIRST AMENDMENT)

SECTION 1.

After one year from the ratification of this article the manufacture, sale, or transportation of intoxicating liquors within, the importation thereof into, or the exportation thereof from the United States and all territory subject to the jurisdiction thereof for beverage purposes is hereby prohibited.

SECTION 2.

The Congress and the several States shall have concurrent power to enforce this article by appropriate legislation.

SECTION 3.

This article shall be inoperative unless it shall have been ratified as an amendment to the Constitution by the legislatures of the several States, as provided in the Constitution, within seven years from the date of the submission hereof to the States by the Congress.

Eighteenth Amendment (1919)
Liquor cannot be manufactured or sold in the United States.

NINETEENTH AMENDMENT — 1920

SECTION 1.

The right of citizens of the United States to vote shall not be denied or abridged by the United States or by any State on account of sex.

Nineteenth Amendment (1920)
No citizen may be denied the right to vote because of sex.

SECTION 2.

Congress shall have power, by appropriate legislation, to enforce the provisions of this article.

Twentieth Amendment (1933)
Presidents start their new terms on January 20. Congress starts its new term on January 3.

TWENTIETH AMENDMENT — 1933

SECTION 1.

The terms of the President and Vice President shall end at noon on the 20th day of January, and the terms of senators and representatives at noon on the 3d day of January, of the years in which such terms would have ended if this article had not been ratified; and the terms of their successors shall then begin.

SECTION 2.

The Congress shall assemble at least once in every year, and such meeting shall begin at noon on the 3d day in January, unless they shall by law appoint a different day.

SECTION 3.

If, at the time fixed for the beginning of the term of the President, the President-elect shall have died, the Vice President-elect shall become President. If a President shall not have been chosen before the time fixed for the beginning of his term, or if the President-elect shall have failed to qualify, then the Vice President-elect shall act as President until a President shall have qualified; and the Congress may by law provide for the case wherein neither a President-elect nor a Vice President-elect shall have qualified, declaring who shall then act as President, or the manner in which one who is to act shall be selected, and such persons shall act accordingly until a President or Vice President shall have qualified.

SECTION 4.

The Congress may by law provide for the case of the death of any of the persons from whom the House of Representatives may choose a President whenever the right of choice shall have devolved upon them, and for the case of the death of any of the persons from whom the Senate may choose a Vice President whenever the right of choice shall have devolved upon them.

SECTION 5.

Sections 1 and 2 shall take effect on the 15th day of October following the ratification of this article.

SECTION 6.

This article shall be inoperative unless it shall have been ratified as an amendment to the Constitution by the legislatures of three fourths of the several States within seven years from the date of its submission.

TWENTY-FIRST AMENDMENT — 1933

SECTION 1.

The eighteenth article of amendment to the Constitution of the United States is hereby repealed.

SECTION 2.

The transportation or importation into any State, territory, or possession of the United States for delivery or use therein of intoxicating liquors, in violation of the laws thereof, is hereby prohibited.

SECTION 3.

This article shall be inoperative unless it shall have been ratified as an amendment to the Constitution by conventions in the several States, as provided in the Constitution, within seven years from the date of submission hereof to the States by the Congress.

TWENTY-SECOND AMENDMENT — 1951

No person shall be elected to the office of the President more than twice, and no person who has held the office of President, or acted as President, for more than two years of a term to which some other person was elected President shall be elected to the office of the President more than once.

But this Article shall not apply to any person holding the office of President when this Article was proposed by the Congress, and shall not prevent any person who may be holding the office of President, or acting as President, during the term within which this Article becomes operative from holding the office of President or acting as President during the remainder of such term.

TWENTY-THIRD AMENDMENT — 1961

SECTION 1.

The District constituting the seat of government of the United States shall appoint in such manner as the Congress may direct:

A number of electors of President and Vice President equal to the whole number of senators and representatives in Congress to which the District would be entitled if it were a State, but in no event more than the least populous state; they shall be in addition to those appointed by the States, but they shall be considered, for the purposes of the election of President and Vice President, to be electors appointed by a State; and they shall meet in the District and perform such duties as provided by the twelfth article of amendment.

Twenty-first Amendment (1933)
This repeals, or cancels, the Eighteenth Amendment to the Constitution.

Twenty-second Amendment (1951)
A President is limited to two terms in office.

Twenty-third Amendment (1961)
Residents of Washington, D.C., have the right to vote for President.

SECTION 2.

The Congress shall have power to enforce this article by appropriate legislation.

TWENTY-FOURTH AMENDMENT — 1964

Twenty-fourth Amendment (1964)
Citizens cannot be asked to pay a tax in order to vote in national elections.

SECTION 1.

The right of citizens of the United States to vote in any primary or other election for President or Vice President, for electors for President or Vice President, or for senator or representative in Congress, shall not be denied or abridged by the United States or any State by reason of failure to pay any poll tax or other tax.

SECTION 2.

The Congress shall have power to enforce this article by appropriate legislation.

TWENTY-FIFTH AMENDMENT — 1967

Twenty-fifth Amendment (1967)
If the President becomes too ill to carry on the job, the Vice-President will take over as Acting President until the President is better.

SECTION 1.

In case of the removal of the President from office or his death or resignation, the Vice President shall become President.

SECTION 2.

Whenever there is a vacancy in the office of the Vice President, the President shall nominate a Vice President who shall take the office upon confirmation by a majority vote of both houses of Congress.

SECTION 3.

Whenever the President transmits to the president pro tempore of the Senate and the speaker of the House of Representatives his written declaration that he is unable to discharge the powers and duties of his office, and until he transmits to them a written declaration to the contrary, such powers and duties shall be discharged by the Vice President as Acting President.

SECTION 4.

Whenever the Vice President and a majority of either the principal officers of the executive departments or of such other body as Congress may by law provide, transmit to the president pro tempore of the Senate and the speaker of the House of Representatives their written declaration that the President is unable to discharge the powers and duties of his office, the Vice President shall immediately assume the powers and duties of the office as Acting President.

Thereafter, when the President transmits to the president pro tempore of the Senate and the speaker of the House of Representatives his written declaration that no inability exists, he shall resume the powers and duties of his office unless the Vice President and a majority of either the principal officers of the executive department or of such other body as Congress may by law provide, transmit within four days to the president pro tempore of the Senate and the speaker of the House of Representatives their written declaration that the President is unable to discharge the powers and duties of his office. Thereupon Congress shall decide the issue, assembling within 48 hours for that purpose if not in session. If the Congress, within 21 days after receipt of the latter written declaration, or, if Congress is not in session, within 21 days after Congress is required to assemble, determines by two-thirds vote of both houses that the President is unable to discharge the powers and duties of his office, the Vice President shall continue to discharge the same as Acting President; otherwise, the President shall resume the powers and duties of his office.

TWENTY-SIXTH AMENDMENT — 1971

SECTION 1.

The right of citizens of the United States, who are eighteen years of age or older, to vote shall not be denied or abridged by the United States or by any State on account of age.

SECTION 2.

The Congress shall have power to enforce this article by appropriate legislation.

TWENTY-SEVENTH AMENDMENT — 1992

No law varying the compensation for the services of the Senators and Representatives shall take effect, until an election of Representatives shall have intervened.

Twenty-sixth Amendment (1971)
No citizen 18 years of age or older may be denied the right to vote because of age.

Twenty-seventh Amendment (1992)
This amendment states that any law passed by senators and representatives to increase their own salaries will not take effect until after the next election for representatives.

Some words in this book may be new to you or difficult to pronounce. Those words have been spelled phonetically in parentheses. The syllable that receives stress in a word is shown in small capital letters.

For example: Chicago (shuh KAH goh)

Most phonetic spellings are easy to read. In the following Pronunciation Key, you can see how letters are used to show different sounds.

┌─ **PRONUNCIATION KEY** ───┐

a	after	(AF tur)		oh	flow	(floh)		ch	chicken	(CHIHK un)
ah	father	(FAH thhur)		oi	boy	(boi)		g	game	(gaym)
ai	care	(kair)		oo	rule	(rool)		ing	coming	(KUM ing)
aw	dog	(dawg)		or	horse	(hors)		j	job	(jahb)
ay	paper	(PAY pur)		ou	cow	(kou)		k	came	(kaym)
								ng	long	(lawng)
e	letter	(LET ur)		yoo	few	(fyoo)		s	city	(SIHT ee)
ee	eat	(eet)		u	taken	(TAYK un)		sh	ship	(shihp)
					matter	(MAT ur)		th	thin	(thihn)
ih	trip	(trihp)		uh	ago	(uh GOH)		thh	feather	(FETHH ur)
eye	idea	(eye DEE uh)						y	yard	(yahrd)
y	hide	(hyd)						z	size	(syz)
ye	lie	(lye)						zh	division	(duh VIHZH un)

└──┘

A

abolitionist (ab uh LIHSH un ihst)   A person opposed to slavery and in favor of ending it. p. 243.

acid rain (AS ihd rayn)   Rain with a high concentration of acid produced by burning fossil fuels. p. 550.

activism (AK tuh vihz um)   Participation in working for change. p. 512.

advertising (AD vur tyz ing)   The art of getting someone to like or want a product. p. 325.

affirmative action (uh FURM uh tihv AK shun)   A program for correcting the effects of discrimination. p. 552.

agent (AY junt)   A person who acts for or represents another. p. 259.

annex (uh NEKS)   To add on or attach. p. 242.

apprentice (uh PREN tihs)   A person who works in return for instruction, room and board, or payment. p. 102.

aqueduct (AK wuh dukt)   A structure that carries water to an area from a distant site. p. 65.

armistice (AHR muh stihs)   A halt to fighting by agreement between warring nations. p. 384.

arms race (ahrmz rays)   When countries compete to have more firepower than one another. p. 380.

artisan (AHR tuh zun)   A worker in a skilled trade. p. 569.

assembly line (uh SEM blee lyn)   A process in which each worker in a factory performs a different step or job in putting together the product. p. 419.

assimilate (uh SIHM uh layt)   To become absorbed into another culture. p. 224.

Axis Powers (AK sihs POU urz)   The countries that fought against the Allies in World War II. p. 459.

B

baby boom (BAY bee boom)   The period between 1946 and 1964, during which there was a great increase in the number of babies born. p. 502.

barbed wire (bahrbd wyr)   A type of wire that has barbs, or sharp points, every few inches. p. 303.

basin (BAYS un)   A wide, deep area bounded by higher elevations. p. 16.

Berlin airlift (bur LIHN ER lihft)   The program undertaken by the United States to deliver supplies to West Berlin in 1948 and 1949. p. 496.

Berlin Wall (bur LIHN wawl)   The wall built to separate East Berlin and West Berlin. p. 519.

Bessemer process (BES uh mur PRAH ses)   A method of making steel by blasting air through melted iron to burn away impurities. p. 304.

bill (bihl)   An officially suggested law. p. 202.

Bill of Rights (bihl uv ryts)   The first ten amendments to the Constitution. p. 191.

black codes (blak kohdz)   Southern laws passed after the Civil War, aimed at limiting the rights and opportunities of African Americans. p. 283.

blockade (blah KAYD)   A blocking of a port or region to prevent entering or leaving. p. 269.

borough (BUR oh)   A distinct self-governing area that is part of a larger city. p. 351.

boycott (BOI kaht)   An organized campaign in which people refuse to have any dealings with a particular group or business. p. 179.

bracero (bruh SER oh)   One of a group of Mexican farm workers who took the place of American farm workers during World War II. p. 469.

broadcast (BRAWD kast)   A program sent to a large audience. p. 422.

buffer zone (BUF ur zohn)   An area of safety between people in conflict. p. 118.

C

Cabinet (KAB uh niht)   A group of advisors to the President. p. 191.

Camp David Accords (kamp DAY-vihd uh KORDZ)   The treaty signed by Israel and Egypt that brought peace between the two countries for the first time in 30 years. p. 540.

carpetbagger (kahr put BAG ur)   The name given to a Northern white person who moved to the South after the Civil War. p. 284.

cartographer (kahr TAHG ruh fur)   A map maker. p. 54.

cash crop (kash krahp)   Something that is grown for a profit. p. 115.

causeway (KAWZ way)   A roadway built above water. p. 65.

certificate of freedom (sur TIHF ih kiht uv FREE dum)   Paperwork that proved that a slave had been freed or had bought his or her freedom. p. 256.

charter (CHAHRT ur)   An official paper in which rights are given by a government to a person or company. p. 97.

civilian (suh VIHL yun)   A person who is not a member of the armed forces. p. 389.

civil rights (SIHV ul ryts)   Personal freedoms of citizens. p. 447.

civil war (SIHV ul wor)   Armed fighting between groups within the same country. p. 267.

climate (KLYE mut)   The pattern of weather in a place over a period of years. p. 10.

closed shop (klohzd shahp)   A business or factory that agrees to hire only union members. p. 487.

cold war (kohld wor)   Sharp conflict between countries without actual war. p. 494.

common (KAHM un)   Land available for use by all people of a village or town. p. 100.

common man (KAHM un man)   The "average" American citizen, whose concerns are represented in government. p. 251.

communism (KAHM yoo nihz um)   The common ownership of lands and industries by people as a group. p. 494.

community action (kuh MYOO nuh-tee AK shun)   The act of supporting the needs of the neighborhood, state, or nation. p. 575.

competitor (kum PET ut ur)   A company in the same industry that wants the same customer's business. p. 322.

compromise (KAHM pruh myz)   An agreement in which each side gives in a little. p. 198.

conductor (kun DUK tur)   A person on the Underground Railroad who helped runaway slaves to hide and escape. p. 257.

Confederacy (kun FED ur uh see)   The nation formed by the states that seceded from the Union. p. 267.

conquistador (kahn KEES tuh dor)   A Spanish conqueror of America in the 1500s. p. 54.

conservation (kahn sur VAY shun)   The care, protection, or management of natural resources. p. 18.

consolidation (kahn sahl uh DAY-shun)   The combining of many small companies into fewer large companies. p. 319.

constitution (kahn stuh TOO shun)   A set of laws governing a state or nation. p. 188.

consumer (kun SOOM ur)   Someone who buys or uses a product. p. 325.

consumerism (kun SOOM ur ihz um)   The buying of goods and services. p. 417.

containment (kun TAYN munt)   The policy of limiting the expansion of communism. p. 495.

Contra (KAHN truh)   A member of a group seeking to overthrow the Sandinistas. p. 546.

Contract With America (KAHN trakt withh uh MER ih kuh)   A pledge signed by Republican members of Congress to seek a balanced budget. p. 543.

cooper (KOOP ur)   A person who makes or repairs wooden barrels, tubs, or casks. p. 138.

corps (kor)   A group of people who act together. p. 221.

Crusade (kroo SAYD)   A Christian expedition to take the Holy Land from Muslims. p. 50.

Cuban missile crisis (KYOO bun MIHS ul KRYE sihs)   The conflict that occurred when the Soviet Union built missile bases in Cuba. p. 518.

cultural borrowing (KUL chur ul BAHR oh ing)   The exchange of ideas, languages, customs, and ways of doing things among different groups of people. p. 139.

culture (KUL chur)   The ideas, values, tools, skills, arts, and ways of life of a certain people. p. 29.

D

decade (DEK ayd)   A period of ten years. p. 493.

Declaration of Independence (dek-luh RAY shun uv ihn dee PEN duns)   The document that stated the reasons for the desire of the American colonies to be independent of British control. p. 166.

defensive war (dee FEN sihv wor)   A war in which an army fights to defend its own territory. p. 268.

deficit (DEF uh siht)   The amount of spending that exceeds income. p. 541.

delegate (DEL uh gut)   A representative. p. 97.

descendant (dee SEN dunt)   A person descending, or coming from, a certain ancestor. p. 577.

dictator (DIHK tayt ur)   A ruler with absolute power in a country. p. 459.

direct democracy (duh REKT dih-MAHK ruh see)   A principle of American government that allows citizens to participate in making laws. p. 107.

disarmament (dihs AHR muh munt)   Cutting back or totally eliminating the weapons a nation has. p. 411.

discrimination (dih skrihm ih NAY-shun)   Action or policies against a minority group. p. 255.

displacement (dihs PLAYS munt)   The process of forcing people to move off of their land. p. 566.

dogfight (DAWG fyt)   A battle between two or more planes within close range of each other in the air. p. 393.

downtown (DOUN toun)   The main business section of a town or city. p. 555.

draft (draft)   A process of randomly choosing young men for military service. p. 382.

drought (drout)   A long period of extremely dry weather. p. 302.

dry farming (drye FAHRM ing)   A farming technique, used in areas of little rainfall and no irrigation, that is designed to keep moisture in the soil. p. 304.

dugout canoe (DUG out kuh NOO)   A boat that is made by hollowing out a log. p. 122.

dune (doon)   A hill of sand formed by winds. p. 439.

Dust Bowl (dust bohl)   An area in the Great Plains that had large dust storms in the 1930s. p. 436.

E

East Indies (eest IHN deez)   The islands of Indonesia; in older times the East Indies also included India, Indochina, and the Malay Peninsula. p. 56.

economy (ih KAHN uh mee)   The way in which natural resources and workers are used to produce goods and services. p. 55.

ecosystem (EK oh sihs tum)   A group of plants and animals and their environment. p. 21.

elevation (el uh VAY shun)   The height of land above sea level. p. 14.

Emancipation Proclamation (ee-MAN suh pay shun prahk luh MAY-shun)   An order that declared freedom for slaves in all states that had left the Union. p. 271.

embargo (em BAHR goh)   A government order that stops or slows trade with a particular nation. p. 216.

emigrate (EM ih grayt)   To leave one's country. p. 577.

empire (EM pyr)   The lands and peoples ruled by a powerful ruler or group. p. 51.

energy conservation (EN ur jee kahn sur VAY shun)   Using energy wisely or preventing it from being wasted. p. 549.

environment (en VYE run munt)   The physical setting of a place, including everything that affects the way people live there: the land, air, water, plants, animals. p. 29.

epidemic (ep uh DEM ihk)   The spread of disease to a large number of people in a short period of time. p. 275

escalation (es kuh LAY shun)   The act of becoming more involved. p. 519.

executive branch (eg ZEK yoo tihv branch)   The part of government that carries out laws. p. 201.

export (eks PORT)   To ship a product to another country to sell it there. p. 115.

F

famine (FAM ihn)   A time when there is not enough food for everyone. p. 233.

federalism (FED ur ul ihz um)   A system of government that divides powers between the national and state governments. p. 203.

First Lady (furst LAY dee)   The President's wife. p. 204.

forty-niner (FORT ee NYN ur)   A person who went to California in 1849 to find gold. p. 295.

fossil fuel (FAHS ul FYOO ul)   A nonrenewable energy source found underground. p. 19.

Frame of Government (fraym uv GUV urn munt)   William Penn's plan for the government of the Pennsylvania colony. p. 135.

Freedom Ride (FREE dum ryd)   A bus trip taken in order to integrate buses during the civil rights movement. p. 523.

frontier (frun TIHR)   A newly settled area that separates older settlements from the wilderness. p. 81.

Fugitive Slave Law (FYOO jih tihv slayv law)   A law that made it easier for slaveholders to get runaway slaves returned to them. p. 243.

G

geography (jee AHG ruh fee)   The study of the earth and how people use it. p. 7.

geyser (GYE zur)   A hot spring that shoots steam. p. 21.

GI Bill of Rights (jee eye bihl uv ryts)   The Servicemen's Readjustment Act, which ensured benefits to returning World War II soldiers. p. 477.

gorge (gorj)   A narrow pass or valley between steep heights. p. 149.

Great Depression (grayt dee PRESH-un)   Economic hard times in the United States, 1929–1941. p. 432.

Great Plains (grayt playnz)   A region west of the Mississippi River that stretches westward to the Rocky Mountains. p. 296.

Great Society (grayt suh SYE uh tee)   President Johnson's plan to improve life for all Americans. p. 514.

gristmill (GRIHST mihl)   A structure in which grain is ground into flour. p. 137.

H

Hessian (HESH un)   A German soldier hired to fight for the British in the Revolutionary War. p. 175.

history (HIHS tuh ree)   The study of past events and people. p. 7.

Holocaust (HAHL uh kawst)   The mass murder of millions of Jews and other people by the Nazis. p. 461.

homesteader (HOHM sted ur)   A person who received land under the Homestead Act of 1862. p. 301.

hornbook (HORN book)   A piece of wood with the letters of the alphabet, often protected by a thin layer of transparent horn. p. 147.

hostage (HAHS tihj)   A person taken and held prisoner by an enemy until certain conditions are met. p. 546.

I

immune (ihm MYOON)   To be protected from an illness because of previous exposure to it. p. 122.

impeach (ihm PEECH)   To charge a public official with having done something illegal while in office. p. 201.

imperialism (ihm PIHR ee ul ihz um)   The policy of extending the rule of one country over other countries or lands. p. 366.

inaugural address (ihn AW gyoo rul uh DRES)   The speech made at the start of a term of office. p. 277.

indentured servant (ihn DEN churd SUR vunt)   A person who sold his or her services for a period of time in exchange for free passage to America. p. 116.

Industrial Revolution (ihn DUS tree-ul rev uh LOO shun)   The period of great change in how people lived and made products, brought about by power-driven machines. p. 218.

inflation (ihn FLAY shun)   An increase in price, causing a decline in purchasing power. p. 487.

innovation (ihn uh VAY shun)   A newly introduced product, idea, or custom. p. 568.

installment plan (ihn STAWL munt plan)   A credit system where purchased items are paid for at regular intervals. p. 417.

integration (ihn tuh GRAY shun)   Bringing together people of different racial or ethnic groups. p. 474.

interchangeable parts (ihn tur CHAYN-juh bul pahrts)   Parts that can be used in place of each other. p. 230.

internal improvement (ihn TUR nul ihm PROOV munt)   The building of transportation and communications systems to help a country's economy. p. 218.

internment camp (ihn TURN munt kamp)   A prisonlike place in which people are held during a war. p. 471.

interpreter (ihn TUR pruh tur)   A person who helps people or groups understand the languages and customs of each other. p. 221.

interstate highway (IHN tur stayt HYE way)   One of the network of highways connecting the regions of the United States. p. 21.

iron curtain (EYE urn KURT un)   A barrier of secrecy isolating the Soviet Union and other countries in its sphere of influence. p. 495.

Iroquois League (IHR uh kwoi leeg)   A political union of Iroquois nations. p. 136.

isolationism (eye suh LAY shun ihz-um)   The policy of staying out of international affairs. p. 459.

isthmus (IHS mus)   A narrow strip of land joining two larger bodies of land. p. 369.

J

Jim Crow laws (jihm kroh lawz)   Laws that segregated and discriminated against African Americans. p. 285.

jobless rate (JAHB lihs rayt)   The percentage of workers who are unemployed. p. 450.

judicial branch (joo DIHSH ul branch)   The part of government that decides the meaning of laws. p. 201.

L

labor union (LAY bur YOON yun)   An organization of workers that tries to help its members. p. 342.

legislative branch (LEJ ihs layt ihv branch)   The part of government that makes laws. p. 201.

legislature (LEJ ihs lay chur)   A group of people who make laws. p. 124.

literate (LIHT ur iht)   Having the ability to read and write. p. 231.

long house (lawng hous)   A large house built by Native Americans in which a number of families live. p. 31.

Louisiana Purchase (loo ee zee AN-uh PUR chus)   The purchase in 1803 of French lands in North America that doubled the size of the United States. p. 215.

Loyalist (LOI ul ihst)   A colonist who was a supporter of Great Britain and King George III. p. 164.

M

majority rule (muh JOR uh tee rool)   Rule by more than half of the population. p. 106.

Manifest Destiny (MAN uh fest DES-tuh nee)   The belief that America should expand its territorial limits. p. 242.

market (MAHR kiht)   A place where a buyer meets a seller to purchase a product or service. p. 228.

Marshall Plan (MAHR shul plan)   A plan of economic assistance from the U.S. to European nations after World War II. p. 477.

mass production (mas proh DUK-shun)   The ability to produce many goods of one kind quickly and efficiently. p. 230.

mass transit (mas TRANS iht)   Public transportation, including trains, trolleys, buses, subways, and streetcars. p. 338.

Mayflower Compact (MAY flou ur KAHM pakt)   An agreement to obey the rules of Plymouth Colony, signed aboard the *Mayflower*. p. 95.

meeting house (MEET ing hous)   A building used for both public and religious meetings in colonial times. p. 100.

megalopolis (meg uh LAHP uh lihs)   A heavily populated area that includes a number of cities. p. 566.

melting pot (MELT ing paht)   The idea that the characteristics of different peoples could meld together and form an "American" identity. p. 340.

mercenary (MUR suh ner ee)   A person hired to be a soldier. p. 175.

mesa (MAY suh)   A flat-topped hill or small plateau with steep sides. p. 30.

metropolitan area (ME troh PAHL ih-tun ER ee uh)   An area made up of a large city or several large cities and the surrounding towns, cities, and other communities. p. 8.

migrant worker (MYE grunt WURK ur)   A worker who travels from place to place to harvest crops. p. 395.

migrate (MYE grayt)   To move from one place to another. p. 28.

minimum wage (MIHN uh mum wayj)   A wage established by law as the lowest that may be paid to an employee. p. 489.

Minuteman (MIHN iht man) A member of a militia of citizens who claimed to be ready to fight the British at "a minute's notice." p. 165.

mission (MIHSH un) A settlement of religious teachers. p. 75.

missionary (MIHSH un er ee) A person sent to teach religion to people of a different faith. p. 75.

Missouri Compromise (mih ZOOR ee KAHM pruh myz) The 1820 ruling that admitted Missouri as a slave state. p. 219.

mobilization (moh buh lyz AY shun) The organization of people and resources to help a cause. p. 388.

monopoly (muh NAHP uh lee) The complete control of an industry. p. 320.

N

national debt (NASH uh nul det) The total of monies owed by the government of a nation. p. 541.

national park (NASH uh nul pahrk) An area of scenic beauty maintained by the federal government for the public to visit. p. 16.

nationalism (NASH uh nul ihz um) A feeling of pride, loyalty, and devotion to one's country. p. 41.

natural resource (NACH ur ul REE-sors) Things, such as coal, water, or farmable land, provided by nature that are useful to people. p. 9.

Nazi (NAHT see) The political party that came to power in Germany in the 1930s. p. 459.

New Deal (noo deel) Programs introduced by President Franklin Roosevelt to fight the Great Depression. p. 434.

nisei (NEE say) A United States citizen born in America to parents of Japanese descent. p. 470.

no man's land (noh manz land) The land separating opposing armies. p. 392.

nomad (NOH mad) A person who moves from place to place. p. 29.

nonrenewable resource (nahn rih-NOO uh bul REE sors) A resource of which there is a limited supply. p. 18.

northwest passage (north WEST PAS-ihj) A northern water route, sought by early explorers, that would link the Atlantic and Pacific oceans and shorten the trip to Asia. p. 54.

O

Operation Desert Storm (ahp ur AY-shun DEZ urt storm) The common name for the Persian Gulf War. p. 547.

Oregon Trail (OR ih gun trayl) The trail blazed by pioneers moving from Missouri to Oregon Country. p. 246.

P

pacifist (PAS uh fihst) A person who does not believe in fighting or going to war. p. 140.

pardon (PAHRD un) To forgive for a crime. p. 538.

Patriot (PAY tree ut) A person who supported the American cause for independence from Britain. p. 164.

Peace Corps (pees kor) An American program for volunteers to help people in developing countries. p. 514.

piecework (PEES wurk) Work done and paid for by the piece. p. 346.

Pilgrim (PIHL grum) A person who travels for religious reasons. p. 95.

plain (playn) A wide area of flat or gently rolling land. p. 14.

plantation (plan TAY shun) A large farm where one main crop is grown. p. 119.

political party (puh LIHT ih kul PAHR-tee) A group of people who hold certain beliefs about how the government should be run. p. 192.

pollution (puh LOO shun) Environmental damage from harmful materials. p. 550.

pop culture (pahp KUL chur) Entertainment, such as art, music, books, and television, that is aimed at masses of people. p. 504.

prairie (PRER ee) A large area of level or rolling grassland. p. 300.

prejudice (PREJ oo dihs) The dislike or distrust of people just because they are of another race, religion, or country. p. 424.

presidio (prih SIHD ee oh) A Spanish military base on the edge of a settlement. p. 76.

primer (PRIHM ur) A simple book for teaching reading to beginners. p. 102.

prisoner of war (PRIHZ un ur uv wor) One who is captured and held by an enemy during a war. p. 474.

privateer (prye vuh TIHR) A privately owned armed ship having a government's permission to attack enemy ships. p. 176.

proclamation (prahk luh MAY shun) An official announcement. p. 163.

prohibition (proh ih BIHSH un) A law making it illegal to make or sell alcoholic beverages. p. 396.

prosperity (prah SPER uh tee) A time of economic well-being. p. 407.

protectorate (proh TEK tur iht) A place or country under the protection of another country. p. 360.

Puritan (PYOOR ih tun) A person in the 1600s in England who thought the English church should be made "pure." p. 94.

Q ───────────────

Quaker (KWAYK ur) A member of a religious society whose beliefs include equality and nonviolence. p. 140.

quota (KWOHT uh) The number of people that are allowed to enter a country. p. 409.

R ───────────────

Radical Republican (RAD ih kul rih-PUB lih kun) A member of the Republican party who wanted to punish the South after the Civil War and give land to black citizens. p. 283.

ratify (RAT uh fye) To formally approve. p. 190.

ration (RASH un) To limit the amount of something that each person can get. p. 389.

Reconstruction (ree kun STRUK shun) The name given to the plan to rebuild the South following the Civil War, 1865–1877. p. 283.

Red Cross (red kraws) An international society for the relief of suffering in times of war or disaster. p. 280.

reformer (rih FOR mur) A person who works for a cause such as improved conditions for workers. p. 343.

region (REE jun) An area with one or more common characteristics that make it different from surrounding areas. p. 10.

represent (rep rih ZENT) To act and speak for another in a lawmaking body. p. 125.

republic (rih PUB lihk) A government in which the power to govern comes from the people, not a king. p. 188.

Republican party (rih PUB lih kun PAHR tee) A political party made up of people who wanted to keep the western territories free of slavery. p. 245.

reservation (rez ur VAY shun) A piece of public land set aside by the government for the use of a particular group of people. p. 299.

revolution (rev uh LOO shun) A sudden, complete change. p. 165.

Rough Riders (ruf RYD urz) Volunteer soldiers in the Spanish-American War, led by Theodore Roosevelt. p. 361.

S ───────────────

Sandinista (san duh NEES tuh) A member of the Communist group that took power in Nicaragua in 1979. p. 546.

satellite (SAT uh lyt) An object rocketed into orbit around the earth, moon, or other planets. p. 491.

scrap drive (skrap dryv) A call for discarded material to be used to support the war effort during World War II. p. 468.

secede (sih SEED) To withdraw from an organization or nation. p. 267.

sediment (SED uh munt) Matter that settles to the bottom of a liquid. p. 15.

separatist (SEP ur uh tihst) A person who wished to separate from the Church of England. p. 94.

service job (SUR vihs jahb) A job that provides a service instead of producing goods. p. 542.

sharecropper (SHER krahp ur) A person who farms land owned by another and gives part of the crop in return for seeds, tools, and other supplies. p. 285.

sit-in (SIHT ihn) A protest in which people sit down in a place and refuse to leave. p. 522.

skyscraper (SKYE skray pur) A very tall, many-storied building, with elevators and a steel frame. p. 338.

slave (slayv) A person who is enslaved and owned by another person. p. 35.

social revolution (SOH shul rev uh-LOO shun) A dramatic change in the way that people relate to each other within a culture. p. 572.

society (suh SYE uh tee) People living together as a group with the same way of life. p. 36.

sod (sahd) A layer of turf containing grass plants and matted roots. p. 300.

speculator (SPEK yoo lay tor) Someone who takes great financial risks, hoping to make a huge profit. p. 321.

sphere of influence (sfihr uv IHN-floo uns) Area or country where another nation has gained special privileges and rights for itself. p. 363.

stampede (stam PEED) To cause a herd of animals to panic and run. p. 83.

staple crop (STAY pul krahp) The most important crop grown in an area. p. 123.

stock market (stahk MAHR kiht) The place where business shares are bought and sold. p. 432.

strike (stryk)   To refuse to work until certain demands, such as higher wages or better working conditions, are met. p. 233.

suffrage (SUF rihj)   The right to vote. p. 343.

Sunbelt (SUN belt)   Most of the states of the South and Southwest, where the climate is warm and sunny. p. 501.

surveyor (sur VAY ur)   A person who determines the location, form, and boundaries of a tract of land. p. 172.

suspension bridge (suh SPEN shun brihj)   A bridge whose roadway is suspended by steel cables supported by two high towers. p. 351.

sweatshop (SWET shahp)   A place where workers work long hours at low wages under poor conditions. p. 346.

T

tapestry (TAP us tree)   An elaborate, heavy cloth with designs and scenes woven into it. p. 40.

Tejano (te HAH noh)   A Texan of Mexican descent. p. 241.

temperance (TEM pur uns)   Moderation in drinking alcohol or total abstinence from drinking alcohol. p. 251.

tenement (TEN uh munt)   An apartment building shared by several families. p. 338.

terrain (ter RAYN)   Land and landforms, including deserts, mountains, and valleys. p. 246.

territory (TER uh tor ee)   An area of land that has not yet become a state. p. 216.

tipi (TEE pee)   A Native American tent made of animal skins. p. 83.

topsoil (TAHP soil)   The upper layer of soil. p. 33.

trading post (TRAYD ing pohst)   A place where people trade goods with the people who live in the area. p. 77.

Trail of Tears (trayl uv tihrz)   The name given to the removal of Cherokees from their homelands to what is now Oklahoma. p. 225.

treaty (TREET ee)   A formal agreement between two nations. p. 298.

tributary (TRIHB yoo ter ee)   A stream or river that flows into a larger one. p. 149.

Truman Doctrine (TROO mun DAHK-trihn)   A program by the government to aid any nation threatened by communism. p. 495.

U

U-boat (YOO boht)   A German boat that travels underwater. p. 381.

Underground Railroad (UN dur-ground RAYL rohd)   A system set up by opponents of slavery to help slaves flee from the South to the North. p. 257.

union shop (YOON yun shahp)   A business or factory that requires workers to join a union after being hired. p. 487.

United Nations (yoo NYT ihd NAY-shunz)   An organization of world nations pledged to promote peace and security. p. 477.

urbanization (ur bun eye ZAY shun)   The process through which cities expand their boundaries. p. 338.

V

vaccine (vak SEEN)   A preparation that prevents a disease from occurring in humans and animals. p. 502.

vaquero (vah KER oh)   A Mexican cattle herder. p. 297.

veto (VEE toh)   To reject a proposed law. p. 125.

victory garden (VIHK tur ee GAHRD-un)   A garden planted by people to show that they could be self-sufficient during wartime. p. 468.

Vietnamization (vee et nuh muh-ZAY shun)   The plan to turn the fighting over to South Vietnamese troops during the Vietnam War. p. 520.

W

war crime (wor krym)   A crime that violates accepted laws of war or norms of humane behavior. p. 461.

work ethic (wurk ETH ihk)   A belief in working hard. p. 114.

INDEX

Page numbers in italics indicate illustrations.

ACKNOWLEDGMENTS

Grateful acknowledgment is made to the following publishers, authors, and agents for their permission to reprint copyrighted material. Every effort has been made to locate all copyright proprietors; any errors or omissions in copyright notice are inadvertent and will be corrected in future printings as they are discovered.

from *A Boy Becomes a Man at Wounded Knee* by Ted Wood with Wanbli Numpa Afraid of Hawk. Copyright ©1992 by Ted Wood. Reprinted by permission of Walker & Company.

from *La Causa: The Migrant Farmworkers' Story* by Dana Catharine de Ruiz and Richard Larios. Cover illustration by Rudy Gutierrez. Copyright ©1993 by Dialogue Systems, Inc. Reprinted by permission of Steck-Vaughn Company.

from *Flight* by Robert Burleigh. Text copyright ©1991 by Robert Burleigh. Cover illustration copyright ©1991 by Mike Wimmer. Reprinted by permission of Philomel Books.

excerpt from "Free at Last" from *The Worlds of Martin Luther King, Jr.,* selected by Coretta Scott King. Copyright ©1983 by Coretta Scott King. Reprinted by permission of the agent, the Joan Daves Agency.

from *Grandpa's Mountain* by Carolyn Reeder. Copyright ©1991 by Carolyn Reeder. Reprinted by permission of Simon & Schuster Books for Young Readers.

from *The Great Migration* by Jacob Lawrence. Copyright ©1993 by The Museum of Modern Art, New York, and The Phillips Collection. Used by permission of HarperCollins Publishers, Inc.

from *An Introduction to Williamsburg* by Valerie Tripp. Copyright ©1985 by Pleasantry Press, Inc. Reprinted by permission of Pleasantry Press, Inc.

from *Journey to Topaz* by Yoshiko Uchida. Copyright ©1971 by Yoshiko Uchida. Reprinted by permission of Creative Arts Book Company.

from *Lincoln: A Photobiography* by Russell Freedman. Copyright ©1987 by Russell Freedman. Reprinted by permission of Clarion Books/Houghton Mifflin Co. All rights reserved.

excerpt from "Molly Pitcher" by Laura E. Richards from *Hand in Hand,* collected by Lee Bennett Hopkins. Text copyright ©1994 by Lee Bennett Hopkins. Cover illustration copyright ©1994 by Peter M. Fiore. Reprinted with the permission of Simon & Schuster Books for Young Readers.

from *Panama Canal: Gateway to the World* by Judith St. George. Copyright ©1989 by Judith St. George. Reprinted by permission of G.P. Putnam's Sons.

from *Pedro's Journal* by Pam Conrad. Text copyright ©1991 by Pam Conrad. Cover art copyright ©1991 by Peter Koeppen. Reprinted by permission of Boyds Mills Press.

from *Sacajawea, Guide to Lewis and Clark* by Della Rowland. Copyright ©1989 by Parachute Press, Inc. Used by permission of Dell Books, a division of Bantam Doubleday Dell Publishing Group, Inc.

"This Land Is Your Land" from *This Land Is Your Land* by Woody Guthrie. Copyright ©1956 (renewed 1984), 1958 (renewed 1986) and 1970 by TRO-Ludlow Music, Inc. Used by permission of TRO-Ludlow Music, Inc.

CREDITS

Front Cover *Design, Art Direction, and Production:* Design Five, NYC; *Photo by* Dana Sigall. *Details by* Steve Elmore/Tom Stack & Associates; Brian Parker/Tom Stack & Associates; Comstock; Ron Klein/Panoramic Images; Kunio Owaki/The Stock Market; Kim Heacox/DRK Photo; NASA; E.R. Degginger/Color-Pic, Inc.; Thomas Kitchin/Tom Stack & Associates; Brian Parker/Tom Stack & Associates; Terry Donnelly/Tom Stack & Associates; Joanne Lotter/Tom Stack & Associates; The Granger Collection, NY; E.R. Degginger/Color-Pic, Inc.

Maps Mapping Specialists Limited.

All Photographs by Silver Burdett Ginn (SBG) unless otherwise noted.

Photographs 1 *bkgd.* Bill Ross/Westlight; *t.l.* Superstock; *t.m.* Art Resource; *t.r.* Valerie C. Santagto for SBG; Courtesy of: "Wings" of America, Santa Fe, American Indian youth running organization; *b.* Robert Frerck/Odyssey Productions. 2–3: *bkgd.* Sean Arbabi/Tony Stone Images. 6–7: *bkgd.* Randy Wells/Tony Stone Images. 8: Kunio Owaki/The Stock Market. 11: Hank Brandli. 12–13: *bkgd.* Eric Schweikardt/The Image Bank. 14: *t.* Brian Parker/Tom Stack & Associates; *b.* John Henley/The Stock Market. 15: *t.* Mel Lindstrom/Tony Stone Images; *b.* Phil Degginger. 16: *t.* Barbara Filet/Tony Stone Images; *b.* Grant Heilman Photography. 17: Ken Biggs/Tony Stone Images. 18: *t.* Wide World Photos; *b.* Bob Daemmrich/Tony Stone Images. 23: David Young-Wolff/PhotoEdit. 24: *inset* Elliott Smith for SBG. 27: Werner Forman Archive, Maxwell Museum of Anthropology, Albuquerque, NM/Art Resource. 29: *l.* Breton Littlehales/© National Geographic Society; *r.* Robert Frerck/Odyssey Productions. 30: *r.* The Field Museum, Chicago, Neg.# A109998c. 31: *t.* Nathan Benn/© National Geographic Society; *b.* The Granger Collection, New York. 34: George Gerster/Comstock. 35: © Dirk Bakker NR: 39. 36: *t.* Werner Forman Archive/Art Resource; *b.* Superstock. 37: *l.* © Gianni Tortoli/Photo Researchers, Inc.; *r.* Superstock. 38: *l.* Robert Frerck/Odyssey Productions; *m.* Fowler Museum of Cultural History, UCLA; *r.* Fowler Museum of Cultural History, UCLA. 39: Giraudon/Art Resource. 40: *l.* Scala/Art Resource; *r.* Art Resource. 41: Giraudon/Art Resource. 43: Fowler Museum of Cultural History, UCLA. 46–47: *bkgd.* Westlight © Adamsmith Productions. 50: Scala/Art Resource, NY. 51: The Bettmann Archive. 52: *t.l.* Stock Montage, Inc.; *t.r.* The Granger Collection, New York; *b.* Daniel Aubry/Odyssey Productions. 54: © 1995 North Wind Picture Archives. 55: E.T. Archive. 56: *t.* Scala/Art Resource, NY; *b.* Library of Congress. 57: Giraudon/Art Resource, NY. 58–59: *bkgd.* Cradoc Bagshaw/Westlight. 64–66: Robert Frerck/Odyssey Productions. 67: *t.* British Museum, London/Superstock; *b.* Robert Frerck/Odyssey Productions. 68: © 1995 North Wind Picture Archives. 70–71: *bkgd.* Peabody Museum-Harvard University, Photograph by Hillel Burger (detail). 73: Superstock. 75: Courtesy, Museo de America, Madrid. 76: Peabody Museum-Harvard University, Photograph by Hillel Burger. 77: *l.* North Wind Picture Archives; *r.* Smithsonian Institution, Department of Anthropology. 78: *t.* Courtesy, The Association For The Preservation of Virginia Antiquities; *b.* Ira Block/Courtesy, National Geographic Society. 79: The Granger Collection, New York. 80: Courtesy, State Library of the Czech Socialist Republic. 81: Courtesy, Archivo de Indias, Sevilla. 82: *t.* Courtesy, New York Public Library; *b.* Smithsonian Institution. 83: Courtesy, The Royal Ontario Museum, Toronto, Canada. 84: *t.* Culver Pictures; *b.* Peabody Museum-Harvard University, Photograph by Hillel Burger. 90–91: *bkgd.* Courtesy, the Day Collection. 95: The Bettmann Archive. 96: *t.* Courtesy, American Antiquarian Society; *b.* Ted Curtin/Plimoth Plantation, Inc. 97: The Granger Collection, New York. 100: Courtesy, Museum of Fine Arts, Boston. 102: *t.l.* The Bettmann Archive; *t.m.* The Bettmann Archive; *t.r.* Courtesy, Peabody Essex Museum, Salem, MA; *b.* North Wind Picture Archives. 103: © Michael Powell. 106: Culver Pictures. 110: *inset* SBG/The Girdler Collection. 110–111: *bkgd.* John Turner/Tony Stone Images. 114: The Granger Collection, New York. 116: The Granger Collection, New York. 116–117: The Granger Collection, New York. 119: The Granger Collection, New York. 122: Courtesy, North Carolina Division of Archives and History. 123: "The Banjo Lesson," by Henry O. Tanner/Hampton University Museum, Hampton, VA. 124–127: Colonial Williamsburg Foundation. 132: *t.* Historical Society of Pennsylvania; *b.* Courtesy, Alethia Carter. 133: *l.* Courtesy, Judy Mahoney. 135: The Granger Collection, New York. 136: Creation Legend, by Tom (Two Arrows) Dorsey/The Philbrook Museum of Art, Tulsa, Oklahoma. 138: The Granger Collection, New York. 139: *t.* National Museum of the American Indian, Smithsonian Institution/photo © 1994 Pathways Productions; *b.* Library of Congress (detail). 140: Historical Society of Pennsylvania. 141: *t.* Yale University Art Gallery, Gift of Robert W. Carle, BA, 1897/Photo by Joseph Szaszfai; *b.* Stauffer Collection--MEZD Print Collection/Miriam & Ira D. Wallach Division of Art, Prints and Photographs/The New York Public Library/Astor, Lenox and Tilden Foundations. 144: *t.* Courtesy, Historic Speedwell; *b.* Courtesy, Peter Gregg. 145: *t.* Michael Powell; *b.* Breton Littlehales/© National Geographic Image Collection. 146: Courtesy, Peter Gregg. 147: The Rare Book Department of The Free Library of Philadelphia. 155: Georgiana Silk/Silk Photography. 156–157 *bkgd.* A&J Verkaik/The Stock Market; *t.l.* Tom Green/Colonial Williamsburg Foundation; *t.r.* Tom Green/Colonial Williamsburg Foundation; *inset* Superstock. 158–159: *bkgd.* Picture Perfect USA. 162: *t.* "Washington in Conference with Iroquois Cheifs," by Junius Brutus Stearns, #0126.1514/From the collection of The Gilcrease Museum, Tulsa; *b.* Ted Spiegel. 164: *t.* Courtesy, Massachusetts Historical Society; *b.* The Granger Collection, New York. 165: North Wind Picture Archives. 166: Private collection/Photograph courtesy, Hirschl & Adler Galleries. 167: The Granger Collection, New York. 168: *t.* Colonial Williamsburg Foundation; *b.l.* Courtesy, Massachusetts Historical Society; *b.r.* Stock Montage. 169: *t.l.* Nawrocki Stock Photo; *t.r.* Courtesy, Bostonian Society/Old State House; *b.* Courtesy, Christopher Day Collection/Girdler Collection. 170: *t.* The Granger Collection, New York; *b.* Chip Fanelli/Courtesy, Concord Museum, Concord, MA. 171: North Wind Picture Archives. 172–173: Library of Congress/Hand-colored © 1995 North Wind Picture Archives. 174: SBG/Hand-colored © 1995 North Wind Picture Archives. 175: *t.* Guilford Courthouse National Military Park; *b.l.* Courtesy, Concord Museum, Concord, MA; *b.r.* Courtesy, Concord Museum, Concord, MA. 176: Ted Spiegel. 177: The Granger Collection, New York. 178: SBG/Hand-colored © 1995 North Wind Picture Archives. 179: The Granger Collection, New York. 180–181: *bkgd.* © H.D. Thoreau/Westlight. 184–185: *bkgd.* Superstock. 188: *t.l.* Larry Stevens/Nawrocki Stock Photo; *t.r.* Nawrocki Stock Photo; *b.* Larry Stevens/Nawrocki Stock Photo. 189: The Granger Collection, New York. 190: Ted Spiegel. 192–193: North Wind Picture Archives. 196–197: Nawrocki Stock Photo. 198: Courtesy, The New York Public Library, Research Collections. 199: *l.* The Granger Collection, New York; *r.* Brown Brothers. 204: *t.* Nawrocki Stock Photo; *b.* Mt. Vernon Ladies Association of the Union. 205: Brown Brothers. 207: Superstock .208–209: *bkgd.* Nowitz/Stock Imagery. *t.l.* The Bettmann Archive; *t.r.* The Bettmann Archive; *b.l.* John Paul Endress/The Stock Market. 210: *inset* SBG/The Girdler Collection. 210–211: *bkgd.* Ed Young/Viesti Associates. 212: Joe McDonald/Animals Animals. 215: *t.* The Granger Collection, New York; *b.* Courtesy, University of Virginia. 216: Courtesy, Missouri Historical Society. 218: The Granger Collection, New York. 222–223: *bkgd.*

Steven Bly/Tony Stone Images. 224: The Granger Collection, New York. 225: Woolaroc Museum, Bartlesville, Oklahoma. 229: Culver Pictures. 230: The Granger Collection, New York. 231: Detail of "Entering the Lock," by E.L. Henry, 1899/Collection of the Albany Institute of History & Art/Gift of the Estate of Catherine Gansevoort Lansing. 232: *t.* The Granger Collection, New York; *b.* Museum of American Textile History. 233: The Granger Collection, New York. 234: North Wind Picture Archives. 235: SBG/The Girdler Collection. 236–237: *bkgd.* The Granger Collection, New York. 238: The Granger Collection, New York. 241: Randall Hyman. 243: The Granger Collection, New York. 244: Charles L. Blockson Collection. 245: *t.* Museum of Political Life/Sally Andersen-Bruce; *b.* Culver Pictures. 246–247: The Kansas State Historical Society, Topeka, Kansas. 248: *t.* Archives Division - Texas State Library; *m.* Archives Division - Texas State Library; *b.* R.W. Norton Gallery. 249: *t.* The Bettmann Archive; *b.* History Collections, Los Angeles County Museum of Natural History. 250: Handcart Company, by C.C.A. Christensen/The Church of Jesus Christ of Latter-day Saints. 251: The Granger Collection, New York. 252: *t.* The Granger Collection, New York; *b.* Culver Pictures. 252–253: The Granger Collection, New York. 254–255: Schomburg Center, New York Public Library. 256: *t.* Chicago Historical Society; *m.* The American Numismatic Society; *b.* Schomburg Center, New York Public Library. 257–258: The Granger Collection, New York. 260: *t.* The Granger Collection, New York; *b.* The Bettmann Archive. 266–267: The Granger Collection, New York. 268: Culver Pictures. 269: Brown Brothers. 270: The Bettmann Archive. 271: The Granger Collection, New York. 272–273: United States Postal Service. 274: Brady Collection/Library of Congress. 275: Courtesy, Dale Cyrus Wheary. 276–277: The Bettmann Archive. 280: *t.* Brown Brothers; *b.* Jim Enos/United States Army Military History Institute. 281: *t.* The Granger Collection, New York; *b.l.* Brown Brothers; *b.r.* The Bettmann Archive. 282: Valentine Museum, Richmond, Virginia. 283–284: The Granger Collection, New York. 285: Courtesy, William Gladstone .288–289: *bkgd.* Carl Kurtz; *t.l.* Edward S. Curtis/Courtesy, National Geographic Society Image Collection; *t.r.* Photoworld/FPG International; *b.l.* Brown Brothers; *b.r.* Nawrocki Stock Photo, Inc.290–291: *bkgd.* Joe Viesti/Viesti Associates. 292: Superstock. 295: North Wind Picture Archives. 296: Archive Photos. 297: The Bettmann Archive. 299: Edward S. Curtis/Courtesy, National Geographic Society Image Collection. 300: Baker Library/Harvard Business School. 301: *t.* Culver Pictures; *b.* SBG/Courtesy, the Day Collection. 302: National Archives. 304: North Wind Picture Archives. 305: *t.* National Archives/Courtesy, National Geographic Society Image Collection; *b.* SBG/Courtesy, the Day Collection. 306–307: *bkgd.* Craig Aurness/Westlight. 312–313: *bkgd.* Luciano Gagliardi/The Stock Market. 314: Robert Frerck/Odyssey Productions. 316: The Bettmann Archive. 317: Archive Photos. 318: *t.* The Bettmann Archive; *b.* Archive Photos. 319: Archive Photos/Lass. 320: Brown Brothers. 321: Herbert/Archive Catalog. 325: *t.* The Bettmann Archive; *b.* Culver Pictures. 326: Archive Photos. 327: *t.l.* The Bettmann Archive; *t.r.* Harold Dorwin/Smithsonian Institution, Anacostia Museum; *b.* The Bettmann Archive. 328: *t.* Michael Freeman; *b.* The Bettmann Archive. 328–329: Archive Photos. 329: The Bettmann Archive. 332–333: *bkgd.* M. Angelo/Westlight. 336–337: Brown Brothers. 339: *t.* The Granger Collection, New York; *b.l.* Nawrocki Stock Photo; *b.r.* Brown Brothers. 340: Schomburg Center, The New York Public Library. 341: The Bettmann Archive. 342: Brown Brothers. 343–344: The Granger Collection, New York. 345: Brown Brothers. 346: *t.* The Granger Collection, New York. 347: Brown Brothers. 348–349: The Granger Collection, New York. 350: *1* The Granger Collection, New York; *2* The Granger Collection, New York; *3* The Granger Collection, New York; *4* The Granger Collection, New York; *5* Edwin Levick/Archive Photos; *6* The Granger Collection, New York; *7* Brown Brothers; *8* Wildlife Conservation Society, Bronx Zoo. 353: The Granger Collection, New York. 354–355: *bkgd.* The Granger Collection, New York. 356: *l.* The Bettmann Archive; *m.* The Bettmann Archive; *r.* Nawrocki Stock Photo. 359: The Granger Collection, New York. 360: Culver Pictures. 361: Chicago Historical Society. 362: National Archives. 363: Culver Pictures. 366: *l.* Archive Photos; *r.* National Portrait Gallery, Smithsonian Institution/Art Resource, NY. 367: *t.* The Bettmann Archive; *b.l.* Brown Brothers; *b.r.* Culver Pictures. 370–371: *bkgd.* Robert Frerck/Odyssey Productions. 374–375: *bkgd.* Cameron Davidson/Comstock; *l.* The Bettmann Archive; *m.l.* The Bettmann Archive; *m.r.* Brown Brothers; *r.* The Bettmann Archive. 376–377: *bkgd.* Viesti Associates. 378: Abbe Boon for SBG. *r.* 381: *t.* The Granger Collection, New York; *m.* The Bettmann Archive; *b.* Library of Congress. 382: *t.* The Granger Collection, New York; *b.l.* Culver Pictures; *b.r.* Courtesy, Christopher Day Collection. 383–384: Culver Pictures. 386: The Granger Collection, New York. 387: *t.* Culver Pictures; *b.* New York Times. 389: *t.* The Granger Collection, New York; *b.* Picture Research Consultants. 390: The Bettmann Archive. 391: *t.* National Archives; *b.* New York State Historical Association, Cooperstown. 392: Imperial War Museum, London. 393: National Archives (Signal Corps). 394–395: Brown Brothers. 395: The Bettmann Archive. 396: The Granger Collection, New York. 397: Culver Pictures. 406: The Bettmann Archive. 407: Culver Pictures. 408–409: The Detroit Institute of Arts/Diego Rivera, "The Detroit Industry". 410: Library of Congress. 411: *t.* Culver Pictures; *b.* Brown Brothers. 412: *t.l.* The Granger Collection, New York; *t.r.* The Granger Collection, New York; *b.* Archive Photos. 413: *t.* Brown Brothers; *b.* The Bettmann Archive. 414–415: Viesti Associates. 416: Brown Brothers. 417: *t.* Archives Division-Texas State Library; *b.* Brown Brothers. 418: *t.l.* Brown Brothers; *t.r.* The Granger Collection, New York; *b.* The Bettmann Archive. 419: The Granger Collection, New York. 420: United States Department of the Interior, National Park Service, Yellowstone National Park. 421: *l.* Brown Brothers; *r.* United States Department of the Interior, National Park Service, Yellowstone National Park. 422: *b.* The Bettmann Archive. 423: *t.* Brown Brothers; *b.* The Granger Collection, New York. 424: *l.* International Tennis Hall of Fame; *r.* Culver Pictures. 424–425: The Granger Collection, New York. 425: Brown Brothers. 428–429: *bkgd.* Carl Rosenstein/Viesti Associates. 431: *t.* Mark Richards/PhotoEdit; *b.* Randy Kalisek/F-Stock. 432–433: *bkgd.* Culver Pictures. 433: The Granger Collection, New York. 434–435: The Bettmann Archive. 436: *t.* Culver Pictures; *b.* The Granger Collection, New York. 437: *l.* Amateur Athletic Foundation of Los Angeles; *r.* Culver Pictures. 438: The Granger Collection, New York. 440: *t.* Culver Pictures; *b.l.* The Bettmann Archive; *b.r.* Brown Brothers. 441: *t.* The Bettmann Archive; *b.* Tom Lea 1939/Pleasant Hill, MO Post Office/Bruce Mathews. 442–445: *bkgd.* Bill Terry/Viesti Associates. 446–447: The Bettmann Archive. 448: Brown Brothers. 449: *t.* The Granger Collection, New York; *b.* Archive Photos. 450: *t.* San Diego Historical Society - Ticor Collection; *b.* Archive Photos. 451: *t.* Courtesy, Judy Girdler Collection; *m.* The Bettmann Archive; *b.* Culver Pictures. 454–455: *bkgd.* Courtesy, Christopher Day Collection. 456: Library of Congress. 459: *l.* AP/Wide World Photos; *r.* Brown Brothers. 460: *t.* Library of Congress; *b.* U.S. Signal Corps from Gendreau, NY. 461–463: Archive Photos. 464: *t.* Culver Pictures; *b.* The Granger Collection, New York. 465: *t.l.* Corbis-Bettmann; *t.r.* The Granger Collection, New York; *m.,b.* UPI/Corbis-Bettmann. 466: *t.* The Bettmann Archive; *b.* Culver Pictures. 467: The Granger Collection, New York. 468: *t.* Archive Photos; *b.* Culver Pictures. 469: *t.* The Granger Collection, New York; *b.* The Bettmann Archive. 470–471: Elliot Elisofon/Life Magazine/© 1942 Time, Inc. 471: Archive Photos. 472–473: *bkgd.* Brown Brothers. 474: *t.* Department of Defense - Heraldry; *b.* United States Air Force Museum. 475: Jeffery Ethell. 476: *l.* Norman Rockwell/The Curtis Publishing Company; *r.* The Bettmann Archive. 477: The Bettmann Archive. 478: Archive Photos. 479: The Granger Collection, New York. 480–481: *bkgd.* Bill & Sally Fletcher/Tom Stack & Associates/Digital Image Build; *l.* Eric Bouvet/Liaison International; *m.* Archive Photos; *r.* NASA. 484: Archive Photos. 486–489: The Bettmann Archive. 490: Archive Photos. 492: *1* Archive Photos; *2* Superstock; *3* Archive Photos; *4* Archive Photos/Graham; *5* Archive Photos. 494: Culver Pictures. 495: Archive Photos. 496–499: The Bettmann Archive. 500: Culver Pictures. 501: Superstock. 502: *t.* Superstock; *b.* Albert Fenn/Life Magazine/© 1955 Time, Inc. 503: Archive Photos. 504: *t.* Culver Pictures; *m.* Photofest; *b.l.* The Bettmann Archive; *b.r.* The Bettmann Archive. 505: *l.* Superstock; *m.* The Bettmann Archive; *r.* The Bettmann Archive. 511: *t.* AP/Wide World Photos; *b.* Bruce Davidson/Magnum Photos. 513–514: The Bettmann Archive. 515: *b.* AP/Wide World Photos. 516: *t.* Ellis Herwig/Archive Photos; *b.* Courtesy, Sue Ligertwood. 517: *l.* FPG International; *r.* Fred Ward/Black Star. 519: *t.* The Bettmann Archive; *b.* Archive Photos/DPA. 520–521: © 1997 Wally McNamee/Woodfin Camp & Associates. 521: The Bettmann Archive. 522: Superstock. 523: The Bettmann Archive. 524: Archive Photos. 525: The Bettmann Archive. 526: *t.r.* AP/Wide World Photos; *b.* The Bettmann Archive. 527: *l.* Frank Johnston/Black Star; *r.* Archive Photos. 528–531: Viesti Associates. 534–535: *bkgd.* TPL/Jacobs/Leo de Wys. 539: Arthur Grace/Stock Boston. 540: *t.* Archive Photos; *b.* Dennis Brack/Black Star. 541: Najlah Feanny/Saba Press. 542: *t.* AP/Wide World Photos; *b.* The Bettmann Archive. 543: The Bettmann Archive. 544: *t.* Eric Bouvet/Liaison International; *b.* Chip Hires/Liaison International. 545: Baldev/Sygma. 546: Sygma. 547: *t.* AP/Wide World Photos; *b.* Dennis Brack/Black Star. 548: Fred Ward/Black Star. 549: Lara Jo Regan/Saba Press. 550: Patrick Forden/Sygma. 551: *bkgd.* Peter Gridley/FPG International; *inset* Mario Villafuerte/Saba Press. 552: *t.* Frederick Pitchal/Sygma; *b.* Dennis Brack/Black Star. 553: *t.* Jim Brett/Archive Photos; *b.* John Chiasson/Liaison International. 554–555: *bkgd.* Gabe Palacio/Leo de Wys. 556: *t.* The Bettmann Archive; *b.l.* Fred Ward/Black Star; *b.r.* Alain Keler/Sygma. 557: *t.* Malcolm Denemark/Liaison International; *b.r.* Carol Bernson/Black Star. 558: John Van Hasselt/Sygma. 559: Harry Schaefer/Black Star. 560–561: *bkgd.* Ken Ross/Viesti Associates. 565: *t.* "Lewis and Clark on the Lower Columbia," by Charles M. Russell, w/c on paper, 1905, 1061.195, Amon Carter Museum, Fort Worth, Texas. 566: Robert Freck/Odyssey Productions. 567: Bob Firth/International Stock Photo. 568: *l.* Myron J. Dorf/The Stock Market; *r.* Superstock. 570: *l.* Emory Kristof/© National Geographic Society; *r.* Joe Viesti/Viesti Associates. 571: *t.* Lewis W. Hine/George Eastman House; *m.* Superstock; *b.* William Taufic/The Stock Market. 572: *r.* The Bettmann Archive. 573: *t.* Bill Stanton/International Stock Photo; *b.* Superstock. 574: *l.* © Timothy Greenfield-Sanders/Life Magazine; *r.* Courtesy, The Oakland Museum . 575: *t.* Gary D. Landsman/The Stock Market; *b.* Archive Photos. 576: *t.* Philip & Karen Smith/Tony Stone Images; *b.* © Will & Deni McIntyre/Photo Researchers, Inc. 578: *l.* National Archives; *r.* Collection of the Blue Ridge Institute & Museums/Ferrum College/Picture Research Consultants, Inc. 579: Superstock. 580–581: National Museum of American Art, Washington, D.C./Art Resource, NY. 583: National Park Service, Statue of Liberty National Monument. 584–585: Tom Van Sant/The Geosphere Project/The Stock Market. 605–611: White House Historical Association.

Illustrations m12–m21: Tim Haggerty. 19: Tom Pansini. 28–29: Phil Wilson. 32–33: Stephen Bauer. 60–63: Eldon Doty. 86–87: John Suh. 89: Eldon Doty. 99: Pamela Hamilton. 100: Tony DeLuz. 104–105: Jeff Shelly. 106–107: Steve Wells. 107: Stephen Schudlich. 120: Nina Laden. 121: Nina Laden. 128: Amy Bryant. 129: Amy Bryant. 146: Wendy Smith-Griswold. 148–152: Carlos Ochagavia. 194–195: Peter Bono. 200–203: Gary Torrisi. 216–217: Rick Farrell. 220–221: Chet Jezierski. 226–227: Chris Van Dusen. 228: Patrick O'Brien. 242: Martucci Studio. 255: Martucci Studio. 261: Joe Boddy. 274–275: Bill Maughan. 292: Eldon Doty. 304: Laszlo Kubinyi. 308–309: Lane Yerkes. 314: Yee, Josie. 322–323: Fred Ingram. 330: Dale Glasgow & Assoc. 331: Joe Boddy. 341: Martucci Studio. 357: Meryl Rosner. 364–365: Greg Newbold. 373: Stephen Schudlich. 379: Jack Unruh. 392: Irena Roman. 393: Phil Wilson. 409: Martucci Studio. 437: Gary Torrisi. 447: Robert Roper. 481: Mike Harper. 488: Carloyn Vibbert. 513: Martucci Studio. 604: Martucci Studio.